POLICE
TECHNOLOGY

Raymond E. Foster

PEARSON

Prentice
Hall

Pearson Prentice Hall
Upper Saddle River, NJ 07458

Library of Congress Cataloging-in-Publication Data

Foster, Raymond E.
     Police technology / Raymond E. Foster.
         p. cm.
     Includes bibliographical references and index.
     ISBN 0-13-114957-1
      1. Information storage and retrieval systems--Law enforcement. 2. Law
enforcement--Technological innovations. 3. Criminal investigation--Technological
innovations. 4. Police communication systems. 5. Electronic surveillance. 6.
Police--Equipment and supplies. I. Title.

HV7936.A8F67 2004
363.2'3'0284--dc22

2004050515

Executive Editor: Frank Mortimer, Jr.
Assistant Editor: Korrine Dorsey
Production Liaison: Brian Hyland
Director of Production & Manufacturing: Bruce Johnson
Managing Editor: Mary Carnis
Manufacturing Buyer: Cathleen Peterson
Design Director: Cheryl Asherman
Senior Design Coordinator: Miguel Ortiz
Cover Design: Jill Little; Design, Inc.
Cover Photo: Getty Images Thinkstock

Pearson Education Ltd.
Pearson Education Singapore Pte. Ltd.
Pearson Education Canada, Ltd.
Pearson Education—Japan

Pearson Education Australia Pty. Limited
Pearson Education North Asia Ltd.
Pearson Educación de Mexico, S.A. de C.V.
Pearson Education Malaysia Pte. Ltd.

10 9 8 7 6 5 4 3 2
ISBN: 0-13-114957-1

Acknowledgments

This work would have been impossible without the support and advice of a great many people. First, I would like to thank Frank Mortimer and Joseph Murray of Prentice Hall for their initial spark of insight. Along the way, I met several extraordinary people who provided invaluable insight and assistance— Captain Wayne Eveland (Retired New Jersey State Police), Vice President, Law Enforcement Marketing, Motorola; Dr. William Tafoya, Police Futurists International; Dr. Sam Nunn, Indiana-Purdue University; John D. Abbey, Abbey and Associates; Alec Gagne, President, CrimeStar; Sam Wagner, President, Video-ID Technologies; and Dr. Barbara McMahon, McMahon and Associates. In addition to their support, I received a ton of technical support in the business of writing from Rhonda Prime, Dorothy Delaney, and Korrine Dorsey, Prentice Hall. I would like to thank Heather Stratton Williams and the entire production team at The GTS Companies, Inc. I would also like to thank three outstanding people from the Los Angeles Police Department—Detective II Maria Teague, Detective II Andrew Malkhasian, and Police Officer Robert Frutos. Finally, I would like to thank my family for their sacrifice when the demands of this project were overwhelming.

Contents

Foreword

Over the course of the eleven years that I was honored to serve on the faculty at the FBI Academy (1980–1991), I asserted, extolled, and in many instances cajoled FBI National Academy students (local law enforcement executives) of the need to "get with" high technology. In an earlier foreword to another text, *Computers in Criminal Justice,* I declared and lamented that "a majority of police executives either do not care about 'high tech' crime investigation or do not know enough to have forced the issue" (in Schmalleger 1990: iii), to make it happen, as it were. Today, on the leading edge of the twenty-first century, in this foreword, I am happy—delighted, in fact—to express the opinion that we've made substantial progress in the use of high technology and the investigation of computer-related crime! Since I retired in 1995, I have had the opportunity to visit a number of law enforcement agencies nationwide. In that nine-year time frame, I have been very impressed with the law enforcement use of high technology that I have witnessed in operational settings. Especially in small- to mid-level agencies, the majority of law enforcement, I have seen the *routine* use of many of the technologies addressed in this outstanding book.

The significance of this observation is twofold. First, the author of this text is a practicing local law enforcement executive. He is a member of one of America's most renowned and highly respected agencies, the Los Angeles Police Department. In the decade of the 1990s and earlier, one would have been hard-pressed to find a text that addressed the same subject matter, and almost none of those were authored by a police practitioner. There could, of course, be an array of plausible explanations for this lack of practitioner representation in an important but narrow niche of the policing literature. I will contend that most local law enforcement executives could not and did not then author texts of the kind you are now reading because few practitioners had the skill set to do so. Today that is not the case. Raymond Foster is proof positive. Second, in that earlier time frame there would have been a limited call for this kind of text. Today not only is there a noteworthy audience for this book, but there are also now a significant number of individuals, preservice and practitioners, hungry for the information in this book that will be transformed into knowledge and applied in operational settings.

A number of chapters discuss cutting-edge issues: major incident and disaster response, the Internet (still not fully exploited), geocoding, and wireless, for example. A chapter on crime analysis has also been included. This evidences the author's understanding of the importance of integration. That is, the value-added benefit of augmenting one capability with another. That a chapter, not merely the closing page, addresses emerging technologies reflects the forward thinking of this author.

Police Technology is a clarion call that announces a move in the direction of a new, positive era for American policing in the near-term future.

William L. Tafoya, Ph.D.
Forensic Computer Investigation Program
University of New Haven
January 2, 2004

POLICE TECHNOLOGY

PART ONE
Introduction to Theory and Basics

Chapter One
Introduction to Police Technology

Learning Objectives

- The student will understand the layout of this text.
- The student will understand the difference between tactical and strategic information.
- The student will understand what is meant by technology in conjunction with this textbook and why technology in law enforcement should be explored.
- The student will understand the difference between efficiency and effectiveness.
- The student will understand the community policing model.
- The student will understand the connection between situational crime prevention and technology.
- The student will understand the concept of fragmentation.

Introduction

He was wanted for thirteen murders. A sophisticated ex-convict had ruthlessly taken over the leadership of a street gang. One detective referred to him as a monster who enjoyed killing. One murder was a tagger from another neighborhood; next, the homeless man who was unfortunate enough to witness the tagger's demise. Then there was the casual girlfriend he sent back to a third murder scene to get his cellular telephone; he had dropped it during that murder. He murdered her because she knew too much. The others were drug rip-offs, robberies, and grudges.

For the first six months after he was connected to the murders, his warrant for arrest languished. One federal agency and one local agency made an effort. But he was protected, hidden behind the fear in his neighborhood—and technology. His gang monitored the police radio. They used cellular telephones because the telephone calls were digital and more difficult to intercept. They used night-vision devices to watch for the police. They used a sophisticated call-forwarding scheme that involved a virtual private telephone number—it insulated the murderer so that he could control the gang without concern his number was being traced. They used the Internet to post messages and e-mail, when driving outside of their neighborhood, they used sophisticated counter-surveillance driving techniques.

Even though he was wanted, the murders and other criminal activity continued. Then a different group of police officers, from another federal agency and a separate local agency, formed a task force to stop him. These officers were different. Sure, they were good cops, but they were also patient and technologically savvy. They brought technology into the search.

They used high-powered optical equipment linked to a video monitor that allowed them to read the label on a pair of pants from more than a mile away. In the dark they used night-vision and thermal-imagining gear. They scoured government, commercial, and Internet data sources. Telephone switching boxes were rerouted to outside the gang-controlled neighborhood, and telephone traps were hung to gain the number called back and forth between residences and businesses

Figure 1.1 The Searchcam 2000 IR is a state-of-the-art tactical surveillance device designed to enable law enforcement and military personnel to covertly observe tactical situations from a secure position. The system combines a high resolution video camera, an invisible infrared light source, a sensitive microphone, and a speaker into a fully articulating, remote-controlled, telescoping probe. On-screen system status graphics insure that the operator can monitor the system without diverting either sight or attention from the task at hand. *Photograph provided by Search Systems Inc.*

associated with the murderer. The officers obtained wiretaps on the cellular telephones and monitored calls originating in California that were dumped by satellite to a Florida location and then forwarded via the Internet to a wire-monitoring station in yet a different Southern California city. They searched government databases for information. They organized their information into a central database and began to analyze the link between the information. The officers used crime-mapping technology to plot the crimes, sightings, and associates. More technology surfaced—remote video cameras, special radios that transmitted on little-known frequencies and in an encrypted manner, and specially equipped aircraft and vehicles. When they served search warrants, they had advanced weapons systems, soft body armor, flash bang devices, and special communications gear.

They used the technology to flush out the murderer. A fugitive on the run is more readily caught than one burrowed deep into the mass of humanity. But it wasn't just the technology. It was the cop work, too. It was working all through Thanksgiving weekend, using their laptops and radio equipment to triangulate and track cellular telephone conversations. It was cop work—talking to people and using media interest to keep the pressure up—newspapers, television newscasts, and *America's Most Wanted*. Their technology allowed them to break down the protective technological barrier the gang had erected. The technology allowed for the easy access to and organization of evidence. The technology made their operations more secure and safer. But in the end, it was diligent, solid police work that paid off.

The murderer was wanted in Los Angeles, tracked to Las Vegas—actually tracked to the Apache Indian Reservation in Arizona—and tracked back to Los

Angeles. And finally, in a small city on the Arizona side of the Colorado River, the cop work and technology paid off. The officers sat for a few hours, watching an apartment building. The murderer came out and was taken into custody without a whimper.[1]

The technology did not apprehend the murderer. It did not bring him to justice—people did. Computers don't solve crimes, arrest violators, or find missing children—courageous, dedicated people do. Certainly the technology gave the officers an edge. But the real advantage they had was their knowledge of what the technology could and could not do. Moreover, as we shall see throughout the text, technology is not a substitute for good judgment, it cannot compensate for insufficient training, provide leadership, or replace the street savvy of veteran police officers.[2]

The officer's advantage was in their acceptance, understanding, and use of the technology because technology can only help gather, organize, and analyze data; computers can't solve the crimes.[3] Their advantage was their team leaders, leaders who bridged the gap between the techies and the street cops. It was making decisions about how far to allow a technology to gather information before taking action. It was making decisions on when using a technology, because it was sexy or glitzy, impeded an investigation. The power of the technology was released by integrating the cultures, tactics, and technologies of the separate teams so they could work as one. I should know; I was one of the team leaders.

Text Design

This text is for people interested in how technology affects the criminal justice system. By the end of the text, you will not be a programmer or engineer, but you will be a more informed student or practitioner of criminal justice—specifically in the area of law enforcement. For that purpose, as technology in law enforcement is explored, we will be interested in technical explanations of a technology for three reasons. First, a technical explanation may help to understand how the technology impacts law enforcement. Or we may delve deeper into the technical aspects in order to understand the potential and limitations of a technology. Finally, certain technical explanations are helpful to build a base from which to understand other developments.

Although we are going to examine a great many technical aspects of technology, especially in the first section of the text, to gain a true sense of the potential, limitations, and challenges associated with technology we have to look at it in context of how it is used. The more interesting questions concerning technology are about how it is used, not what it is. Our study of technology will be infinitely more valuable if we look at it as a background to vital themes in law enforcement today.[4]

As a means to examine how technology is used by and impacts law enforcement, we will follow themes that cut across the study of criminal justice such as criminological theories, policing models, and practical problems. By using the framework of traditional criminological theories and practical problems, the text will convey the challenges, potential, and limitations of technology in law enforcement.

We will also explore three distinct points of view: the line employee, the supervisor, and the police manager. While these three points of view are at times similar, they often diverge significantly. When discussing line employees, we are referring to both police officers and civilian police employees. Indeed, work traditionally performed by uniformed officers has increasingly been given to civilian employees. Usually these are jobs that don't require law enforcement, such as repairing motor vehicles, programming computers, analyzing forensic evidence, and operating radio-dispatch systems. Indeed of all police employees 27 percent in the United States, 35 percent in Great Britain, 20 percent in Canada and Australia, and 12 percent in Japan are now civilians.[5]

Police officers are commonly referred to as **sworn employees** because they have taken an oath of office and generally have the authority to arrest under circumstances that are different from the civil population. In essence, a civilian can only make an arrest for a felony if a felony has actually been committed, whereas police officers can make an arrest for a felony if they have sufficient probable cause to believe a felony was committed.[6] It is necessary to consider the role of both sworn and nonsworn because many of the technology-related assignments in law enforcement are performed by nonsworn employees. Moreover, according the Bureau of Justice Statistics (BJS) 2000 Census of State and Local Law Enforcement Agencies, of the 1,019,496 state and local law enforcement employees, who are employed by 17,784 organizations nationwide, 311,474—or just over 27 percent—are nonsworn employees.[7] So the term *line employee* includes both sworn and nonsworn police employees.

At times, police officers will be specifically identified in the task because the technology relates to the duties normally performed by a sworn employee. Moreover, at times we will differentiate between a detective who is doing investigative work and a police officer who is a first responder in the field. However, it is important to remember that many of the technologies involved in the police service are used, maintained, and managed by nonsworn employees.

All three points of view are similar in that a greater understanding of technology will lead to a better understanding of the challenges, potentials, and limitations of technology in law enforcement. However, the points of view do diverge at a number of points. For instance, when information systems are used to track potential problem officers, the point of view of the line employee may be different than that of the supervisor or manager (the technology used to track problem officers is discussed in Chapter Nineteen). Moreover, line employees and supervisors are primarily the **end users.** End users would benefit from an understanding of the technology because they would probably become more proficient with it. Also, technology changes rather rapidly. An educated end user, who has had successful experiences with technology, is probably going to be more open to use new or upgraded systems. Indeed, there have been cases wherein the deployment of substandard equipment and/or inadequate training has soured line employees to future technological changes.

For the police manager or executive (who could be either sworn or nonsworn), the text has significant value because the manager who is more educated on the types of technologies available—and their potentials and limitations—is in a much better position to make decisions about acquisition and implementation. Technology can be expensive. And technology that does not meet expectations or has undesirable unintended consequences can have even greater expense to the agency. Indeed, one survey indicated that 75 percent of police departments were less than satisfied after a technology had been introduced and that 25 percent of the technologies did not function as expected.[8] A police manager who is better educated is in a position to ask the right questions, make better decisions, and lead his or her agency to a full realization of the potentials of a technology.[9] Finally, police managers themselves are end users of some of the technologies we will explore.

The police supervisor (again, who could be either sworn or nonsworn) has duties that fall somewhere in between those of the line employee and the manager. The supervisor is probably more of an end user than the manager but has the

An **end user** is the primary user of the technology, the one for whom it has been designed.

responsibility to provide daily training to and supervision of the employees and the technology. Prior to the advent of high technology, workers did one thing, supervisors did another, and managers did yet a third. Now, as we enter the twenty first century, we find that workers, supervisors, and managers have many common concerns regarding technology.[10] So with a variety of themes and points of view, we will explore police technology.

The text is organized into four sections. The first section is a collection of chapters whose primary goal is set the stage by explaining a variety of fundamental technological concepts. We move out of the first section with a brief look at the history of technology in law enforcement. The next two sections broadly separate police technology into strategic and tactical tools. Later in this chapter those concepts will become clearer. The final section looks at technology as it specifically relates to the management of the police service. Now this is a very broad field with developments occurring simultaneously. In order to bring some sense to the chaos of creativity, the text begins at the very basic and builds forward. But at times we will delay discussing part of a technology until later in the text because it might be better explored in the context of other themes.

The themes and the points of view are lenses for us to view how the technology has impacted the everyday functions of law enforcement. The focus is on what has happened and the intended and unintended consequences of technology. There are essentially four overriding themes in this text: community policing, efficiency and effectiveness, situational crime prevention, and fragmentation. These themes make sense because community policing is the most widely used model, efficiency and effectiveness are continuously used as arguments for implementation, situational crime prevention is the foundation for many of the current uses of technology, and fragmentation is probably considered the most vexing problem in police technology.

At the beginning of every chapter you will find Learning Objectives. These objectives should give you an idea of what to expect in the chapter and assist you in determining if the learning experience has been successful. As the text develops, terms and concepts with which you may not be familiar are introduced. New terms and concepts will be explained in one of three ways. First, the term or concept's definition may be woven into the text at the point of introduction. Second, there may be a quick explanation of the term in a marginal note on the page where the term or concept is introduced. Third, an explanation of the term or concept may be delayed until later in the text. Some terms and concepts are given explanations in other chapters because their stories require wider explorations.

Throughout the text you will find Try This boxes. Sometimes things are more easily demonstrated by practical experience. We hope they will help to demonstrate what you have read. At times these Try This boxes may be links to Web sites that provide more information about a subject.

The last two items at the end of each chapter are discussion questions and a list of the key terms discussed in that chapter. The discussion questions are often questions the author pondered while researching and writing the chapter. At the very end of each chapter you will find a collection of key terms. You can check your understanding of the information with a quick check of those terms. If you understand them, you probably understood the chapter. The final learning tool you will have at your disposal is a Web site that is a companion to this textbook—www.hitechcj.com. At that Web site, you will find a variety of educational tools, text updates, and links to other sources of information.

The text begins with some very basic information, which is developed into some very complex technologies in later chapters. Consequently, the discussion of the impact of technology will become increasingly more complex and interesting. The last section of the text is about the future. The future, or emerging technologies, is best explored after the past and present have been examined. Information about past performance is the guide we will use in an effort to forecast possible futures.

What Is Technology?

Before technology in law enforcement can be understood, the term technology should be defined. At the most basic level, technology is any tool. Indeed the root word of technology refers to the Greek word for the skill or craft of making tools.[11] Technology has also been defined as a system, as information and as knowledge.[12] For our purposes, technology can be any tool. Technology can be a hammer, the wheel, or a desktop personal computer. But it is important to consider that technology in the twenty first century is not defined by what it is or does, but more by how it is used. It is the context of use that defines technology.[13] Since most work done by police employees involves information, we will concentrate on information technology, or, as in the parlance of the industry, IT.[14]

When a police officer is interviewing a victim or witness, interrogating a suspect, or cultivating an informant, he or she is gathering information. At the line employee level, police work is primarily about communication—talking with people. Indeed the best police officers are those who can talk to anybody. But how do police officers know with whom to talk? They use information. Sometimes that information comes in the form of a **call for service.**

A **call for service** is a specific activity a police officer is directed to perform based upon information received from an official source. Generally, a call for service is based upon a citizen's call to the agency requesting assistance. For instance, a citizen reporting a burglary in his home would contact the police station and some sort of dispatch center (dispatch centers are explored in Chapter Six) would generate a call for service to a police officer. A **call for service** might also be based upon another police officer's request for assistance in the field.

A **self-initiated activity** is anything done by a police officer based upon his or her own observations.

Other times they stop and talk to people such as a traffic violator or a suspicious person. When police officers conduct self-initiated activities (the traffic violator, for instance), many times they are using information they gained from their own observations. In the instance of the traffic violator, the police officer saw a speeding vehicle. However, some **self-initiated activities** are based on information a police officer receives from another source, or the activity the officer initially undertook is modified based on information received from another source. Take the traffic violator, for example. As the police officer begins to stop the car, he or she may check the car license plate via radio or computer in order to establish ownership. Sometimes that check reveals the car is stolen. This information dramatically changes the police officer's response to the situation. The police officer is relying on information, but where does it come from? How does the police officer receive the information? How accurate is the information? These are a few of the questions the text will seek to answer.

In addition to using information, police officers gather information. In the original scenario, the traffic ticket issued to the violator has the potential to become important information to other parts of the criminal justice system. For example, if the violator does not go to court, the information on the citation may be used for the issuance of a warrant for the violator's arrest. Or the traffic violator may have been speeding away from a more serious crime she had just committed. The police officer, unaware of that crime, simply issued a ticket. Later, during a criminal investigation, that ticket may be the evidence that solves the crime. Again questions arise—how does the citation information get to the court or to the state department of motor vehicles? Just as important, how does the officer working on the more serious crime find out about the traffic citation? What if the officers work for adjacent yet separate law enforcement agencies? How is the information exchanged between all of the different parts of the criminal justice system?

A police officer is constantly using and gathering information. And the way that a police officer uses, transmits, and receives that information has changed. For instance, in 2000 32 percent of state and local police departments were using computers to dispatch **calls for service.** Moreover, because the 32 percent of the state and local police departments using computers to dispatch calls for service tended to be larger organizations, in total they employed 78 percent of the law enforcement employees nationwide.[15]

Information from people or about people is not the only kind of information police officers collect. Evidence collection and analysis is also information gathering. The most common type of evidence is testimony presented at a trial. A police officer or detective is usually the person who initially interviewed the witness. A witness's or victim's statement is information that is later presented in court, becoming evidence to prove or disprove a fact surrounding a crime. This is, of course, fairly consistent with the information gathered from the traffic violator.

The physical evidence, such as a fingerprint, that line employees recovered from a crime scene is generally circumstantial evidence. With the fingerprint, it is forensic evidence or information that proves someone touched an object and may be developed into a logical inference that a person was at the scene of the crime. As technology has become more sophisticated, the types of forensic evidence that line employees gather and analyze has become more complex (collection, analysis and preservation of evidence is explored in Chapter Thirteen).

Because so much of the job of the police involves the collection, transmission, retention, and organization of information, we will concentrate on information technology. Technologies other than information management cover a wide spectrum from concealable body armor to vehicle tires. At times our text may diverge from the path of information and examine another realm of police technology. This will become especially true during the tactical information section of the text. The technologies examined in that section are only representative of the types of technologies being used, developed, and implemented to assist line employees in field situations that are peculiar to law enforcement.

Why Examine Information Technology?

The use of IT in law enforcement is rapidly expanding. Indeed, in 1996 it is estimated that state and local governments spent an estimated $3.5 billion on information technology goods and services, and they were expected to spend as much as $4.5 billion in 2001.[16] The use of computers by local law enforcement agencies is an increasing trend. Figure 1.2 compares the total number of officers in local police departments nationwide in 1997 and 2000 who used computers for a variety of information functions. Between 1997 and 2000, the number of local police departments who used computers for Internet access more than doubled, increasing from 24 percent to 56 percent. If the information from the Bureau of Justice Statistics (BJS) report is further examined, you would find that the trend to incorporate information systems (computers) into the police service is increasing at the greatest rate for smaller agencies. For instance, between 1997 and 2000, local departments serving less than 10,000 people nearly tripled their use of computers for Internet access. The BJS data also shows that between 1997 and 2000, the percentage of local police officers working for an agency with some type of in-field computer more than doubled.[17]

The use of computers to manage information is clearly pervasive and increasing in state and local police departments. Now you might think that this information management is simply a function that concerns police managers. As we

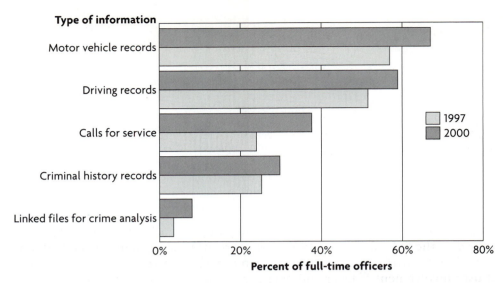

Figure 1.2 This graph shows the increase in the use of in-field computers by state and local law enforcement agencies.

continue to examine technology, we will see that the technology is having a significant impact on all levels of the local police agency. For instance, not only are police officers obtaining information in the field from the radios and computers in their vehicle, but the trend for police officers to report information directly into a database from the field via computer is increasing.

Although the increasing pervasiveness of technology in the police service is a good reason to explore the various technologies, there is another substantial

	Percent of agencies using computers for—										
Population served	Records manage-ment	Internet access	Crime investi-gations	Personnel records	Dispatch	Crime analysis	Inter-agency information sharing	Automated booking	Fleet manage-ment	Crime mapping	Resource allocation
All sizes	60%	56%	44%	40%	32%	30%	28%	18%	16%	15%	10%
1,000,000 or more	93%	100%	93%	93%	100%	86%	53%	47%	87%	86%	67%
500,000–999,999	88	94	88	85	85	91	83	56	85	82	65
250,000–499,999	98	98	88	90	100	98	78	48	60	90	58
100,000–249,999	89	89	80	69	90	92	61	51	50	80	41
50,000–99,999	89	88	75	67	85	76	51	50	38	53	35
25,000–49,999	86	80	72	60	79	58	51	40	33	34	22
10,000–24,999	81	72	65	54	63	48	36	32	30	22	16
2,500–9,999	66	57	50	43	32	29	29	16	17	12	10
Under 2,500	40	42	25	27	8	13	17	7	5	6	3

Figure 1.3 This table looks at the use of how local police agencies used computers in 2000. The table is organized by the size of the population that the police department serves. Overall, 60 percent of all local police departments, which employed 85 percent of the local police officers nationwide, used computers for records management. And 56 percent of the local police departments, which employed 83 percent of all local police officers nationwide, used computers for Internet access.
Source: Department of Justice, Bureau of Justice Statistics, 2000 state and local law enforcement statistics.

reason. In some instances, overall satisfaction with technology after implementation is troubling. One study found that a quarter of the agencies implementing a new technology considered it a failure. When the reasons for low satisfaction and failure are examined, there is one glaring consistency—a lack of knowledge and understanding of the technology chosen. As an example, managers failed to evaluate and redesign critical processes, they failed to align the technology with organizational policies and procedures, and they simply misunderstood the potential and limitations of the technology.[18] For end users satisfaction and failure have also been associated with agencies having unrealistic expectations regarding the potential benefits of a technology. Moreover, in many instances end users did not utilize the technology because they did not have the technical skills necessary to implement or operate the technology.[19] Simply put, by studying technology and educating end users we ultimately have a better chance of successfully implementing and using new IT. Indeed, at the federal level, in 1992 cost overruns totaling more than $7 billion were directly attributed to poor management, ineffective planning and a lack of user involvement.[20] Over and over again, the literature in the field returns to one overriding reason for IT failure—a lack of education and understanding at all levels.

In addition to improving the chances for successful use and implementation, an education about law enforcement IT can enhance the prosecution of offenders. If a police officer finds himself in court, testifying about how he used a technology in a criminal case, the court has an expectation that the police officer will know something about how the technology works. In one case, the court refused to allow the introduction of evidence because the officer's testimony about the technology was lacking. The overriding lesson from the court was that police officers should be provided training in technologies, or police agencies should be prepared to call expert witnesses.[21]

Simply installing advanced IT does not guarantee that employees will use it. And if employees won't or can't use a technology, the gains in performance and productivity will not occur.[22] Normally, when an employee can't or won't do something, the manager or supervisor provides the employee with training or finds some means of motivating her.[23] However, what many organizations are finding out is that if the supervisor or manager doesn't know the technology, he cannot effectively lead, train, or supervise.[24]

At other times the potential and limitations simply were not understood. Clearly, all of these reasons for low satisfaction and failure are connected to knowledge. The primary reason police technology should be studied is that as end user and decision-maker knowledge increase, success and satisfaction with technology is likely to increase. The more the nature of a technology is understood, the more likely that its design and implementation will be consistent with organizational goals and requirements. This requires informed decision makers, or police managers. The more a technology is understood, the more likely an end user will make full use of the technology.

In many cases there are significant advances in these other types of technologies. Indeed, as technology develops and it becomes less expensive to implement and end users become more knowledgeable, the amount of technology in the law enforcement workplace will likely increase. Although the table only looks at nine types of special technologies, it is clear from the information that the larger the agency, the more likely it is to be using or experimenting with different types of technologies. And these special technologies tend to be more field orientated than information-management technologies.

	Percent of agencies using—								
	Night vision/electro-optic			Vehicle stopping/tracking			Digital imaging		
Population served	Infrared (thermal) imagers	Image intensifiers	Laser range finders	Tire deflation spikes	Stolen vehicle tracking	Electrical/ engine disruption	Mug shots	Suspect composites	Finger-prints
All sizes	11%	6%	6%	26%	5%	—%	29%	16%	11%
1,000,000 or more	73%	53%	40%	47%	73%	20%	87%	60%	80%
500,000–999,999	47	36	26	38	62	9	83	53	79
250,000–499,999	58	33	23	60	35	5	63	45	68
100,000–249,999	40	17	19	56	37	2	70	55	66
50,000–99,999	27	17	19	52	25	1	71	41	52
25,000–49,999	28	14	15	45	22	0	58	43	29
10,000–24,999	16	10	9	40	10	—	50	27	13
2,500–9,999	11	4	5	27	3	0	28	13	5
Under 2,500	4	3	2	15	1	—	13	7	6

—Less than 0.5%

Figure 1.4   This table looks at three classifications and nine types of special technologies used by state and local law enforcement agencies.
Source: Department of Justice, Bureau of Justice Statistics, 2000 State and Local Law Enforcement Statistics.

There are also public or community expectations that law enforcement agencies are involved in the use of technology. Everyday experiences people have with computers in their own lives and the bevy of television programs that demonstrate law enforcement's use of technology has created an expectation that the police are hi-tech. The people expect us to use technology to protect them.

The final reason there is value in studying IT is the explosion of IT related crimes. In Chapter Sixteen we will look specifically at hi-tech crimes. But consider that the fundamental problem associated with investigating technology-related crimes is a lack of training and understanding about technology.[25] Consider that technology enables $500 billion to be laundered globally each year.[26] How can law enforcement officials investigate technology-related, technology-created, and technology-enhanced crimes without a basic knowledge of technology.

Tactical and Strategic Information

The focus on information technology in law enforcement is primarily about computer-processed information. As technology has progressed, some of the ways in which police officers receive, transmit, and record information has changed. Those changes have caused changes in the way that police officers respond to situations and the decisions that they make. Decisions that police officers make in the field, those required to be immediate, can be thought of as tactical decisions. For instance, in the not-too-distant past a police officer conducting a field interview of a suspect had to rely on her experience to judge the veracity of the information that was given by the suspect. Today, most police officers can double-check information via radio or computer terminal in the field. Finally, with the better information, an officer is less likely to be surprised or overwhelmed by a situation.[27]

In some cases police officers have other technological resources in the field to further determine a suspect's identity. They may have scanning devices in their patrol cars that allow them to scan fingerprints and nearly instantaneously compare those fingerprints with a wide variety of databases (currently, approximately 49 percent of the local police officers employed nationwide are members of a department that is implementing or experimenting with this type of technology[28]). In the future, police officers will probably have many other technological tools available for field identification.

In addition to receiving information about a suspect, police officers now receive information about situations via a variety of technologies. For instance, the way in which police officers are dispatched to calls for service has changed. During the first fifty years of the twentieth century, police officers were assigned to specific beats (geographic areas of responsibility). They sometimes received information about crime or social problems during a preshift briefing. Other information they received during their shift came from direct contact with the public.

Now police officers receive information in a variety of means—from the radio, computer dispatch, and databases. As we will see, these advances in technology also created new challenges and problems to the police service. For instance, the greater reliance on information from official sources (radio, computer, etc.) resulted in reduced public contact and as a result, may have reduced public confidence. For purposes of our examination of police technology, we will view devices that can be used in the field for immediate decision making as **tactical information** technologies. They provide information to a police officer in the field, enhancing her ability to make an immediate decision or take an immediate action.

The way in which information gathered by police officers is used has also changed dramatically. Information gathered, processed, analyzed, and retained by the police service is beginning to serve a strategic purpose. **Strategic information** can be thought of as information used in planning. As the power of computer processors has increased, so has ability to use the information gathered about what *has* happened in order to make some predictions about what *may* happen. This is the primary focus of crime analysis—looking at what has happened in order to make judgments about what may happen. This, too, has undergone dramatic change in the past decade. Later in the text, when we examine crime analysis, we will see the strategic implications of information gathered by police officers.

Information is used strategically by police officers, detectives, and police managers in a number of other ways. Sometimes detectives use information tactically, to make an immediate decision. However, most of the time detectives work with strategic information. In the opening paragraphs of this chapter the information gathered during the search for the murderer was used strategically to break down the barriers protecting the murderer and to plan for direction actions like search warrants and surveillance operations. It was also used tactically during the field operations. In this instance, the information was used both tactically and strategically. For detectives, information (statements, evidence, and their own observations) is organized and analyzed in order to determine what happened and who did it.

For police managers, issues like deployment, scheduling, training, and risk management have been greatly affected by technological developments. The police manager is able to get more complete and timely information than ever before. Indeed the information needed to perform complex management functions like cost benefit analysis or forecasting of trends is readily available.

As we further examine police technology we will find that some information has both tactical and strategic value. For instance, Geographic Information Systems (GIS) (GIS will be explored in Chapter Twelve) can provide police officers with useful information during the field incidents. A police officer responding to an overturned tanker truck can access information about the surrounding geography that may help in establishing a command post, conducting evacuations, and securing a perimeter around the location. In a strategic sense, the same GIS systems are powerful tools for planning for potential disasters and analyzing crime trends.

Police work is about information.[29] Indeed the skill that separates the outstanding police officer from his peers is his ability to gather information with his communication skills. As we will see, technology has at times enhanced the police's ability to use the information that is gathered, retained, and analyzed. Yet the police service's march into the information age has not been without missteps, costs, and unintended consequences.

Efficiency and Effectiveness

An existing technological system can also be referred to as a **Legacy System.**

One of the major arguments used for the implementation of a new technology or the upgrade of an existing system is that the organization will save money.[30] It is generally recognized that the initial costs can be high (most IT projects are expensive[31]), but the potential long-term savings provide a substantial return on the initial investment. According to the argument, the savings are realized by a reduction in the number of employees because the technology will allow fewer people to do the same job. Moreover, in many instances personnel costs can be more than 80 percent of an agency's budget, so it sounds like fewer people equals less money spent. In essence, increased efficiency, created through technological advances, increases productivity savings.[32] Sounds great—maybe. Before we explore that argument further, let's define **efficiency** as doing something cheaper. For instance, in a factory, before a technological innovation, a worker could make three shirts an hour. Now with the new technology, she can make ten shirts an hour. But the worker doesn't get more money, so the cost of producing the shirts decreases, and efficiency has increased. Now consider that costs include direct (such as salaries), indirect (such as maintenance of a new technology), and opportunity (such as choosing to do one thing instead of another, e.g., an agency can choose to use budget money to install new computers instead of buying new cars).[33]

So our first step in determining if an IT project is efficient is to look at cost, and the second step is to compare those costs against benefits. This is called cost-benefit analysis. Estimating benefits is generally much harder in public service because many of the benefits are intangible or difficult to quantify.[34] From a theoretical point of view, measuring the impact of a technology in business is somewhat more straightforward than measuring its impact in government service. For the business, the technology may reduce the cost of inputs or increase the demand for the product. Both can result in an increase in profit. While the calculations necessary for a business are more complex, at least the business has an idea of the output.

For the government, specifically law enforcement, businesslike economic models can still be used to determine the impact of a technology. However, there are several inherent difficulties. First, what is success? What is the output? What is the goal of law enforcement? Is it public satisfaction? Is it a reduction in crime? Is it a reduction in the perception of public disorder? Police managers have considerable guidance regarding measuring and evaluating police performance. Among the recommendations are measuring patrol services, investigations, traffic services, drug control, and crime prevention.[35] Let's take a look at the goal of a reduction in crime.

There are a few problems with measuring crime rates. Later in the text we will look at the Uniformed Crime Reporting Act and National Incident-Based Reporting System (NIBRS), but for now it is enough to know that some small jurisdictions don't even self report crime to a national reporting authority. So on a national level the crime rate may not be completely accurate. Issues with self-reporting aside, there is the issue of unreported crime. Murders are probably consistently reported—dead bodies are difficult to conceal. What about car burglaries? You probably know someone who has not reported a minor crime. Did he say, "it just wasn't worth the trouble"? Or, "the cops can't do anything anyway." Now consider some very violent crimes. Because of the nature of crimes such as rape, domestic violence, and child abuse they go unreported. So for even the smallest jurisdiction, what is the true crime rate? How much crime is there? In an effort to judge our ultimate success, how true is the measurement? And in addition to not really knowing how much crime there is, there is research that indicates improvements in police performance may cause an increase in crime reporting.[36] Sometimes crime really doesn't go up; people just feel more comfortable reporting it.[37] So we can measure if we are more efficient—that is to say, if our IT project made it easier for an employee to do something. We can measure some types of efficiency. For example, a typical efficiency measurement for a police officer is response time, the time between receipt of a call and arrival on the scene. In this case, efficiency would be measured by the speed with which police officers respond to the calls.[38] In essence, we can measure actvitiy.

But in addition to the difficulty in knowing exactly the output or goal, there is often a tenuous link between police activity and the goal. Therefore, in addition to not always knowing the desired result (did crime decrease?), we may not be able to follow the chain of outputs (faster response to call) and determine if a police activity actually contributed to the goal (crime decreased).

Let's revisit the traffic violator. Suppose that a police department realizes that serious traffic collisions have increased along a specific stretch of highway. The department, by looking at the collision reports, determines that the primary reason for a majority of the collisions is speeding motorists. In response to this analysis, the police manager decides to deploy an officer on that highway for the purpose of enforcing the speed law.

Now for the sake of our example, suppose that the department does not have any speed-detection technology, like radar. The police officer has two basic choices: she can sit along the highway and estimate the speed of passing vehicles, or she can enter and exit the highway, trying to pace behind speeding vehicles. A well-trained and experienced officer can do either with a fair degree of accuracy. But compared to the technology available, both techniques are more time consuming than a radar gun.

So our hypothetical police department realizes that the police officer can only issue so many citations in a single day using the first two methods. The department, desiring to reduce traffic collisions by enforcing the speed law, decides that it should purchase a radar gun. Now the police officer is equipped with the latest technology and is now efficient because she is issuing better-quality citations and has the ability to issue more of them.

Essentially, efficiency is the ability to complete an activity using fewer inputs. Generally speaking, in this instance, the inputs were the police officer's salary, equipment, and support systems. Presume that the cost per day of the police officer (all costs associated with deploying one officer) is $500 and that before the radar gun they were able to issue ten citations for speeding each day. The cost per citation would be $50. Now with the radar gun, the police officer is able to issue thirteen citations a day. For simplicity, presume the cost of the radar equipment adds $10 a day to the cost of the officer. So now the officer who costs $510 a day issues thirteen citations. Now the per-citation cost is lowered to around $38 per day. That's a fairly straightforward look at technology increasing efficiency, right? Well, no.

In this traffic violation example we are focusing on cost efficiency. But there are several problems with this measurement. First, most things the government is supposed to do are not by their nature efficient.[39] Second, efficiency is not the ultimate goal of government. Efficiency is using the least amount of inputs (resources) to conduct an activity or process that moves the government organization toward attainment of an ultimate goal. Recall, we didn't want to issue more tickets; we wanted to reduce traffic collisions. If we lose sight of the ultimate goal, we can end up being efficient in the activity but ineffective in meeting our goal.

The real goal is **effectiveness** in the attainment of some goal. Did the number of traffic collisions decrease? Is there a direct correlation between the activity of issuing citations and the reduction in traffic collisions? Let's be positive and say that as the traffic enforcement increased, traffic collisions decreased. But several questions remain. Was the decrease when the police officer issued ten citations per day, or did it not decrease until there were thirteen citations per day. How many would it take for motorists to understand that the speed laws were being enforced. It is quite possible that the number of accidents would go down at five citations issued per day. Perhaps that would be sufficient, meaning ten had no appreciable difference and thirteen certainly did not.

These numbers are fictitious, but the concepts are valid. The research linking police activity (like issuing citations) to the goal (like reducing traffic collisions) is mixed. Consider before implementing the radar the department may have put up a sign that warned motorists of the radar enforcement. Did that cause people to slow down? Did a major employer change their shift schedule, causing traffic patterns to change? Or perhaps at the time the traffic collisions were measured, there was some weather-related issue that was not fully taken into account. Finally, what happens if the police officer's efforts do directly result in fewer collisions? Doesn't that mean fewer speeding cars? Fewer speeding cars means fewer citations in the future, increasing the cost per citation.

As we examine technology we will constantly ask two questions: Does this technology impact efficiency, and does this technology impact effectives? Clearly the concepts of efficiency (how well do we perform an activity) and effectiveness (did we obtain our goal) overlap. They must both be examined because an organization can be effective but not efficient, or efficient but not effective.

Let's reconsider the traffic violator. A police department could respond to the problem of an increase in traffic collisions by deploying every available police officer to the problem stretch of highway. We could use so many police officers that every speeding motorist would be stopped. That would be effective in that traffic collisions resulting from speed violations would decrease. But that would be as impractical as it would be inefficient. In fact, that solution to the problem of traffic collisions could result in unhappiness in other parts of the jurisdiction (an opportunity cost issue) and very likely an unpleasant backlash from the motorists. Effectiveness is possible (in the short term and with specific goals) at the expense of efficiency.

Likewise, an organization can be efficient but ultimately ineffective. Think back to the radar example. It is very possible that even though we are efficiently issuing citations, the collision rate remains unchanged. Do you have a headache, yet? Take heart; police managers nationwide are vexed by the problem of balancing efficiency and effectiveness. But as we shall see later in the text, there are some very powerful technological solutions to determining what is the most efficient means to be the most effective.

Now we have looked primarily at being cost-effective and cost-efficient. The introduction of a new technology has benefits that are more difficult to demonstrate, but they exist and add to the overall effectiveness of an organization. In the radar scenario, the agency is likely to reap benefits that are outside the strict efficiency and effectiveness constructs. We must also examine technology and its "side" benefits for two reasons. First, managers and supervisors who introduce new technology must sell it to a number of **stakeholders.** Those stakeholders might be the other city government officials (the council, city manager, etc.), the community, and the line employees who must learn and implement the new technology. Second, a consideration of the benefits outside efficiency and effectiveness might give insight into the potential problems with the technology.

Let's look again at the radar. Radar (the technical aspects of traffic enforcement technology, including radar, will be covered in Chapter Eighteen) is more accurate and has a longer detection range than a human. Speeding vehicles could be detected outside of other considerations (for instance, the race of the driver is likely to be unknown to the police officer). Also, radar enforcement is safer to the officer and the public than pacing a vehicle. These two technological edges could translate into greater public confidence and better morale of the police officers. Both are important and yet nearly intangible.

Is there a downside to radar enforcement? If the police officers begin to exclusively use radar, will they ultimately lose the skills associated with pacing vehicles and estimating speed? This, too, is a recurring theme with technology. We will see examples of technology replacing that which was once done by human beings, and the skill is lost. This can have grave consequences. Also, could the use of radar cause the officers to ignore other types of violations. We will see a recurring theme in the implantation of technology: instances of technology that was so easy to use, glitzy, or sexy that it distracted police officers from other tasks.

With the introduction or upgrade of every technology there is some kind of change. Technology is a natural change agent and thoughtful consideration of the potential organizational changes may help us head off, or at least minimize, unintended negative consequences. Questions about effectiveness and efficiency should be primary considerations when contemplating new technologies.

A few last words on efficiency and effectiveness—some equipment clearly makes police officers more efficient. That technology increases efficiency by reducing costs, as with the radar example. However, effectiveness can increase while efficiency decreases because advanced technology requires support personnel.[40] This raises questions of whether IT shifts the cost of police operations from one thing, such as staff, to another technology. So maybe costs stayed the same, or if the technology fails, costs worsened.[41] In a later chapter we will broach the effects of shifting costs.

Our different points of view and our consideration of efficiency and effectiveness are representative of how we are going to explore technology. Another important question is how does technology fit into our model of policing? As was previously mentioned, the vast majority of local police officers work for an organization that practices some type of community policing. Therefore, we are going to use the most common model of policing as a lens through which to view technology.

Community Policing

As of 2000, 68 percent of the state and local police departments had a community policing plan.[42] Moreover, because those agencies that reported a community policing plan tended to be larger, the agencies with a community policing plan employed 90 percent of the state and local police officers in the United States.[43] More interesting, approximately a third of the state and local police departments nationwide reported that they had upgraded their technology to support their community policing efforts.[44]

There are theories, and there are models. In essence, a theory is an effort to explain why something happens, whereas a model is a prescription of what we should do. **Community policing** is a model that is supported by a number of social and criminological theories. If you are looking for a standard, one-size-fits-all community policing model, you won't find it. Although the models are as different as the communities wherein they are practiced, there are several core elements to most community policing models.[45]

As the text progresses we will see how technology has the potential to significantly enhance an agency's community policing efforts. As with life, it's not all roses. Some technologies have the potential for working against our efforts at community policing. We will find that these pitfalls might be avoided with an understanding of technology.

The United States Department of Justice (DOJ) Community-Oriented Policing Services (COPS) offers some general guidelines concerning community policing. According to the DOJ, community policing has ten core elements that fall under three distinct categories of elements—organizational elements, tactical elements, and external elements.

The first of the organizational core elements defines a department that is completely involved in the community policing effort. This means that from the agency head to the newest police officer, everyone practices the community policing model. This is a fairly practical element because, as we delve deeper into community policing, it will become clear that if everyone isn't practicing the model, some elements just won't realize their full potential. Now most criminal justice practitioners realize that the evolution toward community policing will take place incrementally in organizations. Some agencies may at first devote only a certain part of their organizations to total community policing. But as we examine community policing, it will be fairly clear that the full potential of the model can't be realized until it is an organization-wide philosophy.

The next organization element specifies that decision making and accountability be decentralized, allowing employees at all levels to make decisions within their areas of responsibility. This should have the effect of increasing interaction with the community, enhancing problem solving, and improving the quality of police service. However, this is counter to many bureaucratic cultures where it is safer to ask than act. Moreover, we will see that as technology improves and supervisors and managers have more real-time information, the

Chapter Six concerns the history of technological development in the police service. The development and implementation of technology takes place against the backdrop of three distinct policing models or eras. The policing models don't de-velop separately from other government styles or the rest of the criminal justice system. Indeed the evolution of policing and the evolution of govern-ment, particularly civil service, share many of the same elements.

tendency may develop for managers and supervisors to supercede line em-ployees' autonomy.

The third organizational element is that police officers and other personnel are assigned to specific geographic boundaries. In community policy it is key that long-term relationships develop between the police officers and the community. Moreover, police officers assigned to specific areas on a long-term basis will prob-ably gain a greater understanding in the geographic area or community they serve.

The use of volunteers is relatively straightforward. Volunteers can open the door to forming positive partnerships; open new lines of communication be-tween the community and the department; and perform some police services, freeing up police officers for other tasks.[46]

Enhancers, the final organizational element, are primary technologies that en-hance a department's community police. Enhancers would be technologies that improve the efficiency and effectives of a department's community policing.

Recall our earlier conversation of strategic versus tactical information. Organi-zational elements are essentially the strategic components of community policy. As we examine information technology in a strategic sense, we will see many of the systems described in the following chapters can enhance a department's or-ganizational or strategic community policing efforts.

The next set of elements are tactical elements. As with tactical information, the tactical elements are oriented toward the line employee and immediate actions. The first of the tactical elements is enforcing the law. Public safety is the para-mount goal of law enforcement. How an organization measures its effectiveness at reaching the goal of public safety varies from agency to agency. One of the means for attaining increased public safety is enforcement of the law.

The second tactical element, like the first, is a tool for increasing public safety: crime prevention. It is far better to prevent a crime than to arrest a violator. Crime prevention targets the root causes of crime and disorder in two ways: education and problem solving. Typically, crime prevention education centers on teaching the community how to reduce the likelihood they will become victims of crime. Traditional crime prevention education concerns things like what you can do in your home to reduce the likelihood that you will be burglarized. The second method of crime prevention, **problem solving,** is also the third tactical element.

In the opinion of some criminal justice scholars and practitioners, problem solving is the centerpiece of community policing. There are a variety of reasons for this opinion. For instance, it is ultimately more efficient and effective to fix a problem than the alternative of repeatedly responding to the symptoms of a problem—the calls for service. In addition to potentially minimizing repeated calls for service, problem solving efforts are very likely to create new partner-ships and bonds between the community, the police, and other service providers. This is because an in-depth look at most problems reveals that the

In law enforcement, **problem solving** is the use of the scientific method (observe, hy-pothesize, experiment, conclude) as a means to remedy or mitigate com-munity problems. For police officers the scien-tific method is often re-stated as the problem solving model SARA (Scan, Analyze, Respond, and Assess). *Source:* Bair, et al., "Advanced Crime Mapping Topics," 8.

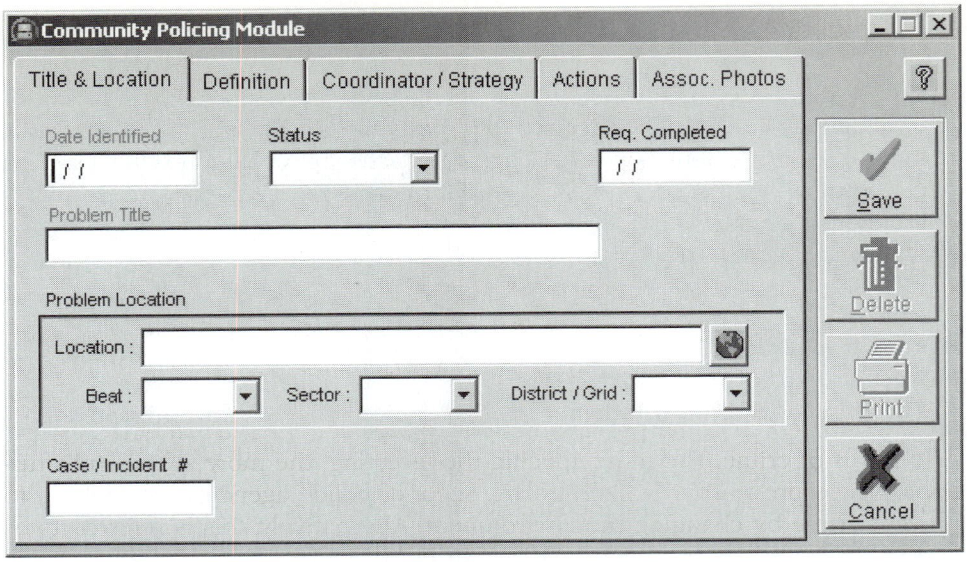

Figure 1.5   A Look Ahead: In future chapters, after we have gained a basic understanding of computer information technology, we will explore how technology is being used as an enhancer to the community policing model. We will find that some technology is being specifically designed and/or adapted for community policing. In this photograph, a computer program has been designed to provide a convenient method of tracking community situations and problems that may or may not relate to criminal activity. The designer's premise is that the specific identification of problems is inherent in community policing. Each problem is identified by a common name and is tracked from the date the problem was originally identified. This software involves detailing the exact definition of the problem, identifying a coordinator and a specific strategy to be implemented regarding the problem, and tracking each activity performed in conjunction with the defined strategy.
Permission for screen capture provided by Crimestar Corporation.

police cannot solve the problem without the community and other service providers. If the police officers are going to solve problems, they will have to force new relationships; seek input, advice, and assistance; and work with a variety of community members and service providers. Again, the alternative is the cycle of calls for service.

As we explore technology, we will find that a wide variety of the technologies have the potential to significantly enhance problem solving. The final category of core elements is external elements. By external we mean external to the bureaucracy of the agency—not external to the community police model. External elements are core to the success of the community policing model. The first of these elements is the public. As discussed, the partnership with the community is key and integral to the community policing model. The second external element consists of other agencies and organizations that provide service in the community. It doesn't take long for a new police officer to realize that many of the calls for service he receives and many of his observations about community disorder are not at their root solvable by the police alone. In reality, the police officers are often ill equipped to solve these problems. As was mentioned, involving other agencies and organizations in the problem solving process is essential for the success of community policing. Here, too, technology can play an important role.

This was a very brief overview of a complex and important issue. The purpose of the review was to provide us with some common ground from which to learn about police technology. You may bring other ideas about community policing to the text, perhaps practical experience or another, more in-depth class of the subject of community policing. As you read about police technology, you are encouraged to compare the information from those other experiences with the technology.

Situational Crime Prevention

The primary focus of most state and local police agencies is the prevention of crime. One of the common operational strategies used by police agencies to prevent crime is called **situational crime prevention.**[47] Later in the text, knowing about situational crime prevention will become important to us. There are three parts to situational crime prevention. First, police activities are directed as specific forms of crime. The more specific the targeting, the more successful situational crime prevention is likely to be. Second, police agencies are looking to prevent crime by changing the environment. Alternatively, this is referred to as hardening the target or increasing offender effort. It could be something as simple as adding lighting in a park to discourage loitering and associated crimes, essentially making in more difficult for the offender. The final tactic of situational crime prevention is to increase the likelihood that the offender will get caught. This is generally referred to has increasing offender risk.[48] Later in the text, such as in Chapter Twelve on crime analysis, the application of situational crime prevention will be obvious. But as you read about other technologies, ask yourself these questions. Does it specifically direct police activities at a certain crime? Does it increase offender effort? Does it increase offender risk?

Fragmentation

Think about our traffic violator again. Remember that as our police officer issued a citation, she might not know that the violator had just committed a more serious crime in another jurisdiction or that the violator was wanted by the court of another jurisdiction. The fact that many adjoining and overlapping law enforcement jurisdictions cannot communicate on the radio or readily exchange data is called a lack of interoperability (we will look at interoperability issues in depth in Chapter Eleven, Information Exchange). Interoperability is caused by a phenomenon known as **fragmentation.**

Most of the governments around the world have centralized law enforcement. However, the founders of the United States feared a strong central government, so many police functions and authorities were invested in numerous fragmented and semiautonomous law enforcement agencies. Today this has resulted in an overlapping and fragmented law enforcement scheme. Although a federal law enforcement system having authority over all state and local agencies would probably provide better efficiency, fear of abuse of authority has resulted in strong resistance to such a centralized law enforcement system in the United States.[49] Criminal justice is intentionally fragmented in order to maintain the checks and balances essential to our democracy. This fragmentation also serves to protect the privacy of incriminating information about the people who come in contact with the criminal justice system. Finally, some people believe that criminal justice is fragmented because of institutional paranoia; agencies don't want other agencies to know what they know and thereby be in a position to challenge their decisions.[50]

As we know (from our traffic violator), this fragmentation has led to agencies maintaining their information in different and incompatible databases.[51] They have different radio types and frequencies, so information exchange is stymied. But fragmentation has also retarded technology in law enforcement. Most technological advances and applications to law enforcement come from the private sector. With seventeen thousand agencies, all with different needs and standards, the market for law enforcement technology is insufficient to attract some private firms. Equipment and technology acquisition are completed on an agency-by-agency basis. Because state and local agencies acquire new technologies at different rates, they also develop expertise at different rates. The problem of fragmentation is often most severe when agencies with contiguous or overlapping jurisdictions obtain incompatible technologies. These incompatible technologies severely hamper information sharing. Fragmentation of local policing is the source of many of the obstacles to technological application.[52]

Most criminal justice practitioners realize that the system performs IT functions poorly primarily because each agency enters crime information repeatedly and separately from one another. Moreover, if information sharing were improved, all levels of the system could make better, more informed decisions.[53] As we look at various aspects of police technology, you will see examples of fragmentation and efforts to improve the information environment.

Chapter Summary

You should have an understanding of how this textbook was designed. The learning objectives, key terms, and discussion questions should assist you in determining if the learning experience was successful. Throughout the book, we will be looking primarily at information technologies because the primary function of a police officer usually involves information gathering. Moreover, we will look to see if information technology has tactical or strategic value—can it be used for immediate decision making or for long-term purposes, or both?

Points of view are generally helpful in understanding all the ramifications of a technology. We will ask ourselves, how does the line employee (whether sworn or nonsworn) view his technology? What are the issues for the supervisor or manager? We will also view technology against the backdrop of efficiency and effectiveness, community policing, situational crime prevention, and fragmentation. With every technology, we should ask if it makes us more efficient in our use of resources. Does it add to our goals, thereby making us more effective? How does it enhance our community policing? Does it add or detract from situational crime prevention? How has fragmentation affected it?

One of the most important things to carry from this chapter is the concept that by becoming more knowledgeable and educated, we can be better end users, supervisors, leaders, and street cops.

Discussion Questions

1. As you go about your daily activities, can you think of a situation wherein someone provided you with tactical information that required immediate action? Strategic information that you used to plan? Information that was both tactical and strategic?
2. This textbook is primarily concerned with information technology. Is information technology the primary technology you use? What other types do you use?
3. Efficiency and effectiveness are important considerations in all walks of life.

Can you describe a situation wherein someone was efficient yet ineffective? How about effective yet inefficient?

4. Of the core elements of the community policing model, which do you think is the most important? Why? Which is the least important? Why?

Key Terms

Call for Service

Community Policing

Effectiveness

Efficiency

End User

Fragmentation

Legacy System

Problem Solving

Self-Initiated Activity

Situational Crime
     Prevention

Stakeholder

Strategic Information

Sworn Employees

Tactical Information

End Notes

1. As of August 2003, the suspect, Timothy McGee, awaits trial for murder in Los Angeles, California.
2. Evolution and Development of Police Technology, 15.
3. Boyle, "Detective Case Management: How to Make It Work for Your Department."
4. Geisler, *Methodology, Theory, and Knowledge,* 127.
5. Bayley and Shearing, "The Future of Policing," 590.
6. Heffernan, "Fourth Amendment Privacy Interests."
7. Department of Justice, Bureau of Justice Statistics, 2000 State and Local Law Enforcement Statistics.
8. Ford, "Can You Keep What You've Got?"
9. Cresswell, et al., *"And Justice for All,"* 15.
10. Shafritz, *Public Policy and Administration,* 1220.
11. Staley, "Writing, Teaching, and Researching," 3.
12. See note 4 above.
13. Staley, "Writing, Teaching, and Researching," 4.
14. Cunningham, *B2B,* 179.
15. See note 7 above.
16. Enos, "Technology Mega-Deals."
17. See note 7 above.
18. See note 9 above.
19. Korsching, Hipple, and Abbott, *All the Right Connections,* 167.
20. Brown and Brudney, "A 'Smarter, Better, Faster, and Cheaper' Government."
21. Markowitz, "Legal Challenges and Market Rewards."
22. See note 20 above.
23. Kurke and Scrivner, *Police Psychology,* 83.
24. Jorgensen and Cable, "Facing the Challenges of E-Goverment."
25. Huey, "Policing the abstract."
26. California High Technology Crime Advisory Committee, "Annual Report on High Technology Crime in California," 34.
27. "The Evolution and Development of Police Technology," 65.
28. See note 7 above.
29. Blumstein, Young, and Granholm, "Development of Policy," 1.
30. Danziger and Andersen, "Information Technology," 591.
31. Dawes, et al., *IT Innovation in Government,* 6.
32. Shafritz, *Public Policy and Administration,* 1761.
33. Cresswell, *And Justice for All,* 62.
34. See note 31 above.
35. Coe and Wiesel, "Police Budgeting."

36. Department of Justice, Bureau of Justice Statistics, "Effects of the Redesign on Victimization Estimates," 2.

37. See note 35 above.

38. Shafritz, *Public Policy and Administration,* 2426.

39. Evolution and Development of Police Technology," 61.

40. See note 35 above.

41. Nunn, "Police Information Technology," 221.

42. During 2000, the BJS began conducting its ongoing Law Enforcement Management and Administrative Statistics (LEMAS) program. The statistical survey contains data from 13,000 local police agencies in the United States. The Bureau of Justice Statistics conducted similar LEMAS surveys in 1987, 1990, 1993, 1997, and 1999. The complete report is available at **www.ojp.usdoj.gov/bjs.**

43. See note 7 above.

44. See note 7 above.

45. Shafritz, *Public Policy and Administration,* 442.

46. Tonry, *Crime and Punishment,* 383.

47. Tonry, *Crime and Punishment,* 380.

48. Ibid.

49. Shafritz, *Public Policy and Administration,* 163.

50. See note 29 above.

51. Ibid.

52. "Evolution and Development of Police Technology," 13–14.

53. See note 29 above.

Chapter Two
Computer Basics

Learning Objectives

- The student will understand the basic hardware and software components of a **desktop personal computer** (PC).

- The student will understand the difference between **operating systems** and **applications** software.

- The student will understand the difference between **flat file** and **relational database**.

Introduction

In this chapter we are going to look at some basic computer operations and terminology. Our explanations will be deep enough to accomplish only two tasks: enable you to minimally operate a **desktop personal computer** and provide you with a foundation from which to explore other more complex technologies. To that end, some computer-related devices and concepts will be explored somewhat in depth. However, there are other devices, terms, and concepts that we may identify but not necessarily explore thoroughly. In the end, more than a mention would not serve our two primary purposes.[1]

Many of you probably have some, perhaps even extensive, experience with computers. If so, you may want to turn to the key terms at the end of this chapter. If you can define all of the terms and understand their purposes, you should probably advance to Chapter Three.

When you walk into a dark room, you probably turn on a light. When you turn on a light, you are completing a circuit, allowing electricity to flow through the circuit to a light bulb. When a light is on, electricity is present at the light bulb. Conversely, no light means the switch is open and no electricity is present at the bulb. At the very basic level, this is something like what is going on inside a computer.

As you know, our primary mathematical system is based on ten digits—0, 1, 2, 3, 4, 5, 6, 7, 8, 9. Our development of a ten-digit mathematical system is probably because we have eight fingers and two thumbs, or ten digits. Very early in the development of computing, there were attempts to construct computing devices on a ten-digit mathematical framework. Essentially, scientists and engineers during this early development period tried using multiple vacuum tubes with varying amounts of voltage to represent our ten-digit system. For a variety of reasons, this did not work out very well. An alternate to the ten-digit system has actually been around for a very long time. In 1679 Gottfried Wilhelm Leibniz described the binary number system and its operations in writing. Leibniz, who is also credited with inventing calculus, set in writing what would become the basis for all

A Look Ahead

In Chapter Ten when we look at the Internet, we will expand on the skills necessary to successfully navigate the Net. In the meantime, if you lack sufficient skills to navigate the Net, you might want to finish this chapter and then skip ahead to Chapter Ten.

computer programming. The binary number system is a mathematical counting scheme that has only two digits, zero (0) and one (1). These two digits are combined in various ways to ultimately represent our ten-digit counting scheme. This turned out to be the solution that eventually led to today's computer. Recall the light switch, on or off is the presence or absence of electricity. Today's computers use this off/on scheme to represent the **binary digits**, commonly referred to as **bits**, 1 and 0.[2]

Our computers hold information in a series of bits. Of course, reading binary digits would be difficult for human beings. Interestingly enough, it is difficult for our computers to translate binary bits into ten-digit-based information. However, it is relatively simple for computers to translate binary digits into a sixteen digit-based code called hexadecimal. Ultimately hexadecimal information is easier for human use than binary information. This coding system is a compromise between our abilities and the computer that allows us to **interface**.

The standard computer code configuration that works with computer bits is called the **American Standard Code for Information Interchange (ASCII)**. ASCII assigns characters, A through Z for instance, and converts them to an eight-digit code called a **byte**. So there are eight bits, or a series of eight ones and zeros, to a byte. Of course, computers deal with a tremendous amount of information. So we use terms in Figure 2.1 to describe the amount of information related to a computer operation. Note in the table that one kilobyte is 1,024 bits, but kilo means only 1,000. This is because one kilobyte is mathematically represented and as 2^{10}, which is 1,016 (two to the power of ten). But we round off to a thousand because it is simpler. Um, enough math.

The devices that make up a computer can be broken down into three essential broad categories of components: **Hardware**, **Software** and **Firmware**.[3]

Hardware

Essentially, hardware[4] can be defined as the physical components of a computer. Let's look at the outside first. A computer is a system, and like any system it has some basic characteristics, as shown in Figure 2.2. First, there is a way to put information into the system. The input is then manipulated, stored, or converted during throughput. The throughput produces output that provides the user with feedback on the throughput. The user then provides more input or feedback about the output. This is almost the perfect closed system but as we will see, not quite. In this system, the **user** is a human being like you or me. The input devices are the computer **keyboard**, **mouse**, and **microphone**. The **output devices** are the **monitor**, **speakers**, **printer**, and various storage media. These

Interface is one of those technological terms that are "in your face" a lot. Essentially, interface means to interact. When there is a systems interface, hardware or software are interacting in some manner through a shared boundary or control point. For people, you may hear the term "user interface." User interface is simply how we interact with the computer—the keyboard and mouse are user interface inputs, and the monitor is the computer's user interface output.
Sources: U.S. Congress, Office of Technology Assessment, "Electronic Surveillance," 72; Band and Katoh, *Interfaces on Trial*, 319.

Name	Abbreviation	Size in Bytes
Kilo	K	1,024
Mega	M	1,048,576
Giga	G	1,073,741,824
Tera	T	1,099,511,627,776
Peta	P	1,125,899,906,842,624
Exa	E	1,152,921,504,606,846,976
Zetta	Z	1,180,591,620,717,411,303,424
Yotta	Y	1,208,925,819,614,629,174,706,176

Figure 2.1 This table outlines the various descriptions of computer bits and bytes.

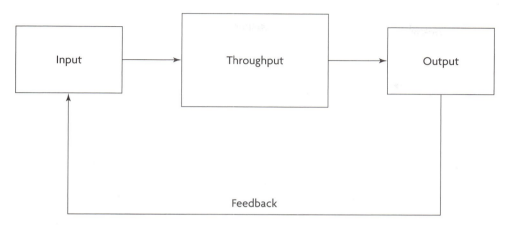

Figure 2.2 A basic closed system.

input/output devices are referred to as **peripheral devices**. Think of a peripheral device as any device not inside the computer case. They communicate with the main part of the computer (our systems throughput) using **ports**. On the back of a computer case you will see a variety of places where cables can be attached to the computer. These places are called ports.

The monitor is the device we use to visually display computer output. Computer monitors display small dots or units of color called a picture element, or

Figure 2.3 This photograph depicts a few typical desktop computer configurations.

pixel for short. Each pixel is assigned a value, which represents a certain color. The pixels are arranged in a horizontal and vertical grid called a raster. We interact with raster-based technology every time we view a computer monitor. The size of this raster matrix is determined by multiplying the number of rows by the number of columns on the monitor. A common setting for a monitor, or resolution, is 480 by 640. Multiply 480 by 640 and you have the number of pixels on the screen (307,200). Current technology in computer hardware can produce monitors that display more than two million pixels and several million color shadings.[5]

While the monitor provides us with a temporary visual representation of our efforts, the printer provides us a permanent, or hard copy, of that information. There are two common varieties of printers in use today: ink jet and laser. The final common output device is speakers. There are a wide variety of speakers whose purpose is to provide us with audio output, or sound. The sound could be music, voice, an alert tone, or some sort of sound effect. Indeed just about any sound you can think of can be emitted from the speakers. Also, most desktop personal computers have an internal speaker, which many users supplement with external speakers.

We put information into a computer through the keyboard, mouse, and microphone. At first glance, a computer keyboard looks much like a typewriter. It is fairly obvious that the computer keyboard concept evolved directly from a typewriter. However, your computer keyboard has a number of other keys, as shown in Figure 2.4. You will notice that in addition to numbers along the top of the keyboard (like a typewriter), there are the same numbers on the right side. These numbers are arranged in the same configuration as a basic calculator. If you push either the number one key along the top or the one on the right side, the computer will perceive your input as the number one. Because much of the information input into a computer is numerical, the configuration of the right-hand

Figure 2.4 This photo depicts a qwerty keyboard, which is used in countries with a Latin-based alphabet. Notice that the six letters on the top row spell QWERTY.

set of keys makes numerical input easier for a skilled user. Thus far, the keyboard has combined the features of both a typewriter and basic calculator.

Between the typewriter-like alphabet and the calculator-like numbers, you will see navigation keys. These keys allow users to move around on the computer screen. There are two other types of keys: control keys and special symbol keys. The control keys allow us to do certain fairly routine computer operations. The symbol keys were probably added for two reasons. First, certain symbols are inherent in the operation of a computer, such as backslash (\) and forward slash (/). Later we will explore more of these symbols. Second, language continues to evolve and keyboards with it. So some of the computer keys represent an evolution in our language since the development of the typewriter—specifically computer language. Now some keyboards have "jump" keys or buttons along the top. These allow for special navigation, particularly with respect to the Internet. While the keyboard is the primary source of user input, it has a helper called the mouse, two examples of which are shown in Figure 2.5.

When you move a mouse around, a corresponding indicator, generally an arrow, moves around on the monitor. This allows the user to point to things on the monitor. There are many varieties of the mouse. The two primary varieties differ in how they sense movement. One uses a roller ball and the other uses an optical sensor. Both of these sensing devices translate the user's movement of the mouse to an electrical signal that the computer recognizes as a movement of the arrow on the monitor. But all mice, in addition to allowing the user to point, allow the user to "click" on an object on the monitor. When the user clicks the mouse button, the mouse is signaling the computer that the user wants to do something with that object, such as open it or move it.

Figure 2.5 The mouse on the right is a typical roller ball mouse; the mouse on the left uses an optical sensor.

Microphones are primarily used to record or send voice signals on the computer. As computers continue to advance in their abilities, software and hardware programs that allow a user to give the verbal computer commands are becoming more common and reliable. This is generally referred to as **speech recognition**. The keyboard, mouse, and microphone are not the only types of input devices. In the text we will see that police employees are using other methods of input, such as stylus and touch screens. The primary reason for this has to do with the nature of field law enforcement. As we will see in later chapters, there are a variety of functions with which a computer could assist a field police officer. Of course it is impractical to bring a desktop computer into the field. The size and the somewhat delicate nature of the desktop make this impractical. We are concentrating on the desktop only as a means to ensure we understand some basic concepts. However, as demonstrated in Figure 2.6, we will eventually see that the laptop computer is currently the most widely used device for field operations, and the laptop computer has a great many similarities to our desktop.

As an input device, the keyboard is restricted in size by the size of the human hand. Past a certain point, our fingers would find input on a very small keyboard ineffective, if not impossible. There are three common methods around the size problem. One is to use a stylus to touch objects on the computer monitor, acting much like a mouse. The second is to touch a small modified keyboard with a stylus. Finally, one might use the stylus to write directly onto the computer screen. Personal digital assistants and notebook computers use a combination of these stylus approaches.

Figure 2.6 This photograph shows a typical laptop configuration in a police vehicle. *Photograph provided by Havis-Shield Corporation.*

In subsequent chapters we will see that some agencies are experimenting with integrating the computer components into the police vehicle.

Additionally, our final chapter will look at the use of handheld computer devices and their applications in law enforcement.

Most computer devices share the characteristics we have thus far looked at: input, computing, and output. But computers can also receive information in a few other ways, and they have the ability to store information. Computers can receive information, other than from the user, in two ways. First, the front of a desktop personal computer has one or more horizontal or vertical openings. These openings are for several types of media, including floppy disks, CD-ROMs and DVDs. Data can be obtained from these storage media and imported or copied to a personal computer. Or as in the instance of watching a movie on your computer monitor, the information is only viewed. Just as a computer can receive information in this manner, it can also store information to a variety of media. In addition to receiving information from the user and storage media, computers can receive information from other computers. This is done via a network. The most recognizable network is the Internet. In two later chapters we will look at networks and specifically the Internet. Moreover, network information can come to the computers through hard lines (like a standard telephone line) and in a wireless nature via radio signals. Both of these methods of accessing one computer through another computer have significant law enforcement applications. Again, later chapters cover this technology in some detail.

All of the computers that we are going to be interested in share these basic characteristics. They have an input, throughput (or computing), and output devices. We have looked at the components that are visible to the user, let's turn the computer around and look at a fairly typical system arrangement. Figure 2.7 is a view of the back of a desktop computer. A variety of cables are running into the computer. Generally, the computer, monitor, and printer each have their own power supply, while the keyboard and mouse obtain their power from the computer. In some instances, power is the electricity that is eventually going to become our series of ones and zeros, or binary data. There is usually a cable from each peripheral device to the computer. They enter the rear of the computer through a port and are one of three basic types: serial ports, parallel ports, and universal serial bus (USB) ports. Various types of ports are illustrated in Figure 2.7.

Ports and cables are referred to as either male or female. Male connectors have one or more small pins that slightly protrude for insertion into the female connector. Parallel ports are female ports that transmit binary data, eight bits at a time, in parallel. A serial port is a male connector used to transmit data as one long stream of information. Generally, parallel ports are used for printers, while serial ports are used for the mouse or a hardware link to a handheld device. Later as we look at other peripheral devices, we will identify the types of ports they use. For now it is enough to know that parallel ports transmit and receive data in parallel while serial ports complete a data transmission task in one long stream. A universal serial bus or USB port is fairly new. It is essentially an upgraded serial port. To use a USB, your computer and the peripheral device must support the USB technology. USB has four wires inside the cable, two for data transmission and two for power. So, like its cousin the serial port, it can exchange data with and provide power to a peripheral device. However, it has several additional advantages.

Figure 2.7 This photograph shows the various ports you find on the back of a desktop computer.

First, it is much easier to use a USB cable and port because they fit together with greater ease than either a parallel or serial port. Moreover, a USB can carry data faster than a serial port.

You will also typically find on the rear of the computer a telephone jack and speaker jack. These are designed to be similar to a standard telephone or stereo speaker connection in order to simplify interface between these devices. Figure 2.7 also shows **expansion slots** and an exhaust for the computer's internal fan. Expansion slots enable a user to add new internal components to a computer without changing the entire case. The exhaust opening allows the computer's internal fan to access the fresh air. The electrical components of a computer inside the case generate heat. Extreme heat and cold are bad for computers, especially heat. Later in the text we will see that compensating for temperature extremes is a major challenge in implementing technology into field operations.

Inside the Computer

We have reviewed the very basic external parts of the typical desktop computer. We are now going to turn our attention inside the computer and look at some hardware components that are found in nearly every modern computer. The systems board, or **motherboard**, is the brain of the computer. The motherboard, like any other circuit board, contains a series of microchips that are connected together by circuitry.[6] Circuits, like wires or cables, transmit electrical signals containing binary data between the various microchips. Computers are designed to store information electronically and the circuits in the computer can detect the presence or absence of electronic impulses.[7] We are going to look specifically at six items on the motherboard: the central processing unit, CMOS chip, flash bios, read-only memory (ROM), cache memory, random access memory (RAM), and expansion slots.

The motherboard contains three types of memory chips: the **central processing unit (CPU)**, the **read-only memory (ROM)**, and the **random access memory (RAM)**. The CPU is essentially the brain of the computer. The CPU—or as it is also called, the microprocessor—is present in all computer technology. Everything from cellular telephones to automobiles have small CPUs inside. It is also one of the features generally advertised in computer sales. When you see an advertisement for a Pentium 4™, they are advertising the qualities of the CPU.

The first CPU was produced in 1971, and it was the Intel 4004. At that time, all the Intel 4004 could do was add and subtract. A microprocessor is a very tiny, prefabricated silicon chip that contains thousands of transistors. Without going too far into it, a transistor is the most basic and essential part of today's microelectronics. The basic idea is fairly simple. Transistors are based on solid substances known as semiconductors. There is a large variation in the amount of electricity that can pass through an object. For instance, you have probably seen rubber gloves that electrical workers wear for protection. Rubber is a poor conductor of electricity; it won't conduct it or let it pass along its surface. Now as you probably know, metal is a good conductor, and certain types of metal are better. Transistors essentially control the flow, or amount of electricity.[8] Moreover, the transistor replaced the old-style vacuum tubes. For comparison's sake, in 1974 when the first home computer was introduced, there were six thousand transistors on the microprocessor. Today a Pentium 4™ chip has forty-two million transistors incorporated into it. Moreover, in the same period of time, the clock speed of the microprocessor has increased from 2 MHz to 1.5 GHz. Just as important, the MIPS, or millions of instructions per second, speed of the CPU has increased dramatically. While the CPU components perform some very complex functions, it has three core sets of instructions that it carries out: mathematical computations such as addition, subtraction, and division; moving data or information from one memory location to another; and making decisions and moving to a different set of instructions based upon those decisions.

The motherboard has two other sets of memory chips: random access memory (RAM) and read only memory (ROM).[9] The ROM chip contains what is known as BIOS, or basic input/output system instructions.[10] When your computer first starts, the microprocessor goes to the ROM chip. The ROM chip contains the basic set of instructions that are required to start the computer.[11] We will return to the computer startup procedure later in this chapter. The ROM chip's memory, or the set of instructions it contains, were installed during the manufacturing process. It is read-only memory because, generally speaking, the uninitiated user shouldn't attempt to modify it.

While both the ROM and the RAM chips are considered primary memory storage, ROM is nonvolatile memory, whereas RAM is volatile memory.[12]

RAM chips contain information only when your computer is on.[13] When you turn off the computer, the memory in the RAM disappears. On the other hand, as mentioned, ROM (BIOS instructions) are a permanent part of the chip.

The motherboard also contains a **complementary metal oxide semiconductor (CMOS)** configuration chip. The CMOS chip is responsible for remembering what hardware is in your computer. When you turn on your computer, it looks to the CMOS for instructions on how your computer is configured or setup. Like the ROM chip, CMOS is necessary for your computer to initially organize itself. But while the ROM information is rarely changed, CMOS information might change somewhat regularly. If you added a new drive, card, or peripheral device, your CMOS information, or the organization of your basic computer hardware, would change. Even though the CMOS might be updated, it still must be preset for startup. In order to get around the problem of the volatile nature of CMOS information (recall, volatile information is lost when your computer is shut off), the CMOS has its own small battery supplying it with constant power.

A computer motherboard also contains a system clock. The system clock makes sure that all the functions of the motherboard are completed in a properly timed sequence. The motherboard also contains expansion slots. These slots are for other circuit boards that allow the motherboard to interface with certain types of peripheral devices. For instance, the computer might have an internal modem. This modem would be one of the circuit boards or cards connected to the motherboard.

The last two components of the motherboard we are going to look at are the RAM and the **cache memory**. Recall that we discussed that computers could store information. This information is stored on hard drives within the computer or on removable media like a floppy disk or compact disc (CD). Later we will look more at drives, but for now consider that they are secondary nonvolatile storage. In other words, if you turn the computer off and come back in a month, any information you stored on a hard drive or external media should still be there. When your computer is actually working with or displaying information (as on the monitor) it has taken that information from the secondary nonvolatile storage and has placed it in the RAM or perhaps the cache. RAM contains information your computer is working with now, and cache memory essentially contains information your computer anticipates you might need.

A computer has this feature and components as a means to speed up information processing. Later as we discuss secondary information storage, we will find out that it has a mechanical aspect to it. Suffice to say that if your computer had to go to a secondary storage device for all information, it would be much slower, and you definitely wouldn't be able to play video games. Think of your brain consisting of secondary storage memories and random access memories. The human brain has features that are similar to the computer information secondary storage and random access memory. What did you lave for dinner last night? I hope you can remember. You always had information about last night's dinner in your brain, but you weren't thinking about it so it took longer to access that information. The computer works similarly. As soon as you ask a question about information that is in secondary storage (last night's dinner), your computer (or your brain) determines its location and brings it to the random access memory. So now you are thinking about last night's dinner, but as soon as you become further enchanted by this text, your thoughts of last night's dinner will recede to your secondary storage. Your computer is somewhat like that. While you are working with information, it is in RAM. But for RAM to be effective, it has to be somewhat limited in the amount of information in can contain. As soon as your computer determines that it is unlikely that you are going to use information in RAM, it disappears. This can also happen when you close down a program you are using. Say you finish working on the term paper in Underwater Basket Weaving 301 (obviously, an upper-division class). So you close your word processing program and start to play a video game. When you close out the word processor and begin to import the video game, RAM dumps the information on the term paper and gets the game, which probably hogs all the RAM.

We users work out of the computer RAM. Another feature of the RAM/cache chips that is similar to the human brain is that in addition to retrieving from secondary storage the information you are working with, it makes assumptions about what information you might need. Think about driving your car. While you're driving, all the information needed to drive the car is enough to keep the car at a constant speed and in your lane. Your brain is programmed to put other information into the "cache" for immediate retrieval. Perhaps the brain knows that you should have defensive driving techniques in cache and available for immediate use. That way, when the moron in the next lane tries to change lanes into you, the information necessary to avoid the collision is not delayed by the physical properties of secondary storage. So RAM is the memory you are working with right now, and cache is what you might need based upon certain programming.

Now this is a huge simplification, but it is an accurate description of what is going on. Your computer and your brain have one other RAM/cache similarity. What did you have for dinner? Probably you had to think about it again, but the information came a little quicker. Depending on a lot of factors, your brain might have sent the information to cache because it wasn't using it right then. This happens because like you and me, a computer can only work with so much information at one time. Whatever it doesn't need now, it keeps in secondary storage. The next time you see a video game for computers, look at the system specifications. A certain amount of RAM is needed because for the complex graphics to work, your computer needs the information readily available; it must be in cache or RAM.

So far we have looked at six of the features of a motherboard or central processing unit. The final feature of a motherboard that we should discuss for our purposes is the **bus**. Simply put, a bus contains the electrical pathways and directions for use of those pathways that the information uses while inside a computer. If you looked at a circuit board, you would see small metal tracings in the circuit board. These take the place of wires to conduct electricity. The bus is these traces and the instructions for their use. A bus has a range or size that indicates the number of binary digits that can travel simultaneously along a path. Think of a public bus. Say the bus had a RAM of four bits (none do!), which would mean four binary digits could travel side-by-side—like seats in a bus. Today typical bus ratings are 16 bits, 32 bits, and 64 bits. So if the public bus were a good representation, it would have 16, 32, or 64 seats across. Note that bus sizes are multiples of eight, and recall that there are eight bits (binary digits) to the byte.

While the motherboard is a very cool invention, it would be useless if the information couldn't get to you or other users in a way you could understand the information. Thus far, we have seen that the input comes from the keyboard and that the motherboard is essentially the throughput of the system. But on the way back out, the information may pass across a bridge, such as a network interface card, Ethernet card, or video card, on the way to the output device. In Chapter Four these devices will be explained.

Long-Term Information Storage Hardware

On the motherboard we looked at what is considered primary data storage. And with the exception of the ROM chip, we discovered that the information on the motherboard was volatile; that is, when we shut off the computer, the information is lost. Whenever we want information to be kept, even if the system loses power or is shut off, we must transfer that information to long-term, nonvolatile storage. There are five common methods of long-term or secondary storage: **hard disks**, **zip disks**, **floppy disks**, **cassette tapes**, **CD-ROMs** and **DVDs**.

The hard disk is more commonly referred to as the hard drive. Figure 2.8 is a hard drive with the cover removed. As was mentioned earlier, a hard drive has a mechanical aspect to it. By mechanical, I mean a moving part. The hard drive consists of a disk that spins at a very high rate of speed and an arm that can reach across the disk. At a simple level, it looks and operates much like a record player, at least mechanically. As the disk spins, the arm has a head on the end of it that allows it to read and write information. We are not going to explore how the hard drive reads and writes the information. However, unlike the record needle, which touches the record, the head of the hard drive does not touch the disk. In fact, if the head comes into contact with the disk, the hard drive can be damaged. This is why computers should not be bumped or moved while they are on. Today's hard drives also contain their own circuit board, microchips, and software that control the operation of the mechanical arm, head, and disk. Naturally, this circuit board is called a controller. Hard drives come in a variety of sizes, but today it is uncommon to find one smaller than twenty gigabytes. The size refers to the amount of binary data (bits) the hard drive can retain. Using the table on page 000, we know a 20 GB hard drive would retain 21,474,836,480 bits. A computer can have more than one hard drive. In this chapter we will talk a little more about

Figure 2.8 This is a photograph of a typical hard drive that would be inside a desktop PC. While there are five fairly common methods of storage, new methods of data storage like USB storage and optical storage are being introduced and becoming more common.

multiple hard drives and in later chapters examine computers whose internal workings consist of multiple hard drives linked together in sequence.

The next type of secondary storage for information is the floppy disk. A hard disk or hard drive is a sealed, nonremovable device in the computer. The floppy disk and its floppy drive work just as the hard drive, except the disk can be removed. A floppy disk is inserted into a slot on the front of the computer. That slot leads to a mechanical device that spins the disk and has an arm with a read/write head and its own circuit board as a controller. Once the disk is inserted, it acts much like the hard drive. Floppy disks come in two sizes, $5^1/4$ inch and $3^1/2$ inch. You don't see the $5^1/4''$ disk much anymore. But if you found one, you would see that it is "floppy." If you waived it rapidly in your hand, you would see that it is somewhat bendable, and seems to "flop" back and forth. The more common disk, a $3^1/2''$, is in a hard plastic case and is not bendable. Of course, the $5^1/4''$ came first, giving it and its little brother, the $3^1/2''$ disk, the name "floppy." A $3^1/2''$ disk can retain 1.44 megabytes, which is much less than a hard drive, but significantly more than the older $5^1/4''$, which could hold only 360 kilobytes. The main advantage of a floppy disk is its portability. For instance, in the writing of this book, rough notes were given to an assistant for typing. Then the notes were saved to a floppy disk and were given to me. I could then merge notes and edits into the master copy of the text on the hard drive. So the notes could be typed on any computer and the information could be accessed on any other computer. A second, and sometimes huge, advantage to floppy drives is the ability to store information outside and away from your computer. These are commonly referred to as backup copies. So if your computer is damaged, fails, is corrupted, or is stolen, your information, on a backup floppy, is safe (assuming you didn't leave the disk in the computer!). Later in the text when we look at the management of huge databases, we'll see the need to back up and secure information is critical. However, the principles are very similar on a small scale; perhaps a video game crashes your computer and you lose the term paper on underwater basket weaving you didn't back up.

A zip disk or drive is like a very large floppy. It has similar characteristics to the operation of your hard and floppy drives. The zip drive contains the arm, head, and spinning capacity along with a controller. Some computers have a zip drive internally installed. The front of these computers would have a slot to insert a zip disk. Another configuration, is to have the zip drive outside the case as a peripheral device. It has the safety and convenience of a floppy disk, but the capacity to retain substantially more information. Where the $5^1/4''$ floppy could retain 360 kilobytes and the $3^1/2''$ floppy 1.44 megabytes, the zip disk is available in styles that can retain 250 megabytes.

Cassette tapes and tape drives are usually used to make a backup copy of an entire system or a large database. Generally, you will not see cassette tape systems on most consumer and business desktop personal computers. Moreover, tape systems work substantially different than disk systems. A disk system that spins and has a moveable arm is able to access data anywhere on the disk. Later in this chapter when we look at how disks are organized, this will become clearer. A tape system, however, is recorded and accessed in sequence. This means that in order to obtain information from anywhere on the tape, you must start at the beginning. Think of the difference between watching a movie on a DVD player and a VCR. If you want to watch a certain scene on a VCR, you must fast forward to that scene. However, most commercially produced movies on DVD have the ability to jump straight to the scene. So the information on the video tape, like the cassette tape backup, is strictly sequential. You must go past the parts you don't

You can have an external floppy disk drive that connects through a USB port. This is a common arrangement with laptop computers.

want to get to what you do want. However, when backing up huge amounts of information, a cassette tape with a 4.0 GB volume is an option. Later in the text when we examine large systems, the tape will have a place.

Increasingly, the most common type of information storage is the compact disc-read-only memory, or CD-ROM. Compact discs are so inexpensive and easy to use that a wide variety of companies send CDs by the millions to prospective new users of their products. In addition to being very common for computers, they are just as common as a medium to purchase commercial music. Because CDs are becoming so common, we will spend a little extra time on their construction. A CD is 12 centimeters (4.8 inches) in diameter and has a capacity to hold 793 megabytes of data, which is 783,216,000 binary digits in each CD.

The process of manufacturing a CD involves impressing microscopic bumps on 1.2 mm–thick piece of plastic. The bumps are arranged in single lines beginning in the center of the CD and spiraling outward. The bumps on a single CD are so small that if they were stretched end-to-end, they would reach more than three and a half miles. After the bumps are impressed on the plastic, the CD is coated with an aluminum acrylic substance. Once data is written to the CD, the bumps are recognized as binary data, ones and zeros.

Like our other drives, the CD spins around in the slot on the computer, but it does not have the mechanical arm and head. It has a sophisticated tracking device that keeps a small sensor focused on the appropriate portion of the CD. Essentially, the bumps in the CD reflect light differently than the smooth area between the bumps. The bumps on a CD are referred to as lands. A sensor detects changes in the reflection of light from the CD. Ultimately, these changes in reflection are translated into binary data and then, by the computer, into information for the user. Although a CD can hold significantly more information than a floppy disk or a zip disk, data on a CD is difficult to overwrite. In other words, once you have recorded that data, it is difficult to change.

The final secondary data storage that we will discuss is DVDs. Most people are familiar with playing a DVD in order to watch a movie, and more and more desktop personal computers contain a DVD drive. However, DVDs were primarily for reading or viewing the information. Very recently devices to enable a home/business desktop computer to write information to a DVD were introduced. A digital versatile disc, or DVD, can hold seven times more information than a CD. Indeed a double-sided, double-layered DVD can hold up to 15.8 GB of information—that is larger than some personal computer hard drives.

While DVD technology is similar to CD technology, there are big differences in data capacity. First, the medium used to record binary data onto CDs and DVDs is the same; except the bumps or pits are considerably smaller. But the DVD technology does not stop there. CDs are single-sided; information is only recorded and accessed on one side. But a DVD can contain information on both sides. Moreover, the manufacturing process for the DVD allows for information to be layered on both sides. Essentially, there can be an upper and lower information level on each side of the DVD. So, since the bumps that represent the information are smaller, the DVD is said to have a higher density for data storage, and the DVD has up to four "sides" of information if you use both layers on both sides.

The way in which information is encoded on a DVD is different from a CD. Compact discs have an error correction code that is used to protect the information and ensure data is properly transmitted from the CD to the computer. On the other hand, DVD technology uses a different, more up-to-date method for error protection. Simply put, the DVD error correction scheme uses less disc space than the CD, allowing for more real information.

The methods of data storage, primary and secondary, that we have reviewed are not the only means that a user can use to access and store information. Sometimes, especially in field police work, information is accessed from some type of secondary (nonvolatile) storage that is remote to the user's computer. As we shall see in the subsequent chapters on data communications, external systems, and networks, there is a huge amount of information available—if you're connected and know where to look.

Software

As we have seen, hardware consists of the physical components of the computer. Some of the hardware, like the keyboard and monitor, is visible to the user. Some of the hardware, like the motherboard, is not generally visible to the user. The hardware we have explored is as reliable as it is sophisticated. But without instructions on what to do when, hardware does not work. The instructions that tell hardware what to do are called software.[14]

There are two broad classifications of software: **operating systems** and **applications**.[15] Software is a set of instructions, written in a language that the computer can understand. Operating systems software (also called the **platform**[16]) tells the computer what to do; applications software allows the user to work with information in the computer. The operating system is the computer software that controls and coordinates the interaction among the hardware elements and between the hardware and the application programs.[17] All computers have operating system software embedded on the ROM chip. Applications are specific programs that allow the user to do specific tasks such as word processing. As we look at software, this difference between operating systems and applications will become much clearer.[18]

When you look at a computer that is turned off, the information on the hard drive is sitting there like a music CD on a shelf. With a music CD, the CD must be put into the player so that the music can be heard, but the music is always there in the form of binary data. So it is with the information on your hard drive. But your computer needs instructions on what data from the hard drive you want to work with. Recall that the data from the hard drive must be put into the RAM and the cache. As we know, the RAM and cache are volatile primary storage—when the power is turned off, the data is lost. In addition to your hard drive needing to know what you want, the peripheral devices—your monitor, keyboard, and mouse—need instructions from your computer. This is where the CMOS and the ROM come into play.

The CMOS chip, with its own small battery, continually holds the information on the configuration of your computer. It knows your ports, memory, keyboard, monitor, etc. When you turn on the computer, the startup process is called "booting." When a computer is booted from the power-off condition, it is called a "hard boot." However, if you push the reset button on your computer, you are performing a "soft boot."

While the CMOS knows where everything should be, including your operating system, the ROM contains a set of permanent instructions known as the basic input/output system, or BIOS. The ROM chip is sometimes referred to as the ROM BIOS or Flash BIOS. As your computer starts, the ROM BIOS reads the CMOS information and begins the process of obtaining your operating system from the hard drive and importing it to the RAM and cache. We know that the information on the ROM chip is embedded at the manufacture—this is what allows it to begin the booting process and the power-on self test. So far, we have looked at hardware and are beginning to look at software. ROM chips are a hybrid of both. It is hardware, a physical component, with embedded software. Because it shares the characteristics of both hardware and software, ROM chips are sometimes referred to as **firmware**.[19]

Now, there is a lot of other stuff going on. For instance, your peripheral devices are being assigned addresses in the computer. And it is more complex because certain other device drivers and interface cards have their own BIOS instructions, etc. But we are going to stop at this depth. The information we have looked at thus far will serve us well later when we look at police technology.

There are a variety of operating systems like Macintosh for Apple computers, UNIX, OS/2, and a variety of Windows versions. For the moment, we are going to concentrate on using a DOS-based operating system because that seems to be the prevalent operating system for which police employees are the end users. Later in the text, other operating systems will be looked at in conjunction with larger network systems.

When a human being is using a computer, he is said to be interfacing. A user interfaces with a disk operating system (DOS) in one of three ways: a command-driven interface, a menu-driven interface, or an icon-driven interface. Most police employees work with an icon-driven interface that is also called a **graphical user interface (GUI)**.[20] For our purposes, we will look at a Windows XP icon-driven interface to explore some of the different uses of a computer. MS-DOS-based Windows systems are the most widely used in the United States.[21]

After your computer has booted and hands your computer over to the operating system, your operating system has two primary jobs. First, it manages the hardware and software of your computer. In addition to making sure the hardware and software work together, your operating system manages the competitive software and devices as they all try to use the CPU. The operating system's job as the manager is to make sure that every part does its job in the right sequence and that one part doesn't inadvertently crowd out another part. The second job is to provide application program interface (API). One of the things that makes computers so useful is the ability to add to them. We can add memory; we can add different peripherals like printers, monitors, and speakers; and we can run a huge number of application programs from word processing to video games. All of these different hardware and software products are produced by different companies. If the operating system does not provide API, which is essentially "the ability to work well with others," then we would have a difficult time using hardware and software from different companies.

After your computer boots up, the monitor will show you what is called the desktop screen. The desktop opening screen of Windows XP is shown in Figure 2.9. At the bottom of the desktop, you will find a taskbar. Generally, on the left-hand side of the taskbar, you will see the word "start." On the right-hand side, you will see the time and perhaps a few icons. On the main portion of the desktop there are small icons, called shortcuts. Now the screen has a background that can be adjusted by the user to suit the individual's taste. Finally, you will see a small white arrow. By moving the mouse around, the arrow makes corresponding movements.

Your Windows operating system is controlling what you see on the screen and how you interface with your various programs. A Windows operating system works with files. Think of a room with five filing cabinets in it. Each of the filing cabinets is a location to store a file. Your hard drive, floppy drive, zip drive, CD-ROM drive, and DVD drive are the five filing cabinets in your computer. Each of them has files in them. Your hard drive most likely contains all of your program files. These are the program applications that allow you to write a term paper, forecast trends from statistical data, surf the Internet, and play games. Your operating

Figure 2.9 The desktop opening screen on Windows XP.

system allows to you go to the filing cabinet (the hard drive) and open a specific file (a word processor). If you are going to work with a document that has been stored outside the hard drive, you open that file while in your program, but the operating system is facilitating this. Later in the text when we look at networked systems and external sources of information, you can think of files contained on those systems as being in rooms or filing cabinets in another building.

With respect to applications, there are several terms that are going to come up quite frequently. An **algorithm** is a set of instructions that tells a computer what to do. When you use the calculator on the computer to balance your check book, you are using a computation algorithm. Someone programmed the algorithm to perform a set of instructions every time you asked the calculator to multiply two times two so the answer would be four. As you can see, an algorithm is a step-by-step set of instructions for performing a specific task.

Databases

A **database** is a collection of organized information that is centrally located and designed to meet the needs of users.[22] It is organized so that we can ask questions about the information. A database on drivers' licenses would enable us to ask questions like the number of men over eighty who have a valid license. We might also ask the same database to identify a certain record. For instance, recall our traffic violator from Chapter One. The police officer in the field could check the database on drivers' licenses in order to determine if the violator's license were valid.

There are essentially two classifications of databases. The first is the flat file, which is a long string of text information called a **tab-delimited file**. If the driver's license information were in a flat file, each piece of information about the

Let's say you were going to write an algorithm for going to the grocery store. It might look something like this:

1. Check groceries in the house.
2. Determine what is missing.
3. Make list of what is missing.
4. Get check book and car keys.
   a. Insert subalgorithm for driving.
   b. Insert subalgorithm for directions to grocery store.

person issued the license would be separated by a special character in that file. The flat file might look something like that shown in Figure 2.11. If we wanted to search a flat file, we would have to search the information sequentially. Recall how cassette taped information is searched—from beginning to end. The second type of database is a **relational database**.[23]

In a relational database, the information is entered into tables that are organized by rows and columns. In the relational database table each row is a set of columns with only one set of values. The rows are the record that has been

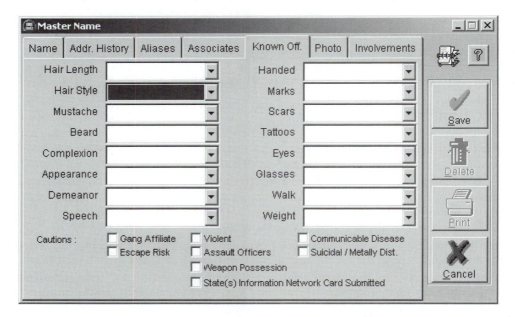

Figure 2.10 Many state and local police agencies use software that allows them configure data entries to match their specific data dictionary. Through the use of **forced-choice formats**, GUI software restricts data entries to previously determined attributes (properties or characteristics). For instance, color is an attribute of hair. In a forced-choice format configuration, the person completing the data entry would use a pull-down menu to choose the attribute that most closely matched the observation. The use of forced-choice formats speeds data entry and standardizes the internal database. However, in many instances the fragmentation of technological development has caused even adjoining or overlapping jurisdictions to choose different attributes. In Chapter Eleven we will take a closer look at the problems of information exchange and some potential solutions. For now, take a close look at this screen capture. If you were going to determine the attributes for the pull-down menu, what would you choose? Handed seems fairly obvious—either right or left. Would you include ambidextrous? What attributes would you assign to Hair Length? How about Complexion?
Permission for screen capture provided by Crimestar Corporation.

Flat File Structure

License No.	Last Name	First Name	Date of Birth	Address
N546987;	Smith;	John;	01-01-59;	123 Maple Avenue, Anytown
N546988;	Jones;	Mary;	02-15-72;	546 Main Street, Anytown
N546989;	Mallory;	Robert;	03-15-67;	1875 1st Street, Anytown

Note: To search for any data, the driver's license number must be known.

Figure 2.11   If driver's license records were kept in a flat file, they would look something like this.

entered into the database. Now, we can search this type of database by just the field identifiers, or columns, and we can begin to compare information within the fields. In the flat file scheme, asking the number of men over eighty with licenses is problematic. In the relational database, it is relatively simple.

In law enforcement we are working with huge databases. In subsequent chapters we will explore relational database management systems (RDBMS) further.[24] Although we are not becoming programmers, it is important to know that one of the most common ways of programming this information is called structured query language (SQL). We will see in future chapters that the use of SQL may be key to web-based solutions aimed at enabling law enforcement agencies to exchange information.[25]

Of course, a database contains data. One of the most important parts of a database is how the information is classified or defined. When deciding how to define information, we are said to be creating a data dictionary, or a file that defines the basic organization of a database. The data dictionary must contain a list of all the files, the number of records in each file, and most important, the names and types of files.[26]

Other Computer Configurations and Necessary Concepts

In this chapter we have concentrated on the personal computer (PC), which is defined as a general purpose device designed for a single user. There are several versions of the PC: the desktop, a nonportable version; the laptop, a portable version of the PC; and the handheld device, or palmtop. We will look at each of those variations later in the text. In addition to those types of computers, there are workstations, which are essentially high-powered PCs designed for a specific task. When we look at communications dispatch centers, we will look at several workstation designs. In Chapter Four we will look at the computer configuration known as a server. Two types of computers we really won't be exploring are mainframes, a term that is rapidly being overtaken by the term enterprise server, and supercomputers. Supercomputers can cost millions of dollars and are used for very specific, high-intensity, mathematical problems, such as finding prime numbers. Lastly, you probably are wearing or carrying a computer. If you have a watch, cellular telephone, or calculator, you are carrying a microprocessor.

There are some computer-related terms in the text that you are going to come across that we can define for you now. Moreover, as you talk to people who are heavily involved in IT, you will find they have their own language. It is almost like a secret handshake; if you know what they are talking about, they may actually switch back to English for you. Part of our job is to find those mystic terms and put them in some sort of context so that you can translate tech into English. For instance, "multimedia term" is used to describe different forms of media being used

In Chapter Four, Network Communications, we will be looking at quite a few computer-related devices such as modems, servers, and middleware.

Recall from the last chapter we learned that legacy systems are older hardware/software systems that are still being used by an organization. It is also important to know that most legacy systems are proprietary. Proprietary means that the system (either hardware, software, or both) manufacturer will not reveal the systems specifications so that other firms may not duplicate the product. This is also known as a closed architecture. Alternately, some companies produce products that are considered open architecture. In essence, these allow for peripheral devices and programs produced by other manufacturers to work with their product. Just remember, if the system is a closed architecture, other manufacturers can't get it. This concept of open versus closed architectures will become very important in subsequent chapters.

by any particular application. Multimedia applications can include graphics, animation, sound, and video elements.[27] So if someone tries to sell you a multimedia program, you know the computer output is going to be more than text on a monitor. Then there is the ever-popular technical term "scalable." A scalable system is one that can be adapted and expanded to meet increased needs.[28] If something is scalable, it has the ability to have new hardware or software installed to meet your growing abilities, tasks, or even a growing workforce. Indeed, one of the keys to the successful implementation of an IT project is to start as small as possible with a scalable system. You can always get bigger if it works. One of the very popular peripheral devices we didn't look at is a document scanner.[29] After a document scanner captures an image, it is stored and can be manipulated by different software. In Chapter Six, we will look at the actual process of scanning because it is important to the growing field of automated fingerprint identification.

Chapter Summary

As you look around you there are many devices that you probably use everyday that contain a microprocessor, the heart of a computer system. It is very important that you understand the concept of binary language as we proceed through subsequent chapters. Binary code plays a big part in the development of police technology. We looked at the basic forms of software—operating systems and applications. This led us to a discussion on the storage of information. We found that most storage is considered nonvolatile, after it has been saved to the selected medium. Data can be stored in two basic types of databases: flat file or relational. As we proceed to explore police technology, relational databases are going to play a huge part.

Key Terms

Algorithm
American Standard Code for Information Interchange (ASCII)
Applications
Binary Digit or Bit
Bus
Byte
Cache Memory
Cassette Tapes
CD-ROM
Central Processing Unit (CPU)

Complementary Metal Oxide Semiconductor (CMOS)
Database
Desktop Personal Computer
DVD
Expansion Slot
Firmware
Flat file
Floppy Disks
Forced-choice formats
Graphical User Interface (GUI)

Hard Disks or Hard Drives
Hardware
Interface
Keyboard
Microphone
Monitor
Motherboard (or Systems Board)
Mouse
Operating Systems
Output Devices
Peripheral Devices
Pixel

Platform
Port
Printer
Random Access Memory
   (RAM)

Read-Only Memory
   (ROM)
Relational Database
Software
Speakers

Speech Recognition
Tab-Delimited File
User
Zip Disk

End Notes

1. For those of you desiring an in-depth look qt personal computers, I recommend Peter Norton's *Inside the PC.*
2. Imel and Hart, *Understanding Wireless Communications,* 34, 113.
3. Band and Katoh, *Interfaces on Trial,* 3.
4. "Toward Improved Criminal Justice."
5. Bair, Sean, et al., "Advanced Crime Mapping," 52.
6. Laidler, *To Light Such a Candle,* 230.
7. Imel and Hart, *Understanding Wireless Communications,* 34.
8. Laidler, *To Light Such a Candle,* 225.
9. Cunningham, *B2B,* 182.
10. See note 3 above.
11. See note 4 above.
12. Band and Katoh, *Interfaces on Trial,* 4.
13. Ibid., 3.
14. Ibid., 4.
15. Ibid., 5.
16. See note 4 above.
17. Band and Katoh, *Interfaces on Trial,* 2.
18. Ibid., 4.
19. Ibid.
20. See note 4 above.
21. See note 17 above.
22. Judd, "Database Management and GIS," 1.
23. See note 4 above.
24. Judd, "Database Management and GIS," 2.
25. See note 4 above.
26. Ibid.
27. Cunningham, *B2B,* 180.
28. See note 4 above.
29. Wood, "GIS Terminology," 1.

Chapter Three
Wireless Communications

Learning Objectives

- The student will understand basic radio wave theory including radio waves and frequencies.

- The student will understand the difference between **analog** and **digital** communications and the basic parts of radio frequency communications.

- The student will understand how digital communications are possible through a variety of schemes; including **Time Division Multiple Access (TDMA), Frequency Division Multiple Access (FDMA), Code Division Multiple Access (CDMA),** and **Cellular Digit Packet Data (CDPD).**

- The student will understand how the cellular telephone system works and its application to law enforcement.

Why Study Radio Communications?

The older white Cadillac sped recklessly through the city streets. Behind it, a trail of red and blue police followed. From the vantage point of the helicopter, it was a unique visual experience. Probably unknowingly, the four robbery suspects careened into another police jurisdiction, off the major boulevard and into residential streets. The driver of the Cadillac seemed to know where he was going, until he turned into a dead-end. Out the robbers jumped, fleeing in separate directions; even from the helicopter, one could see two of them were running with handguns. The helicopter focused on one suspect in particular. He ran into the rear yard of a house and crouched near a brick wall. With the gun in hand, the suspect looked alternately back the way he had come and up at the helicopter. The brick wall separated the yard of the house from another street. As the helicopter orbited tighter and tighter around the armed man, the police inside saw disaster in the making.

On the street side of the brick wall, a lone officer from the other jurisdiction stopped and exited his police car. Neither the helicopter, nor the officer from the other jurisdiction had radios that were compatible with each other. There was no way for the helicopter to tell the officer that he was a few feet from a deadly possibility. The lone officer was fortunate, just as he was about to peer over the brick wall, the suspect surrendered. This is one of many consequences of a failure in radio communication. In this instance, incompatible systems nearly had disastrous consequences.

For line employees, understanding the problems and limitations of the radio system their agency uses can save their lives. For the police manager, an understanding of radio communications can help her make better decisions about implementation and improvements. Finally, an understanding of radio communications will ease our exploration of information technologies reliant on this medium of transmission. In this chapter we will review some basic radio theory and radio equipment that makes radio broadcasts possible. You will see that there are two basic forms of radio wave communications—**analog** and **digital**. From there we will examine how analog and digital communications schemes work, their benefits and their limitations. This chapter will also introduce the concept

Recall in Chapter One we talked about fragmentation and its consequences. This chapter is an introduction to the basics that will provide us a foundation to explore solutions in Chapter Eleven.

of a public safety organization owning its radio communications infrastructure or buying the service from a private industry source.[1]

Electronic Information

This chapter is about how electronic information is transmitted from point to point. As with Chapter Two, some of this information is fairly technical. We will be adding to the technical information you learned in Chapter Two. There are two medias for the transmission of electronic information. The information can be transmitted over a wire, like most telephone conversations, or it can be wireless, transmitted through the atmosphere, like the signals your car radio receives. As we shall see, there are many instances where both media are necessary to complete the information exchange. Consider your home. Do you have a cordless telephone? The handset of a cordless telephone transmits wireless information to a base station in your home. At the base station, the information is processed and sent along its way over telephone lines. Actually, this is a fairly common configuration.

Wireless communication has an advantage over hardwired communication in that wireless can be broadcast over a wide area and to a large number of users. Because wireless communication uses radio frequencies, it is often referred to as RF communication.

Electronic information can be either a voice or data communication. A conversation between you and a friend over the telephone is a voice communication. When you are listening to the traffic report on your car radio, you are receiving a voice communication. An example of data communication would be your use of the Internet. Of course, you can receive voice communication over the Internet, but typically, as when you access your e-mail, you are receiving a data communication.

Voice and data communications can be transmitted as either an analog signal or digital signal. However, voice is typically an analog signal. An analog signal, shown in Figure 3.1, is one that varies between the values -10 volts and $+10$ volts.[2]

Figure 3.1 An analog signal.

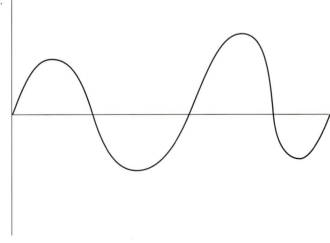

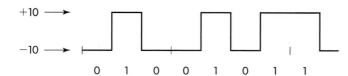

+10 ⟶

−10 ⟶

0　1　0　0　1　0　1　1

Figure 3.2 A digital signal. If you could hear a digital signal, it would sound like a radio clicking off and on.

A digital signal, shown in Figure 3.2, returns us to the binary digits of Chapter 2. Recall binary digits "1" and "0" are the presence and absence of an electronic signal. Digital signals are either off or on, and by combining the off/on or "1" and "0" we can build up the binary code necessary for communication.

A typical analog radio system consists of a microphone that modulates (changes) the human voice to an analog wave, which is processed and sent to an antenna for transmission.[3] The return signal is passed through the **antenna** to a receiver, processed, and broadcast out a speaker, as in Figure 3.3.[4]

An analog radio system can carry digital signals, but first the digital signal must be converted from its analog configuration to a digital configuration. This is accomplished by a modulater-demodulater unit, or **modem**. Generally, for this transmission scheme to work, both the sender and receiver must have a modem.[5] The differences between analog and digital schemes of transmission have some important considerations for the field and management. As you move farther away from the antenna that is broadcasting an analog signal, the signal becomes weaker. Ultimately, the strength of the signal is lost in background static, and the transmission cannot be heard. On the other hand, a digital signal can be broadcast only up to a certain distance.[6] Once that distance is reached, the signal for transmission is effectively gone (Figure 3.4). If we were going to design, upgrade, or simply try to understand a public radio system, the choice of digital or analog communication would impact all subsequent equipment, maintenance, and training decisions.[5]

We know that there are two modes of data transmission: digital and analog. We must also understand that either the digital or analog signal is carried by the fundamental building block of wireless communication—**radio waves**.[6] Like light and sound, radio signals travel in waves. (Light has particle characteristics, too, and in Chapter Fifteen we will look at a technology that takes advantage of those.) If you throw a stone in a pond, small ripples or tiny waves visibly emanate from the stone's point of impact. The pond ripples are different from radio waves in two ways. One, you obviously cannot see radio waves; they are invisible to us. Two, pond waves or ripples tend to get farther apart from each other as they distance themselves from the point of impact. Radio waves do not; they stay constant. This is very important because that characteristic of the radio wave gives us insight into its capabilities.

A radio wave is measured from one peak to the next, or from one valley to the next (Figure 3.5). The drawing of a radio wave represents how we would measure

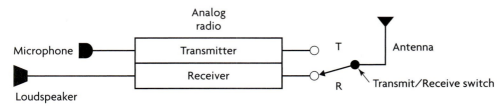

Figure 3.3 A simple radio system.

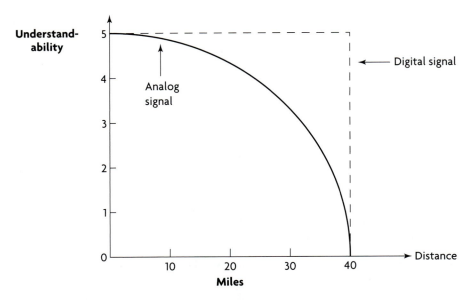

Figure 3.4 Analog versus digital signal performance.

a radio wave in order to determine its wavelength. So if someone told you that a radio signal had a short wavelength, you would know that the distance between either the peaks or the valleys (both measurements are the same) is relatively short. Conversely, if someone told you that a radio wave had a long wavelength, you would know that the measurement between the peaks or the valleys is relatively long. As you look at the radio wave drawing you should notice that the wavelength pattern repeats and that unlike the ripples in a pond, the wave stays constant. A constant pattern, measured through one peak and one valley is known as a **cycle**. The number of cycles occurring each second is called the **frequency**. Essentially, this is how frequent the pattern, or cycle, occurs each second. If you search your car radio for a specific radio station or song, each time you change the station, you change frequency.[7]

Frequency is measured in units called **Hertz** (Hz).[8] Recall that in Chapter 2 when we first examined binary data or bits, we found out that because the numbers of bits used were so large, we used the measurement prefixes kilo, mega, giga, etc. The same thing is done with radio frequencies because the number of

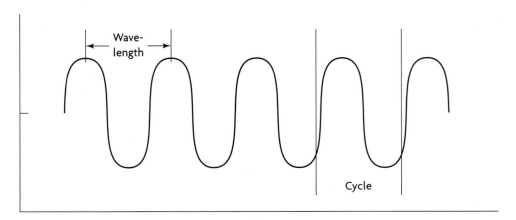

Figure 3.5 Measuring Radio Waves

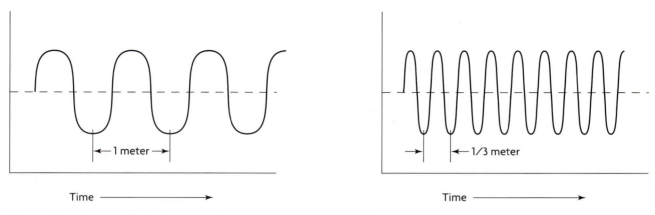

Figure 3.6 Wavelength and frequency are inversely related: the higher the frequency, the shorter the wavelength.

cycles per second can be in the billions. So a frequency of one thousand cycles per second would be a kilohertz (kHz); one million cycles per second would be a megahertz (MHz); and one billion cycles per second would be a gigahertz (GHz). If someone told you a radio station broadcast on a frequency of 800 MHz, you would know that the frequency had a pattern on 800 million cycles per second. Another way to firm up your understanding is to return to your car radio. The AM radio stations generally transmit in the megahertz range. So if you tune in 640, that station is transmitting at 640 megahertz, or 640 million cycles per second.

Recall that wavelength is the measurement between peaks and valleys, and that frequency is the measurement of the number of cycles per second. These two measurements are inversely related, as shown in Figure 3.6. In other words, the higher the frequency, the shorter the wavelength; the lower the frequency, the longer the wave length. If a radio wave had a frequency of 300 MHz, it would have a wavelength one meter long. However, if you triple the frequency, to 900 MHz, the length of the radio wave drops to one-third of a meter.

Radio waves and sound waves share many common characteristics. Humans can hear sounds in the frequency range of 20 to 18,000 cycles per second. For wireless communication (radio and data), the practical frequency range is 30 kHz up to in excess of 300 GHz. You and I can hear a range, or **spectrum**, of cycles. We can see a certain spectrum, or range, of light.[9] Radio frequencies have a practical spectrum. However, the channels that make up the spectrum are finite in number. No more can be discovered or created.[10]

Return to your car radio. You probably have an AM and FM dial or button. In fact, years ago, only AM radios were installed in cars. As time progressed, people bought FM radios and added them to their cars. Eventually, an AM/FM radio became the standard. But why AM and FM? A simple explanation is that AM and FM radios work in ranges that are significantly different from each other. These ranges of frequencies, called **bands**, have very different characteristics.[11] Within the frequency spectrum of 30 kHz to 300 GHz, there are distinct frequency bands that share certain broadcast characteristics (Figure 3.7).

Recall in the opening paragraphs of this chapter, a helicopter pilot from one agency was unable to communicate with an officer on the ground from another agency. That is because they were each on a different group of frequencies, called a **channel**.[12] For everyday operations this makes sense. After all, if you call the

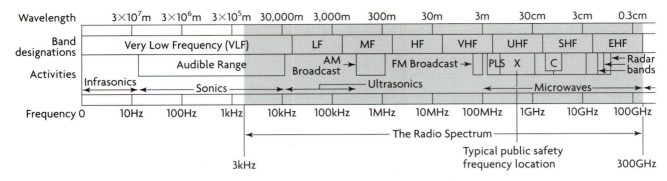

Figure 3.7 This chart lists the frequency bands radio engineers use to describe the general characteristics of those frequencies.

police, you don't want the police to have to wait to receive your call from their headquarters because another agency is using the channel.

The practical radio frequency spectrum is grouped by bands because of shared characteristics. But who decides how frequencies are grouped into channels? Who decides which business, government, or private person can use which frequency? Surprise—the government organization called the Federal Communications Commission (FCC) decides the channel grouping and the number of frequencies in a channel.[13] The number of frequencies in a channel is referred to as the channel's **bandwidth**.[14] The more frequencies allocated to a channel, the larger or higher the channel's bandwidth. Bandwidth considerations are important because the more bandwidth, the more information a channel can handle. Let's move back to your car. Think of the channel as a large highway you are driving on. This highway has four lanes in each direction. The lanes going your way are one channel, and the ones going the opposite direction are another channel. The lanes are the individual frequencies that constitute your channel of travel. The more lanes there are, the more cars that can be accommodated. It is thus so with wireless communications; the more frequencies in a channel, the greater the bandwidth and the greater the amount of information that can be transmitted. If your highway reduces to two lanes because two were blocked by an accident, what happens? Traffic slows. In fact, the more crowded the four lanes, the worse the congestion caused by the blocking. In a sense, this is what happens when we try and push too much information into a channel with insufficient bandwidth—it slows to a crawl. As we shall see, bandwidth is becoming a more and more critical issue as large segments of information are being used by field police officers.

For a moment, let's stay with the highway analogy. As you are driving down the highway, you have probably seen three other highway features that are analogous to radio channels. First, between the opposite directions of travel, you have seen a center divider. This divider is to keep the opposite directions of traffic from colliding with each other. Channels have a similar protection between them called a **guard band**.[15] It is preventing the channels from overlapping and confusing

In the United States, telecommunications policy is primarily determined by the FCC, an independent agency established by the Communications Act of 1934.

TERM DEFINITION

A **license** is a "legally enforceable right to use a part of the radio spectrum for a specified purpose in a limited geographic region." The purpose is to keep multiple users from using the same frequencies. Moreover, the licensing, done through the FCC, enables the government to plan for use of the radio frequency spectrum. The planned use of the radio spectrum gives us the different parts of the frequency continuum that are dedicated to specific users. Although the FCC is the primary regulatory agency, with more than seventeen thousand state and local law enforcement agencies using a limited number of frequencies, frequency coordination is nearly as important as spectrum efficiency. Currently, four agencies are responsible to coordinate public safety radio frequencies. This means that a state or local law enforcement agency that wanted new frequency allocation would work through one of these four agencies:

- Association of Public-Safety Communications Officials (APCO), **www.apcointl.org**
- International Municipal Signal Association (IMSA), **www.imsasafety.org**
- Forestry Conservation Communication Association (FCCA), **www.fcca.info**
- American Association of State Highway Transportation Officials (AASHTO), **www.transportation1.org/aashtonew**

Sources: Banks, "Wireless Communications;" Imel and Hart, *Understanding Wireless Communications*, 75.

the ongoing information exchange. As you have driven, you have most likely seen that highways have a different number of lanes. Channels are just so. Some have multiple frequencies and, consequently, a wide bandwidth. Others are like country lanes—not very much is going to travel over them. Finally, you have probably seen those detestable carpool lanes. Carpool lanes are supposed to encourage more people to ride in single vehicles, thereby increasing transportation efficiency. I am not so sure the transportation theory plays out in practice. But in wireless communication, if you can increase the efficiency of information exchange within the physical properties of the individual frequency, you can push more information with less bandwidth. Later we will see that spectrum efficiency has been greatly improved by technological advances in microcomputers and software. Essentially, spectrum efficiency is increased if we create a highway of carpool lanes by putting more information into the cars, the cars representing each time you transmit a signal.[16]

Recall that we noted that frequencies were banded together based upon some general characteristics. These characteristics are important when choosing a wireless communications system, and they can have devastating consequences if the end user doesn't understand the characteristics that may limit the use of a communications device. The first characteristic of frequency bands is effective radiated power. That is how far away from the source a signal can be received and interpreted. Generally speaking, the lower the frequency, the higher the effective radiated power for a given transmission power.[17] This means that wireless signals sent out in the very-high frequency (VHF) band provide a wider area of coverage. As late as the early 1980s, the United States Coast Guard used low frequency via carrier wave (Morse code) to send and receive position reports from merchant vessels on the high seas. This is because the signal reliably traveled back and forth over a long distance, in many instances in excess of a thousand miles. While there are ways to assist with coverage other than using a lower frequency, in general terms, a wireless communication system that seeks to cover a large area is well served by lower frequency usage. Earlier we looked at frequency bands in general; now as we talk specifically about law enforcement, it would do to limit our consideration to those

State and local law enforcement agencies are assigned to the public safety frequencies, 800 MHz. There are about three hundred channels located in the 800 MHz spectrum band. Because 800 MHz is a higher frequency, it has the disadvantage of less coverage, so an agency needs a larger infrastructure. Moreover, there have been some problems of incompatibility between different 800 MHz trunked systems built by different vendors.

Source: "Toward Improved Criminal Justice."

frequencies and bands allocated by the FCC to public safety (Figure 3.8). One of the functions performed by the FCC is an administrative process to reduce change bandwidths called refarming. The purpose of this process is to gain greater spectrum efficiency.[18] The next consideration, especially in urban areas, is building.[19] The shorter wavelengths of the ultra-high frequencies (UHF) go through building windows better than VHF. If you were a police officer responding to a robbery call inside a large mall, the ability of the radio signal to penetrate the mall could alter your tactical response. As we shall see, there are ways to get around dead spots in radio communications, even ways to overcome signal penetration. However, not all agencies can afford these techniques, and in a large city 100 percent radio coverage in all buildings and terrain is probably impractical. So if you are managing, designing, or using a radio system, you need to take the penetration characteristics of your assigned frequency into consideration.

The next characteristic that radio frequencies within a band share is the propensity to skip.[20] A skip transmission occurs when a broadcast that is generally in the VHF low band reflects off the Earth's ionosphere.[21] The ionosphere's ability to reflect VHF transmissions is associated with sunspot activity. This can

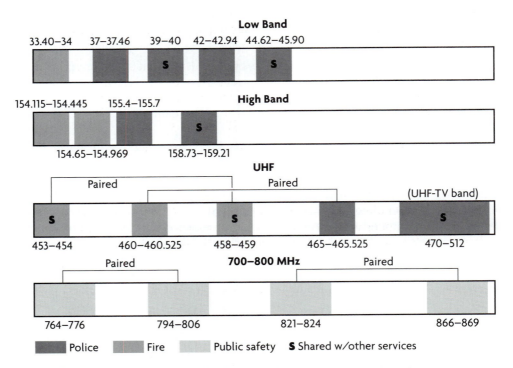

Figure 3.8 This chart outlines the FCC-allocated bands and their general uses. **Allocation** is defined as the process of determining radio spectrum use.
Source: U.S. Congress, Office of Technology Assessment, "Electronic Surveillance," 72.

cause a variety of problems for the agencies using low band VHF. Consider that there are more than seventeen thousand state and local police agencies in the United States. Each of them needs channels with the bands allocated by the FCC. The number of agencies needing a communication channel is significantly increased when you consider the FCC allocates channels within the public safety bands to all manner of public safety agencies, not just state and local police. Because of the large number of agencies (including public safety entities such as fire departments) who need communication channels from a limited number of available bands, there is channel duplication around the country. As we know from earlier in this chapter, radio signals, digital or analog, travel only so far effectively.[22] This means that as long as the agencies who share a channel are geographically farther apart than the effective radius of transmission, there is no problem, except when skip occurs. The problem was demonstrated rather starkly several years ago when a transmission from an Idaho agency was monitored by units in Southern California. The unfortunate call was for a backup officer. Of course, this caused some pandemonium in Southern California.

The next issue involves noise.[23] Return for a moment to your car. Have you ever experienced small interference on your AM radio as you passed under high-voltage power lines? If you did, did you try the FM stations? If you had, you probably found that the noise present on an AM station was absent or significantly less on the FM station. Although noise and interference is more of a problem for lower frequencies (as in AM radio) than higher frequencies, other ways to reduce static have been developed. One of them was to produce a different type of modulation. Whereas AM radio changes a signal by changing the degree of energy attached to a signal, an FM radio changes a signal (like a voice) by moderating the frequency.[24] OK, that's kind of technical; it is enough to know there is a difference and why.

The final consideration for understanding the characteristics inherent to frequency bands relates to antenna size. Earlier we saw that a simple representation of a radio involved an antenna from which to send and receive radio waves. The larger the frequency, the larger the antenna required. Later in this chapter we examine antennas more thoroughly.

Basic Communications Hardware

We now have an understanding of some of the very basic theories that make all wireless communication possible. Now we are going to move into some basic hardware requirements for all radio frequency (RF) communications. It is important to understand that while the basic radio theory applies to all wireless communications, including cellular telephones, the hardware we are going to examine now concerns RF communications. Later we will learn about cellular communications and then be able to compare the strengths and weaknesses of the two communication schemes in the venue of law enforcement. Basic RF communications equipment falls into three broad classifications of types: the base radio station, mobile radio units, and handheld radio units.[25] Generally speaking, base stations are the types of radio equipment housed in police stations and dispatch centers. A mobile radio system such as that shown in Figure 3.9 would be found in a police vehicle, such as a car, motorcycle, helicopter, or boat. Finally, a handheld radio would be the type of radio an officer might wear on his or her equipment belt. Recall the radio in your car, it is designed to only receive radio waves; therefore, it is called a **receiver**. The radio station that you listen to is designed to broadcast, so it is called a **transmitter**. Today police radios are designed

Figure 3.9   Radio equipment in a police car.
Photograph provided by Havis-Shield Corporation.

to both transmit and receive radio waves. As we can see from the example of our car radio, transmitters and receivers can be two different pieces of equipment.[26] However, in order to facilitate two-way communications, mobile units and hand-held units combine the technology to create a **transceiver**. On the other hand, base stations can be separate units, and as we shall see, this may be the most effective configuration, especially for larger agencies. In order to understand what a radio does, we will examine transmitters and receivers separately.

The job of a transmitter is to generate the radio wave, called the signal. As we know, the basic characteristic of a radio wave is its frequency, and that frequency is a series of oscillating waves. Essentially, oscillation means the waves peak and valley in a predictable and uniform manner. Naturally, the part of the transmitter that generates these waves is called the **oscillator**.[27] In order to obtain the desired frequency, the oscillating wave is passed on to a frequency multiplier. Now we have a continuous wave at the right frequency. This continuous wave will be the vehicle that will ultimately carry our information. The signal produced that carries the information is called a carrier. The job of the receiver is to receive the radio wave and change it back into the form originally modified by the transmitter.[28] So if you transmitted a voice signal, the receiver would process the modulated carrier wave and return it to its original form.

Recall that data, or computer information, is made up of binary digits, or bits. The simplest method of transmitting data via a wireless system is to use what is called a **frequency shift key** (FSK) method.[29] Two separate frequencies are used to represent the ones and zeros of binary data. Using this scheme, a transmitter would transmit a carrier wave signal at a certain frequency to represent a one, and at another frequency to represent a zero. At the other end of the transmission, the receiver would interpret the shift between frequencies and ultimately produce binary data for a computer. Simply put, a transceiver combines the function of a transmitter and receiver into a single device. Conversely, when we want to change a voice into digital we use a voice coder, or **vocoder**. It is pretty much the reverse of a modem.[30]

So far, we have learned some basic radio theory and looked at the components of transmitters and receivers. However, we have not discussed nearly all of the physical components of a radio. We should, however, have enough to shortly begin to figure out the problems, challenges, and potential uses of RF communication.

Coverage is one of the most common and often vexing problems with public safety wireless communication (this includes both radio frequency and cellular telephone). The term *coverage* refers to the reliability of a base station and mobile unit being able to communicate within all parts of the anticipated operational area. In essence, can your police department use its mobile radios in all areas of your city? Return to your car radio for the moment. Have you ever driven beyond the reception of your favorite radio station? Have you ever driven into an underground parking and lost the signal from the radio station? How about your cellular telephone—have you ever received a "no service" indication in a particular place? Public safety radio systems face the same coverage issues. Typically, for a police department, the coverage issues revolve around terrain and structures. For instance, a certain ravine or valley or a large wall or factory may present a coverage issue.

In our look at radio components, we briefly referred to antennas. An antenna is the component of a radio transmitter that ultimately sends the signal into the atmosphere. Conversely, the receiver's antenna takes the signal from the atmosphere. Different antennas have different propagation characteristics. **Propagation** means the way in which the antenna sends out the signal. The size, configuration, and location of an antenna affects its wave propagation. For instance, an antenna on a high hill would provide wider coverage than an antenna placed in a valley. Think back to the stone we threw into a pond. From the point of impact, ripples or small waves emanate. What if there were a large rock that protruded about the surface of the pond between you and the point of impact, what would happen to the ripples? The rock would likely deflect them. It is just so with radio waves. The location of the antenna can be critical to ensuring communications or wireless coverage. The basic type of antenna is called a dipole. It is a straight wire or piece of metal. For an antenna to have the best propagation characteristics, it must be a certain length relative to the frequency of transmission. The formula to determine the proper length is that the antenna must be half the length of the wave. Don't confuse radio towers with antennas. The tower's purpose is to get the antenna as high up as possible. The antenna theory is more important than its physical length because there are radio components that essentially compensate for the length of an antenna.[31]

If our antenna is straight up and down, or perpendicular to the earth's surface, the broadcast of the radio waves is said to be omnidirectional.[32] The radio waves are radiating in a complete and even circle on a horizontal plane. The pattern of the signals that are radiating from our vertical dipole antenna are not just on a horizontal plane; some of them are traveling up and down from the antenna. This gives the signal radiation pattern a shade something like a doughnut all around the antenna. An antenna can also be placed in a horizontal position relative to the surface of the earth. In these two examples, a vertical antenna would be said to have a vertical polarization whereas an antenna placed horizontally to the Earth's

Figure 3.10 This antenna array contains many different types of antennas, including several versions of a dipole.
Photograph provided by Robert Eplett, California Governor's Office of Emergency Services.

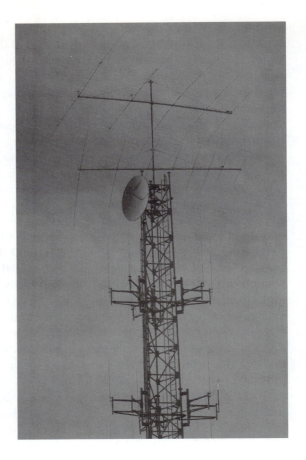

surface would be said to have a horizontal polarization. As we continue to look at how antennas affect coverage, you will find that nearly all mobile and handheld radio units use an antenna with a vertical polarization.[33]

With dipole antennas, you can increase the range of transmission of the radio waves by adjusting the gain. **Gain** is essentially directing the antenna's radiating energy (radio waves) in alternate directions. This has the effect of requiring less transmission power to reach a longer distance in one direction and decreasing radio interference from signals not emanating from the direction to which one has adjusted the gain.

Most base station antennas (like those transmitting a signal from a police station or dispatch center) are omnidirectional antennas like the dipole.[34] In order to increase gain, a series of dipole antennas configured at the base station transmission point can be used. There are also directional antennas that can focus an antenna's radiating energy toward a specific direction or object. Typically, police agencies with problems in coverage can use a combination of antenna configurations. For instance, the base station might have an omnidirectional dipole antenna on the highest building in the town it serves and directional antennas that repeat the signals in areas where the terrain or other structures block base station radio waves. When a scheme involving multiple antennas is used, the secondary antennas are referred to as repeaters.[35] Can you imagine how complex it would be for a large city or state to build and maintain a system of antennas to ensure the most complete coverage possible?

Some police departments are large enough to require multiple radio channels in order to operate efficiently. Even smaller agencies may have multiple channels

Law enforcement agencies that cover a large area often have a complex radio infrastructure that involves scores of repeater antenna sites. In order to facilitate large networks, technology is used to filter and isolate components so that radio transmissions will not interfere with other systems, or even the operation of the host system. Some of these are du-

plexers, combiners, and multicouplers. Essentially, these are the technologies necessary to connect multiple transmitters and receivers to antennas.

Source: Imel and Hart, *Understanding Wireless Communications,* 54.

of broadcasts. For instance, they may have one transmitter for local dispatch, one for tactical use, and perhaps another to push binary data to field units. Moreover, not only do the police need radio frequencies, but local fire departments and emergency medical services are constantly in need of RF communications. And what of the mobile units and handheld units that may want to transmit and receive on more than one frequency? A way around a city government sprouting a forest of dipole antennas is to use devices known as combiners and multicouplers.

These devices allow multiple transmitters, receivers, and transceivers to use a single antenna. A combiner is just that. It is a device that combines the output from multiple transmitters and receivers with computers and manages the multiple transmitter input to a single antenna. On the other hand, a multicoupler is used by receivers to manage the signal input for multiple receivers that obtain radio signals from a single antenna. We now have a sufficient foundation of radio theory and radio components to look at RF.

Radio Frequency Systems

Radio frequency systems can be either privately owned or commercially owned. When we refer to privately owned, we mean the system's primary user built and maintains the system. The example of this would be a city that plans, builds, and maintains its own radio frequency communication system infrastructure, the permanent installations required for radio communications.[36] If an RF system is commercially owned, we mean a private company planned, built, and maintains a radio frequency communication infrastructure and sells the service to the users.

We are going to look at three types of RF systems. However, each of them could be privately or commercially owned. Moreover, after exploring the systems, we will examine the strengths and weaknesses of each, especially as compared to each other, and we will look at the potentially positive and negative aspects of choosing either a private system or commercial system.

In simple voice radio systems there are two schemes. In the first, all users transmit and receive information on a single channel or frequency. This means that if you are a police officer in the field, you cannot use the radio until the dispatcher or other field units have finished. In a later chapter we will examine dispatch centers using a base radio system and sending information out to field units from a central location. Of course, in a large city this could be a complex command center carrying out multiple tasks, or it could be a small agency with a single employee using the radio from the police station. In any event, this first simple voice RF system is called a simplex system.[37] There are obvious drawbacks. If one user is broadcasting nonemergency information while a second is attempting to report an emergency, public safety could be compromised by the emergency information not being received or being garbled. A garbled transmission is one that is partially received or not understood due to radio interference. This radio interference could be caused by an equipment malfunction, a skip transmission, an outside interference, or two users attempting to broadcast on a simplex system simultaneously.

A somewhat improved simple voice radio system involves the use of one frequency to transmit and one frequency to receive. Typically, the dispatch center transmits to all mobile units on one frequency; the mobile units broadcast on another. The signal from the mobile units is receiving a lone police signal that is intended to be picked up by a repeating antenna. These repeating antennas are strategically placed around the coverage area to pick up RF signals. They are then repeated at a higher point and on another frequency to the base station. Similarly, repeaters can be used to increase the coverage by broadcasting signals from the dispatch center. Both the simplex and the repeater system share the disadvantage of "first come, first served." However, a repeater system can greatly expand coverage and provide a constant clear channel for dispatch.[38]

A simple voice radio system has the advantage of allowing users with equipment provided by different manufacturers the ability to communicate as long as the radio equipment has the proper frequencies. For instance, three small adjacent communities could have separate police departments, radio systems produced by different manufacturers, and even different operational channels, and still communicate via radio. This is often accomplished on what is referred to as a mutual aide frequency. The different agencies would decide to have a frequency in common for use during an emergency.

Another disadvantage to a police agency using a simple voice system is that of all the radio systems available to the police, this one is the most easily monitored by radio users outside the agency. Typically, this is a citizen enthusiast who enjoys listening to police radio traffic. However, not only is communications security an issue during covert police operations (such as surveillance), but the police often broadcast sensitive and somewhat confidential information. For example, return to the speeding violator of Chapter One. While issuing a citation to the violator, the police officer may decide to check the validity of the driver's license, or check him for warrants. This information relayed between the field officer and the dispatch center could be fairly easily monitored.

The last RF radio system in widespread use is a trunked radio system.[39] For a larger police agency that has multiple frequencies, a trunked radio system is a scheme that allows for larger spectrum efficiency by using all of the frequencies. Consider that a large agency has four specific geographic areas that are defined as beats. At any one time, five police cars are patrolling those beats. Because the agency has twenty field users, in a repeated voice system they might decide to allocate a channel to each beat. Recall that an RF channel in a repeated scheme is composed of two frequencies. To service the city, ten frequencies with a trunked radio system microprocessor and software are integrated into the base station units and the mobile units. In this system each of our four beats would become a talk group. Of the ten frequencies, one is a control frequency. When an officer in one of the beats uses the radio, his radio system first sends a message on the control channel to the software and microprocessor incorporated into the base station. The microprocessor looks at the other nine frequencies and decides which one is not being used. It then sends a message back to the police officer and every officer in his talk group and tells their radios which frequency the officer is about to use. This generally occurs so rapidly that if there is an open frequency, users do not experience any delay between pushing a microphone button and talking. Essentially, a trunked radio system operates like a telephone trunk system by locating an empty line and assigning it to the caller for the duration of the call.[40]

This scheme gains spectrum efficiency by opening up all frequencies to use by all groups. It can reasonably be expected that some areas of the city will be, at times, busier than others. Therefore, rather than have one channel (a set of frequencies) overburdened, the trunked radio system makes equal use of all RF resources. On the face of it, this seems more efficient than a simplex or repeated system. However, the system requires hardware and software that are significantly more complex.

The first systems for wireless communications we looked at were essentially analog radio frequency systems used to transmit voice data information. However, the trunked radio system is also used with computer data transmission. When we first looked at RF equipment, we described base stations, mobile units, and handheld units. At first, because we concentrated on using RF systems to transmit voice information, we viewed these devices as being primarily the typical radio. However, law enforcement is increasingly relying on computers to enhance field operations.

Typically, these computers in the field are very much like the laptop devices available to the public. However, as we look at computers in the field, we will see that in some ways they have been specifically adapted for law enforcement. Most commonly, these devices have been ruggedized. In addition to laptop computers, a number of law enforcement agencies are experimenting with a variety of handheld computers such as notebooks and personal digital assistants (PDAs). As we continue throughout the text, we will see examples of these devices.

We have seen that at the most basic level, computer information is a series of binary digits and that binary data can be transmitted over radio waves. We also know that in addition to binary data traveling over radio waves, voice communications can be translated into binary digits and attached to a radio wave. So digital communications can be voice or data or both. The trunked radio system can be used to transmit both voice and data information. Moreover, a trunked radio system can be either privately owned or commercially owned. In the instance of a privately owned system, the agency planned, built, and maintains the system. In the commercial model, the agency pays a fee for use to a business that developed the radio system infrastructure.

As we know, the amount of broadcast frequencies is limited by the usable radio frequency range. Therefore, the large numbers of public, private, and commercial users of radio frequencies are in competition for limited space. The short-range capabilities of the higher band frequencies mean that users who are far enough away from each other can use the same frequency with little interference from each other. The trunked radio system is one technology that allows for greater spectrum efficiency, allowing more use of the available resources. There are several others. Another radio system that increases spectrum efficiency is the **Frequency Division Multiple Access (FDMA)** system.[41] With this device in place, the typical radio frequency of 30 kHz is divided into three channels, each 10 kHz wide. Agencies using this system benefit by a three-fold increase in the number of frequencies they can use in conjunction with their trunked radio systems. The next two systems are for use with digital transmissions. However, as we know, voice, as well as typical computer binary data, can be transmitted as a digital signal.

Some police agencies rely on commercial radio systems for their communications ability. While a commercial system can be a simple voice, repeater, or trunked system, an increasingly common system in use is cellular technology to transmit voice and data for police officers.

Cellular Technology

Cellular telephones are everywhere today. Indeed before a movie is shown in your local theater, there will no doubt be a short advertisement developed by the theater requesting everyone turn their telephones off. Moreover, you probably cannot walk into a courtroom today without passing a sign on the outer door that reminds you that your cellular telephones must be turned off. The use of cellular technology is increasing at extraordinary rate. For instance, in 2000 more cellular telephones were shipped than automobiles and PCs combined.[42] Moreover, according to the Cellular Telecommunications and Internet Association (CTIA), in 1993 there were just over sixteen million cellular telephone users (called subscribers) in the United States. As of December, 2002, CTIA reported that there were more than 140 million subscribers of cellular service in the United States.[43] We are going to take a brief look at the historical development of cellular technology, a look at how the technology generally works, and then we'll look at several applications in the police service.

The beginning of cellular telephone services and wireless data transmissions can be traced back to the 1940s, when commercial radio telephone service began. The basic principle of using radio waves to transmit an analog signal for radio was used so that private citizens could use the telephone. In fact, the use of analog signals for cellular service did not completely die out in this country until very recently.

In June of 1946 American Telephone and Telegraph (AT&T) and Southwestern Bell introduced the first commercial mobile radio-telephone. In essence, a private vehicle was equipped with a large radio that transmitted a signal to a receiver, which passed the signal through to a telephone operator, who then connected the radio signal to the landline telephone system. This system was not very successful for two primary reasons. First, the vehicles contained relatively low power transmitters, so in order for the signal to be continuously received and sent as one drove through the service area, the signal had to be handed off from one receiving antenna to another. Now this handoff principle is one of the primary characteristics of cellular systems, but at that time, the technology lagged behind the idea. Second, this was a "push to talk" system. In other words, in order to talk, the person using the mobile telephone pushed a talk button much like the button on a police vehicle microphone. The button was released to listen. This sounds much like a simplex radio system, but it was not. With this system there were two frequencies in use (from the vehicle to the transmitter and from the transmitter to the vehicle). Additionally, one of the primary problems with radio telephone service at this time was the lack of channels for use.

So between the early development of mobile telephones and about 1968, mobile telephones were essentially radio equipment that looked like telephones and could be linked through an operator with the regular telephone system. Part of what eventually made the cellular telephone system ultimately work was other technological developments. The invention and mass production of the transistor, the development of the integrated circuit board, and the creation and mass production of the microchip gave us the technological tools that make all of today's technology, including the cellular telephone, possible.

From the end of World War II until 1968, mobile telephone technology was also being developed in Europe and Japan. In January, 1969 AT&T began cellular telephone service using the two unique characteristics that essentially define cellular service—signal handoff and frequency reuse.[44] However, this system was still an analog system that would eventually be replaced by a digital system.

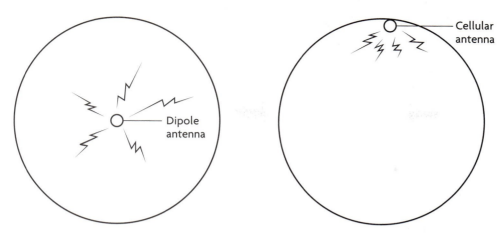

Figure 3.11 This drawing provides us with a visual representation of the difference between the coverage provided by the dipole antenna and the cell site antenna array. Notice that the dipole antenna provides coverage in a circle around the antenna, whereas a hexagon is the base shape to represent the cellular coverage. Simply put, a dipole antenna is in the center of its coverage area, whereas a cellular telephone antenna (the cell site) is at the edge of its coverage area.

One of the keys to how cellular telephone service operates is found in its name. A network of cell sites properly distributed over any specific geographic area can provide coverage to that area. It is very important to understand the difference between a **cell site** and a **cell**. A cell site is a physical location that contains a cellular telephone antenna array and a base station controller. It is the physical location of the hardware. The cell is the area of coverage provided by the cell site antenna array.

Earlier in this chapter we looked at antennas. We saw that the standard dipole antenna provides coverage in essentially a 360-degree area around the antenna. As we know, the total coverage area the antenna provides is dependant upon the frequency that is used and the other radio system components. We also looked at directional antennas. We found that in addition to increasing broadcast gain (or power) in a direction, they also improve reception in the same area.[45] A cellular telephone array is a series of between two and six directional antennas. Therefore, as in Figure 3.11, the cell site is at the edge of coverage cell.

The configuration of cellular sites has some of the same characteristics of the repeater antenna configuration. Multiple antennas are deployed according to their propagation qualities throughout a coverage area. So when you are listening to the car radio, you are receiving a signal from one antenna that broadcasts in a large area. When you are using a cellular telephone, the signal is from a particular cell site, and if you are moving in a vehicle, you are probably moving from cell to cell. This means your signal is handed off between the cells. The coverage of a cell site depends on several factors, but the average area of coverage is between two and ten miles. Moreover, because we know that radio waves bounce off of objects they cannot penetrate, small cell sites can be used to increase coverage in areas where traditional radio transmitters cannot. For instance, in a city with high buildings, cellular sites have to be located in order to ensure wave propagation into the canyons created by the buildings.

A cell site has a variety of channels for communicating with mobile units. The number of channels depends primarily on the amount of traffic anticipated to

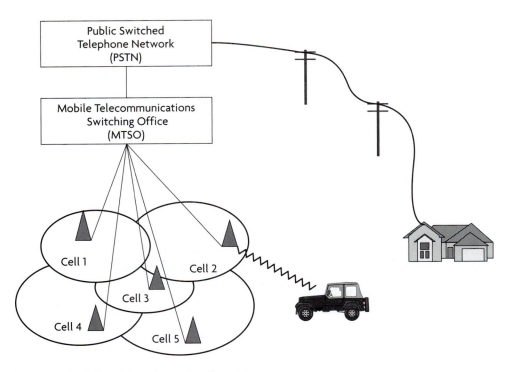

Figure 3.12 Cellular Telephone Configuration.

pass through the cell site. Recall that a channel consists of a pair of frequencies—one for transmitting and the other for receiving. For cellular communications the channel that is coming from the cell site is the forward path and the information coming from the mobile unit is said to be on the reverse path. However, some of the channels have specific purposes. For instance, each cell site has a control channel. The control channel is responsible for setting up the exchange of information (in the instance of a cellular telephone, the call) between the mobile unit and the cell site.

Because the transmitters used by mobile units (as in a cellular telephone or a police communications device) are low-powered transmitters, the cell sites in a large coverage area can use the same frequencies at once for multiple devices. In other words, while you are talking on your cellular telephone, the frequency you are using to get your voice from you cellular telephone to the cell site can be in use somewhere across town from you. This is the essence of frequency reuse in order to obtain greater spectrum efficiency. Cellular systems use a variety to software, hardware, and techniques to handle the connecting, completing, and routing of telephone calls and data exchanges.

The easiest way to demonstrate how cellular technology works is to follow a cellular telephone call. Keep in mind that the technology involved in making the call is very similar to that used for police communication schemes that are cellular in nature. When you first turn on a cellular telephone, the telephone sends an electronic signal out into the atmosphere, seeking the nearest cell site. Because cell sites overlap, your telephone scans around and finds the strongest signal. It is looking for the strongest forward path signal it can find radiating from a cell site. Once your telephone finds the strongest cellular site, it sends information to the site, essentially registering itself. The initial information the cellular telephone sends is its dialing number, the electronic serial number (ESN) of the cellular telephone itself, and information concerning the cellular telephone's home service.[46]

The dialing number is fairly straightforward. That is the number you give to people to call your telephone. The information concerning the home service would be the company you signed up with to provide you the cellular service. The ESN is a little more complex. Recall from Chapter Two that certain types of computer equipment are considered firmware. This is hardware with preprogrammed or embedded software. Typically, in the computer, we are talking about the ROM chip that contains the BIOS information. Your cellular telephone contains a small microprocessor that has ROM BIOS–like information and functions. If it didn't, each time the battery died, the cellular telephone would have to be reprogrammed. Additionally, each cellular telephone as an electronic serial number embedded by the manufacturer on the firmware chip. Over the life of the telephone, the dialing number and the home service can change, but the ESN never changes.

When someone refers to their cellular telephone as having been cloned, they are saying that someone with sophisticated electronic equipment monitored their cellular telephone sending its ESN to the cell site. The cloning of the ESN is the essence of cellular telephone fraud.

In both analog and digital systems, this registration process is continuous. As you move from cell to cell, your cellular telephone registers with that cell site. Now, although most of the cellular telephone service today is digital, there are a few analog systems still operational. Once you place a call from a cellular telephone, your telephone call is sent from the cell site you are using to the Mobile Telephone Switching Office (MTSO).[47] The cell site relays the signal to the MTSO via trunked telephone lines, fiber-optic cables, or microwaves. The MTSO eventually sends the signal into the hardwired telephone service network. This explanation assumes that you are in the home service area of your provider. However, when you are not, your cellular telephone roams, finding a service not your own.[48]

During the call, the MTSO continually monitors the signal strength from your cellular telephone to the cell site and other adjacent cell sites. If the signal begins to fade at the primary cell site and get stronger in another cell site, the MTSO requests that another cell site take over reception of the call. As we looked at earlier, the process is somewhat similar, but inherently more complex, than your cordless telephone in your home. Both systems, cellular communications equipment and the cordless phone, transmit a radio frequency containing information to a base station that sends the signal along into the hardwired telephone system.

Recall in the case of an analog system that is going to transmit in a digital scheme the voice information is changed into a digital format using a frequency shift key (FSK). The information leaving a cellular device is in what is referred to as a data package. In other cellular-type schemes the data leaves in a package of a slightly different configuration. But essentially the package (which is only a piece of your telephone conversation, or the data that you are transmitting via a cellular scheme) has the job of telling the receiver where the information came from and is going to, what the information contains, the information, an error-checking scheme (like bit parity), and a message at the end of the package that

Try This

You can identify the wireless carriers that operate in any area at CITA's Web site—**www.wow-com.** **com.** How many wireless carriers are operating in your area?

identifies that the package is complete. Finally, in order to achieve spectrum efficiency, the data can be compressed within its package. In cellular technology, that data package is a frame.[49]

The primary characteristic that identifies a cellular system is frequency reuse. Recall that our trunked radio system is an example of frequency reuse, as is frequency division, but there are others. The first example of a technique to enable frequency reuse is a **Time Division Multiple Access (TDMA)** system.[50]

When you are speaking with someone on the telephone, there are natural gaps in the conversation. For example, you or the other party might pause to find the right words to express an idea. There is space between your words. TDMA is somewhat similar to taking advantage of the space between words. Since the cellular system has put the voice or data information into small, compressed packages, as it sends the information from or to a cellular device, there is plenty of room on the frequency. Indeed there are up to six frames available on any one frequency. That means that with compressed digital information (again, voice or data), multiple conversations can take place on the same frequency. In essence, each user is allowed a small portion of the broadcast cycle, in a timed sequence. They are simply timed not to interfere with one another. Of course, this takes precision timing, sophisticated equipment, and complex software. But with today's technology, spectrum efficiency (the number of conversations we can have at the same time) is increased by sharing minute portions of time on the same frequency.

Time Division Multiple Access, like Analog Mobile Phone Service (AMPS), is a fading technology. The type of technology used to increase frequency spectrum is **Code Division Multiple Access (CDMA)**.[51] In CDMA each of the available frequencies at a cell site are used for every call. In our trunked radio system, whenever there was a frequency shift, all of the users shifted to receive or transmit information. In the CDMA scheme, each transmission of digital information is spread out among all of the available channels. The digital frames move from one frequency to the next in milliseconds. While this allows for complete usage of all available frequencies, it does require very precise and sophisticated timing. Because the information is spread out among a variety of frequencies, the information must be put back together, each with a unique code (called a direct sequence) to each call.

Data compression is one of the aspects of digital communications that assists us in spectrum efficiency. Think of an empty aluminum can. You are a responsible citizen, so you decide to recycle your aluminum cans. In your garage, you have a large plastic bag that fills very rapidly with the cans. In order to get more cans in the bag so that you don't have to make as many trips to the recycling center, you crush the cans before you put them in the bag. By crushing them, or compressing them, you are removing the empty space in the can so that more cans can fit in the bag. Data compression does many of the same things. However, there are a variety of compression algorithms. One such method is akin to the aluminum can crushing. It simply removes the blank spaces in your data. Other methods take often repeated words and letters and assign them an abbreviated binary code. There are several other methods of compression, some of which will be looked at when we examine hard-line networks.

These three techniques that are used to gain spectrum efficiency can be slightly confusing. Let's summarize:

- Frequency Division Multiple Access transmits information on a different frequency.
- Time Division Multiple Access transmits the information in a certain time frame on each frequency.
- Code Division Multiple Access assigns the information a unique code and then spreads the information over all available frequencies.

Source: Banks, "Wireless Communications."

The cellular telephone is an interesting marriage of telephone technology and radio technology. Indeed the grandparents of the modern cellular telephone are the radio telephone. Moreover, our modern commercial mobile systems were finally in place during the early to mid-1980s. However, these early systems were based on analog technology. During the 1990s the second generation of mobile networks was deployed. These networks, using digital technology, solved many of the problems faced by early models.[52]

In addition to the three methods mentioned so far, another method for transmitting information via a cellular network is being used by law enforcement agencies. This scheme, known as **Cellular Digit Packet Data (CDPD)** is being marketed specifically to law enforcement agencies.[53] CDPD is transmitted over cellular communication technology.[54] In other words, the information from a CDPD system is relayed like a cellular telephone call through a commercial carrier.[55] The first noticeable difference between CDPD and traditionally cellular service is that in a traditional cellular service scheme the user pays for all of the time he or she is connected to the cellular network. Think about the TDMA and FDMA schemes. If you are a cellular subscriber, you are paying for the entire time you are connected to the cellular network, even though other people's conversations and data transmissions are mixed with yours. Of course, this means that TDMA and FDMA not only increase spectrum efficiency, but the same "airtime" is being sold to multiple users. With CDPD, the subscriber only pays for the packets of data sent over the network.[56] So from a financial standpoint, this can have benefits to a law enforcement agency. However, some state and local agencies have negotiated contracts at a fixed rate, thereby improving their cost-to-message ratio.

The second feature of CDPD is that it is a data network, not a voice network. So a device using CDPD does not have a telephone number; it has a Internet Protocol (IP) address. Chapter Four will cover more information on networks. A CDPD system, instead of sending a voice transmission to the hardwired telephone network, sends the CDPD data to the Internet or to another internal network.

Recall that in a cellular telephone scheme digital information is sent in frames, which are called packages. In a CDPD system, data is sent in similar blocks called packets. A typical data packet has five sections.[57] The first and last section of the data packet naturally tell the receiving device (cell site, MTSO, network, etc.) where the beginning and end of the packet frame are. The second part of the data

Typical Packet Data

Start flag	Address	Message/ information data field	Error check	End flag

Figure 3.13 Typical data packet.

To date, law enforcement organizations make little use of satellite technology as a means of communications. Generally, those law enforcement applications for satellite communications have been limited to the purchase and use of a satellite telephone. Satellite communications achieve spectrum efficiency through Spatial Division Multiple Access (SDMA). A satellite in orbit around the Earth can receive signals from locations that are very distant from each other. A satellite using dish antennas can focus its transmission to a very specific and relatively small geographic area. This ability to send and receive signals on the same frequency from multiple areas and to transmit signals on the same frequency to multiple areas is the essence of SDMA.

packet contains the address for which the data is intended. Return to the speeding motorist we discussed earlier. A police officer in the field might use a CDPD-connected device to check the driver's license history of the traffic violator. The address section of the CDPD packet might contain the network address of the state Department of Motor Vehicles. The police officer sends the request, and the address received directs the packet through a network to the computer handling the database. The middle section of the packet is the information that is being sent. In this example, that would be the driver's license number of the violator and a request to check the DMV database. Then, as with all good network communications, the packet contains an error-checking protocol. And finally the end flag appears. This transmission from the field to the DMV computer might take many packets to actually accomplish. In Chapter Four, when we look at networks, this information will become clearer. For now, it is important to understand that CDPD provides access to data networks.

Now, with a basic understanding of how radio frequency technology works, we can begin to look at putting together a radio system. State and local police agencies have a two basic options: they can use a dedicated system (which could be a simplex, repeater, or trunked system), or they can contract a cellular scheme.[58]

With a dedicated system, the agency can design a radio scheme that fits its needs. There is also the opportunity to work with adjacent jurisdictions and design a combined, dedicated system. However, when an agency designs and installs a radio system, it must be prepared for long-term maintenance and improvement costs. Moreover, initial costs associated with dedicated radio systems may be too expensive for some local agencies.

Quite a few state and local agencies are using cellular service to supplement their dedicated radio system. They may simply have issued cellular telephones to field officers, or they may be using cellular technology for their data transmissions (laptop computers in their vehicles) and a dedicated radio system for their voice. There is also the option of using cellular technology as the basis for all communications. Cellular technology is attractive because it is becoming less expensive and is modular in that users can be added to the system fairly simply. Additionally, digital communications add a security level to the system because unauthorized listeners are generally eliminated. However, in rural areas, there may not be sufficient cell sites to provide complete coverage. Finally, with cellular tech-

A Look Ahead

In Chapter Twenty, Implementing and Managing Technology, we look at some of the management issues involved with technology projects like designing a radio system.

nology, the vendors do not provide law enforcement officials with frequency priority. This means that during an incident wherein there may be extraordinary cellular usage by civilians, law enforcement transmission may have to wait its turn.

As we shall see in subsequent chapters, a huge amount of information is available to state and local police officers. As we will see in Chapter Six, much of the information could be tactical if it were immediately available to police officers in the field. State and local police agencies are increasing the tactical value of information by providing their field police officers with wireless data systems. Whether through a mobile data computer (MDC), like a laptop, or a mobile digital terminal (MDT), field police officers are gaining ready access to databases that include information about vehicles, people, and locations. Because of the rapid spread of technology and the usefulness of the information, MDCs and MDTs are becoming standard field equipment for police officers.[59]

As with voice communications, state and local agencies have two broad options. They could design, implement, and manage a wireless network. Agencies with their own dedicated voice systems often choose this route. Or the agency can contract the service. One of the commercial options is CDPD. CDPD technology allows the field officer to directly connect to the relevant database without going through the communications dispatch center. Because CDPD is a commercial cellular service, in most urban and suburban areas, the networks are in place, which means the agency's expenses are for hardware such as laptop computers, software, and modems. Moreover, because CPDP uses standard TCP/IP protocols, the hardware and software costs are more competitive. If the agency chooses CDPD, there is no need to have hardware in place for reception because the field police officers are directly accessing data. Since the CDPD service is in addition to whatever voice system an agency uses, the CDPD can be used as a backup network for voice communications. Although some CDPD providers are capable of giving law enforcement agencies frequency priority, during an emergency the network may not have the capacity to handle heavy volumes of information. Currently, CDPD technology has a relatively low data exchange rate, around 19,200 bps. This may make the transmission of data-intense objects, such as photographs and fingerprint scans, problematic. Finally, CDPD is probably a good solution for small- to medium-sized agencies because the costs to access the network are generally based on the number of users (vehicles in the fleet) and the amount of data sent over the network. A large agency would probably find it ultimately more fiscally sound to develop, implement, and maintain a dedicated wireless data network. However, a jurisdiction, like a state agency, would probably find it more sound to develop and maintain their own network. Simply put, many private companies may not have a large enough service area.[60]

As with voice systems, wireless data systems could also be maintained by a private data network or through some regional data network configuration. In addition to the state or local agency not having control over the network, many of the private data networks and regional networks have a slower data transmission speed than the CDPD network. Private data networks and regional data networks have many of the same advantages and disadvantages of the other wireless networking solutions.

A **mobile data terminal** is a "dumb" terminal. It provides the field officer with only the ability to gain input/output access to a computer at headquarters. Whereas an MDC, like a laptop, has actual computing power in the field.

A Look Ahead

In Chapter Twenty-One, Emerging and Future Police Technologies, we will look at several other possible options to voice and data networking, such as Bluetooth and satellite communications.

Chapter Summary

Radio waves are the way in which both analog and digital signals are carried as wireless communications. While both voice and data information can be carried by either analog or digital signals, both have advantages and disadvantages. As we learned, there are a limited number of channels available for wireless communications. In order to obtain the maximum use out of this finite resource, several transmission schemes have been developed, such as Frequency Division and Time Division. In an effort to create a "carpool lane," compressed digital packets are used in the CDPD scheme. Taking all that has been developed in radio theory and practice, cellular telephone communications are being used to supplement and sometimes replace police wireless communications. In the following chapters, we will build on the basics of police technology and ultimately see how bytes, radio waves, and other basic science has led to the development of modern police technology.

Discussion Questions

1. If you were the chief executive of a law enforcement agency who had to make a decision concerning the development of a new communications system, which system would you choose? Why? Would the size of the agency affect your decision?
2. In what kind of place have you experienced interference on your car radio? If you were a police officer and you knew there were problems with radio coverage in certain areas, how would that change your response to a call for service?

Key Terms

Analog
Antenna
Bands
Bandwidth
Cell
Cell Site
Cellular Digit Packet Data (CDPD)
Channels
Code Division Multiple Access (CDMA)

Cycle
Data Compression
Digital
Frequency
Frequency Division Multiple Access (FDMA)
Frequency Shift Key
Gain
Guard Band
Hertz
License

Modem
Oscillator
Propagation
Radio Wave
Receiver
Spectrum
Time Division Multiple Access (TDMA)
Transceiver
Transmitter
Vocoder

End Notes

1. Imel and Hart, *Understanding Wireless Communications,* 8.
2. Ibid., 34.
3. Ibid., 47.
4. Laidler, *To Light Such a Candle,* 224.
5. Imel and Hart, *Understanding Wireless Communications,* 35–36.
6. Ibid., 39.
7. Ibid.
8. Ibid., 41.
9. Ibid.
10. "Toward Improved Criminal Justice."

11. Imel and Hart, *Understanding Wireless Communications*, 42.
12. Ibid.
13. Phipps, "Order Out of Chaos," 57.
14. Imel and Hart, *Understanding Wireless Communications*, 41.
15. Ibid., 43.
16. Ibid.
17. Ibid., 44.
18. Ibid., 115
19. Ibid., 44
20. Ibid.
21. Laidler, *To Light Such a Candle*, 185.
22. Imel and Hart, *Understanding Wireless Communications*, 36.
23. Laidler, *To Light Such a Candle*, 223.
24. Ibid., 224.
25. U.S. Congress, Office of Technology Assessment, *Electronic Surveillance in a Digital Age*, 72.
26. Imel and Hart, *Understanding Wireless Communications*, 45.
27. Ibid., 46.
28. Laidler, *To Light Such a Candle*, 223.
29. Imel and Hart, *Understanding Wireless Communications*, 47.
30. Ibid., 117.
31. Ibid., 47.
32. Ibid., 48.
33. Ibid., 50.
34. Ibid., 49.
35. Ibid., 54.
36. Ibid., 114.
37. Ibid., 60.
38. Ibid.
39. Ibid., 63.
40. "Evolution and Development of Police Technology," 66.
41. Imel and Hart, *Understanding Wireless Communications*, 57.
42. Clarke, "Emerging value propositions."
43. CTIA provides a daily tally of cellular subscribers based on their survey. The tally can be found on the home page of their website at **www.wow-com.com**.
44. See note 25 above.
45. Imel and Hart, *Understanding Wireless Communications*, 48.
46. See note 25 above.
47. Imel and Hart, *Understanding Wireless Communications*, 69.
48. U.S. Congress, Office of Technology Assessment, *Electronic Surveillance in a Digital Age*, 73.
49. Imel and Hart, *Understanding Wireless Communications*, 59.
50. Ibid., 57.
51. Ibid.
52. Banks, "Wireless Communications."
53. Imel and Hart, *Understanding Wireless Communications*, 58.
54. Ibid., 71.
55. See note 10 above.
56. Cunningham, *B2B*, 181.
57. See note 25 above.
58. Imel and Hart, *Understanding Wireless Communications*, 87.
59. Ibid., 93.
60. Ibid., 93.

Chapter Four
Networks

Learning Objectives

- The student will understand the importance and use of **networks**.

- The student will have an understanding of the different types of technologies necessary to establish a network, such as **nodes**, **modems**, **routers**, and **switches**.

- The student will be exposed to several different types of networks, such as **local area networks**, **wide area networks**, and **wireless local area networks**.

- The student will understand the necessity for network security and several of the means of providing network security.

Introduction

At the most basic level, a **network** is about two or more people establishing a way to communicate. In our lives, we establish quite a few human networks. Some of these networks might be very formal, and some of them, informal. A formal human network would be any of the number of clubs and associations on a college campus. The purpose of these groups is generally for people of similar interests and needs to come together and exchange information. You have probably attended an event billed as a networking opportunity. If you have, you were attempting to establish relationships with other people so you could exchange information. That information you exchanged might be as simple as your business card or as complex as a business proposal. As we look at networks, we should remember that the purpose of any network is to allow people to exchange information.

This chapter on networking is about the exchange of information by electronic means. In previous chapters we were exposed to some network concepts. For instance, we looked at radio frequency (RF) transmissions and cellular telephone technology. In an upcoming chapter, when we look at global positioning satellite (GPS) technology, we will again visit network information. We also looked at a variety of concepts that are used in electronic networks, from the basic information concerning binary digits to data packets. In this chapter we are going to explore technological devices and concepts primarily necessary for the exchange of data information. By data information, we mean getting computers to work together. While most of the information in this chapter refers to hardwired networks, we will also supplement some of the information we already know about wireless communications.

Starting at the simplest level, a network connection is established whenever two or more computers begin an exchange of information.[1] If you look around, you can probably spot several networks. There may be one in your home; you may have established a network between two different desktop computers in your home. Or perhaps you have the ability to link your laptop to your desktop and exchange information. In Chapter Ten, when we look at the Internet, we will find that a large number of people are linking up with the biggest network of them all, the Internet. You may find a network at your job or in your school. As you drive, you can see telephone wires stretching across the sky; they, too, are part of a network.

Figure 4.1 Any time people are getting together to exchange information, they are forming a network.
Photograph provided by Robert Eplett, California Governor's Office of Emergency Services.

State or local law enforcement agencies are interested in creating networks larger than the one in your home and smaller than the Internet. Moreover, many state and local agencies have to link a variety of systems, using a combination of hardwired and wireless technology. This chapter is about looking at the technology that makes networking possible. The primary purpose of a network is the transmission of data.[2] That data, or information, could be writing, an image, a message, a sound, raw data, or virtually any information.[3]

Although state and local law enforcement agency networks are smaller than the Internet, they do, in many ways, take advantage of the Internet. For that reason, an entire chapter is devoted to law enforcement's use of the Internet. In Chapter Ten, when we look more closely at the Internet, we will explore several concepts in far greater detail. But in that chapter we are primarily concerned with the effect the Internet can have on state and local law enforcement agencies. That leaves us with a bit of a dilemma. We have to look at some Internet-related concepts now in order to explore networking. At times, we are going to give a brief description of a technology or process and delay full exploration until Chapter Eleven. For instance, networks are founded on the concept of **client–server architecture**.

Recall from Chapter Two, architecture refers to the design of a system or technology. In the client–server architecture, the individual workstation, called a **node**, is provided networking services by a **server**. Under this scheme, the server is a computer that provides files, printers, and processing power to the individual workstations. Under some configurations, the clients are simply dumb terminals; they have a keyboard and monitor but not their own microprocessor. Under other configurations, the workstations may have a computer, but draw other resources and programs from the server. A server is a special type of computer linked into a network; it is used only to manage the network, shared data, and shared resources.[4] For now, just remember a network is a way to connect computers.

Why Network?

A computer network provides us with several advantages. There are more than seventeen thousand state and local law enforcement agencies in the United States. Some of them are very large and cover a wide geographic area. In many

Figure 4.2 A server is another type of computer, but even though it is a computer, for users it is a peripheral device. It is a device outside the computer that one is using. Servers can be either dedicated or undedicated. A dedicated server would be used to manage data traffic on a network. Generally, we don't use servers as a workstation, but if we do, they are considered to be an undedicated server. One is dedicated to the network; the other is not. Servers are very expensive when compared to desktop computers. But as we shall see in Chapter Ten, a server can be used to do very complex and data-intensive tasks, such as manage multiple Internet Web sites.

instances, a single state or local law enforcement agency has many buildings associated with its agency. There might be a headquarters building, different station houses, administrative offices, and even a crime lab, each in a different physical location. A network allows them to share computer, data, and information resources. Moreover, in subsequent chapters we will see that much of the information state and local law enforcement agencies use comes from outside their organizations. Conversely, state and local agencies provide information to external organizations. Recall our traffic violator from Chapter One. When a police officer decides to run a check on a driver's license or a check for warrants, she is usually checking for information that comes from outside her organization. Before the advent of computer networks, a police officer might radio or call the station, and if it were during business hours, a clerk at the station could call the motor vehicle department to check for license information or, as in the case of a check for warrants, the clerk might call the Federal Bureau of Investigation. Today, because of networking, many of these types of inquiries are made right from the field, from a computer terminal in the police officer's vehicle. Also, after the citation has been issued, information about the violator must be exchanged with the motor vehicle department and potentially a court. Networking simplifies, speeds up, and increases the accuracy of these transactions. Even the smallest of police agencies can benefit from networking. Very small agencies probably use networking to receive external information—like driver's records and warrant information. But they can still use networks even in a single police station.

Figure 4.3 This communications dispatcher is a "human hub." She receives and routes information over radio, computer, telephone and paper mediums.
Photograph provided by Robert Eplett, California Governor's Office of Emergency Services.

As we progress in the text, particularly when we look at agency systems in Chapter Eight, you will see the value of networking for even the smallest of agencies.

Networks also provide organizations with the capability to back up data. Recall from Chapter Two that saving and backing up data is critical. In a network configuration, if one computer fails, the network can take over the processing load. If files and data are stored properly, even an agency that experiences the physical destruction of data (as in a fire) can still access the information. Additionally, networks can provide an organization with a greater degree of flexibility. A networked organization can have its employees perform some of their work just about anywhere. One of the operational strategies of the community policing model is to decentralize operations. In many organizations, this decentralization and move to get closer to the community is actually a physical relocation of staff. Think of the community substations that can be found around the country. Networking makes these substations possible; gives us the opportunity to decentralize operations; and as we shall see in Chapter Ten, can increase citizen participation, foster partnerships, and enhance problem solving.

Finally, networks can increase efficiency. Consider that it is the network that makes it possible for police officers to take computers into the field. It is networks that make it possible for them to query databases, complete reports, and check offenders—without having to return to the station. According to the Bureau of Justice Statistics, in 2000 40 percent of departments, employing 75 percent of all officers, were using in-field computers or terminals. Moreover, between 1990 and 2000, the percentage of local police officers employed by a department providing at least some officers with access to information via in-field computers increased by eight. As you look at larger organizations, you find those serving a population of greater than fifty thousand used in-field computers 80 percent of the time. And those computers weren't just dumb terminals. In 2000 29 percent of all local police officers in the United States had access to criminal history information via a network. So it is fairly common for a police officer to use a computer in the field, and the trend is increasing rather rapidly.[5] Whatever the benefits of these computer networks, in their simplest form, efficiency is enhanced by the reduction in drive time. OK, so networking is here to stay. Let's see how it works.

Back to Analog and Digital Signals

In Chapter Two we looked at digital information. In Chapter Three we were introduced to the concepts of analog and digital signals. We primarily talked about the differences when using wireless communications. There are some important factors to consider in relation to hardwired networks. Recall from Chapter Three that analog signals tend to dissipate as they move away from their sources. In hardwired networks the same phenomenon occurs. Think of water flowing through a garden hose. When it initially comes out of the faucet, the water has more force than it does when it comes out a lengthy hose. One of the reasons that this occurs is that the hose is flexible. As the water flows through the hose, the flexing hose absorbs some of the force of the water. An analog signal weakens as it travels through wire because of the resistance the signal meets in the **medium** that is carrying it. So, whether an analog signal is traveling through the air, a simple copper wire, or a coaxial cable, it is going to lose some strength. To get around this problem, an analog signal that is traveling a long distance might pass through an amplifier so the signal can be increased. However, the amplifier doesn't know the difference between the signal and the noise the signal has picked up as it travels through the medium, so the data signal is boosted, but so is the noise associated with it.

For this chapter, when we refer to medium we mean how a signal, analog or digital, is carried from point to point. For hardwired communications, the medium might be a coaxial cable or a fiber-optic line. For wireless, the medium is an RF signal.

Digital signals are subject to the same decrease in strength as analog signals, but as the digital signal weakens, instead of passing through a signal amplifier, it can be passed through a digital regenerator. The purpose of the digital regenerator is to repair the digital signal and send it on its way to its ultimate destination. So digital signals, the primary means of transmitting data communications, have several advantages over analog. Digital signals contain fewer errors, they can be transmitted at higher speeds, and as we shall see, the peripheral devices are less complex. For instance, analog modems can transmit at about 56,000 (56K) bits per second (bps) and receive at about 33.6 kbps. Our digital signal can far outpace the analog signal because with the right equipment, digital signals can travel at terabits per second. Recall from Chapter Two, a terabit is one trillion bits.

One more piece of technical information about analog data transmission. In Chapter Two we looked at how binary data is converted to the characters that we see on the monitor by commonly using ASCII. Thus far, our conversation has been primarily about the bits. Recall from Chapter Three that the bits are essentially added to the analog wave. The analog wave is called a **baud**. Public networks tend to run at about 2,400 baud, or 2,400 waves per second. Public networks would be really terrible if they could only attach one bit to each baud. That would give you a transmission speed of 2,400 bps. Our technology gets around this by adding more bits to each baud—generally in multiples of four. So a 2,400 baud analog signal that adds 12 bits to each baud would give you an effective transmission rate of 28,800 bps ($2,400 \times 12 = 28,800$).

In Chapter Three we also looked at packet data. Packet data is the essence of network transmission. When you send a request out over a network, the information is broken down into small packets. Networks that use this configuration are said to be packet switching, that is, breaking down a message into very small units, individually addressing them, and routing them through a network.[6]

So far we haven't addressed the possibility that as data travels over a network it can become corrupted. We did mention that as electrical signals move through wire, the signal is degraded or reduced. Remember when we talked about materials having the ability to conduct electricity in Chapter Two. Generally conductivity works in our favor; it gives us variable electrical charges necessary for transistors and it keeps the electricity where it should be—in the wires and not touching us. But as we have mentioned, as our signal or data passes through a wire, it is subject to the resistance of the medium and degrades. There are other things that can cause data to become corrupted. For instance, there could be a problem with your computer. Whatever the reason, it remains that data sent over a network can be potentially corrupted.

Making sure the information received is the information transmitted has vital importance. For instance, imagine you are paying your bills over the Internet. You decide to make a car payment of $200. The consequences could be huge if the information were corrupted and your bank received instructions to pay $2,000 toward your car payment. In law enforcement, what if the binary data that made up a digital fingerprint were corrupted. The wrong person could be identified, or perhaps a dangerous fugitive, released. One of the schemes commonly used to prevent these catastrophes is **bit parity**. As we know, binary data is a series of ones and zeros. If you take any stream of binary and add the numbers up, you will get either an odd or even number:

$$10111010 = 5(1+0+1+1+1+0+1+0)$$
$$10011010 = 4(1+0+0+1+1+0+1+0)$$

As you add a series of ones and zeros, the sum of any particular byte must be an odd or even number because there is no other choice. The error-checking device in bit parity is the addition of a digit at the end of the data to indicate if the sum is an odd or even number. A one is added for even-numbered sums, and a zero, for odd-numbered sums. So 10111010 becomes 101110100 and 10011010 becomes 100110101. The receiving computer compares the sum of the data stream to the bit parity digit. If there is a discrepancy, the receiving computer asks the sending computer to send the information a second time. In addition to bit parity, there are other error-checking schemes, such as cyclic-redundancy checking. For us, it is enough to know that error checking occurs and the basic workings of one such scheme.

Information travels between computers in a network in one of three ways. It could be a simplex transmission where the information travels in only one direction. We examined simplex data transmissions in the previous chapter; recall our simplex radio transmission. You have probably experienced a simplex transmission in the past twenty-four hours—television broadcasts and commercial radio broadcasts are examples of simplex transmissions. As far as computer networks go, you probably won't experience a simplex transmission.

In a half-duplex scheme information flows in both directions. This is a fairly common setup for most networks. In this scheme a network user makes a query on the system and must wait for the reply. It is a give-and-take transmission. In a half-duplex information can go only one way at a time. A full-duplex system allows for the transmission of information simultaneously in both directions.

That means there is no stop-and-wait aspect as with the half-duplex system. You get really fast throughput and response in a full-duplex system.

If we were going to design a network, there are three things we would want to look at. First, we would want the fastest throughput and response time possible. The faster it moves, the more advanced the applications that can be employed. For instance, if we want to have highly interactive sessions on the network, we need the maximum possible amount of data moving through the network. Second, recall from junior high school that the shortest distance between two points is a straight line? Well, if we were designing a network, we would want what is called the least-cost path. That is, we want the data on our network to flow through the fewest devices possible. Network security, physical configurations, and bureaucracies don't always make this possible, but it is a consideration. Least cost also refers to moving higher-priority information over faster lines and lower-priority data by other means. For public safety this might have a number of applications. For instance, we might have our in-field computers sending and receiving data via a CDPD scheme because we want the police officers to have the quickest response to inquiries concerning wanted offenders and stolen cars. But what about routine traffic? Maybe the least-cost path for voice is a radio system and not the relatively expensive CDPD. Our final requirement in design is reliability. After all, if the data doesn't get pushed around the network because the network goes down, the network is useless. So we want networks that are fast, cheap, and reliable. Now how do we connect it?

Things That Connect

In this section we are going to take a look at the ways of connecting and working in a network. A network starts somewhere, and the transmission of data ends somewhere; in between it can take quite a trip. In most networks the starting point and ending points of network transmissions are called nodes.[7] A node can be a computer workstation, a dumb terminal, a printer, or a server on the network. The thing to remember is a node is where the works starts and ends. Today in most networks when information leaves a node, it has to find a path to its final destination, the other node. When some people think of a network, they believe that the data moves in a straight line between the two points, or nodes. I suppose

Figure 4.4 This photograph is of an old-style, 300 bps modem.

they have a mental picture like two tin cans connected by a string. Although we said earlier that we want a network to be cost effective, in that data takes the most direct and cost-efficient route, we did not mean that it always travels to its path in the same manner. Networks would be really slow if everyone's data passed the same way all the time.

Generally, networks accomplish data transfer with a concept called packet switching.[8] In a packet-switching configuration, unused (available) portions of a network are chosen and the data passes through the most efficient available means. Recall from Chapter Three that we discussed packet data. When you send information on a network, the information is broken into the packets and routed on the network based on which path is most efficient. A message you send over a network may take many paths, as individual pieces of information, before it reaches its final destination. Of course, once at its final destination, the packets are reassembled and the message or data transfer is complete.

Many years ago, I played chess by mail. My opponent and I lived several thousand miles apart. Each of us kept a chessboard that had the previous moves made by both players. The chessboards were our nodes. They were, for both of us, the final destination that recorded the play. We could send only one move at a time, so we used postcards. Each postcard recorded the next move, a piece of data about the entire game. As I received my opponent's postcard, I recorded her move on my board, thought about it, moved my piece, recorded my move on a postcard and sent it to her. After I deposited the postcard in the mailbox, I had no idea which route the postcard took to travel thousands of miles. Sometimes I put the postcard in the mailbox in front of my home; sometimes I took it to the post office; sometimes I mailed it from work. I know the postcards always took a different route. I also know that the post office, based upon their workload, decided the best means to carry my piece of data thousands of miles and put it in her mailbox. Networks are like that. Your packets of data are the postcards, your computer is the chessboard, and the post office is the network. Each piece of data

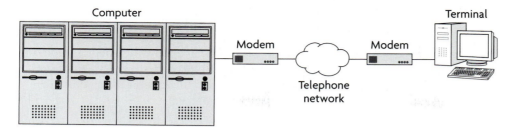

Figure 4.5 In this configuration, a computer dials into a large, central computer. The signal is passed through the central computer, along to the other modem, where it is translated back into a digital signal.

leaves, takes the best route, and is assembled at the other end. If you follow this analogy, each of your data packets has an address, just like my chess postcards. The address is so the network knows where to ultimately send the information.

Let's stay with the chessboard analogy for a while. When you mail a postcard, you must put it somewhere the post office will pick it up. If you leave a postcard in your bathroom, it is unlikely that the post office will pick it up and send it along their network. You must put it in a place where it can be picked up. The mailbox is your connection point between you and the post office. In networks, the connection point between your computer and the network is commonly a **modem**.

The word *modem* is a contraction of the words modulator and demodulator.[9] A modem is typically used to send digital data over a phone line. However, modems are also used to send data signals through radio waves on a wireless network. The important point so far is that modems change your digital signal into a form that can be transmitted over an analog medium. In essence, the sending modem modulates the data into a signal that is compatible with the phone line, and the receiving modem demodulates the signal back into digital data. Wireless modems convert digital data into radio signals and back. Modems came into existence in the 1960s as a way to allow terminals to connect to computers over the phone lines.

The 1960s were the age of time-shared computers. At that time, a business would buy computer time from a time-share computer and connect to it via a 300 bps modem. As we know from Chapter Three, a dumb terminal is a keyboard and a screen. From the dumb terminal, the user typed a character on the terminal, and the modem sent the ASCII code for the character to the computer. The computer then sent the character back to the terminal so it would appear on the screen. This is a good example of how simplex transmissions worked.

For a long time 300 bps was a pretty good speed because that meant you could transmit about 30 characters per second and no one could type or read that fast. So the speed of early modems was good for dumb terminals and simplex network transmissions. In a relatively short period of time, this speed became way too slow because people wanted to transmit large amounts of data. Imagine trying to play any modern game at 300 bps over the Internet. You would get kicked off the server! In 1984 the modem speed kicked up to about 1,200 bps and eventually it would reach 9,600 bps in the early 1990s. Today, with telephone and cable companies offering direct services, network speed for the home computer cooks at more than 8 Mbps.

Recall from Chapter Three that data is transmitted in a wireless fashion using a frequency shift key (FSK). Well, that is how modems started out. They used FSKs to convert your digital signals to analog and back to digital. So your modem

A Look Ahead

In Chapter Ten, when we look at the history of the Internet, we will see that in the 1970s, as personal computers entered the marketplace, bulletin board systems (BBS) were used for connections. A person would set up a computer with a modem or two and some BBS software, and other people would dial in to connect to the bulletin board. The users would run terminal emulators on their computers to emulate a dumb terminal.

is essentially converting the binary code 1 and 0 into two different tones. You have probably heard that NeeNaaNeeNaa sound as your modem at home connects (assuming you are still in the dark ages and using dial-up service). To make the modem scheme even faster, the dialing modem and the answering modem each use different tones, so the transmission can be a full-duplex transmission scheme.

But we needed more speed! In order to create faster modems, modem designers had to use more sophisticated technology than FSK. First, designers used to phase-shift keying (PSK) and then quadrature amplitude modulation (QAM). These techniques allowed a lot of information to be packed into the available bandwidth of a telephone line. We aren't going to drill down any deeper into PSK or QAM; it is beyond the scope of our task. Now, these techniques peaked at a transmission speed of about 48 kbps, or technology more commonly referred to as 56K modems.

But we wanted more speed! The technological evolution of the modem moved to asymmetric digital subscriber line (ADSL) modems. The word *asymmetric* is used because these modems send data faster in one direction than they do in another. An ADSL modem takes advantage of the fact that most homes, apartments, and offices have a dedicated copper wire running between them and the telephone company's central office. The telephone company's copper wire can carry far more data than the 3,000 Hz signal needed for your telephone's voice channel. If both the phone company's central office and your house are equipped with an ADSL modem on your line, then the section of copper wire between your house and the phone company can act as a purely digital high-speed transmission channel. The capacity is something like 1 million bps between your home, apartment, or office and the telephone company. Because the copper wire can carry enough data at once, the same line can transmit both a telephone conversation and the digital data. Essentially, an ADSL modem takes the 1,100,000 bandwidth of the copper wire and divides it into 249 4,000 Hz-wide virtual modems. So, with 249 modems working in your favor, the speed is really fast.[10]

While a modem is used in many homes and businesses, there are other ways of connecting to a network. One of the most common configurations is through the use of a **hub**. If you have traveled through an airport, you may have experienced a hub. Many airline flights are not direct flights. This is because it is cheaper to fly people into a central location, where they can pick up connecting flights to their ultimate destination. If you have ever changed planes to catch a connecting flight, you probably went through an airline's hub. A hub is a central location where things come together. In networking, the hub is the place that the data comes together from different nodes.

Most hubs include a device called a **switch**. There are networks that use switches not really hubs, but if you have a hub, you probably have a switch. The

Figure 4.6 This photograph represents a typical hub.

job of a switch is to determine how data will travel along its path to the intended destination. It is the job of the switch to look for the optimal route—perhaps the most direct, perhaps the least used, or perhaps avoiding a line that has a problem. The cool thing about hubs, switches, and routers is they only determine the data path, they do not record any information about the data that is passing through them. Because they are responsible for handing-off data to the network and not keeping information about the network, they are less complicated, more efficient, and cheaper.

A few sentences ago we mentioned routers. A **router** is like a switch, except a switch is generally thought of to be involved in a single network, whereas a router is a **bridge** between two networks.[11] The router determines the best path between the two different networks. In our chapter on the Internet, we will see that the Internet is not one big network, but rather it is a collection of networks made possible by technology like modems, hubs, routers, and switches.[12]

You may also hear network connection terms like **remote switch**. A remote switch is one that is controlled by a different location. In other words, the switch may be at your facility but is actually controlled by someone else. The control of remote switches will make sense after you have read through the chapter on the Internet.[13] There are also service switching points that work in conjunction with special networks. Finally, there are trunks. We looked at the operation of trunks in Chapter Three. A **trunk** is a circuit between different types of switching equipment. It may be located at the site of the network or between different physical locations.[14]

Before we move on, there is one other concept in making connections that we should know about. So far, we have seen physical technology that makes connections. However, in Chapter Two, we mentioned that there are legacy systems and proprietary systems that are difficult to merge into newer products. If you are running a new application but want to access a legacy database and you find out that your software cannot interface with the databases, what do you do? In some instances a connection can be made between the two applications by using **middleware**. Middleware is a catchall phrase that describes a software program that is used to connect different applications. It is the translator between the two. Now that we have seen how networks are connected, let's look at what passes through them.

Bandwidth

The fire department does not use garden hoses to put out fires. They use fire hoses because they have a greater capacity to throw water on a fire. **Bandwidth** refers to just that. In both wireless and hardwired communications, bandwidth refers to the capacity of the medium that carries the signal.[15] In hardwired analog communications the bandwidth of the medium, such as the coaxial cable, is measured in Hertz. Recall from Chapter Three, that Hertz refers to the number of cycles per second in a frequency. In this application, Hertz also is the number of cycles per second that the medium is capable of carrying. In hardwired analog signals, the bandwidth, or capacity, of a medium is the difference between the highest and lowest frequency that medium is capable of carrying. So a hardwired analog medium that could carry signals between 200 MHz and 600 MHz would have a bandwidth of 400 MHz (600−200=400).

The bandwidth of hardwired media carrying digital signals is measured in the number of bits per second the medium is capable of carrying. For instance, a typical T-1 line has a bandwidth of 1.54 megabits per second, or 1.54 million bits per second. Bandwidths are either narrowband or wideband. For instance, a T-1 line is a narrowband, whereas a T-3 line is a wideband. The T-3 line has the capacity of twenty-eight T-1 lines and runs at 44.7 million bits per second.[16]

Bandwidth is one of the major technological challenges for the future development of computer networks because it determines the speed data can be moved through a network.[17] Recall that when we looked at modems there was initially very little need for high bandwidth because a small amount of information was passing through the network. Now our needs have changed. When we say we want more speed, we mean we want more bandwidth. Some applications are bandwidth hogs. Try downloading a huge file like a detailed photograph. If you are working with a 56K modem, you can spend an hour downloading. But if you are working with ASDL and high bandwidth, it might take seconds.[18] As more information is passed to police officers in the field (like digital photographs, fingerprints, or maps), agencies are going to need high bandwidth or methods of reducing the size of data packets. Recall tactical information; is information tactical if it takes you forty-five minutes to download it? Finally, recall that the radio frequency spectrum is a finite resource. We can't make more. We know how networks are connected and what passes through them, but what makes it possible for all the different computers to use networks?

Protocols

There is a **protocol** for just about everything we do in life. A protocol is an agreement between people on how a transaction should take place. Think about going to the movies (instead of studying). There is a distinct protocol for admission. You must stand in line to buy a ticket, tell the cashier which movie you want to see, tell the cashier in a language he or she can understand, and pay the cashier in United States currency. You, on the other hand, expect to be told the price of

There are a variety of protocols in use. While we do not need to examine them in detail, we should have a quick definition of them.

- Simple Mail Transport Protocol (STMP): This protocol is used for sending Internet-based e-mail.
- *Point-to-Point Protocol (PPP):* This is an Internet set of rules and languages used to transmit packets of data. It is the standard routing technique used by a modem.[23]
- *Post Office Protocol (POP):* This is a common protocol used for the transmission of e-mail messages.
- *Multi purpose Internet Mail Extensions (MIME):* Although e-mail is the most common

form of transmission on networks, it has the limitation of only transmitting ASCII characters. As we know from an earlier chapter, ASCII is only 128 characters. Although most computers support an advanced ASCII, which gives you 256 characters, this is insufficient for the transfer of more complex information via e-mail such as spreadsheets and photographs. To get around this limitation, MIME adds instructions and rules to the e-mail that allow the receiving computer to open the attachments and view the information, such as graphics, programs, sound, and video files.

Source: Cunningham, B2B, 179.

the movies and given the proper change and a ticket for admission. If either of you violate the protocol, your admission to the movie will be delayed until you reestablish the proper protocol. For instance, would you get into the movie if you tried to pay in dinars, francs, shillings, or pesos? Probably not. Would you accept change in any of those currencies? Probably not. The protocol for computers to communicate with each other is similar.[19] There is a distinct language and set of rules you must follow to establish a link to the network.

Here are some of the rules for communications between computers. How is an error in data transmission repaired? What type of data packages can be used? Which devices transmit first? It is becoming very common for many networks to use the **Transmission Control Protocol/Internet Protocol (TCP/IP)**.[20] Moreover, if you want to use the Internet, your computer must use the TCP/IP. In Chapter Three we briefly looked at Cellular Digit Packet Data (CDPD). CDPD uses the TCP/IP to allow field officers to make requests from databases outside their own agency's network.[21] A communications application should have options, so the user can interface with different equipment.[22] Since we are not going to be programmers, we are just going to look at some very basic definitions of the various types of protocols in use.

Basic Network Types

The most common configuration of a network is called hierarchical, or a vertical or tree structure. It is a common structure because it is the most simple and provides for a common location for the control of errors and problems. But because of the common control points, it can also get bottlenecked with data flow. You might set this type of network up in your home or small office.

The most popular network configuration is a **local area network (LAN)**. It is considered a horizontal network that allows for data flow between devices. A LAN allows each device on the network to receive every network transmission. A LAN has the disadvantage in that since all devices share a single data channel, if the channel fails, the LAN is out of business. So many LANs use redundant or backup networks in case of channel failure. Since the LAN does not have a single control point, it is difficult to isolate problems with devices on the network.

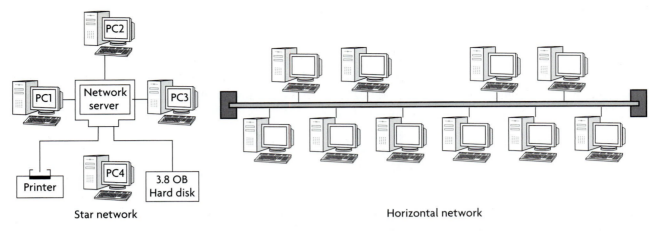

Star network   Horizontal network

Figure 4.7 These drawings represent two types of network configurations–horizontal and star.

A third type is a star configuration. The software for a star configuration is relatively simple. As you can image, all transmissions come from a hub, or the center of the star. While this is similar to the tree, or vertical, network the hub is responsible for sending information to other nodes and isolating problems. For our purposes, we will leave exact network configurations alone and describe networks as a LAN, **wide area network (WAN)**, or **wireless local area network (WLAN)**.

Imagine you are in school at the humanities building. The building is very large, say eight stories, with many offices and classrooms. Each of the offices and classrooms has access to a network, and in that building the network is considered a LAN.[24] Your school has many other buildings. It can join all of the networks together and create a large LAN for the entire school, or it can create a LAN in each large building and link those LANs together in a WAN. Succinctly described, a LAN is a network that operates in one specific location.[25] That location can be each large building or the entire campus. The problem with putting the entire campus on one LAN is that the more devices or nodes you add, the more data you begin to push through limited bandwidth. You can probably guess that this slows down the network. If a LAN, WAN, or Metropolitan area network (MAN) uses Internet protocols (the rules of transaction) it is considered an intranet.[26]

On the other hand, a WAN is usually used to connect geographically separated networks together.[27] Moreover, WANs are almost exclusively Internet-protocol (IP) based and, therefore, intranets.[28] Different LANs are connected together to create WANs through the use of telephone lines, dedicated high-speed lines called T-1 lines (with speeds up to 1.5 Mbps) and T-3 lines (with speeds up to 45 Mbps).[29] A T-3 line is really fast and can handle data-intensive transmissions such as real-time video.

The final network configuration we are going to look at is a wireless local area network (WLAN). A WLAN uses radio waves to connect among the mobile node,

If you really have the need for speed, you can use asynchronous transfer mode (ATM), fiber channel, or an Integrated Services Digital Network (ISDN). While ATM is a relatively new technology and still has to develop standards, it looks to be very promising for the data-intensive organization. Fiber channel is a method of transmission developed from fiber optics. ISDN combines voice and digital into a single medium that allows for the rapid transfer of information.

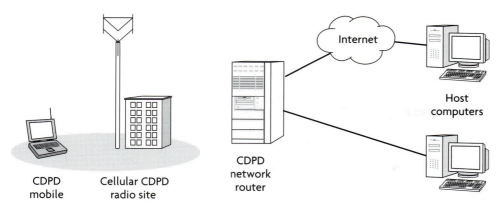

CDPD mobile **Cellular CDPD radio site** **CDPD network router** **Internet** **Host computers**

Figure 4.8 The combinations of hardwired and wireless technologies provide powerful tools for the exchange of information.

mobile computer, and the hardwired network.[30] We saw how the bulk of wireless works in Chapter 3. It is important to remember that for nearly all police technology functions, wireless and hardwired networks are joined at some access point so police officers can access and, in some cases, input data. The access point is the connector between wireless and hardwired networks.[31] Moreover, the difference between the RF configurations we saw in Chapter 3 and WLANs is distance. An RF-configured network that exchanges data, like those in Chapter 3, is capable of covering much larger areas than a WLAN, which covers an area with a radius of about 300 feet.

Data Security

In the past two decades, a multitude of networks have been built and are being used. Many of these networks provide access to databases that contain confidential or sensitive information. In Chapter 16, when we look at Hi-Tech crime, we will revisit and expound upon some data-security issues. For now, there are some issues, terms, and technologies that we need to examine to continue to build our foundation.

This section of the chapter could alternatively be called network security, or computer security, but in reality what we are most trying to protect is the information contained in the various systems. We back up data because sometimes when data is lost, it is not recoverable. In writing this textbook, I backed up the chapters every night and physically stored the zip disk elsewhere. It is the information that is most valuable. That is not to say that the destruction of the physical components of the networks is not important. Indeed physical security is often overlooked. Physical security of a network is protecting our IT systems from natural disasters and bad humans. Protection could consist of placing servers, routers, and switching equipment behind locked doors. Physical security

The purpose of the text is not to make you a programmer, engineer, or systems analyst. The point is to make you a more educated user of police technology. Every once in a while I have to point out the secret tech speak—industry consultants love to use the term "802.11b" in a conversation. They also use the term Wi-Fi (pronounced WHY-FY). Both terms refer to the industry standard in wireless networking. Don't let them dazzle you!
Source: Swope, "Guide to Wireless Security."

is also backing up data in one or more locations. By having data in two places, a fire or flood in one will not kill the backup copy; this is a physical aspect of security. So physical security can be defined as anything we do to physically protect our systems and information.[32]

Wireless networks provide interesting security problems. First, they are fairly easy to set up. Many organizations use **commercial Off-the-shelf (COTS)** technology. A laptop user simply installs a wireless modem (handheld PDAs have these built in), the modem sends RF transmissions back and forth to an access point, and bingo—the user is in the network. Since access points have a range of about 300 feet, WLANs are particularly vulnerable. After all, you are sending the signal and getting the signal right out of the atmosphere. Basically anyone can do it.

So WLANs are fairly vulnerable, but so is the rest of the network. Recall, most large LANs and certainly WANs are intranets and, therefore, IP based. In Chapter Ten we shall see that the greatest asset of the Internet is the open communication standards. Anyone can play. If your network is IP based, your transmission protocols are known. This means we have to come up with some other methods to keep bad people out. In addition to the physical aspects of network security, it has the aspects of access, data, protocols, information, and transactions. Each of those different parts can have a mechanism designed to keep out those who should not be in.[33]

One of the first lines of defense is called a **firewall**. A firewall can prevent unwanted users and data from getting into a network. A firewall operates by controlling access to the network based upon the contents of the data packets being transmitted on the network.[34] A firewall can be a separate device or an internal software/hardware combination. In addition to firewalls, network data, especially network data that is being transmitted onto the Internet or via a wireless device, should be encrypted. **Encryption** is changing text or data into a form that is unreadable without a key. Nearly everyone as a child had a secret code that only their friends knew about. Encryption is basically the same. Once data is encrypted, if you don't know the key, you cannot easily access the information. This is done through a mathematical process.[35] The mathematical process is based upon using an algorithm (a set of instructions) and a key. The algorithm encodes the message; the key (often a single word or code) decodes the message. If a single key is used, the encryption is said to be a single-key system. There are also dual-key systems.[36] In addition to using encryption, one of the simplest and often the most effective means of protecting a network is the use of a password to log into the network.[37]

All of the security aspects of firewalls we have looked at thus far are somewhat passive. They are there to prevent a security breach. But many organizations are taking a much more active role in security by employing **intrusion detection** software. Intrusion detection is a security management system that gathers and analyzes information from different parts of the network. It looks to identify security breaches from outside and inside the network. Intrusion detection software scans a network, performing a vulnerability assessment of the network and devices on the network, looking for user and system activities, typical system configurations that make a network vulnerable, file and system integrity, and any pattern of abnormal behavior. The parts of an intrusion detection system that look to analyze a system configuration are also considered passive security measures. The parts of the intrusion detection system that are considered active systems are those that react to known methods of attack and protect the system.

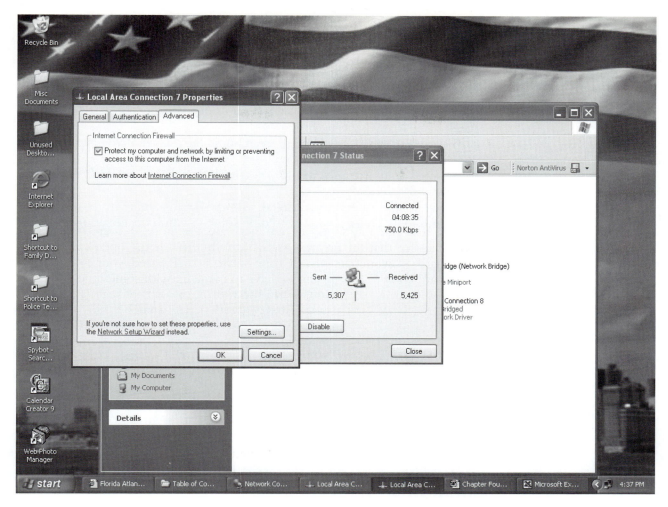

Figure 4.9 Today most operating systems come with a firewall available in the software. This screen capture shows the location in Windows XP where a user would enable/disable the firewall protection.

Chapter Summary

Networks are valuable ways of exchanging information. Whether a human network at a convention or a computer network, the concept of a network is the same—it is a method of exchanging information. We learned that networks consist of nodes, or workstations. These are places that users like you and me enter the network. From our node we are connected to the network by a variety of technologies—modems, routers, and switches. Our network connection can be into the Internet, as at home; or we can be at work or school, enter a local area network, go through a wide area network, and then out into the Internet. These transitions are possible because most of our networking is done through a standard system of protocols like TCP/IP. Or we might enter a network in some RF form, using a laptop or palmtop computer to exchange information.

The open architecture, standard protocols, and RF technology used in networks make our information vulnerable. Since much of the information we exchange, especially in law enforcement, is sensitive, there is a need to protect the security of networks. That vulnerability can be offset by using passwords, firewalls, and intrusion detection software.

Discussion Questions

1. Look around you; what networks do you use? Can you identify a LAN or a WAN?
2. How would your work, school, or even home life change if you had to depend on a 300 bps modem?
3. What types of information would you consider sensitive and need to protect from unauthorized users?
4. If you were on a committee charged with the responsibility to set up a LAN at a community college, what would be some of your considerations?

Key Terms

Bandwidth
Baud
Bit Parity
Bridge
Client–Server Architecture
Commercial off-the-Shelf (COTS)
Encryption
Firewall
Hub

Intrusion Detection
Local Area Network (LAN)
Medium
Middleware
Modem
Network
Node
Protocol
Remote Switch
Router

Server
Switch
Transmission Control Protocol/Internet Protocol (TCP/IP)
Trunk
Wide Area Network (WAN)
Wireless Local Area Network (WLAN)

Endnotes

1. "Toward Improved Criminal Justice"
2. Qureshi, Hartman, and Siegel, "Computer Networks."
3. U.S. Congress, Office of Technology Assessment, *Electronic Surveillance,* 74.
4. See note 1 above.
5. Department of Justice, Bureau of Justice Statistics, 2000 State and Local Law Enforcement Statistics.
6. U.S. Congress, Office of Technology Assessment. *Electronic Surveillance in a Digital Age,* 73.
7. Cunningham, *B2B,* 181.
8. Ibid.
9. Imel and Hart, *Understanding Wireless Communications,* 114.
10. *Electronic Crime Needs Assessment,* 41.
11. See note 2 above.
12. Cunningham, *B2B,* 182.
13. See note 6 above.
14. See note 3 above.
15. Cunningham, *B2B,* 172.
16. Imel and Hart, *Understanding Wireless Communications,* 113.
17. See note 2 above.
18. Cunningham, *B2B,* 171.
19. See note 2 above.
20. Imel and Hart, *Understanding Wireless Communications,* 71.
21. Cunningham, *B2B,* 184.

22. See note 2 above.
23. See note 7 above.
24. See note 1 above.
25. Cunningham, *B2B,* 179.
26. See note 1 above.
27. Ibid.
28. Cunningham, *B2B,* 178.
29. Ibid., 185.
30. See note 1 above.
31. Swope, "Guide to Wireless Security."
32. See note 1 above.
33. Cunningham, *B2B,* 103.
34. Ibid., 104.
35. See note 1 above.
36. Cunningham, *B2B,* 104.
37. Ibid., 181.

Chapter Five
Geographic Information

Learning Objectives

- The student will understand the basic parts of a map and how they are used.

- The student will understand the theory of trilateration in conjunction with **time difference on arrival (TDOA)**.

- The student will understand how **global positioning satellites** operate.

- The student will understand the difference between a map and a **geographic information system**.

- The student will understand the different types of information contained in a geographic information system and the general uses of that information.

Introduction

As we have discussed, much of police work is about information. Some of the information line employees, supervisors, and managers work with concerns geography. There are many definitions for the word *space,* but for law enforcement purposes geography refers primarily to two things: the distance between two objects and the physical characteristics of those objects. The objects could be natural terrain, the streets the officer patrols, or locations that require police response. As with all information the police work with, information about geography can be either tactical or strategic.

An example of the tactical nature of geography would be the driving distance between an officer's current location and a call for service. The tactical information the officer would require is the driving route. In another instance, officers responding to a robbery call at a bank would benefit from having information about the interior of the bank, the locations of exits, and the surrounding area. The tactical uses for geographic information apply to every call for service or self-initiated activity an officer is involved in. As we progress further in the text, we will find that geographic information also has a wide variety of strategic purposes. It is used in determination of beats or patrol areas, the planning for natural and man-made disasters, and crime analysis.[1]

There are a wide variety of technologies that are used to assist law enforcement personnel with geographic information. These technologies range from simple maps to complex software and hardware that allow for detailed analysis of geographic information, but maps are the fundamental component of geographic information. In this chapter we will be looking at some of the technical aspects of technologies that relate to geographic information. Although we are going to look at some very sophisticated technologies, such as global positioning satellites and geographic information systems software, there are a variety of basic terms and skills we need to understand.

What Is a Geographic Information System?

Geographic information systems (GIS) are a combination of computer hardware, computer software, data, and people producing visual displays of

This is the last chapter where we are specifically concentrating on building our understanding of basic science and technology. In the next chapter we will begin to explore how technology works in law enforcement.

information.[2] The software and hardware involved in GIS allow the people to store, display, analyze, and create these visual representations. But as with all technology, it is the people who ultimately make the magic.[3] You can think of GIS as a relational database designed to help store, organize, and use spatial information.[4] In a GIS database we are storing information on the space around us. It is information about streets, parks, buildings—anything that occupies physical space on the planet, including moving vehicles.[5]

GISs are a combination of technologies that enhance our understanding of geography. By collecting, storing, analyzing, and displaying geographic information, we can use real-time information to assist us with tactical field problems, or we can use the information for longer-term planning and decision making.[6] Since GIS is a branch of geography, we need a little information on maps and map reading.

Cartography Basics

Cartography is the science of map making. All of us have looked at a map at one time or another, but did we really understand what we were looking at; did

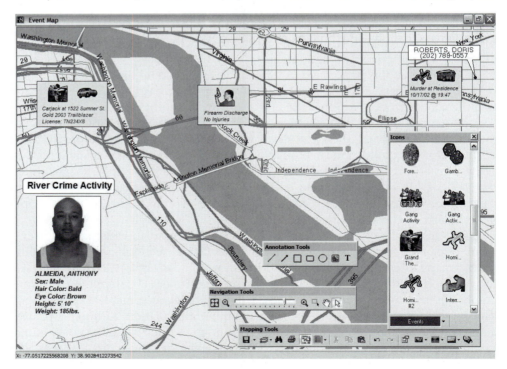

Figure 5.1   GIS is commonly referred to as a mapping system. There are a wide variety of commercially available mapping systems ("Computer-Aided Dispatch," 2.). The screen capture here represents a visual display of how information about geography is used in conjunction with an investigation.
Permission for screen capture provided by Pen-Link™, Ltd.

COMMON MAP TERMS

For a map to enable the reader to quickly and accurately use the information, it must have these basic components:

- *Title:* A map must tell the reader what, where, and when.
- *Orientation:* Cartographers normally place North at the top. However, if there is a deviation, the map should have a symbol to orient the user.

- *Scale:* Scales allow the reader to make judgments about distances and spatial relationships.
- *Legend:* The legend is essentially an explanation of the symbols used to represent objects on the map.
- *Grid:* Maps should have a coordinate system, in the form of parallels of latitude and meridians of longitude.

we find the information we were looking for? Essentially, a map is a visual representation of a defined space. Because today a map could be made of paper or viewed on a computer monitor, it is a visual representation. And because a map could be of a large area (like the map of a city) or a smaller area (like a map of a circuit board), it represents the space we are interested in. It is not uncommon for people to have difficulty in reading and using maps. Once out of the academy, the first thing a new police officer is taught is the importance of always knowing his location.[7] Most field training officers spend hour upon hour drilling this into the new police officers' heads. The implications of not knowing the location in an emergency can be devastating. For instance, a police officer who is driving down the street, unaware of her present location might come across some kind of life-threatening situation—anything from a person who is having a heart attack to a robbery in progress. The first few seconds are critical, and taking time under pressure to figure out her location can have very dire consequences. With map reading, knowing your location is the starting point.

Map reading in the wilderness is somewhat different than map reading in an urban area. In the wilderness, once you're lost, there are no sign posts. Generally speaking, anywhere you are in an urban area, you can find a street sign. Once you know your location, it is time to start using the map. To properly use a map, it must be oriented. Most maps are oriented with the direction of north at the top. For navigating urban areas, we don't have to worry about an exact orientation to north, nor do we have to worry about the differences between true and magnetic north.

So you are sitting in your car and somewhat lost. You know where you are and the address of your intended destination. You pick up the commercial map you bought at the supermarket, and it is a confusing mass of symbols, lines, and street names. Even though you know where you are physically, you don't know where you are on the map. The first thing is to find the orientation symbol and move the map in your hands until the orientation symbol is actually pointing in the direction of north, relative to where you are sitting. Of course, if you were outside the car, you could turn around, but because later we have to learn to use geographic information that is on static displays, like a computer monitor, it is best to learn to move the map around in your head.

Now that you have orientated the map, you need to remember what the orientation is. If you don't, you will do what thousands of hapless map readers do every year, you will find your location, find your destination and work out your route, only to find that because the map was not orientated properly, you followed the directions upside down and went in the wrong direction. Of course, you get more lost and much more frustrated. Most commercially available maps have an alphabetical listing of the streets the map covers somewhere on the map or in an index in the large book-type maps. You look around to find your location. Let's presume that you find you are at the intersection of Main Street and Broadway. You look at the alphabetical listing and find Main Street listed. If Main Street is a lengthy street on the map, you may see several listings. You will note that after Main Street there are a number of single letter and number combinations, like B4, A6, and so on. These number combinations correspond to the grid that is overlaying the street information on the map. A grid is several parallel lines that crisscross the map. The lines are horizontal and vertical, and correspond to X and Y coordinates in a two-dimensional graph. Moreover, the lines are similar in nature to the horizontal and vertical lines cartographers call latitude and longitude.[8]

On a global scale, latitude is measured in degrees from the equator, with positive values going north and negative values going south. In comparison to our commercial map grid, latitude lines are the lines moving horizontally across the paper. On the other hand, longitude is measured from the Prime Meridian, which is the line of longitude that runs through Greenwich, England, with positive values going east and negative values going west. In comparison to our commercial map, longitude is the vertical lines. The Earth is a sphere, so it is 360 degrees from one point all the way around the Earth back to that same point. Latitudinal lines measure up, from the equator to the North Pole 90 degrees and down from the equator to the South Pole 90 degrees. Longitudinal lines measure east 180 degrees and west −180 degrees. Together, longitude and latitude form a grid system that can locate any position on our planet. In order to make these measurements more precise, the grid is broken into degrees, minutes, and seconds. By knowing information to this precise measurement, buildings can be located.

Back to our commercial map—the combination of letters and numbers following the street you are looking for is the grid on the map wherein the street is location. Let's presume that the map tells us that Broadway is located in B4. We turn back to the map and see that there are numbers across the top and letters along the side. The numbers across the top indicate the horizontal portion of the grid and the letters along the side give us the vertical portion of the grid. By finding the grid B4, we have limited our search for Broadway to a much smaller area.

We now know our location and the location of our destination. The next task is to determine our route. As we determine the route to our destination we may decide to stop at a certain location along the way in order to verify we are going in the right direction. Often people unconsciously pick out this point where they double-check their progress. This is known as a **waypoint**. From our commercial map, we have learned about latitude and longitude, grids, destinations, and waypoints.

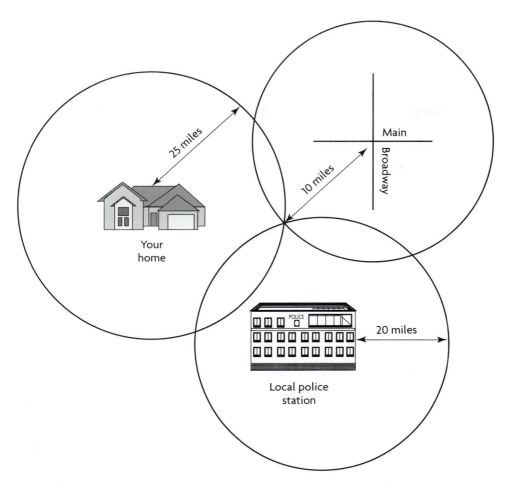

Figure 5.2 Suppose that I was trying to describe my location to you in terms of trilateration. First, I told you that I was twenty-five miles from your home. By using your home as a the first known location, you would draw a circle around your home with a radius of twenty-five miles. The drawing is a visual representation of the information I have given you. I am somewhere on that circle. I then told you that I was twenty miles from the local police station. The second drawing shows the second circle with a radius of twenty miles drawn around the police station. Furthermore, it displays that the two circles intersect, telling you that I am on one of the two points where the circles overlap. Finally, the third drawing demonstrates what occurs when I give you a third piece of information concerning my distance from another stationary location. The third circle shows that I am also ten miles from the intersection of Main Street and Broadway. My present location is at the point where all three circles intersect. In trilateration, we discover the precise location of an object by determining its distance from three points.

Increasingly, law enforcement organizations are using a variety of computer hardware, software, and radio frequency devices to determine location and navigate the surrounding geography. The reference to **www.mapquest.com** in the previous Try This box is an example of software designed to provide geographic information. However, the schemes being used today in relation to urban navigation not only have aspects of software that already knows the basic geography, they can also tell a police officer's location and provide a recommended route, along with waypoints. Generally speaking, any device that provides real-time information on a vehicle's location is described as an automatic vehicle locator

Real time refers to a piece of technology that is able to report information as it changes. If you were watching a news report that included live video feed of an event, you would consider this information to be reported in real time, or as it happens.

(AVL) technology. A fundamental mathematical concept called trilateration is at the foundation of most AVL technologies. Trilateration is similar to the navigational technique of **triangulation**. While both methods can determine relative position between points, triangulation uses measurements of both distances and angles, whereas trilateration uses only distance.

Global positioning satellites (GPS) use this mathematical technique in conjunction with a second mathematical formula to provide users with very precise information as to location. A system that is integrated with GPS technology is actually using a receiver designed to receive radio frequency (RF) signals from a constellation of satellites. This receiver is the first of three components of the GPS system. The second component is a network of satellites.

Navstar

In 1978 the United States began launching a series of twenty-four satellites into orbit around the earth. Ultimately, in 1994 the complete series of satellites was operational, completing the Department of Defense Navigation Satellite Timing and Ranging (NAVSTAR) system.[9] Twenty-one of the satellites are actively used in the system and three are considered spares.[10] Positioned twelve thousand miles above the Earth's surface and traveling at approximately seven thousand miles an hour, this network of satellites circles the globe every twelve hours. Moreover, the satellites are positioned in such a manner as to allow any GPS receiver on the surface of the Earth to receive signals from at least four of the satellites at any one time.

The satellites themselves weigh between three and four thousand pounds. They are solar powered with a battery backup system. Each includes an atomic clock and transmits a continuous signal on several frequencies.[11] Because the orbits of the satellites are subject to forces like the gravitational pull of the moon that can change their precise orbits, they are equipped with rocket boosters so adjustments can be made. Finally, the satellites have a life expectancy of about ten years.

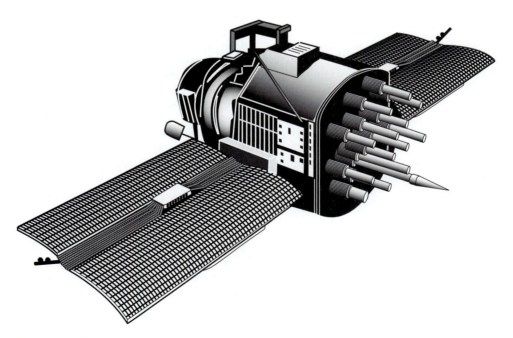

Figure 5.3 The GPS system is composed of twenty-four satellites much like the one shown in the drawing.

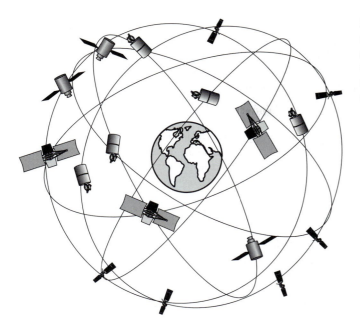

Figure 5.4 The satellites are spaced around the globe so that any point on the Earth can receive a signal from at least four satellites.

The final component of the GPS system is a ground control station. There are four ground monitoring stations that receive information from the satellites and send information such as orbit correction to them. The monitoring stations are controlled by one central control station. These three components (receiver, satellite transmitters, and control stations) use trilateration and the concept of **time difference on arrival (TDOA)** to give the user a precise location.[12]

We know that radio waves travel at the speed of light, or 186,000 miles per second. If we can measure how long it takes for a radio signal to go from a transmitter to a receiver, we can calculate the distance between the two. Although a simple formula (speed multiplied by time equals distance), it is a complex operation. The basic principle of GPS is that location is determined by calculating how long it takes for a radio signal from a series of satellites to reach a GPS receiver.[13] Let's look at a few particulars.

In our example on trilateration we used circles to determine location. With the circles, we were working in two dimensions. In reality, GPS satellites are transmitting in spheres. This is more difficult to visualize, but think of the satellite transmitting a circle all around itself. The satellite is a three-dimensional object, therefore the transmissions are three-dimensional spheres. For TDOA to work, not only must we know the exact location of the satellite, but all of the clocks in the system must register the same time. First, let's look at determining the exact position of the satellite.

The orbits of the satellites that make up the GPS system are very predictable. Because the orbits are predictable, their probable locations are known in advance. Information on their locations is based upon a prediction of the orbital path in a software database that is known as an **almanac**. Yet satellites are subject to the force of gravity and although their paths have been well predicted, they occasionally deviate from the prediction (this is called an **ephemeris error**). The job of the monitoring station and the master control station is to track the satellites and detect deviations from their predicted orbital paths. When a deviation is noted, the deviation is taken into account, the orbital path is recalculated, and the almanac is updated. The almanac information and the precise location of the satellites are updated about every six hours.[14]

For the TDOA to work, it is critical that the receiver's and the transmitter's clocks be precisely synchronized. The satellites accomplish this by having atomic clocks. These clocks are not only extraordinarily accurate on their own, but are constantly updated by the monitoring stations and master control. So just as in adjusting for variations in orbit path, the on-board atomic clocks are synchronized throughout the network of satellites. However, that leaves the ground-based receivers. Commercially available GPS receivers do not have atomic clocks because of clock's size and expense. In TDOA, the measurement of time is in very small nanoseconds. Even the smallest deviation between the satellite transmitter time and the receiver time will result in an error in the calculated position of the receiver. This makes the mathematical formula slightly more complex. Now we must solve the time difference among the receiver and transmitter and the TDOA for the three satellites in our trilateration. In order to solve for four unknowns, we need four sources. The GPS system solves this by using a fourth satellite in every GPS calculation. With this fourth satellite signal, the GPS prediction of the receiver is now accurate.

Although the GPS system as we have explored is designed to be as accurate as the technology will allow, it does have an error. By understanding the errors, technology has been developed to compensate for the errors and increase the accuracy of the system. When these errors occur together, they can make the GPS system off by 150 to 300 feet. The errors in GPS location determination are referred to as the **error budget**.

We have already discussed one of the possible errors—**clock drift**. Another factor that can potentially cause errors in the predicted location of the receiver is the nature of radio waves. Recall from Chapter Three, radio waves can be affected by the atmosphere. For instance, we discussed the possibility of communications occurring in the low end of the very high frequency band being subject to interference from skip transmission. Just as those RF signals can be refracted by the ionosphere in unpredictable ways, so can a transmission from a GPS satellite be affected by passing through both the ionosphere and troposphere.[15]

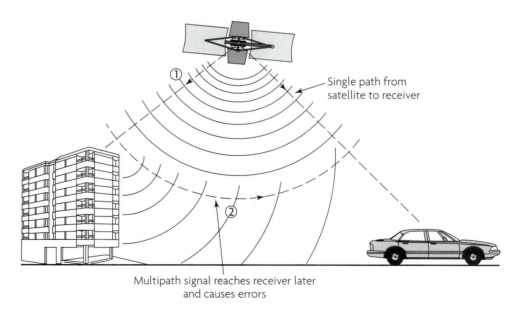

Figure 5.5 Terrain and buildings can distort a GPS signal because if a signal is deflected off of them prior to being received, distance and, thus, time are added to the GPS calculations. In this drawing, 1 represents the original path of the signal, and 2 demonstrates how the signal path is changed and lengthened when the satellite signal bounces off a building.

A Look Ahead

In law enforcement, this can give the police officer an edge in knowing where he or she is located. In future chapters we will see how this technology can be used by dispatch centers to assist in sending police officers to an emergency call.

In addition to clock drift and atmospheric conditions, GPS data can be significantly distorted by the Department of Defense (DOD). Global positioning satellites are part of a passive system and transmit their information to anyone with a receiver. For military operations, GPS technology has significantly improved navigation on land, on sea, and in the air. Were it not for GPS technology, many of the precision munitions used in recent conflicts would not be as precise. Prior to May 1, 2001, the DOD employed **selective availability (SA)** so that the GPS signals were not as accurate for receivers not in the use of the United States government.[16] Since that time, SA has been removed so that civilian signal reception is improved so that receivers can calculate position to within meters; however, military applications can determine location to within centimeters.[17]

The final possible error involved in GPS signals involves the nature of radio waves. In addition to the GPS signal being refracted by the atmosphere, it can bounce off the terrain and buildings. When a GPS receiver captures a signal that has bounced off of something it is said to have captured a multipath signal. Figure 5.5 shows a signal bouncing off a skyscraper in a city. Because the signal is reflected before it is received, it has taken a longer path. Of course, in a TDOA measurement, this longer path could distort the receiver's calculation of its location.

Although not an error, another factor of GPS technology that can impact the accuracy of the receiver's reading is the alignment of the satellites themselves. Generally, the farther apart the satellites are, the greater the precision of the reading the receiver can make. This alignment factor is referred to as the **dilution of precision (DOP)**. Moreover, the alignment of the satellites used for the reading can magnify or minimize the other errors. Certain GPS receivers use the almanac information to select the best satellite alignments for their readings. Indeed, some receivers allow users to deselect readings from some predetermined DOP alignments. Finally, certain GPS receivers take input from all GPS satellites in their view, not just the nearest four. In essence, GPS is a satellite navigation system that uses position, velocity, and time to compute position.[18] One of the uses of GPS is to track the exact location of vehicles.

Automatic Vehicle Location

One of the primary applications of GPS technology in law enforcement is the inclusion of GPS receivers in patrol cars communications packages. This allows for the communications dispatch center (refer to Chapter Seven for more information on dispatch centers) to know the location of the patrol cars; it is an **automatic vehicle locator (AVL)** system.[19] We saw earlier that there can be some location errors in the GPS data. Of course, the more accurate our information, the more exact our response. If a law enforcement agency is using GPS for AVL, it can improve the accuracy of the GPS system with a technique called **differential correction**.

Differential correction involves having a stationary source of GPS signal reception in order to compare to the mobile signals. Since the stationary GPS receiver's location is known and precisely determined, the signals can be compared

On the face of it, GPS technology seems rather benign. But what if you are the police officer whose location is always known by his supervisor? And what if a GPS device is attached to a suspect's vehicle in order to enhance surveillance? As we shall see in subsequent chapters, GPS technology can be as controversial as it is useful.

and distortion removed. By having this benchmark location, all of the errors except multipath and ionosphere distortion are completely removed.

For law enforcement agencies, there are three types of GPS receivers from which to choose. Each offers differing levels of accuracy, but there is a cost in the time it takes to calculate the position of the receiver. So far we have looked at the technology associated with the GPS receiver type considered a coarse acquisition (C/A) GPS receiver. Working in conjunction with a base station to provide a differential correction, C/A receivers are accurate to approximately three to fifteen feet. Because it takes the GPS receiver approximately one second to provide this level of accuracy, it is probably most suited for the general law enforcement purpose of AVL. The other two types of commercial GPS are carrier phase and dual-frequency. These GPS receivers can provide extremely precise location information; however, it may take the receivers up to thirty minutes to develop the precise calculations necessary to give a location within centimeters.[20]

There are other technological methods of determining location. There are commercially available products that use cellular telephone signals (in Chapter Seven we will look at time difference on arrival (TDOA) and angle on arrival (AOA) as it relates to cellular technology) and those that use their own antenna systems to conduct trilateration and triangulation.[21] However, the concepts are generally the same and because GPS technology can be used anywhere in the world, it is becoming the dominant method for AVL.

Global Positioning Satellite Technology and Geographic Information Systems

So far we have looked at some mapping basics and how technology can be used to provide us with precise locations. In law enforcement the use of geographic information is far more than knowing where you are and where you are going. By having the ability to ask questions about the objects represented by the map, we can examine the role they play in crime. For instance, are the instances of accidents wherein alcohol is involved related to the location of a specific bar or liquor store? If so, is traffic enforcement the best way to reduce the number of accidents, or should the police be concentrating their efforts on how the bar or liquor store conducts business?

The use of geographic information systems (GIS) by police agencies to analyze crime is a relatively new technology. As of 2000, only 6 percent of the state and local departments, who employed approximately 8 percent of all officers, had GIS information linked to an in-field technology for officers.[22] By having the ability to ask questions about how things are related to each other, law enforcement may increase public safety by fixing causes instead of responding to a problem after it has occurred. Before we can examine these possibilities, we need to establish a stronger foundation of the basics of geographic information.

We have looked at methods of recording an object's location—the first was the grids on the commercial map, and the second, the use of latitude and longitude.

In Chapter Twelve, when we look at how GIS technology is used to analyze crime, we will be exposed to considerably more information on how these subjects relate. However, examination of spatial data of alcohol-related traffic crashes has suggested

that characteristics of one neighborhood, like the density of locations that sell or serve alcohol, may affect another area's rates of traffic collisions.
Source: Lipton and Gruenewald, "Spatial Dynamics," 187.

GISs use one of two alternative methods: **universal transverse mercator (UTM)** or **state plane coordinates**.[23]

The UTM scheme is also available as a means for GPS receiver coordinators to be determined. The UTM scheme divides the entire would in sixty zones each containing six degrees of latitude. In the UTM scheme, the location of an object is measured in meters from one of the corners of the zone and the longitude.

To give a reference to the size of the zones, the United States is covered by ten of the zones. The important thing to remember is that instead of using the complicated degrees, minutes, and seconds of latitude and longitude, the UTM scheme uses meters from a corner of the zone.[24] State plane coordinates are a system that divides the United States into more than 120 zones. It was developed during the 1930s to assist in surveying. Positional data from all three types of spatial coordinate systems can be used in GIS applications. The most important thing to remember is that when downloading data from one system to the next, the coordinate system used must be the same or converted.

GISs are a combination of maps (knowing where an object is precisely located) and knowing information about the objects detailed on the map. In essence, a GIS system is a combination of two kinds of information or data. A GIS database contains information on the location of an object and data on the features of an object. So GIS systems are complex databases that allow users to store, analyze, and display geographic information.

In a GIS system, the objects or **features** of a map become **spatial data**. They are spatial data because we can not only analyze information about their location and specific information about the object, but we can also analyze information about their relationship to other features mapped in the GIS system. There are three kinds of spatial data contained in a GIS system: **points**, **lines**, and **areas**. A GIS system combines points, lines, and areas to map complex objects like buildings, roads, or political jurisdictions.[25]

Recall that we discussed latitude and longitude. When we used latitude and longitude information to find the location of the landmark object in the Try This box earlier, we were using an X-Y coordinate system. Similarly, when we looked at the commercial map and used the grid system on the map to locate the general area of our destination, we were using an X-Y coordinate system. A point on a map or in a GIS is any object to which we can assign X and Y coordinates or a specific location. Points can be any object on the face of the Earth, whether a natural occurrence like a mountain or a structure like a house, bridge, or fire hydrant.

Try This

Go to **www.ngs.noaa.gov/cgi-bin/spc_zones.prl**. This Web site is maintained by NOAA. Use the Web site to determine the state plane coordinates for the state and county you live in.

Lines are features that represent objects that have a length which runs between two points. One of the most common line objects would be a street. In our earlier commercial map, the number of line features made it difficult to find a single point (our destination or an address). Lines stretch between X and Y coordinates, and in most cases, the lines continue off the map face or GIS visualization with which we are working. Lines can also be natural terrain features such as rivers. So lines are features that stretch between points.

The final feature of a GIS system is areas or polygons. Generally, areas are defined by a continuous boundary that surrounds a certain feature. The most common areas we usually deal with are ZIP codes, census tracts, city limits, and political districts.[26] But a GIS system can also be used to map out a more specific location. In GIS, a specific location for which a map is produced is called a **discrete site**. A discrete site might be a park, shopping mall, or a housing project. It is essentially an area or structure with characteristics that make it different from its surroundings.[27] For law enforcement, a common area might be a particular beat or precinct to which an officer is assigned. You have probably noticed that features, lines, and areas are the basic parts of a map. For a GPS system, this is referred to as spatial data and can be thought of as traditional map information. What makes GIS significantly different from traditional maps is the ability to add information about the features, or **tabular data**, for analysis.

What we know about a feature is the information contained in a GIS database. What we know about the traits or qualities of a feature is known as an **attribute**. For instance, take your residence. If your residence is a feature in a GIS database, what information could we add to the GIS information that might be useful to a law enforcement application. First, is the feature an apartment building or a single-family dwelling. Let's presume it's an apartment. What attributes of the feature of an apartment building might we add? Let's use the number of apartments, the color, the number of car ports, and the size of the units. Once we have decided what attributes we would like to assign to the apartment building, we must come up with a way to answer the questions concerning the attributes.

Clearly, not all apartment buildings are the same. In the creation of a GIS database, we want to be able to gain useful information about all of the apartment buildings in a certain area. Therefore, when we ask the question, "What are the attributes of my apartment building?" we are assigning the same attributes to all of the apartment buildings in our GIS database. Because we want to be able to work with the information, not only are the questions concerning the features (the attributes) predefined, but also the answers are predefined because we must limit them. The answer to the question about attributes is called is the **value**.

We want to limit the values because if we don't, our database will grow so large and confusing it will be difficult to use. When we say the answers are predefined, we mean that all of the possible answers are predefined. Consider when you are taking a multiple-choice test. You must answer with one of the choices on a list. You cannot choose something that is not predefined. The Scantron device won't read a different choice. The point is the possible answers are predefined, so your teacher can more easily assess your performance on the examination.

Think of the color blue. How many shades of blue can you think of? If you were going to assign a feature the attribute of color, blue would probably be one of your values. But, in constructing your GIS database, how valuable would it be to know that a feature's attribute of color was royal blue as opposed to dark blue? More important, if the values are not fairly easy to define, input will likely be different from user to user. If the input is inconsistent, the answers the database will provide would be inconsistent. Recall the computer maxim—garbage in, garbage

Try This

On the Web, go to **terraserver-usa.com** and look up a satellite image of a famous landmark.

out. So defining the features, attributes, and values beforehand is critical. An apartment is an object, but you can also assign attributes and values to the features of lines and areas. Tabular data is information concerning the attributes and values of the features contained in our spatial data.

A third type of data that is occasionally found in maps created with GIS technology is **image data**. Increasingly, image data is taken from satellite photographs. However, it can be aerial photographs or photographs scanned into the software. Another use of image data would be to link tabular data to an image. For instance, imagine that a law enforcement agency decides to use GIS to track and monitor parolees. The spatial data would be a map of the law enforcement agency's operational boundaries. The tabular data would be the information on the parolees. The image data could be a photograph of the parolees linked to the tabular data.

When GIS maps are produced, spatial data and tabular data can be represented in one of two ways. We have looked primarily at the **vector data** method of representing GIS. In law enforcement a common vector data map shows the locations where crimes have occurred. The other common format for GIS-created visual displays is called **raster data** (recall our discussion on raster images from Chapter Two). The raster format works well with image data. Using the X and Y coordinates on the map it is producing, raster data is placed into cells.

What GIS has the capability to do is create and overlay for comparison **thematic maps**. Thematic maps are maps with a certain theme. For instance, police often create maps showing where crimes have occurred. Of course, this map theme is rather large because it doesn't contain parameters that would be useful in distilling the information down to a point where it is useful. Did we want crimes over the past ten years? Crimes over the past month? What types of crime? A thematic map on crime could have a variety of variables that would make it valuable to different users. For instance, a researcher might want information comparing crimes by area over the past ten years, whereas a field police officer is probably interested in what has happened in the past month.

Police agencies have a ready source of daily information that can be used for GIS analysis. Police agencies have calls for service, crimes, arrests, warrants, traffic accidents, and citations, just to name a few. All of this information can be input into a GIS system for analysis. As we progress further in the text, we will see that some police agency computer systems are significantly more integrated than others. Some agencies have the ability to take information directly from

A Look Ahead

Later in the text we will look at systems integration and emerging technologies. But with just what you have been exposed to thus far it is possible to integrate AVL technology, GIS technology, and the computer in the officer's vehicle. Imagine you are a police officer driving down the street and when you near a location, the combination of the AVL, GPS, GIS, and the computer in your car automatically flash a picture of a person on parole, a missing child, a fugitive, a person on probation, or even someone who is chronically mentally ill and a constant source of police calls.

There is a national resource of freely available GIS data from the U.S. Census Bureau, called TIGER data. The TIGER data is created for a national demographic count of the population. It usually does not have enough detail to be used in a GIS without extensive updating.

other internal sources and update their GIS automatically. However, most agencies take the information that they gather on a daily basis and enter it into a separate GIS database. In Chapter Eight, when we take an in-depth look at agency systems, this will become more clear.

Getting the Data

The most difficult part of IT is getting and maintaining good data. GISs do not contain maps or graphics; they create maps, or visual representations, of relational databases. A GIS program is not just a mapping program; it is a combination of display technology, analysis tools, and relational database management.[28] When an event, like a crime, is entered into a GIS database, it must be **geocoded**. Geocoding is the process of determining the proper coordinates of an event's location. Normally this is done by entering an address into a GIS software system. The software converts the address into the coordinates necessary to create a new feature on the map.

Although an agency must somehow input a considerable amount of information into their GIS tabular data, most basic information is commercially available in prepackaged software. Moreover, a host of other state and local agencies have geographic and demographic data. Indeed, a city police agency may find that their own planning department has a tremendous amount of information. Once an agency has a GIS database with information about objects, points, and lines, they can begin to ask a variety of questions like those concerning the causes of crime and the deployment of their officers and make analyses that may assist in the arrests of those committing crimes.

The first step in working with a GIS is developing a database of the general information about the location of all objects that can potentially be mapped. Although there are commercially available products and there are other sources of information for this base data, this is the most labor-intensive part of starting up a GIS. Indeed, this is usually the most expensive part of a GIS—organizing the basic data.[29]

Even with input from other sources, a good analyst is going to spend a considerable amount of time making sure that addresses and locations match—that the product of spatial data makes sense. The ultimate key to a good GIS analysis is how well the analyst works with unmatched records caused by incomplete, incorrect, or changed address and location information. The process of building up the first part of the database is not only labor intensive, but also somewhat complex. This first step is often referred to as address matching. We are going to leave the subject of building up the database here.[30] Once a GIS system has been geocoded

Try This

Some states have been completely mapped for GIS. Others have partial mapping data available. Check the status of your state at **www.nsgic.org**.

(the addresses and locations are matched and verified), the second step is to create our relational database of attributes and values. These are tabular data fields that contain information about the locations and the events at those locations.[31] All of the information we input into a GIS is referenced to a specific location. Our data can consist of images, aerial photography, photographs of location, floor plans, and text and attribute information. But the most important point is all the specific information tied directly to a specific location in the GIS database.[32]

Recall our mention of discrete sites. It would be at this point you might begin to identify those areas or structures with unique characteristics. Think of a place where there is considerable community activity. A discrete site, one that would require special GIS analysis might be a school, airport, or sports stadium.

The final part of the GIS process is the application of the GIS tools for the display and analysis of the database. For example, either the entire database or any user-specified subset can be displayed as a pin map by placing a symbol at the location of each event, or different symbols can be used for different types of events. One of the nearly magical aspects of GIS technology is the production of maps. Depending on how sophisticated your software is, a number of different types of maps can be created; different information can be analyzed for its spatial relationship to other data. Each layer of the map, each type of detail or data, can be turned on or off as you need.[33]

The critical aspect of GIS technology is managing the data input.[34] You cannot check the data often enough. Moreover, as more information is collected for analysis, more reports and users are involved. Of course, this usually adds to the complexity of the databases and the overall management of GIS technology.

Chapter Summary

We looked at a variety of technologies that support the use of geographic data in law enforcement. It is important to remember that GIS is a collection of data about geography that is ultimately visually displayed. GIS has two broad applications for state and local law enforcement agencies. First, it has tactical uses for the field officer. It may help a police officer to find the best route to respond to a call for service. It might be used by the central dispatch to find the closest police unit. Once the police arrive, detailed information about discrete sites could have great value in formulating a response to a tactical problem.

GIS technology also has strategic value for a state or local law enforcement agency. As we shall see in Chapter Twelve, it can be used for crime analysis. In Chapter Nineteen we will see how GIS can be used in the allocation of personnel resources.

The technical explanations of GPS, TDOA, and ADOA are going to be further explored in Chapter Seven when we see how a dispatch center receives a typical 9-1-1 call and when we look at the impact of civilian use of cellular telephone technology in law enforcement.

Discussion Questions

1. Go to the Web site of the National Oceanic and Atmospheric Administration (NOAA) at **www.noaa.gov/**. How is the Search and Rescue Satellite Aided Tracking System (SARSAT) different from GPS?
2. Construct a GIS feature table describing your campus. What features would you include? What attributes would you assign those features? What value choices would you include for your features? How could the GIS data you have defined be used in your campus?
3. Go to the Census Bureau Web site for the American Factfinder at **factfinder.census.gov/servlet/BasicFactsServlet**. You will see that census information from the 1990 census is available in thematic map form. Try your hand at creating a few thematic maps. What kind of information does the Census Bureau have at this Web site that you think might be important for a local agency's GIS?

Key Terms

Almanac
Attribute
Automatic Vehicle Locator (AVL)
Clock Drift
Demographics
Differential Correction
Dilution of Precision (DOP)
Discrete Site
Ephemeris Error
Error Budget

Features
Geocode
Geographic Information System (GIS)
Global Positioning Satellite (GPS)
Image Data
Orientation
Points, Lines, and Areas
Raster Data
Real Time
Selective Availability (SA)

Spatial Data
State Plane Coordinates
Tabular Data
Thematic Maps
Time Difference on Arrival (TDOA)
Triangulation
Universal Transverse Mercator
Value
Vector Data
Waypoint

End Notes

1. Brown and Brudney, "Smarter, Better, Faster."
2. Markowitz, "Legal Challenges."
3. "Public Safety," 8-9.
4. Judd, "Database Management," 1.
5. "Toward Improved Criminal Justice."
6. Mansell and Wehn, *Knowledge Societies,* 88.
7. "Public Safety," 1.
8. Bair, et al., "Advanced Crime Mapping," 53.
9. Wood, "GIS Terminology."
10. "Evolution and Development of Police Technology," 109.
11. Ibid.
12. Ibid.
13. Bair et al., "Advanced Crime Mapping," 54.
14. Ibid.
15. Ibid.
16. Ibid.
17. On March 28, 1996, the Interagency GPS Executive Board (IGEB) was established to manage the United States government GPS policy. This is a high level executive board of the government that sets policy regarding the use of GPS. The use of Selective Availability is

an on-going issue. Visit their Website at **www.igeb.gov** to review the latest policy decision.

18. See note 5 above.
19. "Computer-Aided Dispatch," 3.
20. "Police Technology" NIJ: 109.
21. See note 19 above.
22. Department of Justice, Bureau of Justice Statistics, 2000 Survey of State and Local Police Agencies.
23. See note 8 above.
24. Ibid.
25. Wood, "GIS Terminology."
26. "Public Safety," 8.
27. Bair et al., "Advanced Crime Mapping," 51.
28. See note 26 above.
29. Ibid., 8-10.
30. If you are going to be a crime analyst, there are any number of excellent books on the subject of building a GIS database. I recommend Steven Gottlieb's *Crime Analysis from First Report to Final Arrest.*
31. Drummond, "Address Matching."
32. See note 26 above.
33. "Public Safety," 11.
34. Judd, "Database Management."

Chapter Six
A Brief History of Police Technology

Learning Objectives

- The student will explore the development of police technology against the backgrounds of the policing models—**political**, **professional** and **community-based models**—thereby gaining a perspective from which to examine police technology.

- The student will expand on his or her understanding of **tactical** and **strategic** information by looking at how technology changed the nature of fingerprint evidence.

- The student will understand the difference between **policy** and **procedure** and look at how technology may impact policy and procedure.

- The student will further explore fragmentation and the market-place.

Introduction

One of the greatest attributes you can develop is a sense of perspective. The ability to put things in perspective, or context, gives you a greater understanding of problems and their potential solutions. We are going to look at the history of technology in two ways. The first is a fairly straightforward look at what happened and when. Along the way, we will look at some of the consequences of the introduction of new technologies. However, most of our historical exploration takes place in subsequent chapters. For instance, in Chapter Seven, when we look at dispatch centers, we take a look at the development of the telephone and cellular communications and the universal emergency number 9-1-1. In the future, as users or decision makers, if you can put a technology in perspective, you can understand its limitations and potential.

The second method of exploration is by following a specific piece of information that has been critical to solving crimes for more than a hundred years. Yet it has been technological changes in the past five years that have unleashed its true potential. Even though this information was used by law enforcement for nearly a hundred years, a lack of technology cost lives and in one instance allowed a cop killer to roam free for almost fifty years after a rape and the murder of two police officers.

One of the important functions of government and business management is forecasting. In simple terms, forecasting is effort to predict future events based upon past events. There are some rather sophisticated mathematical models that allow fairly accurate predictions on what is to come based on what has occurred. In business you might use forecasting in an effort to predict sales so you could manage production. In law enforcement you might use calls for service or crimes to determine personnel deployment. While the most common type of forecasting uses numbers of something in the past to predict the future, a look at how police technology has developed in the past can help us make some assumptions about the future, or forecast.

A look at the historical development of technology in law enforcement can aide us in understanding some of the current challenges. For instance, recall from Chapter One that a core element of the community policing model is the use of enhancers. As we discovered, enhancers are the technologies used to further the other core elements. Although technology is an enhancer in the community policing model, technology was present during the political era and to a greater extent in the professional era. By looking at how technology enhanced those eras, it is quite possible that we will gain some insight into the current era of community policing.

History can help us out in a couple of other ways. First, the way in which technology has been implemented nationwide has produced a significant problem. And, as we know from Chapter One, that problem is referred to as fragmentation. Although Chapter Eleven is going to take a look at some of the potential solutions to the problem of IT fragmentation in American law enforcement, to understand the problem and participate in the discussion about solutions, we need a historical perspective.

Finally, history is an excellent way to demonstrate how information management has changed. A historical view will further strengthen our understanding of how information is both tactical and strategic. Later, when we are practitioners, this foundation will enable us to make better decisions about information and information management.

Police Technology in Time

Today most criminal justice scholars tend to divide the history of American policing into three eras—the **political**, the **professional** and **community-oriented**.[1] As those eras progressed, technology took on a greater role in policing. Just as policing progressed, so did the general development of technology. However, toward the latter half of the twenty-first century, technological advancements occurred very rapidly. At first, during the early history of American policing, the police were fairly rapid in their incorporation of a new technology. For instance, police organizations would experiment with the automobile and radio very soon after their commercial introduction, and within a decade they would fully embrace the technology. But as the speed of technological change increased, the police adoption of new technologies did not keep pace.

Some of the earliest accounts of policing in America point to the establishment of a night watch in Boston.[2] Of course, information technology (IT) of the day was the printing press. The first recorded use of the printing press in policing was the publishing of the "Constables Pocket-Book" in 1710.[3] In the 1850s Samuel Colt began the mass production of a multiple-shot revolver. For the next nearly seventy-five years, the revolver and a night stick remained the primary technology used by police officers.[4] In 1867 Allan Pinkerton, the famous American private detective, spy, and originator of America's first private security force, again used the printing press to publish a manual on private policing for his agents titled "General Principles of Pinkerton's National Police Agency."[5] Most police forces established in the late nineteenth century consisted of men who had been appointed for limited terms by local politicians. Thus, the early part of American policing is typically referred to as the **political policing** era.[6]

Much like the rest of American government, the policing system was one of patronage. A police officer's primary source of information came from the people who lived in the community, or in the beat they walked. During this era, one of the first uses of a new science in law enforcement occurred around 1854 when San Francisco began to use photography for criminal identification. Information technology began to creep into law enforcement in 1877 when the police in Albany, New York, began using a police telegraph. In 1878 Washington, D.C., saw the first use of the telephone by a police agency.

Figure 6.1 For the police officer on the beat, the first form of electronic communications was a simple telegraph system. The system was a one-way form of communication originating in the police headquarters wherein an officer moved a dial with about ten choices to let headquarters know what type of assistance he needed. Others were a simple signal that told headquarters that the police officer had arrived at his assigned beat. In 1880 telephones were put in call boxes, allowing two-way communications between the officer on the street and headquarters. Early in the twentieth century in Washington, D.C., police officers began using a telephone handset, which plugged into the box for voice communication with headquarters, as seen here in about 1910 at the intersection of Pennsylvania and 7th Street, N.W.
Source: U.S. Congress, Office of Technology Assessment, Criminal Justice, *12. Photograph provided by Cultural Tourism DC; image from Washingtonian Division, MLK Jr., Public Library.*

One of the first sciences to become actively involved in criminal investigations was fingerprints. This began in the early 1900s and by the mid-1920s had greatly increased a police officer's ability to solve a crime. During the 1930s, police use of automobiles became a fairly standard practice; shortly after that, in 1934, Boston, Massachusetts, installed the first two-way radio in a police vehicle. The effect of the automobile and the two-way radio was to increase police productivity in responding to incidents. At about the same time, the government and policing evolved out of the patronage system into a civil service system. Moreover, many of the ideas on bureaucracy and organizations from Wilson, Von Weber, and Taylor began to take hold. The advent of a civil service system and organization models that prized hierarchy, centralization rules, and standards became the professional policing model. What early twentieth century reformers accomplished was the movement of control of day-to-day operations of the police from politics

No technology changed policing like the combination of the automobile and the radio. Police mobility may have been a force in changing policing from the political to the professional. It is interesting to consider that in 1911, August Vollmer, whom many consider the father of modern policing, put his police department in Berkeley, California, on bicycles. Apparently not satisfied with the speed of the bicycle, he instituted motorcycle patrols in 1912. Of course, our search today is for the speed of data.

Vollmer must have wanted response time because in 1913 he started automobile patrols. Although Detroit is credited with the first full-time use of the radio, Vollmer had experimented with a radio in a police vehicle nearly seven years beforehand. It seems that for Vollmer, technology was a driving force for professionalization of policing.

Source: Vila and Morris, *Police in American Society,* 75–76.

to professional police managers. After police officers had gained civil service status, patronage and political influences in hiring and firing were significantly reduced. Under the professional management of the new era, police officers began to concentrate on crime control.[7, 8]

Police reformers clearly saw technology as a key part of the drive for better police efficiency and greater crime control.[9] It is likely that police reformers were influenced by the technological advances of the day. They could look around and see the automobile, the radio, and other science and technology. The reformers tended to be chief executives of police agencies, businesspeople, public administrators, and scholarly people.[10] They tended to be pretty smart people who saw a new development and how that development enhanced their model of policing—**professional policing**.

In 1923 Los Angeles Police Department established the first crime laboratory in the United States. In the same year, the Pennsylvania State Police initiated the use of the teletype. It wasn't until 1928 that police first began to experiment with the use of the radio. The first city to use one-way radios was Detroit, Michigan. With the one-way radio, police could receive calls, but not acknowledge them, nor request information. As more and more police departments began to use automobiles, police officers began to leave their foot patrols. When someone wanted a police officer, they could no longer find him walking his "beat." They began to call police headquarters. The situation wherein the community called a central location and the police were dispatched to the scene was accelerated and enhanced by the proliferation of the private telephone and the installation of radios in police vehicles. By the second half of the twentieth century, police being dispatched from a central location became the standard.

Before the commonplace use of automobiles and radios, a police officer on the beat was pretty much on his own. The central dispatching fed into the idea of a central bureaucracy—one of the hallmarks of the professional era. Through the 1950s and 1960s, the idea that police supervisors and managers should control the production of service began to take hold. In 1950 an influential police administrator and educator, O.W. Wilson, published a textbook called *Police Administration,* which became the Bible for police administrators in America.[11] Supervisors and managers began to count the numbers of calls for service an officer handled and how fast he arrived at the scene of a call.

This professional model of policing was about mobility and bureaucratic control of officers. During this era, any problems that were noncriminal tended to be viewed as social work by police officers and police managers.[12] It is likely that the axiom, "you get what you count," significantly affected the police service. Not only were police officers not walking the community any longer, they were being

Different
transistors

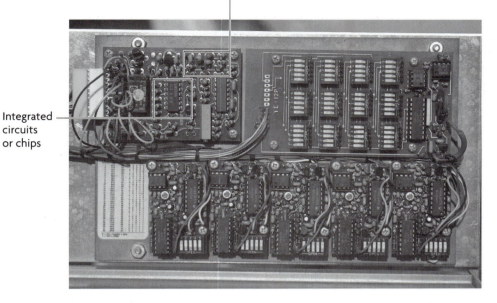

Integrated
circuits
or chips

Figure 6.2   During the last half of the twentieth century, most IT inventions and innovations have developed largely based upon two inventions—the transistor in 1947 and the
microprocessor in 1971. It is difficult to tell where the transistor will ultimately take us.
One observer said that trying to forecast where the transistor and microprocessor will
take us would be like the person who invented the wheel being able to predict the
automobile.
Source: Laidler, *To Light Such a Candle,* 224. *Photograph provided by Robert Eplett, California
Governor's Office of Emergency Services.*

evaluated on the number of calls they handled and how fast they got to the call.
This is somewhat of a simplification, but if you were being judged on the number
of calls for service you handled, would you be more interested in developing a
long-term solution to the problem or moving on to the next call as rapidly as
possible?

In addition to placing the maximum number of police officers in patrol vehicles, the professional model developed a belief that random patrol was an efficient

It may very well be that the use of a radio in apprehending a criminal actually ushered in the era of
commercial radio entertainment. In the early part
of the twentieth century, radio was not used much
commercially because people had the telegraph
and the telephone. The first commercial uses of
radio were for ship to shore communications—
obviously there are no telegraph or telephone
wires for ship to shore. But because everyone was
happy with hardwired communications, radio was
seen as an interesting phenomenon. Then in 1910,
Dr. Hawley Crippen murdered his wife in London
with poison. After burying her body in the cellar,
he and his young mistress got on a steamship for a
trip to Canada. Of course, during the cruise, the
body was discovered. Meanwhile, on the ship, the
captain became suspicious of Crippen and his dis-
guised mistress. The ship's captain used the radio
and contacted the authorities in England. Well, by the
time the ship landed at Quebec, Scotland Yard had already taken a faster ship and was waiting for Crippen. Eventually, they would hang Crippen. However,
the publicity from the trial helped to push commercial radio into the forefront.

Source: Laidler, *To Light Such a Candle,* 198.

Probably sometime between the 1940s and the 1960s, the implementation of technology in the police service began to lag behind commercial applications of technology. Interestingly enough, just two years before the President's commission would observe that police technology was stuck, Gordon E. Moore, co-founder of Intel, predicted that the processing power of integrated circuits would double every eighteen months for the next ten years. Known now as Moore's law, it has remained a truism for nearly thirty years. So technology begins to zip ahead without the police.

Source: Cunningham, *B2B,* 180.

strategy for preventing crime. Moreover, the centralized bureaucracy placed a very high value on the rapid response to calls for police service in the belief that speed was necessary to apprehend criminals.[13]

Through the 1970s there continued to be a reliance on what was to be seen as **incident-driven policing**. The technology was definitely enhancing the police's ability to respond rapidly. Moreover, the advent of the computer made it possible to organize and review this information on incidents and response. Although computers were on the horizon and would make their debut in the late 1970s and early 1980s, it is interesting that between the 1920s and the 1970s police technology did not really change all that much. In response to public concern about crime, President Lyndon Johnson appointed the President's Commission on Law Enforcement and Administration of Justice. In 1967 the Commission published "The Challenge of Crime in a Free Society." That same year, the President's Commission on Law Enforcement and Administration of Justice made the observation that while police were using crime laboratories and radios, the technology was essentially unchanged for the previous thirty or forty years.[14]

Although this era is called the professional era, it is alternately described as incident-driven policing. American police had become very good at responding to incidents, primarily calls for service. As we shall see in Chapter Seven, the development of the universal emergency number, 9-1-1, only added to the police's ability to handle incidents. At the same time the police were becoming incident driven, a ton of statistics was being captured about policing in America.

The professional policing model which relied on science, technology, standards, and centralized bureaucracy did produce professionals. As the police officers who were judged on the number of calls and arrests they made began to rise through the ranks of the police service, the concept of professionalism increased. If you spend a major portion of your life becoming an expert in your field, you are probably going to believe that you know what you are doing. This phenomenon, for the police, had unintended consequences. Police managers, who as police officers took direction from the radio and headquarters, did not rely on community input in the same manner or degree to which the beat officers of the earlier era did. At this point, in the late 1960s and early 1970s, the idea that the police were the professionals who knew best, responded quickly, and handled incidents became organizationally entrenched.

A hundred years ago, if you got into a fight, you were more likely to rely on someone from the community coming to your assistance. With technological changes, you could call other officers to the scene. After all, if you didn't need the community's help in a fight, did you really need their advice about a problem? So the model, enhanced by the technology, likely distanced the police from the community. During the 1960s this became a recurrent theme in cities across the country—the demands for the professionalism of the police. Essentially, the different model and the technology changed the relationship between the police and the community (with the heavy reliance on efficiency, mobility in the field, and centralized bureaucratic control) and introduced a new problem of the growing distance between police officers and the communities they served.[15]

So technological change, primarily in the form of the automobile and the radio, also presented the police with some serious challenges. As officers moved from the intimacy of foot beats to the isolation of the radio car, casual day-to-day contact with the average citizen diminished substantially.[16,17] Worse still, when officers did come in contact with the "noncriminal" general public, it was often while issuing a traffic citation.[18] With increased involvement by police in traffic enforcement, many people who previously regarded police officers as their protectors came to see them as adversaries.

Throughout the last half of the twentieth century, as the police were able to collect more and more statistical information about crimes and incidents, these statistics began to be used for some meaningful and often dynamic research. The research and some scholarly ideas began to change the nature of policing. One of the primary research projects of the 1970s was the Kansas City Preventive Patrol Experiment. During this project, three controlled levels of policing were used. One area had no random patrol, a second experienced twofold and threefold increases in police presence, and a third area received the normal level. The final analysis revealed no significant differences in the level of crime or public attitudes toward police.[19] With the president's commission, the civil unrest in the 1960s, the rapidly rising crime rate, and the acknowledgement through research that some professional era concepts such as random patrol did not work, people began looking for an alternative model.

In the late 1970s something happened that I suspect most cops instinctively knew. It was realized that police officers were responding to many of the same problems repeatedly. While the technology was enhancing the professional model and quite possibly further distancing the police from the people they served, it was also opening another door. That door was the new model—**community-oriented policing**.

Between 1979 and the mid-1980s, two projects were conducted that would lead the way to the development of community-oriented policing. The first, conducted by Michigan State University was called the Neighborhood Foot Patrol Program. The second was a problem-oriented policing program in Newport News, Virginia. In both cases, the research found that solving crimes and arresting offenders alone did not solve a particular community problem. What solved problems was an analysis followed by actions designed to work on the conditions that created the problem.[20]

In March of 1982 James Q. Wilson and George L. Kelling published an article in the *Atlantic Monthly* entitled "Broken Windows." Their discussion revealed that

---

The 1960s and 1970s were certainly decades of change. Not only did the President's Commission and many scholars look at policing, but a number of important court decision changed the nature of policing. The Warren Court rendered a number of significant decisions. For example:

- *Mapp v. Ohio* established the exclusionary rule prohibiting the use of illegally obtained evidence.

- *Escobedo v. Illinois* established that an offender has the right to an attorney when questioning turns to accusation.
- The ever famous *Miranda v. Arizona* where the right to an attorney and against self-incrimination were established.

Source: Shafritz, *Public Policy Administration*, 725.

daily incivilities disrupted neighborhoods. What they said was that an unrepaired broken window can send a message to people in the neighborhood that nobody cares about the building. If nobody cares, this can lead to further and ultimately more serious vandalism. Just as with windows, negative behavior in a neighborhood can signal to others that the behavior is acceptable and lead to more serious consequences.[21]

Community-oriented policing is founded on two social science theories: **normative sponsorship theory** and **critical social theory**. In normative sponsorship, we believe that most people are good and willing to cooperate. It tells us that people will work together if the goal is within the normal standards of the community. So for people to become involved in community-oriented policing, they must agree that it is worthwhile based upon their attitudes and values. Critical social theory looks at the way the community comes together in order to analyze a problem that is preventing the attainment of their goals or needs.[22] Of course if community values, needs, and standards are different from community to community, their police technological needs are also different. We will look at how this may be increasing fragmentation later in this chapter. Community-oriented policing isn't the only modern theory of policing. The **problem-oriented policing** theory shares many of the same characteristics of community-oriented policing. However, problem-oriented policing concentrates on situational crime prevention. Where community-oriented policing efforts generally define community based upon geography, problem-oriented policing looks more at the community of the problem. In problem-oriented policing, communities of interest would shift as problems were solved or new problems become apparent.

Changing the Value of Information

By looking back at developments in the past and examining how problems with information have been resolved, we are able to put the current state of information technology into perspective. Although a time line would provide us with some interesting information, it helps little in showing how technology changed the way in which law enforcement officers gather, organize, and use information. By somewhat closely following the development of a specific type of information and viewing how technology enhanced its use in both a strategic and a tactical sense, we should garner further insights into the concepts of **strategic** and **tactical information**. Moreover, we may begin to observe some common themes emerging.

The use of scientific methods of conducting criminal investigations has had a long, and sometimes controversial, history. One of the hallmarks of the professional policing model is a reliance on scientific investigation. One of the earliest forms of scientific criminal investigation, which is still used today, is **fingerprint** classification. The use of fingerprints in criminal investigations has significantly changed as it has been impacted by information technology. Because of its longevity, the history of the use of fingerprints in law enforcement is an excellent vehicle to view how information technology has changed the use of fingerprints.

As early as the seventeenth century, it was noted that fingerprints had specific patterns. Around 1880 it was suspected and later confirmed that no two individuals' fingerprints are alike. Fingerprints are tiny valleys and ridges on the human hands. Their biological purpose is to make gripping objects easier.

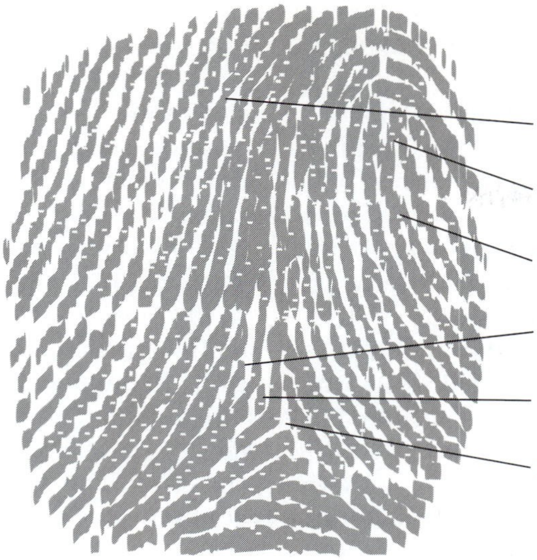

Figure 6.3 Arrows pointing out distinctive parts of fingerprint.

Crossover

Core

Bifurcation

Ridge ending

Island

Delta

While the basic pattern for human fingerprints comes from their genetic coding, the fingerprints are also affected during development by the conditions in the womb. The position of the fetus, condition of the amniotic fluid in the womb, and other environmental factors affect the formation of the fingerprints. The combination of the vast number of possible genetic combinations and the unpredictable and endless combinations of the environmental factors mean that no two individuals are going to have the same fingerprints, not even twins. Once found to be a positive way to identify individuals, fingerprints had a number of uses in the police service. Fingerprints can be either visible, plastic, or latent. Visible prints would be those left by touching a substance before touching a surface, like a bloody fingerprint; plastic fingerprints would be prints left in a soft substance like wood putty. **Latent fingerprints**, or hidden fingerprints, are left behind by the natural oils from our hands. These oils stay on an object, in the pattern of the fingerprint.[23]

In 1880 Dr. Henry Faulds published an article in a scientific journal. The essence of his article was about how fingerprints could be used for personal identification. He also introduced some of the earliest technology of the recovery of fingerprints—printing ink. During the late nineteenth century and early twentieth century there was work to develop classification systems for the prints. For instance, in 1888 Sir Francis Galton developed a system of classification that is still in use to today. A few years later, Sir Edward Richard Henry would develop the Henry Classification System; it also is still in use today.[24]

Around the turn of the twentieth century, the use of fingerprints in police work and criminal justice rapidly evolved. In 1902 the New York Civil Service began using fingerprints as a means of identification. In 1903 the New York State Prison System began the first organized use of fingerprints for prisoners in the United States. In 1904 the Leavenworth Federal Penitentiary and the St. Louis

---

Try This

Wrap a small piece of medical tape around you fingertips and try to pick up a large glass of water. Caution: Use a plastic glass!

Police Department began to use fingerprints. For the next two decades, more and more police agencies in the United States implemented fingerprints in their criminal investigations.[25]

As the trend to use fingerprints accelerated, police agencies throughout the United States began to send copies of their fingerprints to the National Bureau of Criminal Investigation, which had been established by the International Association of Chiefs of Police. Finally, in 1924 Congress established the Identification Division of the Federal Bureau of Investigation (FBI). By the end of World War II, the FBI had 100 million fingerprint cards on file from agencies around the United States.

For the next twenty-five years, the FBI continued to amass fingerprint cards from police agencies throughout the United States. In that time the number of paper files doubled to 200 million. By this time, the FBI had the beginnings of a huge database (databases will be explored in Part Three on information systems), but that database was millions of paper files in an untold number of filing cabinets. In 1967 the FBI organized the **National Crime Information Center (NCIC)** (NCIC will be explored in Part Three on information systems) to handle fingerprint cards and requests for comparison. In 1971 the NCIC began to incorpo-

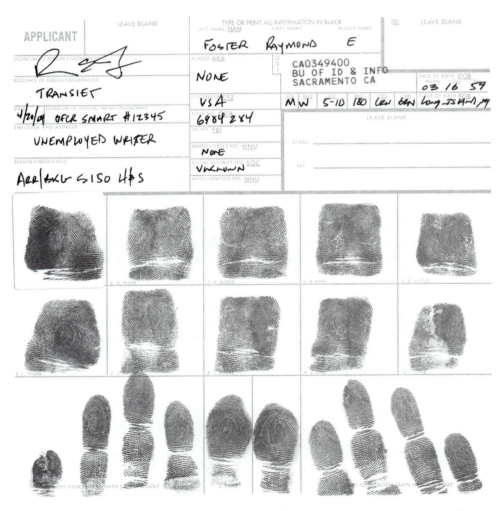

Figure 6.4 Imagine how many file drawers would be necessary to maintain these files and, even with a classification system, how long a comparison could take.

rate criminal histories and correlate them to offender fingerprint cards on file. The medium of transmission for all of those fingerprint cards and criminal histories was the U.S. mail—what is referred to today as "snail mail."

At this point, through most of the 1970s fingerprints had no value as tactical information and little value as strategic information. Consider a police officer in the field. He has stopped a motorist who does not have identification, and that motorist is a fugitive who is actively trying to conceal her identity. Through skillful questioning, the police officer might be able to determine the individual's true name, and thus, her status as a fugitive. But even though the suspect's identity is at the tip of her own hands, there was no way to use the information tactically because the officers in the street had no way of comparing the information (the fingerprints) to official files.

If the police officer were able to determine probable cause sufficient to arrest the suspect and take her to the police station, the police officer might be able to confirm the suspect's identity but not ascertain her identity. Consider that NCIC held in 1971 200 million fingerprints. If a police officer sent the prints to NCIC (at this point the mail would take some time), which card would they compare the fingerprints to? It would probably take a fingerprint expert years of doing one-to-one comparisons to find a match.

Shortly after it was founded, NCIC came up with a partial solution to this problem. The Henry Classification system was mentioned earlier. It is a complex system and not, at this point, necessary to understand. NCIC, however, came up with a system to classify fingerprints that is much simpler. Both the Henry Classification system and the NCIC Classification system are based on patterns of loops, swirls, and ridges (see Figure 6.5) and the finger on which those classifications occur. The NCIC Classification code is a twenty-digit code, ten sets of two numbers. The ten sets represent the eight fingers and two thumbs. Each of the numbers indicate the pattern type on the finger.

As you can see from the chart, by examining each fingerprint and assigning the specific print a pattern type, you end up with a twenty-digit code. However, because this code is about pattern types, more than one person can have this code.

Codes	Definitions and Information
01–49	Ulnar Loop
51–99	Radial Loop
AA	Plain Arch
TT	Tented Arch
PI	Plain Whorl–Inner Tracing
PO	Plain Whorl–Outer Tracing
PM	Plain Whorl–Meet Tracing
CO	Central Pocket Whorl–Outer Tracing
CI	Central Pocket Whorl–Inner Tracing
CM	Central Pocket Whorl–Meet Tracing
DO	Double Whorl–Outer Tracing
DI	Double Whorl–Inner Tracing
DM	Double Whorl–Meet Tracing
XI	Accidental Whorl–Inner Tracing
XO	Accidental Whorl–Outer Tracing
XM	Accidental Whorl–Meet Tracing
XX	Amputation

Figure 6.5 NCIC Pattern Chart

This is a filing scheme that makes it easier and quicker for prints to be compared. It would be akin to looking for someone in the telephone book. You would first turn to the appropriate last name and then begin your search for specific identifiers. Although this scheme made it easier to compare fingerprints, there were still more than 200 million on file. A fingerprint expert, doing one-to-one matches on an unidentified suspect might take only days. However, the NCIC classification system required fingerprints from all eight fingers and both thumbs. Few full sets of fingerprints are recovered from crime scenes. Therefore, the NCIC classification system wasn't much help in identify suspects from fingerprints left at crime scenes.

At this point, NCIC began to correlate fingerprint cards with criminal histories. In the early 1970s a police agency could send a teletype or make a telephone call to NCIC and, based upon the fingerprint classification scheme, begin to make preliminary identifications of suspects. Moreover, as duplicate cards were submitted (primarily from repeat offenders), NCIC began to uncover aliases that suspects used.

In the mid-1970s another technology was introduced into this scheme—the facsimile machine, or fax. This technology allowed agencies to send facsimiles of fingerprint cards directly to NCIC. Once there, not only could they be classified, but the fingerprints could be examined (reintroducing the complex Henry system) so that an exact match could be made. However, the fax machine only sped up the transmission of the information, it did not help to organize it or improve the speed of classification. Moreover, because fax machines rapidly became popular, the use of the technology (which sped up transmission of information) created a bottleneck because technology had not improved the speed of comparison.

The next technological innovation was the **Automated Fingerprint Identification System (AFIS)** project. In the late 1960s and early 1970s the FBI began working with other federal agencies to develop algorithms for searching and matching fingerprints using computer technology.[26] As we have seen, prior to this point, fingerprints had a huge untapped potential. There were millions of fingerprints, many of them from repeat offenders. At the same time, all around the nation, police officers were recovering fingerprints from crime scenes. Yet there was not an efficient means to bridge the gap between the police officers and the information contained in the fingerprint files. Up until this point, the fingerprints were of no value as tactical information (for the police officer in the street) and of little value as strategic information (for solving crimes).

The process of analyzing fingerprints is known as **dactylography**. The AFIS technology further advanced fingerprint information toward becoming true strategic as well as tactical information by comparing fingerprint features known as **minutiae**. Moreover, they concentrate on details where ridge lines end or split in two. These splits are known as bifurcations. Together, these and other features are known as **typica**.

The computer software then uses sophisticated and complex algorithms to recognize and compare minutiae. A simple explanation of what the computer is doing is a connect-the-dots game. The computer determines that the minutiae are a point, or dot. It then draws a straight line between the dots, completing a geometric shape or pattern. It then searches the other fingerprints in the database for a shape with the same size and dimensions. So if fingerprints have the same pattern, there is a great likelihood that the two fingerprints are a match. For most of the United States, matching points of comparison are necessary to consider the match positive.

Use of Automated Fingerprint Identification Systems (AFIS) in local police departments, by size of population served, 2000

Population served	Percent of agencies with AFIS ownership or remote access		
	Total with access	Exclusive or shared ownership	Remote access terminal only
All sizes	20%	5%	15%
1,000,000 or more	100%	93%	7%
500,000-999,999	85	59	26
250,000-499,999	95	60	35
100,000-249,999	85	41	44
50,000-99,999	58	25	33
25,000-49,999	39	13	26
10,000-24,999	26	8	18
2,500-9,999	17	2	15
Under 2,500	13	2	11

Figure 6.6 The use of AFIS is steadily increasing. As of 2000, Americans living in the largest cities were provided police service by a local agency that had some type of access to AFIS.
Source: Department of Justice, Bureau of Justice Statistics, 2000 Law Enforcement Management Statistics.

Although this work in the 1970s was moving toward making the fingerprints on file useful information, there were a number of stumbling blocks. The relative processing speeds of computers at that time was slow. It took a long time for a search. Moreover, in addition to the development of the algorithms, hardware, and software needed to store the information needed to be developed. Finally, there were 200 million fingerprints that needed to be computerized.

While NCIC was developing their national database, the local government agencies forged ahead in developing their similar applications. The efforts of local and regional agencies to develop AFIS technology created successes and highlighted a recurring theme in the development of police technology—fragmentation. Fragmentation will be discussed later in this chapter. However, the introduction of AFIS technology did unleash the potential of fingerprints as strategic information.

Police officers, especially detectives, had a new and powerful tool in solving crimes. AFIS technology began to be used routinely, especially in the investigation of cold cases.[27] Essentially, a cold case is a criminal investigation wherein all leads have been exhausted. Recall that while detectives, for nearly a hundred years, might have a suspect's fingerprint from a crime scene, they were unable to match it to the suspect, unless they already knew the suspect's identity. Technology changed this. Now the real potential for fingerprint evidence was beginning to be unleashed.

Try This

Take a look at the Web site of this regional network: Western Identification Network, **www.winid.org**.

In 1999 the FBI launched the Integrated Automated Fingerprint System (IAFIS). At that moment, the fingerprints of 33 million people who had committed crimes were now available to law enforcement agencies nationwide (although by the 1970s the FBI had more than 200 million fingerprint cards on file, many of them were duplicates, the cards were for some reason unusable, or the fingerprint cards were noncriminal in nature). Additionally, NCIC was replaced with NCIC 2000 (NCIC 2000 will be fully explored in Chapter Nine). Recall that beginning early in the twentieth century, law enforcement agencies had been sending fingerprint cards to NCIC, and now, with the advancements in technology, those records were available for relatively easy comparison. IAFIS made fingerprint evidence true strategic information.

Advances in technology have also begun to make fingerprint information tactical in nature. For fingerprints to be tactical, police officers in field situations would have to be able to examine and compare them against databases in the field. In order to be available in the field, a number of technical challenges remained. The information transmitted between local agencies and the NCIC's IAFIS was conducted along existing networks (networks were explored in Chapter Four). However, for the information to be used by the field police officer, the information would have to be transmitted in some wireless mode (wireless communications were explored in Chapter Three). Moreover, it required a computer in the police vehicle, optical scanning equipment compact enough and rugged enough for the field, and a variety of other hardware and software. In 2000 much of this technology came together, enabling fingerprint information to become tactical information. While some of the technologies that made it possible for fingerprint evidence to become tactical information are subjects of subsequent chapters, this chapter looks at two devices; the optical and the capacitance scanners give us a good overview of how fingerprint information can be viewed and used as tactical information.

There were other developments in the area of fingerprints over much of the twentieth century. In addition to how fingerprint evidence is stored (now as data), compared, and retrieved, there were advances in how fingerprints were taken from suspects and lifted from crime scenes. The way that fingerprints were taken from suspects had not changed in almost one hundred years. The ink was rolled onto the suspect's fingers and hands, and then the fingers were rolled or pushed against paper, as required. The rolling of the finger onto paper was necessary in order to get the most area of the finger and the clearest print for comparison.

The problems with taking a suspect's fingerprints using the ink technology were improved by digital scanning devices. Recall that the AFIS technology examined the minutiae on the fingerprint in order to detect a searchable pattern. The digital scanning device is the other half of the technology.[28] The first task of a digital scanning device is to obtain an image on the fingerprint, it then begins its examination and comparisons.

In January 2003 two 45-year-old partial fingerprints led to the arrest of Gerald F. Mason, a man from South Carolina. Mason eventually pled guilty to murdering two El Segundo police officers in 1957. Authorities believe that the police officers stopped Mason shortly after he had committed a rape. The prints linking Mason to the murder scene were critical. The fingerprints Mason left at the scene had lain dormant for nearly fifty years. It was AFIS technology that solved this cold case.

While there are a number of different ways to obtain a fingerprint from a human being (as in the case of an officer taking a suspect's fingerprints), the two most common methods of digital scanning are **capacitance scanning** and **optical scanning**. While they both obtain the image, they use vastly different technologies.

The optical scanner uses the same technology you would find in a digital camera or camcorder. It uses a charged coupled device (CCD). A CCD is a collection of light-sensitive diodes called photosites. Now, there is significantly more technology involved in the details of the workings of a optical scanner. For instance, we did not even look at, or need to look at, the "analog-to-digital converter." Suffice it to say, there is a lot going on inside the technology, but now let's look at its use.

For our officer who is fingerprinting a suspect, the process typically begins by the officer inputting some basic information into the scanning device, such as the name and date of birth the suspect has given. The information is generally input by using a keyboard and monitor. The suspect's fingers are then placed on a glass plate. A light source inside the optical scanner illuminates the suspect's fingertips and the CCD camera takes a picture. In reality, the CCD system creates an inverted image of the fingers, with darker areas representing more reflected light (the ridges of the fingerprints) and lighter areas (less reflected light) representing the valleys.

Prior to the introduction of optical scanners, the clarity of the fingerprint was judged by the officer. For a variety of reasons, a large number of fingerprints were unusable for later classification or comparison. The fingerprints might have been smudged, too light, too dark, or lacking in detail. Some even had the left-hand fingerprints printed onto the side of the fingerprint card for the right hand. Because officers were required to complete a manual task and the subject of the collection was at times uncooperative, some of the information gathered (the fingerprints) was essentially corrupted data. The fingerprint information that was being taken manually was a paper file. The AFIS technology would eventually convert the paper file to a computer file. Because the fingerprinting was being done manually, the error rate was substantial, and ultimately, the corrupted files were worthless.

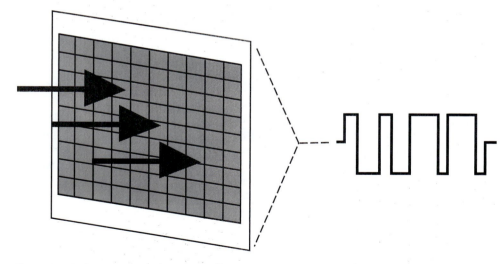

Figure 6.7 The photosites respond to light photons by generating an electrical signal. The electrical signal is recorded as a pixel. Together, the pixels form the image of the fingerprint.

Another way to measure the actual distance of the ridges and valleys of fingerprints is through the use of sound waves. Ultrasonic fingerprint scanners are not as common as their electrical cousins, but because they measure actual distances as opposed to taking a photograph, they are more difficult to deceive, or "spoof."

With optical scanning, the scanner processor makes sure that the CCD has obtained a clear image. In other words, the error rate of manually fingerprinting suspects was all but defeated. Essentially, the fingerprint scanner checks to see if the overall image is too dark or too light. After that check, the scanner looks at the fingerprint definition. In this instance, definition is how sharp the image appears. The digital scanner checks the definition by moving straight lines horizontally and vertically across the scanned image. If the definition is good, the straight line passed over the ridges of the fingerprint will have alternating dark and light pixels. After the digital scanner determines that the image is good, the fingerprint is captured and added to the agency's fingerprint file. In some instances, the fingerprint is compared against local, regional, and national databases.

The second type of digital scanner used to record fingerprints is a capacitance scanner. Like their cousins, the optical scanners, capacitance scanners also make an image of the ridges and valleys of the fingerprint. However, instead of using light, like the optical scanners, the capacitance scanners use electrical current. The sensor that actually views the fingerprint consists of one or more semiconductor chips that contain tiny cells.

How the capacitance scanners actually take an image of the fingerprint involves some fairly technical science like the operations of an inverting amplifier, a capacitor, and an integrator circuit. It is enough for us to know that when a fingerprint is placed against the glass of a capacitance scanner, the device is constructed in such a way as to recognize the fingerprint as a third capacitor.

A capacitor is a device that can store an electrical charge. Therefore, the amount of electrical charge it can store, or is storing, can be measured. Recall the fingerprint is a series of ridges and valleys. When placed against the capacitance scanner, the valleys of the fingerprint are ever so slightly farther away from the device than the ridges. This difference in distance (and the air in the ridges, which acts as an insulator) means that the valleys and ridges, when viewed as a third capacitor, have a very slight difference in the ability to store an electrical charge. The capacitance scanner measures this difference and produces a map, or image, of the fingerprint.

The differences between an optical scanner and a capacitance scanner are important for two reasons. First, the capacitance scanner does not contain the CCD and is more readily miniaturized. Second, because the capacitance scanner is actually taking measurements, it is more difficult to fool. When we examine the science of biometrics, the ability to fool scanning systems will become an important consideration. Prior to the introduction of digital scanning devices, there were a number of drawbacks with the ink technology. First, taking fingerprints from a suspect who was under the influence of drugs or alcohol or was hostile was exacerbated by the time it took to take the fingerprints—rolling ink on their fingers and hands and then the fingerprint cards. With digital scanning technology, the ink is removed from the equation, and the time it takes to complete the task is usually much less. In essence, digital scanning technology has made the process of fingerprinting a suspect some-

Automatically obtaining digital fingerprints and then comparing them to a database of stored fingerprints is a key component of the science of biometrics. In essence, biometrics is the science of automatically identifying people based upon physiological characteristics (such as fingerprints, facial structure, thermal image, gait, speech, and handwriting). We will take a more in-depth look at biometric applications in Chapter Twenty-One.

what safer for the individual police officer. Secondly, it takes some skills to take a "clean" set of fingerprints. Taking fingerprints is a perishable skill. In other words, if you don't perform the task often enough, your ability to perform the task degrades. One of the common problems with the fingerprint cards received by NCIC was the quality of the initial fingerprinting. Smudging, distortion in correct fingers, was a common problem. The digital scanning technology significantly improves quality because the digital scanner will not accept the fingerprinting task as completed unless the clarity of the fingerprints meet minimum quality standards—the computer has become a quality control inspector of sorts. Finally, the digital scanning technology significantly

Figure 6.8 Many law enforcement agencies are transitioning from traditional ink on paper fingerprinting to digital fingerprinting. In this photograph, the police officer is using Cross Match Technologies' ID 1000 Live Scan to fingerprint an offender.
Photograph provided by Cross Match Technologies, Inc.

Figure 6.9 Mobile wireless fingerprint capture devices can be used in the field during traffic stops or at crime scenes to determine in a matter of minutes whether or not an individual is wanted or has outstanding warrants. If an offender is determined to be dangerous, this new knowledge heightens the officer's awareness, improving his or her ability to remain unharmed. Moreover, the technology can increase police efficiency by reducing the number of offenders taken to the station for their identification to be verified. In this photograph, the police officer is using Cross Match Technologies' MV-5 Mobile Wireless Capture Device.
Photograph provided by Cross Match Technologies, Inc.

increased the speed of identification. Police agencies with this type of technology are at the very minimum immediately checking their own records to verify identity. Many agencies are accessing regional and national databases.

With the introduction of fingerprint scanning devices, fingerprint information was becoming tactical information. Consider the police officer who is taking the fingerprints of an arrested suspect. The suspect is being booked (booking is the process of intake into the jail). Generally, it involves a search of the suspect's person, fingerprinting, photographing, and the recording of the suspect's personal information for a minor charge. With the ink technology, the officer might not have any means to verify the name the suspect was giving. In many instances, fugitives from other jurisdictions would use an alias, be booked on a minor charge, and be released before the true identity and status as a fugitive were known. This was a very common occurrence.

Police agencies using digital scanning devices to verify suspects' identities and determine if they have any warrants are using the fingerprint information tactically. The digital scanning device improved the quality of information input into the system (better prints), made the process quicker and, thus, safer for the officer, and improved public safety by reducing the number of fugitives released before their identities could be ascertained.[29]

So far we have looked at fingerprint scanners that are used in the police station. There have been a number of other technological innovations that allow scanners to be used in the field. Later in the text, we will look at NCIC 2000, as it is being used in the field. However, the idea is to use a mobile imaging unit inside police vehicles that will contain a handheld fingerprint scanner, a digital camera, and perhaps even a small printer.[30]

Policy and Procedure

The differences between **policy** and **procedure** are important for any student of police science, and technology may have a role in changing how we think of the differences between the two. Procedures are a set of instructions on how to do something. Like an algorithm, there is very little room for deviation. On the other hand, policy is a broad statement on how things should be done. In field police work, policy is necessary because no two situations are ever exactly the same. No one can give you an exact algorithm on how to handle even the most basic radio call. Policy is a set of organizational guidelines about how we want human beings to exercise judgment. Computers do not exercise judgment, they follow a set of rules. Whenever we insert technology into the decision-making process, we reduce human interaction and turn over our decision-making ability to computers.

Somewhere between organizational policies and implementation in the street, policies sometimes get modified by the person carrying out the task to meet the demands of a particular situation. In other words, people make judgments. We want police officers to have good judgment. We want them to make decisions about situations in the broad framework of organizational policy. At times, the way in which organizational policies are acted out at the line level has been called street-level bureaucracy.

Recall our traffic violator scenario from Chapter One. Not every traffic violator receives or probably deserves a traffic citation. I could come up with scenario after scenario where justice would be better served by a warning or education than a citation. However, police agencies are increasingly relying on cameras, sensors, and computers to monitor traffic at problem intersections. In some instances, police agencies have installed devices that take pictures of vehicles that run red lights or speed. Remember computers can only follow a set of instructions. They cannot make judgments. Every time we insert a technology into the decision-making process (automated databases of fingerprints and DNA, for example), we remove human judgment. This phenomenon of replacing human judgment with computer procedure has been called screen-level bureaucracy. As we look at technologies in subsequent chapters, consider if we are replacing human judgment with computer algorithms.[31]

Fragmentation

Fragmentation of technological development and implementation in law enforcement is such a critical issues that we should return to it momentarily.[32] As we know, the United States has more than seventeen thousand state and local law enforcement agencies, and from Chapter One, we know that this phenomenon is due in part to how our country was founded. In addition to the founding principles of our democracy, fragmentation is caused by a number of other factors. Key among them are the differences among communities.

The vast majority of law enforcement agencies in our country are small, local jurisdictions providing service to some type of municipal political subdivision—a town, a city, and the like. In many instances, these small municipalities have very different community expectations and standards. One of the more interesting sociological and political theories, Tiebot's Law, examines how people group themselves together based on common expectations.[33]

For our police departments, these different expectations play out in vastly different equipment acquisitions. For instance, one community may have a problem, a major thoroughfare running through it and thusly be concerned with speeding. That police agency may choose to purchase technology, like radar, in order to meet the community expectations. Another community may have a large number of young people, so the police agency concentrates its available budget on youth programs.

For the local agency, the budgets are small and most devoted to personnel costs. Technologies are chosen to meet basic officer safety needs and community standards. Add to the problem that many police technologies are drawn and adapted from the commercial marketplace and you have a situation wherein the marketplace cannot make a profit by responding to technology needs of local agencies.[34] Fragmentation causes equipment and technology acquisition to be on an agency-by-agency basis. Therefore, in addition to having different equipment, state and local agencies develop expertise at different rates. The problem of fragmentation has the most dire consequences when state and local law enforcement agencies with contiguous or overlapping jurisdictions have incompatible technologies. The result is that local agencies are generally very poor at the tactical and strategic exchange of information.

In Chapter Eleven, when we look at information exchange, we will look at several possible technological solutions to the problems associated with fragmentation. Moreover, we will look several times at the creation of regional authorities. Many times, by pooling resources, there are organizational and technological solutions to the problems associated with fragmentation. One organizational solution was the founding of the technology section of the National Institute for Justice (NIJ) in 1986. It acts as a technological clearinghouse for law enforcement. They test products (from tires to radios), conduct research, and provide direct assistance to state and local agencies in solving technological problems. Later in the text I will give you the Web site.

Chapter Summary

In this chapter we looked at the development of police technology against the backgrounds of the policing models—political, professional, and community based. Our job was to gain a historical perspective of the different developments and how they affected the models. It is fairly clear from the literature that many scholars believe that the introduction of early technologies like the automobile and the radio enhanced the development of the professional model.

We saw where the professional model ultimately produced incident-driven policing and community dissatisfaction with the police. However, the professional model, with its emphasis on record keeping, did give researchers plenty of information from which to explore the nature of American policing. Out of the research, a primary new model, community-oriented policing, and a secondary model, problem-oriented policing, emerged. As we explore police technology further, we should look for technologies that continue to reinforce the professional model and those that do, or could, enhance the community-based model.

By looking at the development of fingerprint technology, we were able to see the tactical and strategic value of information in law enforcement. Moreover, we saw how technology significantly enhanced the value of this information. It was transformed to true strategic information and ultimately will be of significant tactical value.

We introduced the new concepts of policy and procedure primarily to think about what happens when we substitute computer decision making for human decision making. Certainly computers are much better at storing, organizing, and recalling vast amounts of data. But we should be on the lookout where we may want to insert human judgment in any criminal justice loop. If someone mistypes a name, your name could end up in NCIC as wanted. We don't want our police officers acting solely on that information. We want them to exercise judgment.

We also looked at fragmentation again. Fragmentation is an overriding, constant theme in police technology. The more we understand its causes and effects, the more able we will be able to deal with the problems and search for solutions.

Discussion Questions

1. Law enforcement is not the only field that has been changed by technology. What other fields have been changed by technology?
2. Other technologies and sciences were applied to police work in the past fifty years. How did technologies such as radio communications impact the professional policing model?
3. When we looked at the difference between policy and procedure, we introduced the concept of screen-level bureaucracy. What other examples of screen-level bureaucracy have you experienced?
4. Throughout the professional era, the implementation of police technology was primarily concerned with enhancing the model by speeding up the response times to calls and improving communications and technologies for criminal investigations.[35] How can technology be used to enhance the community-based model?
5. Police agencies are not the only organizations that may be unintentionally removing human judgment. Can you think of situations you have seen where a computer is making a decision that used to be made by a person? What are the positives of this? What are the negatives?

Key Terms

Automated Fingerprint
  Identification System
  (AFIS)
Capacitance Scanning
Charged Coupled Device
  (CCD)
Community-Oriented
  Policing
Critical Social Theory
Dactylography

Fingerprint
Incident-Driven Policing
Latent Fingerprint
Minutiae
National Crime Information Center (NCIC)
Normative Sponsorship
  Theory
Optical Scanning
Policy

Political Policing
Problem-Oriented
  Policing
Procedure
Professional Policing
Strategic Information
Tactical Information
Typica

End Notes

1. "Evolution and Development of Police Technology," 34.
2. Miller, *Policing America,* 29.
3. Vila and Morris, *Police in American Society,* xxxi.
4. See note 2 above.
5. See note 3 above.
6. Shafritz, *Public Policy and Administration,* 1678.
7. "Evolution and Development of Police Technology," iv.
8. Shafritz, *Public Policy and Administration,* 1678.
9. See note 2 above.
10. Vila and Morris, *Police in American Society,* 74.
11. Vila and Morris, *Police in American Society,* xxxiv.
12. Shafritz, *Public Policy and Administration,* 1679.
13. Ibid., 444.

14. Shafritz, *Public Policy and Administration,* 442.
15. See note 2 above.
16. See note 7 above.
17. Shafritz, *Public Policy and Administration,* 444.
18. Vila and Morris, *Police in American Society,* 77.
19. Shafritz, *Public Policy and Administration,* 445.
20. Ibid., 445.
21. Ibid.
22. Ibid.
23. "Evolution and Development of Police Technology," 72.
24. Ibid., 71.
25. Ibid.
26. "Toward Improved Criminal Justice."
27. U.S. Congress, Office of Technology Assessment, *Criminal Justice,* 19.
28. U.S. Congress, Office of Technology Assessment, *Criminal Justice,* 18.
29. See note 26 above.
30. Ibid.
31. Bovens and Zouridis, "Information and Communication Technology."
32. Evolution and Development of Police Technology, 40.
33. Shafritz, *Public Policy and Administration,* 1297.
34. See note 7 above.
35. Ibid., 14.

POLICE
TECHNOLOGY

PART TWO

Strategic Information Systems and Technologies

Chapter Seven
Communications Dispatch Centers

Learning Objectives

- The student will understand how hardwired and wireless **universal emergency number**, or 9-1-1, calls reach a **public safety answering point (PSAP)**.

- The student will understand what kinds of information are automatically included in a 9-1-1 call and how that information is used, including **enhanced 9-1-1 (E911)**.

- The student will understand the basic functions of **computer-aided dispatch (CAD)** systems.

- The student will understand the need for and design of alternative, or **routine universal service numbers**.

- The student will understand the basic functions of an **intelligent transportation system** and its relation to law enforcement.

Introduction

In the first six chapters we examined some of the history, theory, hardware, and software that are the foundation of police technology. From this point forward, the text is about how the technology can enhance public safety. It is about how people interact with the technology. By viewing how people and technology have interacted in law enforcement, we should get an idea of what is possible, what is not possible, what we might want to avoid, and the future of police technology.

At one of the most visible levels, police technology starts to come together in the dispatch center. It has been estimated that about 85 percent of state and local police activities are based on calls to dispatch centers.[1] Dispatch centers can be very complex or relatively simple. The complexity of a dispatch center is probably proportionate to the size of the law enforcement agencies. The primary purposes of the dispatch center are to manage calls for service from the public and provide communication and information support to field police officers. As we shall see, some complex dispatch centers are beginning to be the first point of collection of police statistics, like crime information, and they are increasingly beginning to take on the ability to manage community traffic control systems flow, particularly in large urban environments.

The Universal Emergency Number

Whether complex or simple, the first task of the dispatch center is to be the **public safety answering point (PSAP)**. Essentially, when you or I use the telephone to call the police, we generally get the PSAP, or communications dispatch center (Figure 7.1). No view of PSAPs and dispatch centers would be complete without an overview of how citizens use the telephone to contact the police.

It's fairly common knowledge that Alexander Graham Bell invented the first working telephone. Moreover, in what may have been an indication of the future, the first telephone call he made was an emergency call. So the story goes, on March 10, 1876, in Boston, Massachusetts, Bell was going to call his assistant Thomas Watson on the first working telephone. As he was making the first call, he knocked over a container of acid, splashing some onto himself. Reportedly, the

Figure 7.1 This photograph was taken inside the Police Department Dispatch Center in Walnut Creek, California. It shows a typical dispatch center workstation. Using a dual-screen monitor, the dispatcher is able to receive incoming 9-1-1 information, monitor the computer-generated information from patrol officers and query a variety of systems. *Photograph provided by Randolph Larson, Editor,* 9-1-1 Magazine.

first telephone message was, "Mr. Watson, come here, I want you!" Ninety-one years later, the first 9-1-1 call would be made in the United States.

In 1957 the National Association of Fire Chiefs (NAFC) recommended that a single number be used to report fires. The NAFC recommendation would ultimately result in the universal emergency number 9-1-1. In 1967 the Federal Communication Commission met with American Telegraph and Telephone Company (AT&T) and discussed the development of the universal emergency number.[2,3] Prior to 1984, AT&T was the telephone service supplier to nearly all Americans.[4]

The digits 9-1-1 were eventually selected as the universal telephone number for two reasons. First, when commercial telephone systems were being developed, the second and third digits of a telephone number were reserved by the telephone companies so that any number dialed that had the digit one as its second and third digit would be automatically routed to the business office. Early on in the development of commercial telephone service, 4-1-1 became Directory Information and 6-1-1 became Telephone Repair. Since the number one as the second and third digits of a telephone number were essentially reserved, any three-digit number that was going to be the universal emergency number would end in 1-1. In the 1950s, long before serious efforts to develop a universal emergency number in the United States, officials in Great Britain had designated the three-digit number 9-9-9 for reporting fires. So the second reason that 9-1-1 emerged as our universal emergency number is probably because of the numbers chosen across the Atlantic.

Today nearly 93 percent of the population, covering 96 percent of the area of the United States, has 9-1-1 as the universal emergency number.[5] This means that in addition to providing the public with immediate contact with the police, it is also the number called for fire and emergency medical services.[6] Because PSAPs handle police, fire, and emergency medical services, the complexity of the dispatch center is increasing.

Before the advent of 9-1-1, people calling the police had essentially two choices. The most common occurrence was for people in an emergency to dial the operator and ask for the police, the fire department, or an ambulance. At that point in time, the telephone operator was the de facto public safety answering point. While the telephone company operators did not ask questions or take action like today's 9-1-1 professionals, they did have to make decisions. For instance, the telephone company operator had to decide which agency the emergency call should be transferred to. After all, AT&T was the one company providing primary service, and within AT&T's customer service areas there were thousands of law enforcement agencies that could be responsible for the emergency. Each telephone operator did not have to choose from thousands, but in urban areas it is quite possible that even though the calls went through local exchanges, the commercial telephone operator would have to make a decision between two or three.

The second way for the public to contact police, fire, or emergency medical services was to have the correct number memorized or handy. They could then dial the number directly. When 9-1-1 service began, if you called the police, you were immediately connected with your local PSAP. So your emergency telephone call went to the right location, but the PSAP operator would only know the information you told him or her. In January 1979 AT&T deployed **Enhanced 9-1-1 (E911)** systems. When you make a telephone call from a hardwired telephone line, your telephone number is not the only information being sent over the telephone wires.

Recall from our discussion on cellular telephones that each cellular telephone has an embedded electronic serial number (ESN). While your telephone does not have an embedded ESN, it does send out an **automatic identification number (AIN)** signal to the telephone carrier network. The AIN is an eight-digit number consisting of the seven-digit telephone number of the subscriber and a single digit that is an abbreviation of the area code from which the call is being made. This eight-digit is called the numbering plan digit (NPD). Originally the AIN was developed to help the telephone company assess the proper charges when a long distance call was placed.

When a 9-1-1 call is made, the voice signal and the AIN pass through the local exchange carrier switch and are routed to a telephone company device referred to as the 911 tandem. The 911 tandem reads the AIN and, based upon the software programming, forwards the call to the appropriate PSAP, or dispatch center. Once the call is received by the PSAP, a PSAP with Enhanced 9-1-1 automatically queries a telephone company database that converts AIN information into the physical location of the telephone. A check of the telephone company database is necessary because there are instances where the telephone is located at one place and the bill is sent to another. Typically someone will have a telephone in a residence or business but have the bill sent to a Post Office box. When the information on the physical location of the telephone returns to the PSAP, it is called **automatic location information (ALI)**. Generally, this happens so quickly it appears as if the telephone call and the ALI arrived at the PSAP at the same time. Because the PSAP receives the ALI at virtually the same time as the call, the call-taking process is simpler and the possibility of human error in the entry of the caller's address is reduced.[7]

But what about cellular telephone 9-1-1 calls? According to the Cellular Telecommunications and Internet Association, in 2001 more than 156,000 cellular 9-1-1 calls were made on a daily basis.[8] Since a cellular telephone has no permanent physical location, how can PSAPs obtain critical ALI? The essence of cellular technology is that the telephone moves from site to site. So the telephone number of the cellular telephone and its electronic serial number are of little use in querying a database to determine the cellular telephone's location. Conceivably, the cellular telephone subscriber could live in Los Angeles and be making an emergency 9-1-1 telephone call in New York.

The Federal Communications Commission (FCC) has required that cellular providers develop technology to enable the PSAP to have a fairly accurate ALI when their products are used to make emergency calls to PSAPs.[9] The cellular providers have come up with a number of schemes for complying with the FCC regulations.[10]

Recall from our chapter on geographic information systems (GIS) the concepts of trilateration and time difference on arrival (TDOA). As we know, cellular telephone signals are constantly being monitored by more than one cell site. This is primarily to facilitate the signal handoff of a moving cellular telephone. However, it can also be used to combine trilateration and TDOA for the purposes of locating a cellular telephone.

Presume that the cellular telephone signal that is making an emergency telephone call is being monitored by three cell sites, as in Figure 7.2. As we know, cellular telephones and cell sites are constantly trading information with each other. The cellular telephone sends a signal that it is on, including its ESN. The cell site, through the control channel, is telling the cellular telephone a variety of information, including the correct time, according to the cellular system.

Since your cellular telephone's clock is in sync with the cellular system clock, the cell site is able to determine your location in the same manner as global positioning satellites (GPSs) did in Chapter Five using the TDOA formula. Moreover, one of the alternate manners that cellular providers are using to comply with FCC regulations regarding ALI information and Enhanced 9-1-1 is the inclusion of a GPS system in each cellular telephone. With the GPS configuration, the cellular telephone can essentially have a GPS device added to it and thereby make its own

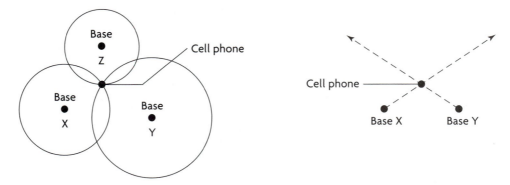

Figure 7.2 This drawing represents how cellular telephone triangulation typically operates. The drawing on the left represents cellular technology using TDOA like trilateration while the drawing on the right depicts more simple triangulation.

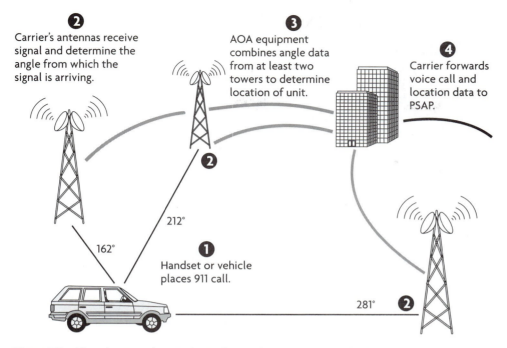

2
Carrier's antennas receive signal and determine the angle from which the signal is arriving.

3
AOA equipment combines angle data from at least two towers to determine location of unit.

4
Carrier forwards voice call and location data to PSAP.

2

212°

162°

1
Handset or vehicle places 911 call.

281° **2**

Figure 7.3 This drawing depicts how the angle on arrival is calculated.

determination as to location. Or in the cases of what is called wireless-assisted GPS (WAG), the cellular telephone receives the GPS signals and forwards them to the cell site. The cellular provider's equipment then makes the location determination based upon the signals forwarded from the cellular telephone.

In addition to the TDOA and GPS schemes, cellular providers are commonly using one other scheme that can determine the ALI of a cellular telephone. Moreover, this scheme can be used in conjunction with TDOA to make the determination of the ALI information more exact. The third scheme for determining a cellular telephone call's ALI is called **angle on arrival (AOA)**. This scheme uses the antenna at the cell site to determine the angle that a cellular telephone call signal arrived. Using the principle of trilateration, the AOA can be used to calculate a more precise ALI. Many cellular systems, like the one depicted in Figure 7.3, use AOA in conjunction with TDOA in order to obtain as precise an ALI as possible.[11]

It is a fairly safe assumption that every police agency in the United States has a telephone and, therefore, a PSAP of some kind. However, as of 1999, only 7,195 of the more than seventeen thousand state and local law enforcement agencies in the United States actually had communications or dispatch centers.[12] So we can state that all agencies have a telephone and most have 9-1-1, but less than half have a formal communications dispatch center. At many smaller local agencies, the PSAP, even though 9-1-1 configured, may only be someone who answers the telephone at the local station. The point is the PSAP may not necessarily be a dispatch center. It is also fairly safe to state that the larger an agency is, the more likely it is to have a formal dispatch center. But just because they have a dispatch center doesn't mean they have **computer-assisted dispatch (CAD)**. Moreover, the presence of CAD does not mean that the agency will be using all of the CAD, functions possible. Therefore, as we begin to discuss dispatch centers and CAD, we will be looking at what is possible, given necessity and funding, at any police agency.

Computer-Aided Dispatch

Computer-Aided Dispatch is a term used to describe software applications and hardware that assist in the management of dispatching calls for service. In fact, the best way to look at a CAD system is as a management tool that automates the many functions of a dispatch center. For state and local law enforcement agencies, CAD also provides access to other databases and acts as interface software in the two-way voice communications between the dispatch center and field units. Computer software designed to assist with the management of vehicles, communications, and dispatching is not peculiar to public safety. Many private firms, such as trucking companies, use similar types of software to manage their day-to-day vehicle-related functions. Private firms may track the locations of their trucks, or they may coordinate deliveries. In the private sector, CAD software has many uses. However, there are aspects to a fully integrated CAD that are law enforcement specific (Figure 7.4).[13]

In reality, the most important part of CAD is the software and various other systems with which CAD can interface. Before we look at the software and additional interfaces, let's briefly describe the hardware that comprises the workstation. A CAD workstation's operating system is typically either UNIX or Windows based. The workstation is outfitted with the communications equipment (like radio transmitter/receiver, headphones, and microphone) necessary for contact

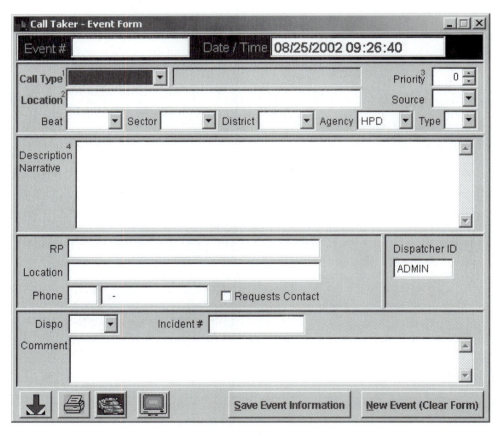

Figure 7.4 During an initial call to the PSAP, the 9-1-1 operator would use GUI-based software similar to that represented by this screen capture.
Source: "Computer-Aided Dispatch," 1.
Permission for screen capture provided by Crimestar Corporation.

with the field units. Moreover, as we will go into in some detail, the workstation is in some way connected to the commercial telephone network. In addition to a traditional desktop PC hardware configuration, the hardware can include one or two monitors, and in some cases touch screens.[14]

While CAD does assist police agencies with the management of their field resources, public safety CAD also captures and retains information about all of the 9-1-1 calls and field-generated incidents. This means that for the public safety organization, a huge relational database is being constructed that can be used for a variety of other information-related tasks.[15] For instance, CAD should be able to tell the user that the police have responded to a location previously. This can have great tactical benefit to the field officers because they might receive information that the call they are responding to was handled on a previous shift and, for instance, the person at the location is mentally ill.

On the strategic side, a fully integrated CAD system can be used to assesses deployment needs, provide information on problem locations, and provide the initial incident number that will be used to reference all subsequent evidence, reports, and police activities. Although we are going to look at CAD as a software product, the more complex the CAD program, the more complex the hardware that is involved in executing the CAD functions. Additionally, an advanced CAD system interfaces with complex hardware and software systems.

There are other possible combinations of PSAP responsibilities in the dispatch centers nationwide. Some PSAPs handle emergency calls for police, fire, and emergency medical services. Other PSAPs may handle the police, but if the call is regarding a fire or medical emergency, the call is transferred to a fire/medical

Figure 7.5 This photograph demonstrates how a computer-aided dispatch system can also support the use of telecommunications devices for the deaf (TDD). A deaf or hearing-impaired caller can communicate with the PSAP by using a keyboard device that is attached to the caller's telephone.
Source: "Computer-Aided Dispatch," 4. *Photograph provided by Positron.*

Figure 7.6 This is the dispatch floor at the San Jose, California, police department. Calls for service for most state and local law enforcement agencies can be recorded with CAD. Most CAD systems automatically record the following information for each incident:

- Incident number
- Source of the information
- Nature of incident
- Location of the incident
- Date and time of the incident
- Receipt of the call by the PSAP and the assigned unit
- Dispatch of each unit

- Arrival at the incident of each unit
- Clearing from the incident of each unit
- Closing of the incident
- Disposition of the incident (a disposition would be a brief summary, usually a single word, that describes the outcome of the call, such as "Arrest" or "Citation."

Source: Bair, et al., *"Advanced Crime Mapping,"* 97. *Photograph provided by Randall Larson, Editor,* 9-1-1 Magazine.

emergency services dispatcher. As we explore dispatch centers, we will concentrate on calls for service as they relate to police emergencies. Keep in mind that a request for fire or emergency medical service might either be handled by the same PSAP or be transferred to a second PSAP.

Of course, dispatch centers, as in Figure 7.6, not only receive 9-1-1 calls, but also provide communications support for police officers in the field. In some smaller agencies, the dispatcher may also be responsible for routing business calls throughout the police station. For ease of examination, we will look at the functions of receiving emergency calls and providing communications support to field police officers as if they were separate. In some larger and mid-sized agencies this is probably true. But in the vast majority of occasions, the one or two people responsible for these two functions perform both simultaneously. To observe what happens inside a PSAP, let's follow an emergency call.

As of 1996, in the United States there were approximately 268,000 calls made to 9-1-1 PSAPs daily.[16] Moreover, a large percentage of these calls were not emergencies. They may have been a request for information, the report of a nonemergency

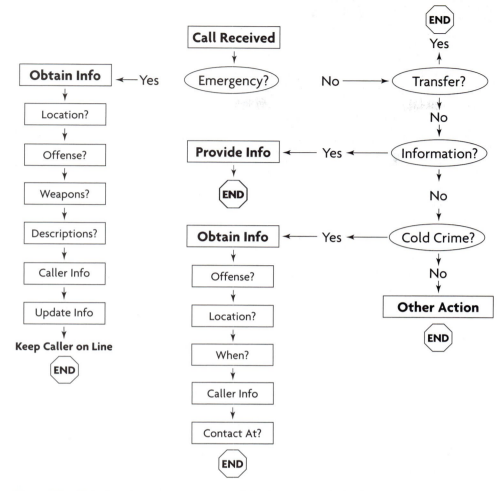

Figure 7.7 This drawing represents one of the recommended call-taking processes. It was developed based upon information provided by the National Emergency Number Association.

situation, or some other type of call that is not even related to public safety. The estimates on the percentage of 9-1-1 calls that are nonemergency in nature range from 35 percent up to 90 percent.[17] Whatever the true figure, it is clear that many of the calls received by a PSAP operator are not emergencies. In order to minimize the time that nonemergency calls take up and to minimize the potential that a nonemergency call will keep an emergency call waiting, most PSAP operators screen the calls on arrival.

Figure 7.7 is a call-taking process recommended by the National Emergency Number Association.[18] In this process, the first question asked by the PSAP operator is something like, "9-1-1 Emergency, what are you reporting?" Fortunately, PSAP operators are generally well trained and highly experienced at determining whether a call is of an emergency nature. If the call is an emergency, the PSAP operator takes some basic information and begins the process of generating a call for service to a field unit.

If the call is not of an emergency nature, in smaller agencies, the PSAP operator may continue to handle the call and provide the caller with the requested information, service, or a transfer to more appropriate person. In larger agencies, the PSAP operator may immediately transfer the person to someone else in the dispatch center who is tasked to handle nonemergency calls. In the second scenario the 9-1-1

PSAP operator has cleared the call off his workstation and is ready for the next 9-1-1 call. The nonemergency caller may have to wait on hold until the nonemergency PSAP operator is available. For the moment, let's presume that the call is an emergency and that the police agency has Enhanced 9-1-1 and a fully integrated CAD and communications system. Remember, all of the functions we are going to explore are not used by all agencies. As we have mentioned, the technology used by the thousands of PSAPs is as fragmented as most police technology, for a variety of reasons.

Our example PSAP answers the telephone at 3 A.M. and states, "9-1-1 Emergency, what are you reporting?" The caller tells the PSAP that she believes her neighbor's house is being broken into. This type of call, a report of a possible burglary in progress would be an emergency call. Once our PSAP operator determines that the call is an emergency, the information provided by the Automatic Identification Number (AIN) provided in E911 is converted to the basis for the call for service. Public safety CAD should have the ability for direct interface with the 9-1-1 system. This means that when a 9-1-1 call comes into the dispatch center, the CAD automatically displays the ANI.

The PSAP is going to do a number of things simultaneously, and in order for this emergency call to be processed efficiently and for the process to be more effective, the design of the PSAP/CAD console is important. Notice that in Figure 7.1 the PSAP has two computer monitors. The first monitor is displaying the ANI information, and is an input screen so that the call for service can be generated. The second screen displays status of the police agency's various resources. This second screen tells the PSAP how many police officers are on duty and their current status.

Let's examine some of the CAD features. It should be able to interface with the ANI and ALI information coming through the Enhanced 9-1-1 network. A complete interface means that when the 9-1-1 ANI and ALI information arrives with the 9-1-1 emergency call, the proper fields on the opening screen of the PSAP operator's CAD screen are populated or contain the ANI/ALI information. This would mean that the location or address the 9-1-1 call is coming from could be transferred into the CAD system as the location of the call for service by clicking an icon. As with our current example, many times a neighbor or passerby will call the police. The location of the call for service would be the location the call was made from after determination by the PSAP operator, or under circumstances such as an open line. So the location the 9-1-1 call is coming from may or may not be the location of the emergency. This type of interface increases efficiency and effectiveness because the call is broadcast to the field units quicker and the opportunity for human error has been reduced because the PSAP operator does not have to type in information; it can be automatically transferred from the ANI/ALI to the CAD call for service information.

Because emergency information needs to be entered into CAD quickly while the operator is under pressure, a CAD system should be easy to use. Most people consider a graphical user interface (GUI) system with pull-down menus and transaction icons the simplest and most efficient way to input critical information under pressure. For most of the local agencies, the PSAP operator is also the dispatcher who is in radio and data communication with field units.

Returning to our burglary in progress, the PSAP operator has imported the caller's location into a field that describes from where the call is coming. As the PSAP questions the caller, it is determined that the house in question is directly next to and south of the caller's location. When most people call 9-1-1 they are under extreme duress. They are nervous, scared, or even injured. The information they give is sometimes confused or incorrect. The value of a good PSAP operator cannot be overemphasized. In addition to being able to calm a distraught caller, a good PSAP operator can illicit information that will make the responding officer's

INCIDENT NUMBERS

The incident number tracks the call, reports, arrests, and evidence. In Chapter Eight, when we look at agency systems, the importance of a single number will become clearer. For now, realize that most agencies do not have this capability. Each subsequent police report is given a report number and the incident number created by CAD is referenced in the report, but not cross-indexed in some kind of automated system. An incident number usually consists of a modified Julian Data, and the sequential number of the call.* Therefore, the first call after midnight on January 1, 2003, would have an incident number something like 000100103. The first four digits are the sequential number, the next three numbers are the day of the year, and the last two digits are the year. The fiftieth call on March 1, 2003, would look like 005006003.

* The Julian Date was invented by Joseph Scaliger in 1853. It is a system of converting the calendar date into an integer, or whole number. Scaliger's system used a 7,980-year cycle which began January 1, 4713 BC. Most CAD programs create a modified Julian date that combines the date and time in order to create an incident number. The pure Julian date for May 29, 2003 at 7:54 P.M. Pacific Daylight Time is 2452788.6210380443371832. However, a modified Julian Date for May 29, 2003, at 7:54 P.M. might be a combination of the number of days in the year that May 29, 2003, represents (159) plus the time in military time 1945; or 031591945.

task much safer. In this instance, the caller could have confused directions and said that the house being burglarized is to the north instead of the south. This information could change the tactical response by the police, perhaps they would inadvertently park directly in front of the location or approach the wrong house, alerting the suspect to their presence. The point is that the technology is valuable, but it is the people who make it work.

While most PSAPs are outstanding, the tools an advanced CAD system can provide them can make their job easier and their performance better. For instance, an enhanced CAD system with a fully integrated GIS database gives the PSAP more tools in trying to determine the exact location of the emergency. The GIS system gives them the ability to query by street address, intersection, and landmark, to name a few. In the event that the call to 9-1-1 does not contain ANI/ALI information—as in the case of a cellular telephone call—the PSAP can, with GIS and the caller's help, determine the location of the call. Although some CAD programs do not have GIS programs integrated into them, with the FCC requirements that cellular providers use some system to report ALI on cellular emergency calls, there will be a push to have existing CAD systems upgraded to incorporate GIS. This is because cellular ALI information is going to be reporting to the PSAP in the form of latitude and longitude, and GIS software is the only efficient way to convert this data into a location that our dispatcher can use.[19] As we shall see later in the chapter, the GIS function of CAD can have other critical functions.

Our PSAP has now used a mouse to click an icon, causing the caller's information to be become a call for service. The CAD computer will recognize that a call for service is being generated and assign an incident number to the call. An incident number is a critical part of CAD. In a fully integrated system, not only does the incident number track the call, but it is used for all record keeping in the police agency. For instance, if this call results in someone being arrested or a report being taken, the incident number is also the report number.

Now that the call has been generated by CAD, the PSAP has some choices. The PSAP operator must tell the CAD system what type of call and what priority to assign the call. Because police agencies get such a large volume of calls for service, they are each given a priority—in essence, a recommended order that the field officers should handle calls. In some CAD configurations, the software predetermines

Up until the early 1990s, the law enforcement services provided by state and local agencies were generally considered a public good. A public good is something produced by the government, generally paid for by taxes, and freely provided to all members of the community. In contrast, a private good is something produced by a private firm and paid for and consumed by an individual. So the services of the police are a public good, and a hamburger is a private good. However, the view on police services, particularly as they relate to alarm calls, is changing. Some public administrators are taking the view that if a private firm benefits from a police action, they should pay for the benefit. Generally, we think of the many local ordinances that are being enacted so that a fee can be charged when the police respond to a false alarm. However, there are other instances of the state and local law enforcement agencies seeking compensation for actions they took that benefited a private firm.

Source: Bayley and Shearing, "Future of Policing," 589.

the call priority or at least makes a recommendation to the PSAP. For instance, a burglary in progress call would have a recommended higher priority than a call for service complaining about barking dogs.[20] Additionally, most CAD systems are programmed with icons to select the type of call. Our PSAP in this example would select the icon for burglary, and CAD might ask if the burglary was in progress, the suspects had just left, or if this was only a report call. Our PSAP operator selects the icon that denotes the burglary is in progress and the CAD software recommends that the call be given a high priority. Our PSAP accepts the high priority and continues with the interview of the caller.

Our enhanced CAD system includes a GIS interface, so when the PSAP checks the address of the caller, the PSAP can access the addresses that are next door to the caller. The caller tells the PSAP the house is to the south, when our PSAP enters that address, CAD automatically checks for other calls to the location. At this moment, our PSAP is alerted by CAD that another operator has just taken a call from an alarm company stating that a silent burglary alarm was recently activated at the location in question.

In many agencies, silent alarm calls are generally a low priority call because the vast majority of them are false.[21] Moreover, in a large agency that did not have CAD, it is likely that the two calls for service would not be referenced until it was too late for their relationship to have any tactical value. Now not only does the neighbor believe a burglary is in process, but there is an alarm activation at the location. These two calls, taken together, increase the likelihood that there is indeed a break-in occurring. Moreover, the fact that there is another call confirms the directions to the location the neighbor has given. If the neighbor gave the wrong direction or did not know what direction to give (many people can't tell direction), an advanced CAD system would find fresh calls in a predetermined area around this call.

The ability of CAD to create a buffer zone around a call location is extremely valuable. In this instance, imagine that the neighbor behind the house being broken into heard glass breaking, but he cannot tell from which direction the noise came. Since it is 3 A.M., the neighbor decides to call 9-1-1. It is a large agency, and that call was handled by a third PSAP. Because an advanced CAD system has the ability to alert users to duplicate calls, and calls in the same general area as other calls, it adds value to the tactical nature and strategic nature of the information. In the tactical sense, the information on the burglary is now confirmed from three sources—the next-door neighbor, the alarm company, and now the neighbor behind.

In a strategic sense, before CAD, the breaking glass call would not have been related to the other two until after the fact. So a third call would have been generated and unnecessary police resources dispatched to the incident. Of course, the officers in the field might hear the three calls for service and begin to put the information together, but in this day and age when many calls come via the in-car computer, it is likely they would not have. Moreover, by incorporating the breaking glass call into the first call to the police, police managers get better data on the actual number of calls for service. In the pre-CAD dispatch center, the managers would have unwittingly counted three calls for service. In the CAD dispatch center the basic statistics of police calls for service are significantly more accurate. So CAD has already increased the tactical and strategic value of this call for service—and we're not finished.

At this point, our PSAP has enough information to get the field units responding to the burglary, but in our large dispatch center the PSAP is not the person who is in constant and direct communication with the field units. That person is the radio operator. In a large agency, it would be impossible for someone to take 9-1-1 calls and handle the requests from the field units. There would just be too much work. So our PSAP clicks an icon to select a unit for dispatch. Our state-of-the-art CAD system includes an interface with an **automatic vehicle locator (AVL)** system on the patrol cars. It combines information on the closest police units and the status of those units to create a picture of the available field resources. However, the closest unit may be police officers who have a suspect in custody or are for some other reason unavailable to respond. Like all computer systems, the value of the information output is directly influenced by the input.

In other words, unless the field police officers and the dispatchers constantly update the information in the CAD, the information becomes stale. The closer any computer system moves toward an effort to provide real-time data, the more critical the continuous update of the information becomes. Now our CAD system selects and recommends that the closet available unit to the burglary call is Unit 5. Our PSAP accepts the recommendation by clicking an icon and selects another icon to broadcast the call to the field units. At this point, the PSAP has probably told the caller to remain on the line so he can get additional information, but for now, the important task is to get the field units responding.

When our PSAP selects the icon to broadcast, the radio operator who is handling the field units radio traffic is alert that a PSAP has an emergency call broadcast. If our radio operator is transmitting, she ceases to transmit, allowing the PSAP frequency time. Again, we are looking at a large agency with multiple people in the dispatch center. In a large agency, there might be dozens of people working simultaneously. Because of the size and complexity of the task, the PSAP and radio operators often cannot see each other, much less verbally communicate. At the moment the PSAP transmits, the call is also sent to the console of the radio operator. Now the field units and the radio operator, who can hear the PSAP's transmission, know there is a burglary in progress.

Our PSAP waits to hear Unit 5 acknowledge the call and then goes back to interviewing the caller. In our situation, the caller gives the PSAP further information that there is a man in dark clothing climbing in the window of the neighbor's house. Because the PSAP knows the location of the caller and the location of the burglary, the side of the house can be determined. Our caller does not have any more information. So our PSAP tells the caller that the police are en route and hangs up. At this point, the PSAP enters the additional information concerning the description of the suspect into CAD and would probably broadcast that information to the field units in the form of a supplemental information broadcast. Now finished with this call, the PSAP selects an icon to close out the call. The call is now the responsibility of the radio dispatcher and the field units. Our PSAP goes on to the next 9-1-1 call.

But CAD's job is not finished. In this instance, when the police officers in the field receive the call, they would get the information over the voice radio and on their in-car computers. In Chapter Eight on agency systems, we will look more closely at the in-car computers, but for now, the information, along with driving directions and waypoints, appears on the officers' computer. It is important to note that CAD is not the GIS nor the GPS system that is at the heart of our agency's AVL.[22] CAD is the interface between these systems.

The mapping aspect of CAD is considered a software subsystem. As we noted, we are describing how an advanced CAD system might work. In our scenario, the CAD mapping system shows the current geographic information and status of the field units. By having this information, our dispatcher can look at the current call location, any other pending calls, and the active units. Many advanced CAD systems also look at the same information and, based on their programming, make recommendations to the dispatcher. The advanced CAD system might highlight the nearest available unit.[23] Recall from Chapter Six, if our dispatcher allows the CAD system to actually make the decision on which unit to send, the dispatcher is defaulting to screen-level bureaucracy.[24] The CAD system is making a recommendation; the dispatcher has to make the decision, and other factors may influence that decision.

While the PSAP and CAD determined that Unit 5 was the closest available unit, this may not be practically true. It may be that another unit is closer because of traffic conditions. Of course, at 3 A.M., traffic conditions probably don't have the impact they might have at 3 P.M., but it is a consideration. Moreover, Unit 5's status in CAD might have been available, but in practicality, they may have just taken a suspect into custody and may not be available to respond. Our point is that while AVL information is updated by the system as frequently as every fifteen seconds, CAD unit status information is only as accurate as the last thing people entered into the system. So our radio operator, who now has responsibility for the call in the dispatch center, must be able to change the status of the call and its information. In our scenario, let's presume that Unit 5 was available, and that Unit 2 and Unit 6, along with a supervisor, have also told the radio operator that they are on their way to the call.

Recall that CAD has a history of all the calls for service that have been generated by the dispatch center. Depending on the requirements of the agency, that history can go back as far as ten years. In some instances, CAD will tell the PSAP information about the location from which the call was generated.[25] For instance, perhaps the location's history was that several false calls to 9-1-1 had come from it, or perhaps the person living at the location was mentally ill. All of this information in CAD has tactical value to the field officers. In an instance where a location had a relevant history, the PSAP or the radio operator might make the field units aware of the history by broadcasting a synopsis of the information. For instance, a radio operator might broadcast to the responding units, "use caution at 123 South Main Street; the person at the address was previously reported as mentally ill." Such a history at a location might change the response by the field units. Almost certainly, a field supervisor hearing this kind of supplemental history would respond to the location.

In addition to enhancing the tactical value of communications information, an advanced CAD system can have significant positive impact on the strategic aspect of police information. A fully integrated system is going to allow users to find out what happened to a call for service. It is going to be able to tell users if a crime did occur, if an arrest was made, or if no action was taken. This enhanced system already contains geocoded information. In other words, since the GIS system is being used for AVL and dispatch, our potential crime-mapping information is also available. In Chapter Twelve, when we look at crime mapping and crime analysis, it will become clear that a fully integrated CAD system, with its ability to directly interface to GIS for crime mapping, is hugely valuable.

As our officers arrive at the scene, they begin to make plans via one of their tactical frequencies. While the radio operator probably has the ability to monitor the in-field tactical radio frequencies, they probably do not. The radio operator has all the radio traffic of the other field units to work. Presume for an instant that while Unit 5 was available and acknowledged she was going to the call, on the way she observed a major traffic accident. Unit 5 would probably stop at the accident scene in order to determine if their were injuries and so on. Unit 5 would report to the radio operator that she was at the scene of a traffic collision and unable to respond. The radio operator would now update the CAD information to show that Unit 5 could not handle the call for service. Since another unit is already on the way, the radio operator would probably assign the call to that unit. However, if no other unit was on the way, the radio operator would query the CAD system and AVL in order to determine the next closest available unit. Moreover, the radio operator would probably receive information regarding the traffic collision and have to contact the fire department and emergency medical services dispatch so the proper resources could go to the scene of the traffic collision Unit 5 happened upon.

In large agencies, just as the PSAP and radio operator functions are separate, generally, the fire department and emergency medical services dispatch are also performed by different personnel. In a large city, it would not be uncommon for the PSAP to be working for the police department and other dispatchers to be working directly for the fire department.

The first unit on the scene is Unit 2. Unit 2 decides that prior to approaching the house that may contain the burglar, he would like to speak to the person who made the initial 9-1-1 call. However, instead of approaching the caller's residence and possibly alerting the suspects, Unit 2 requests that the radio operator "patch" a call through to the original caller. An advanced CAD system has the ability for the radio operator to place a call to the original caller and then link the police radio system directly to the telephone system so that the field officers may interview the caller.

While Unit 2 is interviewing the caller, a man exits the residence that is reported to contain a burglar. The man, with his hands raised, approaches the police officers and tells them that he lives at the address and had to break a side window because he lost his house keys and wallet while on a short vacation. This scenario, or one much like it, is very common. Now the police officers must determine the man's identity and verify his story.

Police officers in the field have access to a tremendous amount of information. In most police agencies, the officer obtains that information directly from the dispatch center. The police officer might obtain that information via the voice radio or via the in-field computer. As we examined in Chapter Three on radio communications, there are also communications schemes that allow the officer direct access to databases from his vehicle. Most commonly, that is a cellular data packet device (CDPD) system. However, in a dispatch center with advanced CAD capabilities, the PSAP and the radio operator have access to all the information databases that the in-field officer does. This is for two purposes. First, many times, a police officer in the field is unable to use the in-field computer. For instance, the police officer may be inside a building conducting an investigation and be unable to return to her vehicle to use the in-field computer. In another instance, the field situation itself may prevent the police officer from using the in-field computer.

At times, a police officer's use of technology in the field can be unsafe. The computer in the police officer's vehicle is one of the devices that if used at an inappropriate time, can comprise a police officer's personal safety. For instance, recall our speeding violator from Chapter One. As we noted, the traffic violator to whom the police officer is issuing a citation may be wanted for some unrelated crime. In this example, each time the police officer uses the radio or in-field computer, the suspect is naturally going to believe the police officer is attempting to verify the suspect's identity and may uncover the crime the suspect knows about but the police officer does not. Because the suspects always have perfect information about themselves—they know if they have just committed a crime or if they are wanted or believe they may be wanted—the police officer is at a disadvantage. Moreover, each time a police officer—especially one working alone—uses technology he must take his eyes off the suspect. So the question for the police officer issuing the traffic violator a citation is: do I verify the violator's information via the radio—where I can stand outside of the car, or do I sit in the car and type on the in-field computer? The former is always safer. This type of situation is fairly common and is one of the reasons that the dispatch center must have complete access to all databases.

We also learned in Chapter Three that communications schemes like CDPD that rely on commercial systems may not be able to give priority to law enforcement data traffic. And with sophisticated communications systems there are going to be times that the in-field computer is inoperable. The system will go down. Our second reason that the dispatch center must have access to all databases is because they are a backup system to the in-field communications system.

In review, an advanced CAD system is completely integrated into enhanced 9-1-1 and the agency's overall records management system; it can produce reports, can provide a tracking number for all reports, and is the basis for GIS analysis of crime. It increases the efficiency and effectiveness of dispatch by providing up-to-date, AVL-assisted locations and statuses of all field units. It has a history of the calls for service.

In Chapter Four we looked at networks and discussed some general precautions that can be taken to ensure the safety and security of a computer system or network. A CAD system should also be treated as any vital information system. At the very least, a CAD system should be protected by a series of passwords so that only authorized users have the ability to use the system. Moreover, depending on how integrated an agency has become, the system may need other security systems such as firewalls.[26] And, as we noted in Chapter Two, information should always be backed up early and often.

Nonemergency Points of Contact

A large portion of the interaction between public safety (police, fire, and emergency medical services) is of a routine, or nonemergency, nature. The public has a need to contact these services under circumstances that are not time sensitive. Probably because of the ease of dialing a three digit number and always being assured that one would reach police, fire, or emergency medical services, the

The San Diego Police Department in California has created a direct-dial nonemergency number for the public. Go to their Web site at **www.sannet. gov/** **police/video/index.shtml** and view an online video presentation about the number.

number of nonemergency 9-1-1 calls has steadily increased. Indeed, as we saw, the number of nonemergency calls may be very large. A number of different organizations and individuals have called for the creation of a three-digit method of contacting pubic safety officials other than 9-1-1. Thus, in some areas—particularly large urban areas—the 3-1-1 number was created to give the public an alternative to jamming the 9-1-1 lines with nonemergency telephone calls.

Earlier we looked at the basic call-screening process and saw that a larger organization may have PSAP operators dedicated to handling nonemergency telephone calls. In some of those large agencies, 3-1-1 systems have been implemented that ring directly to the nonemergency operators. Other agencies have the 3-1-1 configured to ring the front desk of the police station and not the dispatch center.

Intelligent Transportation Systems

At the beginning of the chapter we noted that although we are concentrating on the law enforcement aspects of dispatch centers, many dispatch centers (Figure 7.8) also handle fire and emergency medical services calls. A relatively new

Figure 7.8 Inside the Park City, Utah, Police Communications Center dispatchers use a variety of technology. In addition to using the computer (of which a keyboard is visible), dispatchers use radios and telephones, monitor closed-circuit televisions, and write with pen and paper. Clearly, the job of a dispatcher is very demanding.
Photograph provided by Randall Larson, Editor, 9-1-1 Magazine.

phenomenon has been to incorporate **intelligent transportation systems (ITSs)** into CAD functions. An advanced CAD with an ITS capability might allow the dispatcher access to real-time traffic information from **closed-circuit television (CCTV)** cameras along major thoroughfares.[27]

In addition to the CCTV images, real-time traffic data is sometimes collected from sensors under the street. All of this information can be imported into an advanced CAD system, giving the dispatcher a tremendous amount of valuable information. The traffic information could be used to provide field officers with information concerning the traffic conditions or best routes to calls for service. With the CCTV systems, it is likely that dispatchers may actually see traffic collisions before they are reported. In those instances wherein a situation is visible by CCTV, the dispatcher can provided the field officer with additional information or even send additional resources before the arrival of the first responder.[28]

Chapter Summary

We learned that by dialing the universal emergency number, 9-1-1, we reach a public safety answering point. As our call reaches the dispatch center, information about our location is also known. An agency using a computer-aided dispatch (CAD) system would take our caller identification information and import it into the agency system. A CAD system is used by a state or local law enforcement agency to manage the intake of calls for service and the activities of the field units. While doing so, an advanced system, with the combination of GPS data and GIS data would be creating a powerful relational database.

Computer-aided dispatch systems not only manage field resources, but also add to the information retained in an agency record management system, thereby creating a source of data for crime and management problems. Although we concentrated on law enforcement's use of dispatch centers, we know that both fire and emergency medical services can either be dispatched from the law enforcement dispatch center or from a separate system.

Because the large percentage of the calls for service received via 9-1-1 are of a nonemergency nature, many agencies are creating alternate, universal service numbers like 3-1-1. Additionally, as technology increases, dispatch centers have access to intelligent traffic systems, which could provide valuable information in real time about field situations.

Discussion Questions

1. Are the services provided by state and local law enforcement agencies always a public good? If not, other than alarm calls, can you think of a situation wherein a private firm or an individual should be charged a fee for the services rendered by a state or local law enforcement agency?

2. Now that you know that your cellular provider can know your location, does that raise privacy concerns for you?

3. If you were responsible for upgrading a basic computer-aided dispatch system but had a limited budget, what order of priority would you give enhanced systems? Why?

4. Visit your local police department or campus security office. Do they have a computer-aided dispatch system? If so, is it advanced? If not, what would you add? Why?

Key Terms

Angle on Arrival (AOA)

Automatic Identification Number (AIN)

Automatic Location Information (ALI)

Automatic Vehicle Locator (AVL)

Closed-Circuit Television (CCTV)

Computer-Assisted/Aided Dispatch (CAD)

Enhanced 9-1-1 (E911)

Intelligent Transportation System (ITS)

Public Safety Answering Point (PSAP)

End Notes

1. Gaines and Miller, *Criminal Justice in Action*, 118.
2. American Telephone and Telegraph (AT&T) was founded in 1877 by Alexander Graham Bell and initially named Bell Telephone. By 1983, AT&T provided telephone service to the lion's share of Americans. AT&T's dominance in the telephone market resulted in an anti-trust lawsuit that ultimately resulted in AT&T retaining long distance service and being broken up into separate regional telephone companies providing local service.
3. An excellent source for information concerning 9-1-1 issues is the National Emergency Number Association at **www.nena.org**.
4. Bonnet, "ISP-Bound Traffic," 187.
5. National Emergency Number Association, **www.nena.org**, (May 15, 2003).
6. A source of current information affecting public safety dispatchers is the online magazine, *Dispatch Monthly Magazine*. Its home page is **www.911dispatch.com**. To view a list of the 231 counties that did not have 9-1-1 services as of November 2001, visit this page on the Web site **www.911dispatch.com/911_file/counties_no911_state.html**.
7. "Computer-Aided Dispatch," 4.
8. The Cellular Telecommunications and Internet Association provides a variety of information about the use of cellular telephone and Internet technology, including a constantly updated count on the number of cellular telephone users at **www.wow-com.com**.
9. "Computer-Aided Dispatch," 3.
10. You can view the Federal Communications Commission's decisions relative to E9-1-1 and wireless communications at **www.fcc.gov/911/enhanced/**.
11. See note above.
12. Department of Justice, Bureau of Justice Statistics, "1999 Survey of State and Local Agencies."
13. "Computer-Aided Dispatch," 1.
14. Ibid., 7.
15. Ibid., 2.
16. "Fact Sheet on the 3-1-1 National Non-Emergency Number" Department of Justice, Community-Oriented Police Service.
17. A number of publications and sources give figures for the number of nonemergency calls received by PSAPs. The figures on the number of calls were strictly self-reported and varied widely between agencies. However, there did appear to be a trend that the percentage of PSAP calls that were of a nonemergency nature was larger in urban areas.

18. The Web site address for the National Emergency Number Association (NENA) is **www.nena.org**.
19. "Public Safety Answering Point," 9.
20. The Union City Police Department, in California, uses a typical call priority scheme. You can mview the call priority scheme at **www.ci.union-city.ca.us/police/dispatchPD.html**.
21. In 1996 police officers nationwide responded to more than 38 million alarm activations. It is estimated that between 94 percent and 98 percent of the alarms were false activations. Moreover, alarm calls accounted for approximately 25 percent of all calls for service rendered by the police. The Department of Justice, Office of Community-Oriented Policing Services, sponsors "Problem-Oriented Guides for Police Services." For an excellent look at some solutions to the alarm call problem, take a look at "False Burglar Alarms by Rana Sampson" at **www.cops.usdoj.gov/pdf/e05021556.pdf**
22. "Computer-Aided Dispatch," 4.
23. Ibid., 2.
24. Bovens and Zouridis, "Information and Communication Technology," 174.
25. "Evolution and Development of Police Technology."
26. Ibid., 8.
27. Ibid., 5.
28. McEwhn, "Intelligent Transportation Systems."

Chapter Eight
Agency Systems

Learning Objectives

- The student will understand the reasons that good record keeping is critical to law enforcement.

- The student will understand the concept of **operator security**, including the concepts of **right to know** and **need to know**.

- The student will understand the purpose of **record management systems (RMSs)**, **jail management systems (JMSs)** and **evidence management systems (EMSs)** and how they generally work.

- The student will understand the impact of concepts like the **Freedom of Information Act** on police records.

- The student will be introduced to the concept of digital images in law enforcement.

Introduction

In the first chapter we developed the idea that police work is primarily about the gathering, analysis, retention, and use of information. State and local police agencies collect a vast and varied amount of information. For instance, we saw in the previous chapter that most computer-aided dispatch (CAD) programs retain information about calls for service. Consider that the millions of calls each year received by a public safety answering point (PSAP) become millions of individual records. Moreover, each of those records could have subpieces of information like the location, disposition, and officer(s) handling the call, etc. A police record system is how that and other information is retained and organized.

The information retained by police agencies runs the spectrum from crime reports to personnel records. Because of the type of information the police collect, the information needs to be readily available, kept for a long time, and held confidentially. Arrest reports are good examples of documents that must be available yet confidential. Presume that an arrest ultimately leads to a conviction. Even though the person has been convicted, there is always the possibility that something will occur and the original arrest report will be needed for review. For instance, say ten years after someone's conviction, evidence comes to light that may tend to prove his or her innocence. What if the police can't find the original report? What if the court file is incomplete or missing? Do we just say we are sorry?

Many individual law enforcement agencies have very sophisticated records systems capable of producing the full range of statistics on their own activities.[1] However, a 2000 Bureau of Justice Statistics report indicated that less than half of all local police agencies maintained computerized files on warrants. Think back to our traffic violator from the first chapter, if the violator had been wanted by an agency that did not keep computerized files on warrants, how would the police officer issuing the citation ever find out that the traffic violator was wanted?

In reality, the situation on warrants and police records isn't all that dismal. A closer look at the BJS report shows that although only 43 percent of the agencies have computerized files on warrants, when you look at state and local agencies that have a service population of more than ten thousand, the majority of the

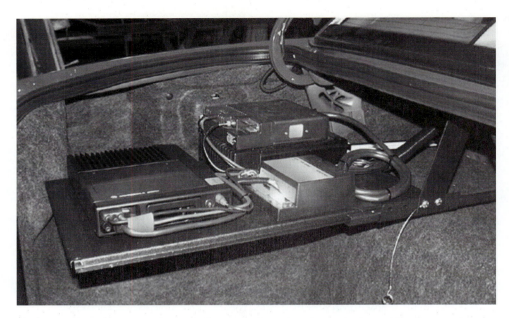

Figure 8.1 Both digital data and voice pass through radio equipment like this trunk-mounted radio transceiver.
Photograph provided by Havis-Shields Equipment Corporation.

agencies have computerized files on warrants, alarms, traffic stops, and criminal histories. That means that most police officers in the country have access to computerized records. The problem of a lack of record automation becomes more acute as one examines the very small police agency. The problem of fragmentation is probably most acute in the area of police records.

A little later in the chapter, when we take a look at the benefits of record automation, we will see that even small police agencies and the communities they serve can reap huge benefits from records automation. Of course, the people working in the small agencies have already discovered this, and their efforts to join the information age have somewhat added to the problem of fragmentation. If you are ever in a position to make decisions about systems design, purchase, or implementation you will learn about **first tier** and **second tier** manufacturers.

If you were designing a system for a large agency and you had great pots of money, you would probably contract with a first tier manufacturer. One of the primary reasons for this is that when government is spending a lot of money, it has a cumbersome procurement procedure that requires a bidder to complete often very complex and lengthy bid forms. In Chapter Twenty, Implementing and Managing Technology, we will go into this in a little more depth. For now, realize that there is a direct relationship between the amount of money government is going to spend with one provider and the amount of paperwork, approval cycles, and politics connected to the purchase.

Any manufacturer that wants to bid on a large project is going to have to spend a considerable sum of money just to bid. Moreover, large projects tend to be complex and users from large state and local police agencies tend to want their systems custom designed. So first tier manufacturers (of both hardware and software) are large companies. Those large companies are set up to produce quality, custom-designed software and hardware configurations. Because of the large amount of money first tier companies have spent on just getting in the door and

Figure 8.2 In the last chapter, we looked at CAD and 9-1-1 as a means for civilians to contact the police. However, CAD and 9-1-1 can be used for the police to contact the community. One of the relatively inexpensive tools they can purchase is a telephone notification system that, through their dispatch center, has the capability identifying and telephoning thousands of people with emergency instructions. Using GIS and CAD, an area is selected, numbers are dialed, and a prerecorded message is delivered. It can be used for neighborhood crime alerts, evacuation instructions, and neighborhood watch notifications. This system might be simpler for a small- to medium-sized local agency than a large local or state agency to implement. *Source:* "Evolution and Development of Police Technology," 113.

maintaining their own internal infrastructure to design large systems, there is little or no profit for them to make with the small agencies. This does not mean that small agencies don't purchase equipment from large companies—they do have vehicles, computers, and software from major firms—but generally, when they do purchase from major firms, they purchase off the shelf and not custom designed (Figure 8.2). This is more true with hardware than software.

If you were a large firm that spent millions of dollars developing a sophisticated software application designed to automate police records, and you could sell the product to large agencies and make a profit, would you sell the product for less to a smaller agency because they were small? Return for a moment to the hamburger stand. When you purchase a hamburger, does the hamburger stand ask you how much money you have? Would they sell it to you for less because you had less than the person in line behind you? The analogy may become more clear if you think of a fancy restaurant and a hamburger stand. In both you get food. In the more expensive restaurant, you get personal service, there is a wider variety on the menu, and it is cooked to your exact tastes, etc. In the hamburger stand, even though they tell you they will cook it the way you want it, there are only so many variations to a five-minute hamburger. The fancy restaurant is first tier; the hamburger stand is second tier. Both are filling, but the experiences are different.

Many second tier products are very good, but when you talk to second tier manufacturers they will tell you that small agencies struggle to purchase even from a second tier manufacturer. In one conversation I had with a second tier manufacturer, they told me a story of a small agency that held a bake sale to purchase the manufacturer's product. So as the small agencies struggle to implement second tier products, the large agencies have different struggles with first tier products. The result is that many of these systems are incompatible, and the smaller agencies do not gain the expertise that the larger agencies have; the problem of fragmentation and the resulting effects continue to grow.

We are not the first ones to struggle with fragmentation. The problem has been long recognized. Realizing the importance of local police records and the problems with fragmentation, between 1995 and 1999, the United States Office of Criminal Justice Programs (OCJP) granted more than $265 million dollars to state and local governments for the purposes of upgrading their criminal records.[2] Moreover, the literature is replete with information and case studies on local law enforcement agencies that have used grants from state and federal authorities for the purpose of upgrading their records systems. The growing attention paid to state and local law enforcement records management is because of the value of the information gathered by police agencies.

Much of the focus today is on **criminal justice information systems**. It is important to realize that there is a difference between criminal justice information systems and police records management. Criminal justice information includes every piece of information gathered in and used by the criminal justice system. It might be court transcripts of testimony, parole or probation records, state drivers' licenses records, privately gathered information, or police calls for service. It is information used for decision making at every level and stage of the criminal justice process. On the other hand, when we refer to police records management, we are primarily concerned with information gathered, retained, and organized solely by the police. However, a fully integrated police records management system is going to have access to all of the other records maintained by different criminal justice organizations.

The primary purpose of retaining and organizing information is so we can make better decisions. In criminal justice good information is critical in good decision making.[3] At the most basic level, police records have two basic roles. The first is to supply information, so good decisions can be made about offenders. The second purpose is to supply information for management decisions. Information about offenders might be crime reports, evidence, and their location in a jail. Management information might be crime data used for tactical and strategic planning, calls for service data to be used for resource allocation, or personnel records for use in personnel decision making.[4]

It should be fairly clear that criminal justice organizations, including the police, operate on information. In addition to the need for good information, that information needs to be accessible and timely. Recall our traffic violator—if the police officer doesn't know the offender is wanted, the police officer cannot take action on the warrant. The police officer might not know because his agency's system is incompatible with the agency that holds the warrant. The information simply is not accessible to the police officer. The agency responsible for updating a database that contains warrants might not do so in a timely manner, so the police officer in the field lacks the information. Accessibility and timeliness are two of the motivating factors behind the need to automate police records.

There are many benefits to record automation—detectives can track gangs, ensure the chain of custody of evidence, and coordinate the recovery of stolen property.[5]

Figure 8.3 Generally speaking, state and local police agencies can be grouped into four stages of information management development. The first is the paperwork stage, wherein all records are processed manually. In the photograph here, we see that prior to electronic information management, the millions of records required hand filing and searching. The second stage can be thought of as the personal computer (PC) stage. In the PC stage law enforcement agencies have desktop computers but no plans or capability to network them. In the third stage, the law enforcement agency has developed an internal network and is beginning to run a complete record management system of its own records. The final stage of development would be considered full integration with the entire criminal justice system. In the final stage the fully automated agency record management system is an integral part of a regional, state, and national criminal justice information system.
Source: "Evolution of Police Technology," 96. *Photograph courtesy of the Social Security Administration.*

Police officers in the field are safer because they have better information. Police managers can make better decisions about resource allocation. Moreover, automation generally means less paper and can reduce staff costs (Figure 8.3). Police officers can access policy and reference manuals in searchable, online databases. References and referrals as sources of solving neighborhood problems become more available. Simply put, ready access to good data can improve decision making.

As we look at agency systems, the importance of total information resource management cannot be overemphasized.[6] In addition to automation, there are security and privacy issues that are important for a state or local law enforcement agency to consider. The information has to be accessible, but only to those who are authorized.

Information Security and Accuracy

Before we begin to look at agency systems, we need to understand the concept of **operator security**. In Chapter Four, we briefly looked at encryption as a means to prevent unauthorized access to transmissions. What we learned was that if encrypted data was intercepted by an unauthorized party, the likelihood that the data could be understood was reduced, and different levels of encryption provided different levels of protection. However, what we find in law enforcement is when information is compromised, authorized users primarily do it intentionally. It is far easier to protect the system from being compromised by technology than it is to protect the system from being compromised by our own.

Generally, information collected by law enforcement and to which law enforcement users have access is considered privileged information. That means that the information is for official use only. There are a variety of reasons that information is privileged or confidential. Perhaps the general dissemination of the information would compromise an investigation. For instance, let's say that you are investigating a murder. You, as the investigator, are privy to all information and evidence about the crime scene, and as you may find out as an investigator, not all information is introduced in a trial. There are a variety of reasons that evidence won't be introduced or that the defense lawyer will successfully suppress the evidence. That means that the jury should only hear the evidence that is lawfully presented. If the details of your crime scene become public knowledge, there is a possibility that the jurors will hear evidence that will not be admitted in the trial. The result could be that the suspect does not receive a fair trial. If the information is damaging enough, it might mean that the suspect who actually did the murder will not be punished.

Law enforcement personnel also have general access to a wide variety of information about the average person that is confidential and protected by law. For instance, recall our traffic violator from the first chapter. Our officer could have accessed the state driving records in order to determine if the traffic violator's license was valid (Figure 8.4). At the same time, the police officer would have obtained the traffic violator's home address. The information contained in the driving record is confidential because the information could be used to harm the traffic violator. Prior to stricter regulations in California, driver's license infor-

Figure 8.4 The ASTRO Saber™ digital radio is an example of a state-of-the-art portable radio designed to work in both a digital and analog environment. Police officers in the field who do not have access to an in-car computer often use portable radios to request information about traffic violators.
Photograph provided by Motorola.

mation that was released to a private party resulted in someone stalking and killing an aspiring actress.[7]

The idea of operator security introduces two concepts with regard to police access to information, whether a document or an information database: the **right to know** and the **need to know**. In the first chapter, when our police officer stopped the traffic violator for speeding, the police officer had the right to know information about the violator's driving records. As a part of the police officer's job, he has the right to know information that will further an investigation. So the right to know is derived from the police officer's occupation. Police officers have the right to know certain privileged information.

The second part of the concept on operator security is the need to know. The need to know is derived from the situation. In the instance of the traffic violator, the officer had the right to know based upon his occupation and the need to know based upon the traffic violation. What if the police officer was off duty, and his next-door neighbor wanted to know if her long lost Aunt Sally was still alive. Put yourself in that situation—all your neighbor wants to know is the home address of her Aunt Sally. Do you have the right to know that information? Yes. You are a police officer. Do you have the need to know that information? No. What if Aunt Sally doesn't want to be found by your neighbor? She is not going to be happy you gave out the information. Indeed if you passed the information to your neighbor, you probably committed an illegal act. The circumstances of your neighbor's request were an insufficient reason for you to need to know.

Information that police officers seek to further an investigation can have an additional layer of protection for the individual. Sometimes a police officer needs a search warrant to obtain information. Information that generally requires a search warrant or court order includes telephone company records (the numbers called from and incoming to a telephone), live conversations of any electronic medium, and certain commercial credit information, just to name a few. In Chapter Nine we will look at some external sources of information that require a search warrant. We will find that there is a tremendous amount of commercial information that does not require a warrant. Moreover, in Chapters Fourteen and Fifteen, when we look at the technology involved in covert operations, we will see that sometimes a search warrant is required and sometimes not. For now, think of a search warrant as the judicial review of a police officer's right to know and need to know. That is the simplest definition of the probable cause necessary to gain a search warrant or court order.

So the first protection for the security of police data is training people to realize their ethical responsibilities with confidential information. But as we know, networks and computer systems have some vulnerabilities of which we should be aware. Although we touched on many of these network and systems security issues in Chapter Four, looking at them in the context of their practical uses will give us a greater understanding of their value. For instance, one of the best attributes of twenty-first century information technology (IT) is its size and portability. Computers on desks, in vehicles, and held in users' hands are networked together and provide the ability to access information just about anywhere. We have seen that if our mythical police officers had access to information about a traffic violator, he or she could make better decisions. But in addition to being accessible and portable, these systems are at risk because they are small enough to be easily lost or stolen. One research paper on e-government found that 80 percent of security breaches in wireless government networks occurred because someone's device was lost or stolen.[8]

Flagging records is a common technique used with advanced criminal justice information systems and other government-maintained databases. In computer programming, a flag is a predefined bit or bit sequence used to remember something or to leave a sign for another program. In our context, if you were a police officer and you ran the name and date of birth of a past or present President of the United States for driver's license information, you would be visited by the managing authority and quite possibly the Secret Service because that information is likely to be flagged as sensitive.

Security breaches via lost or stolen equipment can be minimized by educating employees, having clear rules and regulations concerning the field use of equipment (like locking the police vehicle doors when away from the vehicle), and using passwords. As we know from Chapter Four, passwords are a valuable method of keeping unauthorized users out of databases. In addition to passwords, networks and databases are usually designed to keep a log of use. In other words, each time a user accesses a database via a network, the database records the node that requested the information, the time of the request, the user who was signed on, and the nature of the request or data that was provided. Data logs provide managers with a means to audit information databases for unauthorized use. Moreover, a good database will monitor use and make notifications to the managing authority when users make an unusual number of inquiries, or in some cases certain records are flagged if the information is accessed.

In addition to needing a password for access, some password systems provide for different levels of access to databases. Most police officers have access to agency information, but they cannot add, change, or delete information. A password scheme that provides levels of access ensures database integrity. It is protected from unauthorized tampering. One last security measure that is similar to passwords is the process of authentication. Authentication occurs when a user enters a password and the password is checked by the database. More sophisticated authentication procedures may include the database checking to make sure that the node requesting the information is an authorized node. So when you access a database using authentication, your computer is examined by the computer managing the database to ensure your node is a registered and authentic requestor.

One of the primary reasons that database security is critically important for state and local law enforcement agencies is the type of information those databases contain. Police databases are capable of storing a tremendous amount of information, and most of that information is about people.[9] Whenever information about individuals is stored, questions concerning their privacy need to be considered and respected.[10] **Privacy** can be defined as information that, if exposed, could create a sense of nakedness for the person the information concerns.[11] There are lots of things about us that are not bad, but if other people knew them, we would feel exposed. Those things are private matters. One of the most common issues for law enforcement is divulging information about victims, witnesses, and offenders to the news media.

The name of a victim of sexual assault is routinely protected from being divulged to the public. There are a variety of state laws that require that law enforcement agencies do not release the names of victims of sexual assault. Moreover, failure to protect the victims' privacy can result in civil litigation. In one instance, an agency accidentally released the name of a victim of sexual assault. The victim's name was subsequently published in a newspaper, along with a variety of details regarding the assault. The law enforcement agency settled out of court for $2,500; the newspaper lost the trial, and the jury awarded the victim $100,000.[12] Subsequent to the trial, the state appeals court upheld the award, but the United States Supreme Court eventually overturned the decision.

For state and local law enforcement agencies, there are four areas of concern regarding the data they collect. First, information about someone can be considered their personal property. If information is property, it could be subject to the restrictions of police seizure as outlined in the Fourth Amendment of the United States Constitution. Second, when state and local agencies collect information about victims, as in the case of sexual assault victims, the victim trusts that the

In Chapters Fourteen and Fifteen, when we look at the various technological means of surveillance, we will explore the constitutional restrictions on data gathering in more depth.

agency will not reveal the information. Third, if the person's information is revealed, it could cause the person to suffer, as in defamation. Finally, using a person's likeness, as in a booking photograph, raises issues of ownership.[13]

There are so many uses for information that can improve state and local police efficiency and effectiveness, information collection is very likely to increase.[14] A possible opposite view is that the mass of information collected by state and local police agencies is tantamount to an invasion of privacy. It could be that just as incident-driven policing drove a wedge between the community and the police, twenty-first century information gathering may cause the community to lose confidence in police agencies. The goal of state and local law enforcement agencies is to seek a balance between privacy and the use of information.[15]

One of the ways that public confidence in police information gathering can be balanced is to provide mechanisms whereby people can access the information about them. There are a large number of cases where the United States Supreme Court has addressed the right to know information about oneself. When these cases are examined in total, they provide three situations where a private person has the right to know what information the government has collected about her. The first situations simply are the times in which state and local law enforcement agencies are prevented from intercepting communications by private citizens. Situations that fall under the first category are the Fourth Amendment–related subjects we will examine later. The next situation is where the government must fulfill a citizen's demand to know what information the government has obtained. This obligation is commonly referred to as the **Freedom of Information Act (FOIA)**. The FOIA relates specifically to the federal government. However, many states have similar disclosure laws. The final requirement that the government balance information with privacy involves situations wherein there is a

One option for an agency to consider when developing a policy to balance data and privacy is to adopt the Code of Fair Information Practices, which was the central contribution of the HEW (Health, Education, Welfare) Advisory Committee on Automated Data Systems, established in 1972.

The Code of Fair Information Practices is based on five principles:

1. There must be no personal data record-keeping systems whose very existence is secret.
2. There must be a way for a person to find out what information about the person is in a record and how it is used.
3. There must be a way for a person to prevent information about the person that was obtained for one purpose from being used or made available for other purposes without the person's consent.
4. There must be a way for a person to correct or amend a record of identifiable information about the person.
5. Any organization creating, maintaining, using, or disseminating records of identifiable personal data must assure the reliability of the data for their intended use and must take precautions to prevent misuses of the data.

Source: "Report of the National Task Force," 11.

requirement that the government take affirmative acts to inform people of information. Again, in Chapter Fourteen we will see an example of this when we look at wire intercepts. For now, remember these three situations.[16]

The last thing that should be reemphasized is that data systems must be backed up very often.[17] By keeping a backup in a different location than the main system, data security is enhanced.

Turning Data into Information

When organizations first started to collect information, a number of systems were created to organize this information so that it could be recalled and used. One of these schemes was referred to as indexing. There are some police agencies that still use this scheme. An example of indexing can occur when someone comes into police custody. The original report about the arrest is sent to a records person. That person creates a three-by-five card, which has the offender's name and other identifying information. The card is assigned a master number, and the number of the arrest report is recorded on the card. If the person is arrested again, the card is pulled and the number of the new arrest report is recorded; the police reports themselves are then filed separately. If you were an investigator and wanted to know about an offender's prior criminal history, you would go to the index file, pull the card, and write down the numbers of the previous arrest reports. With those numbers, you could go to the original report file, pull the reports, and gain your information. This type of indexing has been done with offenders, victims, witnesses, evidence, and just about all police data. Of course, now we have indexes in databases and looking up information is simpler.

In Chapter Two we briefly looked at relational databases. One of the primary things to remember is that relational databases consist of records that are broken down into fields.[18] The relationships between records depends on the accuracy and dependability of the information entered into the fields.[19] The relational database is the foundation of modern police **records management systems (RMSs)**.[20] As with Chapter Seven, we are presuming the agency we are examining is fully integrated and, therefore, all other software and systems eventually report data to and obtain data from our RMS. Moreover, an RMS can be the agency's

Unfortunately, many local law enforcement agencies have existing records management systems that are unable to report the new National Incident-Based Reporting System (NIBRS). Sometimes they cannot comply with new federal standards because they continue to follow an old, hierarchy-based reporting system, or their systems are simply antiquated and unable to be updated. In Chapter Nine on external systems, we will explore NIBRS and the importance of an incident-based reporting system will become clearer. In that chapter we will also take a much closer look at the National Crime Information Center. Moreover, in Chapter Twelve, when we look at crime analysis, you will see how a fully integrated, incident-based reporting system has the potential to significantly increase state and local law enforcement agencies' efforts in problem solving.

Source: "Implementing National Incident-Based Reporting System," 9.

---

link to external sources of information like the National Crime Information Center (NCIC) or state stolen vehicle systems.[21]

How we choose to initially organize a relational database will greatly affect its future usefulness. Remember in Chapter Seven when we looked at computer-aided dispatch (CAD), we saw that CAD automatically creates an incident number. In most police agencies, that incident number is different from any crime or arrest report number. So a relational database would have to cross-reference those numbers in order to obtain all the information about a particular incident. If the agency is fully integrated and the CAD-created incident number is also the crime, arrest, or incident report number, then a query of the relational database by incident number would give you all the information available.[22]

The importance of field description in a relational database cannot be overemphasized. Let's presume that you want to query a relational database about all of the activities of a particular officer. Would you query by name? Badge number? Employee number? All of the queries could be successful, but if you query by name, especially in a large agency with an in-depth historical database, you would need a full name and probably date of birth, and chances are you would come up with more than one record. If you queried by badge number, you would find that badge numbers are often reissued. If a police officer gets promoted to sergeant, he gets a new badge—most likely with a different number. If you query by employee number, that number should be the only one ever issued—like your social security number. A query by employee number would give you full name, date of birth, all badge numbers, and all incident numbers involving that employee.

So in most instances when we ask a database a question, we have to define the parameters of our search. A parameter is simply a value that we send to the computer. Say you want to find out about police reports at 123 North Main Street. If you queried a relational database, it would return all reports at that location. In a large agency, that could be dozens of reports. So you refine your search by asking the database to tell you about all of the reports that occurred in the past thirty days. You would send the values of "123," "North," "Main," "Street," and your inclusive dates.[23] Depending on the program, your computer could give you just the specific information you asked for. So no reports that did not have all of those values would return to you. What if the person who entered the data forgot to include North, or confused North with South. The point is, when working with databases, you must consider the programming (will it only answer what I ask?) and the data entry.

People provide police officers with misleading information in many situations. However, they try to make up information about themselves that they can remember—like using a relative's name instead of their own. However, dates of birth are tricky for offenders. Police officers check date of birth information during a field interview by asking confirming questions at different points in an interview. For instance, the year of a date of birth can be verified by asking someone's age. If he tells you he is 40 but born in 1959, something is amiss. The month of his birth can be verified by asking the confirming question, "What is your Zodiac sign?" If someone tells you he was born in October, but his sign is Aquarius, something is wrong. The important point is the technology is much more effective when the users are better trained in getting good data for inquiry. Try these interview techniques on someone.

In a fully integrated agency, the record management system is likely to consist of several smaller systems (like CAD and GIS) that exchange information with a master server. However, when you ask questions, you may also only ask questions of a specific database within the agency. For instance, if you were a police officer in the field, and you were checking a traffic violator for warrants, you would only be interested in querying your agency's warrant file and perhaps a regional database and the national database. When parameters of a search are defined, often the first decision is which database to turn to. Luckily for us, those decisions are made by programmers before we have to use systems. In other words, if you want to know about warrants, an agency system probably has predefined query fields that only check the warrant system (Figure 8.5).

Return to our traffic violator for a moment. In many instances, when the police have contact with someone, that person does not have identification, or the police officer has reason to suspect the identification. This means the people are often checked for traffic warrants based upon information they provide—and people can be misleading, both intentionally and unintentionally. An unintentional way that people provide misleading information can be their weight. Presume our traffic violator doesn't have any identification and when he reports his weight to the police officer, he gives his current weight. Unbeknownst to our police officer, the violator's current weight is correct, but it doesn't reflect the fifty pounds he lost while in prison. There could be a warrant for the violator that reports the preprison weight. Software designed to circumvent this problem searches for things like height and weight within predefined parameters. It asks the database something like, "give me all wanted persons between the weights of 150 and 170."

Of course, then there are people who intentionally mislead. Sometimes an offender who believes she is wanted will give a different spelling of her name. For instance, a person named "Walker" might give the name "Wacher." Her hope is that by providing a derivative of her name she can both remember her lie and escape detection. Some want and warrant software employs a search technique not specifically designed to uncover falsehoods, but to handle the many different spellings of words that sound the same.

Names and words that are misspelled can be a problem for database designers. Names can have different spellings, and they are not unique. Some names have a diversity of ethnic origins, which give us similar pronunciation but different spelling. This problem is solved by phonetic algorithms that can find similar-sounding terms and names. These algorithms are often called **SoundExes**. They are named after the original patent design created by Margaret O'Dell and Robert C.

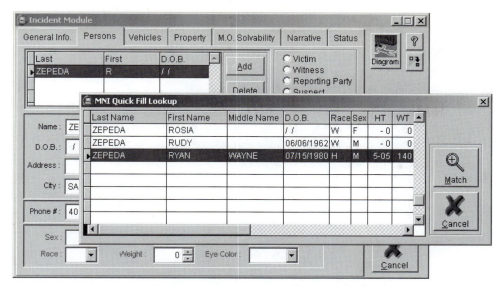

Figure 8.5 As we know, a small number of people cause the lion's share of law enforcement problems. It is not uncommon for a local agency to come into contact with the same offender on a fairly constant basis. A fully integrated relational database gives an agency the ability to take information from previous contacts and import the information into current contacts. It gives the agency the ability to complete multiple forms with a single data entry, reduces the error, and improves overall efficiency. This screen capture is an example of GUI-based software that assists in the management of integrated relational databases.

Permission for screen capture Provided by Crimestar.

Russel in 1918.[24] Most variations of the software work in a relatively similar manner. They convert the name into a code, or key, consisting of the first letter, followed by several numbers that are assigned based upon a predetermined grouping of consonants. The result is the ability to search a database that contains words that sound the same but are spelled differently.

In addition to allowing us to obtain information on individual offenders, relational databases can be used for a number of strategic purposes such as deployment and crime analysis.[25] Two types of inquires are often made when working on strategic matters. The first is a conditional query—find all white males who were victims of crimes. The second is considered an ad hoc query—find all radio calls at 123 North Main Street, before October 1, 2002.[26]

The final aspect of relational databases is their ability to populate other related documents. Take, for instance, our radio call from the previous chapter. Once the dispatcher entered the information about the call into CAD, that information could be used to populate the fields of subsequent systems. For instance, if our police officers in the field arrested someone, some information from CAD could populate the police officer's laptop in her vehicle.[27] During the booking process, once the CAD incident number was accessed, information about the radio call could be automatically put into the other systems, such as jail management or evidence management. This transference of information is handled by the agency's record management system.

In a fully integrated agency, RMS data is imported to and from a central server. There are as many configurations of networks, systems, databases, and computers as there are agencies who set them up. The important thing to

Figure 8.6 This photograph shows a typical arrangement inside a police vehicle. Both the police radio and the dash-mounted laptop computer are visible.
Photograph provided by Havis-Shields Equipment Corporation.

remember is that RMS is the software umbrella to and from which all other database systems report.[28]

Police Hardware and Software

Most police employees don't directly access the agency's RMS. Under some configurations, a police clerk might update records or data directly in the RMS, but generally speaking, state and local police officers access and update information through a variety of subsystems. Many of those systems are increasingly accessible to the police officer in the field through what is being referred to as the mobile office (Figure 8.6).[29]

The field police officer's mobile officer consists of the vehicle, the mobile radio system, and increasingly a mobile data computer (MDC). An MDC is a microcomputer, either much like a laptop or a laptop, installed in the vehicle. Using the MDC, a police officer can access driver's license, local, state, and national wanted persons databases and databases concerning stolen vehicles (Figure 8.7). Moreover, an MDC can receive calls for service and allow the police officer to exchange e-mail-like transmission with the dispatcher.[30] A few police agencies are beginning to test systems that will dramatically expand the capabilities of the mobile officer. In addition to receiving dispatch information and having the ability to make system inquires, new systems allow the officers to access mugshots, fingerprints, GIS maps, and even aerial photographs. All of these functions have the

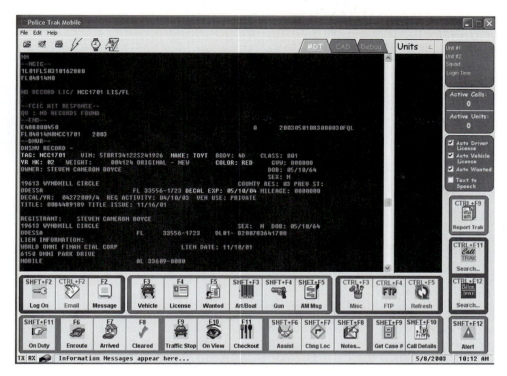

Figure 8.7   In 1983 the Institute of Police Technology and Management, University of Florida, established a computer section. The IPTM computer staff develops a variety of software products for use in the criminal justice field. One GUI-based software application developed by IPTM is Police Trak Mobile, a wireless communications system. Using CDPD, GPS, or radio frequency data communications equipment, Police Trak Mobile gives the officer in the field the ability to query state and national crime information systems, run vehicle registration checks, run driver's license checks, run wanted person checks, and much more. The system also combines an interface for CallTrak, IPTM's CAD system, whereby officers can be dispatched at the touch of a button. Officers in the field can see current activity of all other officers in real time, check out calls and traffic stops, request case numbers, query both the CallTrak and Police Trak systems, and communicate with others on the system via instant messaging and e-mail. The text to speech capabilities minimize distractions while driving.
Permission for screen capture provided by the Institute of Police Technology and Management.

potential for enhancing officer safety and efficiency.[31,32] It has been estimated that the mobile office concept can reduce the time a police officer spends in the station on paperwork by 37 percent.[33] However, as we know from our earlier chapters, one of the challenges for these new, powerful systems is going to be bandwidth. Transfers of files containing images are going to have the potential for clogging the bandwidth and slowing the system. In the next chapter, when we look at external systems, we will see how these new mobile offices will allow officers to take full advantage of NIBERS and NCIC 2000.[34]

If our police officer in the field took the traffic violator into custody, once at the station the police officer would interact with other software, such as a **jail management system**. Most local agencies do not house offenders for long periods of time, but they do house offenders while there are awaiting arraignment in court. During these two- or three-day stays, an agency assumes responsibility for

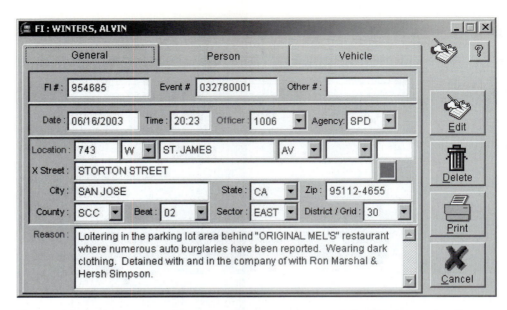

Figure 8.8 Field interview (FI) reports are among the most valuable pieces of police information. However, their potential is often unrealized for a variety of reasons. When a police officer stops a person in the field, the FI is often used to document the detention, and it places a person (including associates and vehicles) at a particular place and time. In Chapter Twelve, when we look at crime analysis, we will further explore the value of being able to associate potential offenders with locations, vehicles, and associates. One of the reasons that the FI is underutilized is lack of computerization of FI information. FI information that is input into a relational database has tremendous potential for solving crimes. Some agencies are beginning to use advanced methods of recording FI information such as PDA devices, driver's license scanning, and force-choice formats. These schemes make FI information gathering somewhat simpler. On the other end, there is computer input. Many agencies (large and small) take the handwritten FI information and input it into some type of relational database like the one depicted in this screen capture. *Source:* Bais, et al., "Advanced Crime Mapping," 62. *Screen capture provided by Crimestar Corporation.*

the care and well-being of the offender. This means meals, medical care, and visitors. Failure to properly administer this responsibility can lead to expensive litigation. Recall the Livescan fingerprinting device from Chapter Six, one integrated booking and jail management technology combines Livescan fingerprinting, automated fingerprint identification, and digital photography.[35] Once the offender has been booked into the jail, the police officer then must complete the reports and secure any evidence. Again there is a software technology, connected to the RMS relational database that can ensure evidence is properly secured and documented (Figure 8.9).

Image Processing

A picture is said to be worth a thousand words. For the field police officer, having the ability to take photographs of offenders, traffic collisions, and crime scenes can be valuable years later when testifying in court. Look at your old family photographs, especially ones where you were present during the event. I am sure that they will bring back memories, and often by looking at a photograph

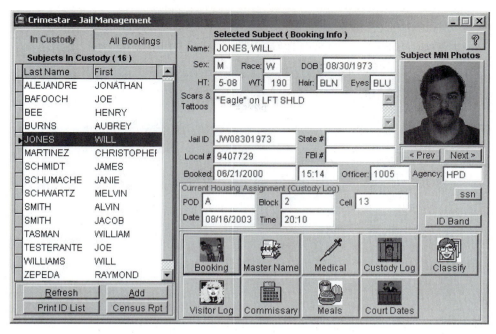

Figure 8.9 While most local agencies do not hold prisoners for long periods of time, they may house an arrested offender until the offender can be transported to court or to the jurisdiction responsible for long-term custody. Nevertheless, during the period that an offender is housed by an agency, they have a number of responsibilities to fulfill. Medical care and feeding are two obvious functions. Depending on local laws and policy, they may have to allow visitation. Moreover, since offenders are often repeat customers of the system, any jail management system should be fully integrated into the agency's overall record management system.
Permission for screen capture provided by Crimestar Corporation.

closely you will remember long-forgotten details. Photographs used as evidence in court can have the same impact on witnesses (Figure 8.10).

Image processing systems are part of police technology. Documents, photos, fingerprints, and crime scene photographs can be scanned, digitized, and stored in the agency's database. In the field, police officers can take photographs of suspects and crime scenes with digital cameras. With a digital camera, a picture is transferred to a color monitor and appears as an electronic image. One of the advantages of a digital camera is that the police officer can decide when the best possible picture is on the screen and then instruct the camera to capture that evidence. When the cost of film and developing is taken into account, digital photography can also be less expensive than regular photography. Moreover, because the image is a data file, it can be stored as part of an agency's RMS, available for recall from a variety of subsystems. Initially, there was some reluctance to use digital photographs because digital photographs can be manipulated. We have all probably received an e-mail where someone has taken a celebrity or political figure and placed his or her face on some unflattering body. However, digital cameras have mechanisms that can make the file unalterable. More and more, these photographs are being accepted in court as valid representations of evidence.

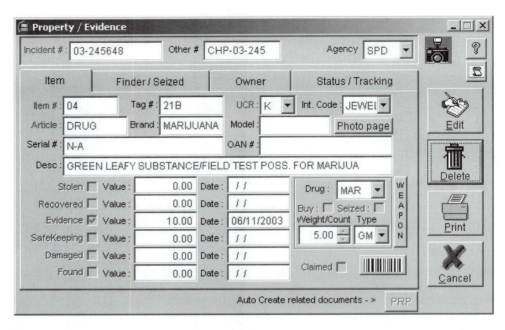

Figure 8.10 A Look Ahead: In Chapter Thirteen, when we look at technology in investigations, we will explore how the technology of recovery and analysis of evidence has changed. However, two of the most common mistakes made with evidence have little to do with the technology or science involved. When we look at DNA in Chapter Thirteen, we will see that the science itself is unequivocally accepted by the court. The common mistakes with evidence generally revolve around the management of the evidence. In other words, when evidence is rejected by the court, it is commonly rejected because it was mislabeled or the chain of custody was improperly or incompletely documented. Simply put, the chain of custody involves documented the handling and storage of evidence so that when it is introduced in court, the court is confident that the evidence hasn't changed since it was taken into police custody. No one tampered with it. It is becoming fairly standard for state and local agencies to use GUI-based software products for the management of evidence or, an **evidence management system** (EMS). A good product would have features like bar coding, photographs, tracking, and security measures to make tampering with the database itself difficult.
Source: Kay and Sensabaugh, "DNA Evidence," 511. *Permission for screen capture provided by Crimestar Corporation.*

Chapter Summary

In this chapter we examined a number of aspects of police record keeping. While there are technical challenges to implementing an integrated record management system, there are other issues that are equally important. Among those issues are the concepts of operator security, the right to know, and the need to know. Essentially, the purposes of those concepts are to maintain data security and individual privacy in government databases. We spent a considerable amount of time talking about privacy and describing some of the ways users and policy makers should consider privacy.

A state or local law enforcement agency's record management system is an umbrella system that allows the capture of information from multiple sources, bridges the agency to outside sources of information, and allows for different types of information queries. By and large, police data systems are relational databases. By placing information in tabular fields, agency employees can use the same data for multiple purposes. Data might be used for a single investigation, to

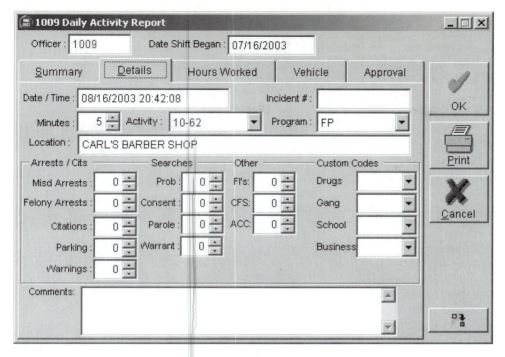

Figure 8.11 In Chapter Three, when we looked at wireless systems, we saw that the number of state and local law enforcement agencies that are using in-field computers is increasing, becoming fairly commonplace. In addition to police officers using the computers to make inquiries into databases (we will look at external databases like the National Crime Information Center and State Motor Vehicle information in the next chapter), they can prepare reports and log their activities. Among the information a police officer might log would be calls for service, self-initiated activities, and arrests. But computer logs can also be used to record information on the hours a police officer worked, the status of their police vehicle, and supervisory approval.
Permission for screen capture provided by Crimestar Corporation.

speed the booking process of a multiple offender, to do crime analysis, or for an analysis of workload and deployment. All of these different purposes are possible because of the way in which police data is captured, organized, and retained.

Discussion Questions

1. What other circumstances can you think of where a police officer may have the right to know information but not the need to know the information?
2. Visit your local police department or campus security office. Evaluate their record management system. What stage of record management development are they in? Are they paper driven? Do they rely on nonnetworked personal computers? Do they have an integrated internal network? Is their record management system integrated with the wider criminal justice system?
3. If the victims of sexual assaults should have their names kept confidential, how about the victims of other crimes? For example, what about a man who fell prey to an Internet financial scam or a woman whose home was burglarized? Should these people receive privacy protection similar to victims of sexual assault? If so, why? If not, why?

4. What other relational databases can you identify? Does the local college use one?
5. On the Web, go to **ftp.rootsweb.com/pub/usgenweb/mo/ andrew/ census/1860/indxjeff.txt**. This is the 1860 census report of Andrew County, Missouri. On your Web browser, click Edit, Find on this page, and enter "Robert." How many did you find? That is very similar to the actions your computer takes when it searches a flat file. Go to the Bureau of Justice Statistics online database at **www.ojp.usdoj.gov/bjs/dtd.htm**. Click on the online statistics. Here you can compare a large number of variables on crime in the United States. Try your hand at it. This is an example of the ability of a relational database.

Key Terms

Criminal Justice Information Systems

Evidence Management System

First Tier

Flagging Records

Freedom of Information Act

Jail Management System

Need to Know

Operator Security

Privacy

Record Management System (RMS)

Right to Know

Second Tier

SoundExes

Endnotes

1. "Overview of NIBRS"
2. Pastore and Maguire, eds. *Sourcebook of Criminal Justice Statistics*.
3. U.S. Congress, Office of Technology Assessment, Criminal Justice, "New Technologies," 45.
4. Ibid.
5. "Evolution of Police Technology," 81.
6. Shafritz, *Public Policy and Administration,* 1138.
7. In 1989 Rebecca Schaeffer, a twenty-one-year-old actress, was murdered by Robert Bardo, a mentally ill man who stalked her. Bardo obtained Schaeffer's home address for $250 from a private investigator. At the time of the murder, anyone with one dollar could get the Department of Motor Vehicle (DMV) records on any other person. Since that time, the law has been changed in California, so that DMV records are not so readily obtainable. However, there are still other methods using commercial databases that home addresses can be found (refer to Chapter Nine in this text). More information about Schaeffer's murder can be found at **crimemagazine.com/stalkers.htm**. You can find a review of measures the California DMV has taken to protect individual privacy at **www.dmv.ca.gov/dl/authority.htm#protects**.
8. Swope, "Wireless Security."
9. Shafritz, *Public Policy and Administration,* 627; Myers and Miller, "Ethical Dilemmas in the Use of Information Technology: an Aristotelian Perspective," 155.
10. Moore, *Mass Communication Law,* 422.
11. Heffernan, "Fourth Amendment," 2.
12. See note 10 above.
13. Myers and Miller, "Ethical Dilemmas," 156.
14. Shafritz, *Public Policy and Administration,* 628.
15. Ibid., 628.
16. Foerstel, *Freedom of Information,* 14.
17. "Toward Improved Criminal Justice," 53.
18. Judd, "Database Management and GIS," 2.
19. See note 17 above.
20. Ibid., Appendix.

21. "Computer-Aided Dispatch," 2.
22. Ibid.
23. Drummond, "GIS Technology," 240.
24. "Understanding Classic SoundEx Algorithms."
25. See note 21 above.
26. Judd, "Database Management and GIS," 3.
27. "Toward Improved Criminal Justice," 50.
28. See note 21 above.
29. Ibid.
30. "Toward Improved Criminal Justice," 53.
31. "Evolution of Police Technology," 96.
32. See note 8 above.
33. Blumstein, Young, and Granholm, "Commentaries," 9.
34. "Evolution of Police Technology," 96.
35. Garipoli, "Offender Identification."

Chapter Nine
External Systems

Learning Objectives

- The student will understand the history of and newest developments at the **National Crime Information Center (NCIC)**.

- The student will understand **uniform crime reporting (UCR)** and the **National Crime Victimization Survey (NCVS)**.

- The student will understand the **National Incident-Based Reporting System (NIBRS)**.

- The student will explore other potential sources of government information available to state and local police officers, such as the **Financial Crimes Enforcement Network (FinCEN)** and individual state motor vehicle departments.

- The student will understand the difference between a government database and a commercial database.

- The student will review several regional information sharing schemes such as the **Bureau of Justice Assistance Regional Information Sharing Systems (RISS) program**.

Introduction

In the previous chapter we looked at some of the systems inside a state or local law enforcement agency. We saw how a police officer could input and access information relative to the agency's systems. Several times throughout the preceding chapters we alluded to external organizations and systems. In this chapter we will look at many external sources of information that state and local police officers can use in the field for investigations and for management of their organizations. As you will see, some of those sources are government based and some are commercial firms.

In addition to there being both government and commercial sources, there are essentially two broad classifications of records that a police officer might access. There are **public records** and **investigative records**. Public records are those records that could be available to the public. The best way to think of a public record is that it is a record about something that has happened. On the other hand, investigative records are about things that are going on. Access to investigative records is often more restrictive, so some aspect of an ongoing law enforcement operation or case will not be compromised.

There are several reasons that external sources of information are often more extensive than local sources. The first is that offenders move around. As offenders move from jurisdiction to jurisdiction, they leave an information trail about their activities. This was realized very early in the twentieth century and led to the formation of centralized national information repositories. Secondly, many small agencies do not have the resources to maintain large or extensive databases. However, as we shall see, much of the information contained within national repositories is data from state and local law enforcement agencies. A third reason for the external databases is related to both of the previous reasons. Many crimes are complex and cross-jurisdictional. In some instances, special agencies or task forces have been formed to investigate these crimes. Drug trafficking and

The National Law Enforcement Telecommunications System (NLETS) is a high speed communications network and message switching system that connects nearly every state and local law enforcement agency in the country. Agencies can make inquiries into state and national databases accessing criminal histories, vehicle and driver information and NCIC files.

Source: "Toward Improved Criminal Justice."

Internet-related crime are examples of these multijurisdictional crimes. Federal authorities maintain almost two thousand databases that include information about immigration, bankruptcy, Social Security, and military personnel, to name just a few.[1]

While federal authorities certainly maintain a large amount of information, state and regional government agencies are not far behind. Many state and regional authorities maintain information on births, marriages, divorces, property ownership, voter registration, and workers' compensation claims. Moreover, many state and regional authorities are licensing agencies, so they maintain records on professionals such as doctors, lawyers, engineers, insurance agents, and accountants.[2]

Information concerning individual offenders or groups of offenders is not the only information available to state and local agencies. Information that can assist in the management of an agency and resources for research into criminal justice issues is also available from a wide range of databases. In addition to this information, there is commercially available information that state and local agencies can find useful in investigating individual and serial crimes and in managing their resources.

National Crime Information Center

In the 1960s the United States began to experience a nationwide increase in crime. One of the ideas to combat this crime was the establishment of a nationwide database of wanted persons, stolen vehicles, stolen license plates, stolen handguns, and other stolen property that could be identified by a serial number. In 1965 in order to accomplish the task of establishing a nationwide database, the Federal Bureau of Investigation (FBI) created a working group that consisted of state and local law enforcement personnel from around the country. The working group established the first nationwide standards for a database that could be added to or queried by any law enforcement agency in the United States. In January of 1967, fifteen computer terminals in several states and metropolitan areas went online with the **National Crime Information Center (NCIC)** database.

When NCIC first started, there were ninety-five thousand records in the database. By 1971 all fifty states and the District of Columbia had access to NCIC.[3] In addition to being available to agencies nationwide, one of the things that make NCIC unique is that each participating agency is responsible to enter, update, and delete their own records. This is a means of ensuring accuracy and timeliness. The premise is that the agency that makes the entry into NCIC has the most up-to-date information. If the authority to enter, update, or delete information were centralized, the NCIC staff would be many times its size and probably the slowest bureaucracy imaginable.

Return for a moment to our traffic violator from the first chapter. Prior to NCIC, if our police officer, during the routine traffic stop checked the violator for warrants, the information available would have probably been only local warrants and perhaps state warrants. Prior to NCIC, if the traffic violator had been wanted in another state, our police officer probably would not have known about it. Now, with NCIC, our police officer can use the police radio to ask his dispatch center to check the person for warrants. Most agencies with a formal dispatch center automatically include a check of NCIC files when a police officer makes a request for a warrant check. Although the NCIC database is maintained by the FBI in Clarksburg, West Virginia, all requests from state and local agencies go through a state control terminal that is run by the individual state. The state control terminal checks for state warrants, and if there are no warrants within the requesting police officer's state, the NCIC computer is queried. Using all the technology on computers and networks we have discussed, this transaction takes seconds.[4] Today NCIC has ten million records in seventeen files and maintains millions of individual criminal histories. Moreover, in addition to all fifty states and the District of Columbia, NCIC participants now include Canada, Puerto Rico, and the United States Virgin Islands.

The National Crime Information Center computer is indeed a huge and increasing enterprise. In 1967, during its first year of operation, NCIC conducted 2 million computer transactions. By 1995 NCIC was conducting 600 million computer transactions annually. As NCIC continued to grow, so have the available technologies. As of 2000, NCIC was receiving about 1.7 million inquiries each day, from more than 500,000 users.[5] In response to the huge number of records and transactions, and the changes in technology, the FBI has redesigned NCIC.

While NCIC is thought of as a federal-level database, it is actually a system wherein the data is contributed and maintained by the individual state and local law enforcement agencies.[6] Today state and local law enforcement agencies contribute information to NCIC through a multilayered network. Although there are thousands of state and local agencies contributing and using information, their contribution is done through approximately one hundred control agencies. Typically a small police department will submit arrest information to NCIC through a state **control terminal agency (CTA).** Some larger agencies actually send their information directly to NCIC. Overall, the policies of NCIC are governed by a board of directors, which has a goal of reducing the number of agencies that directly input information into NCIC so that each local agency submits its information through a state CTA. Currently, about one hundred state and local agencies share responsibility for the multilayer network that provides access for the agencies using NCIC. [7]

When an agency makes an arrest, it enters all applicable arrest information into the CTA within twenty-four hours.[8] As an arrestee makes her way through the system, different agencies are required to update the NCIC information. The updated criminal history information might show that a case was not filed, the offender was found innocent at trial, or that she served a prison term. One of the most serious problems with NCIC information is receiving complete and timely dispositions of arrests and cases.

The system that receives the offender information from the different CTAs is called the **Interstate Identification Index (III)**. State and local agencies use this system to determine if a record for an offender exists. If a record exists, the system serves as a referral service. So if our police officer on the traffic stop was in Vermont and subsequently arrested the violator, our police officer would take the offender to the station and query the III to see if the offender had a record. In our example, if the III returned that the violator had a record in California, our Vermont police officer would receive all information entered about the offender by California and know not to enter the arrest information as a new arrest, but rather under the offender's existing III number. This system of inquires was established in order to prevent the duplication of effort between the various states.[9]

NCIC 2000

Throughout previous sections of the textbook we have seen how different technologies have advanced and how many of those advances have been incorporated into the daily functions of law enforcement. The National Crime Information Center, in addition to adding different types of databases, has also advanced. In Chapter Six on the history of police technology, we caught a brief glimpse of NCIC's advances in technology when we followed the progression of fingerprint information. Moreover, we saw how **NCIC 2000** enhanced the effectiveness of local agency submission of fingerprint records.

The improvements incorporated into NCIC 2000 seek to enhance the reliable and effective traditional NCIC functions of allowing end users (state and local law enforcement agencies) to input and manage their information so that law enforcement agencies nationwide are aware of their wanted persons, stolen vehicles, etc., with digital technology.[10] Moreover, the projected improvements in NCIC 2000 will enhance the information's tactical value. It should make it easier to use and provide a wider variety of uses for field personnel.

Basically, NCIC has reduced fingerprint and photographic information on wanted persons to digital information. Furthermore, the system, as we have discussed, allows for agencies to submit fingerprint and photographic information in a digital format. Ultimately, NCIC 2000 aims at bringing digital fingerprints and photographs into the patrol car. According to NCIC 2000's plans, field officers will ultimately be able to check people's fingerprints, photographs, or other identifying images (scars, marks, and tattoos, for instance) right from their patrol vehicles.[11] The NCIC 2000 system will then compare that digital information to the national files, looking for hits in a variety of databases, such as the wanted persons database.

While NCIC 2000 provides the software application to run this system at no charge to state and local agencies, the end users must acquire the hardware necessary to run the software. In addition to publishing hardware specifications, NCIC 2000 has designed the system to run with fairly standard computer and communications equipment so that agency acquisition should be less costly and complex. For instance, network access uses Transmission Control Protocol/Internet Protocol (TCP/IP). As we shall see in Chapter Ten, that is the Internet standard. The NCIC 2000 system has been tested and data can be transmitted via various communications technologies such as cellular digital packet data (CDPD) and 800 MHz radio frequency (RF).

While NCIC 2000 technology has the potential to be enormously valuable, there are several considerations. First, we know that the development and implementation of technology in law enforcement has been fragmented because of the type of market that state and local agencies create. Both the very small and the very large agencies are having difficultly incorporating this technology. For the very small, it is a matter of other priorities competing for a fixed amount of funding. To realize the full benefit of NCIC 2000, the very small agency might have to purchase and maintain equipment far beyond its current state of technological development. Going from a simple voice radio system to having computers in the vehicle that are networked to NCIC may be problematic. For the larger agency, in addition to having to purchase more of the equipment than the smaller agency, they have the problem of incorporating these improvements into their existing infrastructure.

The use of fingerprint scanners in the field brings additional problems to the field officer. Return to our traffic violator from the first chapter. The United States Supreme Court has long settled the question concerning checking people for warrants during the brief detention that occurs while a traffic citation is being issued. While a police officer can perform a warrant check and query the state motor vehicle records to determine the status of a license during the detention of the traffic violator, can the police officer take the person's fingerprints? If the traffic violator has a driver's license, is the police officer escalating the detention by taking the violator's print? Does the taking of the fingerprint constitute a seizure, and thus is the information protected by the Fourth Amendment of the United States Constitution. In the instance wherein the traffic violator has a valid license, the taking of a fingerprint in the field may indeed be viewed as a seizure. However, in the instance wherein the traffic violator does not have identification, the detention has already escalated and the officer has more leeway in determining the person's true identity.

In addition to legal questions, there are safety questions. Recall that during our imagined traffic stop, the traffic violator has more prefect information about himself than the officer has about him. The traffic violator knows if he was speeding because he was fleeing the scene of a double murder or if he was simply late getting home. However, our police officer does not know why the traffic violator was speeding. Because of this imbalance in information, the police officer is at greater risk.[12] We previously discussed how, in this instance, it would be poor field tactics for the police officer to complete the warrant check via a computer because the police officer would have to take her eyes off the traffic violator. But now, with the in-field fingerprint scanner, at this critical point in the imbalance of information, our police officer is going to have to approach the traffic violator and come within arm's length to take the fingerprint scan. Moreover, the police officer is probably going to have the scanning device in her hands. This is very dangerous. If the traffic violator believes that the police officer may uncover some other more serious offense, the traffic violator may take this opportunity to assault the police officer and flee the scene.

So police agencies are going to have to develop protocols and field tactics so that the NCIC 2000 technology can be used legally (so that no violations of constitutional rights occur) and safely (so that no police officers are unnecessarily injured). The potential benefits of NCIC 2000 are huge. However, in addition to acquiring hardware and software, they are going to have to train people on how the equipment works and how and when to safely use it.[13]

Uniformed Crime Reports and the National Crime Victimization Survey

The United States Department of Justice (DOJ) has two programs that gather statistics on crime; the **Uniformed Crime Report (UCR)** and the **National Crime Victimization Survey (NCVS)**. In 1929 the FBI began the self-reported compilation of national crime statistics.[14] By self-reporting we mean that UCR statistics are voluntarily compiled and sent by state and local agencies, on a monthly basis, to the FBI. As of 2001, approximately sixteen thousand state and local law enforcement agencies, which provided law enforcement services to 255 million people and covered about 89 percent of the total area of the United States, participated in UCR.[15,16] In an effort to obtain a complete picture on crime in the United States, the FBI uses Census Bureau information to extrapolate crime in jurisdictions that do not participate in UCR.

The statistical information that is reported consists of crimes categorized as Part I or Part II (Figure 9.1). There are eight Part I crimes that are reported; homicide, forcible rape, robbery, aggravated assault, burglary, larceny/theft, motor vehicle theft, and arson.[17] Twenty-two additional crimes are included in the Part II category. The FBI publishes these statistics on an annual basis for use by law enforcement managers to aid in the determination of their agencies' effectiveness. UCR statistics are meant to be only one of the factors that are considered in making judgments about effectiveness and efficiency. The FBI continually cautions in various publications against the wholesale ranking of jurisdictions against one another.[18]

There are a variety of reasons that UCR information should be considered only one factor in the analysis of law enforcement services. First, crime and punishment is sometimes vastly different from state to state. In order to compensate for these differences, the FBI provides general guidelines concerning which category

1 CLASSIFICATION OF OFFENSES		2 OFFENSES REPORTED OR KNOWN TO POLICE (INCLUDING "UNFOUNDED" AND ATTEMPTS)	3 UNFOUNDED, I.E., FALSE OR BASELESS COMPLAINTS	4 NUMBER OF ACTUAL OFFENSES (COLUMN 2 MINUS COLUMN 3) (INCLUDE ATTEMPTS)	5 TOTAL OFFENSES CLEARED BY ARREST OR EXCEPTIONAL MEANS (INCLUDES COL. 6)	6 NUMBER OF CLEARANCES INVOLVING ONLY PERSONS UNDER 18 YEARS OF AGE
1. CRIMINAL HOMICIDE a. MURDER AND NONNEGLIGENT HOMICIDE (score attempts as aggravated assault if homicide reported, submit Supplemental Homicide Report	11	1	1	0	0	0
b. MANSLAUGHTER BY NEGLIGENCE	12	0	0	0	0	0
2. FORCIBLE RAPE TOTAL	20	2	0	2	2	1
a. Rape by Force	21	1	0	1	1	0
b. Attempts to commit Forcible Rape	22	1	0	1	1	1
3. ROBBERY TOTAL	30	1	0	1	0	0
a. Firearm	31	0	0	0	0	0
b. Knife or Cutting Instrument	32	0	0	0	0	0
c. Other Dangerous Weapon	33	1	0	1	0	0
d. Strong-Arm (Hands, Fists, Feet, Etc.)	34	0	0	0	0	0
4. ASSAULT TOTAL	40	35	1	34	29	2
a. Firearm	41	0	0	0	0	0
b. Knife or Cutting Instrument	42	1	0	1	1	0
c. Other Dangerous Weapon	43	4	0	4	3	0
d. Hands, Fists, Feet, Etc. - Aggravated Injury	44	19	1	18	15	2
e. Other Assaults - Simple, Not Aggravated	45	11	0	11	10	0
5. BURGLARY TOTAL	50	14	0	14	5	0

Figure 9.1 A typical form generated by a records management system to voluntarily provide the FBI with UCR information.
Report provided by Crimestar Corporation.

a particular type of crime should be reported under. The UCR refers to determining the proper crime category as classification. Let's consider murder. What if a nine-months pregnant woman is stabbed in the stomach? At the hospital, the baby is removed from the mother but unfortunately dies as a result of the stabbing. The mother survives, but the baby dies. Is this murder? For the purposes of UCR reporting, fetal deaths are not homicides.[19]

While the FBI takes measures to adjust for errors in reporting (such as shifting boundaries and nonparticipating agencies), it is clear that UCR information is not a complete picture on crime in the United States. As we mentioned in Chapter One, a large percentage of crime probably goes unreported. The estimate on the percentage of unreported crime is has high as 64 percent.

The primary goal of UCR is to produce reliable statistics for use in law enforcement administration. However, over the years UCR has become one of the leading social indicators.[20] This is despite the Federal Bureau of Investigation's continued advisements not to use the data for comparisons. There are a number of problems associated with the use of UCR data as comparisons between cities, one of them being that the information is voluntarily self-reported.

National Crime Victimization Survey

In addition to the UCR, information about nationwide crime trends is also provided by the Department of Justice, Bureau of Justice Statistics in their National Crime Victimization Survey (NCVS). Whereas the UCR statistics are self-reported by state and local agencies, the NCVS statistics come from the victims themselves.[21] The information gathered by NCVS is designed to be complementary to the UCR information. The idea is that by using two distinctly different data collection methods, a more comprehensive picture on crime will emerge. However, while

Try This

You can view the entire National Crime Victims Survey at **www.ojp.usdoj.gov/bjs/pub/pdf/ncvs1.pdf**.

the collection methods are different, the two programs have similarities.[22] For instance, the Part I crimes that UCR reports are nearly identical to the Part A crimes that NCVS reports.

While the crimes that both UCR and NCVS report on are very similar, there are some important differences and those differences highlight the value of both instruments. For instance, when UCR reports on rape, it only looks at those crimes wherein women were the victims. On the other hand, NCVS looks at crimes against both sexes. The NCVS does not look at homicide, arson, commercial crimes, and crimes against children under twelve. When you realize NCVS is a survey instrument directed at victims, the exclusion of those four crimes makes sense. Homicide victims are impossible to interview. Since the NCVS surveys households, it would not normally be contacting people who are the victims of commercial crimes—occurring at places of business. Interviewing children under the age of twelve is problematic.

The definitions of certain crimes are also different because of the differences between the collection methodologies. For instance, UCR defines burglary as the unlawful entry into a structure to commit a felony or theft, whereas NCVS defines burglary as entry into the residence by a person who has no right to be there. Again, because the UCR information comes from police agencies, legal definitions are important. Many types of crimes require that the offender have the specific intent to commit the crime. Burglary is a specific-intent crime. However, the NCVS is surveying laypeople and the NCVS definition of the crime of burglary precludes the victim from having to speculate as to the intent of the offender. So NCVS asks the questions and defines the terms in a way it is believed that they will be understandable by the laypeople they interview.

The data sets are also different because of the methodology. When UCR publishes its statistical report on property crime, it talks about the number of crimes per one hundred thousand people. Conversely, NCVS reports the number of property crimes per one thousand households. The total population, and the subset of the number of households in the United States, does not grow at the same rate. Therefore, trend analysis may not be comparable. Finally, as we discussed, the FBI makes a statistical estimation of those areas that do not voluntarily report. On the other hand, the NCVS relies on a survey instrument that has its own margin of error. While both the UCR and the NCVS use well-established methods for correcting for margins of error, it is important to remember when

Try This

The New York State Division of Criminal Justice Services completed a comparison of UCR and NIBRS crime definitions. You can take a look at the differences at **criminaljustice.state.ny.us/crimnet/ojsa/fbicccc.pdf**.

making comparisons between the products of both agencies that their methodologies are distinctly different.

Twice a year, personnel from the United States Census Bureau interview members of forty-two thousand households, which include approximately seventy six thousand people across the country. The households are selected so that the information produced from the survey will be representative of the United States population at large. Each household stays in the survey for three years, and new households are rotated into the survey process on a continuous basis.

The NCVS concentrates on issues about the victims and their experiences. For instance, the NCVS survey asked typical background questions (sex, age, education, etc.) and questions about their relationships with the offenders, the weapons used, and the economic consequences of the crime. Between 1972 (the program's inception) and 1992, the NCVS redesigned the survey. One of the primary changes in the NCVS survey was the inclusion of questions designed to enhance a victim's recall of crime.[23] This last improvement was substantial in improving the results of the reporting of family violence.

Both the UCR and NCVS give law enforcement personnel information that can be used strategically. The data is often used in the long-term planning and budgeting process and provides valuable research data for criminal justice issues. However, unlike the NCIC data, the UCR and NCVS data have little or no tactical value. Certainly, having an understanding of crime and the nature of victimization aids the line police officer in his or her overall duties, but it has little value for use in a specific incident.

Recall in earlier chapters we looked at the differences between flat files and relational files. In practice, the information provided by UCR and NCVS is a flat file. Certainly, the information can be used for statistical comparisons and a search for significance in relationships, but that tends to be an academic or perhaps a management function. Information that can be used for academic and management purposes is strategic in nature. However, what if we combined some of the facets of the UCR and the NCVS and then collected and reported the information in a relational table.

Certainly the UCR and, to a lesser extent, the NCVS, were conceived prior to the advent of computational technology. I know that statement seems like a no-brainer, but it has serious consequences. The integration of existing systems into new technology is an overriding theme in the implementation of all technology. It's referred to as "paving the cow path." Think back to the second chapter; we looked at the computer keyboard and noticed that it looked very much like a standard typewriter keyboard. Using the template of the standard typewriter to produce the computer keyboard made sense. After all, a lot of people had learned to type, and introducing a new keyboard would put them off computers. Also, if you looked at keyboards over time, you would see that they are very much evolving with the rest of computer technology. Yes, the letters are still in the same place, but keys and functions are being added as the technology changes.

Ask around and find out how many people use the computer for word processing. You will probably find quite a few who can open a file, type a document, and get it to print. Now ask the same people if they can track changes, do a mail merge, or hyperlink a chart or graph. Fairly soon you will realize that for many people, the desktop computer is a convenient, sophisticated typewriter. They are doing everything that could be done on a typewriter, only a little faster and with greater accuracy. But they are only using a very small percentage of the potential of the computer.

The very bright people at UCR have realized that the computer technology is woefully underutilized in the reporting of crime. For the most part, it is used to add stuff up. But what could you do with the information about crime if you could begin to show its relationships to other things? Could you better deploy police officers? Could you identify things that are causing crime and formulate plans to solve the underlying problems? What if you could combine relational information about crime with what we learned about GISs? Chapter Twelve is about crime analysis, and while we don't want to give too much away, we can answer many of those questions, or at the very least we can learn to ask better questions. Let's set GIS aside for a moment and look at a primary component of crime analysis.

National Incident-Based Reporting System

The **National Incident-Based Reporting System (NIBRS)** (Figure 9.2), like the UCR, is a program run by the FBI's, Criminal Justice Information Service (CJIS). With UCR, crimes are classified and voluntarily reported by state and local police agencies. Many times, when a crime occurs, the offender does not commit just a single crime. You may have read or heard a news report wherein an offender was indicted or charged with three counts, yet all of the counts stemmed from a single incident. For UCR purposes, only one of the counts is reported using the **hierarchy rule**. In essence, the hierarchy rule states that only the most serious crime is reported to UCR.[24]

The first difference between UCR and NIBRS is that NIBRS looks at criminal incidents. With the NIBRS scheme, the first difference you would see is that NIBRS reports all of the crimes that occurred during the single occurrence or incident. In the bank robbery example noted in the text box at the bottom of the page, UCR tells us a bank robbery occurred. In the NIBRS scheme, we know that there were three victims (the bank, the teller, and the car owner), the offender used a firearm, and the offender, for some reason, did not have transportation away from the crime scene. Just in itself, that is a lot more information.

While we do not want to get too far ahead in looking at crime analysis, consider if you were looking at all of the bank robberies that occurred in a large urban jurisdiction. Now, using UCR, you would not be able to see the differences between the crimes. For instance, there were 1,337 robberies in Los Angeles in 2002.[25] Using UCR, you wouldn't know if they were committed by a single person or many people. It is a fairly safe assumption that all of those robberies were not committed by the same person.

However, in an NIBRS scheme, you would see the bank robberies where the offender used a gun or a demand note. You might see other incidents where the offender struck a bank employee or needed getaway wheels. With NIBRS-like information, you would be able to see patterns that could affect strategic as well as tactical decisions.

AN EXAMPLE OF THE HIERARCHY RULE

Imagine a crime wherein an offender robs a bank, pistol whips the bank teller, and after exiting the bank steals a car at the curb to make his or her getaway. You have three crimes: the robbery, the assault, and the car theft. UCR states that the robbery is the most serious and, therefore, it is the crime reported. *Source:* Federal Bureau of Investigation, *Uniform Crime Report Handbook,* 16.

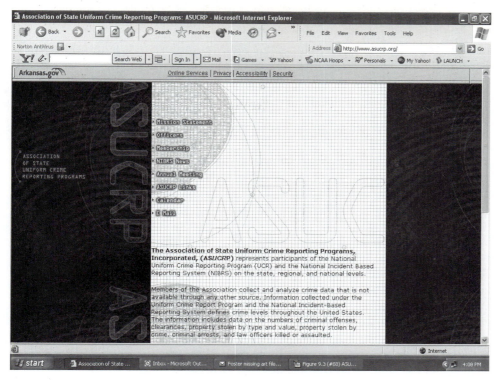

Figure 9.2   The Association of State Uniformed Crime Reporting Programs, Incorporated (ASUCRP) represents participants of the National Uniformed Crime Reporting Program (UCR) and the National Incident-Based Reporting System (NIBRS) on the state, regional, and national levels. Members of the Association collect and analyze crime data that is not available through any other source. Information collected under the UCR and the NIBRS defines crime levels throughout the United States. The information includes data on the numbers of criminal offenses, clearances, property stolen by type and value, property stolen by crime, criminal arrests, and law officers killed or assaulted.
Screen capture provided by the Association of State Uniformed Reporting Programs.

With NIBRS we are looking at a crime and all of it components as an incident. NIBRS also borrows from NCVS is a number of ways in that in addition to recording facts about the number of individual crimes occurring in an incident, it also asks questions regarding the relationships of the victims to the offenders. What NIBRS seeks to do is have the investigating police officer record the **elements** of the incident. Recall from Chapter Two, that relational databases have elements

To begin regular submission of NIBRS data, a state program must meet the following FBI certification requirements:

- Error rate of less than 4 percent for three consecutive months.
- Statistical reasonableness of previously submitted data (in other words the FBI looks at trends,

volumes, and fluctuations to determine if the submitted information looks reliable).

- The ability to update records, meet deadlines, and respond to error messages.
- Systemic compatibility with the national hardware and software.

Source: "Implementing National Incident-Based Reporting System," 7.

that are filled with information called **values**.[26] In the NIBRS scheme, the investigating police officer asks questions (elements) about the crime and reports the answers (values). One of the elements might be the use of a firearm—a simple value would be "yes" or "no."

Although as of 1997, less than 6 percent of the population is represented by NIBRS contributing agencies, it is likely that NIBRS will eventually replace UCR information gathering.[27] However, because NIBRS information is much more comprehensive than UCR data, it will require state and local agencies to eventually computerize their collection of crime statistics. There are several likely byproducts of the implementation of NIBRS. First, because NIBRS is significantly more detailed, as more agencies participate, there will be more common information available to analyze cross-jurisdictional crimes. However, some law enforcement executives are concerned that the type of detailed information required by NIBRS will require police officers to spend additional time completing reports and reduce their available time.[28] There is definitely a trade-off between spending more time collecting detailed information and the ultimate ability to use the data for crime analysis and management purposes. At first, police officers might become less efficient in their response to calls for service, but eventually the agencies would probably become more effective at reducing crime. Currently, there is a dearth of research to support either contention.

As with NCIC and UCR, NIBRS information is sent by local agencies to information collection points within the state. Moreover, the states are providing training and technical assistance to local agencies in NIBRS. NIBRS dictates a minimum number of data elements, but some states have chosen to add to the information they want collected by the local agencies. Some states have increased the number of data elements from 53 to 75.[29] This may actually be adding to the problem of fragmentation. Consider the response of a software company that produces products for smaller agencies. To meet the additional state requirements, they would have to do custom programming, thereby driving up the cost of software. If software is more expensive, very small agencies with limited funds are less likely to purchase software and hardware for NIBRS collection.

Government Databases

There is a tremendous amount of information available about nearly every American. The information can be obtained easily and either at a very low cost or for free. For instance, the U.S. Postal Service will provide a police officer with a person's address, including forwarding addresses. Courthouses retain a tremendous amount of public information about case dispositions, civil actions, divorces, child custody, and the ownership of personal property. By visiting a county assessor, you can find out how much a property was sold for. At a county hall of records you can get birth, death, and marriage records and find tax liens, bankruptcy records, etc. Much of the information is computerized or on microfilm.[30] Of course, going to each of these locations would take time. However, there are a number of government sources and commercial sources wherein a police officer can access this information very easily.

The **Regional Information Sharing Systems (RISS)** program uses a secure Internet connection to provide a network that connects six regional centers and member agencies. As of 1998, there were a total of 4,739 member agencies. The regional intelligence centers provide information sharing among the agencies, analytical services, and investigative support such as confidential funds. Moreover, they have specialized investigative equipment and can provide training and technical assistance.[31] Their Web site is **www.iir.com/RISS**.

Through the secure Internet connection, member agencies can access information like the Intelligence Database Pointer System, a criminal intelligence database that contains data about suspected criminals and criminal activity; RISS National Gang Database, a database that has information on gang members and gangs; and RISS Investigative Leads Bulletin Board, a bulletin board where agencies can post information regarding a criminal case.

In addition to RISS, there are a number of other information sources such as the **National Drug Pointer Index (NDPIX)**. In 1992 the Office of National Drug Control Policy gave the Drug Enforcement Agency (DEA) the mission of establishing a national drug pointer system. In 1997 the DEA launched NDPIX. The system runs through NLETS; NATIONAL LAW ENFORCEMENT TECEIYPE SYSTEM however, information can be entered directly by a state or though RISS. The purpose of the system is for state and local agencies to have a pointer system for suspected drug offenders currently under investigation.[32] Their Web site is **www.usdoj.gov/dea/programs/ndpix.htm**.

The Bureau of Alcohol, Tobacco, and Firearms (ATF) established the **National Tracing Center** in West Virginia. This is a nationwide database on all guns used during the commission of a crime. Through the tracing center, state and local agencies can trace gun ownership. Currently, the ATF is working on the means to make this information available via network communications. The ATF also operates the National Explosives Tracing Center, which provides state and local agencies with assistance in tracing the origins of explosive materials. You can visit both Web sites via the ATF homepage at **www.atf.gov**. The Bureau of Justice Assistance sponsors the **National White Collar Crime Center**. Here, state and local law enforcement agencies can obtain information about criminal cases involving individuals or organizations involved in white collar crimes, such as fraud. Their Web site is **www.nw3c.org**. The FBI and the DEA merged 4.4 million FBI records and 4.1 million DEA records into a massive database on past and present drug-related investigations. This database is called **DRUGX**.

A **pointer system** is an index identifying information about a suspected offender, location, or crime. An agency opening a case can add to the index and check to see if other agencies have opened a case on the same offender, location, or crime. If there is a match, the two agencies are provided the names and telephone numbers of the other case agents. It is designed to increase police officer safety, improve interagency communication, and improve efficiency through the exchange of information.

In 1990 the Department of Treasury created the **Financial Crime Enforcement Network (FinCEN)**. Many criminals are motivated by money, so by looking at certain banking transactions, a police officer can get an idea of the extent of a criminal enterprise and develop information necessary for an arrest. However, the primary purpose of FinCEN is to assist in uncovering money-laundering schemes and practices. Using federal legislation commonly referred to as the Banking Secrecy Acts, FinCEN can provide information like forms filed by banks whenever an individual deposits a large sum of money and casino transaction reports, those reports made by casinos whenever someone wins a large amount of money. Moreover, later in this chapter we are going to examine commercial sources of information, and FinCEN has access to many of these sources of information (Figure 9.3). You can visit their Web site at **www. fincen.gov**.

Driver's License and Motor Vehicle Registration Information

A very common source of external information is driver's license and vehicle information. Currently, approximately 228 million drivers' licenses and identification cards have been issued by state (including territories) motor vehicle departments.[33] The configuration of the identification, the rules for application, and the amount of information taken from applicants varies from state to state. There was one state that did not require a photograph until very recently. Because of the highly mobile society we live in, state and local police officers come into contact with identification issued from all around the country.

A state or local police officer accessing driver's license information in his or her own state probably does so through the agency RMS and directly to the state authority. In most instances, the police officer can find out a considerable amount of information about an individual, including personal identifiers, former addresses, vehicles owned, and driving history. In some states, digital photographs are available by calling or sending a network message over a special secure network. Moreover, the driving history often links to previous citations and accidents, which can provide valuable investigative information.

A police officer requesting driver's license information from another state typically uses NLETS as the method of communication. Because there is such a difference in driver's license regulations from state to state, a police officer has to be wary about the information. The American Association of Motor Vehicle Administrators (AAMVA) Special Task Force on Identification Security has issued recommendations and sought federal legislation that would standardize many of the features of a state driver's license. The legislation would require states to conform to standards for driver's license eligibility, proof of identity, license content, and document security. An improvement in those features would enhance information sharing between jurisdictions. Moreover, the AAMVA standards recommend biometric identifiers, like fingerprints. The inclusion of fingerprints, digital photographs, and eligibility requirements would not only improve information exchange, but likely prevent many forms of fraud, including offenders who seek licenses in different states under different names and identifiers.[34]

Ideally, a state driver's license system should be able to transmit and receive accurate real-time data. An ideal license would have a magnetic stripe on the back to be used for querying records and to populate incident report fields.[35] In other words, our police officer would take the driver's license from the violator, swipe an e-ticket book, and the driver's information would be recorded in the proper citation fields. In the future, data systems like warrants would be automatically queried.

Commercial Sources of Information

The beginnings of commercial sources of information can be found in the history of catalog sales. About a 125 years ago, the advent of a national railroad system vastly improved mail delivery. As the mail became more reliable, East Coast retail establishments began catalog sales nationwide. Nearly a hundred years later, the catalog sales, or direct marketing, began to be supplemented by telephone sales. For years, direct marketing remained a small portion of actual retail sales because it had an extraordinarily high failure rate. After all, how many times have you hung up on a telemarketer?

Direct marketers knew that if they could achieve a greater focus on people likely to buy their products, they would have to make fewer calls to make more

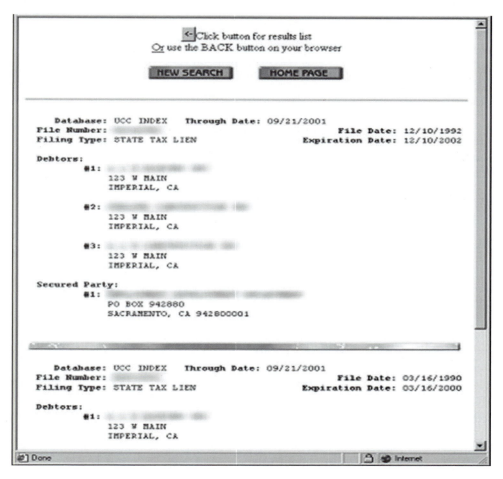

Figure 9.3 Private industry information can be invaluable when performing tasks from locating witnesses to determining property ownership for a search warrant. This screen capture is a typical return on a request for private industry information. Some of the information was intentionally blurred in order to maintain privacy.
Permission to reprint provided by Merlin Information Services.

California Searches		National Searches	
Birth Index (1905-1995)	$5.00	Merlin Cross-Directory NEW	$0.00
Board of Equalization and Alcohol Beverage Control Licenses	$5.00	LINK TO AMERICA™ More Information	
		Credit Headers	
Brides and Grooms (1960 to 1985)	$5.00	Legal Phone Break	$10.00
Corporations and Ltd Partnerships	$5.00	BusinessFinder America	$3.00
Criminal Indexes	$10.00	PhoneSource	$0.25
Death Index (1940-1999)	$5.00	National Criminal 🔒	$10.00
Professional Licenses	$6.00	Sex Offender Multi-State Registry NEW	$15.00
Statewide Fictitious Business Names	$10.00	Date of Birth File	$2.00
Statewide Property	$5.00	National Bankruptcies, Judgments and Tax Liens	$3.00
Superior Civil Indexes	$6.00	National Fictitious Business Names	$15.00
UCC Index	$5.00	National Property	$5.00
Los Angeles Municipal Criminal Index	$15.00	Social Security Administration Death Master	$2.00
		TraceWizard National Business Locator	$3.00
		TraceWizard National Residential Locator	$3.00
		PeopleFinder America 🔒	$3.00

Figure 9.4 Commercial databases can provide police officers with a wide variety of information. For instance, on this search page, a query of the "Date of Birth File" would give a state or local police officer access to 1.5 billion records containing names, addresses, and dates of birth from dozens of public record sources.
Permission to reprint provided by Merlin Information Services.

sales. Computer technology gave direct marketers this opportunity. Initially, by putting customer information into a relational database, direct marketers could see who had purchased what and when. They could begin to focus their efforts on the people who had previously purchased their products, either through the mail or by telephone.

Recall in Chapter Six we discussed the theory that people tend to live among people of similar socioeconomic and cultural backgrounds. For police technology, this has had a hand in creating some of the problems with fragmentation of technological development among law enforcement agencies. For direct marketers, it meant that if people from one ZIP code were buying their product, others—who probably shared a similar background—might purchase the product also. Moreover, in the 1970s the Census Bureau made census information available in a format more easily input into the direct marketers' relational databases. With the combination of the direct marketers' own sales data, ZIP codes, and Census Bureau information, direct marketers were able to more sharpen their focus on customers. Eventually, direct marketing would be further focused by market surveys. Essentially, direct marketers, realizing that people with similar backgrounds and beliefs tend to live together, conducted research on specific areas and were able to use their information, government information, and now their research to focus their sales to an extraordinary level of precision. In 1995, direct marketing efforts combined to a staggering $600 billion in sales.[36]

Somewhere along the line, direct marketers began to share and sell their information with other direct marketers. Most likely, the first information exchange took place between direct marketers of noncompeting goods. Eventually, companies formed that did nothing but collect, organize, and sell information. Information about us became an industry all its own (Figure 9.4). There are more than five hundred firms, with yearly sales in the billions, who sell personal information. Moreover, these personal information firms do not include credit data firms who collect credit history information reported by retailers, banks, and credit card companies. One of these credit information firms monitors the credit history of more than 205 million people in the United States.[37]

In addition to marketing data, personal information firms have collected information from public records. Marriages, births, deaths, criminal convictions, and civil actions are public records. You can go to the county courthouse, hall of records, or registrar's office in your local area and get information about people in your area—just by asking. Furthermore, many of the state and local governments who collect this information provide it to personal information firms in computerized form. The personal information firms simply merge the public records with their market research. The result is that the typical consumer ends up on about one hundred mailing lists and in more than fifty databases.[38] Some of these commercially available databases contain more than sixty-five million unlisted telephone numbers and one billion residential names and addresses. How many databases do you think you are on?

What Can You Get Commercially?

- National Fictitious Business Names contains more than ten million records from government filing offices such as Secretaries of State, Fictitious, DBA, AKA and Assumed Name Filings, Boards of Equalization, and various licensing offices, as well as Yellow Pages listings and newspapers. More than 150,000 new businesses are added to this file each month. Historic records go back to 1989, although the file is comprehensive from 1994.
- More than 200 million records that contain business names, addresses, telephone numbers, contact persons, business types, dates added to file, and dates last validated for more than 95 percent of the businesses in the United States.
- Bankruptcies, judgments, and tax liens.
- Miscellaneous records indicating the name, birth date, date of death, Social Security number, and ZIP code for the last residence of each subject file.
- 1.5 billion birth records from literally dozens of public record sources.
- Compiled marketing data that can give you property ownership; current and previous addresses; relatives including addresses, phone numbers, property ownership, and personal details; and associates including addresses, phone numbers, property ownership, personal details, and aliases.
- Comprehensive Loss Underwriting Exchange (CLUE) Report is an insurance claims registry. If you make a claim against your automobile or home owner's insurance, it is recorded in CLUE. Initially designed to help fight fraud, the system has been used by insurers to qualify customers. Its use for that purpose has been controversial.

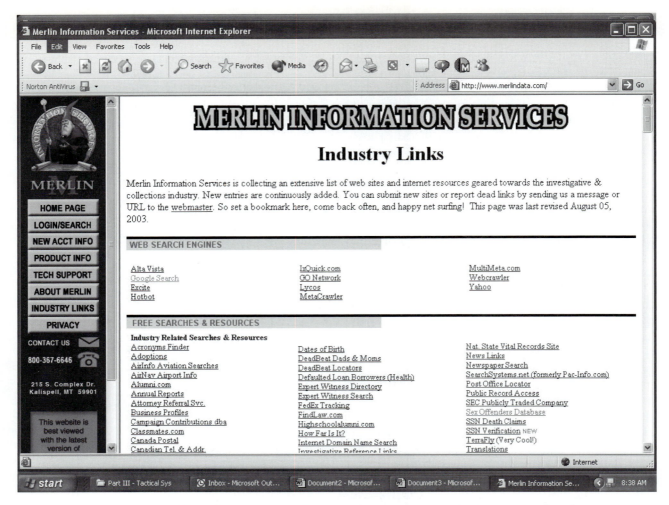

Figure 9.5 In Chapter Ten we are going to explore the Internet. In that chapter, we will find that a tremendous amount of information is available—if you know where to look. Try this: go to **www.merlindata.com/** and examine the wide variety of sources of information available.

Permission to reprint provided by Merlin Information Services.

Chapter Summary

In this chapter we looked at sources of information that are external to a state and local law enforcement agency. Recall in the previous chapter that we looked at some of the privacy issues and questions commonly asked. Although state and local law enforcement agencies don't generally control the content of external sources (except for their input into NCIC, etc.), each of these databases raised questions concerning fair use and privacy: Is the information accurate? Does the subject of the record have the right to review the information? Does the subject of the record have the right to demand correction of information? Who has access to the information? How can it be used?

The National Crime Information Center (NCIC) is probably the largest source of external information that is used by state and local agencies. Although NCIC is external, the data is made up of the information input by all of the state, local, and federal agencies in the country. NCIC, which has served law enforcement very well for more than thirty years, is being replaced by NCIC 2000, an updated hardware and software system that includes digital photographs and fingerprints. Currently, a few agencies are experimenting with implementing complete access to NCIC 2000 for field officers.

We looked at the Uniformed Crime Reporting (UCR) and the National Crime Victimization Survey (NCVS) for two purposes. First, much of law enforcement data collection and management decision making revolves around information contained within these two databases. Second, UCR is an introduction into the National Incident-Based Reporting System (NIBRS). As we know, NIBRS will eventually replace UCR, but more important, NIBRS should introduce us to the concept of collecting specific data about crime for crime and management analysis. The use of NIBRS-like data will become clearer in Chapter Twelve on crime analysis.

We looked at a variety of government and commercial databases in order to familiarize you with the information available to state and local police officers. I am certain that you now know more about available information than 90 percent of the police officers in the nation.

Discussion Questions

1. Consider the traffic violator scenario, is the scanning of her fingerprint a violation of the Fourth Amendment of the United States Constitution? What if she has seemingly valid identification? What if she does not have identification? What about the passengers in the vehicle, can their fingerprints be scanned?
2. There is a widespread perception among state and local law enforcement executives that reported crime will increase with the adoption of NIBRS, largely as a result of the elimination of the hierarchy rule, and that this could represent a potential public relations problem.[40] Proponents of NIBRS argue that the increase in crime is merely an artifact effect from previous reporting inaccuracies. The perception that crime is increasing does generate fear and could have significant negative consequences on a community. How should state and local law enforcement executives handle this problem? Is the potential that reported crime will increase a valid reason for not adopting NIBRS? The technological issues of implementation aside, does NIBRS have advantages that outweigh the concerns regarding the perceived increase in crime?
3. Some have argued that the standards proposed by the American Association of Motor Vehicle Administrators will create a de facto national identification card. Go to their Web site at **www.aamva.org** and review the standards. Will the national standards proposed create a national identification card? Are you opposed to a national identification card? If so, why? If not, why?
4. Take a look at the different agencies listed under Key Terms. Which of them do you think provide public records? Investigative records? There is some overlap in the types of records that are kept. Why do you think that is?

Key Terms

Control Terminal Agency (CTA)

DRUGX

Elements

Financial Crimes Enforcement Network (FinCEN)

Hierarchy Rule

Interstate Identification Index (III)

Investigative Records

National Crime
    Information Center
    (NCIC)
National Crime Victim-
    ization Survey (NCVS)
National Drug Pointer
    Index (NDPIX)

National Incident-Based
    Reporting System
    (NIBRS)
National Tracing Center
National White Collar
    Crime Center
NCIC 2000

Pointer System
Public Records
Regional Information
    Sharing Systems (RISS)
Uniformed Crime Report
    (UCR)
Values

End Notes

1. Solove, Daniel "Privacy and Power," 1393.
2. Ibid.
3. Imel and Hart, "Understanding Wireless Communications," 82.
4. According to the Federal Bureau of Investigation (FBI), the average NCIC transaction takes approximately twenty seconds. The FBI states that in one year, NCIC was responsible for identifying 81,750 "wanted" persons; resulted in 113,293; 39,268 missing juveniles and 8,549 missing adults were located; and identified 110,681 stolen vehicles. The NCIC website is **www.fbi.gov/hq/cjisd/ncic.htm**.
5. See note 3 above.
6. Buckler, "NCIC 2000."
7. Ibid.
8. "Toward Improved Criminal Justice."
9. Ibid.
10. See note 6 above.
11. See note 3 above.
12. Indeed, the Court noted in United States v. McRae, 81 F.3d 1528, 1535–36 n.6 (10th Cir. 1996) that considering "the tragedy of the many officers who are shot during routine traffic stops each year, the almost simultaneous computer check of a person's criminal record, along with his or her license and registration, is reasonable and hardly intrusive."
13. See note 3 above.
14. "The Nation's Two Crime Measures," Department of Justice, **www.ojp.usdoj.gov/bjs/pub/ascii/ntcm.txt** (June 7, 2003).
15. Ibid.
16. The Association of State Uniform Crime Reporting Programs (ASUCRP) is an excellent source for information and updates on UCR and NIBRS.
17. The crime of arson was not one of the original indexed Part I crimes. In 1978 in response to a congressional mandate, arson was included. In 1982 with the passage of the Anti-Arson Act, Arson permanently became the eighth, indexed Part I crime.
18. The January 2002 to June 2002 UCR report is available at **www.fbi.gov/ucr/cius_02/02ciusprelim.pdf**.
19. Federal Bureau of Investigation, UCR Frequently Asked Questions, **www.fbi.gov/hq/cjisd/ucrfaq.pdf** (June 7, 2003).
20. "Overview of NIBRS."
21. Department of Justice, "Nation's Two Crime Measures."
22. Ibid.
23. The Bureau of Justice Statistics maintains a summary page on National Crime Victimization Survey results at **www.ojp.usdoj.gov/bjs/cvict.htm#summary**.
24. Federal Bureau of Investigation, "Crime Reporting," 2.
25. Los Angeles Police Department Crime Statistics, Year ending 2002.
26. Federal Bureau of Investigation, "Crime Reporting," 16.
27. Implementing National Incident-Based Reporting System, 6.
28. Ibid., 11.
29. See note 27 above.
30. Moore, *Mass Communication Law*, 384.
31. See note 8 above.

32. Ibid.
33. Electronic Privacy Information Center "Your Papers, Please: From the State Driver's License to a National Identification System" Watching the Watchers–Policy Report No. One: February 2002, 1.
34. Ibid.
35. See note 8 above.
36. See note 1 above.
37. Ibid.
38. Ibid.
39. "Implementing National Incident-Based Reporting System," 10.
40. Ibid.

Chapter Ten
The Internet and Law Enforcement

Learning Objectives

- The student will have an understanding of the historical development of the Internet.

- The student will have increased skills in navigating the Internet.

- The student will be exposed to how law enforcement organizations have used the Internet.

- The student will understand how the Internet can increase a law enforcement agency's efficiency and, possibly, effectiveness.

- The student will understand how the Internet can be used as a technological enhancer of the community-oriented policing model.

Introduction

In this chapter we first look at the historical development of the **Internet**, then begin to build on our skills and knowledge of police technology by exploring different methods of navigating and searching the Internet. In the place of case studies, we will look at a variety of law enforcement agencies' Web sites as a means of exploring and understanding the potential of the Internet. Throughout this chapter we will be asking these questions. How can the Internet increase a law enforcement agency's efficiency and effectiveness? How can the Internet be used as a technological enhancer of community-oriented policing?

Recall from Chapter One, technology is seen as an integral part of community policing. However, the part that technology plays is as an enhancer to the core elements of the model. For instance, in this chapter we will examine ways in which the Internet is being used in problem solving, increasing community partnerships, and increasing community participation. In Chapter One, in addition to looking at the COP model, we looked at how state and local law enforcement agencies are developing crime prevention operational strategies that fall into three broad categories. As we examine state and local law enforcement's use of the Internet, we should be looking for ways that Internet technology has enhanced or can enhance situational crime prevention, community crime prevention, and criminality prevention.[1]

The History of the Internet

In 1994 nearly 94 percent of American homes had telephones and just over 24 percent had computers.[2] Interestingly enough, in 1994 the United States Census Bureau did not even ask Americans about their use of the Internet. By 1997 the percentage of American households with a telephone remained constant, but the presence of a computer in the home had grown to more than 38 percent and nearly 19 percent of Americans had Internet access.[3] By 2000 the presence of a telephone grew slightly, but the personal computer was now in 51 percent of American homes, and Internet access had more than doubled to nearly 42 percent.[4] The growth in access to the Internet has been exceeded only by the growth in what is available on the Internet. In 2003 Internet users had access to more than three billion pages of information, and approximately three million new web pages are added daily.[5,6] Although today the Internet is very large, it did not start out that way. The idea was always big, but the actual network started out comparatively small and stayed that way for a relatively long time.

In 1962 J. C. R. Licklider wrote a paper at the Massachusetts Institute of Technology (MIT) entitled "On-Line Man Computer Communication." In that paper he described the "galactic network," an idea that in theory operates like our Internet of today.[7] Throughout the early 1960s and into the 1970s, the precursor to the Internet was called the ARPANet, after the Advanced Research Projects Agency within the Department of Defense, which provided the funding for the project.[8] Essentially, the United States government needed a way for the government employees, researchers, and contractors to communicate effectively.[9]

The early development of a worldwide communications network was undertaken for military communications. The "urban legend" that the Internet was designed so that a communications network could survive a nuclear attack does not appear to be the driving force behind development and implementation. However, in the minds of some, it may have eventually had that characteristic, but it does not seem to have been a driving motivator.

The ARPANet was developed by United States government employees and people working in the academic field. In fact, the first communication hookups were between two academic computers linked into the ARPANet. The first two computers were located at the University of California at Los Angeles (UCLA) and Stanford University, California. Among the greatest early technology challenges that ultimately made the Internet successful was the development of data packets. Recall from our earlier chapters we discussed that digital data moves across wireless and hardwired networks in small packages. In 1972 the development of the ARPANet went public when it was premiered at the International Computer Communications Conference. It was also at this conference that e-mail was introduced.

As it developed, the primary foundation of the Internet became that it is an open architecture network. This means the Internet grew from multiple networks of different designs that could be linked together using some basic principles. Today's Internet is not one big network. Rather, it is many networks that are linked together. In Chapter Three ("Wireless Communications") we briefly looked at the history of the development of cellular telephones. We mentioned in that chapter that before 1984, American Telephone and Telegraph was the primary carrier for telephone service in the United States. There was, in essence, one big telephone company. Recall from our chapter on networks, we saw that there were local area networks, wide area networks, and even metropolitan area networks. By using the right protocols, these privately owned networks can become part of the Internet. Any computer or network that has Internet access has become a small part of the huge, global network. The point to remember is that there is no one big company, enterprise, or network that is the Internet. The success of the Internet is that everyone who gains access becomes part of the global network. You and I are the Internet.

Recall in Part One ("Introduction to Theory and Basics") we discussed packaged data several times. In Chapter Four, on networks, we looked at the Transmission Control Protocol/Internet Protocol (TCP/IP), which is essentially software that divides information into packets and then transmits this information in its divided form. Packaged data and TCP/IP protocols are essentially all that is required for computers on the Internet to communicate.[10] There can be other protocols involved in a network connection—for instance, Serial Line Interface Protocol (SLIP) or Point-to-Point Protocol (PPP) connections.[11]

Earlier we learned that protocols are the rules and language we must use to complete electronic transactions. We also learned that TCP/IP is the Internet standard. This protocol gave us four principles from which the Internet flows. First, as we have said, each network is its own design. It does not have to comply with some global Internet standard. Second, if your data gets to its destination corrupted (recall error detection coding in data packets from Chapter Three), you, the sender, would retransmit the data. Third, the access points (gates and routers) to the Internet would be only access points; they would not keep information about the data that passed between them. The third point is important. When compared to most of the technology that makes up the Internet (such as servers), the access point technology is relatively simple. It would be significantly more complex if it did much more than foster access. Fourth, there would be no central Internet control point. There is no Big Brother engineered directly into the Internet.

A Look Ahead

Although there is no "Big Brother" engineered directly into the Internet, there are a number of means by which the transfer of data is monitored by the government. Some people have argued that although there is no Big Brother, there is a series of "little brothers." Our text focuses on state and local governments, and Internet monitoring is done by the Federal Bureau of Investigation (FBI). In Chapter Fourteen, when we look at wiretaps, we will examine how Internet communications can be monitored by the government. Moreover, in Chapter Sixteen on hi-tech crimes, we will look at how the Internet is used to facilitate certain crimes and how law enforcement and private industry are responding to these crimes.

For the next decade or so, the Internet remained primarily as a resource used by the government and increasingly by the academic community. In 1987, there was a significant development in the standardization of software technology that ultimately gave us today's Internet and **World Wide Web**. As more and more networks became part of the larger Internet, a new protocol was needed for the management of the access points (routers). Ultimately, the Simple Network Management Protocol (SNMP) was adopted. In addition to TCP/IP, SNMP became standard rules and languages our computers would use to communicate.

Some people use the terms *Internet* and *World Wide Web* as if they are interchangeable. In some sense they might be interchangeable, but they are different concepts. The Internet is the system of protocols and architectures that allows the vast number of different networks and, ultimately, different computers to communicate. Because we use telephone lines and direct service lines (DSL) to connect in a wired mode, radio frequencies to connect in a wireless mode, and dedicated lines to connect between networks—the Internet is virtually every means of transmitting digital information around the planet. Because the Internet does use satellite signals and we can view images from other planets, the Internet is arguably solar system—wide. Essentially, the Internet is the information super highway. On the other hand, the World Wide Web is a way in which most of us use the information super highway.[12]

The World Wide Web is based on client/server computing.[13] In this arrangement, the client is a Web browser that can communicate with any Web server on the Internet. Moreover, the Web server shares resources with all of the Web browsers.[14] Think of a drive-through hamburger stand. As you drive through, you are the client. You place your order into the speaker. At the other end of the speaker, the server is taking your order. At the same time, the server is quite possibly doing other things. For instance, he might be recording your order on a touch screen, filling sodas, making change with the person ahead of you, or passing your order to the cook in the back. Moreover, the speakers and the wires that connect them are the network between you, the client, and the server in the hamburger stand. As more people put demands on the server, your service slows. Our server in the hamburger stand is like a computer in that he can multitask, but as we noted in Chapter Two, a computer can do only one thing at a time, and the appearance of multiple things going on is an illusion of speed. Your Internet client/server relationship is similar. The client (your computer) makes requests to a server through a network of connections. The server is receiving and managing other requests from different clients.

The World Wide Web consists of pages of information that are linked together.[15] These electronic links between pages are called **hyperlinks**. Hyperlinks make it possible to jump from one document or Web page to another.[16] For instance, you may be on one Web site and see that they provide a link to some document that provides more information on a subject. Many of the endnotes in this text provide you with Web site addresses for additional exploration. If this textbook were a Web page, you could click on those links and would be taken to another Web site. By using a link on a Web site, you are never really sure where you are going. The Web site might be maintained by the person in the house next to yours, or it might be all the way around the world from you. The linkages between the pages are what make them a distinctive web of information.

In 1988 the commercialization of the Internet began to take hold. The people who had been responsible for the development of the Internet up to that point began to hold tradeshows that introduced the technology and concepts they had developed. At this point most private individuals who gained Internet access probably did so through an **access service provider (ASP)**. Many ASPs provide a variety of other services to their clients like newsgroups and chat rooms.

Throughout the 1990s the Internet began to increase in size and scope as more people joined the Net. Today, the Internet is nearly everywhere. It has grown beyond the early government and academic uses to a tool for all.[17]

Navigating the Internet

Now that we know how the Internet and World Wide Web were created, we need to learn how to navigate the Net. The Web consists of millions of cyberlocations created by people to exchange information. Some of the Web sites are commercial information—someone is trying to sell you a product or service. Some are governmental, academic, or not-for-profit sites that have a number of purposes. Finally, there are the thousands upon thousands of personal sites dedicated to a hobby, a family, or some personal interest.

Although some of the Web sites consist of a single page, most consist of multiple Web pages. The first page (and occasionally the only page) is considered the Web site's **home page** or, as it is increasingly referred to, **index page**.[18] The Web would not be as we know it today if each of the Web sites' owners had to have their computer constantly connected to the Web. In other words, if each time you visited a Web page you were actually going to the Web site owner's computer, there would be far fewer Web sites and the system would be significantly slower. When you visit most Web sites, the physical location you are going to is an **internet service provider's (ISP)** Web server. In Chapter Two ("Computer Basics") we discussed servers. A Web server is a computer dedicated to managing the information flow associated with the Internet.[19] ISPs provide a large variety of services to individual users and organizations. For instance, an ISP might provide Internet access, Web hosting, electronic mail, and e-commerce services.[20] The physical location of the ISP Web server is called the **point of presence (POP)**.[21] Although an ISP can provide many services, many ISPs center on hosting Web sites. In order to be an ISP, one would have to have high-speed access of at least the capability of a T-1 line and a server. Companies like America Online who primarily provide access to the Internet, are referred to as access providers. However, just as an ISP can provide access, an access provider can provide Web hosting.[22]

If you have Web access at home, you are using an ASP. That ASP can be dial-up, cable, an asymmetrical digital subscriber line (DSL), or some direct access scheme. The ASP you use for access probably will also provide you with limited space for a personal Web page.

Today most people are using one of two **browsers** as a means to explore the Internet—Internet Explorer or Netscape.[23] These browsers are graphical user interface (GUI) software applications that simplify Internet **navigation**. As we know from Chapter Two, a GUI scheme is one that provides the user with icons to complete certain tasks. The body of the browser is the Web page that the browser has accessed (Figure 10.1). When you connect to the Net using a browser, your browser has a predetermined home page. If you are using an ASP like America Online (AOL), this configuration with your browser is different. We are going to work with an ASP that is unlike AOL, one that only provides you with access to the Web. We are doing this because most law enforcement Internet access is through an ASP that provides access only and not the myriad of services available through an ASP like AOL. Depending on how your Internet service is configured, there may be some type of authentication

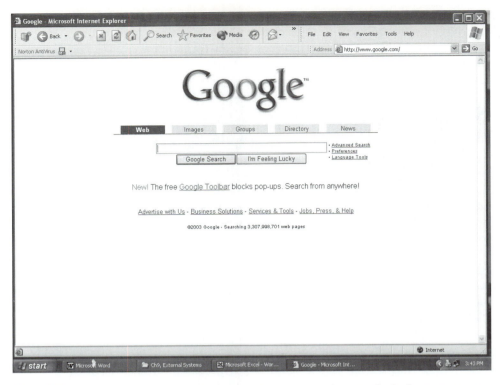

Figure 10.1　The opening page of the browser Internet Explorer with the homepage set to Google.

Permission to reprint provided by Microsoft Corporation and Google.

process that allows access to the ISP. If you are using the Internet at school or in a large organization, the Internet is probably accessed by simply clicking the browser icon on your computer screen. However, if you have dial-up service, you may have to enter a user name and password to gain access to the Internet.[24] Additionally, when you first open the browser, if you are using a computer at home, the browser will default to the software manufacturer's home page. If you buy a computer that is specifically manufactured for you, from Gateway for instance, they may set the browser default to their home page. We, however, have control over this. With Internet Explorer, click Tools, Internet Options, General, and you will see the place where you can change the home page (Figure 10.2).

On the Internet, each Web site that you visit has an address. We are used to accessing an address like **www.prentice-hall.com**. This address is to the Web site is called a **domain name**.[25] However, in reality, the domain name, or Web site address, is actually a number.[26] In this instance the actual address for Prentice Hall, the publishers of this textbook, is 192.251.135.15. Recalling a bunch of numbers so that we can access different Web sites would be cumbersome. We would end up keeping an address book nearby so that we could visit our favorite sites. The browser simplifies this by giving us an address line (at the top of the browser in Figure 10.1) that translates the number into the domain names with which we are familiar. This address line software application is called the **universal resource locator (URL)**.[27] You have probably noticed that before the domain name is the URL, there are the letters *www*—rather obviously, the World Wide Web. Preceding those letters you will find—*http,* which stands for **Hypertext**

Figure 10.2 You can set your browser home page any page on the Web.
Permission to reprint provided by Microsoft™ Corporation and Google™.

Transfer Protocol; this is the protocol used to transfer information within the World Wide Web.[28]

When you visit a Web site, your computer actually downloads the page you are viewing and saves it to a temporary file. It is not like television where you are receiving a continuous signal. When you open a Web page, the contents of that page are now on your computer. That is why if you move to another page, and then a short time later go back to the original page, the original page will appear much faster. Your computer knows that the content is still there, it checks the Web site to make sure nothing has changed and then shows you what you have already seen. Recall in Chapter Two ("Computer Basics"), we looked at the functions of cache. When your computer places the Web site information into a temporary file, it is caching the information in order to speed up the operation of

Don't be confused. The domain name is the plain language name we commonly use. The **Internet Protocol (IP)** address is the number the computers use to find each other. Also, it is important to note that Web sites have static IP addresses, they never change. However, when ever you access the Internet, your home personal computer is assigned a dynamic IP address. Your ISP assigns this address to you based upon what is available.

The domain name has an extension that generally describes the general function of the organization. The six most common extensions are:

- Commercial organizations (.com)
- Educational institutions (.edu)
- Military (.mil)
- Government (.gov)
- Miscellaneous organizations (.org)
- Networking organizations (.net)

In the United States, an organization called Internic is the governing body controlling the issuance and control of Internet domains and addresses. The management of domain names is done through a partnership between the United States government and a private firm, Network Solutions, Inc.

Source: Cunningham, *B2B,* 100; 179.

your computer. Although temporary files have a preset lifespan, you can change the settings on your computer to delete them earlier or you can delete them yourself.

The browser is also translating the program language used to design the Web site into the images on the page you are viewing. The most common Web site programming language is **hypertext markup language (HTML)**.[29] HTML uses programming cues called **tags** to tell our computers what we should see on the screens. It gives the Web site developer the tools to add color, lines, and formatting to his or her Web site. For instance, in order to determine the colors that the Web site is going to be, the tags used are six-digit numbers. The color tags use two-digits to identify distinct shades of the primary colors. By combining the two-digit shades of the primary colors, your computer knows what color the programmer intended you to see. As an example, 999999 is the code for black. Conversely, 000000 is the code for white. All of the colors of the rainbow fall between the codes of 000000 and 999999. The programming language HTML can format the text of a document; create links to Web pages; describe the structure of a Web page; and display different kinds of media like images, video, and sound.[30]

With HTML you can create the perfect Web site. The only problem is your Web site is just a collection of pages in a special file on the Internet. With HTML it is static and unchanging. In order to create more dynamic Web sites, developers use programming that tells a computer to execute a program—to do something. The programs, or scripts as they are called, use a computer's common gateway interface, or CGI. With special scripts, the CGI can be used to create interactive maps on a Web site.[31]

One of the common scripts used in conjunction with CGI is Java. Java was created in 1995 by Sun Microsystems.[32] Essentially, when you download an HTML file that requires Java, the Java applet (applet is a term for an application that runs a relatively simple program) is downloaded to your computer and it runs the Java program. The use of Java adds to the dynamic nature of Web sites.[33] Since we are not aiming at becoming Web developers (fancy programmers) we will stop here.

With thousands of ISPs hosting millions of Web pages of organizations and individuals, how can we find anything?[34] One way is to rely on private firms that have designed **search engines** to do the hard work for us. One such search engine is Google. A search engine searches the World Wide Web for keywords, keeps an index of the words it finds, and allows users to look through those indexes for words or combinations of words.

File Transfer Protocol (FTP) is a protocol used on the Internet to transfer many different types of information in the form of files and data. For instance, were you to create your own Web site, you might use FTP to load your Web site from your computer (where you designed it) to your Web host. *Source:* Cunningham, *B2B,* 177.

A Look Ahead

In the next chapter, on information exchange, we will look at another type of Web programming that is becoming increasingly useful and popular, extensible markup language (XML).

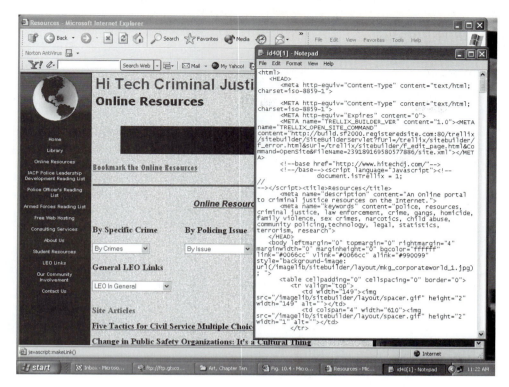

Figure 10.3 While at your home page, in the upper left-hand part of your browser, click View. A drop-down menu will appear. Click Source. Another window will open up in Notepad. You are looking at the programming language that makes up the Web site you are viewing. Note that in the very top left-hand corner you probably see <html>; this tells you that the primary code used to write this Web site was indeed HTML.
Permission to reprint provided by Microsoft™ Corporation and Google™.

Whatever search engine you are using, it cannot refer you to a Web site if it has not visited it, conducted an analysis of the content, and indexed that content. That means that the most popular search engines will have indexed hundreds of millions of pages and will respond to tens of millions of inquires each day. And because the Internet is constantly changing as people update their pages (or fall out of or climb into cyberspace), this is an ongoing process. Search engines accomplish the review of Web pages with software robots called **spiders**.[35] As we shall see, there are good spiders and bad spiders. Furthermore, if you have a Web site hosted by an ISP, you have had good spiders and bad spiders crawling all over it.

The bad spiders do the bidding of the evil **spam** kings. They crawl onto your Web site, devour your e-mail address and take it back to the spam kings. The spam kings in turn take your e-mail address and send you all those messages that you don't need about lowering the interest rate on your home loan. Take heart, though; the good spiders are crawling around the Web, too.

The spiders start at the most commonly used servers and jump onto the most popular Web sites. From there, they look at every word in the Web site and then follow the links those Web sites have provided. By using these heavily traveled cyberpaths, the spiders find their way to the popular parts of the Web. Once on a Web site, the spider looks at two things—the words on a page and the location where the words were found.

Spam is unsolicited e-mail. In most instances, spam e-mail is very much like junk mail, in that it is sent out in huge batches. Spam is not a known acronym for any technical term. Spam is however, the canned meat product produced by the Hormel company. Some say that the term spam (to denote junk e-mail) comes from a Monty Python skit. If you are so inclined, a quick Internet search for "spam Monty Python" will locate a Web site wherein you can hear Vikings singing the "Spam Song." *Source:* Cunningham, *B2B,* 183.

Figure 10.4 Experiment with something like what we older cybernauts used instead of a modern search engine. As we know, before the advent of the Web of today, people used search engines like Veronica, Archie, and Gopher. On your computer, click Start then All Programs. Then select Accessories and Command Prompt or DOS Prompt. Your computer will open a new window that bypasses your GUI and allows you access to the underlying disk operating system (DOS). You will see a flashing cursor. Type "telnet" and hit enter. You now see "Microsoft Telnet." This is Internet access as it used to be. On the command line, type "o." If you are connected to the Internet, type "bbs.fament.com" and hit enter. Once at the Family Entertainment site, you are using the Internet, but not the Web, per se. However, you will be in an "old style" bulletin board system (BBS) that was used for Internet access. You probably noticed that it does not have any of the visual characteristics of today's Net. If you have time (I know that paper on underwater basketweaving is waiting), go into the Tradewars game and compete with the older cybernauts. You will find that it is nothing like the games of today, but we still like it.
Source: Cunningham, *B2B*, 184.

A hyperlink is a way that a Web site developer provides the user with a quick way to jump to another Web site. Sometimes links are underlined or highlighted words on a Web site: *Educational Books*. At other times, a link is the actual Web site address: **www.prentice-hall.com**. In either case, if you select that link with your mouse, you will be redirected to that Web page.

The spiders, for being so small, are pretty smart. They look at every word except articles. So, the spiders crawl past words like *a, an,* and *the,* but they look at every other word and, depending on its location and frequency of use, begin to develop an idea of how to rank the Web site for your search. People who have designed Web sites want the spiders to recognize how applicable they are to your search, so Web site developers use HTML **meta tags** while writing your Web site (Figure 10.3). If you opened up the source code on your Web site you would see **meta tags** at the very beginning of the programming. These meta tags are the programmer's way of helping the spiders decide what the Web site is about.

While spiders like the help from programmers, they don't trust them. The meta tags are especially helpful to the spiders in making a decision about words on your Web site that many have multiple meanings. But the spiders know that some Web site developers are untrustworthy. The evil programmers (who are probably part-time employees of the spam kings) sometimes put meta tags in the HTML programming that have nothing to do with the Web site's actual content. The evil programmers just want you to waste your time looking at their bogus content. Because the spiders are good, they know that sometimes people do not want their Web sites to be crawled over. For instance, if you were running a game server, the spider's interference might be perceived by the game as a really good player and crash your system. So the spiders recognize programming, or scripts, that tell them to go away.

After the spiders have completed their review of the Web site (they will be back constantly in case the content changes), they go back to the search engine owner and divulge all that they have learned. The search engine programs go to work and index the information so that you and I can search the Web and find what we want. Some of the methods for creating an index are rather complex. For instance, information is given different weights depending on its location in the Web site. For us, it's just enough to know that the search engine programmers have designed a way for us to reliably search the Net.

There are three kinds of searches users commonly perform on the Internet. Probably the most common is a search using **boolean logic**.[36] A Boolean search is named after the mathematician George Boole who lived from 1815 until 1864. His mathematical system of logic is not only used for our searches, but also one of the underlying principles of programming that enables mathematical computation by computers. Recall that computers use binary data—off and on. Boolean logic uses the off and on scheme to answer questions as true or false. If you have ever played twenty questions, you know that by answering true or false, or yes or no, you can determine an object. So, our Boolean logic search (by far the most common Internet search), uses Boolean operators like the word *and* to enhance our search capabilities. If at the search engine we type in the words *cars* and *asteroids*, we will only get a search return for Web sites that contain both words. There are six common Boolean operators:

- AND—all words joined by and must appear. For instance, "cars **AND** aster-oids **AND** cats, will reveal only Web sites that contain all three words." There is no limit to the number of times you can join words for your search.
- OR—one of the words is in the Web site. For instance, "cars **OR** vehicles."
- NOT—the word following *not* is not in the Web site. For instance, "cars **AND** asteroids **NOT** cats."
- FOLLOWED BY—one of the words must follow the other. For instance, "cars **FOLLOWED BY** asteroids."
- NEAR—the words must be within a certain distance from each other on the Web site. For instance, "cars **NEAR** asteroids."
- QUOTATION MARKS—By placing the words in quotation marks, they are treated as a phrase and must be in that order. For instance, "car asteroids."

Now we know a little bit about the Internet, Web sites, and searching the World Wide Web. The last technical issue we should look at before we start to see how the Internet is being used by law enforcement is **cookies**. Cookies, like spam, are one of the current hot topics of the Internet. Moreover, cookies, like spiders can be both good and bad. The purpose of cookies is to allow what is called "retaining state information." Let's presume that you have set your browser to open at **www.msn.com**. You are using this as your home page so that you can access your e-mail, newsgroups, and chat rooms. In order for the Web site to recall how you personally configured (set up) this page, it gives your computer a cookie which has a serial number identifying the state of the page you want to retain. Without this cookie, you would have to repeatedly reset how you want the page configured. In essence, a cookie is a very small file that identifies you to the Web site. This cookie is not a program; it cannot do anything on its own. That is the good part—now the bad. Anyone with access to your computer can look at your cookies and see where you have been. You sort of leave a trail of cookie crumbs along the information highway. Moreover, some Internet companies, like Double Click, which provide Web advertising, retain your cookies because they want to develop a shopping profile of you. On your personal PC, you can go to Tools, Internet Options, Privacy and determine when and how you will allow cookies to be placed in your computer.

In addition to storing your personal preferences at certain Web sites, cookies also save information about which sites you visited, when you visited them, if you made a purchase, and any files that you downloaded.[37] There is a second way in which personal information is collected on the Internet. We give it up. Any time we register or complete a commercial transaction on the Web, that information is retained by the firm who owns the Web site. Because Web sites can compile information from our cookies, transactions, and registrations, they can develop a fairly accurate picture of our personal likes and dislikes.[38] Before we look at specific uses, we should take a look at an Internet use that is common to nearly every Internet user—e-mail.

Employee Use of E-mail and Instant Messaging

Electronic mail, or e-mail, is the Internet's most widely used program. In fact, e-mail is so popular, it has surpassed the United States Postal Service in the number of messages delivered daily.[39] When you send an e-mail, you are creating a file that will be transmitted to a recipient's electronic mailbox. In addition to the text message, you can transfer files that contain other documents, photographs, and a myriad of other multimedia information.[40] With the developments in the hardware and software associated with scanners and printers, just about anything you could send via facsimile, you can send via e-mail.

Electronic mail is also far less expensive than either long-distance telephone calls or facsimile transmissions. Moreover, your e-mail address is portable. If someone wants to send you information, a document, or a photograph, with the telephone, facsimile machine, or regular mail, they have to know where you are going to be when you will receive it. With e-mail, you can send someone information, and they can access it from just about anywhere there is Internet service. There are security, privacy, and legal reasons you should use a communications method other than e-mail, but for most communications, e-mail is becoming the preferred choice.

While the security of e-mail is still a concern, encryption (for further reading on how encryption works, return to Chapter Four on networks) technology is increasingly allaying fears about messages being read by unauthorized persons. There are a variety of commercially available products and services that scramble messages between users. In most instances, all an end user has to remember in order to unscramble an encrypted message is a password or confidential phrase. These products guard e-mail against unauthorized intrusion during both transmission and storage.[41] A second form of electronic communication is real-time conversations between people on the Internet using **Internet relay chat (IRC)**.[42,43] The Internet capabilities of e-mail and chat bring up interesting questions for employee–employer relationships. If you were at work and you placed a telephone call using your employer's telephone, would you expect the telephone call to be monitored by an agent of your employer? Would you expect the telephone call to be recorded and potentially monitored from a database of employee telephone calls? What if you were on a break at work and reading a magazine—would you expect your employer to review what you had read? As we know from our earlier chapters on computer basics and networks, it is very possible for an employer to monitor, store, and retrieve e-mail, chat, and Internet activity.

One survey by the American Management Association indicated that 45 percent of firms monitor their employees' e-mail, voice mail, or Internet use.[44] As we know, hardware and software has become so sophisticated that an employer can monitor or record virtually every electronic word an employee utters.[45] It is a fairly safe assumption that many state and local law enforcement agencies are following the lead of private industry and also monitoring their employees.

Essentially, there are two types of electronic monitoring. The first is **interception**. Interception occurs when the electronic communication is examined by the employer as it is occurring between the sender and receiver. With e-mail or chat, a copy of the message might be routed to a supervisor's computer. With a voice communication, a supervisor might listen in on the conversation. The second type of monitoring is **auditing**. Auditing is primarily concerned with e-mail. However, in some instances, telephone conversations are also routinely recorded by an employer. For instance, as we learned in Chapter Seven, on communications dispatch centers, 9-1-1 calls are routinely recorded. Auditing occurs when the employer examines the message after it has been received, stored, or perhaps even deleted. While some employees have challenged their employer's right to monitor their electronic communications, the courts have generally said that auditing was like the employer looking in a filing cabinet. The employer owns the filing cabinet, so he can look in it when he wants. The issue of monitoring is much more complex. However, if the employer has an electronic communications policy (like an e-mail policy that warns of potential monitoring) and the monitoring is done in a reasonable manner, the courts have generally upheld the employer's right to monitor the communications.[46]

Figure 10.5 You can register at their Web site **www.crimeweb.net/home.asp**. *Screen capture provided by CrimeWeb.Net.*

Just as the Internet has brought us new ways to communicate, it has brought us new questions in the areas of employee–employer relationships and privacy. The Internet can cause questions about what is appropriate material for you to read or possess at work. The safest position is for employees to realize that the employer's computer and Internet service is the property of the employer. It is nearly always subject to monitoring and auditing.

Listservs and CrimeWeb

A **listserv,** or a list server, is a program that automatically redistributes e-mail to names on a mailing list.[47] Users can subscribe to a listserv by e-mail, or in some instances, there is a registration process. Once someone has subscribed, the list-serv will automatically add her name and distribute future e-mail postings to every subscriber. The programs can be managed by a human being or a computer program. Commonly, people join listservs because they have some common interest with the other subscribers. One of the common hobbies that take advantage of listservs is genealogy. But there are law enforcement applications.

CrimeWeb (Figure 10.5) is a listserv that generates e-mail alerts to subscribers when a public safety agency makes notification of a missing child, missing adult, major crime, homeland security issue, school information alert, or community information alert. Any member of the public can go to their Web site and register. You enter the ZIP codes for which you are interested in alerts, and if a public safety agency posts an alert pertinent to your ZIP code, you receive an e-mail.

The Internet and Law Enforcement

In previous chapters we have seen how the Internet and Internet protocols have been used to supplement state and local law enforcement communication schemes. From this point forward, we are going to look at how law enforcement agencies have used Web sites on the Internet. The law enforcement–related Web sites listed in the text box on pages 214 and 215 provide information that gives you an idea of what other people are doing, and they can provide statistical and research information so that you can make better decisions or explore other aspects of law enforcement. Although the listing of law enforcement–related Web sites is by no means totally inclusive of what is available, it should be fairly representative. Furthermore, in order to completely understand the potential of the World Wide Web, it must be explored in a hands-on fashion. You will get a lot more out of navigating the Web than you will by reading my descriptions of the Web.

A comprehensive examination of the police function will reveal that there are many police and police-related functions that can be conducted via Web site, or supplemented by an agency's Web site.[48] Much of the research for this chapter was provided from examples of private firms exploring the commercial potential of the Web. That is because the success of some **e-commerce** firms has directly impacted the development of **e-government**.[49] Many police departments are beginning to take cues from commercial firms that have been successful in e-commerce. The first job of a police department Web site is to get users to the Web site and attract them back again. Whether we like it or not, at first it is all about marketing. While it is unlikely that police department Web sites will attract new users to the Internet, they should be designed to attract those people in the community who are users. People visit a Web site because there is something at the Web site they want to see, know, or buy. Furthermore, in many instances, people visit a Web site because they were referred by another Web site.

At first, law enforcement Web sites resembled e-magazines.[50] They were online publications that looked like newsletters or magazines. They sought to tell the reader what was unique about the particular police department that had published the Web site. Today many agencies still use the Web as a means to provide this type of one-way communication to the public. Those Web sites, which are probably the majority, are essentially static. While the information they contain might change on a fairly regular basis, they are static because they remain a one-way form of communication. One-way forms of communication with the public are trademarks of the professional policing model.

With one-way communications, the police are telling the public what they have done and what they are going to do. For community-based policing to be successful, the police must have two-way communications with the public. There must be an exchange of ideas about what is important to the community, and the community must be involved in solving the problems. Now, most police department Web sites have some form for feedback. Generally, there is a method to either submit an electronic feedback form or submit an e-mail to the police department's Webmaster or perhaps to some police department employee designated to handle requests via e-mail. This is certainly a step toward two-way communication.

Recall from Chapter One that in the community-oriented policing model, technology is an enhancer. We have certainly seen that technology has enhanced traditional police functions. There are numerous examples of technology increasing police efficiency, and in later chapters we will see how technology has increased the effectiveness in traditional roles. The question remains, how can the technology of the World Wide Web enhance community-oriented policing? The

E-commerce is the completion of a commercial transaction via the World Wide Web. Essentially, a business sells something that you buy via the Internet.
Source: Cunningham, *B2B,* 176.

A **webmaster** is the person who monitors the content of a Web site. In many instances, the Webmaster is the person who developed the Web site. However, the Webmaster is generally not the Internet service provider who hosts the Web site.

It is likely that you will gain more from this chapter by actually exploring law enforcement on the Internet. The following nine Web sites are a collection of government, not-for-profit, and commercial firms that provide law enforcement–related information. While most of the Web sites listed below contain information that is available to anyone with Internet access, some sites, like the Federal Bureau of Investigation, maintain portions of their Web sites that can be accessed only by law enforcement personnel. As we saw in Chapter Nine, on external sources of information, there is information available via the Internet that law enforcement personnel can access with the proper passwords and secure linkages.

- The Source Book of Criminal Justice Statistics
  www.albany.edu/sourcebook/index.html
  This site annually compiles criminal justice statistics from more than one hundred sources. The information is presented in more than six hundred tables. The information is searchable and available for review and downloads in Adobe Acrobat format.

- National Criminal Justice Reference Service (NCJRS) **www.ncjrs.org/**
  This Web site searches the NCJRS Web site and the Web sites of the U.S. Department of Justice, Office of Justice Programs (OJP) (OJP includes five separate bureaus: the National Institute of Justice, the Office of Juvenile Justice and Delinquency Prevention, the Bureau of Justice Statistics, the Bureau of Justice Assistance, and the Office for Victims of Crime), and the White House Office of National Drug Control Policy. Additionally, this Web site has the capacity to search the NCJRS Abstract Database, which contains more than 160 thousand criminal justice publications. There are a large variety of text documents available in both a plain text format and Adobe Acrobat format.

- United States Department of Justice, Community-Oriented Policing Services (COPS) **www.cops.usdoj.gov/**
  This Web site provides a good overview of community-oriented policing and funding opportunities, and it publishes problem-solving guides for police agencies. There are currently nineteen problem-solving guides that offer information and advice on subjects ranging from rave parties to the use and abuse of 9-1-1.

- The Federal Bureau of Investigation
  www.fbi.gov/
  The FBI Web site offers a reference library on a variety of police subjects. There are also links to a variety of programs the FBI is conducting in conjunction with state and local law enforcement agencies.

- The Bureau of Justice Statistics
  www.ojp.usdoj.gov/bjs/
  The BJS is responsible for the collection, retention, analysis, and dissemination of statistics related to criminal justice. It is an outstanding source for statistical information. Many of the links from other Web sites on statistics actually take you to the BJS.

- National Institute for Justice
  www.ojp.usdoj.gov/nij/
  The NIJ is the research, development, and evaluation agency of the United States Department of Justice. It was created in 1994 as a component of the NIJ's Office of Science and Technology, the National Law Enforcement and Corrections Technology Center (NLECTC). The NIJ serves as the "honest broker" offering support, research findings, and technological expertise for state and local law enforcement and corrections personnel. The NIJ includes regional centers around the United States that are available to assist criminal justice personnel with technology problems. Moreover, the NIJ sponsors research and development when it otherwise will not occur.*

- International Association of Chiefs of Police (IACP)—Technology Clearinghouse
  www.iacptechnology.org/
  The IACP link will take you to their Technology Clearinghouse. It has a wide variety of resources available, including a searchable library,

*"Evolution and Development of Police Technology," vii.

an archive of "Tech Talk" articles that appeared in past issues in their magazine, and links to police technology practitioners.

- The Terrorism Research Center **www.terrorism.com**
  The Terrorism Research Center (TRC) conducts research into terrorism and terrorism-related subjects. In addition to analysis of terrorism trends and counter-terrorism efforts, the TRC, through its Web site, offers information on information warfare and infrastructure protection. It includes a searchable knowledge database on articles, policy analysis, and reference materials.

- The Society of Police Futurists International (PFI) **www.policefuturists. org/index.htm**
  The Society of Police Futurists International (PFI) is an organization of law enforcement practitioners, educators, researchers, private security specialists, technology experts, and other professionals dedicated to improving criminal and social justice through the professionalization of policing. Futures research (long-range planning and forecasting) is the pivotal discipline that constitutes the philosophical underpinnings of PFI. The tools and techniques of this field are applied in order to more accurately anticipate and prepare for the evolution of law enforcement ten, twenty, and even fifty years into the future. Futures research offers both philosophical and methodological tools to analyze, forecast, and plan in ways rarely seen in policing in the past. The strength of PFI lies in the participation of its members as we engage in dialogue and collaborate on research on the future of the policing profession.

answer is fairly straightforward—a police department's Web site should be designed to attract users and increase the two-way communications between the community user and the police.

One move in the direction of creating two-way communication and partnerships might be in community participation in Web site design. Consider that a static Web site is fairly simple and not very expensive. Hosting services for a 350 MB site that includes fifty e-mail addresses is less that $60 a month. Moreover, fairly comprehensive Web development software costs less that $200. The primary stumbling block is development and content.

Even a static Web site can be made more attractive by constantly updating and changing the content.[51] The question for the manager of the agency is, where do we find the talent necessary for site development and management? A Web site can become a technological enhancer for community policing if the community is involved in the development of the site. Even with differing community values and standards, there is little direct community input into the day-to-day operations of a local police agency. Police agencies are restrained and directed in what they can do and what they must do by the Constitution, federal law, state law, case law, etc. In other words, any time a police agency has the opportunity to solicit community input and involvement in decision making, it is a special occasion. A Web site gives an agency that opportunity. A Web site can foster community participation and input if the community is given a strong hand in site development and content. What do they want on their Web site? How should their Web site look?

Following the lead of e-commerce, how can police agencies increase Web traffic? I have not referred you to police department Web sites that are static and dull; you can find those on your own. The point is that you were unlikely to have visited those Web sites without a referral, one of the most basic things a police department can do to increase Web traffic. Referrals come from links with other agency's Web sites, or e-partnerships (Figure 10.6).

One of the tenets of community-oriented policing is partnership with the community. This is not just partnership with individual community members.

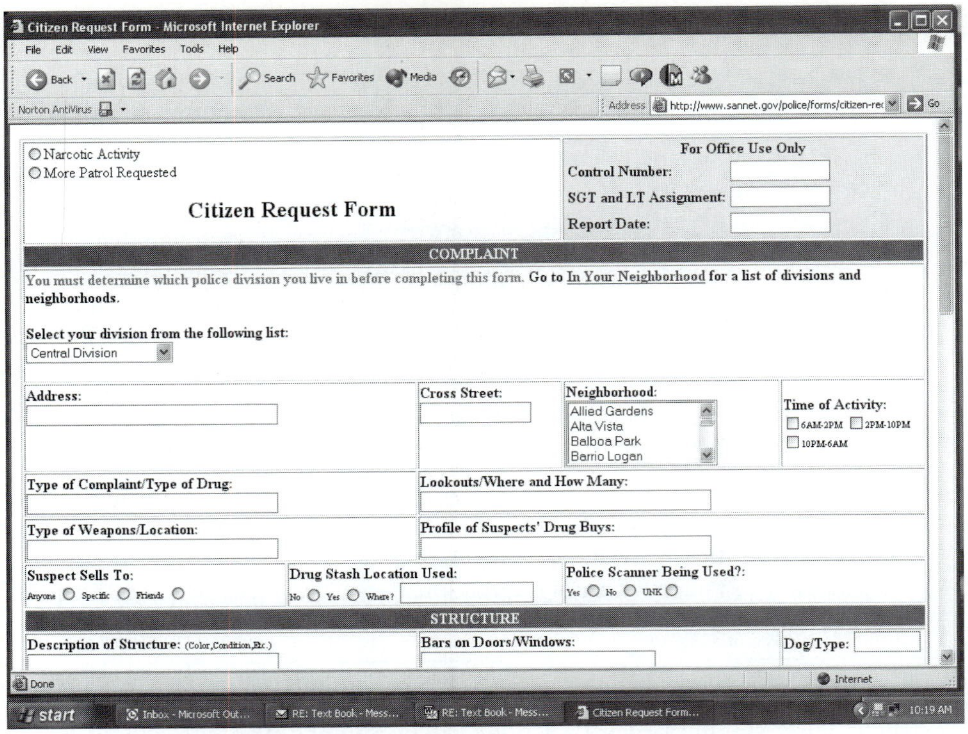
Citizen Request Form - Microsoft Internet Explorer

File Edit View Favorites Tools Help

Back Search Favorites Media

Norton AntiVirus

Address http://www.sannet.gov/police/forms/citizen-re Go

○ Narcotic Activity ○ More Patrol Requested **Citizen Request Form**	**For Office Use Only** **Control Number:** **SGT and LT Assignment:** **Report Date:**

COMPLAINT

You must determine which police division you live in before completing this form. **Go to** In Your Neighborhood **for a list of divisions and neighborhoods.**

Select your division from the following list:
Central Division

Address:	Cross Street:	Neighborhood: Allied Gardens, Alta Vista, Balboa Park, Barrio Logan	Time of Activity: 6AM-2PM 2PM-10PM 10PM-6AM
Type of Complaint/Type of Drug:	Lookouts/Where and How Many:		
Type of Weapons/Location:	Profile of Suspects' Drug Buys:		
Suspect Sells To: Anyone ○ Specific ○ Friends ○	Drug Stash Location Used: No ○ Yes ○ Where?	Police Scanner Being Used?: Yes ○ No ○ UNK ○	

STRUCTURE

Description of Structure: (Color,Condition,Etc.)	Bars on Doors/Windows:	Dog/Type:

Done Internet

start Inbox - Microsoft Out... RE: Text Book - Mess... RE: Text Book - Mess... Citizen Request Form... 10:19 AM

Figure 10.6 In Chapter Eleven, when we look at information exchange, we will explore the value of regional systems. One regional system is the Automated Regional Justice Information System (ARJIS) in the San Diego area of California. Regional information systems not only increase the technological efficiency and effectiveness of the participating agencies by reaping the benefits of economies of scale, but the combined agency resources have the capacity to increase the use of technology for information exchange with the public. The San Diego Police Department, in conjunction with ARJIS, has produced a very interactive Web site (www.sannet.gov/police/). Through the Web site, the community can view interactive crime, traffic, and sexual offender maps; they can obtain information about the San Diego Police Department and other service organizations; and they can submit crime clues and other information online. Go to **www. sannet.gov/police/prevention/index.shtml**. You will find that the San Diego Police Department provide hyperlinks to a variety of community resources, broken down by police beats. *Permission to reprint provided by the San Diego Police Department.*

This is also partnership with other community service organizations. We know that community-oriented policing is about solving problems, and we know, primarily from experience, that the police cannot solve most community problems. Yet as one of the most visible members of the service community, the police are often called upon to solve problems far outside their area of expertise. If you want a test of whether or not a police department is practicing community policing, you need only ask a few basic questions about the operation of that department. Does that police department recognize that many of the root causes of crime, fear, and disorder are outside their area of expertise? Does that police department work to solve those problems by seeking partnerships with the people and organizations who have the expertise to address the root causes? If you can answer yes to both questions, some level of community-oriented policing is occurring.

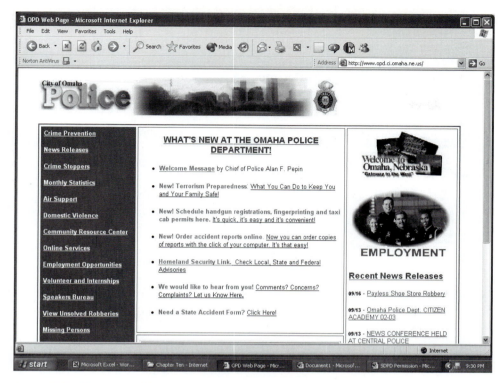

Figure 10.7 Take a good look around this Web site. The Omaha Police Department provides online support for the purchase of some types of reports, online appointment scheduling, and a very comprehensive frequently asked questions section.
Permission to reprint provided by the Omaha Police Department.

Many of the organizations that police departments work with to solve problems have their own Web sites. Creating Web linkages with agencies a police department works with to solve problems is a means of strengthening those partnerships and increasing Web traffic. This can be as simple as modifying the way in which police departments post press releases on their Web sites. Instead of a static press release that tells the public what happened, the press releases should be dynamic and have links to the participating agencies. Conversely, when those agencies post their version of the press release, they should have a link to the police department Web site. Both agencies benefit by having their particular audience jump back and forth between the Web sites.

These types of linkages are very common in e-commerce. Commercial firms whose products are complementary but not competitive often link among each other in an effort to increase market share. That is the essence of partnership; we are complementary and not competitive. While most police service is not a commercial transaction, individual commercial transactions are conducted between the police and some community members.

Generally, police service is a public good that we all pay for in advance through taxes; whether or not we use it, we pay for it. However, there are some transactions for which the police are going to charge a fee to an individual. For instance, let's say that you are unfortunate enough to have your cellular telephone stolen out of your parked car, but you were smart enough to purchase loss insurance when you obtained the telephone. However, the insurance carrier wants a copy of the police report in order to process your claim. Your local police department is probably going to charge you a fee for a copy of the completed report (Figure 10.7).

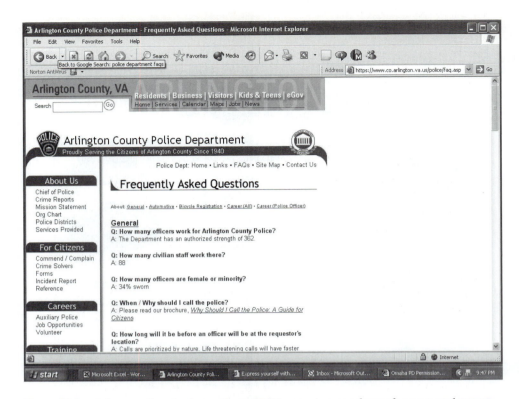

Figure 10.8 A frequently asked questions (FAQ) page is a good way for new and returning users to look at questions that are regularly asked.
Source: Cunningham, *B2B,* 176.
Permission to reprint provided by the Arlington County Police Department.

Term Definition:

E-commerce is a term generally associated with commercial enterprises. Simply put, it is the act of buying or selling goods electronically, primarily over the Internet. However, as the presence of public organizations expands on the Internet, e-commerce, or **e-government**, is the process of conducting transactions between the public and the government, over the Internet. A developing concept is **m-commerce**, which is the ability to purchase goods and services anytime and anywhere through a wireless Internet-enabled device. *Source:* Clarke, "Emerging Value," 133.

Presume that in addition to being savvy with your cellular telephone, you are an Internet wizard. You have learned to purchase all kinds of merchandise via the Internet. So would you rather go to the police station, stand in line, and pay for the report that they will mail to you in seven to ten days, or would you rather go online, pay for the report, and have it mailed to you in three to five days. This is exactly what is happening in many police departments across the nation. They are beginning to use e-commerce to facilitate commercial transactions with individuals. For the Omaha Police Department, e-commerce is becoming more significant as a business-to-business transaction, especially in the realm of traffic collision reports, which are used primarily by automobile insurance companies.

There are several benefits to government-based e-commerce. First, it gets the user to the Web site. That user is likely to look at other services available at the Web site. E-commerce increases Web traffic. Second, e-commerce improves public satisfaction. If the transaction is not quick and simple, there will be no users. If there are users, they are likely to be satisfied because the service was quick and simple. Moreover, think about your perceptions of the police department. If you order the report online, your expectations are fulfilled. However, if you go to the station and stand in line with the collection of people who find themselves in the lobby of a police station and you have to deal with a desk officer or clerk who is handling the telephones and all of the people in the lobby, no matter how efficient that person at the desk is, it is very likely that your perceptions of the experience are going to be less favorable than had you ordered online.[52]

In addition to improving your experience with the police department, e-commerce has the advantage of allowing the police department to more effectively use their personnel's time. Police departments, like all organizations, experience peak staffing times. No matter how much a police manager tries to deploy personnel in order to even out the workload, there are always going to be unexpected peaks, employee absences, and unexpected lulls. Some agencies fill the lulls by having employees complete e-commerce transactions during lulls in the workload.[53]

Let's stop for a moment and consider a question about efficiency and e-government. One study on e-government looked at the annual purchases of federal, state, and local governments. It found that our government purchases goods and services totaling $568 billion annually. Now private industry has found that by putting services online, it can cut costs by as much as 20 to 25 percent. Well, if we use the business model, it looks like our government could save more than a hundred billion dollars a year by going online.[54] Sounds like we ought to wire up the government now, right? Well, maybe not. Strict comparisons between business models and government often lead to serious disappointment. First, the government is responsible for doing things that are by their very nature inefficient. If there were an efficient way to provide a service that people would pay for, a private firm would probably do it. Second, the more complex e-government becomes, the more people and resources (read as money) are going to be needed to support the operation. So there might be some gain in efficiency by going online (as with the Omaha Police Department reports), but we must carefully examine the resources that were shifted away from one area to support e-government. We might find that there was little or no gain in how we spent the public money. Finally, shifting money to support online resources creates questions of equity (at the end of the chapter one of the discussion questions is designed to help you consider the issue of equity).

It is probably fairly clear to you that the main problem with Web sites is the development and maintenance of content. Content is what the Web site says or does. The actual programming, structure, and issues related to hosting are relatively simple when compared with the problems associated with the content. Many law enforcement agencies underestimate the cost of content, especially the need to change content.[55] If it is not interesting or useful, people are not going to come back.

Between links (partnerships) and e-commerce, a police department can probably significantly increase the traffic to their Web site. Now the task is to increase the

A Look Ahead

In Chapter Twenty ("Implementing and Managing Technology") we are going to examine some of the difficulties in planning, implementing, and managing a technology project like a Web site. One common, recurring theme in all law enforcement technology is how well-trained personnel are often lost to the private sector. For instance, if a police agency develops in-house talent for the construction and maintenance of their Web site, they can find themselves in the position of losing good people. A stellar Web site means the agency has a stellar developer or Webmaster, and the better someone is, the greater the lure of private industry. Of course when someone leaves an agency, the agency can find itself in the position of no one knowing how to update their Web site.

Source: Jorgensen and Cable, "Challenges of E-government," 15.

number of times that users return to the Web site. There are a number of ways to increase return visits. The most obvious is to develop a dynamic and well-thought-out Web site. Additionally, people return to a Web site when they are reminded that there is something useful for them to view at the site. Again, taking a cue from commercial e-commerce, police departments are developing the means to alert users when new and useful information has been posted to the Web site. Many organizations are taking advantage of the listserv concept much like CrimeWeb. As we saw with CrimeWeb, the e-mail notification could take on a variety of forms. It could be an actual newsletter or news digest of some sort, or it could an e-mail that provides you with a link to the Web page with new information.

In addition to e-mail notifications or alerts, Web traffic is increased when the information available at the Web site is likely to change frequently. The more real time the information, the more frequently users are likely to access the information (Figure 10.8). If you return to the San Diego Police Department Web site, you will see that they post nearly real-time crime information (taken from the type of relational database we discussed in Chapters Two, Seven, Eight, and Nine). Moreover, the maps are interactive and the view and data can be changed depending on the user's needs.

E-government

Police agencies are not the only government entities that can benefit from Web sites; the term *e-government* is inclusive of all services. Some political jurisdictions, particularly the larger ones, are using the parent jurisdiction Web site (the municipality is the parent of the police department, the county might be the parent to the sheriff's department, and so on) as a **portal** to all government services.

A **portal** literally means a gateway into something. Portals started out as search engines. They grew from an index to a center that could provide information on a variety of related subjects. For e-government, a portal is a gateway to all of the services offered by the particular jurisdiction.
Source: Cunningham, *B2B,* 9.

The portal concept is gaining ground at the federal level where there are reported to be more than twelve hundred different e-government projects in progress.[56] We will probably find that as e-government matures, technology is going to force us to reorganize our government structure to meet demands. Linkages within portals should allow the community one-stop access to government services. As we know, many community problems cannot be solved by the police themselves. The portal concept relies on hyperlinks to other resources and other organization's resources in a manner that complements the problem solving process. For instance, Web-based mapping like the type you can view at the San Diego Police Department site supports a wide variety of applications, such as resource management, crime prevention, urban planning, education, and community participation.[57] However, this is going to require redesigning service delivery and significant coordination. Just getting different departments within a jurisdiction

As technologies mature and begin to converge, the challenges and opportunities for creative law enforcement increase. For instance, one of the emerging business models concerns the convergence of cellular and Internet technologies. In the private sector, this convergence is providing customers alert notifications to business transactions such as auctions and stock price changes. We are not very far from the day when the CrimeWeb concept could be combined with cellular technology. In the business model, the combination of the Internet-based CrimeWeb service and cellular technology is thought of as location-based marketing. Note that subscribers to CrimeWeb identify the alerts they are interested in by ZIP code. Recall from Chapter Three, one of the defining features of cellular telephone service is the network's ability to keep track of the cellular telephone and hand off service among cell sites. A true convergence of the CrimeWeb technology and cellular technology would entail the subscribers getting notifications based upon which cell site they were currently using.

Source: Clarke, "Emerging Value," 133.

to share the same standards and systems so that everything fits together and offers users the same look and feel is a huge task.[58]

So far we have seen how law enforcement agencies can use the Internet to increase two-way communications with the community, form and strengthen partnerships, and facilitate problem solving. The Internet also has the capability to facilitate situational crime prevention. Recall that situational crime prevention can be defined as reducing the opportunities for a criminal offender. If we can make it more difficult to commit a crime, thereby increasing the effort an offender must expend, crime may be prevented. Typically, we think of this as 'hardening the target.'[59] By using the listserv concept; providing crime prevention information on their Web site; and through nearly real-time, interactive mapping, police agencies can provide the community with information necessary to protect themselves.

Chapter Summary

We have seen that in the beginning the Internet was a big idea that actually started out relatively small. From government efforts to improve communications between defense contractors, employees, and researchers, the idea of a global communications network grew. The two key ideas that finally launched the Internet were determining standard protocols that allowed different networks to communicate and the concept of sending information in data packets. From the Internet, the World Wide Web evolved as people used hyperlinks to create connections to information they determined was consistent and complementary to their information. Essentially, the information highway (the Internet) enabled the creativity that has become the World Wide Web.

The technology of the Internet and the creativity of the World Wide Web spawned the explosion of commercialization. As e-commerce became possible and profitable, government organizations began to look for ways to use the Internet as a means of providing information, communication, and individual transactions. Somewhat slowly, e-government is learning from e-commerce that the power of the Internet is to deliver the content to the community that the community wants. For law enforcement agencies, the content the community wants is Web sites that enhance the community-oriented policing model—two-way communications, partnerships, and problem solving.

As we have seen, a static Web site resembles the professional model of policing in that it is primarily a one-way form of communication. Therefore, law enforcement agencies are increasingly turning to the use of dynamic Web applications that allow them to increase two-way communications, partnerships, and problem solving. Some of these applications are:

- Multimedia applications that enhance text, graphics, audio, and video.
- Relational databases that allow nearly real-time information in the form of text, tables, and maps.
- Multiple means of communications including listserv capabilities, feedback forms, and e-mail to specific officers.
- Hyperlinks to other service organizations and resources.

Although the Web can enhance an agency's community policing efforts, there are challenges. With a finite budget, police executives must make tough decisions about where to spend public money. Dynamic Web sites can be costly to develop and maintain. The shifting of public funds to Web sites brings tough questions about efficiency and equity. The money comes from somewhere. Does it create more public value when it is applied to Web development and maintenance?

In the next chapter, when we look at information exchange, we will build on our knowledge of the previous chapters while looking at some of the problems associated with information exchange in a fragmented environment. We will explore some of the consequences of the inability to communicate on a tactical level and the inability to exchange information about offenders.

Discussion Questions

1. A 1999 study by the National Telecommunications and Information Administration (NTIA) found that a rural, low-income household has a less than one in thirty chance of having Internet access in the home.[60] Because law enforcement agencies have limited budgets, when funds are used to develop a Web site, they can reduce funding to other areas of the department or the parent agency. Because the people who arguably need police services the most have less access to e-police services, do law enforcement agencies unintentionally create service inequities? If so, what do you think a law enforcement agency, or the parent organization, should do to minimize the inequity?

2. It is estimated that the number of people who have Internet access via a mobile communications device, such as a cellular telephone, increased more than 700 percent between 1999 and 2003 (from 7.4 million to 61.5 million).[61] Traditionally, most law enforcement Web sites have targeted the citizens who live in their jurisdiction and have Internet access. Given that mobile Internet users may just be passing through a jurisdiction, are there content or configuration changes law enforcement agencies should consider in order to capitalize on the number of people with mobile Internet access?

3. Surf the Web and find several state and local law enforcement agencies' Web sites. There are some common questions we ask about Web sites in an effort to determine what, if any, standards the organization developed.[62]
   A. Is the site accessible? What meta tags did they use? Are they linked to other organizations?
   B. Is the site easy to use?
   C. Is the site well maintained; do there appear to be constant updates?
   D. Is it interactive?
   E. Is the presentation attractive and effective?
   F. Does it have any e-commerce attributes?

4. If you were building a law enforcement Web site, what would you include and why?

Key Terms

Access Service Provider (ASP)
Auditing
Boolean Logic
Browsers
Cookies
Domain Name
E-commerce
E-government
Home Page
Hyperlink
Hypertext Markup Language (HTML)

Hypertext Transfer Protocol
Index Page
Interception
Internet
Internet Protocol (IP)
Internet Relay Chat (IRC)
Internet Service Provider (ISP)
Listserv
M-commerce

Meta Tags
Navigation
POP (Point of Presence)
Portal
Search Engines
Spam
Spiders
Tags
Universal Resource Locator (URL)
Webmaster
World Wide Web

End Notes

1. Tonry, *Crime and Punishment*, 380.
2. Ibid., 100.
3. Cunningham, *B2B*, 100.
4. Ibid.
5. On July 27, 2003, the Search Engine Google reported that it was searching 3,083,324,652 Web pages.
6. Fletcher, "Government Paperwork Elimination Act," 723.
7. The Internet Society (ISOC) is an organization composed of private individuals, government agencies, commercial companies, and foundations that are a primary force in the past and current development of the Internet. The members of the society also comprise several other organizations such as the Internet Engineering Task Force (IETF) and the Internet Architecture Board (IAB). For a view on the development of the Internet from people who were involved in its creation, a look at current standards, and a glimpse of the future, visit their Web site at **www.isoc.org**/.
8. Cunningham, *B2B*, 100.
9. Ibid., 7.
10. Ibid., 178.
11. Ibid., 174.
12. Ibid., 185.
13. Ismail, Patil, and Saigal, "When Computers Learn to Talk," 71.
14. Zhu, "Web-Based Mapping Applications," 249.
15. Ibid.
16. Cunningham, *B2B*, 178.
17. Bonnett, "ISP-Bound Traffic," 187.
18. Cunningham, *B2B*, 177.
19. Ibid., 185.
20. Ibid., 178.
21. Ibid., 181.
22. Ibid., 171.
23. Ibid., 172.
24. Ibid., 172.
25. Ibid., 175.
26. Ibid., 178.

27. Ibid., 184.
28. Ibid., 178.
29. Ibid., 177.
30. Ibid., 177.
31. See note 14 above.
32. Cunningham, *B2B*, 179.
33. See note 14 above.
34. Cunningham, *B2B*, 182.
35. Ibid., 182–183.
36. Trinkle, *Writing, Teaching, and Researching*, 187.
37. Cunningham, *B2B*, 174.
38. Solove, "Privacy and Power," 1393.
39. See note 17 above.
40. Cunningham, *B2B*, 175.
41. Mccullagh, "Technology as Security," 129.
42. See note 17 above.
43. Cunningham, *B2B*, 178.
44. Watson, "Private Workplace," 79.
45. Spykerman, "E-mail Monitoring."
46. See note 44 above.
47. Cunningham, *B2B*, 179.
48. Cisar, "Police Department Website."
49. Cunningham, *B2B*, 176.
50. Ibid.
51. Ibid., 141.
52. See note 48 above.
53. Ibid.
54. Al-Kibsi, "Putting Citizens On-line," 65.
55. Cunningham, *B2B*, 147.
56. See note 6 above.
57. See note 14 above.
58. See note 54 above.
59. Tonry, *Crime and Punishment,* 380.
60. Jorgensen and Cable, "Facing the Challenges of E-government," 15.
61. Banks, "Wireless Communications," 585.
62. See note 6 above.

Chapter Eleven
Information Exchange

Learning Objectives

- The student will understand the value of information exchange between state, local, and federal agencies.
- The student will understand the issue of **interoperability**.
- The student will understand the various factors that make information exchange difficult.
- The student will understand some of the potential solutions to information exchange, such as XML and various information exchange schemes.

Introduction

"I wish I'd known that." How many times have you heard, said, or thought that? Many times we make decisions based on erroneous or incomplete information. Of course, we only find out about the missing information after the decision has been made. So far we have seen that much of police work and, by extension, the entire criminal justice system is about information.[1] People make decisions all of the time based on the information that they have, and in many instances people are not even aware that other information exists.

In this chapter we will look at information exchange in two primary ways. The first is the exchange of tactical information. As we know, tactical information is the type of information that a police officer uses to make an immediate decision. As we look at tactical information, we will focus primarily on the exchange of tactical information between separate agencies during a tactical occurrence. Recall from Chapter Three the incident wherein at the end of a vehicle pursuit the police officers from different agencies are unable to exchange information about an offender with a gun. This is a tactical exchange of information—concentrating on immediate situations, decisions, and consequences. What we are going to find is that the scenario from Chapter Three is a common occurrence; most state and local agencies cannot communicate at a tactical level, specifically car to car or between field officers.[2]

The other exchange of information is about strategic information. The expectation of the twenty-first century is that information is available at any time and in any place.[3] Information about offenders is held by a wide variety of entities in the total criminal justice system. If you think of criminal justice in a very broad sense, you can find information relevant to individuals in law enforcement databases, court databases, and corrections databases. Later in this chapter we will see examples of how one of the parts of the criminal justice system had information that a separate decision-making part did not. This lack of information can have serious safety consequences for the community and field police officers.[4]

A completely integrated criminal justice system would be a network designed to provide each agency with the information it needs to make a decision. That information, regardless of its source, would be correct, timely, and available in a format compatible with the decision-making entity. So the information would be available to a judge in the court who is making a decision about bail; it is available to the detective who is making a decision about an investigation; it is available to the police manager who is making a decision about deployment; and it is available to the police officer in the street who is making many decisions.[5]

As we explore information exchange, we will see that there are a variety of efforts underway to improve the exchange of justice information. Between 1990 and 2001, the United States Office of Criminal Justice Programs provided state and local governments with more than $184 million to improve information exchange.[6] There are other programs and grants in the hundreds of millions of dollars that have been applied to this problem. Information sharing and exchange is one of the hottest topics in law enforcement. An exploration of some of the consequences of a lack of information exchange will bring the amount of money spent on these projects into perspective.

Why Is the Exchange of Information Important?

Interoperability is the process of connecting different agencies or units with agencies using communication technologies so that they can communicate directly.
Source: "Guide for Selection of Communications Equipment," 11.

On June 1, 1998, the Immigration and Naturalization Service (INS) arrested Rafael Resendez-Ramirez for illegal immigration. Ramirez's arrest occurred at the Sunland Park, New Mexico, border patrol station. After his arrest, the INS agents took his photograph and fingerprints. His fingerprints were run through an INS database for identification. On June 2, since the INS system did not have any information concerning Ramirez, he was returned to Mexico. Unbeknownst to the INS agents, Ramirez was a serial killer who had been dubbed the "railway killer." A few days after his return to Mexico, Ramirez illegally reentered the United States. Between the time of his reentry after INS detention and his eventual arrest, Ramirez is suspected of killing four more people.[7]

In July 1995 a man was arrested in Los Angeles by the California Highway Patrol for a drunk driving–related traffic collision wherein an eighteen-year-old was killed. In California an offender must be charged within forty-eight hours of booking or he is automatically released by the court. In this case, Los Angeles County Sheriff's officials followed the law and released the man because they believed that the CHP officers had not filed charges within the time limit. In Los Angeles County thousands upon thousand of people are arrested by the eighty-plus state and local agencies who have jurisdictions within Los Angeles County. There are more than fifteen million people living in the county. Almost all of the arrests are at some point processed through the Sheriff's Office. Moreover, it is not uncommon for people to be released because charges were not filed. Unfortunately, in this case, local prosecutors had indeed filed charges and placed a warrant in the countywide system, but this is not the normal procedure for notifying the Sheriff's Office. The Sheriff's Office did not check the warrant system, and they released the man.[8]

On April 7, 2000, a man was paroled from the Virginia State Prison. He had just served more than six years for an assault, theft, and obstruction of justice charge. On April 17 he reported to his parole office and was assigned a supervising agent. Later that day, sometime after leaving the parole office, he was arrested in a neighboring county for cocaine possession. By April 19, the man had been released on the cocaine charge and he called his parole agent. He did not tell the parole agent about the arrest on the seventeenth. Sometime during that same day, the man stabbed to death an eight-year-old boy. On April 20, the man failed to keep an appointment with his parole agent, and he failed to appear in the neighboring county courthouse on the cocaine charge. The court immediately issued a warrant, but the parole agent, following office procedures, made several attempts to locate the man. After failing to locate the man, the parole officer sought a warrant for his arrest on May 11. OK, I know this is getting confusing, but this offender is now wanted by one county on a drug charge and by the state for a parole violation, and he has committed a murder for which he has yet to be named as a suspect.

The parole agent got the warrant on May 11, but the agency's policy is that for a parole warrant to be entered into the National Crime Information Center (NCIC) database, the warrant must be approved by the state parole board. So our agent entered the warrant in the first county's local system and sought approval for entry of the warrant into the national system. On June 9 the man was arrested on the court warrant in the second county and released on $2,500 bail; the second county did not know about the parole warrant in the first county, and the state parole board did not ultimately approve the NCIC warrant (which the second county would likely have discovered) until June 19. On June 25 the man was arrested on the parole warrant in NCIC. A few days later, DNA evidence linked him to the murder of the eight-year-old boy.[9]

But data exchange isn't the only problem. The response by different agencies to a tactical incident can also highlight problems with voice integration. On September 11, 2001, after the Pentagon was attacked, Washington, D.C., city officials could not even get a dial tone on the telephone; the mayor and other city officials could contact each other only via e-mail. The vast number of state, federal, local, and regional agencies that responded each had their own radio frequencies. Coordination was difficult. In New York City, the collapse of the World Trade Center destroyed the emergency operations center. Each firefighter in New York City is issued his or her own radio, but those radios broadcast at 400 MHz, whereas the dispatch to the trucks is on 800 MHz. So once away from the trucks, contact with individual firefighters or teams was problematic. The ability for communication among resources responding to an incident has become a "homeland security" issue for government agencies.[10]

However it is not only to major incidents that first responders have difficulty communicating. In Oregon, police, fire, and emergency medical units responded to a shooting call. The police department radios were on a different frequency than the emergency medical services units. At one point while handling the incident, firefighters resorted to using charades-like hand signals to inform the medical personnel of the situation.[11] There are many cases of first responders using outdated or incompatible communications equipment while working at the scene of an emergency.

I wish I could tell you that these examples were isolated and unusual. They are not, and they were chosen as examples not because they were sensational, but because they highlighted different problems with information sharing throughout the criminal justice system. In the first instance, there is the difficulty of federal agencies and state or local agencies sharing information. In the second, there is a large county with more than eighty overlapping jurisdictions—each with its own rules and procedures. Finally, in the third instance, you have two local counties and a state agency, overlapping and contiguous, but unable to share critical information. In these instances, if the people involved had timely and accurate information, they would have made different decisions.

In addition to people not having access to strategic decision-making information, most field police officers communicate tactically with adjoining or overlapping jurisdictions. There are a number of reasons for the inability to share information and tactically communicate (Figure 11.1). As we look at them, some of it will be familiar information from prior chapters. The important point to remember thus far is that the inability to share critical information is

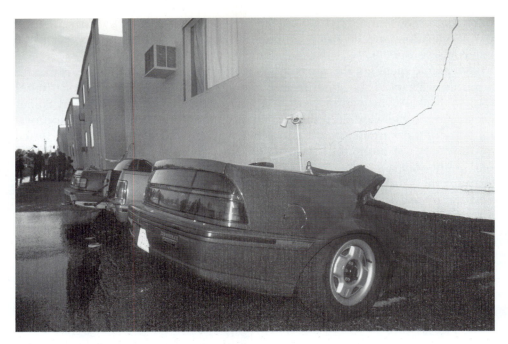

Figure 11.1 Major incidents, like the Northridge earthquake in 1994, tax government emergency communications. Often telephone and power service is interrupted and the problems associated with interoperability are exacerbated.
Photograph provided by Robert Eplett, California Office of Emergency Services.

dangerous. Community members are killed because decisions were made based upon incomplete information. Moreover, police officers are killed because they lack critical information. This isn't a sporadic problem; it is a routine occurrence. Simply put, people would make better decisions with the right information.[12]

Why Can't Agencies Exchange Information?

Recall from Chapters One and Six, we discussed the fact that criminal justice organizations are fragmented for reasons like our desire to maintain a system of checks and balances.[13] We don't need to revisit the reasons for fragmentation. It is here. It is a fact. But the results of fragmentation should be further examined.

In many ways, organizations are like organisms. They are born, they adapt, they grow, and some even die. In fact, there are those who postulate that all organizations, like all organisms, die. Consider that fragmentation has created organizational islands wherein different groups live and adapt. Local and state police agencies are very much like organization islands. Certainly they are influenced by outside forces. New legislations, court decisions, and technology all influence these islands, but the organisms on these islands take that influence and digest it. They accept some of the influence, adapt other parts to fit their schemes, and reject other parts out of hand.

As state and particularly local agencies adapt new ideas and technologies, they tend to adapt them to their ways of doing business. Recall our discussion of the

The Public Safety Wireless Network (PSWN) is a federal government program that started in 1996. The primary objective of the program is to improve public safety wireless communications interoperability. The PSWN is working toward increased interoperability in two primary ways. First, they create partnerships with state and local agencies in an effort to implement interoperability solutions. For instance, they might provide technical assistance in the development of a regional system. Second, they act as a clearinghouse for best practices and technical information. In 2001 PSWN began publishing a national interoperability scorecard that demonstrated the efforts to improve public safety wireless communications across the United States. According to the PSWN scorecard, interoperability had increased 41 percent, from a national score of 40.82 to 57.65, from 2001 to 2003. The PSWN scorecard looks at six issues in interoperability: shared systems, coordination and partnerships, fund, spectrum efficiency, standards and technology, and security. The scorecard is based upon information collected from state-level communications personnel. You can view your state's scorecard on an interactive map provided at **www.publicsafetywins.gov/**.

Source: "PSWN Program."

National Incident-Based Reporting System in Chapter Nine; some states added to the reporting requirements. They adapted the new idea to fit their ways of doing things. So our state and local law enforcement islands end up with an assortment of systems, applications, databases, and communications schemes.[14] Moreover, many of these technologies are proprietary or incompatible with neighboring schemes.

Some technological incompatibility is unavoidable. For instance, as we learned in Chapter Three, there are only so many radio frequencies to go around, and it makes sense that on a day-to-day basis, state and local agencies have their own radio frequencies. So to get the most out of the available frequencies, the government reissues the same frequency to organizations that are far enough apart that they will not interfere with each other. That's a pretty good idea, except if you want to talk to the jurisdiction next door because many radios are designed so they can only broadcast on your frequency.[15]

Characteristically, the entire criminal justice system tends to perform the function of information management exchange very poorly because each island (including courts and corrections) enters information into the system separately, differently, and often repeatedly.[16]

We have different codes and terms, different radio frequencies, and different and often incompatible equipment. These barriers to integration tend to undermine all of our other efforts to capture, organize, retain, and analyze data. A lack of interagency data exchange leads not only to bad decisions, but to users becoming less interested in using computerized systems.[17] Because each state and local agency tends to be a technological island, they are separate organisms, sometimes competing to be successful. An integration effort has to build on current infrastructure and capabilities.[18] While there are a number of programs underway designed to improve information sharing, the most we have are partial efforts and specific solutions.[19] However, there are some common concepts that all law enforcement information sharing schemes should share.

The tables of codes listed below represent two different, albeit common, radio code systems used in state and local law enforcement. Many professions like law enforcement developed their own language. Shorthand terms and phrases can make work more efficient and safe. *Moreover, organizations that are technological islands probably develop even more distinct language peculiarities. One of the problems in communication between agencies, or **interoperability**, is the different languages police officers speak. From state to state, the system of laws (often referred to as a penal code) has different sections for different crimes. When police officers in California talk about a murder suspect, they tend to say a 187 suspect because 187 is the general section of the Penal Code making murder illegal. Murder is illegal in all of the other forty-nine states, but if you told an officer in another state you were looking for a 187 suspect, would she know what you were talking about? The solution is to remind ourselves that during interagency, real-time tactical situations we must use plain language to avoid misunderstandings.

Code 1 – Answer on radio
Code 2 – Proceed immediately w/o siren
Code 3 – Proceed w/ siren and red lights
Code 4 – No further assistance necessary
Code 4A – No further assistance is necessary, but suspect is not in custody
Code 5 – Uniformed officers stay away
Code 6 – Out of car to investigate
Code 6A – Out of car to investigate, assistance may be needed
Code 6C – Suspect is wanted and may be dangerous
Code 7 – Out for lunch

Code 8 – Fire alarm
Code 9 – Jail break
Code 10 – Request clear frequency
Code 12 – False alarm
Code 13 – Major disaster activation
Code 14 – Resume normal operations
Code 20 – Notify news media to respond
Code 30 – Burglar alarm ringing
Code 33 – Emergency! All units stand by
Code 99 – Emergency!
Code 100 – In position to intercept

10-1 – Unable to copy
10-2 – Message received
10-4 – Relay my message
10-6 – Stand by
10-7 – Out of service
10-8 – In service
10-9 – Please repeat message
10-10 – Prisoner present at . . .
10-13 – Agent needs assistance
10-15 – Residence
10-16 – Change frequency

10-19 – Return to . . .
10-20 – Location
10-21 – Call . . . by landline
10-22 – Disregard
10-25 – Respond to . . .
10-28 – Registration check
10-30 – Subscriber information
10-33 – Emergency traffic
10-99 – Emergency! Agent needs assistance
10-100 – Radio silence

* Shafritz, *Public Policy and Administration*, 992.

What Should Integration Look Like?

Before we look at some of the potential solutions to the problem of a lack of integrated justice systems, we need to determine what an integrated system would look like. First, an integrated criminal justice information sharing system must fulfill the needs of the agency employing the system and address the needs of agencies. For instance, an integrated jail management system would not only help the local agency manage its own jail, but be able to pass information on to the next decision-making portion of the criminal justice system. If an offender were being transferred from a municipal jail to a county facility, both the county facility and the offender would benefit from having information concerning the medical needs transmitted, or at least available, to the receiving agency.[20] Any system change must benefit both the agency making the change and the agencies with which it shares information.

For any system integration to be successful, it must be founded on standards in data elements, protocols, policies, applications, and hardware systems.[21] In our examples we saw that agencies in the criminal justice system need information to make decisions at critical points.[22] These exchanges of information can be thought of as transactions between the different agencies. Some of these transactions occur at fairly regular and predictable intervals.[23] When an offender is arrested, a police report is written. That report must go to the prosecuting agency. The prosecuting agency makes a decision to file, and the case appears before the court.

For these transactions to be complete, they need to employ several different concepts. The first is **context**, which is an agreement between the agencies that the exchange is going to be about a certain subject. If you call directory assistance, you are calling to get a telephone number. The context of your conversation is about the telephone number. The next concept is protocol.[24] We learned in Chapter Ten that protocol is the rules for how the information is going to be exchanged. In information sharing between criminal justice agencies, the idea of protocols is somewhat expanded to include an agreement on how the information will be used. Integration of procedures is often the key to successful systems integration.[25] Moreover, protocols would include agreements on minimum security levels and procedures for linked agencies. Generally speaking, issues of security can be taken care of by an agreement on the rules regarding access and various methods to detect breaches. Among the methods we discussed in previous chapters were auditing and user passwords.[26]

In an intergrated system, information would be captured once and reused during subsequent decision-making points.[27] Recall from Chapter Seven, a considerable amount of information is captured in the dispatch center. That information is usually organized by incident numbers created by the computer-aided dispatch. A fully integrated system would use the incident number as a reference number throughout the justice process, so a subsequent criminal filing, court decision, and action by correction officials would always reference that original incident number.

A fully integrated system would have the ability to automatically query databases of other organizations. Recall from Chapter Eight that a good records management system allowed local police officers access to NCIC information. This is an example of an intergrated system being able to pull information from other sources. A good system would have the ability to push data, too. In the example of a prisoner transfer, the medical records of the prisoner are pushed from the local jail to the county facility.

Now the interesting thing about data transfer is you generally don't need all of the information. When you ask someone for their address, do you expect to get their address, telephone number, date of birth, and mother's maiden name? Probably not. If we transferred all the data, agencies would be transferring quite a bit of information that receiving agencies don't need. In our example of a prisoner transfer, the receiving jail probably doesn't need to know the arresting officer, the vehicle the offender was driving, or any information about evidence. However, when the offender's case goes to the prosecuting agency, they need the police officer's information, but probably not the information about medications the offender is taking. In an integrated system, only data that is needed is pushed and pulled. Finally, a characteristic of an integrated system is the ability to receive notifications. An example of a notification might be when an offender fails to show for a court date, the court issues a warrant, which is placed into regional and national warrant systems. The court also sends a notification to the agency that made the initial arrest.

Establishing protocols, procedures, and policies can take care of some of the issues, but information exchange, or interoperability, has two other primary dimensions: **interchangeability** and **connectability**. Interchangeability refers to things being substitute goods. For instance, there are two primary diet colas on the market. If someone wanted a diet cola, you could substitute one for the other. The person may have an argument about taste, but in essence, the two products can be substituted. Connectability is the way that different products can work together without having a third product bridge the operation.[28] If you travel throughout the United States, your clock radio can plug into just about every hotel wall outlet, but if you travel to Europe, where they use 220 volts instead of our 110 volts, you need a third product between your clock radio and the power grid. Without the third product, your clock radio is not connectable. So how do we connect up disparate databases, systems, and networks?

Extensible Markup Language

Those of you who paid attention in the first ten chapters are probably wondering why law enforcement agencies aren't using Web-based standards. After all, the functionality of the Internet is based upon standard network, data, and communications protocols. Recall that TCP/IP standard protocols made the Internet possible.[29] So the question is, if millions of people around the world can access billions of pages of Web-based information, why can't state and local law enforcement agencies use the same methods? Well, we saw in our look at wireless communications and dispatch centers that the exchange of information is becoming more IP-based. Actually, much of the NCIC scheme presumes the use of IP standards. But even the use of IP standards in network and systems development leaves a big hole in the plan.

With IP standards, networks can deliver information. The question is, what information? Recall that agencies need only certain portions of each other's data and that because of fragmentation the databases are often incompatible; the data fields, values, and attributes are nonstandard and even the architecture of the databases is often different. So information in databases can't be passed with just IP standards.

The first thing we need is a programming language that allows us to pick and choose what we want to send and receive. One of the most promising avenues is the use of **extensible markup language (XML)**. Recall from the previous chapter that we briefly discussed how most Web designers use hypertext markup language (HTML) to create Web pages. As we know, HTML is one of the overriding standards that make visual displays of IP-based information possible. Since I have

In 1998 the National Institute for Justice began a program designed to address the issues inherent in voice communication interoperability. The Advanced Generation of Interoperability for Law Enforcement (AGILE) program approaches the problem of information sharing on three fronts. As we saw in Chapter Ten, the NIJ conducts research, development, tests, and evaluations of law enforcement–related equipment. One of the approaches they are using with communications interoperability is to fund projects designed to develop technology for use by state and local law enforcement agencies. The NIJ is also involved in the identification and development of open architecture standards (like XML) that will facilitate the exchange of information with both voice and data transmissions. Finally, the NIJ continues to conduct numerous education programs that provide law enforcement officials with information on best practices and lessons learned.

Source: "Toward Improved Criminal Justice."

a Web browser that can translate HTML into a visual display, I can use the Internet. XML is a root markup language that is derived from and similar in some ways to HTML.[30] XML is intended primarily for the transmission of text information, but it can be used to pass other binary data such as images.[31] The programming language XML makes information exchange possible by using "tags" to identify information so disparate applications and systems can easily recognize the data.[32] Recall when we looked at the source code for HTML-based Web pages, we could see the tags that separated the instructions for our browsers. XML performs a similar task, and these tags can be specifically designed or created for any law enforcement application.

Hypertext Markup Language (HTML)	Extensible Markup Language (XML)
Describes data content only.	Describes data content, format, and presentation and provides for application control over data.
Viewed with a Web browser only.	Can be viewed by a variety of applications.
Nonextensible markup.	Extensible markup enables the creation of client-specific applications.
No context or access control.	Context and access control.

This table outlines the differences between HTML and XML.

Because we are not going to be programmers, our explanation and demonstration of XML is necessarily shallow. There is a quite a bit of knowledge necessary to be a good programmer, but we want to be educated end users. The XML tags to represent that the data is someone's name would be:

```
<subjectName>
<last>Foster</last>
<first>Raymond</first>
<middle>E</middle>
<suffix>Sr</suffix>
  </subjectName>
```

As you can see in the example, the symbols < > mark the beginning and end of the tag and the data. The field identifier for the overall name is <subjectName>; another example would be <eyeColor>, and so on. Recall in the previous chapter that HTML also uses tags, but HTML would identify a name simply as text:

With previous applications security issues were minimized by the nature of the networks and systems. In other words, a closed system had a way of controlling access. But, XML is IP based and proposes that sensitive data be passed using protocols that everyone with Internet access is somewhat familiar. Giving open access through IP based protocols is nearly the opposite of security. One of the ways to further ensure security is through the use of Security Assertion Markup Language (SAML) which is used to define data exchange security measures. SAML was adopted as the Technical Committee of the Organization for the Advancement of Structured Information Standards (OASIS). OASIS is a non-profit group working on e-government and e-business standards. You can visit their website at **www.oasis-open.org**.

Source: Robinson, "Solving the XML Dilemma."

Raymond E. Foster, Sr. You can see that XML turns the concept of the Web-based HTML code from a flat file of text to a relational database of usable information.

For instance, using these tags to separate out the data, an agency could query another agency's database and examine the entire database, taking only the information they need. Essentially, XML codes data so it has meaning and can be easily searched and analyzed.[33] The secret of XML is that it separates style from content. Style is the way in which an agency decides it wants the data presented—what the city jail wants to see as opposed to what the county facility wants to see. The content is the part of the total that each picks for its own style.[34] XML doesn't solve all of the problems of information exchange. There still needs to be context.[35] Rules must still be developed between the agencies that indicate what relevant information is. Recall, context is the subject of the inquiry.

Now one of the things we need to consider is that if agencies are going to use XML, the standards begin with the Internet. That means that as time passes, any new or upgraded system must be IP based.[36] For XML to work, we still need to have a standard data dictionary.[37] Without standards, developing XML tags is just developing another stand-alone system that no one outside your jurisdiction can use.[38] One solution to the problem of national standards is being tackled by the Joint Task Force on Rap Sheet Standardization. This project, which is sponsored by the Federal Bureau of Investigation, has the mission of implementing a national standard for the exchange of criminal history information.

It would be premature to believe that XML applications will solve all data transferring and exchange problems in law enforcement. There are still a number of issues and problems, primary among them the creation of a data dictionary and the acceptance of IP-based communications strategies.[39] However, XML is one of the more promising solutions.

Tactical Communications

There are a significant number of anecdotal stories wherein one law enforcement agency could not communicate with another during a tactical operation. As we have found, this could be because they had different frequencies or incompatible equipment. It is very common during joint operations for agencies to loan radios to each other. Then there is a link between them. Of course, this still becomes a relayed communication, but it helps to alleviate the inability to talk.

As we have seen throughout the text, the differences in radio frequencies and radio equipment are very common. There are a great many reasons for this arrangement, and we have covered most of them. In short, there are two common technological strategies and one operational strategy that can improve communications between different agencies.

The first common technological solution is through the use of trunked radio systems (recall trunked radio systems from Chapter Three).[40] Some trunked radio systems do allow for the programming of other agency frequencies into the radio system carried in a police vehicle. However, the conversion to a trunked radio system may be expensive. Some larger agencies are programming in talk groups that include the frequencies of agencies that overlap or are contiguous. In the instances where a trunked system is used, there should still be operational agreements between the larger agency and the generally smaller agencies.

A second method is to provide some type of gateway interface between different agencies. This gateway could be either a permanently installed technology or one that is used during major tactical incidents. A communications interface system can allow telephones like the one depicted in Figure 11.2, cellular telephones, and radios on different frequencies to communicate together. In essence, the connection system is like a giant switchboard where you connect radios in and the system switches the transmission around depending on the source destination.[41] It is something like the instance where agencies trade radios for joint operations, but instead of trading radios and having human beings act as the interface, it is connected to a gateway that routes the transmissions around.

A third solution involves the use of the Incident Command System (ICS). In Chapter Seventeen, when we look at major incident and disaster response technology, we will spend a considerable amount of time discussing the ICS. It is enough to say that ICS provides common terminology and organizational structures for successful joint field operations.

Figure 11.2 The photograph here depicts interface hardware that can be used for interagency communications during tactical operations.
Source: Kaluta, "New Developments." *Photograph provided by Robert Eplett, California Governor's Office of Emergency Services.*

Agency Partnerships

One of the most popular local-level strategies for crime prevention is the use of agency partnerships.[42] In addition to working on problems directly related to crime, there are ways that agency partnerships can improve interoperability and the exchange of data information. We are going to look at four possible partnership configurations. First, we will look at the direct pooling of physical resources and how that can be used and considered in information sharing. A second and closely related method is to pool just data, not actual facilities. Third, we will look at schemes wherein a smaller agency might decide to contract communications with a larger agency. Finally, we will look at the creation of regional systems.

There are two ways of looking at information-integration partnerships. The first is a horizontal integration between agencies at the same level of government. So if three local agencies come together to form a partnership, this is considered a **horizontal partnership**. The second type is vertical. A vertical partnership is probably more complex because it involves agencies at varying levels of government. For instance, a partnership between local, state, and federal authorities would be a **vertical partnership**.[43]

Almost every discussion about regional systems and related schemes like resource pooling starts off with a commentary on the savings benefits an organization will realize through gaining "**economy of scale**."[44] **Economy of scale** is based upon the economic theory that the more you produce of a good, the less that it costs for each additional unit. Generally, in government service, economy of scale is realized by expanding the geographic boundaries of service.

Take, for instance, three small cities. They are all right next to each other, sharing common boundaries. Each of them has their own aging dispatch center. They decide that instead of each purchasing a new dispatch center, they will purchase one center and run the communications dispatch for all three communities from one location. Instead of three buildings, three base stations, and three computer systems, they need purchase only one. They share the cost, so they achieve economy of scale by enlarging the geographic area of the dispatch center by a factor of three, and realize a savings of two-thirds each. Sounds pretty good. Maybe.

First, upwards of 85 percent of most state and local law enforcement budgets are personnel costs, not equipment costs, so to find out the true savings of this scheme the question has to be how many fewer people will it take to run one center, as opposed to three. There will probably be some savings, but not two-thirds of the cost, over the long term. Second, questions concerning the merging of policies and procedures must be addressed. Among the policies and procedures are work rules, common terms, and even more complex issues like vehicle pursuit policy.

Sometimes, because of the policy and procedure issues, local governments are reluctant to directly pool resources. Consider what would happen after a local agency dispatcher went to work at the three-agency dispatch center. Who does that person actually work for? What if there is a citizen complaint or an employee problem? What if there are union agreements in place for one or more of the agencies, but not the other(s)? Moreover, in addition to these sometimes thorny issues, there is the wider impact of pooling the one resource of communications on the remaining systems. Recall, computer-aided dispatch information is often the source of crime analysis information and information for decisions on personnel allocation. If an agency changes the CAD system, they may have to change or upgrade their records management system, jail management system, or evidence management system. With technology, you can rarely change just one thing. So while it is possible to directly pool physical resources, there are a large number of considerations.

Information sharing is the transfer of information from one system to another via an intermediate system.[45] Instead of actually pooling facilities, agencies just agree to send their data to a central **data warehouse**.[46] Under this scheme, the involved agencies agree to send their information to a central facility, and all of the other participants can use the information. This gets the data pushed and pulled fairly effectively, but it does not address voice communications. Of course, as with nearly all information sharing, there has to be an agreement on protocol, procedures, and policies.

In some instances, a local agency may decide to contract their information services with either a private vendor or with a larger agency. We will look a little closer at contracting with private firms in Chapter Twenty, so let's just take a brief look at contracting to a larger agency. Typically these schemes are used by a small municipal police department that decides to contract certain services with the county law enforcement agency, typically a sheriff's department. Essentially, for a predetermined fee, the larger agency conducts the public safety answering point, computer-aided dispatch, and radio systems maintenance, and controls access to databases. This is probably the least favorite scheme of local agencies because of the perception that they may lose their identity. Imagine you call 9-1-1 and the sheriff's department answers the telephone, who would you think you received law enforcement service from—your local city police or the sheriff? Also, there have been several cases wherein the contracting fee is initially a good bargain. After an agency contracts with the sheriff, they often dispose of their equipment and reassign the personnel. Then the fee creep begins. In one California community it took only five years for the contract fee to exceed the cost of owning and operating a dispatch center.

So far we have somewhat concentrated in this section on a relatively broad cost—benefit analysis of these first three schemes—but we shouldn't be to shortsighted in our evaluation of the benefits. Even if the systems cost more, there is the distinct likelihood that the improvements in information sharing and interoperability will reap unknown benefits. We cannot predict the major disaster or incident that was managed much better because everyone could talk. We cannot predict the number of mistakes that are avoided in the release and incarceration of offenders. But we do know that a failure to share information routinely has dire consequences.

The final configuration we are going to visit is a regional system. An increasing trend in law enforcement information sharing is for agencies to come together and form joint communications projects. These are the true regional systems that are characterized by multiple horizontal and vertical integrations. Sometimes these ventures are referred to as **intergovernmental agreements (IGA)** or **joint powers authorities (JPA)**. In some instances, agencies will form not-for-profit organizations in order to create and manage a regional system.

The best way to explore this increasing trend is to examine one of the more successful regional systems. In the San Diego area of California, the Advanced Regional Justice Information System (ARJIS) is a regional system that combines the resources of thirty-eight local, state, and federal agencies into one criminal justice information sharing network. In the late 1970s a federal grant to the San Diego Police Department resulted in the formation of the ARJIS JPA.

A **special service district (SSD)** can be a private, military, or government organization employing security guards, law enforcement personnel, or emergency medical service personnel who provide services to unique communities or locations. For instance, many colleges and universities have some type of public safety department. Because most SSDs have overlapping jurisdictions with state or local law enforcement agencies, they often work together.
Source: "PSWN Program."

Ten members of ARJIS are considered official members while twenty-eight members are ex officio. The official members represent the local agencies that have actual geographic responsibility for day-to-day police services in the ARJIS area. They consist of nine municipal police agencies and the San Diego County Sheriff's Department. The exofficio members are state and local agencies from all parts of the criminal justice system.

In order to show the complexity necessary for the procedural and policy coordination, a brief look at the structure of ARJIS is necessary. The are actually two agreements that determine the structure and delineate the decision making in the ARJIS regional system. The first is the JPA. The JPA is the general agreement between all of the ARJIS members. It delineates their purpose, rules, procedures, and funding. For instance, the JPA states the composition and authority of the governing board. The board of directors is composed of the two political officials from each of the official member organizations. They are the mayors or city council members of the cities. This governing board meets monthly and makes decisions including the annual operating budget.

Earlier in this section of the chapter we talked about the complex policy and procedure discussions that would be necessary for an agency partnership. It is likely that one of the things that makes ARJIS successful is the involvement of political leadership in a policy-setting role. Through the second document that governs ARJIS activities, the by-laws, the more day-to-day matters are delegated by the board of directors to committees that are composed of law enforcement and technology professionals.

Although a federal grant was the genesis of the project, ARJIS is now funded by all of the participating agencies. The officer-member agencies reimburse ARJIS for expenses based upon their population and usage while exoffico members are billed 50 percent over their actual usage to support the network. In addition, each agency pays for the number of terminals that have access to ARJIS.

So what does it do? ARJIS, in addition to being an information-sharing scheme, is also a powerful investigative tool. Recall that in Chapter Ten ARJIS was one of the Web sites you were encouraged to visit. At their site, you can create nearly real-time crime maps. In the next chapter, when we discuss crime analysis, the value of crime mapping will become more apparent. Additionally, ARJIS, through a secure intranet, integrates more than 2,500 workstations throughout the 4,265 square miles of San Diego County. ARJIS has more than 10,000 users who generate more than 35,000 transactions each day. Through ARJIS, users can query databases of regional crime cases, arrests, citations, field interviews, traffic accidents, and gang information. In addition to the regional information, ARJIS provides users with access to a wide variety of state and local databases like motor vehicle information and the National Crime Information Center.

ARJIS is a composite of a central mainframe and client server applications that are accessible via a secure intranet. The actual hardware and software are located in the City of San Diego. Much of ARJIS data is updated in real time from member agency computer-aided dispatch records. Recent improvements to ARJIS include access to digital photographs and the ability for data entry into the ARJIS system by field units via laptop computers in police vehicles.

One of the things that make ARJIS unique and successful not only in terms of information sharing, but also as a criminal investigative tool, is its membership. In addition to giving ARJIS members access to shared data, it gives them access to people involved in these organizations. It is likely that the personal relationships developed from membership in ARJIS are as important as the technology. A look at the membership will give you a good idea of how comprehensive the membership has become: Carlsbad Police Department, La Mesa Police Department, Chula Vista Police Department, National City Police Department, Coronado Police Department, Oceanside Police Department, El Cajon Police Department, San Diego Police Department, Escondido Police Department, and San Diego Sheriff's Department.

Ex Officio Members of ARJIS: Bureau of Alcohol, Tobacco, and Firearms; San Diego State University Police; California Department of Insurance; San Diego Superior Court; California Department of Justice; U.S. Border Patrol; Donovan Correctional Facility; U.S. Customs Service; Federal Bureau of Investigation; U.S. Drug Enforcement Administration; Internal Revenue Service; U.S. Forest Service; Naval Criminal Investigative Service; U.S. Immigration and Naturalization Service; San Diego City Attorney; U.S. Marshal's Service; San Diego City Schools Police; U.S. Postal Service; San Diego County District Attorney; U.S. Pretrial; San Diego County Marshal's Office; U.S. Probation; San Diego County Probation; U.S. Secret Service; San Diego Harbor Police; and University of California, San Diego.

Chapter Summary

The better the information you have, the better decisions you are capable of making. Time and again, we hear people lament that they would have done something differently if they had only had more information. Yet in criminal justice, especially for the field officer, there isn't time for research. The information to make a decision is either available now or not available at all. Information sharing and interoperability are about getting critical information to people who are making critical decisions.

Justice system integration falls under two broad categories; data integration, such as crime and arrest information, and voice communications. As we have seen from the few examples provided, there can be dire consequences when state and local law enforcement agencies are unable to share information or communicate. There are a variety of reasons for the inability to share information and communicate and most of them stem from the fragmentation of policing in our country. As we saw, this fragmentation is not only a technological issue, but in many ways an organizational culture issue. Moreover, there are many practical reasons, such as the need to have dedicated primary radio frequencies and issues related to frequency spectrum efficiency.

In addition to providing the agencies and community with the benefit of increased safety, information sharing can improve decision making at all levels of the criminal justice system. It can reduce staff and workload by eliminating the need to enter the same information into different systems. Over the long run, increased information sharing and interoperability can make state and local law enforcement more efficient and effective.

There are two basic technological ways to overcome the inability to communicate via radio. One involves the installation and use of trunked radio systems and the other involves the installation and use of a device that trunks disparate systems together. In the case of a tactical incident, there is an organizational strategy that can mitigate some of the communications problems—the Incident Command System.

We looked at XML as a means of providing information sharing via IP standards. The ideas surrounding XML as a means of being able to pull only the data an agency needs are fairly new, and the issues of standards and security protocols remain to be completely solved.

We looked at four types of agency partnerships. In each of those, there are policy and procedural issues that are often more difficult to surmount than the technical issues. We spent most of the time looking at ARJIS because of its governing structure and the resulting network of information services. ARJIS is successful because of the involvement of political leadership, the delegation of practical matters to experts, and the inclusion of different types of agencies.

Discussion Questions

1. The use of Web-based services has the potential to integrate not only law enforcement data, but also data from other sources. It would be possible for law enforcement officials to have ready access to building permits, liquor licensing, and even municipally owned utility records. What new ways to interact with the other aspects of state and local government do you see? What problems and opportunities will emerge?

2. Exercise: In 1996 the Public Safety Wireless Network (PSWN) program was established by the federal government. The focus of the program is to improve public safety wireless communications interoperability. The PSWN Web site has a unique online tutorial program that uses fictional case histories as a means to explore the issues in interoperability. As you use the tutorial, you will be asked to make decisions about the direction the fictional public safety employee should take. You can experience the results of these decisions online. Go to **www.pswn.gov/libdetail.cfm?secid=33** and choose one of their tutorials:
   A. Shared System Development through Coordination and Partnership.
   B. Formulating Successful Funding Strategies for Shared System Development.

3. Visit a state, local, or campus police station. What level of information sharing or interoperability do they have?

4. Discuss an incident wherein you would have made a better decision if only you'd known.

Key Terms

Connectability
Context
Data Warehouse
Economy of Scale
Extensible Markup
  Language (XML)

Horizontal Partnership
Interchangeability
Intergovernmental
  Agreements (IGA)
Interoperability

Joint Powers Authorities
  (JPA)
Special Service District
  (SSD)
Vertical Partnership

End Notes

1. Blumstein, Young, and Granholm, "Commentaries," 1.
2. Kaluta, "New Developments."
3. Clarke, "Emerging value propositions," 133.
4. "Toward Improved Criminal Justice."
5. Geerken, *Consequences,* 3.

6. Pastore and Maguire, "*Sourcebook of Criminal Justice Statistics*."
7. Geerken, *Consequences,* 18.
8. Ibid., 22.
9. Ibid., 23.
10. Perlman, "Can We Talk."
11. Ibid.
12. Blumstein, Young, and Granholm, "Commentaries," 1.
13. Ibid.
14. See note 12 above.
15. See note 10 above.
16. See note 12 above.
17. Nunn, "Police Information Technology," 221.
18. Roberts, "Integration," 12.
19. Cresswell, et al., *And Justice for All,* 12.
20. Roberts, "Integration," 5.
21. Cresswell, *And Justice for All,* 22.
22. Roberts, "Integration," 7.
23. Ibid., 8.
24. Ibid., 9.
25. "Toward Improved Criminal Justice."
26. See note 12 above.
27. Roberts, "Integration," 11.
28. Band and Katoh, *Interfaces on Trial,* 5.
29. Band and Katoh, *Interfaces on Trial,* 41.
30. "Putting Web Services in a No-Spin Zone," 16.
31. "XML Specification," 4.
32. Robinson, *Solving the XML Enigma.*
33. Steins and Chavan, "Technology Trends," 28.
34. Cunningham, *B2B*; 111.
35. Cunningham, *B2B*, 110.
36. Oscar, "E-Commerce Architecture," 11.
37. "Toward Improved Criminal Justice."
38. See note 36 above.
39. "Putting Web Services in a No-spin zone," 16.
40. "Guide for the Selection of Communications Equipment," 11.
41. Ibid.
42. Tonry, *Crime and Punishment*, 379.
43. Roberts, "Integration," 4.
44. Aronson, "Management Police," 79.
45. See note 4 above.
46. Roberts, "Integration," 4.

Chapter Twelve
Crime Analysis

Learning Objectives

- The student will understand the definition of crime analysis and some of its underpinning theories such as **situational crime prevention**, **routine activity theory** and **displacement**.

- The student will understand the applications of crime analysis particularly as a method to identify **hot spots** and as a means to investigate **serial offenders**.

- The student will be exposed to how crime analysis can be used to solve community problems and advanced crime mapping topics like **geographic profiling**.

Introduction

In Chapter Five, when we examined geographic information systems (GISs), we found that GIS has several roles in law enforcement, such as automatic vehicle locator (AVL) systems and crime analysis. In the chapter on GIS, we briefly touched upon the subject of crime analysis. Now, as we take a much more in-depth look at the subject of crime analysis, we will find that while GIS is an integral part of the process, there are other statistical methodologies, theories, and practices that make up the art of crime analysis.

Early on in Chapter One, we talked about community policing and one of its alternative models, problem-oriented policing. It is important to remember that without the component of criminal investigations, neither model of policing is valuable. At the core, the functions of state and local law enforcement remain prevention, investigation, and apprehension. The new models are ways of making state and law enforcements' efforts at their primary mission more efficient. However, both models emphasize that police officers need to develop techniques and tactics that make their efforts at prevention, investigation, and apprehension better.[1] Crime analysis is one of those tactics.

The use of crime analysis by state and local law enforcement agencies is increasing. In 2000 15 percent of state and local police departments, including a large majority of those serving 100,000 or more residents, conducted some type of crime analysis. Moreover, because the state and local police departments that were conducting some kind of crime analysis tended to be larger agencies, in total they employed more than 59 percent of all police officers nationwide.[2] Crime analysis and crime mapping originally started with police officers placing pins in a map on a wall. This gave them a visual representation of what was going on and where they should go to have the greatest impact on crime.[3]

Crime Analysis and Community-Oriented Policing

Recall in Chapters One and Six we briefly looked at the community-oriented policing (COP) model. During our look, we examined two social science theories that are important to COP: normative sponsorship theory and critical social theory. A crucial part of the critical social theory is problem solving. Along with forming a partnership with the community, problem solving is a critical component of the COP model. Through partnerships, problems are identified and

HOT TIP

The chapters in this textbook on geographic information systems, communication dispatch centers, and agency systems have laid the foundation for much of the material presented in this chapter.

A quick review of the main points of those chapters and the key terms will probably help you understand the concepts presented in this chapter.

solutions agreed upon. The lion's share of the literature on COP notes that most of the incidents that the police respond to are simply symptoms of some underlying problem. An essential part of problem solving, and thus COP, is an examination of incidents, their relationships to each other, and their relationships to underlying problems. This type of problem solving requires an examination of a large amount of information and means to organize, store, and retain that information.[4] While community input and assistance with problems are vital, police officers are still the paid full-time employees who the community expects to take the lead in problem solving. One of the ways that police officers use their expertise in problem solving is through the analysis of crime.

Crime analysis starts with crime mapping, which begins with the principle that crime is not as random as it seems. A crime or a series of crimes may be the result of a variety of other factors. By examining the geographic placement of crime, we may be able to see those other factors and find clues to uncover the identity of the offender. Crime mapping is about problem solving, about the identification of the problem and about using the information gained from analysis to mitigate the problem.[5]

Essentially, crime analysis is problem solving. We know that problem solving is an essential component of the COP model. While there are different methods of problem solving, all of them include analysis of the problem as a step in their methodology. For instance, one of the most prevalent problem-solving methodologies used by police departments is **Scanning–Analysis–Response–Assessment (SARA)**. As we shall see in this chapter, the SARA steps of scanning, analysis, and response are in many ways very similar to crime analysis. We shall find out that police departments that are not conducting crime analysis are unlikely to be fully involved in community-oriented policing.

What Are the Benefits of Crime Analysis?

The first benefit crime analysis provides is the ability to show relationships between crime and casual factors. These relationship factors may be **spatial** in nature. In other words, the crime may be resulting from its proximity to a location. Recall our discussion on driving under the influence. An analysis of traffic collisions could tell us that the proximate cause of the collisions was alcohol, and a more in-depth analysis may show that the number of alcohol-related traffic collisions is near a neighborhood bar.

When we looked at that scenario earlier, we presumed that by using GIS information, the traffic collisions were related to the bar solely based upon their geographic proximity. As we get further into detailed crime analysis, we will find that in addition to the geographic information, crime analysts also look at other information. Perhaps in this case, the geographic proximity of the bar to the traffic collisions was supported by statements made by the people involved in the incidents as to the last place they were drinking alcohol. In addition to a

SARA is a relatively straightforward process that involves scanning your area of responsibility for problems, conducting a reasonably in-depth analysis of the source of the problem and resources available to assist with the problem's solution, designing and implementing a response to the problem, and assessing the effectiveness of your solution. Although straightforward, there is substantial literature devoted to a detailed explanation of each of the steps involved in the SARA process.
Source: Shafritz, *Public Policy and Administration*, 445.

spatial relationship, crimes could be related by time, something about the victim, or something about the offender, to name a few.

Crime analysis also promotes information integration and cooperation among different police agencies and among the police and other government agencies. For instance, much of the data a police crime analyst may use can come from other government agencies. The analyst may use information from the local planning department or a regional planning department, like a county. They may use Census Bureau information from the federal government. These uses of information from other government agencies establish liaisons and communication feedback loops. Additionally, criminals don't operate within just one police agency's jurisdiction. They often cross jurisdictional boundaries, from one city to the next, or they may be committing crimes within overlapping jurisdictions. For instance, a car burglar may be operating on a college campus that has its own police department and in the city that contains the campus. Increasingly, crime analysts are forming regional groups to discuss trends, exchange information, and foster professional development. In addition to crime analysts promoting cross-jurisdiction communications, they, unlike their parent organizations, often use similar hardware and software and speak in similar technical terms. All of these factors increase communications and cooperation among agencies.

In addition to lending itself to problem solving, crime analysis and its related technology are a COP enhancer because they can assist in the establishment of partnerships with other non–law enforcement agencies. As you begin to analyze problems, you find that many of the causal factors are outside the control or expertise of law enforcement. For instance, analysis of a crime might find that something about the construction of a location lends itself to crime. Perhaps more lighting at a park will reduce crime. Return to the traffic collisions that are related to the bar. A better way of fixing the problem might be the use of building codes or business codes that are enforced by another city agency. You might even find that a nonprofit community group has some influence or expertise that is integral to the solution.

Crime analysis can also enhance communication within and without the police department. Simply put, a picture is worth a thousand words. Although sophisticated mapping and statistical analysis techniques are used in crime analysis, the product can produce a dramatic visual presentation of a problem. For the police manager, the ability to not only give the number of calls for service, but also visually represent them on a map may be key in arguing for some increase in funding or change in policy. For the line employee, crime analysis and the maps they produce can give the field officers information on where to spend their time.[6] For the community member, maps of the locations of known sex offenders or the types of crimes that are occurring in their neighborhoods may give them information that helps them make better decisions about their personal safety.

Today most law enforcement professionals look at crime analysis and crime mapping as a tool that assists them in the deployment of their personnel. Real-time information, historical trends, and forecasted trends can help police managers make better decisions on how many police officers should be on duty and where. As crime analysis matures, police managers will probably see that crime analysis also provides information on what field officers should be doing.

Increasingly, the crime analysis information is being used to deploy more officers in an area that is experiencing a higher crime rate. This is good, but it is a short-term solution. What commonly happens is the deployment of more officers stops the crime from occurring there and then—it is displaced. This **displacement** can be either spatial or **temporal**. That means the offender either goes somewhere else (spatial) or waits until the cops are gone (temporal). The bad part is that if crime is displaced, one person isn't victimized, but someone else is. Crime analysis is not seen as being reactionary (deploying officers to displace crime); it is seen as being proactive (targeting the offenders and causal factors).[7]

There are a lot of social factors that go into crime. Indeed the causes of crime are the subject of shelf upon shelf of research. While police departments should be looking at causal factors and developing partnerships with organizations that have greater expertise with those causal factors, what the police do best is investigate crimes and arrest offenders. Since most crime is committed by a very small percentage of any community, the police should be targeting their investigating efforts on those individuals. If crime analysis is used to identify **serial crimes** and develop solutions aimed at the arrest and prosecution of the offender, displacement doesn't occur; **incapacitation** occurs. Simply put, a **serial offender** is incapacitated when she is incarcerated or placed under court supervision.

As crime analysis matures, it is moving toward the identification of serial crimes and the targeting of serial offenders. In combating serial crime, the police department moves away from simply deploying more officers to an area experiencing an increase in crime and moves toward deploying police officers to arrest that specific offender. These are two very different schools of thought. Police officers looking for a specific offender might use covert operations, follow different investigative leads, and conduct preliminary crime scene investigations differently.

With serial crimes, resource allocation does not mean how many as much as it means what the police officers are doing. For instance, take your average car break-in. How much time and effort do you think police officers spend during the initial investigation of the average car break-in? A clue can be found in the fact that many police departments take these reports over the telephone. With all of the other crimes, car break-ins are a fairly low priority. How would a police department's response change if the car break-in was seen as the twentieth car break-in, in a series of break-ins. In other words, if crime analysis had determined that car break-ins in a certain area, occurring at a certain time and in a certain manner, were most likely committed by the same offender, how should a police department's response change? Because it is a serial crime, it makes sense for the investigation of this crime to be allocated more resources. The crime scene investigation should move from a telephone conversation to nearly the resources and expertise used during a homicide investigation. The point is that crime analysis allows police departments to become more effective because their efforts can be specifically directed at a serial offender.

Crime analysis can be a very powerful tool for law enforcement professionals. We can see how it enhances community-oriented policing; it is essential to problem solving; it increases communication, cooperation, and partnership with other agencies; it can provide police departments with another communications tool; and it can make police departments more effective.

Rational Choice, Situational Crime Prevention, and Crime Analysis

In previous chapters we briefly looked at **situational crime prevention**. In essence, situational crime prevention is based on two things: offender opportunity and **rational choice theory**. Situational crime prevention theory says that the reason an offender commits a crime is a result of these two factors coming together.[8] He has the opportunity to commit the crime, or the chance to do it, and

A **serial crime** is multiple crimes committed by an offender or group of offenders, which occur over a period of time. In Chapter Nine, when we looked at the National Incident-Based Reporting System (NIBRS) we saw that an offender can commit several crimes at one time, in one location—recall our bank robber who struck a teller and then stole a car. That is not a serial crime. Serial crimes are those crimes committed by the same person or persons and are distinctly separated by time and, usually, geography.

A tremendous amount of research shows a relatively few people commit most crimes. Moreover, for most career criminals, there isn't much specialization in the type of crime they commit. It may be that people who take an anti-social path commit crimes based upon situational factors. For purposes of sentencing, may states have statutes that identify a minimum criminal history for the classification of a career criminal. For instance, some statutes require multiple convictions for serious felony offenses. Moreover, there is a growing body of research into the phenomenon of career criminals. This research has developed concepts like chronic offenders, onset of career, continuation of career, desistance of career, and escalation. It may be that in the future, based upon research into this field, criminal justice practitioners and social service providers may be able to tailor interventions early into an offenders career. It is important to consider that a serial offender might be a career criminal, or not. Generally, a career criminal is someone who has come into contact with the criminal justice system a relatively large number of times over a long duration. A *Serial Offender* is a person committing a series of crimes now.

Source: Tonry, *Crime and Punishment,* 241; 377.

he sees more benefit to committing the crime than the potential risks involved, or he chooses to do it.

Rational choice theory is actually one of the theories involved in the study of economics. In essence, the theory says that people have preferences in outcomes. They know what they want and when given choices among outcomes, they are able to place a value on the various outcomes. Based on which outcome has the highest value to them, they choose that course of action. While rational choice assumes people know what they want and they are making thoughtful decisions, it does not mean that people don't make irrational or stupid decisions.[9] Some people are crazy, and some people don't think things through. Don't forget that most crime is committed by a small number of people who are probably career criminals. They have experience at making choices.

Decisions are made based upon the information available, as we saw in the previous chapter, many decisions are made based upon imperfect information. If someone chooses to commit a car burglary because she wants something in the car, but she did not know that the car was under surveillance by the police, she made a decision based upon imperfect information—and is probably thinking, "I wish I knew that."

With rational choice theory, offenders choose to commit crimes when the opportunity is right, when they have enough information that the value of the crime is more than the risk of punishment. In judging risk versus value, offenders look at the effort involved and the potential for arrest against the reward of the crime. It is important to step back and say that this is not a mathematical formula. People don't go around and assign numerical values to things and make decisions. Rational choice theory is a decision-making model that helps explain why people commit crimes (and make many other decisions).[10]

A close cousin and helpful theory in further understanding why offenders commit crimes and how law enforcement might dissuade them is the **routine activity theory**. There are three parts to routine activity theory: an offender, a victim, and the absence of an interfering force. The offender and victim are self-explanatory. The interfering force is something that adds to the risk of detection.[11] It could be a nearby police officer, the presence of people stronger than the offender who might render assistance to the victim, a video camera, or a witness who knows the offender's identity. In short, an interfering force is anything that the offender perceives as adding risk to the crime. Later in this chapter, as we look at the analysis of a crime, we will see how situational crime prevention, routine activity theory, and rational choice theory work.

The Basic Requirements for Crime Analysis

As with much of the textbook, we are going to look at what is possible if a police department's information system is fully integrated. This allows us to see the full potential of crime analysis and highlights the need to continue efforts at systems integration. As we go along in our look at crime analysis, we should note that most agencies are not fully integrated. Moreover, the lack of systems integration, funding problems, and the lack of technical expertise are poor reasons for not conducting crime analysis. Those are just challenges. Because the potential benefit of crime analysis is so great, getting started even in a small way will probably be extraordinarily beneficial.

Although mapping is not the only thing crime analysis does, you cannot conduct modern crime analysis without mapping capabilities, and you cannot conduct geographic and statistical analysis without minimal hardware and software. The minimal equipment requirements are a desktop personal computer with sufficient processing speed and hard disk storage to accommodate your data and functions. Moreover, at the very least you need a high-quality printer that can handle the color maps and workload. Today, with the relatively low cost and high speed and capacity of off-the-shelf computer equipment, if a small agency spent more than a few thousand dollars, they got ripped off.

What is usually more difficult to obtain than the equipment is the data and the expertise. Let's tackle expertise first. A crime analyst can be either a civilian or a sworn person. There are arguments, benefits, and costs to using either. The most prevalent argument for the use of civilian personnel is that cops should be in the street fighting crime. However, there are some distinct differences between crime analysis and most scientific and technological work in a police agency. With most scientific and technological tasks in police departments, the expertise in the specific task is more important than a general knowledge of police procedure. In other words, a serologist, who analyzes blood, needs to have more skills in a very specific scientific area and little or no knowledge of general police procedures. However, crime analysis requires not only computer skills and analytical skills, but also a general knowledge of the community, an understanding of police procedure, and investigative abilities. As we shall see, crime analysis is not only problem solving; it is conducting a criminal investigation. There are strong arguments that personnel who conduct crime analysis should be drawn from the ranks of sworn personnel.

Whether civilian or sworn, where do they get the expertise? The are a couple of routes to gaining expertise. One would be to contact the National Institute for Justice (NIJ), Mapping and Analysis for Public Safety (MAPS) division. In addition to sponsoring crime analysis training, the NIJ holds conferences and has resources of other organizations that can assist in formal training.

The third and often most vexing issue is obtaining the data necessary to conduct crime analysis. Two types of data are needed: mapping data and crime data. The mapping data necessary is the information that runs the GIS component of crime analysis. As we know from the chapter on GIS, that information allows the user to create layered maps of an area. This data can be obtained from a variety of sources. For instance, GIS data can be purchased commercially, or, depending on the size and resources of the police department's parent organization (city, state, or county government), the information may be already available in the planning department. Additionally, mapping data might be obtained from some regional authority, such as a city police department obtaining the data from the county planning department. So there are a variety of means for obtaining mapping data.

In many agencies, the ability to produce wall-sized maps has a number of applications. These maps are printed by devices called **Plotters**. Although a plotter is not essential to crime analysis, they can improve visual displays and have a number of strategic and tactical usages. For instance, if an agency were planning their response and involvement with the city's annual Founder's Day celebration, a wall map would make planning convenient.

However, as we shall see, no matter where the data is obtained from, the user should be prepared for some challenges associated with the information.

In addition to mapping data, crime data is needed. While police departments routinely collect crime data when they take police reports, getting that information into the data format necessary for crime analysis can be challenging. In the chapter on communications dispatch centers and agency systems, we saw the many police departments are moving toward total system integration. We also saw in the chapter on external sources of information, the National Incident-Based Reporting System (NIBRS) provides a format for agencies to collect crime data in a way that is easily usable for crime analysis. There are some agencies wherein the crime analyst need only import data from an existing system into the computer that is going to be used for crime analysis. To date, this is the exception, not the rule.

In the chapter on information exchange, we noted that one of the hallmarks of good systems and data integration was that information was entered into a database one time. In agencies that do not have systems integration, or do not have a records management system (RMS) that collects information on crimes and arrests, crime analysis is only possible if the analyst enters the information from each crime and arrest report into the computer being used for crime analysis. For many police agencies, this is the case. Crime analysts end up spending an inordinate amount of time entering crime and arrest data into a separate database while the information often sits in an incompatible and unconnected primary database. This scenario highlights the need and advantages of systems integration. For our exploration of crime analysis, we will presume that the police agency has a fully integrated system.

The Analysis of a Crime

Recall in the chapter on communications dispatch centers we used a 9-1-1 call of a possible burglary to explore how dispatch centers operate. Let's return to that same scenario, except in this case, it turns out that a burglary did take place and the suspect escaped before the police arrived. Let's see how crime analysis might work in this scenario. For the purposes of exploration, the imaginary police department we are looking at is a suburban municipal police department for a city of 100,000 people and twenty-four square miles and is surrounded by three other independent municipalities with their own police departments. The department employees 180 full-time sworn officers and thirty civilian employees; for operational purposes, the city is divided into ten distinct **beats**.

As you recall, the burglary call came in at 3 A.M. After taking a police report, the police officer turned the report in at the end of the shift and commented to the watch sergeant that there seemed to be an increase in residential burglaries. Often crime analysis begins from anecdotal information. It could be the comment that our police officer made; it could be a community complaint heard at a block club meeting or a variety of other observations based not on statistics, but on the intuitive judgment of someone in the field. The sergeant tells the police officer that she should speak with the department's crime analyst to see if there is indeed an increase in burglaries. (While any structure can be burglarized, we generally break burglaries down by residential and commercial. Moreover, the types of offenders who commit these different crimes tend to be different themselves. For this exercise, when we talk about burglaries, we are looking at the residential burglaries.) The police officer speaks to the crime analyst and tells the analyst that she seems to be responding to more burglary calls than normal. The analyst agrees to look at the problem.

How the elements of **burglary** are articulated varies from state to state. For our purposes, a burglary is entering a structure with the intent to commit a theft or any other crime.

A **beat** is an artificial policing area within a jurisdiction. Sometimes adjectives are used to describe beats, such as "basic car." These areas are sometimes determined by geography, an area of the city is simply somehow isolated by the rest of the city. Most commonly, police managers analyze factors such as calls for service, population density, street miles, and crime rate in order to create as even a distribution of workload as possible. As straightforward as that seems, beat boundaries and assignments can become very political, especially if the beat in some way mirrors some political or other special district.

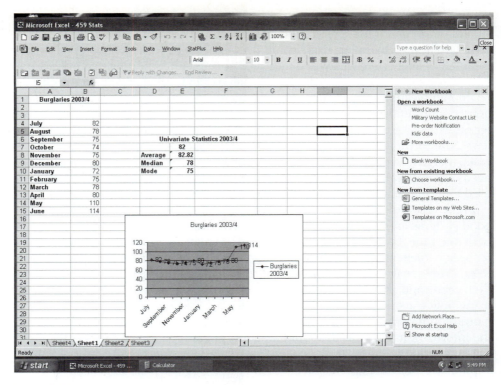

Figure 12.1   A cursory examination of the information shows that there seems to be an increasing trend in the past two months, May and June.

Although mapping is critical to crime analysis, it is not the starting point. As we shall see, good crime analysis begins with a statistical analysis for the purpose of narrowing the scope of the question. Our analyst begins by deciding to look at burglaries over the past twelve months and imports information about burglary reports from the police department's RMS. The information is then put into a spreadsheet and summarized as in the screen capture provided in Figure 12.1.

The next step for our analyst is to conduct a statistical analysis of this information in order to determine the average, or **mean number**, of burglaries; the middle value, or **median number**, in order to be able to view the information from the least number to the greatest number; and to look and see if any of the data repeats itself, or the **mode**. A quick comparison of the mean and median numbers shows that they are fairly close together, so we know that the data is not skewed. Now, armed with information on the average number of burglaries occurring during the past month, our analyst compares the average to the actual and finds that there is indeed an increase, over the average, in May and June. While this is important, we know that there are seasonal increases in certain types of crime. It may be that this increasing trend occurs each year. So, to see if the information is truly significant, our analyst completes a comparison of this year's number of burglaries against last year's number of burglaries. A comparison of the two tables enables our analyst to determine if the number of burglaries has changed, and if so, how much of a change occurred (Figure 12.2). The percentage of change often gives us more of an idea of the seriousness of the change than do the raw numbers. In this instance, there has been a 52 percent increase in burglaries. Our police officer was right.

Our imaginary city is fairly large. Twenty-four square miles is a lot of area to police. What are crime analyst is doing is actually defining the problem. The initial

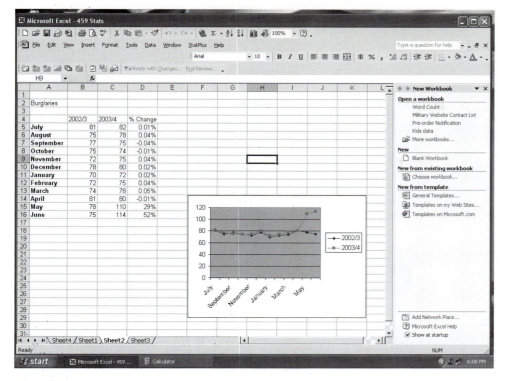

Figure 12.2 If we look at the data, we see that there has been an increase and that our analyst has determined the percentage of the change.

statement was by our police officer—I think burglaries have increased. Our problem definition has now changed and is more focused. The analyst has determined that burglaries in the month of June have increased 52 percent over past year. As the problem statement becomes more precise, the potential answer also becomes more precise.

The next step is to gain an even more precise determination of the problem by breaking the burglaries down to a more defined area of occurrence. Our analyst is looking for a **crime pattern**. A crime pattern is a series of similar crimes occurring within a distinct area. Since our city is already divided into ten beats, it makes sense for our analyst to look at the number of burglaries occurring in each beat. So our analyst takes the crime figures for June and defines the occurrences by the beats (Figure 12.3). At first glance, it appears that our crime pattern may be in two different beats, but because our analyst has some institutional knowledge of

---

HOT TIP

Do not be intimidated by the statistical work a good analyst performs. There are plenty of commercially available software applications, like Microsoft Excel, that perform the calculations easily and reliably. Moreover, there are a variety of software applications written by government-funded organizations that are available to not only tutor the analyst, but also perform the calculations. However, as the field of crime analysis matures, I suspect we will see enterprising people routinely doing multiple statistical regression in order to determine the significance of the relationships between suspected causal factors and crime. But don't try that at home.

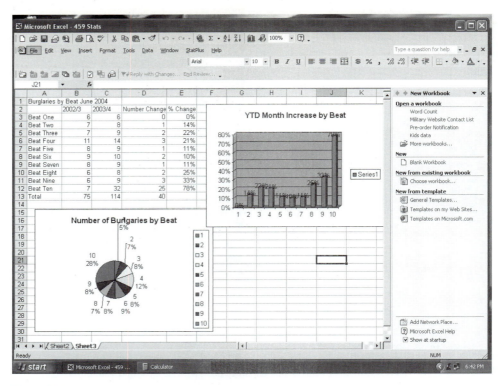

Figure 12.3 Our analyst has now created a table and can see that beats four and ten account for the greatest number of burglaries in the city.

general crime patterns in the city, he knows that beat four has a high-density population and apartment buildings. He further knows that generally speaking, this area experiences higher crime than other areas of the city. Moreover, beats four and ten are widely separated by two other beats. We are not going to automatically discount beat four, but we are going to take another step to see if the percentage of increase is confined to one beat and if that beat is number ten. Doing much the same calculations as before, our analyst compares the percentage of increase over the past year in each of the separate beats. What he finally determines is that while there are a higher number of burglaries in beat four than other beats, that number has not increased substantially. Our analyst has further defined the problem statement to: There has been a 48 percent increase in burglaries over the same month last year in beat ten. Now we have something to work with.

Recall from our chapter on GISs that GIS allows us to map variables and examine their relationships to each other. Moreover, as we learned, GIS allows us to layer information and manipulate information in order to further analysis. Our analyst first decides to do a symbol map to represent the crime pattern of burglaries in beat ten. What our analyst initially produces is a **single-symbol map**—each point on the map is represented by the same type of symbol.

There are drawbacks to a single-symbol map. In our example we are looking at residential burglaries, but residences can be apartment buildings. Therefore, they can have the same address. So when our analyst initially produces the map, he has to be careful that the map is not misleading because two incidents occurring at the same address would be represented by only one point.[12] In our example this is not going to be a problem, but if in analyzing other crimes, this problem occurred, a **graduated-symbol map** could be used (Figure 12.4). With this type

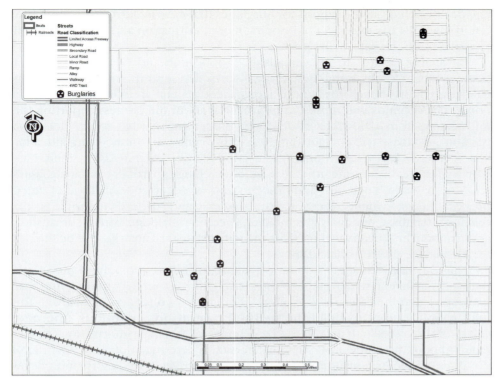

Figure 12.4 Using GIS software, our analyst is able to produce a map showing the spatial relationship of the burglaries.
Screen capture provided by ESRI.

of map, the symbol gets larger or changes color to represent multiple incidents occurring at a single location.

At this point our analyst could publish some type of internal crime alert telling the officers that beat ten has a burglary problem. Although he mapped out the problem, the problem statement is still much too general to really come up with viable solutions. Considerably more analysis remains. At this point we have examined the mapping of the crimes but not an analysis of the information about the crimes that might be helpful in apprehending the offender or offenders. Our analyst now begins to search for information that will point to a **crime series**.[13]

Although there is considerable work left, quite a bit has been accomplished. Instead of having to analyze all the burglaries in the city, our analyst is going to concentrate on the burglaries in beat ten. As was mentioned before, our analyst is fortunate enough to be working in a city with a fully integrated information system. The information he is going to work with next is fairly accessible. However, in a system that is not fully integrated, our analyst would be trudging over to the police department's records unit and looking for the files on the burglaries in June and in the current month of July that occurred in beat ten.

One of the primary purposes of crime analysis is to assist in the deployment of resources in order to prevent crime and apprehend offenders. Our analyst used the last complete month of crime data as a starting point for analysis. This was done because it simplifies things like month-to-month and year-to-year comparisons. However, using the most current data available is key to good analysis. Therefore, after determining that the problem is occurring in beat ten, the analyst decides to include all the reports for burglaries that have occurred thus far in beat ten in July. This has the effect of bringing more information and more current information into the data analysis.

Our analyst returns to his spreadsheet application and creates a small relational database for the burglaries. As we discussed in several chapters, a relational database will have each row of the spreadsheet contain an individual record, or crime. The columns will represent information about the crimes. Importing this information from a NIBRS-based RMS will predetermine what record fields this relational database will contain. But the idea is to enter this limited data into a format so certain factors surrounding the crime can be examined for similarities. Our analyst decides to include the type of dwelling (apartment or single-family residence); victim's age, sex, and descent; time of occurrence; method of entry; property taken; evidence recovered at the scene; and suspect's description. The relational database our analyst is building is commonly done with a spreadsheet application. The spreadsheet used for the initial statistical analysis will be the perfect format for this relational database.

What our crime analyst is doing is looking for information about the crimes that will enable him to determine if there is anything about the crimes, other than geography, that indicates a single offender or group of offenders is involved. This information is used to build the **method operation**, or **modus operandi (MO)**, of the offender. If an MO can be determined from the information (data elements about the crimes), our analyst can make a determination as to whether or not these incidents constitute a crime series. Moreover, if the information develops into a crime series, the problem statement can be further refined, making subsequent plans likely to be more effective. As we shall see, with the information from this relational database, our analyst will be able to forecast the likely times and places for future crimes committed in this series and perhaps create a **profile** of the offender.

In addition to the twenty-one burglaries from the month of June, our analyst finds that there have been three more burglaries in the same area, and those are added to the database. In looking at the twenty-four burglaries, the first information examined is the date and time of occurrence. Our analyst first notes that one of the burglaries occurred at 3 A.M. (our earlier radio call that started this process) and that all of the other burglaries occurred between 9 A.M. and 3 P.M. In this instance, there is such a stark difference between the times of occurrence in the general pattern and the single 3 A.M. occurrence, our analyst decides to remove that case from the database. Our analyst also notes that of the remaining twenty-three burglaries, four were apartments and ninteen were single-family residences.

As our analyst looks at the information, he sees that of the nineteen single-family residences that were burglarized, seven of the points of entry were side windows and twelve were rear sliding glass doors. He also notes that in all four of the apartment burglaries, the point of entry was a rear sliding glass door. Because the burglary of an apartment and a single-family residence may point to a different offender, our analyst was tempted to take the four apartment building burglaries out of the analysis. However, they, too, involved entry through the rear of the structure. The most important point of this is that crime analysis is an art. There is a substantial amount of science, technology, and intuitive experience. Analysts make judgments about some of the information, specifically what to include and what not to include, in the analysis by technological means. However, part of the strength of using computers for analysis of crime information is the ability to easily manipulate the information. In other words, if our analyst felt strongly about the information, he could simply look at it both ways. He could conduct an analysis of

I'll bet everyone has heard the term *MO*. People are creatures of habit, who duplicate their previous successes in their future actions. If you drive to work or school a certain way, it is your MO to drive that route because you are familiar with it and successful with it.

A **profile** is information that portrays the significant features of an offender, or information that tends to demonstrate the offender's different traits or abilities. Based upon evidence, investigators can often determine offender characteristics like gender, race, height, or weight. One of the hot topics in law enforcement is racial profiling. Racial profiling would be detaining an individual based solely on her race, without probable cause. For our purposes, we are using evidence to determine characteristics on an unknown offender.

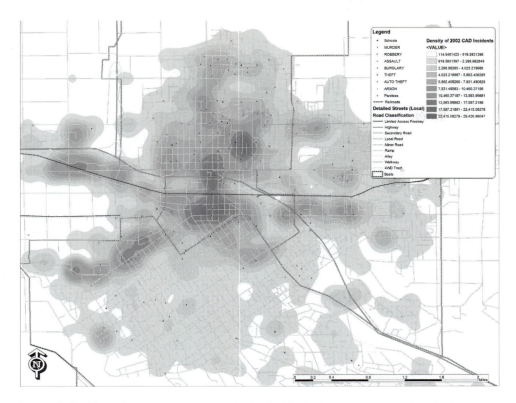

Figure 12.5 There is some controversy in the field of crime mapping and analysis over the term **hot spot**. Most of the controversy centers on whether a hot spot is an area that traditionally has a lot of crime or an area with an unusual increase in crime. The controversy aside, hot spot analysis can also be used to link different areas with related crimes together. For instance, an area where cars are stolen from is typically linked to areas where stolen cars are recovered by the police. Hot spots can also be used to advise police officers of an increasing crime trend. By using threshold analysis, an organization could say that any increase in a certain percentage of crime in a specific area should be examined. This would probably be done mostly by large organizations with large geographic responsibilities.
Source: Russell-Chamberlin, *"Where the Bad Guys Are,"* 34. *Screen capture provided by ESRI.*

the information including and excluding the apartment buildings. In this instance, he decides to include the information.

At this point our problem statement is becoming much clearer: In the past five weeks, there have been twenty-three daytime burglaries, representing a 56 percent increase over the same time last year, occurring between 9 A.M. and 3 P.M. in beat ten, where the offender entered the victim's home through a side window or rear sliding glass door. However, our analysis is not complete.

Our analyst observes that in sixteen of the crimes (one apartment and fifteen single-family dwellings) heavy objects such as computer equipment (ten) and televisions (eight)—(two locations lost computer equipment and televisions) were taken. Because the property taken in the sixteen cases involving heavy objects is unique, our analyst begins to focus on those crimes. Again, his intuitive judgment is used, but nearly every house has a television, and although computers are fairly common objects in homes, they were a larger percentage of the property taken in these crimes than they probably are in the general population.

His observations about these sixteen crimes continues. In two of the cases, a neighbor of the victim reported seeing a suspicious white van. A partial fingerprint was recovered from one location. Shoe prints were observed in three. He further notes that in eleven of the crimes, the investigating officer determined that a flat-head screwdriver was used to pry open the window or sliding door. Moreover, that tool was used twice on the apartments and nine times on the single-family residences, and was fairly evenly distributed between the side window and rear sliding glass door. Based upon an analysis of the relational database, our crime analyst now believes that there is a serial offender operating in beat ten. He takes the addresses from the sixteen crimes and imports the information into his GIS program, creating a map of just these sixteen crimes. Although our analysis is incomplete, there is enough information to take some action. In many police departments, crime analysts publish **crime alerts** or **criminal intelligence bulletins**. In the vast number of state and local police departments nationwide, there are probably other terms used to describe official information given to field police officers.[14] The concept is that during a field police officer's available time, he or she, armed with the information from the crime alerts, will spend time patrolling the designated area. This preliminary crime analysis is telling the officers that there has been an appreciable increase in a certain type of crime in a defined area. Many times, these crime alerts may just tell the field police officers that there has been an increase in all crime in a defined area. Both types of crime alerts would be informing the field police officers of what crime analysts refer to as hot spots. The purpose of determining a hot spot is to increase awareness and patrols in a defined area (Figure 12.5). Probably the most common maps produced by crime analysts are **crime density maps**. These maps simply map the total number of crimes in a specific area. Identification of "hot spots" can be used to allocate resources in a problem area.[15]

Our analyst is fortunate to be employed by a police department with a fully integrated information system. In many organizations, the crime alerts are actual documents produced from a common template, printed, photocopied, and distributed through intradepartment mail. Our analyst is able to create the document in a template and then send an e-mail to the field officers, investigators, civilian employees, and department managers.

Each of the groups of people who receive our analyst's e-mail might take different actions based on the information. For instance, the chief of police might decide that the information should be published to the community; the police officers would increase their activity in the designated area; and the investigators would know that they possibly have a serial offender in beat ten, not a rash of isolated crimes. As we shall see, the investigation, strategic response, and tactical response to a serial crime should be vastly different to the response to a rash of seemingly unrelated crimes.

At this point, our patrol officers and detectives have quite a bit of information with which to work. They have a fairly defined time, area, and method of operation.

A Crime Alert or Criminal Intelligence Bulletin has a map of the sixteen crimes and a narrative like: "In the last five weeks there has been a 52% increase in day time residential burglaries in beat ten. Sixteen of those crimes, all occurring between 9 A.M. and 5 P.M., are probably the work of a serial offender. In each instance, the property taken was a heavy object. Computers and television sets are the likely targets of theft. The offender(s) use a flat head screw driver to pry open a side window or the rear sliding glass door. During the preliminary investigation of two of the crimes, neighbors reported seeing a white van in the area."

While all agencies handle these incidents differently, one thing that could be done is to form a working group that included the analyst, the daytime watch supervisor, the daytime officers who are assigned beat ten, and the investigators who are responsible for following up on the preliminary crime reports. With such a succinct problem statement, there should be a well-formulated plan. Moreover, at this point in the problem solving, it might be good to involve people outside the police department. As you read the rest of the chapter, think about whom you would involve.

In the first chapter, I told you that eventually we would look at the future of technology in police work by using the past. Attempting to predict future events by using past events as a guide is called **forecasting**. If I gave you the series of number 2-4-6-8, what do you suppose would be the next number? If you predicted ten, you were correct. By seeing the pattern of numbers, you were able to predict my next choice. However, crime is not that straightforward and there is the real possibility that the criminal would choose eleven. So in forecasting future criminal occurrences based upon previous criminal occurrences, the results are not going to be exact, but they can be amazingly accurate.

Now our analyst is going to use the data he has in an effort to forecast the date, time, and location of the next residential burglary. Our analyst is going to use his spreadsheet again. He takes the dates that the crimes occurred and lists them in sequence. He figures out how many days there were between each crime and determines the average number of days between the crimes. Then, taking the fewest days between crimes and the most days between crimes, our analyst uses the **standard deviation**. If you took and understood statistics, you know that we can use the standard deviation to state how confident we are that our prediction is going to occur because the standard deviation measures the spread or dispersion of data. By using multiples of the standard deviation, our analyst could say something like the next burglary has a 60 percent chance of occurring on this date, or a 95 percent chance of occurring on these three consecutive dates, or a 99 percent chance of occurring during these five consecutive dates. This is a somewhat complex set of calculations, and we need only understand that it can be done and what is meant by statements like, "I am 60 percent confident that the next burglary will occur on this date."

Next our analyst will conduct nearly the same calculation with time. He will be able to make similar statements concerning the likelihood that the next burglaries will occur within a certain time frame. There is a problem in forecasting an exact time frame for certain crimes. It has to do with when the crime was discovered. For crimes like robbery, where the victim is present, we know to a reasonable exactitude the time of occurrence. But for crimes like burglary, a crime best committed when no one is looking, we usually know when the victim left the residence and when the victim returned and discovered the crime had occurred. Sometimes there are things that can narrow our time frame, like a witness statement, but by and large, for crimes like burglary and auto-related crimes, the determination of the exact time of occurrence is problematic. Now our problem statement has actually changed considerably. Our problem statement was about what had happened, but now we can think of the problem in terms of the future. We could say, "the serial offender committing burglaries in beat ten is very likely to commit another burglary in the next five days, between the hours of 9 A.M. and 3 P.M."

Thus far, our analyst has identified the burglaries as a crime series and done calculations to predict the most likely dates and times of the next occurrence. His next job is to use analysis techniques in an effort to predict the next location likely to be burglarized. The analysis conducted in order to determine the next likely location of occurrence is called **spatial forecasting**; somewhat obviously, the previous calculations to determine date and time are **temporal forecasting**.

A method used in spatial forecasting is **standard distance around mean center point (STAMP)**.

Recall that the crime map of the burglaries our analyst produced is a series of X and Y coordinates on a plane, and each of the locations is a different set of X and Y coordinates. The mean (or average) of these coordinates can be determined by using similar statistical methods that were used to discover the means of the dates and times. All of the X coordinates are added together and all of the Y coordinates are added together. Then by dividing the number of X (or Y) coordinates by the sum of the coordinates X (or Y), the mean is produced. The X and Y values produced by these calculations is the **mean center** for our burglary problem. Once the mapping software translates the mean center X and Y coordinates into an address, the center to all the burglaries our analyst mapped is identified.

Finding the center has a number of useful purposes. For instance, if the police department decided that one of the strategies they were going to use to solve this problem was covert surveillance of the area, the mean center could provide a starting point for the surveillance. The officer who is responsible for patrolling that area could use the mean center as a starting point for his or her patrol. In addition to providing useful information for field uses, the mean center provides our analyst with a starting point for further analysis of the crime series.

Once the mean center is established, our analyst begins the calculations necessary for spatial forecasting. First, our analyst uses the mapping software to measure in linear feet the distance between each crime and the mean center. Those distances are used to calculate the **mean distance** (or average distance) from the mean center to the burglary locations. With the mean distance established, our analyst then calculates the standard distance, which is the most exact measurement of all of the crimes from the mean center. Determining the standard distance (or standard distance deviation) involves a considerable amount of math. Although fairly straightforward, understanding the math beyond the level we have explored is for those of you who want to become crime analysts. For the majority of us, looking at how the previous calculations are completed gives us an idea of how the information is ultimately produced and how valuable it can be.

Recall that by using the standard deviation, we can determine how confident we are that something we are forecasting is likely to happen. Now that our analyst has the standard distance, he can use the standard deviation to determine three buffer zones around the mean center of the burglaries, and he can assign confidence levels to the prediction that the next burglary is likely to happen within one of those buffer zones. The first buffer zone around the mean center has the lowest confidence level. As you look at the buffer zones in Figure 12.6, the first buffer zone encompasses the smallest area, and like the most precise forecasts for date and time of occurrence, the most precise forecast for location has the lowest confidence level. As the buffer zones expand, the total area that the burglary is likely to occur in increases, as does the confidence level.

The spatial forecast means that there is a 63 percent chance that the next burglary will occur in the first buffer zone. There is a 98 percent chance the next burglary will occur in the combination of the first and second buffer zones. There is a 99 percent chance the next burglary will occur in the combination of the first, second, and third buffer zones. Again, the more area the spatial forecasting encompasses, the higher the confidence that the prediction will come to pass. You may have noted that the confidence levels for temporal forecasting are somewhat different than those for spatial forecasting. They are, and there are mathematical reasons for this, but quite frankly, I don't know the reasons and it is more

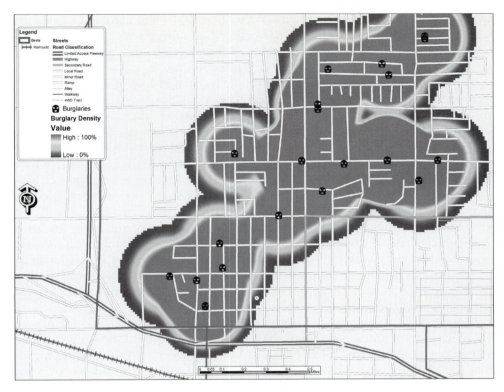

Figure 12.6 Somewhat like temporal forecasting, our spatial forecast gives us probabilities of the next location of occurrence.
Screen capture provided by ESRI.

important for us to know these differences exist when we are working with the product of our analysts than it is to know why.

The buffer zone information has some real consequences for field operations, investigative techniques, and further crime analysis. For the field, we now know the likely area, date, and time of the next occurrence. So if we were planning a covert surveillance of the area, we could decide how many police officers would be needed to gain what level of confidence we would have of apprehending the suspect. For the patrol officer, in addition to starting her patrol at the mean center, she now knows how far from the center to patrol. For our community, if we decided to issue a crime alert to the community, we now know the area within which we should send the alert. Since we are working in a fully integrated police department, we can assume that the mapping software is sophisticated and the geocoded data is fairly accurate. With good software and fairly accurate data, the mapping program can produce mailing address labels for every residence and business in the buffer zones. There are some police departments that have incorporated the GIS and CAD information so well, they could have automated telephone calls made to each household and business in the buffer zone. However we are able, we can now involve the total affected community.

There are quite a few things that can be done by uniformed police officers and community members, but what can our investigators do with the information? Recall that because of limited resources, some crimes are not investigated as fully as other crimes. It is simply a matter of having only so much time to spend on the myriad of issues facing state and local police departments. Just as we saw in the chapter on communications dispatch centers, police departments prioritize their work. Basically, a murder gets the most attention, and a barking dog call gets the least. Residential burglaries fall on the higher side of that scale, but now our investigators know that these are a series of burglaries being committed by the same offender(s), and the offender is going to continue.

The police department's investigators could go back to each of the previous burglary locations and reinterview the victims. They could look for patterns that might relate how the victims were chosen, and that might lead to the suspect. They could intensely canvass the neighborhoods of the crimes for witnesses. When the next burglary occurs that fits the profile of our serial crimes, that burglary crime scene could be handled like a homicide crime scene. The point is that because we have identified a serial offender, more resources should be shifted to solving these crimes.

Let's digress for a moment and talk about a couple of criminological theories that make our spatial and temporal forecasting viable. The first is called a **comfort zone**. In essence, people are lazy; they tend to commit crimes in areas with which they are comfortable. They have become comfortable with the area because they live, work, or socialize nearby. It may be an area they frequently travel through or an area they are familiar with because of some social tie, like family and friends. As with all theories, there are exceptions, but for most crime analysis, it is a good starting point.

The next theory is **routine activity theory**, which postulates that the offenders commit the crimes at the first place they happen upon during their routine activities where it seems relatively safe to do so. Safety for the offender means that the victim is vulnerable in some manner and there is no one to stop the crime, such as the police or an active witness. If these two theories are in play, there is something about the area (the buffer zones) that anchors the offender. The offender probably does more than commit crimes in the area. He or she may live, work, shop, or socialize in the buffer zones or relatively nearby. Once a crime series establishes a buffer zone, we need to consider the space within the zone.

Many times, after establishing the buffer zones, the analyst will realize that although the buffer zones are mathematically correct, the actual locations of the crimes have an orientation that is not circular. In other words, the symbols representing the crimes on the map are not an exact circle around the crime, and indeed have some obvious orientation. By orientation, we mean that they appear to spread from one direction to another, perhaps north to south, east to west, or some other combination of the compass points—but they are definitely not a circle (Figure 12.7).

This phenomenon has been noticed by crime analysts often. In order to give a more accurate picture of the buffer zone of a crime series, the tools necessary to create a **standard deviation ellipse** (or oval) were created. Fortunately, our analyst had already downloaded the software application CrimeStat from the Internet and could use it to draw an ellipse that would encompass the orientation of the crime.

As we know, the GIS software has the ability to layer information over our crime series map. As we have just discussed, there may be something about the space itself that will provide a clue as to the offender's identity. Our crime analyst can add symbols to represent some of the geographic features of the area. What should he include? Should he include churches, libraries, and bookstores? How about pawn shops, drug treatment centers, and the home address of people on parole or probation?

Recall that our crime analyst was going to be part of a working group tasked to solve the problem of the series of burglary crimes in beat ten. The last job of our analyst is to produce a working document for that group. Something that summarizes the detailed information and provides the mapping information and a copy of the crime reports that were generated with each crime. The document for the

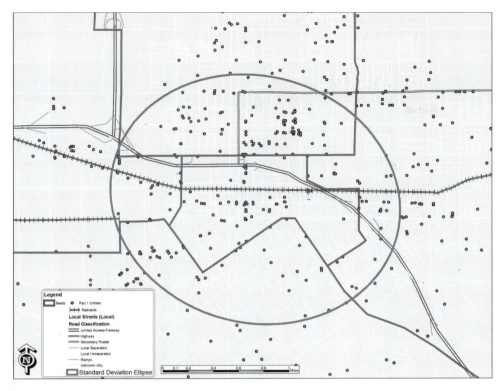

Figure 12.7 Now we have an ellipse over the traditional buffer zones and a better idea of where we should apply our resources.
Screen capture provided by ESRI.

working group would be much more detailed than the information given in our original crime alert.

The purpose of the working group is twofold. First, they should come up with responses to the problem. Some of the responses might involve the field officers; others might be using a variety of investigation techniques to identify the offender(s). The second job is to brainstorm the analysis. What else should be included? What other information would be valuable? Crime analysis is a work in progress. New data (additional crimes) can change the buffer zones; an analysis of the buffer zones can lead to the inclusion of new spatial data; a review of the previous crime scenes may cause an incident to be removed from the data set—also changing the spatial and temporal forecasts.

Crime mapping and analysis is not fortune-telling. It can't tell us exactly where the next crime is going to occur, but it can make police officers both more effective and more efficient.[16] Crime mapping and analysis has uses beyond giving us valuable information on crime; it can be used in the administration of a state or local law enforcement agency. In Chapter Nineteen we will look at some of the uses of crime mapping in the general deployment of personnel.[17] Additionally, crime mapping and analysis can be used for general problem solving.

Crime Analysis and General Problems

We have talked a lot about problem solving without attempting to define a problem. For state and local police officers, a problem is usually anything the community says it is. Community-defined problems can include very small issues or issues that are so large as to be problematic. For our purposes, let's define problem as a cluster of incidents.[18] By looking at the spatial relationships of incidents of crime, public nuisance complaints, or calls for service, police agencies can provide analysis that impacts general community problems.[19] Analysis produced by the police can have uses for other government and nonprofit agencies working in the community. Recall that we stated that we might find a spatial relationship between locations that serve alcohol and traffic collisions. This information might be valuable to city council members who are considering an application to renew, change, or grant alcohol sales.[20] One spatial analysis research project found a relationship between alcohol sales and assaults. Moreover, incidents in crime may have spatial relationships with factors in another jurisdiction.[21] So crime mapping and analysis extends beyond the police station.

Crime mapping and analysis can provide information into why crime occurs. By knowing the location of crime, its relationship to the other factors can be analyzed. As it turns out, many of the other factors are outside the control of most state and local police agencies. For instance, poor lighting, the purview of the street maintenance department, could be a factor in why crime occurs in an area.[22]

In nearly any problem confronting a police agency, the relationship of the problem to space and time may provide information about the solution. The spatial and temporal relationships may indicate that the underlying factors are best handled by another service provider. So a mapping analysis of problems can force police agencies to seek partnerships with other organizations and the community.

Geographic Profiling

The art of crime mapping and analysis is continuing to grow and become more sophisticated. While most agencies are using crime mapping simply to highlight hot spots, or areas of concentrated incidents, other more advanced projects are working on concepts like **geographic profiling**.[23] Geographic profiling is used with serial crimes and typically only with the most serious crimes. Recall from our discussion that a profile is information about an offender, the person's personal attributes. Crime analysis is being used increasingly as a means to determine offenders' geographic attributes—where they potentially live, work, and socialize. The key to geographic profiling is that people tend to follow predictable patterns.[24]

Geographic profiling is a fairly advanced crime analysis technique that takes the attributes of time, space, behavior, target, and offender and analyzes their spatial and temporal information in order to first determine an offender's **activity space**.[25] These methods of analysis use complex algorithms that start with the premise that serial offenders tend to commit their crimes within areas of their own routine activity, but they stay away from areas they would be readily recognized, like their homes. Using a software program, the data indicates a general hunting area. The hunting area is where the offender looks for victims. As we saw with the relatively simple crime analysis, the more crimes in the series, the better the probability of prediction. With crime data, this software seeks to provide a probable location of the offender's home.[26]

The minimum number of crimes needed in the series is five, or the program can use five different times and locations that are related to one crime. For instance, say the offender met the victim at one location, drove to another to commit the crime, dropped the victim at a third, used the victim's credit card at a fourth, and abandoned the victim's vehicle at a fifth. A crime analyst would have five distinct locations to plot. Using the software algorithm, a geoprofile is created. Probability scores are given based on the information. If the crime series occurs over an area of less than ten square miles, the algorithm can predict the location of the offender's home to within a one-half square mile area.[27]

Chapter Summary

In this chapter we saw a further example of how the various systems in state and local policing come together. In this instance, the hardware, software, and data from an agency's system combined into crime analysis. Because crime analysis is essentially a spatial and temporal analysis of crime problems, it can be an integral part of a state or local agency's community policing model.

A theory important to crime analysis is situational crime prevention. In situational crime prevention, there are tactics an agency can use to deter offenders depending on how police resources are applied. Part of situational crime prevention and crime analysis are the theories of routine activity and rational choice. In routine activity it is believed that offenders commit crimes during their routine activities, as targets present themselves. In rational choice it is essentially said that offenders choose to commit crimes based on their assessment of the reward and risk factors involved in the commission of the crime.

There were two key points from the analysis of the burglary problem. First, most agencies rely on crime mapping as a means to point out hot spots of increased crime activity. Second, the more sophisticated use of crime analysis is in giving police officers information about serial offenders. Crime analysis can be used for general police operations, like deploying more officers to a hot spot, and specific actions, like surveillance of an area a serial offender is predicted to strike.

Crime mapping and crime analysis have uses outside the everyday function of the agency. Crime mapping can provide other city services, nonprofit agencies, city leadership, and other jurisdictions with information that may be critical to a wide variety of problems. The use of GIS software in state and local government is not peculiar to police work. It is being used by planning departments, fire departments, and other city entities to assist in the spatial and temporal analysis of problems associated with their particular venue.

As crime mapping and analysis continue to mature, it is likely that the public will hear more stories of the techniques being used for geographic profiling. Once a geoprofile is established on a serial offender, other mapping data can be overlaid and the search for the offender hastened. For instance, imagine that an analysis of a series of sex-related crimes is able to narrow the offender's residence to a relatively small area. An agency could then overlay other data (recall GIS layers can be added and removed), such as the known addresses of registered sex offenders.

Discussion Questions

1. Should crime analysis personnel be drawn from the ranks of sworn or civilian personnel? If so, why? If not, why? Would it make a difference?
2. Thus far, you have learned about quite a few systems. If you were the decision maker in a police organization and had only enough funding to complete one of the three following projects, which would it be? And why?
   A. Establish a crime analysis unit.
   B. Establish a department Web site.
   C. Implement a new records management system.

3. In our scenario of the residential burglar. If you were going to form a working group to solve the problem, whom from outside the police department would you involve? Why?
4. Go to the ARJIS Web site (**www.arjis.org**) and make your own crime maps. What did you find?

Key Terms

Activity Space
Beat
Comfort Zone
Crime Alerts or Criminal
    Intelligence Bulletins
Crime Density Map
Crime Pattern
Crime Series
Displacement
Forecasting
Geographic Profiling
Graduated-Symbol Map
Hot Spot
Incapacitation
Mean Center

Mean Distance
Mean Number
Median Number
Method Operation, or
    Modus Operandi (MO)
Mode
Plotters
Profile
Rational Choice Theory
Routine Activity Theory
Scanning–Analysis–
    Response–Assessment
    (SARA)
Serial Crimes
Serial Offender

Single-Symbol Map
Situational Crime
    Prevention
Spatial
Spatial Forecasting
Standard Deviation
Standard Deviation
    Ellipse
Standard Distance
    Around Mean Center
    Point (STAMP)
Temporal
Temporal Forecasting

End Notes

1. Bayley and Shearing, "Future of Policing," 589.
2. Department of Justice, Bureau of Justice Statistics, 2000 Law Enforcement Management and Administrative Statistics.
3. Russell-Chamberlin, "Where the Bad Guys Are," 34.
4. Shafritz, *Public Policy and Administration,* 445.
5. See note 3 above.
6. "Mapping and Analysis," 1.
7. Tonry, *Crime and Punishment,* 374.
8. Tonry, *Crime and Punishment,* 372.
9. McCarthy, "Sociological Criminology," 417.
10. Tonry, *Crime and Punishment,* 373.
11. Ibid.
12. "Mapping and Analysis," 3.
13. Bair, et al., "Advanced Crime Mapping," 6.
14. "Mapping and Analysis," 3.
15. See note 3 above.
16. Ibid.
17. Bair, et al., "Advanced Crime Mapping," 8.
18. Skogan, *On the Beat,* 3.
19. "Mapping and Analysis," 4.
20. Ibid., 1.
21. Lipton and Gruenewald, "Violence and Alcohol Outlets," 187.
22. See note 3 above.
23. Ibid.
24. Bair, et al., "Advanced Crime Mapping," 11.
25. See note 6 above.
26. Ibid., 6.
27. See note 3 above.

PART THREE

Tactical Information Systems and Technologies

Chapter Thirteen
Technology in Investigations

Learning Objectives

- The student will understand how technology has changed the nature of crime scene protection and evidence gathering for first responders, investigators, and criminalists.

- The student will understand the basic science behind DNA evidence.

- The student will understand how the gathering of fingerprint evidence has been impacted by technology.

- The student will be exposed to some of the issues surrounding DNA databases.

- The student will briefly explore a technical explanation of digital photography.

- The student will see several examples of software being used in investigations.

Introduction

Evidence is left at the scene of virtually every crime. As we shall see in this chapter, the protection of crime scenes and the gathering of evidence is becoming the most important consideration of first responders, investigators, and criminalists.[1] Advances in technology have brought to light evidence that might have been overlooked only a decade ago.

That evidence might be fingerprints, **deoxyribonucleic acid (DNA)**, or even the way in which the crime was committed. Recall from Chapter Six, fingerprint evidence has been recovered, analyzed, and used in the prosecution of crime for almost one hundred years. However, just as technology changed the nature of fingerprint evidence through the creation of databases that could be accessed for comparison, the science of colleting fingerprints has also advanced. Not so long ago, supervisors approving police reports would note that the police officer who had investigated the crime wrote in the report that "there were no printable surfaces." That was true then, but today the science of fingerprint collection has significantly increased the number of surfaces from which fingerprints can be obtained.

A more recent development in evidence has been DNA. As we examine DNA in this chapter, it is important to realize that we are constantly leaving our DNA everywhere we visit. It might be our hair follicles, flakes of our skin, or saliva—but we leave it virtually everywhere. As we saw in Chapter Twelve, through crime analysis, we can learn facts about the offender that may assist in his or her capture. Crime analysis is taking facts about the crime and producing evidence in the form of information that can direct police efforts.

However, the lion's share of this evidence is lost, destroyed, contaminated, or just ignored. Evidence like fingerprints and DNA can be destroyed by the weather or contaminated by an improperly protected crime scene. Evidence is often ignored because it is too costly to recover. For example, while police officers may attempt to lift fingerprints at the scene of a car burglary or even a residential burglary, they rarely employ the more sophisticated fingerprint recovery techniques

Figure 13.1 Many medium to large agencies are investing in mobile crime scene labs. First responders protect the crime scene, detectives coordinate the crime scene, and professional criminalists use a variety of scientific methods to process the crime scene. This photograph represents a typical mobile crime scene laboratory. *Photograph provided by OBS INC., Specialty Vehicles.*

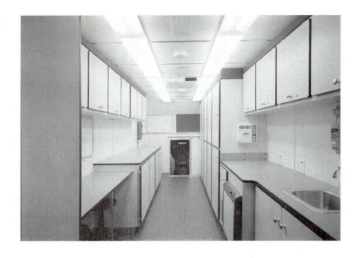

we will look at in this chapter. Sometimes more advanced methods of fingerprint detection are not used because it is simply not cost effective; police technology is a limited resource, and its use is prioritized by law enforcement agencies. Sometimes the agency just doesn't have the technology. In 2000 only 44 percent of departments used computers for criminal investigations. However, because the agencies using computers tended to be larger, they did employ 76 percent of all state and local police officers nationwide.[2]

Except in cases of homicide, major assault, and sexual assault, DNA evidence is not collected from crime scenes. As the technology of evidence is refined, police officers—especially first responders—are going to have to become more cognizant of the need to protect crime scenes. In one study, albeit seventeen years old, found that follow-up investigations by detectives were not as instrumental in solving crimes as information obtained by first responders.[3] With new evidence technologies come new questions and challenges. For instance, the more complex evidence technology of DNA is often analyzed by commercial laboratories. People used to debate victims' rights and offenders' rights; now a new debate—commercial proprietary rights—has entered the criminal justice arena. Questions concerning the use of DNA, especially the creation of DNA databases, abound. As we shall see in this chapter, questions concerning the offenders' rights and the rights of the offenders' families have entered the discussion. Even though you may never commit a crime, your rights may be impacted by DNA databases.

In this chapter, in addition to looking at how technology has impacted the investigation of crimes through advanced methods of evidence collection and analysis, we are going to pursue a number of questions concerning society and the individual. In addition to asking those questions, we are going to see how state and local police officers must become more technologically savvy in the twenty-first century.

The technologies we will look at fall under two broad classifications. The first is **forensic science**. The root of the word *forensic* comes from the Latin term *forensis,* which can be translated into the Roman term for forum, or a meeting place where people get together to discuss public business. Today forensic science is the application of science in our legal system. So any scientific methods that are used in our legal system are considered forensic. Most science used in forensic science is based on the **theory of transfer**, which examines how whenever two objects come into contact, they leave some evidence of that contact.[4]

In 1986 in Flint, Michigan, a college professor was raped and murdered. Although fingerprint evidence was recovered during the criminal investigation, the Michigan state fingerprint file did not contain a match. In 1991 in Romulus, Michigan, a flight attendant was raped and murdered. In 2001 DNA from the 1986 and the 1991 crimes were matched in a DNA database, and fingerprints from the 1986 crime were submitted to the Integrated Automated Fingerprint Identification System (IAFIS), where a match was found. Instead of immediately arresting the offender, the police officers followed him and eventually retrieved a napkin he had used while eating in a restaurant. DNA from the napkin matched both murders. The offender was subsequently arrested and charged.

Source: Adams, *Statement for the Record*.

For police officers, the evidence of that contact could be evidence like fingerprints, DNA, or impressions. As we shall see, because of advances in technology, what police officers once overlooked can be critical if you know what to look for, how to protect it, and who to call to gather it. One last thing before we continue: evidence based on the theory of transfer only tells us that two objects came into contact. If your fingerprints are on this book, you touched it, but we don't know when you touched it. So inferences and conclusions about transfer evidence are made by people.

Scientific Validity in the Courtroom

Before we examine our primary technologies and sciences, let's set the stage a little more by talking about how new sciences and technologies, and the evidence they reveal, are accepted by the court. After all, collecting evidence, even if it leads to a reasonable conclusion about offender guilt, is useless if it is not accepted as evidence in court. For the court, there are two general questions often asked. First, how did the evidence get to court? Second, is the science or technology that produced the evidence or aided in the interpretation of the evidence reliable?

There are a variety of other sciences involved in crime scene investigations. An anthropologist might be called into determine the age, sex, or race of skeletal remains. A tool mark expert can examine marks at the scene of a crime and give investigators an idea of what type of tool or implement was used to create the mark. Later, if a tool or implement is recovered, a tool mark expert may be able to match the tool or implement to the mark. An odontologist could be called to a crime scene to examine bite marks. Typically, we think of bite marks left on a victim, but offenders sometimes leave partially eaten food at the scene of a crime. From the bite marks left on partially eaten food, an odontologist might be able to provide investigators with information about an offender, such as approximate age and stature. Fibers from just about any naturally occurring or manufactured material, such as a blanket, can be examined because they differ dramatically in color, shape, and composition. Impressions and casts of foot prints can tell a great deal about an offender. An expert can determine if the offender was running or walking, if the offender was carrying a heavy object, and sometimes even if an offender was familiar or unfamiliar with the crime scene. In many instances, a tire mark expert can determine the make and model of a tire and, depending on a number of other factors, give investigators leads on possible vehicles that might have been used by the offender.

When evidence is introduced into court, the person offering the evidence must testify to the **chain of custody**, or the whereabouts of the evidence at all times from the moment it came into an agency's custody until the moment it is brought into court. For instance, with DNA, if blood samples from an offender were used for comparison, the nurse who drew the blood from the offender must testify. Whoever took the samples from the nurse into police custody must testify; whoever transported the samples from police custody to the laboratory must testify; the analyst must testify. In this way, the court is reasonably assured that a correct comparison was made between the offender's blood and the DNA recovered at the crime scene.

In the first instance, the court looks at how the evidence was seized. Thus far, we have had some cursory mentions of the Fourth Amendment, and in Chapter Fourteen we will see further examples of the amendment. Whenever a law enforcement agency uses a new technology to obtain evidence about an offender, there can be Fourth Amendment issues.[5] So far, the classic case that is often referred to is *Kyllo v. United States*.[6] In *Kyllo,* a thermal imager was used to determine radiated heat from a private residence. The court found that the officers should have obtained a warrant for the use of the imager. The important issues from *Kyllo* are that if a technology is not in general public use (binoculars are in regular use and therefore generally not an issue) and the technology is used to seize information that would be protected by the Fourth Amendment because without the technology the government couldn't seize the evidence, the evidence is protected by the Fourth Amendment. Think of it this way: the police officers, if they did not have the technology, would not have known about the radiated heat unless they entered Kyllo's residence. So even though the technology enabled them to get the information without entering the location, they still needed a warrant to obtain information using technology not readily accessible to the general public.

In addition to how the evidence came into police custody, the court often asks questions about how the police handled the evidence. Generally these questions revolve around the chain of custody, but the court does on occasion look at whether or not a police officer had sufficient knowledge about a science or technology in order to properly seize evidence. Here's where your study may come in handy. If you were called as a witness police officer who had guarded a crime scene, you could be asked about the measures you took to prevent contamination. You could be asked questions about how you knew to take the precautions. At this point, police officers often testify to their training, education, and experience. If you were testifying, you could talk about your training and experience and the class you took that required reading this portion of the text. The basic information about science and technology you gain in this text could very well help you to ensure evidence is properly received in court.

The last question courts look at is scientific and technological reliability. This is often referred to as the **Daubert test**. For the ninety years prior to Daubert, the courts applied what is referred to as the general acceptance rule.[7] As it says, if the science or technology was generally accepted to be reliable, it was good enough for the court. This changed in a 1993 civil case, *Daubert v. Merrell Dow Pharmaceuticals, Inc.,* when the court decided that the acceptance of scientific evidence depended upon the experts' methods and that those methods must be scientifically valid and reliable.[8] In essence, the Daubert test consists of five parts:

- Is the science derived by the scientific method?
- Has the science been subjected to peer review or publication?
- Does the relevant scientific community generally accept the science?
- What is the error rate of the scientific technique used to gain the information?
- Are there standards for controlling the technology used to obtain the scientific evidence?

The purpose of *Kyllo,* the Daubert test, and court inquires into the chain of custody is to protect the rights of the accused. As we shall see later in the text, the science and technology used in both fingerprints and DNA are well established and accepted by the courts. Now the primary issues raised by offenders in court are generally about chain of custody and if analysts followed established procedures.[9]

Fingerprint Technology

Recall from Chapter Six that the unique properties of fingerprints have been known for a very long time. They have been used in criminal investigations for about a hundred years, but for most of that time, fingerprints were recovered by applying various powders to a surface that would highlight the oils left behind by human contact. The problem was powder could not be applied to many objects with success or without damaging the original object. Science and technology has changed that.

Today the detecting and lifting of fingerprints can be accomplished with powders, chemicals, and lasers. One chemical that can be used on paper is ninhydrin, which is an oxidizing agent that activates the amino acids left behind when one touches an object. Once the ninhydrin comes into contact with an object, the fingerprints become visible. While ninhydrin is an activating agent, some chemicals are designed to restore the moisture to a fingerprint. You have probably used one of these chemicals around the house, cyanoacrylate.

In the 1970s the Japanese invented a process known as cyanoacrylate fuming. Cyanoacrylate is the chemical typically used in superglue. They found that common household superglue could be used to develop prints on smooth surfaces. Superglue fuming polymerizes the print, turning it into a plastic piece of evidence. During the 1980s this fuming process began to be used routinely in crime labs. If an object is placed in a closed container with a small amount of superglue, the vapors from the superglue attach to the chemicals left behind on the fingerprint and turn white. This technique works on most nonporous surfaces such as plastic, metal, glass, enameled or varnished wood surfaces, metal foils, and some fabrics.[10] While this made the fingerprints visible, the size of the fuming chambers meant that the item had to be recovered at the scene and taken to a crime lab for processing.

Of course, as we have seen with many technologies, something starts out large and nonportable and eventually it is miniaturized. At first, a portable vapor pump was designed that allowed crime scene technicians to process fingerprints with superglue vapor in the field in about two hours. Later, the Vapor Wand made the technology even smaller. By combining a butane torch and a small container of methyl cyanoacrylate, a high concentration of "superglue" could be directed at an object and heated at the same time. What was created was a portable and relatively inexpensive way of using the fuming process in the field.

As science and technology progress, more creative ways of developing latent fingerprints are being found. Some of the more exotic and often costlier methods include fuming with iodine vapor and silver nitrate, and the use of radioactive materials. While these methods may eventually reach the average police agency, one method that is finding increasing use is laser technology. **Laser** is an acronym for light amplification by stimulated emission of radiation. Basically, a laser controls the way that energized atoms release photons.

There are many types of lasers, but they share certain technologies. Whatever medium is used to create the laser, energy is excited by various means to the point where the atoms of the medium have energy that is typically two or three times their normal state. The electrons of the atoms in this high energy state are somewhat lazy, and they want to return to their normal energy level. As

Try This

Take a sandwich bag and touch the inside. Take a small amount of superglue and put it inside the bag (not on the area you touched). Seal the bag. Come back in about a half hour. What do you see?

they do, they release protons. Each proton has a certain wavelength and can be very useful to science. If you have ever looked at the heating element glowing inside a toaster oven, you have seen protons being released. The protons make up the beam of laser light. It is different from regular light in that only one wavelength is being emitted. It is essentially one color. The release of these protons is very organized, giving the laser the tight beam effect with which we are most familiar.

Lasers are used in conjunction with chemicals, most commonly in the fuming process. Because the laser light is monochromatic (one color), it can be used to visually enhance fingerprints that have been fumed or treated with chemicals that contain a dye. Because of the color of the dye and the one-wavelength property of the laser, latent fingerprints become more visible. This technique works with even very small quantities of residual chemicals in fingerprint residue and chemicals added through the fuming or treatment process.[11]

Deoxyribonucleic Acid (DNA)

Fingerprint evidence meant that you had to touch an object in order to leave trace evidence of your presence. As you sit reading this text, not only are you leaving fingerprint evidence, but your body is constantly leaving telltale signs that you were in the room where you are reading, and that you were using this text. When you breathe, your breath contains very small particles of water vapor; your skin is constantly sloughing or flaking off; your hair is falling out; and if this subject is really boring you, saliva drools out onto the page. Although we typically think of DNA evidence as being only in blood, semen, and other bodily fluids, it is coming off of us constantly and at the molecular level, in large amounts.[12]

Today in law enforcement, DNA evidence is probably the most powerful investigative tool available.[13] Recognizing the importance of DNA evidence, between 1996 and 1999, the federal government provided state and local governments funding in excess of $31 million for DNA laboratories and analysis.[14] To understand the potential of DNA, especially for first responders and investigators, we have to look at the science. Again, that word of caution: you won't leave here a qualified laboratory technician fully trained in DNA analysis, but if you respond to a crime scene, you will understand the precautions necessary to protect this valuable evidence.

Our bodies contain about one hundred trillion cells. Most of our cells have a center piece called the **nucleus**. The nuclei of our cells each contain twenty-three pairs of **chromosomes** that are the biological instructions for our development.[15] During conception, our parents contributed one chromosome to each of the twenty-three pairs of our chromosomes.[16] Inside our chromosomes, there are as many as hundred thousand paired **genes**, the fundamental building blocks of our hereditary traits.[17] While each gene can also have as many as one hundred different versions, most of them are the same in each of us. As you probably know, the genes your parents passed to you determine your individual characteristics. Your characteristics can be thought of as general or specific. Specific characteristics are traits that you possess, like your eye and hair color, that are not common to each and every other human being. Your general characteristics are those things about you

DNA evidence analysis is now considered routine and has essentially taken a place alongside fingerprinting, fiber analysis, and ballistics analysis in criminal justice. In 1996 the National Academy of Sciences found DNA evidence to be solid science.
Source: "Evolution and Development of Police Technology," 77.

which are common to everyone else—most people have a nose, two eyes, two legs, etc. Our genes are made of up deoxyribonucleic acid (DNA).[18] DNA, whose nature was beginning to be revealed in 1953, is a very small thing with huge consequences.[19] At the root of our growth and development, everything is controlled by our DNA. DNA consists of a long string of four repeating **nucleotides**: adenine (A), cytosine (C), guanine (G), and thymine (T).[20] Because DNA is a long string of repeating units (the four nucleotides), it is defined as a **polymer**.

As you read this sentence, it is the order of the letters that are typed on the page that give meaning to the words. For instance, take the letter O, G, and D. Based on the way the letters are ordered, they could convey different information to you. They could spell either god or dog—same letters, different concepts. DNA works in a similar manner; the information contained in DNA depends on the order the nucleotides appear in the DNA polymer.[21]

A complete DNA molecule has two polymer strands with four bases.[22] Recall from Chapter Three that digital information travels in packets that contain information that determines when the packet of information begins and ends. Just as with our packets of digital information, the DNA information defines the size of the segments within the polymer. In DNA, the two strands are always paired with the A across from the T and the G is across from the C.[23] These pairs are like the heading in a digital information packet; they tell us the size of the DNA segment. Lastly, these pairs connect the two strands together, forming what looks like a spiral staircase with the stairs going in opposite directions, or the DNA **double helix**.[24] DNA is represented in the double helix form in order to show us how replication can occur.[25]

Serology is the study of blood and body fluids. Early work in serology consisted primarily of blood typing. Serologists examine bodily fluids and tissues, like blood, semen, saliva, hair, and skin in order to determine their origin.

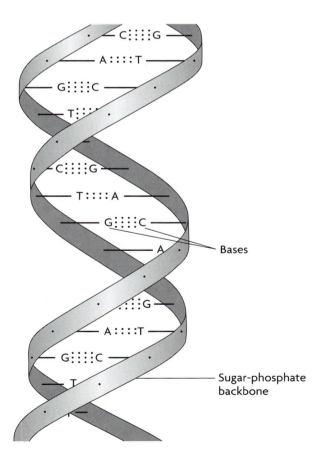

Bases

Sugar-phosphate backbone

Figure 13.2 The DNA double helix, in addition to being very small, is very tightly wound together. Were the 3.3 billion pairs of nucleotides that make up our cells unwound, they would stretch six feet, despite the small size of the nucleotides. Everyone, except for identical twins, has a unique DNA helix or genome.

We were introduced to two technological concepts in Chapter Two that can help us understand how DNA is structured and works. Recall our bits of information, 1 and 0. Instead of a binary coding system that makes up digital information, DNA is information on a four-count system, made up of adenine, cytosine, guanine, and thymine. Just as with the binary information, the biological system varies the combination of the four nucleotides to give specific instructions for cell growth. In Chapter Three we looked at a variety of media for the storage of digital information. One of the storage media we looked at was cassette tape. Recall that digital information on cassette tape is stored sequentially. So if we took three gigabytes, or about 3.3 billion bits of information, and stored them on a cassette tape, we would have a storage system similar in size and structure to DNA. This 3.3 gigs of information contained in a single human cell is enough to store all thirty volumes of the *Encyclopedia Britannica,* several times over.[26]

Just as digital information is often stored in files, our genetic information is organized and retained in our chromosomes. Just as if we were looking for a specific piece of information on a sequential tape, we would look for the file, and then the data place within the sequence. For DNA, the location of a specific piece of information is known as a **locus**.

There is a difference between our digital information and DNA information. The DNA information in each of our cells is actually two merged, and usually identical, copies of information. Recall that our DNA is a result of our parents DNA merging at conception. Most of the information, especially the common characteristics, is identical. Because our parents leave their genetic material behind to create us, we inheret our parents' characteristics, and of course, we can use DNA to prove paternity. Whenever we leave our DNA behind, we can be positively identified through comparison, because only we have that combination of DNA; that makes us unique.

There is only a small amount of DNA that varies from person to person, but one difference in the information per thousand pieces is enough to make us distinguishable from the next person.[27] As human beings, we share most of the same DNA, or genetic code, but that small amount is enough for the DNA to be analyzed and provide the identity of a specific individual. These small differences are referred to as **polymorphisms**. While the polymorphisms make us different,

Toxicology is the science of detecting substances such as drugs, alcohol, and poisons in the blood of offenders and victims.

monomorphisms make us the same. These are the places where all human DNA is the same—we all have two eyes, two hands; they are the things that make us all human beings. Generally, when an analysis of DNA is conducted, two types of polymorphisms are examined. First, an analyst would examine the length of DNA at specific locations, or loci. The variations in length of the DNA at specific locations are called **variable number of tandem repeats (VNTR)**.[28]

When examining VNTR, the analyst is looking at portions of the DNA that are made up of short, repeating patterns. By determining the number of times a DNA pattern repeats within specific loci, an analyst can determine the length of the DNA molecule within the loci. An analyst uses a scientific method known as the **restriction fragment length polymorphism (RFLP)** technique to examine and compare the VNTR. In addition to making comparisons of the length within sections of the DNA, an analyst can simply compare specific base pairs of nucleotides. The comparison of the nucleotides is completed with the scientific method known as **polymerase chain reaction (PCR)**.[29] Essentially, PCR will allow a short stretch of the DNA to be amplified about a millionfold so the analyst can determine the sample's size and nucleotide sequence. The particular stretch of DNA that is being amplified is called the target sequence. An analyst would choose one test over another depending on the amount and quality of the DNA sample.[30] If there is only a small sample, or the quality of the sample is poor, the PCR test is usually used because it requires less DNA and works when the DNA is of poor quality. For instance, a PCR test will work with as little as two-billionths of a gram of material. On the other hand, the RFLP test requires ten to twenty-five

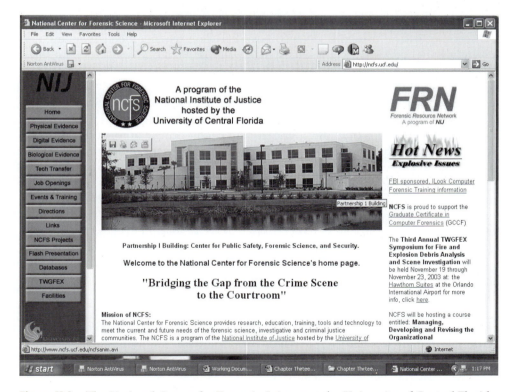

Figure 13.3 The National Center for Forensic Science at the University of Central Florida provides research, education, training, tools, and technology to meet the current and future needs of the forensic science, investigative, and criminal justice communities. View their flash presentation at **ncfs.ucf.edu/index3.html**.

The Southern Blot or transfer method uses a certain enzyme to cut the double helix in half. Each half of the double helix is a fragment called the RFLP. After the RFLP is chemically treated through a very complex process, x-ray film is used to form pictures of the RFLP. If these bands match the offender, or DNA evidence from a crime scene, a mathematical formula is used to calculate the probability of a match. The difficulty in interpreting the sample is the reason that this process is repeated at different locations in the DNA sample in order to confirm and increase the probability of the DNA match. The method of preparing DNA samples for examination in this manner is called *Southern Blotting*. It is named after its inventor.

Sources: "Evolution and Development of Police Technology," 76; Kay and Sensabaugh, "DNA Evidence," 574.

times the amount of sample material. Moreover, a PCR test can be completed in significantly less time than an RFLP test. Typically, a PCR analysis can be conducted in a few days, whereas the RFLP analysis may take several weeks. In PCR analysis there are three basic steps: extraction of the DNA, amplification, and the use of a detection method dependent on the sample type.[31]

Once the DNA evidence is received at the testing laboratory, it is isolated and purified. Then, depending on the type of test chosen, the analyst begins a series of rather complex steps such as cutting the DNA, or **restriction enzyme digestion**; separating the DNA, or **gel electrophoresis**; and transferring the DNA to a surface for examination, or the **southern blotting**. What the analyst is doing is looking at locations where it is known that the human DNA sequence is different. They are not reading the full DNA code of a person.[32]

While most DNA analysis is restricted to the comparison of short strands, an examination of **mitochondrial DNA (mDNA)** is done when a full sequencing test is sought under certain circumstances. Inside almost all of our cells there are small organelles called mitochondria. Their job is to break down the food we eat and the air we breathe into energy for the cell. While our cells each have only one nucleus that can be used for DNA analysis, they contain scores of mitochondria. So while DNA gives us two copies per cell (double intertwined helix), mDNA can give us hundreds or thousands of copies per cell. And each of these mitochondria has its own DNA sequence. Essentially, because there are so many more mitochondria than nuclei, the likelihood of recovering mDNA from a small or degraded sample is greater than for nuclear DNA. But mDNA is passed maternally. Because it is inherited directly from the mother (siblings would share the same mDNA) it is more useful in making comparisons such as associating skeletal remains. For instance, say a family makes a missing person report, and six years later skeletal remains are recovered. One way to confirm that the remains are the missing person is by extracting an mDNA sample from the remains and the possible mother.[33] mDNA testing and analysis are more rigorous and time-consuming than regular DNA analysis. Given the effort and limited applications, it is not as common as DNA analysis.

Two things determine if the DNA analysis of a sample is possible. First, there must be sufficient quantities of the sample present. Although mDNA analysis can be done on much smaller samples than DNA, there are minimum limits. Second, the condition of the sample is of critical import. As with skeletal remains or DNA evidence that has been significantly contaminated, the sample must not be so degraded as to compromise the analysis process.[34] However, even a degraded or contaminated sample can be tested if there is a sufficient quantity of the sample.

What an analyst needs is intact, long DNA molecules. Temperature, oxygen, and water are the primary conditions or substances that cause DNA to degrade.

Clearly, the science of DNA is solid. The difficulties in using DNA evidence in court are connected to the way in which the DNA evidence is recovered from crime scenes and the quality control measures used in DNA-typing results and the DNA evidence's interpretation. On a national level, in order to overcome problems associated with the quality of DNA, the FBI has established two groups charged with establishing guidelines and protocols for the recovery, analysis, and interpretation of DNA evidence. They are the Scientific Working Group on DNA Analysis Methods **(www.fbi.gov/hq/lab/fsc/current/swgdambylaws)** and the DNA Advisory Board (DAB) **(www.fbi.gov/hq/lab/codis/index1.htm)**. The primary action a laboratory can take in order to deter offender challenges to evidence is document its organization and management practices. A review of the common errors made by police officers and DNA analysts reveal that the problem is not with science, but with the way people are trained. Among the common errors are:

- Mislabeling reference samples from the suspect.
- Packaging two wet samples in the same container.
- Mishandling or mislabeling samples in the field.
- Failure to properly document a sample's chain of custody.

Source: Kay and Sensabaugh, "DNA Evidence," 509–511.

With water and oxygen, the problem with contamination is the growth of bacteria. The primary concern here is the storage of evidence that is gathered. If DNA evidence is not stored properly, it will rapidly degrade. Moreover, improper storage methods are one avenue of attack an offender can make on the evidence. An evidence gatherer—often in small agencies that could be the first responder—who does not properly handle, package, and store evidence that may eventually be analyzed for DNA risks rapid deterioration of the evidence. As was stated in the beginning of the chapter, it is the actions of the first responders that often decide the eventual outcome of a scientific investigation. Remember, DNA analysis has to be performed on old blood stains, semen stains, hair, bone, bite marks, vaginal swabs, cigarette butts, urine, and fecal matter. Anything that was touched, left behind, or any place an offender has been can contain trace evidence.

Earlier in this chapter we looked at how forensic evidence is tested by the court for validity. For DNA testing, offenders don't challenge the science, they challenge the application of the science. The most common challenges to DNA evidence in court revolve around which techniques are best used with evidence that has been exposed to the elements, or how a laboratory has followed validated protocols for testing.[35] The final court challenge usually involves the extent to which the chain of custody of a piece of evidence remains unbroken.

At first, DNA was used to link known offenders to specific crimes. In these instances, federal, state, and local police officers obtained a DNA sample from the offender and then had a laboratory compare the offender sample against DNA evidence recovered from a crime scene.[36] As the science and technology matured, DNA samples from offenders were computerized, organized, and stored in DNA databases.[37]

DNA Databanks

It was not long after the value of DNA as evidence was realized that someone started planning a database of DNA samples. England was the first country to establish a nationwide database. Today the English require anyone charged with a recordable offense to provide a DNA sample.[38] In 1990 the FBI began a pilot program called the **Combined DNA Information System (CODIS)**. Around the same time, some states began similar efforts. In 1994 the Violent Crime Control and Law Enforcement Act authorized the FBI to permanently establish a software and hardware system capable of sharing offender DNA information contained in the state and federal databases.[39] Recall that the fingerprint database uses an algorithm to convert the image of a fingerprint into binary code. Of course, this is the only way that a computer can organize the information. CODIS uses an algorithm to organize DNA information in much the same manner.

While IAFIS at the federal level is a single database, CODIS is in reality a combination of databases and is used as a term to describe the federal program that supports that state programs.[40] Currently CODIS is composed of 153 laboratories in forty-nine states and the District of Columbia. Many of the participating states run their own databases and contribute information to the national database, or only run a DNA sample through the federal database if there is no hit in their state database. As of March 2002, CODIS had assisted state and local law enforcement agencies in more than forty-seven hundred investigations.[41]

CODIS is three databases containing DNA profiles of convicted sex offenders, other violent offenders, and missing persons.[42] For instances, if a DNA profile of an offender is gathered during the investigation of a sexual assault and there is no named offender, the state or local laboratory will search the Convicted Offender Index. Presuming there is no match in the Convicted Offender Index, a search of the Forensic Index is conducted. The Forensic Index acts much like a pointer system; it can tell investigating officers that the offender committed another crime wherein DNA evidence was recovered. Often these matches in the Convicted Offender Index are from a different jurisdiction. It is likely that were it not for this index, many cases would never be related.[43]

In 1994 the DNA Identification Act, in addition to creating the national database, offered financial incentives for states to create their own. As a result, all fifty states have legislation requiring different types of offenders to provide DNA samples. At first, most states only required very limited types of offenders to be included in their databases; generally offenders convicted of sexual assault and homicide were required to provide samples. It is said that these two crimes were the predominant classes of offenses chosen because it was believed that there was a higher likelihood that DNA samples in the form of either semen or blood would be left at the associated crime scenes. But as we have seen, as the science and technology in DNA analysis matured, smaller and smaller samples could be used for comparison. Therefore, many states began to expand the classification of offenders required to provide samples.[44] As of 2002, there were more than nine hundred thousand DNA profiles in the Convicted Offender Index and more than thirty-three thousand in the forensic index. As of 2003, the FBI was working on improvements to CODIS that will significantly speed computerized searches and allow for the inclusion of fifty million DNA profiles.[45] Did you read that twice? *Fifty million* DNA profiles. While the DNA database has done a tremendous amount of good work, the nature of DNA is raising social and ethical concerns.[46]

When an offender gives a sample of DNA, he is not giving a sample of just his DNA; he is giving a sample of his entire family's DNA. The closer you are related to someone who has involuntarily given DNA, the more of your personal biological information is being retained by the government. But maybe that's not so bad. After all, a DNA profile is typically a computer algorithm made from a photograph of RFLP banding. The issue becomes more complex when you realize that although the goal is DNA analysis, twenty-nine states are retaining tissue samples after the profiling is completed by the laboratory, and tissue samples can be used to gather information about hereditary traits. The retention of tissue samples is generally justified because it is believed that as the science and technology improves, there will be more ways to test the DNA and more offenders can be connected to crimes.[47]

The increasing abilities of science and technology is also a major part of the controversy. There are some who want to use offender tissue samples for research. They believe that through research they may be able to develop medical therapies and possibly determine genetic traits that may predispose some to commit crime. But doesn't that research apply to you also—presuming you have a relative who has involuntarily supplied a DNA sample? Consider if your child is convicted of a crime and forced to surrender her DNA. Half of her DNA is your DNA.[48] How long will it be before science is able to determine which half belongs to you—and then has your entire genetic profile. What if the therapy that your wayward child could benefit from is found to also be beneficial to you? This is not science fiction, and there are a lot of very smart people working on this science.

Among the other concerns regarding DNA is the way in which it is collected from offenders. In most states, offenders must submit a sample while in prison or before they are released on probation. In at least one state, the government is allowed to take the DNA sample by force. Thus far, courts have upheld statutes authorizing forcible extraction of DNA from offenders for use in offender DNA databases without a search warrant, probable cause, or individualized suspicion.[49] This raises the question of how much force can be used. Generally, the courts look at the taking of blood as minimally intrusive, considering the circumstances. But what if an offender is violently opposed? Should the state knock him down and take it?

Beginning in 1899, when a juvenile court system was established in Chicago, juvenile offenders are treated differently than adult offenders. One of the important differences was the ability to seal or eliminate a juvenile offender's criminal record after a certain period of time. However, in comparison, no DNA database statute requires DNA profiles or samples collected from juvenile offenders to be purged or sealed. In fact, Arizona prohibits the elimination of juvenile DNA records and Texas distinguishes between DNA data and fingerprints and/or criminal records. This scheme makes sense given the potential for juvenile offenders to commit violent offenses as adults, but it is a departure from the concept that the juvenile justice system is primarily designed to rehabilitate the child.

Sources: Siegel, *Criminology;* Kimmelman, "Ethical Insolvency," 209.

The final controversy surrounding DNA databases is their inclusiveness. As we saw, they started out as repositories for information about very violent offenders. We saw that in England every person convicted of a recordable offense is required to submit a sample. The definition of a recordable offense somewhat varies, but generally, that is any offense that could be put on your criminal history. Anything more serious than parking tickets, such as simple battery or drunk driving, is recordable. Who should be in the database? Apparently, there are going to be more than forty-one million vacant spots soon.

Software and Criminal Investigations

In Part Two we looked at a variety of software applications designed specifically for law enforcement (Figure 13.4). For just about any function, someone creative is designing a software system. As we look at a few examples, think about their applications inside law enforcement but outside criminal investigations. In other words, investigating a crime is very much like solving a problem. The correct answer to the criminal investigation problem is the identity of the offender. Much of the software is designed to supplement the crime solving

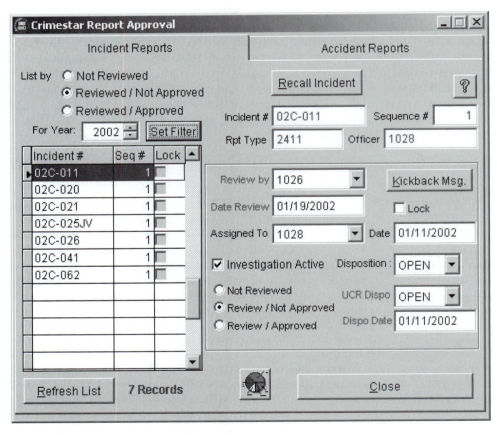

Figure 13.4 Although we have spent a considerable amount of time looking at the collection, analysis, and management of evidence, technology has also impacted the way in which investigations are managed. Both initial crime reports and follow-up investigative reports are generally reviewed by supervisory personnel. As technology nudges state and local agencies toward becoming less paper dependent, new software is being used to review, "kick back," and approve reports.
Screen capture provided by Crimestar Corporation.

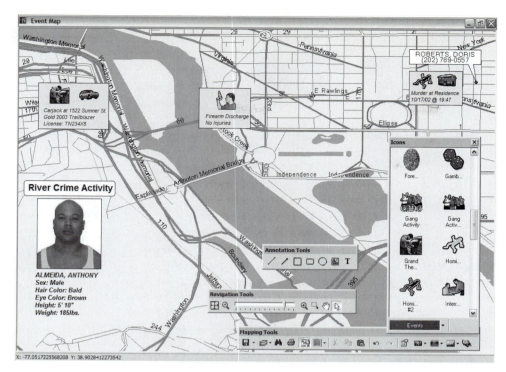

Figure 13.5 By combining GIS technology, link-analysis software, and the information gathered during an investigation, a police officer can use software like this to create a spatial display of case information.
Screen capture provided by Pen-Link™, Ltd.

problem of investigations. But if you look closely, it has applications for problem solving in the general community (Figure 13.5).

Unlike on television, detectives do not carry one case at a time. In one large jurisdiction, the case load backlog (backlog is the number of assigned criminal investigations) is not measured in numbers; it is measured in the number of feet the unassigned cases total when stacked vertically on the floor. So detectives, much like their cousins in uniform, have multiple tasks to perform. One software application in law enforcement is for case management. With a good case load management software program, a supervising detective can review the number of assigned cases, the number of follow-up investigations completed, the status of evidence, and any number of critical tasks. However, case load management software only gives a general idea of real case load. Recall that the computer can count, but unless we tell it to weigh things differently, it will not know the difference between a detective with complex cases and one with relatively straightforward cases. Sometimes, just based on the charge, this is relatively easy to discern. We expect a murder investigation to be more complex than a car break-in. So when looking at the case load, a supervisor could make a pretty good estimate on investigative productivity.

When I first started in police work, when one responded to a traffic collision, one was responsible to draw a picture of the accident scene. One of the first things you bought yourself was a small ruler that had a template of small overturned cars and run-over pedestrians. Even if you were an art moron like me, you could still draw the accident scene. A few years later, someone got the idea of saving the drawings of major intersections when they had been done by someone

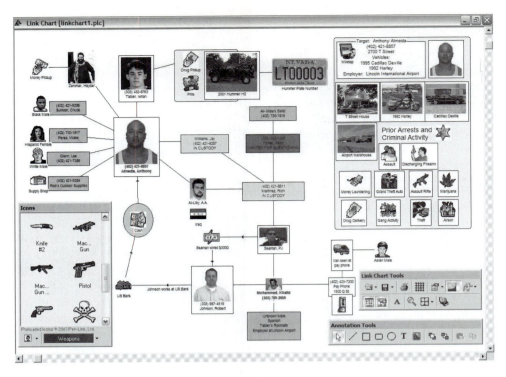

Figure 13.6 Particularly in large or complex investigations, recording, organizing, and using the information can be a daunting task. Software programs, like in the screen capture here, assist police officers in creating visual displays of how information relates to an offender or investigation.
Screen capture provided by Pen-Link™, Ltd.

who was more artistically inclined. So the first thing you did at an accident scene was call the station and see if a template of that intersection was available. If so, after taking preliminary measurements, you went to the station, photocopied the predrawn scene and scribbled your rendering. Now there is software that does it all.

Traffic collisions are the only drawings police agencies produce. At any major crime scene, there is going to be a drawing of where evidence was located and the general layout of the location. There are a variety of software applications available that allow you to draw crime scenes and traffic collisions. Some allow the saving of previously done intersections so all you need to do is click and drag. Not only are the drawings much more efficiently completed, but they are ultimately more professional and useful, especially when you finally get to court.

The more complex the investigation, the larger the amount of information investigators are going to amass. This is especially true about investigations into criminal organizations like gangs. Having the ability to store the information and complete an analysis on the information can be very useful. This is generally called **link-analysis** (Figure 13.6). As an investigator or teams of investigators uncover information, it is entered into the software application, in a relational database. The link-analysis software application allows the police officer to look at the relationships among information through a visual display. This type of software application can prevent duplication of effort, can uncover new investigative avenues, and is very useful for presentations to judges or juries on how the information tends to prove something, like a conspiracy.

Link-analysis software can also be useful in solving community problems. As we have stated many times, there may be many underlying causal factors that create a community problem. By inputting information into a link-analysis software application, you might see relationships to problems that you did not know existed, and you may be able to show how other community and government entities are related to the problem or the solution. Many of the software applications used to solve the crime problem of "who dunnit" can be used to assist in solving general community problems. Only your imagination is holding you back.

Digital Photography

State and local police agencies are increasingly turning to the use of digital photography to replace film. However, as of 2000, only 16 percent of local agencies, employing 47 percent of all police officers, used digital imaging technology.[50] The use of digital photography makes sense because it is much less expensive and because you can look through the screen on the camera and preview the photograph to know you are taking the picture you need. Let's briefly look at how digital photography works and then look at some of the challenges.

A digital photograph is a photograph taken in such a manner as to be in a language that computers understand. Recall from our earlier chapters, computers work with binary language. Therefore, to take a digital photograph we have to convert the image we want to photograph to a digital file. A digital photograph is very much like every other computer file. It is binary data organized in a manner to be recognized by the computers as an image. As we know, the images we view on computer visual displays—such as computer monitors, television sets, and view ports of digital cameras—are made up of pixels.

The simplest explanation of a digital camera is that it takes a sample of the light that is reflected off the image you are viewing and converts it into a picture. Without going too far back into your third grade science class, remember that the real-life images and colors we see are an effect of radiated light reflecting off images. I see a red shirt because the color of the shirt (red) reflects the spectrum of light that represents the color red.

The digital camera focuses the light on a semiconductor where it is then broken down into digital information that a computer can understand. Recall we looked at the essence of a digital camera in Chapter Six—the charged coupling device. The same technology is used in a digital camera as is used in the fingerprint scanner. (There are low end cameras that use CMOS technology, but we will assume that a law enforcement agency that purchased digital cameras had the sense to buy reasonable equipment.)

Recall that the CCD uses photosite technology to capture light images. Well, a photosite is colorblind. It sees light but not color. To get color photography, a filter system must be used to obtain the three primary colors. Once those colors have been recorded by the camera, the spectrum of colors we see can be re-created. One of the ways that digital cameras employ filtering systems is to place a filter over three separate sensors. The light is then directed to different sensors by a beam splitter. The beam splitter sends an equal amount of light to each filtered sensor, and each sensor is responsible for seeing only a certain primary color. This is one of the cool things about splitting a beam of light; each beam, if they are equal, has the complete image. That is counter-intuitive but true. In fact, that is the essence of hologram technology.

The most common challenge to digital photography is that the binary data that makes up the image can be manipulated. Of course, we have all seen examples of someone putting someone's head on a second person's torso. There are two ways for a state and local agency to overcome this challenge. First, cameras can be purchased that are designed to create a file that cannot easily be manipulated without destroying the file. I say "cannot easily," but some claim that it can't be done. Given the time, somebody could. In addition to overcoming this challenge, a state or local agency needs to introduce policies and procedures that are consistent with the technology, such as establishing a chain of custody for the image file as they would any evidence. Second, the image is not evidence. In reality, fingerprints aren't really evidence. Evidence is people's testimony about physical objects and the inferences they draw. A photograph, a fingerprint, or any other evidence cannot introduce itself into court. Someone must do it. Well-trained and well-supervised employees who are following thoughtful policies and procedures should be able to introduce digital images into court without too much resistance.

Chapter Summary

As science and technology advance, the need to ensure proper crime scene protection increases. The actions by first responders, such as crime scene protection, witness interviews, and direct observations, are often more instrumental in solving crimes than the follow-up efforts of investigators. Advances in fingerprint lifting and DNA analysis have made more information available, but at the same time placed more of a burden on first responders to protect the crime scene. Although we concentrated on fingerprint and DNA evidence, all manner of trace evidence can be found at any crime scene. It is up to the first responders, evidence gatherers, and investigators to ensure that all evidence is used to tell the story of what happened.

While fingerprint science and technology have certainly changed from strategic information to more tactical information, DNA evidence is far surpassing fingerprint identification as the primary crime scene evidence. Fingerprint evidence differs from DNA evidence in two important ways. First, to transfer fingerprint evidence, an offender must touch something, but with DNA evidence, an offender has to merely be present at the crime scene. Second, fingerprint evidence tells the police only the offender's identity, whereas DNA evidence can tell the police the offender's identity and provide information about the offender's genetics.

DNA databases are used to make comparisons among offenders and crimes, and among different crimes. As we have seen in the examples in Michigan and Louisana, linking an offender to multiple crimes can provide information that leads to the offender's identity. But some states keep not only the offender's DNA profile, but also tissue samples. A critical question in the future is going to be how we use these samples. Do we allow research? As we get further into the text, it should become apparent that today's information technology experts are becoming less technical people and more policy makers. As science and technology advance, the consequences of those advances must be considered and policy determinations made.

We briefly looked at digital photography. The initial costs of a digital camera can be more than a film-based photography system, but the digital camera, because there is neither film nor developing costs, will probably be a neutral cost item. However, because you see the image before you create the image file, it gives even the novice crime scene photographer the ability to produce quality images. Issues surrounding tampering can be minimized by purchasing the right software applications for the digital camera and establishing good chain of custody policies and procedures. As with almost all evidence, the issues surrounding the integrity of digital photography evidence directly relate to the integrity of the employee taking the photograph and the systems, policies, and procedures of the agency that ensure proper handling of the evidence. Ultimately, someone has to testify that the photograph is a visual representation of the crime scene, tool mark, etc. Nearly always, it is the integrity of that person, not the technology, that is the issue.

While the software applications we looked at have the potential to significantly enhance the investigative ability of a state or local police agency, they can also be useful when applied to general community problems.

Discussion Questions

1. Given that DNA information contained in an offender database contains some DNA information about family members, what potential problems or abuses could occur?

2. Some states have DNA collection and retention statutes that allow for the DNA tissues to be used for research. There is the potential for genetic research to develop educational, therapeutic, or pharmacological inventions that may prevent crime. However, most DNA was collected from offenders without their consent. Do you see a difference between using seized DNA as evidence as opposed to research? What potential problems or abuses could occur?

3. As we have seen, with today's computer technology, fingerprint and DNA evidence have both tactical and strategic value as information. Some have argued that a universal DNA and fingerprint database, which would contain information from every American, would solve crimes and deter crimes because people would be unlikely to commit crimes if they knew their DNA and fingerprint information was not only "on file," but also readily accessible.[51] How much deterrence effect do you think universal databases would have? Are you in favor of universal databases? Why?

4. Clearly, DNA evidence has strategic value to law enforcement in that it can be used for the investigation of crimes. Recall in Chapter Six we examined how technology increased the strategic value of fingerprint evidence and gave law enforcement tactical uses for fingerprint information. Currently the technology does not exist that turns DNA evidence from strategic to tactical information. However, it is quite conceivable that science and technology will develop to the point where DNA analysis can be done rapidly and in the field. At that point, DNA might have tactical value. If the science and technology were to develop to the point that DNA evidence had tactical value (immediate use by law enforcement personnel), what uses would the information have? Do you see any potential problems?

Key Terms

Chain of Custody
Chromosomes
Combined DNA Information System (CODIS)
Daubert Test
Deoxyribonucleic Acid (DNA)
Double Helix
Forensic Science
Gel Electrophoresis
Genes
Kyllo

Laser
Link-Analysis
Locus
Mitochondrial DNA (mDNA)
Monomorphism
Nucleotides
Nucleus
Polymer
Polymerase Chain Reaction (PCR)
Polymorphism

Restriction Enzyme Digestion
Restriction Fragment Length Polymorphism (RFLP)
Serology
Southern Blotting
Theory of Transfer
Variable Number of Tandem Repeats (VNTR)

End Notes

1. "Evolution and Development of Police Technology," 72.
2. The Bureau of Justice Statistics reports to the United States Department of Justice. The complete report is available at **www.ojp.usdoj.gov/bjs**.
3. Shafritz, *Public Policy and Administration,* 445.
4. "Evolution and Development of Police Technology," 70.
5. "Searching and Seizing Computers and Obtaining Electronic Evidence in Criminal Investigations" Computer Crime and Intellectual Property Section, Criminal Division, United States Department of Justice, January 2001: 9.
6. Kyllo v. United States, 533 U.S. 27 (2001).
7. Markowitz, "Remote Sensing and Digital Information," 219.
8. Kay and Sensabaugh, "DNA Evidence," 489.
9. Ibid.
10. U.S. Congress, Office of Technology Assessment, *Criminal Justice, New Technologies, and the Constitution,* 19.
11. Ibid.
12. Kimmelman, "Ethical Insolvency," 209.
13. "Evolution and Development of Police Technology," 74.
14. Pastore and Maguire, "Sourcebook of Criminal Justice Statistics."
15. Laidler, *To Light Such a Candle,* 289.
16. Kay and Sensabaugh, "DNA Evidence," 491.
17. Laidler, *To Light Such a Candle,* 273.
18. "The Evolution and Development of Police Technology," 75.
19. Laidler, *To Light Such a Candle,* 231.
20. Ibid., 273.
21. Ibid., 271.
22. See note 16 above.
23. Laidler, *To Light Such a Candle,* 274.
24. See note 18 above.
25. Laidler, *To Light Such a Candle,* 273.
26. Ibid., 289.
27. Ibid., 290.
28. Kay and Sensabaugh, "DNA Evidence," 492–493.
29. Ibid., 497.
30. "Evolution and Development of Police Technology," 76.
31. Kay and Sensabaugh, "DNA Evidence," 497.
32. Ibid., 493.
33. Ibid., 495.
34. Ibid., 503.
35. Ibid., 489.
36. Ibid., 491.
37. Peterson, "DNA Databases," 1219.
38. Ibid.
39. See note 12 above.
40. Adams, "Statement for the Record."
41. Ibid.
42. "Toward Improved Criminal Justice."
43. See note 40 above.
44. See note 37 above.
45. Adams, "Statement for the Record."
46. See note 12 above.
47. Ibid.
48. See note 12 above.
49. See note 37 above.
50. The Bureau of Justice Statistics reports to the United States Department of Justice. The complete report is available at **www.ojp.usdoj.gov/bjs**.
51. See note 37 above.

Chapter Fourteen
Wiretaps

Learning Objectives

- The student will understand the context and value of gathering information in a covert manner.

- The student will understand the difference between capturing **device-identifying information** and **call-content information**; and, the value of each.

- The student will understand the impact of the **Communications Assistance for Law Enforcement Agencies (CALEA) Act**.

- The student will understand the general legal requirements for a wiretap.

- The student will understand how wiretaps are conducted.

- The student will understand the legal requirements and operational aspects of PEN registries, traps, and traces.

- The student will understand whose Internet communications are intercepted by law enforcement.

- The student will receive a brief overview of the **PATRIOT Act**.

Introduction

In the preceding chapters we established that the gathering, retention, and analysis of information is a key law enforcement task. So far, we have looked at information that comes from official sources. Those sources might be statistical or crime information collected by the agency or collected at some regional level. The information might come from sources external to the agency, such as the motor vehicle department, the National Crime Information Center (NCIC), or the Financial Crimes Enforcement Network (FinCEN). We have also seen some of the information can come from commercial sources, such as credit reports. This type of information can be thought of as coming from official sources. However, there are other ways that law enforcement agencies gather information.

Law enforcement information can also be gathered from the observations of police officers, from citizen reports, and from the offenders themselves. Typically police officers are gathering information through observations when they detect changes to the community wherein they work. For instance, a police officer might observe freshly painted graffiti. Often that graffiti is gang related and can be interpreted by the police officer. It might contain information on gang vendettas, crimes that have occurred, or changes in gang leadership. In another instance, a police officer might observe a crime in progress. The most common occurrence is our traffic violator from Chapter One. In that instance, the police officer observed a speeding vehicle and took action based on that information. The observations and interpretations of graffiti and crimes in progress are typical ways that police officers gather information.

Information about crime can also come from citizens. Recall our 9-1-1 call in Chapter Seven. In that instance, the citizen was reporting what she believed to be a crime in progress. Generally speaking, information coming from citizens is presumed to be reliable. A citizen who reports something to the police is presumed to be making the report out of a sense of civic duty. Experience shows that often citizens report information that they believe to be suspicious but turns out to be quite normal. Take the example of a citizen who observes an unfamiliar motor vehicle parked on his street. If he saw a person sitting in the vehicle, he might be prompted to call the police. In many instances, the responding police officer finds out that the person sitting in the motor vehicle has a reason to be in that neighborhood, which is not criminal. With this example, the police officer who stops and talks to the person in the vehicle is acting on information provided by the citizen.

Police officers also obtain information from the offenders themselves. Information that is obtained from offenders can be divided into two fairly broad classifications. The first is when an offender voluntarily supplies the police officer with information. One of the ways that police officers gather information from offenders is to interview them about crimes for which they are accused. This is done during some type of interview, possibly in the field or in the police station. During instances where police officers are interviewing offenders about crimes for which they are accused, a large body of case law regulates the conduct of the police officer; most typically, we think of Miranda.[1] Police officers also interview offenders for information about crimes for which they have knowledge but are not necessarily involved.

Offenders who provide information about crimes for which they are not necessarily involved are referred to as informants. There is an axiom in law enforcement that goes something like, "If you want to know about sin, you are not going to talk to Angels." With informants, the fact that they are offenders makes their use as sources of information problematic. There are a bevy of problems and potential problems involved in the use of informants, but even though there are inherent dangers, there is nothing like the real-time information they can provide. Typically, when we think of informants, we think of offenders who are providing specific information about criminal conduct to a specific police officer. The fact that informants are cultivated, developed, and used by individual police officers is one of their greatest potentials for problems. In addition to police officers developing informants, there is a move in law enforcement to obtain more general information from offenders.

Some law enforcement agencies are beginning to debrief all offenders that come into their custody. One research project noted that 67 percent of arrested persons are willing to provide information about other crimes. Sometimes this information is specific—the offender knows about another crime that has been committed or that someone is planning to commit. But, most often, the information obtained during these debriefings seems general in nature. For instance, the debriefed offender might comment that he or she has seen "a guy selling stolen computer equipment around the neighborhood." On the face of it, that seems like a fairly general statement that would be difficult to take police action on. However, what if this offender was being interviewed by the same agency that conducted the crime analysis in Chapter Twelve? Could this information be useful in that investigation? Consider two different police officers receiving that information—one who works in a law enforcement agency with a weak or nonexistent crime analysis unit and the second who works in our imaginary law enforcement agency that uses crime alerts or criminal intelligence bulletins. The second police officer would probably key in on the offender's statement and ask questions that might provide at least a general description of the burglary suspect. The point is that debriefing an offender has the potential to develop meaningful information at a very minimal cost.

Law enforcement agencies also gather information from offenders without the offenders knowing. Gathering information directly from the offender, without the offender's knowledge, is the definition of **covert surveillance**. We are centering on covert surveillance, but there is also overt surveillance. An example of overt surveillance would be security personnel assigned to patrol a parking lot in a mall. Their purpose is to watch the activities in the parking lot in order to deter criminal activity. The person conducting this type of surveillance wants to be seen. On the other hand, covert means hidden. The purpose of covert surveillance is to gather information without the person under surveillance realizing it. Don't we all act differently when we know someone is watching or listening?

Covert surveillance can have extraordinary value to law enforcement investigations and operations. Simply put, there is nothing like hearing people talk about what they did or what they are going to do, or watching someone actually commit a crime. Although very valuable, it is at the same time fraught with pitfalls for the police, the offender, and society. Moreover, as technology has advanced, covert surveillance has become increasingly complex and expensive to conduct. Because it can be so valuable and is becoming relatively easy, the amount of covert surveillance conducted by law enforcement agencies is increasing.

In this chapter we are going to look at the technological means for gathering information by listening in a covert manner. By listening, we mean state and local law enforcement agencies intercepting telephone conversations. While we will very briefly look at the ability to intercept Internet communications such as e-mail and instant messaging, our focus is voice. Furthermore, when law enforcement agencies are investigating terrorism and international spying, the rules for intercepting electronic communications are different. Since most state and local law enforcement agencies are not involved in these types of investigations, we will focus on covert surveillance as it relates to the investigation of domestic crimes.

The Electronic Surveillance of Telephone Conversations

When we refer to **electronic surveillance**, we mean intercepting the **content information** and/or the **device-identifying information**. Content information is the substance of the message. In a conversation it is the voices of the parties talking. In an e-mail message it is the content of the message. Simply put, content information is the message. Recall from Chapter Seven that when you make a telephone call from your home, automatic number information (ANI) accompanies that call. In the instance of a cellular telephone call, in addition to the ANI, the electronic serial number (ESN) of the cellular device is sent. So for telephone conversations there are at least two types of device-identifying information, the ANI and ESN.

Electronic surveillance for the purpose of capturing the content information from a telephone is commonly called a **wiretap**. Most wiretaps capture device-identifying information in addition to content information. However, when only device-identifying information is captured, this is done through **pen registers**, **traps**, and **traces**. As we look at the purposes, devices, and techniques used for electronic surveillance, these terms will become clearer.

Since the inception of commercial telephone service, there has always been someone covertly listening to conversations. Much of early telephone service was party-line service where if you picked up a residential telephone, you were likely to overhear your neighbors having a conversation. In the beginning of commercial telephone service, it was much less expensive to put several houses on one line.

Call content information is succinctly defined as "any type of electronic communications sent by or sent to the intercept subject, including transfer of signals, writing, images, sounds, data, or intelligence of any nature."
Source: U.S. Congress, Office of Technology Assessment, "Electronic Surveillance."

As the telephone industry grew, more and more households were given single lines. Eventually, commercial telephone service matured to the point where most people had single-line service. Furthermore, it hasn't always been the police listening to conversations. Wiretaps have been used for governments to spy on each other, commercial espionage, and individual blackmail. Although it probably wasn't long after commercial telephone service was implemented that someone used the telephone in the furtherance of a crime, it wasn't until 1928 that there was a significant court challenge to the use of wiretaps by law enforcement personnel.

The Fourth Amendment of the United States Constitution guarantees that "the right of the people to be secure in their persons, houses, papers, and effects, against unreasonable searches and seizures shall not be violated."[2] A way to look at how this applies to wiretaps is to think of our private communications as our personal property. The government should not be able to seize our private communications without a warrant because they are our personal property. However, in 1928, in *Olmstead v. United States*, the Supreme Court decided that a wiretap did not violate the Fourth Amendment of the United States Constitution.[3] What the Court decided was that a wiretap was not a violation of the Fourth Amendment unless is involved "trespass." At the time of the *Olmstead* decision, there were no statutes dealing with wiretaps.[4] Congress had written no laws, rules, or regulations for the use of wiretaps.

In 1934 Congress passed the Communications Act of 1934. In Section 605 of the act, Congress stated, "no person not being authorized by the sender shall intercept any communication and divulge or publish its existence."[5] A straightforward interpretation of this law could mean that wiretaps were essentially illegal. However, the wording of the law was left open to interpretation and law enforcement officials continued to conduct wiretaps. For the next forty years, there would be a number of court challenges, but it essentially held that as long as law enforcement officials did not trespass onto private property in order to conduct electronic surveillance, the information gained was not protected by the Fourth Amendment.[6]

In 1967 two cases decided by the Supreme Court changed the view on wiretaps.[7] Today our private communications are protected by the Fourth Amendment. We tend to think of this as the right to privacy, which was made explicit in *Griswold v. Connecticut,* a Supreme Court decision striking down a contraceptive law. The concept that the government cannot seize our personal communications being articulated as the right to privacy is a phenomenon of the previous century.[8] Just about everyone would agree that although the framers of the Constitution did not have telephones, they would agree that our personal conversations deserve the same Constitutional protection as our personal letters, papers, and other property.

Because the Fourth Amendment protects private communications, judicial review and court order are required before law enforcement can conduct certain types of electronic surveillance during the course of a criminal investigation. Because of the PATRIOT Act, how the government intercepts electronic signals relative to national security and terrorism issues is different than domestic criminal issues, and we are focusing on state and local law enforcement agencies conducting domestic criminal investigations.[9] However, at the end of this chapter, we will look at some aspects of the PATRIOT Act that can impact state and local law enforcement officers. The judicial review and order comes either in the form of a search warrant or a court order.

IN THE _____ SUPERIOR COURT

COUNTY OF _____, STATE OF CALIFORNIA

RE: ORDER AUTHORIZING [TELEPHONE TRAP] [NUMBER SEARCH] [DIALED NUMBER RECORDER] [LINE HISTORY BLOCK CHECK] [STAR 69 TRACE]

No. _____

ORDER

Having considered the affidavit of [name of affiant], hereinafter "affiant" of the [name of law enforcement agency], this court finds that the information ordered disclosed herein is relevant to an ongoing criminal investigation, and that Pacific Bell, a telephone corporation as defined in California Public Utilities Code § 234, has received notice that this order was being sought. It is hereby ordered that Pacific Bell, through its employees and agents, shall take the following action:

Install, provide facilities required for installation, and provide technical assistance required for installation of equipment commonly known as a "dialed number recorder" which will detect and record the numbers dialed or pulsed by the telephone(s) connected to telephone number [insert target phone number]. Furthermore, Pacific Bell shall furnish affiant with a record of such calls and, upon request of affiant shall furnish it with the name and address of the subscriber of record, whether published or nonpublished, of each telephone number recorded by the dialed number recorder.

RELEASE OF INFORMATION: Pacific Bell shall furnish affiant with all information gathered pursuant to this order at reasonable intervals while this order is in effect.

COMPENSATION: Affiant's employer shall compensate and/or reimburse Pacific Bell for all charges and expenses incurred in complying with this order.

NONDISCLOSURE: Having determined there is probable cause to believe that disclosure of the existence or execution of this court order would impede a criminal investigation, it is ordered that Pacific Bell, and its officers, employees, and agents shall not disclose to any person any information regarding the existence or execution of this court order or any information obtained pursuant to this order unless ordered to do so by this court.

DURATION OF ORDER: Pacific Bell shall begin the dialed number recorder operation required by this order on [insert date] and terminate such operation on [insert date] unless a written extension is granted.

JURISDICTION: This court has jurisdiction to issue this order pursuant to California Penal Code § 1523 *et seq* which gives magistrates jurisdiction to issue search warrants, and California Code of Civil Procedure § § 128, 187 which give the courts authority to carry their jurisdiction into effect.

Date Judge of the Superior Court

Figure 14.1 The document here is a template used for a DNR and telephone trap court order. A typical judicial order encompasses: (1) identity of the person whose conversations are to be intercepted, (2) the identity of the communications facilities to be used, (3) a specific description of the type of information to be intercepted, (4) the identity of the police officer and the law enforcement agency authorized to conduct the wiretap, (5) the period of the order (which cannot exceed thirty days), and (6) an order requiring the law enforcement agency to minimize the interception of conversations not relevant to the investigation.
Source: Dunham, "Carnivore."

In some cases, police officers are seeking telephone records. When police officers are searching for an existing record of telephone calls an offender has completed, the police officer uses a search warrant to obtain those records from the commercial carrier. When police officers are seeking to monitor, intercept, or record real-time conversations and data, they need a court order. In essence, search warrants are used to seize that which the police officer believes to already exist, and court orders are used to seize future conversations and data.

There are some instances wherein state and local police officers can electronically record communications without warrant. For instance, return to our traffic violator from Chapter One; during the issuance of the citation of speeding, our police officer can surreptitiously record the conversation between herself and the traffic violator. The Court has found that we have no reasonable expectation of privacy when speaking with a uniformed police officer. It is also fairly commonplace to transport co-offenders from the location of their arrest to the police station in the same vehicle. Many times the police will walk from the vehicle and allow the offenders a "private" moment. Since there is no reasonable expectation of privacy while you are handcuffed in the rear seat of a police vehicle, the police officers can record anything the offenders say, so if they discuss the crime, that recording can be used against them. Generally speaking, telephone calls made by agents of the police to offenders can be recorded without the offenders' knowledge. Typically the police will have the victim call the offender and attempt to illicit incriminating statements. The final two examples of electronic interception or recording of conversations that do not require judicial review are the use of a body wire and the installation of devices to capture incoming call data when used by the victim of a crime.

In 1968 Congress passed the Omnibus Crime Control and Safe Streets Act. This act specified rules that state and local law enforcement agencies must follow in order to use wiretaps. The regulations decided upon by Congress required that each federal and state judge who reviewed an application authorizing law enforcement officials to intercept private communications to submit an annual report to the Director of the Administrative Office of the United States Court.[10] As we have discussed, a variety of private communications between individuals can be electronically overheard. The 1968 act required that any effort to intercept a communication that infringed on an individual's Fourth Amendment rights required prosecutorial and judicial review.

Subsequent to the 1968 act, forty-three states, the District of Columbia, and the Virgin Islands have enacted similar (and in many instances, more restrictive) legislation enabling the use of wiretaps by state and local law enforcement agencies.[11,12] In the seven states without legislation (Alabama, Arkansas, Kentucky, Michigan, Montana, South Carolina, and Vermont), state and local law enforcement officials do not initiate wiretaps.[13]

Recall from Chapters Six and Seven that at the time of the 1968 act, there was essentially one commercial telephone service provider in the United States—American Telephone and Telegraph (AT&T). In 1968 telephone service was

---

Try This

You can examine your state's wiretap legislation and any additional safeguards they have put in place at **www.constitutionproject.org/ls/ 50statesummary.doc**.

essentially a big network of hardwired telephones. Moreover, because there was essentially only one service provider, equipment tended to be very standardized across the nation. From the inception of commercial telephone service until the mid-1980s, a wiretap consisted of police officials physically clipping wires onto the line they wanted to tap. Very shortly after the breakup of AT&T, telephone service drastically changed in a number of ways.

As we know, with the breakup of AT&T, numerous companies moved into the telephone market. Each of these companies had their own ideas, their own standards, and a variety of protocols and equipment. At the same time, cellular, Internet, and digital communications devoured analog service like Pacman on a binge. In a very short period of time, it became technologically difficult and expensive for law enforcement agencies to employ wiretaps.

By the late 1980s, it became apparent that because of the changes in technology and the fragmentation in technological standards created by the competitive market, law enforcement was going to need some kind of legislation to ensure access to wiretaps. In 1994 Congress passed the **Communications Assistance for Law Enforcement Act (CALEA)**. Essentially, CALEA requires commercial communications service providers to develop equipment, facilities, and services that enable electronic surveillance by law enforcement officials. Initially, the Federal Communications Commission (FCC), which administers CALEA, gave the market until October of 1998 to comply with the act, but that deadline was extended until June of 2002. In addition to establishing standards that commercial communications service providers must meet, CALEA provides $500 million in reimbursement for upgrades, changes, and expenses service providers incur when modifying equipment installed prior to January 1, 1995.

CALEA demands that communications service providers meet certain other requirements. It is important to understand that the service provider is responsible for intercepting the call and routing it to the law enforcement monitoring station. Therefore, the service provider must make sure that both call content and call-identifying information are accurate and not altered and that the intercepted call is routed to the law enforcement agency in a standard format. The service provider must decode, decrypt, and decompress the information before forwarding it and must ensure the call information is routed through a minimum number of states and devices before being transmitted to the law enforcement monitoring station.

Operational security refers to the steps taken by both the communications service provider and the law enforcement agency to ensure that the targets, or unauthorized persons, do not become aware of the electronic surveillance. CALEA requires that the call be transparent to the offender. **Transparency** means that nothing is changed in the means or reception of the subject of the intercepted calls. If the wiretap is transparent, the offender does not know the line is trapped. In addition to transparency, the service provider must prevent disclosure of the existence of the wiretap to unauthorized people and restrict the knowledge of the wiretap to as few individuals as is practical. Operational security is also a paramount concern for the law enforcement agency. As we shall see,

---

Try This

Visit the FCC Web site and take a look at their FAQs on CALEA (**www.fcc.gov/calea**).

the procedure for obtaining a wiretap involves personnel from the law enforcement agency, the prosecutorial agency, and the judiciary agency. While it is unlikely that any of these individuals would intentionally divulge the existence of a wiretap, the more people who know about the operation, the more likely it is that the operation will be compromised. It is important that only people with the right to know and the need to know be informed of even the existence of a wiretap. Sometimes just the knowledge that an agency is conducting a wiretap is enough for the operation to be compromised.

The procedure for obtaining permission to instigate a wiretap is significantly more complex that obtaining a search warrant. For state and local law enforcement agencies, the use of search warrants is fairly common. A search warrant involves a police officer applying directly to a judicial authority. In the search warrant, the police officer (called the affiant in the search warrant) tells the judicial authority about his expertise, the probable cause to believe that certain evidence is located somewhere, and how that evidence tends to prove a certain crime was committed. Presuming the police officer has done a good job, the judicial authority grants the warrant to search a specific place for a specific thing and, usually, within a certain time parameter. The agency policies regarding search warrants vary. However, in most agencies, only supervisory review of the warrant is required before the police officer submits it to the judicial authority.

A wiretap requires that the judicial authority issue a court order. Moreover, the 1968 act requires that the local prosecutor review the wiretap request before it is submitted to the court.[14] Because of the review of the local prosecutor, a wiretap request is often also reviewed at the top levels of agency management. There are considerably more levels of review in the procedure to obtain a wiretap than a normal search warrant. In an effort to understand the rules, regulations, and procedures for obtaining a wiretap, let's follow a typical investigation that might use a wiretap.

A Typical Wiretap Investigation

Let's return to the same agency we watched conduct a crime analysis in Chapter Twelve. Recall that our imaginary police department is a suburban municipal police department for a city of one hundred thousand people, twenty-four square miles and is surrounded by three other independent municipalities with their own police departments. The department employs 180 full-time sworn officers and thirty civilian employees. For operational purposes, the city is divided into ten distinct beats. Law enforcement efforts to thwart drug dealers have been the primary reason for obtaining wiretaps for the past several years. In 2001 78 percent (or 1,167) of the wiretaps were used in narcotics investigations.[15] So let's presume that our agency is investigating a drug dealer.

The local agency has two detectives assigned to investigate narcotics and vice-related crimes. The detectives receive information from an informant that John Smith is a mid-level drug dealer involved in the sales and transportation of methamphetamine.[16] Using the basic information they have received, the detectives positively identify Smith. A review of Smith's criminal history reveals that he has been arrested four times for drug dealing and that one of those arrests resulted in a prison sentence. The detectives follow Smith and observe him meeting with street drug dealers. The detectives are able to arrest several of those street dealers, and they confirm that Smith is their supplier.

During the course of their investigation, our detectives have contacted numerous other sources of information, and through the Financial Crimes Enforcement

Network (FinCEN), they find out that Smith has made several large cash deposits to a local bank. They also know from the state motor vehicle department that Smith owns six new and expensive automobiles. Finally, they determine that Smith, who lives very well, has no job. Based on their investigation, our detectives develop sufficient probable cause to believe that Smith is a mid-level dealer, but the detectives decide that they want to discover the extent of Smith's network and his supplier. The detectives decide to use a wiretap in order to gain further evidence against Smith and determine the scope of his network and supplies.

In order to use a wiretap, the detectives must determine what kind of communications device and service provider Smith is using. What is his home telephone number? Does he have a cellular telephone? Does he have a paging device? Our detectives might rely on the commercial sources of information and some official sources of information to determine Smith's telephone number. But that information is often dated and generally only tells the user the telephone numbers Smith has reported using. Moreover, telephone numbers and service providers are easily changed. So in order to get the most current information on Smith, the detectives need a court order or a search warrant that they will serve on service providers. Generally, commercial communications service providers will not give subscriber information to law enforcement officials absent a warrant.

To which provider do they send the warrant? How do they figure out which service provider Smith is currently using. For hardwired telephone service, this is usually a fairly easy to determine. The officer need only figure out the local telephone company. But it is very likely Smith is also using a cellular telephone. On their surveillance of Smith, they may have seen him use a cellular telephone. Recall in the chapter on external sources of information we looked at the Regional Information Sharing System (RISS). One of the intelligence aspects that RISS can provide to state and local agencies is an exhaustive list of all commercial communications service providers in any region. Our detectives seek a court order for subscriber information and request the court to order each of the known service providers to check their subscriber information for John Smith. Generally, not only RISS will provide the detectives with a form that lists the service providers that can be used as an attachment for the court order, but RISS will also fax the information to the service providers and assist our detectives in determining which service provider Smith is using.

After determining Smith's service provider, our detectives have a number of significant hurdles to overcome before their wiretap can be implemented. Because of the intrusive nature of wiretaps, the legal requirements for authorization are much more stringent than those for search warrants. In addition to establishing probable cause to satisfy Fourth Amendment concerns, our detectives must prove to the judicial authority that the evidence they seek to obtain from the wiretap cannot be obtained in any other investigative technique or that alternative investigative techniques would be too dangerous. In a dire emergency, such as an ongoing kidnapping case, it is possible for state and local police agencies to obtain an emergency wiretap with the assistance of the commercial communications service provider, provided the police officers obtain a court order authorizing the wiretap within forty-eight hours. However, this is extraordinarily rare.

Because the wiretap act requires the purpose of the wiretap focus on gaining evidence, and not just general criminal intelligence or information, the detectives must articulate to the judicial authority the specific offense being committed, the specific place from which the wiretap is to be installed, the types of conversations the detectives believe they will intercept, and the identities of the offender or offenders involved. Additionally, because the wiretap

Recall from Chapter Seven, **subscriber information** is personal information such as name, date of birth, home address, work address, and social security number of the person who subscribed to the commercial communications service. If you have a telephone in your name, your service provider would list you as the subscriber.

request must be reviewed and approved by the local prosecutorial agency, there is likely to be significant bureaucratic review within the detectives' agency and the prosecutorial agency.

Presuming that our detectives are able to justify their wiretap, they now have a number of practical concerns. The rules about how a wiretap is operated provide their own set of challenges for our detectives. For instance, the intercepted conversations must be recorded in such a manner as to be protected from editing, alteration, or deletion. The wiretap must be conducted in a manner that minimizes unrelated and Fourth Amendment–protected conversations from being overheard. For instance, the wiretap is focused on Smith. If Smith's wife is not identified as a party under investigation, her conversations should not be intercepted.[17] Even when Smith's conversations are intercepted, those conversations, such as a conversation with a child, cannot be intercepted unless they are specifically about the drug trade. Moreover, privileged communications such as those between Smith and his attorney cannot be intercepted.[18] The rule for monitoring conversations is that when the telephone is answered, the person monitoring the conversation has thirty seconds to decide if the conversation is relevant to the case or not or privileged. If it is determined that the conversation is not relevant, the person monitoring the conversation must immediately cease monitoring and recording the conversation. However, every two minutes the person monitoring the wiretap may check the conversation to see if it has turned into a conversation relevant to the investigation. Again, the investigator has thirty seconds to make his determination.

The information recorded during a wiretap must be kept in strict confidence. In most states only people with specialized training are allowed to overhear conversations in real time. After a conversation has been recorded, it is evidence and other people (investigators, managers, and prosecutors) can access the information if they have the right to know and the need to know. In addition to the restrictions and regulations regarding monitoring, there are significant reporting rules that must be met.

Every five days our detectives must supply the judicial authority with a thorough recapitulation of the wiretap. They must tell the judicial authority who was monitored, generally what evidence was gained, how many conversations were intercepted, and the length of those conversations. In addition to the five-day report, they must ultimately supply the judicial authority and the prosecutor with a complete recapitulation of the wiretap. Moreover, if the information is introduced into court, it is subject to discovery by Smith's attorney. Within thirty days of the conclusion of the wiretap, the investigators must send a letter to each person whose conversations were monitored.

As exhausting as these requirements can be, they are made significantly less trying by technology. We know that CALEA has forced communications service providers to be able to provide law enforcement with the ability to intercept calls. No longer do law enforcement officials physically hang clips on wires. After we identify the person and the service, our court authorization is served on the service provider, who is responsible to intercept the information and forward it to our detectives. Essentially, the telephone company intercepts the call, not the detectives. Our detectives are then responsible to manage the intercept within the boundaries of the law.

An example of the technological systems that assist in the management of wiretaps is the Advanced Digital Audio Collection System (ADACS). The ADACS provides for the intercepting, decoding, recording, and playing back of both hardwired and wireless communications. It automatically matches **call content** and **call-identifying** information.[19]

Generally defined, discovery is the defendant's right to know all of the information that can be used against him or her during trial. Items that are subject to discovery include arrest reports, scientific reports about evidence, crime scene photographs, witness statements, and the conversations that were intercepted by wiretap.

Furthermore, ADACS allows for the intercepted calls to be stored in a tamper-proof manner on a number of media (e.g., Magneto Optical and DVD). It is also possible to obtain software modules for ADACS that allow for the automatic creation of reports like the five-day report. Finally, ADACS has the capability to export the call-identifying information to other programs for analysis of telephone patterns. During many investigations, the call patterns are just as important as the call content information. Software programs that allow you to correlate call-identifying information with other investigative information and then graphically portray that information can be very important, especially in the prosecution of complex narcotics organizations or racketeering charges (Figure 14.2).

In 2001 there were 1,405 court orders allowing 1,491 communications intercepts (some court orders allowed multiple intercepts).[20] Considering that there are more than seventeen thousand state and local police agencies in the United States, the use of a wiretap by a state or local police agency is still a very rare occurrence.[21] Even for a large state or local agency, an investment in technology like ADACS is probably not cost effective, and in addition to the purchase and maintenance of the system, a control area or space has to be designed to house the "wire room." Fortunately, today's technology is such that the actual physical location of the wire room and the accompanying equipment is not important to the individual case. Since our detective's agency doesn't, and is not going to own or purchase the equipment for their wiretap, our detectives are going to use a regional facility.

There are a number of ways that regional wire room facilities are developed. In some instances, there is a regional drug task force in place, such as RISS, which

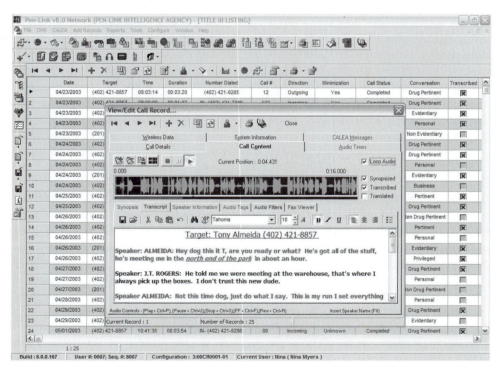

Figure 14.2 This screen capture shows the computer workstation screen that a police officer would use to monitor an intercepted call and include that intercept in the database.
Screen capture provided by Pen-Link™, Ltd.

has wire rooms in addition to information-gathering and analysis capabilities. In other cases, there are regional wire rooms that were developed in response to earlier criminal investigations. Since most wiretap operations are directed against offenders involved in drug trafficking, in makes sense that most wire rooms were established in response to drug control efforts.

Because the communications service provider is going to route the intercepted telephone call to the wire room, the location of the wire room is not important technologically speaking. However, the wire room, the investigation, and the location of the telephone intercept must be in the same state. At the state and local level, you cannot get a wiretap for a telephone that is located in another state. However, as we know, one of the basic features of cellular telephone service is the ability to hand off service within the service provider's area. Moreover, many cellular telephone service providers have nationwide calling features that allow their subscribers to make cellular telephone calls from anywhere in the nation. With nationwide calling, the communications service provider still has the ability to intercept and route the call to law enforcement. However, when subscribers without the nationwide service enter another service provider's area and they begin to "roam," the subscribers' cellular provider may not have the ability to intercept and route the call. In this case, CALEA requires that the service provider be able to provide law enforcement personnel with the name of the service provider to which the targeted offender is "roaming." In that instance, the law enforcement agency would have to modify the court order and obtain the new cellular service provider's assistance in intercepting and routing calls. However, this is a somewhat rare occurrence.

Even though CALEA has shifted some of the burden for making the intercept possible to the commercial service provider, there is still significant cost to the agency when conducting a wiretap. In 2001 the average total cost of a state and local wiretap was $33,650.[22] Now some of this expense are shared costs of running the wire room. Often wire rooms are funded through state and federal grant money, directly by the state or federal government through a task force, or with seized assets from prior narcotics investigations. But there are still the personnel costs. Some wiretaps run twenty-four hours a day, but most are operational only during the hours the investigators believe the offender is active. A wiretap must be monitored by a person. Intercepts cannot be automatically recorded and reviewed at a later time. During 2001, the average length of a wiretap was thirty-eight days. The wiretaps in 2001 intercepted an average of 1,565 conversations from an average of eighty six people over the life of the wiretap. Some wiretaps intercepted more than six hundred conversations in a single day.[23] The point is this is a lot of work. Finally, law enforcement agencies are required by CALEA to reimburse commercial communications providers for some of their equipment and personnel costs associated with both wiretaps and pen registries. These costs vary depending on the scope of the request and the service provider.

Some agencies have their employees attend the training necessary to monitor a wiretap. They then staff the wire room with their own employees who are responsible for monitoring the intercepts and updating the database that maintains the intercept information (an ADACS-like product). Other agencies hire professional wire room monitors. These are civilians who work for a commercial organization who are trained in the use of the equipment and are knowledgeable about intercept rules and regulations. In addition to being well trained and often bilingual, these civilian employees are often less expensive than agency employees. Moreover, our two detectives would have a difficult time monitoring a wiretap twenty-four hours a day for thirty-eight days. Simply put, the bulk of the cost in

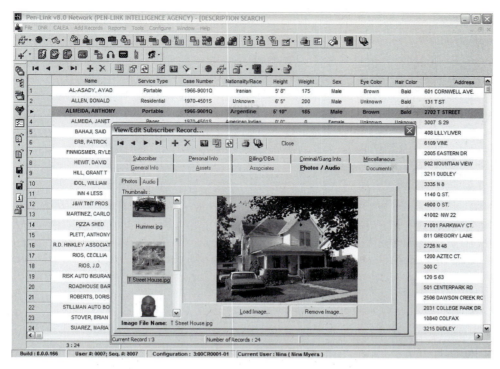

Figure 14.3 As police officers intercept an offender's telephone calls they can also add to a database of information known about the offender. This type of organized intelligence can be invaluable in furthering an investigation and ensuring successful prosecution. In this photograph the ability to add digital images to the database is shown.
Screen capture provided by Pen-Link™, Ltd.

operating a wiretap is personnel costs associated with the monitors. This expense, often as much as a thousand dollars a day, is a major stumbling block for small- to medium-sized agencies. Our detectives are probably going to have to find funding for their wiretap.

After obtaining the necessary authorizations, training, funding, and monitoring location, our detectives are ready to work their wire. A modern wiretap works much like using the telephone—except you listen and can't talk. Let's take a cellular telephone call. As soon as Smith dials his cellular telephone and pushes enter, the call is routed to the monitoring station. The detectives' computer screen tells them the number Smith is calling and they hear, through headphones, the telephone ringing. Our wire is live as soon as Smith activates his cellular telephone by pushing enter. Our detectives can hear any conversations or background noise even before the other party picks up. Once the other party picks up, the detectives hear the conversation. If Smith dials a voice mail, our detectives hear the message, and if Smith is retrieving messages, the computer shows the numbers he dials for access to the voice mail on the computer screen. We now know his voice mail number and access code, and, of course, we hear him pick up messages.

During complex investigations, the numbers that Smith dials may turn out to be just as important as the content of the telephone calls. By using link-analysis software, the detectives may be able to use the device-identifying information and the content of the conversations as a means to outline the hierarchy of a criminal organization (Figure 14.3). For instance, if Smith contacts one person, discusses the results of street sales of narcotics, and is giving instructions to the

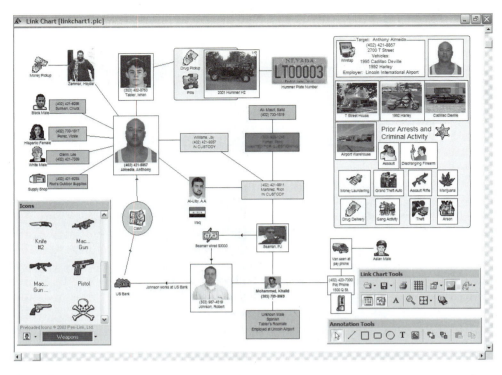

Figure 14.4 Particularly in large or complex investigations, recording, organizing, and using the information can be a daunting task. Software programs, like that in the screen capture here, assist police officers in creating visual displays of how information relates to an offender or investigation.
Screen capture provided by Pen-Link™, Ltd.

seller, we might infer that the person works for Smith. If Smith makes another telephone call and is arranging the purchase of narcotics, we might infer that the supplier is either outside the organization or if the person is giving Smith instructions, we might infer that Smith works for that person. The investigation and final determination of the size, scope, and organizational hierarchy of a criminal organization is significantly more complex, but wiretap information can provide valuable insights into criminal organizations (Figure 14.4). For instance, in 2001 "in New Hampshire, the State Attorney General's Office reported that a wiretap in use for twenty-nine days in a drug conspiracy investigation produced fourteen arrests." Furthermore, during that investigation, not only was the wiretap information critical to the investigation and prosecution, but it prevented a home invasion robbery.[24]

In the New Hampshire example, the police officers were conducting a wiretap for the purposes of furthering a criminal investigation. As we have seen, they developed information about another crime that was being planned—a home invasion robbery. Because wiretaps provide law enforcement with real-time information about criminal actions, sometimes information is received that must be acted on at once, but this creates a dilemma for the police officers. Actions taken on information received from the wiretap might compromise operational security and cause the targets of the wiretaps to change their mode of communication.

Wiretaps are on the cutting edge of the most common law enforcement balancing act—public safety and individual Constitutional rights. Recall that anytime a police officer detains, arrests, searches, or seizes the property of someone in the United States, the police officer has made a decision that the public safety outweighs the individual's rights. Wiretaps push law enforcement officials onto another fine edge, balancing operational security with public safety. How long do you let the wire run? When must you take action that might compromise the operation?

Recall from Chapter One, during the search for a murder fugitive, a wiretap was used. As the police officers monitored the conversations of the gang members, they heard them boasting about riding around in a stolen car. They also talked about having a shotgun and just having committed a drive-by shooting. Although the information was somewhat sketchy, the police officers knew the make of the vehicle (the make is the manufacturer), the color, the general area the gang members were driving around in, and because they had a gang expert on the wire, they knew the names and physical descriptions of the gang members. In this instance, the wire room was not in the city wherein the investigation was focused. A quick call to the central dispatch center of that city revealed that a shooting had just occurred. Even though revealing the existence of the wiretap might compromise the operation—and recall the target of the wiretap was wanted for thirteen murders—immediate action was necessary. The police officers monitoring the wire contacted the local police watch commander. He was briefed on the existence of the wire and the information. Ultimately, he broadcast on the police radio that a citizen had reported the information the police had received from the wiretap.

This provided some level of protection for wiretap and gave the police officers in the field enough information to look for the roving suspects and information for their investigation that would ultimately result in the arrest and conviction of the shooter. However, it had a very immediate effect on the wire. The gang monitored the police frequencies. As soon as the information was broadcast on the police radio, the gang members dumped the stolen vehicle and hid out. Although they were not arrested that night, they were prevented from doing another drive-by shooting that night, and they were ultimately charged with the crime. Because call-identifying information can be important to an investigation, there are alternative methods to capturing call-identifying information without necessarily capturing call content information.

Pens, Traps, and Traces

Pen register is actually an antiquated term used to describe the process of intercepting **device-identifying information** while not being privy to **call content information**.[25,26] The term *pen register* dates back to the days of telegraphs and describes a machine that uses ink and ticker tape to record and display telegraph pulses. Today the pen register essentially references the ability to interpret outgoing information.

Today the device used to record and decode the electronic signal that identifies the number someone dial is called a **dialed number recorder (DNR)**. The dialed number recorder is a law enforcement, not a commercial, tool. It is not the same technical means that telephone service providers use to track device-identifying information for billing purposes.

You have probably seen something similar to a pen register. Anyone who has a caller identification feature on her telephone or attached to the telephone is, in a very real sense, operating a pen register on her own telephone line. The difference is that callers can block their caller identification information to commercially available caller identification devices but not to a pen register. Pen registers differ from wiretaps in a number of ways. Whereas the commercial communications service provider intercepts call content and device-identifying information for law enforcement, a pen register can be attached to a junction box by law enforcement personnel in the target's neighborhood. The information is then either

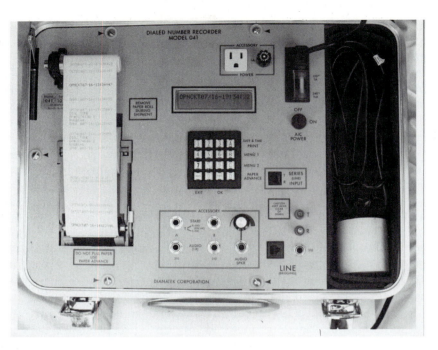

Figure 14.5 This photograph is a typical pen register or DNR.
Photograph provided by Dianatek Corp.

recorded locally at the junction box and periodically retrieved by law enforcement personnel or routed from the junction box to a monitoring station where it can be observed in real time. For cellular communications, in compliance with CALEA, communications service providers have developed an intercept solution that involves the separation of device-identifying information from call content information. After content has been separated out, the device-identifying information is routed to the law enforcement monitoring station over a private TCP/IP network connection. Once it arrives at the law enforcement monitoring station, the device-identifying information is stored and analyzed.

Pen registers also differ from wiretaps in that their threshold for judicial authorization is much lower. In 1986 the **Electronic Communications Privacy Act (ECPA)** established a lower standard of judicial review for capturing telephone numbers through the use of pen registers and trap and trace devices. Although telephone numbers are not protected by the Fourth Amendment, ECPA requires law enforcement agencies to obtain a court order to use a pen register.[27] As we know, a judicial authorization for a wiretap requires probable cause and it must be demonstrated that the information cannot be gathered by other means, but court orders for a pen register require a law enforcement official to certify only that "the information likely to be obtained is relevant to an ongoing criminal investigation."[28]

While you still need a court order, there is no prosecutorial review, nor mandatory judicial reporting of approval. Because state courts do not routinely report their authorization of pen registers, there are no reliable figures on the number of pen registers used by state and local law enforcement personnel. However, there are figures available for federal law enforcement. In 1998 federal law enforcement personnel used 4,886 pen registers; that is more than eight times the number of wiretaps.[29] Presuming that the federal law enforcement ratio of pen registers to wiretaps is somewhat consistent with use by state and local law enforcement, the use of a pen register is probably fairly common.

State and local law enforcement officials are rarely involved in placing listening devices, commonly referred to as bugs, inside locations. In 2001 listening devices, microphones, and eavesdropping made up fewer than 8 percent of the total intercepts used by state and local law enforcement agencies. While federal law enforcement agencies used these devices somewhat less often in 2001 than state and local agencies, the rules and regulations set down for federal agencies are clear. The Department of Justice's Criminal Resource Manual's section on preparing affidavits for electronic surveillance includes pen register information as part of the essential background information and probable cause for the affidavit for a court-ordered wiretap. The manual says, in part, "Any background information needed to understand fully the instant investigation should be set forth briefly at the beginning of this section. The focus, however, should be on recent and current criminal activity by the subjects, with an emphasis on their use of the target facility or location. This is generally accomplished through information from a confidential informant, cooperating witness, or undercover agent, combined with **pen register** or telephone toll information for the target phone or physical surveillance of the target premises. It is Department of Justice policy that pen register or telephone toll information for the target telephone, or physical surveillance of the targeted premises, standing alone, is generally insufficient to establish probable cause." You can view the entire manual at **www. usdoj.gov/usao/eousa/foia_reading_room/ usam/title9/crm00029.htm**.

During a criminal investigation, police officers may want to know who a suspect has talked to on the telephone because the information may help establish a link between two or more suspects. In addition to the information obtained from pen registers that may identify accomplices or coconspirators, it may be useful in demonstrating a link between an offender's actions and a crime. Moreover, the information gathered from a pen register is often used as part of the basis for a search warrant or a wiretap court order.

Traps and traces provide essentially the same information as a pen register, but a trap or a trace is used with the knowledge of the telephone service subscriber.[30] Generally these devices are used during the investigation of obscene, annoying, or threatening telephone call investigations. After a police report has been taken, the telephone service provider is contacted with the consent of the victim, and a trap or trace is placed on their line. This is done to assist in the identification of the offender(s). Because the victim wants the trap or trace placed on his line, no court order or search warrant is required.

Carnivore and Magic Lantern

No, these aren't superheroes. These are methods of intercepting Internet-based information, primarily e-mail. Prior to 1986 there were two basic types of electronic surveillance—wiretaps and bugs. The ECPA added a third category to the types of surveillance. Communication schemes in this third category include pagers; facsimile machines; and some computer transmissions, such as e-mail. Although still a small portion of the overall intercepts conducted by state and local law enforcement agencies, the interception of criminal Internet communications is likely to increase. At this time, a state and local law enforcement agency conducting an investigation requiring the interception of Internet communications must rely on the FBI.

The FBI developed Carnivore (referred to as DCS1000 by the FBI), a software tool designed to facilitate the interception of electronic communications on the Internet.[31] Recall from our chapters on computer basics, networks, and the Internet, that Internet messages travel in digital packets that contain a destination, protocol instructions, and a message. Carnivore uses an IP packet **sniffer** that can select and record a defined subset of the traffic on a network. Packets to be examined by Carnivore can be selected based on IP address, protocol, or in the case of e-mail, on the user names in the TO and FROM fields (Figure 14.6).[32]

In some cases, packets can be selected based on their content. Whenever an investigation seeks to intercept the TO and FROM lines, IP address, or user names of an Internet e-mail message, the investigation is acting much like a pen register in that it is intercepting device-identifying information. This is referred to as the pen mode. However, the Internet transmission can be intercepted in what is called full mode, so the content of the message is also intercepted. Currently the interception of Internet-based communications has been used to further investigations into terrorism, espionage, information warfare (Web site hacking), child pornography, fraud, and other felonies.

Magic Lantern is actually a computer virus developed by the FBI. It is sent to and infects a target's computer. Once the program has manifested itself, every tap of the target's fingers on the keyboard is recorded and forwarded to the FBI. This software was developed in order to defeat an offender's use of encryption technology. While this sounds like something useful against terrorists, the FBI has employed Magic Lantern during the investigation of mob-related gambling crimes.[33] While Magic Lantern currently is not a tool used by state and local law enforcement agencies, it is likely that as technology advances, it will become available to them.

The manner in which Carnivore collects transmissions is abstractly analogous to a law enforcement roadblock, instituted to search for an escaped convict, that stops every vehicle (packet) traveling down a certain road (ISP). If law enforcement is not

Figure 14.6 As with telephone call content and device-identifying information, intercepts of Internet communications must be recorded and organized. This photograph depicts software designed to retain, organize, and analyze Internet communication intercepts.
Screen capture provided by Pen-Link[TM], *Ltd.*

100 percent certain the traveler is the convict (targeted suspect), the traveler is processed through the roadblock (Carnivore) and continues to the intended destination. If law enforcement is 100 percent certain, however, the traveler is detained.[34]

The Telephone as an Investigative Tool

The telephone is one of the most powerful and versatile investigation technologies available to state and local law enforcement agencies. Of course, we know that a detective can gather information about a crime on the telephone from victims, witnesses, and other sources of information, but in some instances, the telephone is also a valuable tool to contact offenders. Nearly everyone is familiar with Miranda. Essentially, the Miranda decision directed law enforcement agents to inform an offender of his or her right against self-incrimination and the right to counsel prior to a custodial interview during which the law enforcement agent intends to ask accusatory questions.[35]

The failure of a law enforcement official to inform an offender of his or her Miranda rights can result in subsequent statements being inadmissible in court. Consider that for the Miranda decision to apply, two conditions must be met. First, the law enforcement agent must be asking accusatory questions. Typically, these are questions about the crime such as, "What is your side of the story?" Generally, they are not questions concerning personal identification information such as, "What is your date of birth?" The second condition is that the offender must be detained.[36] Recall our traffic violator from Chapter One; that is an example of a simple detention. The traffic violator is not free to leave until the police officer has conducted the traffic stop. In most instances, whenever a police officer stops someone and that person is not free to leave, Miranda applies.

This is where the telephone come into investigative work. Presume you are investigating an assault case between a husband and wife. The police officer who responded to the initial radio call took a report because the husband, who has been accused of assaulting his wife, fled the home. You are the detective who gets the report on Monday morning. The wife has provided you with the husband's work telephone number. So you call the husband at work and ask him, "Can you tell me your side of the story?" He then proceeds to make incriminating statements. You did not inform him of his Miranda rights. Are these statements admissible? They resulted from a relatively simple accusatory question, but is he detained? Isn't he free to hang up the telephone at any time? The husband's statements probably are admissible in court.

It is not enough to understand how technology works. It is more important to understand how technology fits into the criminal justice system as a whole. It is also important to ask ourselves how a technology impacts current operating procedures, standards, and our legal rights.

During the Cold War, the National Security Agency (NSA) developed a system for the routine monitoring of global communications. The system, **Echelon**, is capable of monitoring millions of telephone calls, telexes, and facsimile communications. The system "listens" for key words and voices (through a voice recognition program) and separates out electronic messages for review and analysis by a human being. Because the system was designed to gather foreign intelligence, its use is not reviewed by our criminal justice system. However, electronic communications entering or leaving the United States are subject to monitoring by Echelon. While targeting activities outside the country, it is possible that information gathered by Echelon could be used in domestic investigations.

USA PATRIOT Act

Shortly after the events of 9/11, the federal government took steps to strengthen the nation's ability to gather electronic information on terrorists. While this book is about state and local governments, some portions of the PATRIOT Act will change the nature of domestic surveillance. Not only could these changes affect state and local law enforcement agencies during their investigations of domestic crimes, but they will affect their operations any time they are working in concert with federal authorities.

In the two months after the events of 9/11, Congress passed the **Uniting and Strengthening America by Providing Appropriate Tools Required to Intercept and Obstruct Terrorism (USA PATRIOT) Act**.[37] While the PATRIOT Act has changed the nature of many aspects of electronic surveillance, we will look at three issues: lowering the threshold for obtaining permission to intercept electronic communications, clarifications to the interception of Internet-based communications, and the aspect of roving electronic intercepts.

The Foreign Intelligence Service Act (FISA) of 1978 limited the federal government's ability to electronically intercept communications to times when the surveillance orders were made for the "primary purpose" of investigating foreign intelligence activities. The FISA court is a secret court of eleven federal judges who review requests for secret searches and covert electronic surveillance. The PATRIOT Act changed the wording regarding a search's purpose to reflect that the FISA court can grant an order for an electronic intercept if foreign intelligence activities are the "significant purposes" of the surveillance. This has had the effect of allowing FISA approval on domestic criminal cases wherein the criminal conduct may provide support to terrorist or international spying. The difference is critical. In the past, the government had to demonstrate that the intercept was of someone likely to be involved in terrorism; now the government has to certify that the information is relevant to an ongoing investigation.[38]

The PATRIOT Act clarified the debate on packet information in Internet-based communications. Now the statutes on pen/trap issues on telephone communications also apply to Internet-based communications. So just as with telephone communications, the requirements for monitoring caller identification information are different from monitoring call content information.[39] One of the biggest changes brought about by the PATRIOT Act concerns roving wires. In the past, the law enforcement officials had to demonstrate that if they wanted to intercept telephone calls from a different telephone, they had to show that the offender was using that telephone. So if during the intercepts on one approved line, it became apparent that the targeted offender was using a new telephone, a new court order was required. Now the intercept order is not so much for the device as for the offender.[40] This means that if during an investigation, the offender borrows someone else's cellular telephone and makes a call, the government can continue to monitor that cellular telephone. Before the PATRIOT Act, pen/trap orders were only valid within the jurisdiction of the court that ordered the intercept; now the orders are valid throughout the country.[41]

Chapter Summary

There is tremendous value for law enforcement to be able to know what offenders are doing and planning to do in real time. There is no question that in some criminal investigations, especially those involving criminal organizations or conspiracies, that the ability to intercept electronic communications can be critical to the investigation. However, because of the invasive nature of eavesdropping on someone's telephone conversations, electronic intercepts are considered a seizure and protected by the Fourth Amendment. Although the PATRIOT Act targets terrorists and international spys, it has a number of effects of criminal cases. Not only has the threshold for obtaining an order been lowered, but the call identification portion of Internet-based communications is now considered the same as telephone communications.

In this chapter we looked at a variety of technical means to carry out electronic intercepts. We saw the difference between device-identifying information and call content information, pen registers, and technology for the interception of Internet-based communications. One piece of legislation designed to assist law enforcement officials in keeping up with technological changes is the Communications Assistance for Law Enforcement Agencies (CALEA) Act. CALEA requires telecommunications carriers to provide technology (both hardware and software) necessary for law enforcement electronic intercepts.

Discussion Questions

1. Privacy advocates, like the American Civil Liberties Union (ACLU) and the Electronic Privacy Information Center (EPIC), have argued that Carnivore invades the privacy of Internet users because their packets of information are analyzed along with the offender's during Carnivore's filtration process.[42] The FBI counters that "each packet contains very little information and the intrusion—a brief, one-second processing of data—is negligible."[43] Moreover, the FBI states that even if the government collects, stores, or analyzes a nontargeted Internet user, the information would be barred from use in court by the exclusionary rule.[44] Do you think "a brief, one-second" analysis of your Internet data packets violates your Fourth Amendment rights?
2. The PATRIOT Act lowered the threshold for court approval of an electronic intercept of those suspected of involvement in terrorism or activities possibly supporting terrorism. Do you support the lowering of the threshold. If so, why? If not, why?

Key Terms

Call Content Information
Call-Identifying Information
Communications Assistance for Law Enforcement Act (CALEA)
Content Information
Covert Surveillance
Device-Identifying Information

Dialed Number Recorder
Echelon
Electronic Communications Privacy Act (ECPA)
Electronic Surveillance
Magic Lantern
Operational Security
Pen Registers
Sniffer
Subscriber Information

Traces
Transparency
Traps
Uniting and Strengthening America by Providing Appropriate Tools Required to Intercept and Obstruct Terrorism (USA PATRIOT) Act
Wiretap

End Notes

1. *Miranda v. Arizona,* 384 U.S. 436 (1966).
2. United States Constitution, Fourth Amendment.
3. *Olmstead v. United States,* 48 S. Ct. 564, 277 U.S. 438.
4. Heffernan, "Fourth Amendment Privacy Interests."

5. U.S. Congress, Office of Technology Assessment, "Electronic Surveillance," 5.
6. Justice Tom Clark, in writing an opinion in *Berger v. New York,* 388 U.S. 41 (1967), provides a somewhat comprehensive history of the Court's interpretation of the Fourth Amendment and wiretaps between 1928 and 1967.
7. *Berger v. New York*, 388 U.S. 41 (1967) and *Katz v. U.S.*, 347 (1967).
8. U.S. Congress, Office of Technology Assessment, "Criminal Justice," 8.
9. It is not uncommon for state and local law enforcement officers to become involved in task forces with federal law enforcement agencies. Prior to 9/11, these task forces were generally restricted to the investigation of domestic criminal acts. However, post 9/11, state and local agencies are becoming more and more involved in Joint Terrorism Task Forces (JTTF). In many instances, the state and local participants are subjected to background investigations in order to gain a security clearance and in some, they are deputized by the host federal agency. These JTTFs pose a number of challenges for local officials. As we have seen in previous chapters, there is a great difference in how agencies communicate. There is also a great difference between the policies of one agency and another. It can be difficult to reconcile these policy differences at an operational level. For instance, a local agency may have a restriction on how far outside their jurisdiction they allow their employees to travel in order to conduct an investigation. And the JTTF (or any task force operation) investigation may lead the employees very far afield. Moreover, there are many instances where the line employees, through their association with the JTTF (or any task force) garner a security clearance, and because of that clearance, they are privy to information that they cannot disclose to an individual without clearance. The clearance issue becomes difficult when the police manager who the line employee reports to does not have a clearance. Finally, it is critical for state and local law enforcement personnel to recognize that when they are involved in JTTF operations, the rules are different.
10. 2002 Annual Report of the Director of the Administrative Office of the United States Court on the Application for Orders authorizing the Interception of Wire, Oral, or Electronic Communications.
11. Good examples of tougher state restrictions exist in Hawaii and Ohio. In those states, adversary hearings are required before the issuance of a court order. The adversary hearing involves a court-appointed attorney who has the ability to question witnesses and argue against the wiretap.
12. 2001 Annual Report of the Director of the Administrative Office of the United States Court on the Application for Orders authorizing the Interception of Wire, Oral, or Electronic Communications.
13. "Electronic Surveillance."
14. Federal law enforcement agencies seeking a wiretap must obtain a review directly from the United States Attorney General, the Deputy, or an Assistant Attorney General of the Department of Justice. So if federal agents in California want to conduct a wiretap, they must petition through their agency to Washington, D.C., and then go before a local federal magistrate. The bureaucratic process on the federal side of law enforcement is very cumbersome. Often, when working with state and local agencies, federal agents will provide the funding and expertise for a wiretap, but the state and local agency must get the actual court order.
15. 2001 Wiretap Report.
16. For our purposes, a mid-level dealer provides drugs to street dealers. He is not an importer or manufacturer; he is a wholesaler.
17. A somewhat comic and yet fairly accurate portrayal of conversations that should not be intercepted occurs in the movie *Casino,* a movie based upon real-life events. In the movie, the characters played by Joe Pesci and Robert DeNiro are mobsters under investigation and subject to a wiretap by the Federal Bureau of Investigation. Knowing that a wiretap is probable, the characters have their wives initiate conversations and after the time that law enforcement officials can listen to determine the conversations are not subject to the intercept elapses, Pesci and DeNiro conduct their mob business.
18. Privileged communications are statements or conversations made under circumstances of assured confidentiality that must not be disclosed in court. These include communications

between husband and wife, attorney and client, physician or therapist and patient, and religious leader with anyone seeing him in his religious status.

19. "Electronic Surveillance," 72.
20. 2001 Wiretap Report. Director of the Administrative Office of United States Court. "Application for Orders Authorizing or Approving the Interception of Wire, Oral, or Electronic Communications," 2002.
21. Bureau of Justice Statistics, "2000 Law Enforcement Management and Administrative Statistics (LEMAS)."
22. 2001 Wiretap Report.
23. Ibid.
24. Ibid.
25. Although pen registers have been replaced by dialed number recorders, nearly all of the individuals involved in the process of obtaining a pen register (police officers, prosecutors, judges, and industry people) still use the term.
26. "New Technologies," 13.
27. *Smith v. Maryland,* 442 U.S. 735, 742-45 (1979)
28. Title 18 United States Code, Section 3122(b)(2).
29. Electronic Privacy Information Center, **www.epic.org**.
30. "Electronic Surveillance," 74.
31. Dunham, "Carnivore."
32. Ibid.
33. Sullivan, "FBI Software."
34. Dunham, "Carnivore."
35. *Miranda v. Arizona* 384 U.S. 436 (1966).
36. Moore, "Mass Communication Law," 84.
37. "Money Laundering," 839.
38. Henderson, "Patriot Act's Impact," 179.
39. Ibid.
40. Ibid.
41. Ibid.
42. You can visit EPIC's Web site at **www.epic.org**.
43. Dunham, "Carnivore."
44. Ibid.

Chapter Fifteen
Tracking and Surveillance

Learning Objectives

- The student will understand the difference between **passive surveillance** and **interactive surveillance**, certain legal issues surrounding surveillance, and the purposes of surveillance.

- The student will be exposed to the techniques for tracking vehicles and tracking electronic communications.

- The student will be exposed to passive surveillance devices like closed-circuit television, video recording devices in police vehicles, and electronic traffic enforcement devices like **photo red light**.

- The student will be exposed to interactive surveillance devices like body wires and night vision equipment.

Introduction

In Part Two of the text we looked at a variety of methods for gathering, organizing, retaining, and analyzing information about crime and offenders. With relational databases and networks, a tremendous amount of information is available about offenders and offenses. But the information a database has is primarily about what has happened in the past. Often the information, especially as to an offender's whereabouts and current activities, is dated information. By the time the information is collected, input, and distributed, offenders have moved on to something new.

In the previous chapter we looked at the value of having real-time information. By listening to electronic communications, police officers not only hear what is happening now, they often hear an offender's plans for the future. In a great many instances, police investigations are furthered by watching an offender's actions—looking at where they go, what vehicles they use, and who they talk to. This is especially true during complex investigations into criminal organizations.

Surveillance is essentially sustained observations of an offender, a group of offenders, or a location.[1] We are going to break surveillance into two broad categories. The first is **passive surveillance**. Passive means just watching. Watching could be electronically tracking a vehicle or electronic communications device, closed-circuit television monitoring of an intersection, or watching a location through a thermal imaging device. The point is passive surveillance denotes just watching. On the other hand, there is **interactive surveillance**. Just as the term indicates, that is when law enforcement officials are interacting with the suspect. Sometimes during an undercover drug buy, the operation is tape recorded via a **body wire** and possibly video recorded by a covert camera. Interactive surveillance has different technology, tactical considerations, and legal requirements than passive. At times passive surveillance may prompt a police officer to take action. For instance, police officers using night vision equipment to observe a known drug location are conducting passive surveillance. Of course, if they see a drug transaction, the situation may change to highly interactive, but the interaction between the police officers and the offender is no longer surveillance; it is an arrest or detention.

Everywhere you go you are under surveillance. You are under surveillance by closed-circuit television (CCTV) at the corner convenience store, in the department store, while you are pumping gasoline, and while making a withdrawl from the ATM. You are under surveillance as you drive down the street; on the highway you pass CCTV monitoring traffic; you pass through intersections monitored because of crime problems; or you pass the outdoor ATM as someone else is using it. If you have a cellular telephone, as we know from Chapters Six and Seven, it is continuously sending your location from one cell site to the next. You may have a vehicle with the increasingly popular system that will unlock the doors, give you directions, and call the police for you. If they want, they know where you are, too! We are a surveillance and tracking society. Just as these different forms of electronic surveillance are watching and tracking you for their purposes, state and local government can apply some of the same, and indeed more, technology to watch and find you.

In several of the previous chapters we have looked at Fourth Amendment issues as they relate to technology. There are a couple of legal points regarding surveillance that we should know about at the beginning of our examination. First, generally speaking, anything that someone does in public is open to surveillance without court order. Essentially, you have no expectation of the right to privacy in a public forum. So the police can install video cameras on a street light, or in a decoy car, and watch an offender's home. Anything that goes on that would be reasonably visible from the street is open to police surveillance without warrant.[2] This is an extension of what is commonly referred to as the plain sight doctrine. That is that evidence of a crime may be seized without warrant if the police officer is in a lawful position to observe the evidence.[3] So if the curtains are wide open at your house and someone walking by could reasonably see inside, a police officer could also look inside, from the sidewalk, and if you had evidence of a crime, the police officer would not need a warrant.[4]

While it is fairly well settled that the police can conduct a warrantless surveillance of an offender in a public place, surveillance is generally very expensive in terms of staff resources and equipment. Simply put, why do the police need to conduct surveillance and use video technology at all? Primarily, video footage of an offender committing a crime is powerful evidence for a jury.[5] Secondly, during complex investigations, where an offender goes and who she associates with can provide valuable evidence about her activities and uncover associated offenders. Additionally, covert surveillance has a place in community policing. There are many places throughout communities that are problem locations. For instance, a gang may frequent a local park, making it virtually unusable for the community. Sometimes video footage of covert surveillance is used to seek civil injunctions against specific groups of people or in the abatement process of problem buildings. The video can be used as part of the evidence to convince a judge to issue a restraining order against the gang. There are a wide variety of reasons that surveillance of an offender can be useful police work.

In addition to enhancing the likelihood of a criminal filing and conviction, video is a good medium to document police activity. In some instances, video cameras are used at crime scenes to record where and how evidence is found and to demonstrate the condition of the location before and after the police activity. Moreover, video cameras in police vehicles have both evidentiary and liability applications. In addition to actually following someone and watching him, there are ways to track vehicles remotely.

Tracking Vehicles

Vehicle-tracking technology is used in criminal investigations in two manners. The first is when the police install a tracking device on an offender's vehicle. Once this is done, police officers can either remotely view a vehicle's position in

The combination of GPS technology and cellular technology allow for a vehicle to be remote tracked. In a configuration like this, the GPS receiver determines the vehicle's location and the information is relayed to a desktop PC via cellular telephone service.

The Desktop PC contains Geographic Information System (GIS) software which translates the GPS location information into a visual display for police officers. As you can see, this technology brings together the subject matter from Part I and Part II of the text.

real time from a computer terminal in the station, or they can follow the vehicle at a distance. The second type of vehicle tracking is when you have a tracking device on your personal vehicle and it is stolen. In the second instance, you notify your service provider and through a variety of means, law enforcement personnel use the tracking device to locate your vehicle.

Vehicle tracking systems are a combination of many of the technologies that we have already examined. Some of them use global positioning satellite (GPS) technology to locate a vehicle, and there are others that use radio frequency (RF) technology to triangulate a vehicle's position. So the basis for all remote tracking technology is the automatic vehicle locator (AVL) that we looked at in previous chapters. Let's look at consumer-installed AVL first.

Consumer-installed AVL impacts state and local law enforcement agencies in one of two ways. Some systems, once activated, report the location to a central location staffed by the manufacturer. These systems relay the location of the vehicle to the police. So if your car were stolen, you would call the police and the vendor. The police take a stolen vehicle report and the vendor activates the technology. Some devices are GPS based while others are RF based. In either case, the vendor receives a signal from the vehicle and, using GIS software, determines the vehicle's location. That information is relayed to the police, who search for the vehicle.

The other configuration of consumer AVL actually installs the locating technology in police vehicles. In this scheme, you report your car stolen and the manufacturer is notified. They send a signal to your consumer AVL, which is then activated and begins sending a locating RF signal into the atomshere. The specially equipped police vehicles receive the signal. They have a relatively simple indicating system that shows signal strength, direction, and the number of the device that has been located; this number works very much like a cellular telephone serial number in that each device has its own number. That number can be input into the police agency's computer and a description of the vehicle the police officers are searching for is given. Using the signal strength and direction indicator, the police officers track the vehicle. In the first configuration of consumer AVL, the police agency is notified of the vehicle's position. As we know, GPS technology can give a fairly accurate location. In the second configuration, the police officers in the field use a receiver to track an RF signal.

Police officers covertly track a vehicle using one of the two technology configurations. However, both systems require that police officers covertly install a tracking device on an offender's vehicle. Generally, this is done by locating the place the offender parks the vehicle overnight. Usually very early in the morning, the police officers will covertly approach the offender's vehicle and install the device somewhere on the undercarriage of the vehicle. Police officers who are experienced at this will usually find a vehicle similar to the offender's and practice locating a space to place the transmitter. The device consists of a transmitter/power source box that is usually attached to the vehicle by between two and four powerful magnets. Once the transmitter is attached to the vehicle, the police officers plug in the antenna, which is also attached by a magnet. Typically, plugging

In 1990 an off-duty sheriff's deputy confronted a prowler at a neighbor's home. The prowler shot and killed the deputy. The subsequent investigation initially pointed to a specific offender. The investigating police officer did not have enough information to arrest the offender, so one of the investigative techniques they used was to attach a tracking device to the offender's vehicle. Over the space of several weeks, the police officers analyzed the offender's patterns. They noted that he would go several miles away from his home, into another jurisdiction and drive and park his vehicle late at night. The investigating police officers approached the neighboring jurisdiction in an effort to determine what the offender was doing in that neighborhood. It turned out that the offender's travels and stops in the neighborhood correlated to three rapes of women in their homes. The offender was subsequently arrested and convicted for the murders and rapes.

in the antenna activates the system. These systems have a battery life of between forty-eight and ninety-six hours. Generally speaking, if the offender's vehicle is on public property, because no trespass occurs, police officers do not need a warrant or court order to use this device.

The second configuration involves actually installing the covert tracking device in the offender's vehicle, much in the same manner that consumer AVL devices are installed. This presents two challenges. First, this operation probably does require a warrant because you are entering the offender's vehicle (as opposed to crawling under it and attaching something). Second, this takes time, takes tools, and makes noise. One way this is accomplished is by using some pretext to impound the offender's vehicle. When it is released, it has the tracking device installed. This type of installation has a number of technological benefits. First, the power for the unit is drawn from the vehicle, so there are no batteries to replace. Second, because the system is hardwired in a custom manner, signal reception is generally superior.

So there are two ways to get the tracker on board the offender's vehicle and a few ways that the technology allows the police to monitor the vehicle's location. Both schemes somewhat mirror the consumer AVL. In one, GPS technology reports the location via cellular or RF technology to a desktop PC somewhere in a police station. In the other, an RF signal is transmitted to antennas owned or leased by the service provider. The RF (or cellular signal) is used to do time distance on arrival (TDOA) calculations. Once the police officers receive the signal, they can either follow the offender or simply allow the software located on their desktop PC to record the offender's travels.

Tracking Electronic Communications

As we know from previous chapters, our cellular telephones are constantly updating our location so that we can communicate throughout various cell sites. With the advent of Enhanced 9-1-1, the ability to locate a cellular telephone, using either GPS technology or a TDOA-like scheme, will be more exact and commonplace. This same information can be used by police officers to track a cellular telephone. This technology has proven especially helpful during fugitive investigations.

There are a variety of means by which police officers can track cellular telephones. However, there are problems because some of the equipment is not compatible with some cellular providers. Cellular telephone transmissions can be

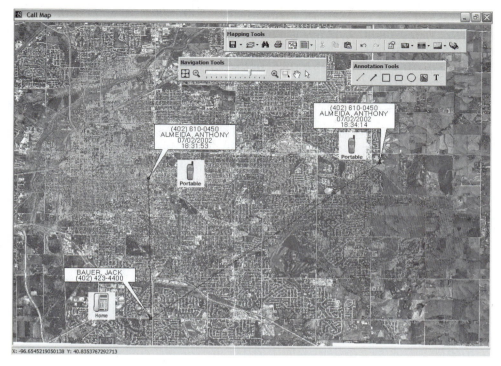

Figure 15.1 The screen capture here is a spatial analysis of a cellular telephone intercept. Note the pie shape of the shaded areas and recall from Chapters Three and Seven the configuration of cellular sites; the shaded areas of the map are the areas from which the intercepted calls must have been made.
Screen capture provided by Pen-Link™, Ltd.

tracked by having the cellular provider forward real-time information on the cell sites the cellular device is using (Figure 15.1). This does require a court order. Police officers tracking these communications use hardware and software combinations like "Triggerfish" to interpret the real-time feed of data from the cellular provider. Second-generation devices (there are second- and third-generation devices being used in the field, but the names and access to the devices are currently classified information) not only take real-time feed from the cellular provider, but they can also locally track the transmission of the device's electronic serial number (ESN). In other words, the real-time data on the cellular telephone will get police officers very close to the device, but in an urban environment, even as close as thirty

Try This

Do an Internet search for the words "skip tracing calling card." You will find any number of companies used by law enforcement, private investigators, and regular consumers to find out who's calling who. Usually a calling card will be sent under the guise of a "promotional product" to a target. Whenever the target uses the card, the number they called from and called to are reported to the person or organization using the technique. This reporting can be real-time via a pager, or the information can be accessed with a password on a Web site. If you were a police officer looking for a fugitive, you might send this card to the fugitive's spouse, child, or some other family member. No warrant is required, and they are relatively inexpensive.

meters could mean that the offender was still not visible to the police officers in the field. By having the ESN and using signal strength and directional equipment, good technicians can pinpoint the offender's location.

Photo Red Light

Photographic traffic enforcement systems, or **photo red light**, have been in use since 1986. The deployment is becoming much more commonplace and widespread. As of 1998, there were more than eight thousand photographic traffic enforcement systems deployed in forty-five countries.[6] A photographic traffic system can be composed of electromagnetic loops buried in the pavement, a terminal block that houses a microprocessor, and a camera on a pole. When the traffic signal turns red, the system becomes active and will detect vehicles passing over the electromagnetic loops under the pavement. If you are unfortunate enough to pass over the loops after the light turns red, your picture is taken.

Photographs are often taken of the rear of the car; or, in cases where two cameras are deployed, both the front and rear ends. The microprocessor used in the system records the data, time of day, elapsed times of the signal and loop activation, and the speed of the vehicle as calculated by how fast it passes over the loops. Generally, these devices are preset to give potential violators a three-tenths of second grace period. The speed calculation is necessary so that low-speed right turners are not photographed (presuming you're in a state that allows right turns on red lights). Of course, you know what is next—a traffic citation is sent to the registered owner.

Photographic traffic enforcement systems use one of three types of film. The most common is an industrial-quality 35 mm film that takes black-and-white or color photographs. Although black-and-white film is the most common, primarily because it is the least expensive, color film can be used to fight claims that the light was not red. The film must be retrieved and processed, often on a daily basis.

Some systems use digital cameras that can produce a higher-resolution photograph than even industrial-quality 35 mm film. A possible benefit of digital cameras is they are easier to service (collect the photographs), and because the picture is in data form, the process of notifying violators is accelerated. Moreover, digital photographic traffic enforcement can be deployed so that the digital image is sent directly to the reviewing person and incorporated directly into the citation itself. So you get a ticket and a high resolution JPEG of yourself!

Increasingly, state and local law enforcement agencies are looking at video cameras as a means to enforce traffic violations. Video cameras can be used to determine a vehicle's speed as it approaches the intersection, predict whether or not the vehicle will stop for the red light, and then track the vehicle through the intersection, recording any violations. Moreover, digital video cameras allow for real-time transmission of images and, like digital still cameras, reduce transport, handling, and reproduction costs. By using full video sequences, an agency can increase the number of detected violations and, therefore, the number of citations.

An advantage of a video system may be its ability to determine a vehicle's speed and predict if a red light violation will take place. In addition to the ability to detect violations, a video system may be able to prevent traffic collisions by adjusting the traffic signals to an all-red configuration. This may prevent cross traffic and record the violation. Moreover, because many of these digital camera schemes have the ability to transmit real-time images, they may have other law enforcement uses.[7] Later, when we look at CCTV, we will explore some of those potentials.

The use of digital photographic traffic enforcement devices often raises some of the questions related with the general use of digital photography in law enforcement—mainly tampering and storage. As we have discussed, tamper-proof files and data storage, along with solid policies usually allay these concerns.[8] Of course, whatever someone comes up with, somebody else tries to get around. There are a number of companies that sell license plate protectors and fogging sprays that are supposed to prevent a photographic enforcement device from reading your license plate.

As was mentioned in the first chapter, photographic traffic enforcement is a technology that takes decision making and discretion away from people and puts it into the hands of a software algorithm.

In-car Video

Increasing numbers of state and local police agencies are placing video recording devices into police vehicles.[9] As of June 2000, 45 percent of all local police agencies were using video cameras.[10] Video recording devices are becoming popular for many of the same reasons they have become a popular item in American homes. They offer visual documentation of an event. While many of the features on police in-car cameras are similar to a commercially available device, there are some important differences and considerations.

In this section, as we concentrate more on the tactical use of technology, we are peering closer at field operations. Police work is a 24/7 operation that takes place in all kinds of weather and under all kinds of conditions. In many state and local police agencies, larger and more expensive pieces of field equipment are pooled resources—everyone uses them. So after one police officer finishes his or her shift, the vehicle and all of its equipment are handed off to the next shift. The car, computer, radio, and—if one is present—in-car video system can be operating twenty-four hours a day. This continuous operation tests ruggedness of the equipment.

Consider the likely environmental conditions a police vehicle and the equipment could be exposed to in the southwest portion of the country during the summer. The day shift police officer checks out the car and equipment. At one o'clock in the afternoon, the police officer handles a disturbance call. While the police officer is inside the location, the car is outside, windows up, doors locked, and motor shut off. The temperature inside the vehicle soars to what—140 degrees? The police officer returns, turns on the air conditioner and the temperature lowers to a balmy 80 degrees. That afternoon, the car is passed to the swing shift police officer. After the sun goes down, convection sucks the heat off the desert and the ambient temperature is in the 40s. While the police officer is handling calls, the vehicle cools. Within a twelve-hour period the electronic equipment inside the vehicle is subjected to extremes of heat and cold, day after day. Of course, then there are rain and snow and coffee and doughnut crumbs, which are all bad for electronic equipment.

As manufacturers design equipment for field police use, they take these conditions into consideration and **ruggedize** equipment. Being ruggedized refers to the engineering process of considering not only potential environmental conditions as they affect the equipment, but other physical aspects of the conditions of use. For instance, try reading a commercial laptop screen in the sun. The screens on most laptops designed for police use have an antiglare component. Consider the placement of equipment in the vehicle. You cannot put radios, computers, and cameras in front of the airbag, particularly on the passenger's side of the vehicle. Some laptops designed for police use claim to be bullet resistant. Any technology introduced into field police work must be able to withstand the conditions of use, which can be extreme and constantly varying.

What would happen if you left your laptop and personal video recorder on the seat of your car for a few weeks (other than it would be stolen)? How long could you leave these items in your car before you would expect them to degrade? What about videotapes? Ever noticed the warning on the label of video rentals—don't leave in the sun? The major point is that if we are going to introduce video cameras into police vehicles, they have to be designed for field use, they have to be cared for, and there have to be organizational policies that make sure the videotapes aren't left in the sun.

We have looked at some of the positive aspects of videotaping a police officer's activities in the field, and we will revisit the positive aspects, but for us to determine the likely benefits, we need to have an understanding of the challenges involved in employing a system to record events under field conditions. How many times have you seen something and thought, "I wish I had my video camera"? Life happens quite spontaneously. When should the police officer in the field turn on the video camera? Should it be running continuously? Should the police officer decide when to turn it on? Before you answer those questions, let's consider the storage medium of videotape.

Recall the local agency that we used as an example in Chapter Twelve. An agency that size is likely to field as many as twenty-five police officers during the peak operational periods—Friday and Saturday night, for instance. If we deploy a videotaping system in each vehicle, and we require that it should be running the entire shift, we have twenty-five videotapes at the end of the night. Some recording schemes can get up to twenty-four hours on one tape. So for a weekend, we have as many as fifty tapes. Let's be conservative and say during the week, the agency produces another 150 tapes. How long should the tapes be kept? Should they be kept only when the police officer says there is something noteworthy on the tape? Every time there is an arrest? Well, unfortunately, most police management problems come to light several weeks or months after the event. A citizen or traffic violator complains, files a civil suit, or there is something else on the tape that might be useful for management or criminal purposes. Again, let's be conservative and say that the agency develops a policy to hold the tapes for ninety days, and if nothing from that shift becomes a problem, the tapes are reused. Ninety days, or twelve weeks, times two hundred tapes equals twenty-four hundred tapes. Think about the size of a commercial videotape. Where are you going to put them? Who is going to manage the rotation—that could be a nearly full-time job. If only 1 percent of those tapes become evidence, you are looking at the long-term storage of one hundred tapes a year, and that will grow year by year.

Clearly, constant videotaping of field activities as seen through the windshield of a police vehicle is probably impractical, which brings up another point—a visual record of what happened can be very important, but it has limitations. Nearly everyone has seen a videotape of an event where most of the action takes place outside the frame. With someone holding the camera, especially someone who knows what he is doing, more of an event can be recorded, but typical in-car

A National Institute for Justice (NIJ) report on technology commented, "Mobile video also protects the public. Officers who know they are on camera are more likely to act in a professional, appropriate manner." It is just as likely that police officers will try and get the "action" in the frame. As it is, they will be motivated to act more appropriately. It is reasonable to presume that if you know you are being watched, you will do your best, and you may try to ensure that your best is actually captured on film.

Source: "Evolution and Development of Police Technology," 91.

video systems are looking forward, out the windshield of the vehicle. One of the effects of the limitations of the frame is that police officers try to move the action into a spot where it can be taped. They get traffic violators out of the vehicle and place them between their cars and the police car, often with their hands on the hood. Being between two cars, especially on a busy highway is a very dangerous place. Having unsearched offenders get out of their cars and place their hands on the hood of the police vehicle looks cool but is tactically unsound. Have you ever seen a videotape where the police officer gets the driver out of the vehicle, places her with her hands on the hood of the vehicle, and returns to talk to the passengers. Even if the officer has a partner, he is turning his back on an unsearched, unknown offender. Sometimes it is clear that the motivation is to place the offender in front of the video camera.

In-car cameras have their limitations and potential problems, but they can be valuable and there are solutions to the problems. In order to reduce the number of videotapes, some agencies have configured their systems to only be activated when the police officer turns on the overheard emergency lights or siren, or at the police officer's discretion. This certainly reduced the number of tapes needed to record field activities. However, if the system is activated after the police officer turns on the emergency equipment, that means there was no chance the video system could have captured the traffic violation that motivated the stop. The ability to record events has so many uses, such as evidence in a criminal case, that other options of recording and storage media are being developed and deployed.[11]

Recall from earlier chapters that we examined the science and technology of both analog systems and digital systems. Videotape systems that use the large tapes you commonly rent from the local video store are of images recorded using analog technology. The DVDs that you rent use digital technology. Recall that long explanation on storage media in Chapter Two? This is one of the reasons that understanding data storage is important. Events in the field can also be recorded in a digital format.

In Chapter Two, when we looked at storage media, one of the technologies we briefly looked at was using tape to back up data storage. The storage of digital video images evolved from that storage medium. **Digital video cassettes (DVCs)** can contain more information than their analog cousins and are considerably smaller. So one option is for a police agency to consider digital video and a DVC storage medium. But you still have lots of tapes, lots of smaller tapes. We know that the digital images produced by a digital camera, or digital video camera, are actually large image files of binary data, and as we saw in Chapter Two, there are several good storage media, besides tape, or binary information. If we are going to use a digital scheme, we can take advantage of the technology and look for a system of storage that has a large, nonvolatile capacity—like a hard drive.

One solution to the problem of taping is to use replaceable hard drives as the storage medium. Essentially, the digital video system records to a small

Figure 15.2 Although many state and local police agencies still rely on standard video recording equipment, the rigors of field work and the necessity of obtaining the best evidence for prosecution have motivated some law enforcement agencies to employ more advanced equipment. This photograph represents a portable, stand-alone video lab that allows for the stabilization and enhancement of images in real time or of recorded images.
Photograph provided by Pyramid Vision Technologies.

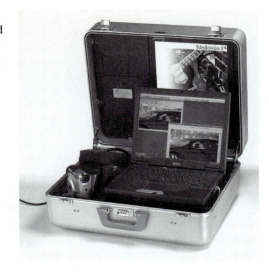

microprocessor and hard drive in the trunk of the police vehicle. Because the hard drive can contain a substantial amount of information, the time between transferring the data from the police vehicle to a secondary storage medium (like taking the tapes out of the machine) can be greatly extended. Consider that in twenty-four hours of constant use you would record about 2.5 gigabytes of data, so the data on a thirty-gigabyte hard drive should be transferred about every fifteen days. Some systems are accomplishing this by using portable, or removable, hard drive systems. On a regular schedule, a supervisor opens the trunk, turns the system off, pulls out the hard drive, puts another in, and reboots the system. That takes a few minutes. Then the agency can either keep the hard drive (which is about the size of a video cassette anyway) for the time period of their policy or transfer the data from the hard drive to a larger, long-term storage and recycle the hard drive back to the street.

As these technologies mature, they have the ability to seemingly anticipate a problem. Recall that earlier we discussed that one of the considerations was when to turn the recording device on. There are a number of schemes, such as continuous event taping (activated by the lights or siren) or a manual configuration. Right now—*my* right now—I am typing on a computer. As we know, that computer is translating my thoughts through the keyboard and displaying them on the monitor. Everything I type gets displayed on the monitor, but sometimes (too often, in fact) I don't save what I have typed. A digital recording system can work in the same manner. It can be on all the time, yet not saving all the time. So, if you set a digital in-car camera to only record certain events, like the activation of the emergency lights or siren, you can also configure it to save all of the information that occurred at a specified time before or after the event; because it is always recording the information, but only saving what you tell it to save. Depending on how you configured this system, the officer's activation of the emergency lights could cue the system to save all data one minute before the activation and one minute after the activation—potentially capturing the event that prompted the officer to activate the emergency lights. I have typed this last paragraph, but I may not save it. The information is permanently recorded only if it meets certain parameters.

In addition to activation schemes that are common to both standard and digital video, the digital system has the capacity to record other information. Anything that is common digital information can be correlated and recorded along with the visual images. So if an agency is using GPS for AVL, the digital recorder can also provide the precise location of the police vehicle when the information was recorded. Moreover, information like radar readings, vehicle speed, brake usage, and air bag deployment can be information included in the digital recording. These systems can be what black boxes are to aircraft.

Someday, as data compression and bandwidth technologies continue to advance, the digital video system in the police vehicle could ultimately be linked to the dispatch center. There the real-time data of the street could be constantly reviewed and stored, but that is probably off into the future.

Some agencies are beginning to multiply the effect of the in-car video systems by making them portable (Figure 15.2). The field police officer can actually remove the camera and take photographs of victims, evidence, and crime scenes. While having the video camera in the car is valuable, making it accessible for other functions can greatly increase its value. Victims' and witnesses' statements could be recorded for use in court. Offender confessions in the field could be presented to juries. The important point to remember is that video evidence is becoming almost incontrovertible in court.[12]

Closed-Circuit Television

Closed-circuit television is noncommercial video recordings that are broadcast on a private network. The network may be very small, such as a camera in a convenience store that networks to a single monitor and recorder. State and local government use of CCTV and video technology has steadily increased in the past decade. Videotape technology is a creation of the 1960s that has matured into a field that includes traditional tape and now digital means of recording, transmission, and storage. Thus far, we have seen CCTV applications in photographic traffic enforcement and in-car camera systems, but the technology is also used for the surveillance of public places and covert surveillance operations (Figure 15.3).[13]

Figure 15.3 This photograph depicts one type of surveillance camera. *Photograph provided by SpectraTek Law Enforcement Technologies.*

Figure 15.4 As we have discussed, a wide variety of video technologies can be used to support covert surveillance. This photograph displays the inner workings of a typical surveillance van. *Photograph provided by SpectraTek Law Enforcement Technologies.*

In 2001 the International Association of Chiefs of Police (IACP) conducted a survey of two hundred law enforcement agencies regarding their use of video technology, specifically CCTV. The survey found that 80 percent of the respondents used some form of CCTV, and the remaining 20 percent were considering the technology. Among the respondents, the top three uses of CCTV were investigative (63 percent), evidence documentation (54 percent), and crime reduction (20 percent). As with most new technologies, it is relatively uncommon for state and local agencies to have devised a method to directly measure either their effectiveness or their contribution to efficiency. However, most of the agencies responding to the survey felt that CCTV and related video technologies positively impacted their agencies in many of the ways we have already discussed.[14]

At this point in the text, we know enough about the related technologies to enable us to concentrate primarily on the applications of CCTV. As the size of cameras has decreased, their capabilities have increased. This phenomenon lends itself to the use of CCTV in covert surveillance operations. As we have noted, little is more convincing to the jury than a video of the offender committing the crime. Surveillance CCTV can be either static or mobile. Many mobile schemes involve placing a variety of equipment into a large van, truck, or recreational vehicle and using the vehicle as a platform for the surveillance (Figure 15.4). The equipment can be any combination of the technologies we have looked at thus far in the text. They can be very complex and permanent installations or they could be a police officer using his own camcorder in the back of a rented van.

One interesting and useful combination of technologies is used to construct a **bait car**. Usually, a bait car is employed as a tactic in areas experiencing a high rate of automobile thefts. This type of project would benefit from some intensive crime analysis because you are looking for a specific type of offender.[15] Because bait cars are fairly expensive to construct, you generally get a one-size-fits-all car that is loaned between agencies. Therefore, if your automobile theft problem is specific to the type of automobile, as in a commercial auto-theft ring working your jurisdiction, a bait car may not catch the offenders you are looking for; you have the wrong bait. What a bait car can do is catch opportunistic joyriders. Sometimes in response to a problem, a bait car is used and will catch the opportunistic thief, but it does not address the real crime problem. A bait car is a vehicle that has a remotely activated "kill switch" that allows the offender to start the vehicle and perhaps move it a few feet, and then police officers can activate the kill switch, stopping the motor. In many configurations, once the kill switch has been activated, the doors lock and the offender cannot easily escape. Moreover, these vehicles have video and audio devices secreted in the dashboard to record the offender and, sometimes more interestingly, the offender's reaction.

In Chapter Seven, when we looked at communications dispatch centers, we briefly mentioned the increasing use of intelligent traffic systems (ITS). An integral part of ITS is the use of CCTV. In this instance, CCTV is used to monitor roadway conditions, but it can be used as a means of crime reduction and prevention. As of 2000, 13 percent of local police departments, employing slightly more than 30 percent of all police officers nationwide, used some sort of fixed-site CCTV for surveillance.[16]

So far we have looked at CCTV applications directed at a certain offender or offender problem. For instance, the use of a bait car, the video surveillance of a home where narcotics are being sold, or even the surveillance of a particular street where the sales of narcotics is a problem. These are examples of the video technology being applied to a specific problem. However, CCTV is also used for the surveillance of locations where there may not be a specific problem, but perhaps the area is just plagued by different problems. The use of CCTV in response to general problems is often justified as a deterrent and as a means of efficiently using resources.[17]

Just as it is presumed that if police officers know they are being videotaped they will behave better, it is thought that if the community knows about CCTV in public places, the offenders will behave better. Some think that just the presence of a camera is enough to induce better behavior. This line of reasoning goes back to the application of the rational choice theory in situational crime prevention. The camera is seen as an additional element of risk, or a guardian that will cause the offender to not commit the crime in the presence of the camera. While there is very little research to support this, it does make sense; however, I would imagine the real effect is for there to be spatial displacement of the offender's bad behavior. Essentially, he will probably go around the corner. Some agencies, believing that the deterrence effect of these cameras is somewhat valuable, have taken to installing dummy, or nonoperational cameras, as a less expensive way to garner the deterrent effect of the technology without the significant investment in the working technology.[18] Another side to the debate on dummy cameras is that it may give the community a false sense of security, thereby increasing the danger to them.

The second reason given to support the use of CCTV is that it is an efficient means of providing police protection to an area. The thought is that instead of having a cop on every corner, you could have a camera on every corner. If the cameras are monitored in real time, one person could conceivably monitor multiple video images. How many televisions could you watch at once? Crime happens quickly; I imagine that watching multiple monitors would be like watching six different games of golf. Nothing would happened for a long time, but just as someone did something, you might miss it. More important, is this the best use of a police officer's time? A possible solution is to have community members monitor the screens. There are plenty of people in the community who have time and would volunteer. The reception point of the images could still be in a police facility, with community members watching the monitors. They could have a direct connection with the dispatch center and alert the dispatch, or perhaps a desk

Entrapment, a criminal defense, is the act of a law enforcement agent convincing someone to commit a crime when he has expressed a desire not to. The core concept of entrapment is whether or not the idea for the commission of the criminal act originated with the law enforcement agent or with the offender. The factual question often asked is: "Would Mr. Smith have engaged the prostitute if he had not been unduly enticed by the undercover officer?" The use of a bait car is usually not considered entrapment.
Source: Law.com.

A Look Ahead

Video technology has a huge role to play in state and local law enforcement training. We will explore that role in Chapter Nineteen.

officer, of unusual activity. While they aren't trained police observers, everyone can probably spot a car break-in or purse snatch.

By having community members involved in the monitoring, and potentially having them consult on the location of monitors (using crime analysis data as the primary decision-making tool), a state or local agency would probably be in a good position to get around some of the community concerns about pervasive surveillance of public locations.[19]

Body Wires

Devices have been developed that miniaturized CCTV and audio reception to the point where devices can be installed into a lamp, clock, radio, duffel bag, purse, picture frame, or even a wrist watch.[20] With body wires, we are primarily interested in audio devices that can be secreted on a person. We won't look at devices that record the conversations themselves; we will look at devices that transmit the audio to a remote recording location. We are restricting our look because the second configuration is far more typical of state and local police operations, while the latter is primarily the purview of federal agencies.

Body wires are often used during interactive surveillance, where the police officer, working in an undercover capacity, has direct contact with the offender. Moreover, the undercover police officer is trying to establish a relationship with the offender, as in pretending to be a fellow drug dealer. The courts have well established that undercover police officers can pretend to be offenders in order to gain the confidence of an offender.[21] The use of a body wire by an undercover police officer does not generally create a conflict with the Fourth Amendment, so no warrant or court order is required.[22]

While the technology is fairly simple—consisting of a transmitter, power source, and antenna—some of the implications are complex. Technically, a body wire is a low-power transmitter, so when they are being used, consideration should be given to the range of reception and interference issues including building penetration. A body wire has two essential purposes. First, it is a police officer safety device. When police officers are involved in undercover operations, they are with offenders and apart from their fellow police officers. This is very dangerous. However, an undercover police officer who has a body wire has a means to call for help either by directly stating there is a problem or through the use of a predetermined code word. The second use of a body wire is to record conversations between undercover police officers and offenders.

Night Vision Devices

Eleven percent of local police agencies, who employ 38 percent of all officers, use infrared (thermal) imagers; while 6 percent of agencies, who employ 26 percent of all officers, use image intensifiers.[23] What's the difference between **thermal imaging** and image intensifying? Night vision technology consists of two major types: **light amplification imaging** (or intensification) and thermal imaging (infrared).

Most consumer night vision products are light amplifying devices. This technology takes the small amount of light from the surrounding area (moonlight, starlight, or street lights) and converts the protons that make up the light energy into electrons, or electrical energy. The electrons are then directed through a thin disk that can be as small as a quarter. This disk has millions of channels through which the electrons pass. As the electrons pass through the channels, they bounce around, and when they strike the walls of the channels, they release even

Figure 15.5 One of the reasons that the night vision device depicted in this photograph is one of the more advanced models available to state and local law enforcement officers is that it has the ability for the user to adjust the gain. Recall from Chapter Three, "Wireless Communications," gain is adjusted to increase signal strength. In the instance of the night vision device, gain would be adjusted, up or down, depending on the amount of ambient light.
Photograph provided by ITT Industries.

more electrons. By turning the light energy into electrical energy, the technology is in a position to increase the amount of electrical energy. The next step is to take the increased amount of electrons, bounce them off a phosphor screen, and turn them back into protons, or visible light energy. This is how light is amplified or intensified in most commercially available products.

Thermal imaging works by using the upper portion of the infrared light spectrum. This portion of the light spectrum is emitted as heat instead of as light. So the hotter an object is, the more heat it will radiate. This radiated heat can be seen as infrared light. Thermal imagers take the infrared light that is emitted by objects and focus it on an array of infrared light detectors. These detectors are used to create a thermogram, or a temperature pattern. The thermal imager then takes the information from the thermogram and converts it into electrical data. These data, or impulses, are sent to a microprocessor that creates an image for display. Thermal imagers are significantly more complex than light amplification devices. You generally see these devices employed by state and local governments on helicopters.

Video Evidence

The primary theme of Chapter Thirteen was how technology has changed the nature of crime scene investigations. This applies to video technology also. Throughout this chapter we have seen instances of the police using CCTV or video technology as a means to gather evidence. However, CCTV is so pervasive

Try This

Visit the National Institute for Justice's Western Regional Center's Web site at **www.nlectc.org/ nlectcwr**. This is the NIJ-associated facility con-

cerned with the restoration and analysis of both video and audio evidence.

in our society that police officers need to be cognizant of other sources of video evidence. This is especially true in retail commercial areas, where there seems to be a greater concentration of the commercial use of CCTV. It may not just be the CCTV inside the location of the crime. Evidence could come from the ATM machine or gas station across the street from the crime. First responders and investigators should look around; perhaps an inadvertent view from a commercial CCTV source around the corner would show a getaway car.

The use of commercial sources of CCTV as evidence has grown to the point where special technologies have been developed in order to enhance CCTV images. The National Institute for Justice (NIJ) funded research into development of a software application that can enhance blurred, grainy, or poorly contrasted photographs.[24] This application, called "Restoretool," is available to state and local agencies. The point in mentioning this is to caution first responders. There seems to be an overwhelming need for people to look at CCTV when they discover it may have information about a crime. Unless there are exigent circumstances, first responders should gather video evidence without reviewing it. Because of the possibility they may inadvertently damage or even erase the evidence.

Chapter Summary

We started out in this chapter by looking at passive surveillance like tracking vehicles, electronic communication devices, and in-car video. What we learned is that passive surveillance is the act of watching or looking. As we looked at the technologies involved in the tracking of vehicles and communications devices, you should have noted that much of the technology we have examined in the previous fourteen chapters was being combined in different ways, to complete different tasks. In this chapter GPS and AVL were not used to track police vehicles in the field and increase response times; the technologies were used to look for stolen cars and track unsuspecting offenders.

There are a vast number of different forms of video surveillance being conducted daily. Everywhere you go, someone, at some point, is creating a visual record of your activities. State and local law enforcement agencies are following the lead of commercial firms by increasing their use of video technology. Video technology can increase the likelihood that an offender will be identified and that the offender will be convicted. Video technology can record the actions of a police agency and potentially reduce false liability claims. Video technology has a place in crime analysis as a means to target specific areas and offenders for investigation. Video technology can likely deter crime and enhance the community-oriented policing model by garnering community involvement in CCTV projects.

Although some privacy groups have raised concerns about CCTV in public places, the courts have continuously found that the right to privacy does not extend to public places.[25] But just because it is legal, a state or local agency would be well served by seeking community input prior to the installation of CCTV. The fact is, few people like being watched all the time. CCTV surveillance of public locations has a use in state and local law enforcement, and the technologies are becoming so inexpensive and reliable that their use is probably inevitable. However, by using crime analysis data to support decisions on placement, seeking community input on placement and installation, and perhaps using community volunteers to monitor the activity, state and local law enforcement agencies might be able to get the gain without the pain.

Discussion Questions

1. In Great Britain the use of CCTV by law enforcement officials is significantly more extensive than in the United States. In one instance, law enforcement agencies have chosen not to post maps displaying the entire police CCTV coverage in the city because it is believed that criminals could potentially use the information to avoid the CCTV system.[26] Do you think you get greater crime prevention by criminals knowing that cameras exist somewhere rather than knowing that a camera is observing a specific location? If criminals do not know the specific locations of cameras, then the general public doesn't either. Although CCTV is used by law enforcement in public places, do you see privacy concerns? Do your personal privacy concerns outweigh any benefit you see of CCTV in public?
2. If you were a police manager responsible to set up a new in-car video system, what technology would you include? How would you configure the activation scheme? How long would you keep the information? Let's make it interesting, presume that you have a limited budget and can afford a fully integrated system for a few patrol cars, or a limited system for all of your patrol cars. Which would you choose and why?
3. If you were responsible for providing training to police officers on video evidence, what would you cover? Why?

Key Terms

Bait Car	Entrapment	Passive Surveillance
Body Wire	Interactive Surveillance	Photo Red Light
Closed-Circuit Television	Light Amplification	Ruggedize
Digital Video Cassette (DVC)	Imaging	Thermal Imaging

End Notes

1. Heffernan, "Fourth Amendment Privacy Interests," 1.
2. *United States v. Jackson,* 213 F.3d 1269 (10th Cir. 2000).
3. "Searching and Seizing Computers," 19.
4. See note 1 above.
5. "Evolution and Development of Police Technology," 77.
6. Ibid., 113.
7. "Guidance for Using Red Light Cameras."
8. Blumstein, Young, and Granholm, "Commentaries," 10.
9. See note 5 above.
10. Department of Justice, Bureau of Justice Statistics, "2000 State and Local Law Enforcement Statistics."
11. "Evolution and Development of Police Technology," 91.
12. Ibid., 77.

13. "Use of CCTV/Video Cameras," 2.
14. Ibid., 3.
15. "Mapping and Analysis," 3.
16. See note 10 above.
17. See note 15 above.
18. "Use of CCTV/Video Cameras," 12.
19. Ibid., 11.
20. Ibid., 13.
21. See note 1 above.
22. Ibid.
23. See note 10 above.
24. See note 5 above.
25. "Use of CCTV/Video Cameras," 7.
26. See note 15 above.

Chapter Sixteen
Hi-Tech Crime

Learning Objectives

- The student will understand the differences among **computer crime**, **computer-related crime**, and **technology crime** and why all three of these broad categories fall under the umbrella of **hi-tech crime**.

- The student will understand some of the possible reasons that hi-tech crime is underreported and the potential effects of underreporting.

- The student will understand how the Internet has facilitated traditional crimes and created new types of crimes.

- The student will understand the different forms of a **system attack** and its potential effects.

- The student will explore how computers and the Internet have facilitated **theft of services**, **software piracy**, and counterfeiting and theft of hardware.

- The student will explore some basic information on searching and seizing computerized records such as the **Independent Component Doctrine**.

Introduction

In this chapter we will explore some of the crimes that have been created or made possible by the introduction into society of computer technology. We will look at three distinct areas: **computer crime**, **computer-related crime**, and **technology crime** and combine them under the title of **hi-tech crime**. What you will see is that there may be overlap in the three categories and at times a single offender may actually commit a crime that could be classified in all three categories, but the clearest way to understand the impact that technology has had on crime may be to look at all three categories as if they were very distinct. Once you have an understanding of the categories, sorting out the crossover will be much simpler.

Throughout this chapter, when we refer to traditional crime, we are referring to crimes that could be committed without a computer. As an example, many of the fraud schemes that are perpetrated on the Internet are only e-versions of scams that have been going on for centuries. A traditional crime like the possession of child pornography was possible before computers, but has definitely been impacted by computers. So a traditional crime is any crime that could be committed without a computer, but the computer makes commission of the crime more efficient for the offender.

Technology is changing crime in the United States. The changes in the way that crime is committed, the objects of the attacks, and the way in which offenders are keeping computerized records of their offenses are going to require that state and local police agencies employ police officers, investigators, and civilians with technological backgrounds.[1] As science and technology advance, new tools, training, and resources are going to have to be developed by police managers.[2] These changes affect the line police officer also. Just as technological changes are forcing line police officers to look at fingerprint, DNA, and video evidence differently, so, too, will first responders have to consider the potential value of computer-related evidence.[3] Basic computer forensics might be a portion of crime scene investigation.[4] Simply put, technology has created new ways of committing crimes, and because of a lack of training and understanding, police officers are having difficulty investigating these crimes.[5]

But how much hi-tech crime is there? Even experts in the field have difficulty in calculating the exact losses. Part of the reason for the inability to determine the extent of loss, and therefore, the amount of resource that should be expended, is because it is difficult to define computer crime. As you will see in this chapter, there is a great deal of crossover and debate as to the nature of the problem. In addition to this problem, you will see that victims of computer crime are often reluctant to come forward, which adds to the problem of determining the extent of the problem. Despite these problems, some experts believe that computer crime, computer-related crime, and technology crime cost us billions of dollars each year.[6] Even with the difficulty in defining computer crime and the aspects of computer crime that make an accounting difficult, steps are being taken to measure the amount of these types of crimes. The FBI amended the Uniformed Crime Reporting (UCR) scheme in an effort to address the different types of electronic crime. Moreover, the FBI has included a question in NIBRS regarding electronic crime.[7] As we look at the different aspects of computer crime, pay special attention to points at which the different classifications cross over, how they all combine to create the problem of hi-tech crime, and some of the proposed solutions.

Approximately half of the states modeled their statutes primarily on the 1977 or 1979 versions of the Federal Computer Systems Protection Act. As a result, most states have enacted legislation that defines computer crime similarly to California Penal Code Section 502 which states, in part, ". . . any person who commits any of the following acts is guilty of a public offense:

- Knowingly accesses and without permission alters, damages, deletes, destroys, or otherwise uses any data, computer, computer system, or computer network in order to either devise or execute any scheme or artifice to defraud, deceive, or extort, or wrongfully control or obtain money, property, or data.
- Knowingly accesses and without permission takes, copies, or makes use of any data from a computer, computer system, or computer network, or takes or copies any supporting documentation, whether existing or residing internal or external to a computer, computer system, or computer network.
- Knowingly and without permission uses or causes to be used computer services.

- Knowingly accesses and without permission adds, alters, damages, deletes, or destroys any data, computer software, or computer programs which reside or exist internal or external to a computer, computer system, or computer network.
- Knowingly and without permission disrupts or causes the disruption of computer services or denies or causes the denial of computer services to an authorized user of a computer, computer system, or computer network.
- Knowingly and without permission provides or assists in providing a means of accessing a computer, computer system, or computer network in violation of this section.
- Knowingly and without permission accesses or causes to be accessed any computer, computer system, or computer network.
- Knowingly introduces any computer contaminant into any computer, computer system, or computer network."

Sources: Jacobson and Green, "Computer Crimes," 273; California Penal Code, Section 502.

Computer Crime

The first type of electronic crime we are going to look at is crime where the computer or the ability of the computer is the object of the attack.[8] The attack can take three basic forms. The first is a **virus** designed to invade the computer or computer network and cause damage, such as denial of service or the deletion of critical operating system files. The second, theft of computer system services, would be an offender **hacking** into a computer and using the computational services of a larger mainframe.[9] A third type of computer crime is a close cousin of viruses, hacking into a Web site for the purpose of defacing the Web site or changing content. The key aspect of computer crime is that the computer, network, or system is the object of the remote attack. There is no physical theft; there is either a virtual vandalism or a virtual theft of services.

Computer-related Crime

A computer-related crime occurs when the offender uses a computer to commit a traditional crime or stores data on a computer that is evidence of a traditional crime.[10] Computers are sometimes used to facilitate what can be thought of as traditional, nontechnological crime such as the manufacture of counterfeit documents; the possession of child pornography; and the retention of any data, such as financial records for crimes like narcotics trafficking.[11] In some instances, computer-related crime relies on the Internet, such as auction fraud, copyright infringement (unlicensed movies and music), distribution of pornography, credit card fraud, and identify theft.[12] You might be thinking that Internet crime is a computer crime and not a computer-related crime, but stop and think of it this way, the Internet is the means, or instrument, that enables these crimes to be committed. All of these crimes, in different forms, were committed before the advent of the Internet. The Internet allows the offender anonymity and a wider reach, but the crimes could still be committed without the use of a computer.

Take an auction fraud crime. You are surfing the Internet and you see a very good laptop computer for sale at a bargain price. You contact the seller and since you are using a well-known e-auction service, you are comfortable wiring the large down payment to the seller. In return, you get either a product well below the capabilities of what you agreed to purchase or you get nothing and the offender disappears into the virtual mist. It sounds like an Internet crime—a computer crime. Well, in reality this is just a version of a very old scam called the "Rocks in a Box." While on the Internet, your confidence is gained by a sleek-looking picture, a cool description, and probably the use of a well-known e-service. In person it works pretty much the same way. Usually you are pumping gas at a gas station and you are approached by a nice-looking white male who tells you that he worked at a computer store and the manufacturer delivered too many of the great new laptops. He shows you one; you can touch it and see it operate. He shows you that he has several others still sealed in the boxes. He offers you a great price and you decide to take the one still sealed in the box, because everyone hates floor models. When you get home, you have a nicely sealed package of rocks. The only laptop the offender has is the one that he showed you, the others are simply empty boxes.

The scams are essentially the same. Someone entices you with a very good deal and then fails to deliver, nearly always intending to deceive you. If you were the victim of the "street scam" would you report it? Most people don't. They are embarrassed by their own greed and gullibility. On the Internet, the scam is slightly different, but versions of nearly all confidence games only change with the technology. So traditional crimes, even if they are modified by technology, are still computer-related crimes. Fraud is fraud no matter the instrument. Unfortunately, nearly every crime committed can have a high-technology twist or aspect.[13]

Technology Crime

A technology crime is a crime that uses or is directed at a technology other than a computer, or a crime that involves the theft of any technology, including computers. For instance, cellular telephone fraud is a technology crime. In cellular telephone fraud the offender either fraudulently obtains a legitimate cellular telephone or she clones a legitimate cellular telephone for fraudulent uses. Cellular telephone fraud is an example of a technology being the object of the crime. Another instance of technology crime where the technology facilitates the crime is fraudulent telemarketing where telephone technology is used to bilk victims. Technology also facilitates crime when offenders use the technology to conduct counter-surveillance.

Another form of technology crime is the theft of computer hardware and software.[14] In computer crime, the computer is the object of an external attack of some type. In a technology crime, the computer is the object of a theft. Of course, if an offender keeps records of computer hardware and software on a third computer, that computer is involved in a computer-related crime. Let's make it messier before we straighten it out. What about **software piracy**? If you illegally download software from the Internet, you are involved in a computer-related crime. You are stealing someone else's property and the computer is the instrumentality of the theft. If you go to a computer store and shoplift software, you are committing a technology crime by stealing the same software, but in person as opposed to over the Internet. If you go home and duplicate the stolen software, your computer is being used for a computer-related crime. If you sell the stolen software on the Internet, you are committing a computer-related crime (selling stolen property). However, if you modify the software and use it as a virus to attack another computer system, you are committing a computer crime.

Many crimes, when you make an effort to put them into categories, can be just as confusing. Take a murder; it seems fairly simple, but recall from our discussion on the Uniformed Crime Reporting (UCR) system that since it is an hierarchical reporting system, only the most serious crime is reported. The murder may involve the sub-crimes of burglary, rape, and robbery. If you start to classify them, murders and rapes are considered crimes against people, whereas robberies and burglaries are generally considered crimes against properties. As with computer crimes, you can go around and around discussing the classification of traditional crimes, but traditional crime has been around a very long time, so our understanding of it is clearer. We know that in a murder investigation, you have homicide detectives as the lead investigators, and they may consult with detectives whose specialty is sexual assaults.

Classifying these crimes under the banner of high-technology crime then breaking them down into computer crime, computer-related crime, and technology crime is a means to help us look at crimes as the individual acts and determine resource allocation by enhancing reporting. So don't get bogged down, they overlap.

To summarize, a computer crime is an offense made possible by the development of computers; a computer-related crime is an offense where a computer enhances the offender's ability to commit a more traditional crime; a technology crime is a crime where computer hardware and/or software is the object of a theft. These three categories of crime are all related to the offenders seizing on the opportunities and capabilities produced by the increasing use of high technology in our society.[15]

All of these types of crimes can be thought of as hi-tech crimes:

Classification	Unique Feature	Types of crime
Computer	Computer system or capability is the object of the crime.	Viruses, theft of system capabilities.
Computer-Related	Computer facilitates crime or keeps records of crime. Some are traditional crimes, others are crimes created as a result of the computer age.	Traditional: Child pornography, narcotics trafficking. Nontraditional: Software piracy, Internet fraud.
Technology Crime	Technology is stolen or other technology services are stolen.	Computer hardware theft, theft of cellular telephone service, theft of cable television services.

Hi-Tech Crime

Although there are several distinct differences among computer crime, computer-related crime, and technology crime, these offenses can be grouped together as hi-tech crime because their commission, investigation, and prosecution share some strong similarities. First, let's look at the problem of reporting hi-tech crime. One of the major reasons that hi-tech crime goes unreported, especially among major computer firms, is they prefer to handle computer attacks and thefts themselves, thereby avoiding the publicity associated with a public investigation.[16] Consider if you were an Internet retailer, if you relied on people sending you their credit card information so you could complete transactions, would you want your customers to know that security had been compromised? Sometimes the loss of consumer confidence can be more devastating that the actual loss involved in the offense.

Reliable statistics regarding hi-tech crime are also difficult to amass because of the problems with defining hi-tech crime.[17] Recall the scenario where you bought the nonexistent laptop via an e-auction. If you reported it to your local police, they would probably take a crime report and classify the crime as grand theft, not as a computer-related crime. This has several interesting effects. Primarily, when decisions concerning deployment of investigative personnel are made, police managers often use crime statistics to make those decisions. If your crime is classified as a grand theft, when the global statistics are used for deployment and resource allocation, more resources will go to the investigators who work traditional theft cases, and fewer, if any, will be devoted to investigators who understand the nature of hi-tech crime. With the loss of your laptop at the local level this may not have a major effect, but consider a larger crime. Let's say that a truck containing semiconductors is hijacked. Today this crime would be investigated by police officers with an expertise in cargo thefts, but these semiconductors are headed for the technology market. Although the thieves who carried out the hijacking might be ordinary street thugs, the people behind the hijacking have a specific market in mind. To eventually prosecute those people, you have to know something about the technology market. Again, more resources would go to cargo theft investigations and less to the investigation of hi-tech crimes.

Moreover, if every state and local jurisdiction reports e-auction fraud as simple fraud or theft, system attacks on Web sites as vandalism, and software piracy as plain theft, the picture on a national scale is skewed. When federal authorities make decisions about resource allocation, hi-tech crime could get the short end of the stick. This misclassification of hi-tech crime means that policy makers and managers have invalid statistics about the problem.[18]

Another reason that hi-tech crimes tend to go unreported is that a considerable amount of hi-tech crime is committed by people inside the victim organization. When a crime is committed by an insider, the firm can usually determine the source and would rather make an example of the person internally. This is also related to the negative publicity aspect of hi-tech crimes for private firms. If the offender is inside the organization, a public admission of the problem can be interpreted as a sign the firm's own security policies and procedures do not work. Also related to the publicity issue is the cost of prosecution. For a firm that has discovered the problem with an insider (or outsider), it is less costly to fix the security problem than to prosecute (Figure 16.1). Prosecution not only means publicity, but also means paying people to respond to requests for evidence or testimony.

Some hi-tech crime simply goes unreported because it is not discovered. Many people have their ATM cards accessed for a few hundred dollars and never know. They keep sloppy personal records and the disappearance of a hundred dollars goes unnoticed. Moreover, many cases of computer-related identity theft don't become known until the offender has stolen thousands of dollars and moved on to another victim. Finally, sometimes a hi-tech crime is so pervasive, reporting on an individual scale is impossible. Consider massive virus attacks that invade commercial networks and home computers. Have you had a virus? How much time did you lose fixing it? Did you lose any data? Even though you were the victim of a crime when your personal system was attacked by a virus, you probably didn't report it to law enforcement.

Even when industry experts attempt to determine the economic loss associated with hi-tech crime, their survey instruments are sometimes unscientific and ambiguous, making the data suspect.[19] With so little information and different local priorities, it is difficult to define the problem, allocate resources, and make decisions on policy and legislation.[20] However, often the first step in preventing crime and apprehending offenders is understanding the nature of their criminal acts. To begin our exploration of hi-tech crime, we start with the definition that high-technology crime is crimes in which technology is used as an instrument in committing—or assisting in the commission of—a crime, or in which technology is the target of a criminal act.[21]

The Internet and Crime

The growth and nature of the Internet have enabled high-technology crime.[22] As we saw in Chapter Ten, the success of the Internet is directly attributable to the open architecture and standard protocols used for information exchange. This success has brought hundreds of millions of users and billions of Web pages of information. Since anyone with access can get onto the Internet, some of the users have been offenders who either found a new venue for their crime, or have decided to use the Internet as a vehicle for their virtual vandalism. In this section we are going to look at how the Internet has impacted two traditional crimes: fraud and child pornography.

The essence of fraud has been changed by the Internet. There are two basic things that make fraud possible. First, the defrauder must gain the victim's confidence. With the traditional, in-person fraud, the offender employs a variety of means to gain the victim's confidence. It may be the way the offender is dressed and carries himself, or it may be that the offender offers to first entrust the victim with something valuable. The second aspect of fraud is the victim has to

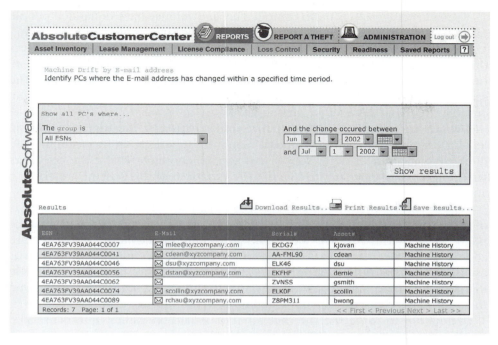

Figure 16.1 One solution to the rise in the theft of computer hardware is to install software on a computer that allows it to be traced. For instance, if an individual's or organization's computer is stolen and it has certain software installed, the next time the thieves use the computer to access the Internet, the computer reports it. Using automatic number identification (recall ANI technology from Chapter Seven) and the IP address (recall IP technology from Chapter Ten), the location of the computer can be determined.
Screen capture provided by Absolute Software.

participate by being greedy. It can't be said any other way. Let's look at how a traditional fraud is carried out in person, and then we'll look at how it is done on the Internet.

The "Pigeon Drop" is worked by two or three offenders. One of the offenders, frequently a woman, will approach the victim and explain that she found a considerable sum of money and is unsure what to do with it. Another version has the victim and the offender finding the money at the same time. Quite often there will be a note in with the money hinting that the money was obtained illegally or is to be used for drugs. The fact that the money comes from some illegal source often helps the victim (or mark in the parlance of the hucksters) get past any guilt over taking someone's lost money.

The second offender comes upon the scene, pretending not to know the first offender. She is soon involved in the conversation and is asked what should be done. She explains that she works for or knows an attorney and says she will ask him what to do then leaves to do so. When she returns, she explains that the money can be legally divided among them, but one of them should hold it for a period of time (usually thirty days).

A conversation ensues, during which the victim is elected to hold the money. One of the offenders objects and explains that whoever holds the money should put up "good faith" money for the others to hold while the victim holds the found money. Once the victim agrees to put up good faith money, the offenders establish how much they can get. Once the offenders have the money, they suddenly have places to go. The victim is left with the found money, which always turns out to be cut-up newspaper.

A **pump and dump** scheme involves the offender purchasing a stock at a relatively low level then posting messages about the stock in chat rooms or creating false press releases and even sending false e-mail messages that indicate the company is on the verge of some "breakthrough." These false messages are intended to create artificial speculation and drive the price of the stock up. Alternatively, bad news is falsified and the offender sells short. Either way, the offender cashes out and the stock collapses. **Touting** occurs when an employee of a legitimate publication publishes false or exaggerated news about a company in exchange for money or stock.
Source: Hittle, "An Uphill Battle," 165.

The Internet version is more complicated, and yet may have defrauded people out of as much as five billion dollars worldwide. It is called the "Nigerian," "Advance Fee," or "419 Scam" (section 419 of the Criminal Code of Nigeria covers this type of fraud, thus the 419 Scam). In Europe, it is called "The Nigerian Connection." However, it is usually just called "419" by the Nigerians themselves. The scam begins with the victim receiving an unsolicited fax, e-mail, or letter concerning Nigeria or some other African nation.

On the Internet, the e-mail contains either a **money laundering** or some legitimate-sounding business proposal. Common variations on the scam include double-invoiced oil or other supply and service contracts where the offenders want to get the overage out of Nigeria. The variations of this scheme are creative and endless.

Very much like the old pigeon drop, the victim is asked to pay an advance fee of some sort. This fee is alternatively referred to as transfer tax or a performance bond. If the victim pays the fee, there are often complications, which require additional advanced payments. This milking of the victim continues until the victim quits, runs out of money, or both. I know a victim who spent $80,000, a few thousand at a time, and he still refuses to believe this is a scam. It has been said that this scam is between the third- and fifth-largest industry in Nigeria.

In addition to using the Internet for traditional con games, Internet-related stock scams are said to cost investors $10 billion a year.[23] Through sham stock offerings, **pump and dump** schemes and **touting**, offenders bilk the nation's online investors at an incredible rate. The Internet is replete with stories of false and sham startup companies. From new earth asteroid explorations to eel farms, people invest their money in companies that don't exist and often for services probably no one would buy anyway.[24] One offender gave a direct public offering for his company on the Internet and raised $190,000 from 150 investors. The offender spent the money on stereo equipment and groceries. Another pair of offenders bilked Internet users out of $3.5 million promising their product would double the users' investments in four months.[25] But, the point is, these are all traditional crimes that are enhanced by the Internet.

Understanding how Internet enables fraud is important for state and local police officers. It enables fraud because offenders and potential victims are anonymously brought together through chat rooms, forum discussions, e-mail, and instant messaging systems. With the in-person fraud of the pigeon drop, the victim at least has a physical description of the offender, whereas Internet offenders can vanish into the virtual mist. Moreover, with the in-person fraud the offense takes place in a physical location, whereas Internet fraud is not only multijurisdictional, it is multinational.[26]

Try This

The Securities and Exchange Commission (SEC) has primary responsibility for policing issues of stock fraud like touting and pump and dump. In July 1998, in response to the growing instance of Internet stock-related fraud, the SEC formed the Office of Internet Enforcement (OIE). The OIE oversees two interesting Internet enforcement programs: Cyberforce and the Online Enforcement Complaint. In addition to being a good method of combating Internet fraud, since people who are victims of Internet fraud must be online users, the Web site is also a good example of possible e-government applications. You can visit their Web site at **www.sec.gov/divisions/enforce/internetenforce**.
Source: Hittle, "An Uphill Battle," 165.

There are a variety of expert recommendations on how law enforcement agencies should respond to Internet fraud. Not surprisingly, just as the crimes themselves are variations of traditional crimes, the solutions are also variations of traditional crime prevention and apprehension strategies. For instance, it has been recommended law enforcement and industry-regulating bodies increase user education.[27] This is a very common situational crime prevention methodology. Educated victims should make it more difficult for offenders. Increased effort is supposed to deter offenders. Other recommendations include increased penalties for offenders and increased cooperation among enforcement and regulatory agencies. All of these recommendations should seem very familiar. Fraud is not the only traditional crime that the Internet has enabled; the anonymity and ready access of the Internet have attracted offenders involved in child pornography and crimes against children.

Offenders are using the Internet to disseminate child pornography and as a means to arrange meetings between pedophile offenders and the victims—children.[28] The crime of disturbing child pornography is further complicated by law enforcement because offenders are increasingly using encryption algorithms as a means to conceal the images that they distribute or transfer. As with stock fraud, the law enforcement approach to this problem has been to employ traditional law enforcement tactics in the Internet environment. For child pornography and to capture those offenders seeking children for the purposes of illegal sexual conduct, law enforcement often uses undercover techniques on the Internet. As an example, some state and local law enforcement vice units and sexually exploited–child units surf the Internet looking for Web sites that contain child pornography. Just as with illegal drugs, undercover e-detectives make buys and follow investigative and prosecution patterns that are remarkably similar to working a traditional crime. Of course, just as with fraud, these crimes are mostly multijurisdictional. Later in the text, when we look at task force operations, you will get a glimpse of how local, state, and federal agencies can work together in a virtual, multijurisdictional environment.

The FBI runs an operation that targets sexual offenders seeking children—Innocent Images.[29] To apprehend and prosecute these offenders, the FBI uses undercover agents who assume the role of a child. Typically, these meetings between the offender and the victim (or, we hope, an undercover agent) take place in chat rooms and discussion forums on the Internet. Instead of undercover agents making a buy, they attempt to arrange meetings between the offenders and themselves in the role of the child.

Fraud and crimes against children are two of the primary traditional offenses that computers and the Internet enable. These types of crimes are considered computer related because of the role the computer and the Internet play in enabling the traditional crime.[30] The computers and the Internet also facilitate computer crime, or attacks against systems.

Try This

Go to the Federal Bureau of Investigation's Innocent Images Web site at **www.fbi.gov/hq/cid/cac/states.htm**. In addition to finding information about the project, you will find a link page to the State Sex Offender Registry Web sites. Visit your state's Web site.

System Attacks

Computer crimes are attacks against computer systems. They are all of the new forms of vandalism that are directed against computers.[31] Most of the time, we think of computer crime as being committed by outsiders who gain illegal access to another computer or system, but some computer crimes are committed by insiders and don't involve the skills we normally associate with hacking and viruses. For instance, in the spring of 2003, I was asked by a nonprofit agency to look at repeated failures of their internal network. Eventually, the problem was traced to a disgruntled employee who was repeatedly deleting operating system files on individual machines. While there are insiders who perform acts of vandalism, the lion's share of problems seem to come from outsiders.

As we look at these crimes, it is easiest to think of them as acts of **vandalism**. For our purposes, **vandalism** is defined as the willful or malicious destruction or defacement of public or private property. We are using the term *vandalism* because offenders who commit these crimes tend to be motivated not by financial gain but by some perverse sense of pleasure, or in some instances they are politically motivated. These offenders commit their crimes by either gaining illegal access to a Web site (commonly referred to as **cracking**[32]) or by disguising a destructive software application (a **virus**) as an innocuous e-mail message or attachment to an e-mail message. Because we are not going to become programmers, we are not going to examine how one "hacks;" "cracks;" or creates a virus, worm, or Trojan horse, but let's look at the effect as a means to understand the seriousness of these types of crimes.

Typically, a hacker breaks into a Web site to deface the Web site or place slogans and disable Web site features. In technical terms, hacking into a Web site or a system is considered an act of **intrusion**. At first glance, this seems like any other act of physical vandalism, like gang graffiti, that just needs to be cleaned up, but with Web sites, you can't just clean it up. Because someone has been into the source code, a programmer must check nearly every line of coding in order to ensure that other surprises weren't left behind by the offender. This can be expensive not only in terms of the programmer's time, but also in terms of lost revenue or confidence by the Web site being hacked. Some time ago, the Central Intelligence Agency's (CIA) Web site was hacked. Did that make you feel more or less confident in the CIA's ability? Once lost, reputation is hard to rebuild, and what hackers often attack is reputation. This may be the reason that as many as nine out of ten computer break-ins are unreported.[33]

While hacking is one form of intrusion, another very serious form is through the use of a virus. A virus is a software application that is designed to replicate itself and spread, like the common cold, through a system or network.[34] Viruses can be designed to not do any real damage, they may just install an annoying screensaver on your computer, but the vast majority of viruses are destructive. They can cause your computer to delete critical operating system files, or they can make your computer participate in another **system attack**. While viruses that

---

Try This

You can read about some interesting computer intrusion cases at the Department of Justice, Computer Crime and Intellectual Property Section (CCIPS) at **www.usdoj.gov/criminal/cybercrime/cccases**.

---

spread via the Internet from personal computer to personal computer are harmful, it is the viruses that shut down government and public networks that cause the most harm. One way that a virus can shut down a network is through a **denial of service attack**, which is a tactic used by offenders to overwhelm a Web site or system with hundreds, perhaps thousands, of incomplete e-mail messages. Sometimes these attacks originate from one computer, but they can come from a virus that has spread to many computers to coordinate an attack. The offender simply writes an algorithm (recall that an algorithm is a set of instructions) that tells the virus to replicate in your PC, invade your mailbox, send its replicated self to everyone in your mailbox, repeat the steps of replication and invasion, and at a specific date and time, all of the infected PCs are to send an e-mail message to the real target. Recall from Chapters Two and Ten, computers don't do two things at once, they only seem to. But too much information arriving at the same time can have the effect of shutting down a system, or denying service.[35]

The writing of viruses has become even simpler because of the Internet. In many instances, novice hackers download small programs, or scripts, already prepared and written to intrude on other systems. With these applications, and a little more knowledge "script kiddies" are on the road to becoming hackers. In fact, experts believe that worldwide, there are fewer than one hundred people actually involved in the active writing of scripts. The rest are copycat hackers who take the basic information and plan their own offenses.[36]

The essence of computer crime is intrusion, the unlawful access, destruction, or entry into private, corporate, or government computers and networks. The purpose of this intrusion is often the theft, destruction, or manipulation of the information contained in these systems.[37] Thus far, we have looked at computer-related crime and seen that it is traditional crime that is enhanced or enabled by the Internet, and we have seen that computer crime is based upon intrusion—or an attack on a computer, a computer system, or a network. The final category of hi-tech crimes is technology crimes. Recall that we defined a technology crime as a crime that uses or is directed at a technology other than a computer, or a crime that involves the theft of any technology, including computers. In the next few sections we are going to look at examples of technology crimes.

Service Theft

In reality, technology crime is a catch-all category. It involves technology-related crimes whose use of technology is not motivated by intrusion or traditional crime. These are crimes that did not exist before the introduction of the certain technology. No one stole computer hardware and software before it existed, and there are certain technology services that are the object of an offense. These services are broadly defined as telecommunications and cable television services. These types of crimes include stealing telephone calling card numbers, stealing telephone or cellular telephone service, and stealing cable television services.[38] Calling card thefts generally involve an offender using binoculars to watch a public telephone from a secret position. From that vantage point, he writes down the calling card number that the victim uses. The number is then resold to other offenders who often call home, overseas. The theft of cellular telephone service was very prominent during the early days of cellular telephone services. Essentially, an offender used a device to capture a cellular telephone's ESN as the victim made a cellular telephone call. Remember from Chapters Three and Seven, the ESN is part of the information constantly broadcasted between your cellular telephone and your service provider. With the ESN, cellular telephones are cloned and illegal calls are made. This type of theft is much less prevalent now because of security measures taken by cellular service providers, and it points out an interesting phenomenon. One of the reasons that hi-tech crimes may go unreported is that private firms realize the difficulties and costs of prosecution are greater than developing security systems, policies, and protocols that can defeat offenders. Today most cellular service theft involves the actual theft of cellular telephones or offenders who obtain service by fraudulently completing service applications.

Cable television piracy generally involves the offender establishing link with a cable television provider without paying. This offender is likely one of your neighbors who enjoys the cable television service that you have without paying for it. The National Cable Television Association estimates that piracy costs more than $6 billion a year.[39] As you can see, these crimes, although in reality plain thefts, did not exist before the technology. In addition to the **theft of services**, some offenders steal intellectual property.

Software Piracy

If you could write music or write a novel that was so well done that someone would pay you for your talent so they could enjoy your creative work, would you appreciate it if it were stolen? This is the essence of theft of intellectual property. It is the theft of creativity. Typically, we think of this as **software piracy**, but it

---

In 2001 the Electronic Crime Needs Assessment for State and Local Law Enforcement, conducted by the NIJ, found ten critical issues in the area of electronic crime. While the NIJ report did not specifically examine some of the areas we are including in hi-tech crime (such as theft of microchips), the ten issues identified by the NIJ report apply to all hi-tech crime:

1. Both the general public and government officials need to be educated on the scope of the threat of electronic crime.
2. The NIJ report identified the lack of data and information regarding the extent of electronic crime. As we have noted, without proper information on the extent of the problem, it is difficult to assign the proper resources and conduct research into methods of prevention and investigation.
3. The NIJ report outlined the need for state and local agencies to receive management assistance in developing electronic crime units. The report also called for regional task forces to investigate and prosecute these crimes.
4. Training and certification in electronic crime investigation was identified as a critical need.
5. As we have seen, there have been many instances where technology has developed

much faster than our laws, rules, and regulations. The NIJ report identified the need for updated and uniform rules.
6. A companion issue to number two stressed the need for cooperation from the hi-tech industry.
7. There was a clear need for special research and publications so that investigators and prosecutors could identify experts, best practices, and trends.
8. A companion to issue number one was the need for agency management awareness of the electronic crime problem. Clearly, without management emphasis on the problem, there will continue to be a lack of personnel, funding, training, and equipment.
9. There is a need for up-to-date tools, equipment, and protocols for the investigation of electronic crime.
10. There was debate over the structure of computer crime units. Some agency personnel investigate computer crime, while others are computer forensic experts. The structure, responsibilities, and duties of computer crime personnel could have significant impact on the outcome of investigations.

Source: "Electronic Crime Needs Assessment," ix.

also includes the theft of trademarks, music, movies, and any other information in a digital format. This is one of those crimes that could be a computer-related crime because the theft of intellectual property has been around for a very long time. But we are concentrating solely on the theft of intellectual property delivered to the consumer in a digital format, or a theft of intellectual property that involves duplication through a technological means. So it could be downloading music or a pirated movie from the Internet, or it could be the purchase of a pirated copy of a movie in video format.

Software piracy is committed in a number of ways. It could be just people exchanging the latest version of software, or it could be duplication and counterfeiting of software products. Many private firms are taking the essence of situational crime prevention deterrence into their own hands by using copy-protection systems and watermarking methods to protect their property. In some instances, software will only work a limited number of times until you register it. So if you register your copy and pass the software on, it will only work a limited number of times. Intellectual property really isn't sold to you, the consumer. When you buy software, you are generally not buying it; you are leasing it. It is being licensed to you under very specific terms. If you were buying it, you could do what you want. One of the reasons that a very major producer of operating systems is so successful is an early court decision, which made software something you lease or rent through license and not something you buy. If you were a police manager for a small police department and you wanted a new or updated version of an operating system for seven desktop PCs, you might actually get one copy of the software and seven licenses. For some products, licenses are not for the number of devices (desktop PCs) but for the number of users. This is a typical licensing arrangement for e-mail applications. You buy licenses based on the number of users because more than one person may use a desktop PC. Most times, when you share software, even if you are a small business and buy one license, but load it onto four machines, you are committing an act of software piracy.

Along with software piracy, there are music and video piracy. Music piracy is usually the downloading or sharing of music files via the Internet. Like a virus, one person pays for the music, converts it to a file, and shares it along the Internet. Video piracy can involve someone converting a videotaped presentation to a digital file and sending it along the Internet, or it could involve someone digitally recording a new release while seated in a movie theater and making copies of the movie available. In addition to stealing software and other intellectual properties, some offenders target hardware.

Hardware Theft

Although shoplifting and e-auction crimes are one source of hardware-related theft, the primary concern is the large-scale theft or robbery of semiconductor chips, microprocessors, and circuit boards like prefabricated motherboards.[40] While the hi-tech crime that we have reviewed thus far tends to be nationwide and distributed (both offenders and victims) solely on Internet access, the theft of computer-related components is a regional phenomenon associated with those areas that are manufacturing centers, import/export centers, or distribution hubs.

Stolen computer components end up being re-marked and often built into well-known labels. Although this is a traditional crime because it simply involves the theft and resale of stolen property, like many crimes, it does require some level of expertise on the part of the investigator. The counterfeiting or re-marking of stolen goods is a huge industry and includes goods well beyond computer components. Often industry-paid security personnel are involved in checking flea markets, computer trade shows, and classified ads for stolen or counterfeit goods. State and local police officers are likely to encounter calls for service involving paid security people who have made private persons' arrests at these venues. In this instance, as in many others, line police officers find themselves in the position of having to rely on the expertise of the industry employee.

Now that we have looked at a variety of hi-tech crimes and should have a basic understanding of the types of crimes and the reasons that they are categorized as computer crimes, computer-related crimes, or technology crimes, we can now look at some issues involving the seizure of hi-tech evidence and one of the potential solutions to this expertise-intensive and multijurisdictional problem.

Evidence and Hi-Tech Crimes

Every major criminal investigation should at least consider the possibility that some sort of high technology was involved in facilitating the crime. Therefore, issues regarding the collection of evidence extend well beyond the police officer who has developed expertise as a technology investigator.[41] First responders and investigators involved in traditional criminal investigations should be cognizant of how technology may have enhanced the particular criminal investigation they are pursuing.

About a decade ago, I was a uniformed supervisor at the scene of a search warrant for narcotics. The warrant called for the investigators to seize all evidence that tended to show the offenders were involved in the sales of narcotics. The warrant specifically stated it was for "Pay and Owe" sheets. As the investigators searched, they continually walked by a new desktop PC. The PC was set up and clearly had been used. As the investigators searched, I pointed to the PC. The lead investigator shrugged and said, "I wouldn't even know where to begin." At that point, desktop PCs were fairly new as household items. Few people within state and local police agencies even knew the first thing about turning them on. So, as evidence, I am certain they were continuously ignored. Today this is less likely to happen, but along the way another phenomenon started.

About five years later, I found myself a uniformed watch commander at the scene of a warrant service into a commercial auto theft ring. Again the warrant called for seizing records. During a search of the location, the investigators discovered a floor safe and a desktop PC. When they found the safe, they made a telephone call for the "safe detail." When they found the PC, one of the investigators sat down and turned it on. As I watched, the PC was obviously password protected. I walked up to the investigator and asked him why they had called the safe detail. He told me that while he and his team could bust open the safe, the safe detail were experts; they could do it much easier and they would not destroy any evidence contained in the safe when they opened it. We had a brief discussion (another example of me making friends), and I explained that the PC was like the safe. The password protection was the lock. Sure, he could maybe bust it open, but even more than with the safe, he risked destroying evidence. More important, if he wasn't a computer expert, he would have a very tough time attempting to introduce computer evidence in court. I explained his options, much in the way I am going to explain them here.

Scenarios that are likely to involve the search and seizure of computer equipment are probably going to be search warrant situations. A computer, like all other personal property and potential evidence, is protected by the Fourth Amendment of the United States Constitution.[42] Although a first responder or investigator may come across a situation wherein she does not have a search warrant but is in a position to see a computer that might contain evidence, the best course of action is to secure the computer from tampering by the offender and seek a search warrant. An exception to the need for a search warrant would be an offender who loses control of a file, perhaps by sending it to a second person who gives that information to the police.[43] Although this is not a search and seizure manual, probably the best way to treat computer evidence is to think of it as any other closed container, like a briefcase.[44]

Recall in both of the scenarios above, a computer was found inside a residence and it was believed that it may contain evidence of the crimes that were under investigation. In both cases a search of the computer was not specifically mentioned in the original warrant. In both cases it would be highly desirable to obtain a second search warrant for searching the computer records.[45] Again, a general rule of thumb is that because searching and seizing computer records is a specialized field and computers often contain a large amount of personal information, if the computer was not the original target of the search, it is better to seek a second warrant.

Searching and seizing computer records is more complicated than most searches conducted by state and local law enforcement agencies. Recall in Chapter Thirteen that the analysis of certain types of evidence is considered forensic science, and forensic science means we are bringing scientific information into the courtroom as evidence. Computer searches and seizures are also a forensic science. It takes special software and hardware tools and expertise to properly conduct a forensic analysis of computer evidence. For this reason, expert advice and expertise in conducting the search is highly recommended so that evidence can be preserved is such a manner as to ensure the court will accept it.[46]

Although our purpose is not to become computer evidence specialists, let's briefly look at some of the aspects of the search of a computer for evidence. Like most forensic science, these searches tend to be complicated. As we know, computer files actually consist of binary data held by electrical charges. If you have ever scanned your hard disk drive, you know that computer data can be stored anywhere on the hard drive. We also know that there are a wide variety of nonvolatile storage media, such as floppy disks and DVDs. In addition to computer evidence being in any number of storage media physically located with the computer, data can be, and often is, stored remotely, and with the Internet, that remote storage could be anywhere in the world. So the most important aspect of searching a computer is planning the search.[47] Based on the information developed for the probable cause for the warrant, investigating police officers should spend time speaking with computer forensic experts and plan how and where the search will take place.

As we have seen throughout the text, what we call computers are in reality a vast combination of hardware and software that enable us to perform certain tasks. One of the key concepts to understand when seizing computer evidence is the **Independent Component Doctrine**. Simply put, when writing a search warrant or seizing computer evidence, a law enforcement official should consider separately each component of the computer system the offender used. For instance, presume you are writing a search warrant on a narcotics offender. Will you seize his printer? What would be your justification? If the offender had written threatening letters, the case for seizing the printer is much stronger. The printer may have been used to print the letters (making it an instrument of the crime) and the printer and letters might be analyzed for comparison.

When developing probable cause for a search warrant of a computer, state and local police officers should be aware of the types of evidence they might find. As we have discussed, a computer might contain financial information about the crime, such as "pay and owe" data. It could also contain the names of other offenders involved in the crime. This is especially true in fraud, narcotics, and child pornography cases. The computer might contain actual evidence of the crime, as in child pornography cases, and the computer might contain information that could lead the investigator to other victims. History data from instant messaging, chat rooms, and Internet Web sites could provide valuable information that might uncover additional, unknown victims.[48]

There are four basic options for searching a computer. One is to search the files and print out the evidence that you seek. Another is to search for the evidence and make a copy of the digital data. A third possibility is to make a complete copy of the hard drive while still at the offender's location and duplicate the hard drive later in the forensic computer lab. Finally, the computer may be seized and the hard drive examined under the controlled conditions of the computer forensic lab.[49] The method that investigators will use depends on their investigation, the role the computer played in the crime, the type of computer, and how the computer is configured as it relates to other systems. However, turning on the computer and simply printing out files is without question the worst way of seizing evidence. Many files are automatically date and time stamped when they are accessed. By opening a file and printing it, you may actually lose or destroy valuable evidence.

Sometimes you have no choice in the method you are going to use. For instance, if in addition to containing relevant information, a computer is also stolen, it must be seized. On other occasions, the offender may be an employee of a company and the criminal information is actually stored remotely on the company-owned and company-run server. Seizing the server could be massively disruptive to an organization. Under those conditions, copies of the files or even a copy of the entire server maybe the best course of action.[50]

While the legal aspects of searching and seizing computers are relatively straightforward, seizing the evidence is often a complex forensic science that can go well beyond the capabilities of a local police agency. Moreover, the cross-jurisdictional nature of hi-tech crime make the investigations often long and complex. One solution is for agencies to pool their resources and form high-technology task forces.

A task force is bringing together people in criminal justice with different types of expertise for the purpose of addressing a single problem. Hi-tech task forces somewhat mirror narcotics task forces. They include local, state, and often federal law enforcement officers, prosecutors, and forensic specialists. By working in a task force configuration, not only do the pooled resources alleviate many of the problems associated with complex investigations, but they also allow for cross-jurisdictional apprehension and prosecution. However, state and local law enforcement officers looking for technical assistance with electronic evidence can turn to the federal government. Many federal agencies that have law enforcement investigators also have technical specialists trained in computer forensics. For example, the FBI has Computer Analysis Response Team (CART) examiners, the Internal Revenue Service has Seized Computer Evidence Recovery (SCER) specialists, and the Secret Service has the Electronic Crime Special Agent Program (ECSAP).[51]

Chapter Summary

Computer crime, computer-related crime, and technology crime are all part of the broad categories of offenses that fall under the umbrella of hi-tech crime. The important element of computer crime is intrusion or a system attack. One of the most common computer crimes is hacking. For computer-related crime, a computer is used as a means to facilitate a traditional crime. One of the most common computer-related crimes is fraud. A technology crime is when a technology other than computers is used to facilitate a crime, or is the object of the offense. A crime that involves the theft of computer hardware and software is also a technology crime. This could be cellular telephone fraud or software piracy.

Much of hi-tech crime goes unreported. It could be unreported because victims are unwilling to come forward, because it is misclassified by law enforcement personnel, or because it goes undiscovered. Whatever the reason for the underreported nature of computer crime, the effect could be that not enough resources are allocated to the problem.

Key features of the Internet have facilitated an explosion in certain types of crime. The Internet can provide the offender anonymity. The fact that the offender may remain anonymous removes some of the barriers to criminal activity that we explored in rational choice theory. If you don't think you will be caught, the potential cost is less and, therefore, the benefit of committing the crime is greater. The Internet also gives offenders access to a huge pool of potential victims. There are millions of users. Additionally, the open nature of Internet protocols makes system intrusion or attack easier for offenders.

The final aspect we looked at was searching and seizing computer evidence. There are two critical points to remember with computer evidence. First, the search and seizure of computers is not much different than the search and seizure of other personal property. Second, searching for computer evidence is a complex forensic science. As such, state and local police officers should seek expert advice whenever dealing with computer and computer-related evidence.

Discussion Questions

1. Some have argued that the best approach to fight hi-tech crime is the use of deterrents.[52] Deterrents to the commission of crime are things like making it more difficult to commit the crime, making prosecution and penalty imposition more likely, and making the benefit of committing the crime less desirable. For instance, it has been argued that high-technology defenses, such as intrusion detection, will decrease the likelihood that a Web site will be hacked. Do you think that deterrents would have a greater effect on high-tech crime than they do on traditional crime? If so, why?

2. As we saw in this chapter, much of hi-tech crime goes unreported for a variety of reasons. One of the primary reasons for not reporting or underreporting hi-tech crimes is the victim organizations' belief that certain types of hi-tech crimes perpetrated against them can undermine public confidence in their products, or at least the security of their Web sites. It has been suggested that legislation is needed to restrict certain hi-tech criminal data from becoming public information (much in the manner that the identity of a sexual assault victim is kept confidential) because it is the only way we will ever have a clear idea as to the extent of hi-tech crime.[53] What do you think of this idea? Do you think it would improve reporting? What could be the unintended consequences to consumers?

3. If a police officer has a warrant to seize a computer, can he seize peripheral devices, such as the offender's printer, in order to facilitate a search of the computer? If yes, why? If no, why?

Key Terms

Computer Crime
Computer-Related Crime
Cracking
Denial of Service Attack
Hacking
Hi-Tech Crime

Independent Component
  Doctrine
Intrusion
Money Laundering
Pump and Dump
Software Piracy

System Attack
Technology Crime
Theft of Services
Touting
Vandalism
Virus

End Notes

1. Kenney and McNamara, "Police and Policing," 53.
2. "Annual Report," 13.
3. "Electronic Crime Needs Assessment," 32.
4. "Annual Report," 27.
5. Huey, "Policing the Abstract," 243.
6. Jacobson and Green, "Computer Crimes," 273.
7. See note 3 above.
8. "Electronic Crime Needs Assessment," 9.
9. Raskin and Schaldach-Paiva, "Computer Crimes," 541.
10. See note 6 above.
11. See note 8 above.
12. See note 9 above.
13. "Annual Report," 7.
14. See note 6 above.
15. Dunham, "Carnivore."
16. See note 9 above.
17. Bakewell, Koldaro, and Tjia, "Computer Crimes," 481.
18. "Annual Report," 24.
19. Ibid.
20. Ibid., 8.
21. This definition of high-technology crime is borrowed from California Legislature's definition.
22. "Annual Report," 8.
23. Dunham, "Carnivore."
24. Hittle, "An Uphill Battle," 165.
25. Steele, "Investment Scams."
26. Dunham, "Carnivore."
27. Hittle, "An Uphill Battle," 165.

28. Dunham, "Carnivore."

29. Ibid.

30. See note 9 above.

31. See note 6 above.

32. There is some distinction between the terms *hacking* and *cracking*. A hacker is a person who has the computer skills necessary to gain access to a system. Not all hackers commit crimes. However, cracking is the use of hacking skills to gain illegal access to a computer system. The illegal access usually results in a vandalism or theft.

33. "Annual Report," 21.

34. See note 9 above.

35. "Annual Report," 24.

36. Ibid., 21.

37. Ibid., 31.

38. Ibid., 35.

39. Ibid., 37.

40. "Annual Report," 40.

41. Ibid., 16.

42. "Searching and Seizing Computers," 30.

43. Ibid., 9.

44. Ibid., 7.

45. Ibid., 54.

46. "Electronic Crime Needs Assessment," 23.

47. See note 42 above.

48. "Annual Report," 16.

49. "Searching and Seizing Computers," 32.

50. Ibid., 33.

51. Ibid., 30.

52. "Annual Report," 20.

53. Ibid., 25.

Chapter Seventeen
Major Incident and Disaster Response

Learning Objectives

- The student will be familiar with the **Federal Emergency Management Agency (FEMA)** and understand the **Incident Command System (ICS)**.

- The student will understand how technology can enhance the different organizational missions, goals, and objectives at a major incident or disaster.

- The student will understand the importance of an **incident command post (ICP)** and how technology can enhance the efficiency and effectiveness of an ICP.

- The student will understand the typical configuration of an **emergency operations center**.

- The student will explore some of the technologies used in the response to major incidents and disasters.

Introduction

State and local police agencies around the nation define major incidents and disasters in different ways. For some, a major incident occurs when a certain percentage of their available patrol force is redirected to an incident. Of course, for a small agency, just about any radio call with the potential for violence can redirect most, if not all, of their available patrol force. For our purposes, we will define a **major incident** as any incident where one police officer assumes the responsibility to direct the actions of two or more officers at the scene of an incident. Our reasons for this definition will become clearer as the chapter proceeds.

The definition of a **disaster** is fairly consistent throughout the nation. A disaster is any unexpected occurrence that disrupts routine life in a community for more than twenty-four hours and causes either the loss of life or the loss of property. There are two types of disasters—natural and human caused. A natural disaster could be an earthquake, hurricane, or some other geological or weather-related event. A human-caused disaster could be something like a chemical spill or major crime. Throughout this chapter, whenever we are looking at technologies relative to both major incidents and natural disasters, we will refer to them as **unusual occurrences**. However, at times, we will specifically refer to technologies that are geared toward one or the other.

The first step in returning to a state of normalcy is establishing leadership over the incident. No matter the size or scope of an unusual occurrence, the first step is always someone taking responsibility for making decisions regarding controlling and responding to the incident. For the fairly small unusual occurrence, leadership might be as simple as one police officer directing the activities of several other police officers at the scene of the unusual occurrence. In the case of the very large, such as natural disasters, leadership is probably established at a predetermined **emergency operation center**.

The first part of this chapter will look at how we establish leadership at the scene of an unusual occurrence through the use of a widely accepted organizational

Figure 17.1 As said in the first chapter, not all of the technology state and local police officers use is information technology. In this photograph, the Los Angeles County Sheriff's Department helicopter is participating in a State of California, Office of Emergency Service—Law Branch swift-water training exercise.
Photograph provided by Robert Eplett, California Governor's Office of Emergency Services.

Just as the name implies, first responders are the emergency personnel— police, fire, and medical— who first reach the scene of any incident.

scheme. Recall that our primary interest throughout the text is on information technology (IT) in state and local law enforcement agencies. In this chapter we will continue with that theme. One of the key features of the organizational scheme that we are going to examine is its ability to enhance the flow of information (Figure 17.1). The organizational scheme itself is a low-tech information technology. Along the way, we will look at some hardware and software applications and devices that can help a **first responder** or the person in charge of the unusual occurrence manage the incident.

The Incident Command System

The **Incident Command System (ICS)** is an organizational model for the command, control, and coordination of an agency's response to an unusual occurrence. The ICS model was developed in the 1970s as a response to a series of major fires in Southern California.[1] It was developed by a group of municipal, county, state, and federal fire authorities who formed the Firefighting Resources of California Organized for Potential Emergencies (FIRESCOPE). One of the purposes of FIRESCOPE was to examine the problems with multiagency response to unusual occurrences.

According to FIRESCOPE, there were several recurring problems whenever multiple agencies responded to an unusual occurrence. Many of the problems identified by FIRESCOPE have been discussed in earlier chapters. FIRESCOPE found that whenever multiple agencies responded, there were communications problems because the agencies had different equipment and different terminology. There was also no predetermined mechanism to expand or contract the organizational structure that coordinated resources response. This meant that as an unusual occurrence grew or contracted, there was no organizational way to grow or contract with the emergency. Just as the different agencies responded with different communications equipment and terminology, they also had different ways of doing things. Finally, FIRESCOPE noted that there was little planning in regard to facilities, resources, and personnel management.

The Incident Command System was developed to mitigate the problems FIRESCOPE had identified. For about a decade after the development of ICS, it remained a tool used primarily by firefighters. During that time, the National Interagency Incident Management System (NIIMS) began to teach and use ICS as the primary model for response to unusual occurrences.[2] While different types of agencies began to adopt ICS (such as the United States Coast Guard and most state agencies who mirror a FEMA model), local law enforcement agencies were slow in adopting ICS.[3,4] As of 2001, few local law enforcement agencies outside the Western United States are familiar with the model.[5]

The reason that law enforcement agencies may be slow to adopt ICS is because of the nature of most law enforcement tasks. For the lion's share of the time, police officers work alone or in pairs. Moreover, even when police agencies respond to major incidents within their own jurisdictions, they would use incident command models that were either developed by the agency or handed down as experiential information from one police officer to the next. Conversely, fire departments always respond to an incident as a team. Each team, often a fire company, has a team leader, or captain. The job of the fire captain is to take charge as the incident commander. Moreover, often fires rage uncontrollably through multiple jurisdictions. Firefighters from jurisdictions that are separated by vast distances often find themselves working together at the scene of a major wildfire. The team concept and the necessity of working with multiple jurisdictions drove the development and acceptance of ICS for the fire service.

In our earlier chapters, especially the chapter on information exchange, we have seen that the development of law enforcement technology has been fragmented. We also know that one of the primary concerns of law enforcement personnel is the ability to communicate with other agencies during an unusual occurrence. As with the issue of interoperability, the fragmentation of incident command models has been a concern of law enforcement professionals. The problems that FIRESCOPE noted existed in the fire service also existed in law enforcement. However, because law enforcement agencies do not have as many **mutual aid** experiences as the fire service, the problem was only highlighted in the most dramatic failures.

In 1991 in Oakland, California, a devastating wildfire raged uncontrolled through the Easy Bay Hills.[6] By the time the fire was controlled, three thousand homes were destroyed, and one police officer, one firefighter, and twenty-five civilians were killed. Although California had the Statewide Fire and Rescue Mutual Aid System, the response of hundreds of emergency workers (police, fire, medical, and public utilities) was uncoordinated primarily because they had different organization structures and command systems. In 1993, in response to the 1991 Oakland fire, the California Legislature mandated the use of the **Standardized Emergency Management System (SEMS)** which incorporates ICS.[7] State law enforcement agencies are required and local agencies are encouraged to use SEMS so they will be eligible for state funding and certain response-related personnel costs. Furthermore, SEMS must be incorporated into all event and incident

Mutual aid is the voluntary provision of services and facilities by an agency not affected by an unusual occurrence when the existing resources of the agency directly affected by the unusual occurrence prove to be inadequate.

In California the Standardized Emergency Management System (SEMS) is a comprehensive major incident and disaster response model that includes five components.

1. The Incident Command System.
2. Multiagency or interagency coordination.
3. The state's mutual aid program.
4. Operational areas.
5. The Operational Area Satellite Information System (OASIS).

Figure 17.2 Many times state and local law enforcement agencies find themselves providing a support function at the scene of an unusual occurrence. In this photograph, a California Highway Patrol car escorts utility crews through a fire zone.
Photograph provided by Robert Eplett, California Governor's Office of Emergency Services.

planning, training, and exercises and there must be documentation that SEMS is used during actual incidents.[8] In 1994 the **Federal Emergency Management Agency (FEMA)** adopted SEMS.[9]

The **incident command post (ICP)** system has become the model for command, control, and coordination of the response to a major incident or disaster. It not only provides the primary agency responsible for the unusual occurrence with a road map for responding to the incident, but also provides outside agencies who are rendering assistance a shared command system, training, and goals. The responding agencies know that common goal is to stabilize the unusual occurrence by protecting life, property, and the environment.

As we begin to examine the workings of ICS, we are using a law enforcement point of view. This means that sometimes, as during a hostage situation, the law enforcement agency is the lead agency, and the incident commander would come from the law enforcement agency. Conversely, if a law enforcement agency responds to the fire department's request to assist in evacuations at the scene of a fire, the law enforcement agency would probably take a role in the **operations section** of the ICS configuration. As we shall see, ICS is a flexible, modular system that allows for the response to the unusual occurrence to expand and contract as necessary.

The ICS model incorporates seven basic emergency management concepts: **unified command**, **modular organization**, **span of control**, common terminology, consolidated action plans, comprehensive resource management, and communication interoperability. The modular organization of the ICS organizational structure has five primary components: command, planning, operations, logistics, and finance/administration. The command component of ICS is the incident commander.[10] Usually, the first police officer to arrive at the scene of a

With the assistance of FEMA, a professional certification program was developed by representatives of several professional associations. Administered by the International Association of Emergency Manager (IAEM), the Certified Emergency Manager program permits individuals to earn professional certification by demonstrating a minimum level of education, specific training in emergency management, and experience in the field. To maintain certification, individuals must continue their training and education. As in most professional certification programs, the process permits the certification of those currently professionally experienced in the field, but lacking the requisite formal education or training. FEMA offers thirty-nine online courses in emergency management, such as "Emergency Man-

ager: An Orientation to the Position," "Radiological Emergency Management," "Special Events Contingency Planning for Public Safety Agencies," "Basic Incident Command System and the Emergency Operation Center's Role in Community Preparedness," and "Response and Recovery Activities." You can enroll, download all materials and take the test online. In about six weeks, a certificate is sent to you or your employer. This is an outstanding tool to improve or refresh your emergency skills. You can view the course catalog and enroll at **training.fema.gov/EMIWeb/IS/crslist.asp**.

Source: Shafritz, *Public Policy and Administration,* 751.

major incident is the incident commander. For widespread disasters, the highest-ranking supervisor on duty usually assumes the role of the incident commander. As a major incident develops, and more personnel arrive, it is not uncommon for the first responder who is the incident commander to be relieved by a higher-ranking or more qualified person. However, the ICS model is clear: the most qualified person should be the incident commander, not merely the highest-ranking individual. In the ICS model, the incident commander is responsible for making the decisions on how resources are going to be used during the event. By having one incident commander, all responders know who they should pass information to, and from whom they should take direction. The idea that there is one incident commander from whom all responders (even those from different agencies) take direction is the concept of unified command (Figure 17.3).

The ICS model is considered modular and flexible because in order to properly manage an incident, the ICS organizational structure need have only as many

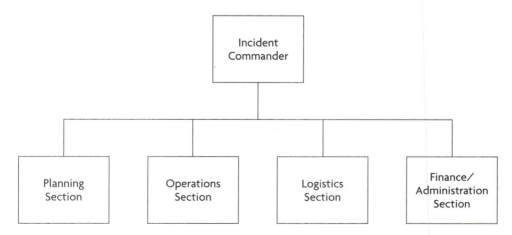

Figure 17.3 All incidents, regardless of type or size, must have an incident commander.

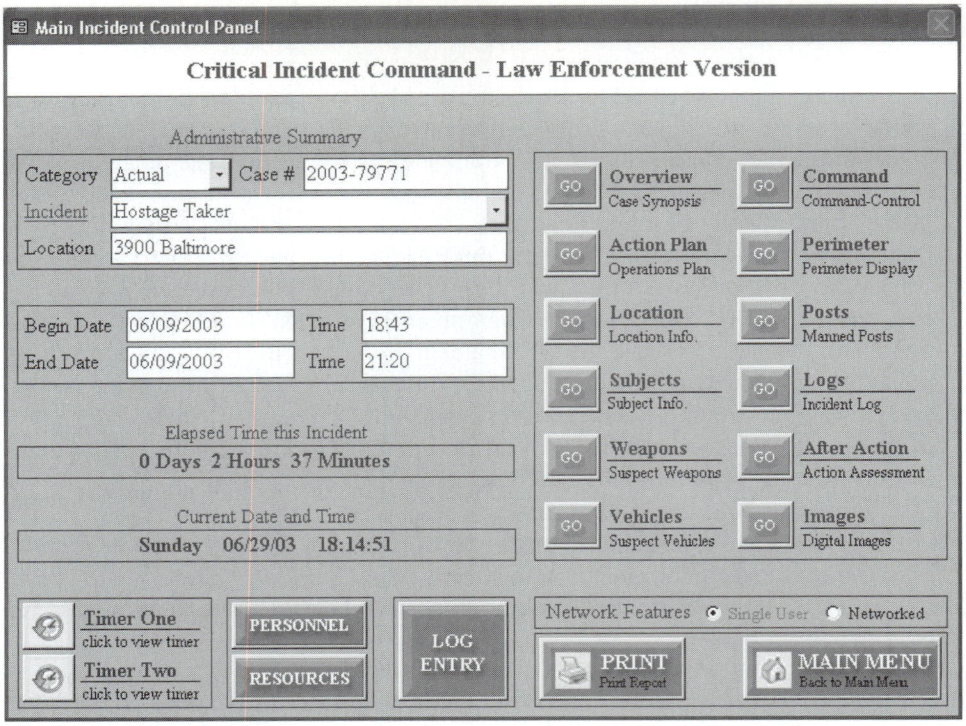

Figure 17.4 In previous chapters we learned the importance of relational databases. Relational databases can be the foundation of software applications that can assist an incident commander in managing an unusual occurrence.
Screen capture provided by 2002 Advanced Police Software Incorporated.

When a police officer arrives at the scene of an incident that he is going to need other resources to handle, the first communication he should make is to the dispatch center is a **situation estimate**. A situation estimate would include the location of the incident and the perceived area involved, the type of incident, special hazards, the types of resources needed, and the ingress and egress routes for the resources. If the incident necessitates a larger ICS structure, later information might include the location of the command post, staging areas, and additional resource requests.

of the components as are necessary to manage the incident.[11] Let's look at a traffic accident on a major state highway in order to explore the concepts and components of the ICS model. The accident may involve the local police, the state police, the local fire department, and the highway department. In this scenario, presume that the first responder is a police officer from the local police department. That police officer assumes the mantel of incident commander, relays a **situation estimate** to his or her dispatch center requesting the state police to conduct an accident investigation, the fire department for fire hazard and emergency medical services, and the highway department to close the on-ramps to the highway (Figure 17.4). When the state police arrive, because they are responsible for conducting the accident investigation, one of the state police officers assumes the role of incident commander. Shortly after the arrival of the state police, it is found that one of the vehicles involved in the accident is a tanker truck and it is leaking an unknown type of liquid. However, on the side of the truck, there is a blue emergency placard similar to the one in Figure 17.5. Because of the possibility that a hazardous material is leaking from the tanker truck, the state police officer decides to expand the ICS model. Our incident commander quickly consults her copy of the *2000 Emergency Response Guidebook* and finds that the placard on the tanker truck identifies the potential chemical as a highly toxic, water-reactive substance.

In order for an incident to be managed in as orderly a fashion as possible, responders must know who the incident commander is and where that individual is located. In the field, one of the first responsibilities of the incident commander

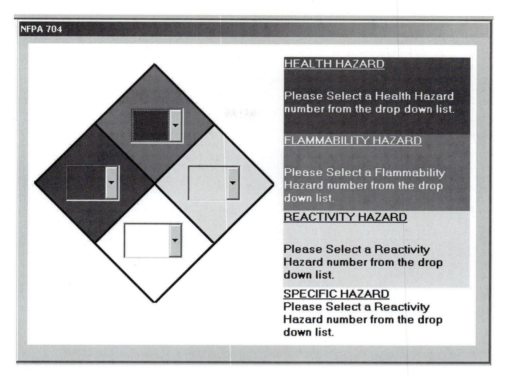

NFPA 704

HEALTH HAZARD

Please Select a Health Hazard number from the drop down list.

FLAMMABILITY HAZARD

Please Select a Flammability Hazard number from the drop down list.

REACTIVITY HAZARD

Please Select a Reactivity Hazard number from the drop down list.

SPECIFIC HAZARD
Please Select a Reactivity Hazard number from the drop down list.

Figure 17.5 Hazard placards are required on all commercial vehicles transporting dangerous, toxic, or flammable substances.
Screen capture provided by CoBRA®.

is to establish an incident command post (ICP). The ICP is the field office from which the incident commander operates. By having a single designated location, responders know where to send information, from where to get direction, and resources that are still responding to the scene have a meeting place.

Our state police officer first selects an ICP site. This is a critical task because the ICP must be close enough to the incident in order to manage the incident, and yet far enough away so as not to become part of the incident. Our state police officer moves the ICP to a part of the highway that is two thousand feet away from the accident and uphill and upwind from the accident. This location is chosen because the closed portion of the highway provides enough room for resources to respond; it is two thousand feet away in case there is an explosion; it is uphill from the accident because liquids flow downhill; it is upwind to prevent potentially toxic fumes from overcoming the ICP staff. Simply put, an ICP site should be selected to manage the problem and minimize the possibility that it will become part of the problem.

As she begins to organize the ICS structure, our incident commander realizes that the incident is becoming too large to handle by herself. Some incidents are

---

Try This

Go to the United States Department of Agriculture Forest Service Web site at **www.fs.fed.us/fire/planning/nist/ics_forms.htm** and look at their ICS forms. Take a look at ICS207, the Organization Chart. It gives you an idea of the potential complexity of disaster management.

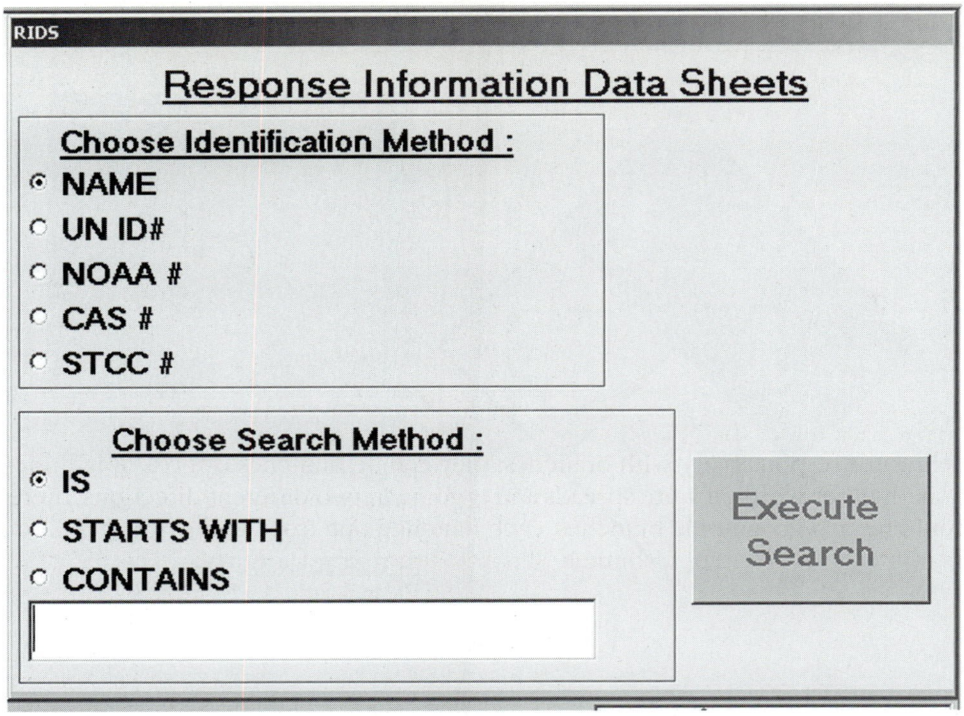

Figure 17.6 The *2000 Emergency Response Guidebook (ERG2000)* was developed jointly by Transport Canada (TC), the U.S. Department of Transportation (DOT), and the Secretariat of Communications and Transportation of Mexico (SCT) for use by firefighters, police, and other emergency services personnel who may be the first to arrive at the scene of a transportation incident involving dangerous goods. It is primarily a guide to aid first responders in quickly identifying the specific or generic hazards of the material(s) involved in the incident and protecting themselves and the general public during the initial response phase of the incident. For the purposes of the guidebook, the "initial response phase" is that period following arrival at the scene of an incident during which the presence and/or identification of dangerous goods is confirmed, protective actions and area securement are initiated, and assistance of qualified personnel is requested. It is not intended to provide information on the physical or chemical properties of dangerous goods. You can find a copy of the guide online at **hazmat.dot. gov/erg2000/unidnum.htm**. Carrying the booklet is a good idea, but a better idea is to have all of the information in a database that can be accessed by first responders and incident commanders. This screen capture is a searchable database of information about hazardous materials. Because the information is in a relational database, it can be searched by placard, as in Figure 17.5, or by chemical name, as in this screen capture.
Source: Department of Transportation, 2000, "Emergency Response Guide." *Screen capture provided by CoBRA®.*

relatively small, and the incident commander does not need any help. However, one of the strengths of ICS is that the incident command structure can grow and shrink as the incident changes; this is the modular nature of the ICS model. So at some incidents there may be only the incident commander, and at others the event may grow to include an ICP staffed by a score of people. Her first steps are to appoint an operations chief, planning chief, and logistics chief.

The operations section of the ICS model is responsible for carrying out the **action plans** decided upon by the incident commander. Action plans identify objectives and strategies decided upon by the incident commander. They can be either oral or written but are essentially the set of directions the incident commander expects to be followed in order to ultimately return to normal. If they are written, they can serve to document the tactical and support activities that were implemented during a specific operational period. For instance, with our tanker truck scenario, the incident commander might decide that one of the objectives is to minimize exposure to any potentially hazardous material leaking from the tanker truck. The strategy would be to establish a two-zone perimeter around the truck.[12]

The ICS model is designed for the coordination of different agencies, departments, and jurisdictions (Figure 17.7). In our tanker truck scenario, we realize that the police are going to play an important role, but not the only role, and possibly not the most important role. The situation may develop to the point where it makes more sense for the fire department to take the lead and become the incident commander. However, until that happens, the different resources that are arriving fall under the operations section.[13] In the operations section, ICS further delineates responsibility with branches; they can be branches by area or by function. In other words, if a fire spreads and is going in two different directions, there could be two geographic branches, each handling one front of the fire. That is an example of a geographic branch. On the other hand, one may organize the branches by function. For our scenario, the operations section would contain a law enforcement branch, a fire department and emergency medical services

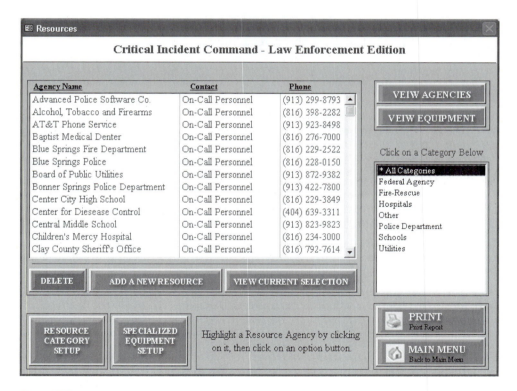

Figure 17.7 Although agency response varies around the country, law enforcement personnel are often called upon to be the first responders to most emergencies. As an example, in DeKalb County, Georgia, the Police Department Hazardous Materials Team is the designated first responder to threats of bioterrorism. This screen capture represents typical software that can assist an incident commander in locating and summoning the proper resources to the scene of an unusual occurrence.
Source: Lichtveld, "Preparedness on the Frontline," 184. *Screen capture provided by 2002 Advanced Police Software Incorporated.*

branch, and a highway department branch. In other words, the incident commander has decided that the best organizational structure is by function. Each of them would answer to the operations chief, who would coordinate their activities in order to carry out the action plans of the incident commander.

As needed, the ICS model expands to meet the emergency. At the same time, you can see that its highly organized nature allows it to maintain a sense of unity of command and a manageable span of control. In essence, unity of command means that everyone has a single supervisor in the chain of command. Having a single supervisor minimizes confusion about directions and orders, and every participant in the incident knows that a single person is in charge. Span of control means that a supervisor does not have too many people working for him or her. Different ICS guidelines suggest span of control ratios anywhere between 1:3 and 1:7; with 1:5 being the most common.[14] So, unity of command is how it appears looking up the organizational ladder, and span of control is how it appears looking down the organizational ladder.

For small unusual occurrences, like our tanker truck scenario, the incident commanders can use people from their own agencies to fill most of the command positions within the ICS structure. However, for large-scale unusual occurrences, the positions are usually filled by leaders from all of the agencies involved.[15] Later in this chapter you will see how the ICS model is very similar to the organizational structure of many emergency operation centers.

The ICS model is an outstanding vehicle for conducting emergency operations. However, how does our incident commander keep track of all of the responding resources? How does she determine the size of the perimeter, quickly obtain information concerning the contents of the tanker truck, and communicate with the different agencies? We can answer these questions and others as we look at technology that enhances the ICS model.

Incident Command Post Technology

Even relatively simple incidents, such as a perimeter around a search for a car theft suspect, can be confusing if the incident commander does not have some method of keeping track of resources. Moreover, the confusion and potential for mistakes increase as the complexity of the incident increases. The earliest way of keeping track of resources and their disposition was writing them down. Some police officers developed notebooks that contained maps, forms, and other paper products that could be used to help manage resources. Furthermore, because the police radio was installed into the police vehicle, the incident commander's vehicle was usually the incident command post. Thousands of perimeters and notes have probably been written on the roofs of black-and-white police vehicles. In the 1980s, my colleagues and I carried grease pencils so we could use the roof of the police vehicle as a portable whiteboard. It was a quick way to sketch out a perimeter or write down who had been assigned what task. The past decades have included development in both software and hardware that enhance the operation of the incident command post.

As we have seen, the patrol vehicle is fast becoming a mobile office (Figure 17.8), and many police departments have taken police passenger cars, sport utility vehicles (SUVs), and specially designed vehicles and outfitted them as mobile incident command posts. In many instances, the trunk-mounted platform has ports that allow an interface with the vehicle's radio and laptop computer equipment. The agency will usually stock the compartments in the trunk-mounted incident command post with maps, forms, and reference guides. For most incidents that require

Figure 17.8 This is an example of a trunk-mounted incident command post.
Photograph provided by Troy Products, Inc.

a small ICP, the trunk-mounted option works well. It provides the incident commander with an excellent platform to manage a relatively small incident. There are a few drawbacks, however. First, only so many people can crowd around the rear of the vehicle. If the incident commander finds himself managing more than four or five subordinates at the ICP, the trunk-mounted configuration is of less value. Also, the trunk-mounted configuration is exposed to the weather and bystanders. Last, the trunk-mounted configuration has limited capacity to carry additional resources such as radios, forms, reference material, and maps (Figure 17.9).

Figure 17.9 Recall from Chapter Eleven, Information Exchange, one of the solutions to agencies having different frequencies was the introduction of a system that could connect or trunk the frequencies. A smaller version of that type of hardware can be installed into a trunk-mounted or SUV-mounted command post. Significantly smaller, it has fewer capabilities than its larger cousin.
Photograph provided by SpectraTek Law Enforcement Technologies.

The next option for the law enforcement agency is to equip an SUV as a mobile ICP (Figure 17.10). Simply because it is larger, the SUV has the capacity to carry more resources to the scene of an incident. Typically, the SUV will not only have more paperwork-type resources, but also contain barricades, lighting, and other tools used to close an area or assist with the incident. Moreover, an SUV configuration can accommodate more technology, such as additional laptop computers and radios. There are even some SUV configurations with a cabana that can be extended over the rear of the vehicle, providing the command post with some protection from the elements. Both the trunk-mounted and SUV configurations share the benefit of usually being immediately available to the incident commander. In some jurisdictions these vehicles are routinely assigned to supervisors as their patrol vehicles. In others, the vehicle is at the station and can be brought to the scene quickly. The SUV configuration shares some of the disadvantages of the trunk-mounted incident command post. Both are restricted in the number of people who can effectively use the tools, and both are still exposed to the weather and bystanders.

The next step up in these tools is the specialty vehicle. A specially designed incident command post can be a converted recreational vehicle, bus, or tractor trailer rig. Figure 17.11 is a forty-five-foot converted bus called the Prevost Mirage XL. It is billed as the largest and most sophisticated self-propelled mobile incident command post in the United States. Currently, the New York City Mayor's Office uses one of these vehicles as its mobile ICP. Clearly, it is private and protected from the elements. The rear of the ICP has a conference room that can accommodate up to fifteen people (Figure 17.11). The forward portion is a command

Figure 17.10 This photograph displays a typical incident command post mounted in an SUV. *Photograph provided by Troy Products, Inc.*

Figure 17.11
A large mobile command post offers protection from the elements and from unauthorized personnel, as well as a wide variety of communication technologies.
Photograph Provided by OBS INC., Specialty Vehicles.

center that has a variety of radio combinations and computer workstations (Figure 17.12). This type of vehicle also has the ability to use hardwired telephone lines and receive live-feed video from a remote location or from its telescoping surveillance cameras. Although this type of vehicle has a number of advantages over the first two, there are a number of concerns. First, depending on the type of chassis used to build the vehicle, a special license may be needed to drive the vehicle. For instance, in most states, a modified bus requires a different classification license. Even if a special license is not required, the vehicle requires special driving skills. Both of these factors mean that only certain agency employees are going to be able to bring the vehicle to the scene of the incident. Moreover, it seems as though the likelihood that an incident will occur is directly proportional to the least convenient time it can occur. If an incident occurs during the vehicle operator's off hours, that person would have to respond from home. Even if she were working, she would have to go to the location the vehicle is stored and bring it to the scene of the incident. In essence, the specialty vehicle usually has a time delay before it reaches the scene.

However, the time delay may not be a significant factor because the larger vehicle would more than likely be used at only major incidents and disasters, and

Figure 17.12 A larger mobile command post allows for planning conferences to take place out of the weather and the chaos associated with a major incident and away from unauthorized persons.
Photograph provided by OBS INC., Specialty Vehicles.

they usually take a long time to conclude. All three vehicles have their place in the response to incidents and in an agency's planning of community events. In those instances where an agency knew that a parade or demonstration was going to take place, one of these vehicles could be used as a tool to police those community events. The last factor is cost. Just as they go up in size and capability, these three types of mobile ICPs increase in price. Moreover, the size and complexity of the specialty vehicle is probably going to require someone to be assigned to conduct care and maintenance of the vehicle and its systems (Figure 17.13).

We know from our earlier chapters that in a short period of time, computer processing power has increased tremendously. Based upon our previous readings, we should have a basic understanding on how the radios and laptop computers would operate in either of the three mobile incident command posts. Just as computer hardware and vehicle technology have been adapted for the ICS model, so has computer software.

If you visited the United States Forest Service (USFS) Web site and looked at the ISC forms, you saw there were twenty different forms that could be used during an incident. Many of the USFS forms are particular to fighting wildfires.[16] However, there are still about ten necessary ICS forms. The first type of software available is the ICS forms in a template format. For instance, the USFS provides all twenty of its

Figure 17.13 Additional command post technology includes portable, briefcase-sized command and communications systems. In the photograph here, a police officer is using a portable communications device that allows him to access a variety of technologies such as the Internet; the capture and transmission of video, radio, and cellular telephone communications; and GIS map creation.
Photograph provided by 308 Systems.

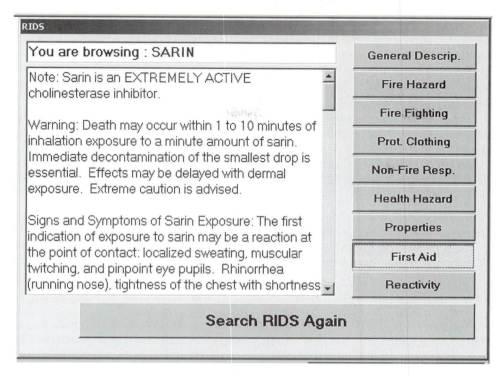

Figure 17.14 This database has been queried for information concerning Sarin, a highly toxic poison.
Screen capture provided by CoBRA®.

recommended ICS forms in template form for free. The USFS will provide software that allows an agency to complete and edit ICS forms using templates developed in MS Word 6.0 and WordPerfect 6.1, and documents developed in Lotus Word Pro 97. Although this is a big step up from handwriting everything that could occur during an incident, it is not fully realizing the power of the computer.

Recall in Chapters Two ("Computer Basics"), Eight ("Agency Systems") and Eleven ("Information Exchange"), we explored the power of relational databases. Software has been developed that unleashes the computing and organizing ability of the computer. Some software has been developed to assist state and local police agencies with managing the personnel and resources that respond to an incident. In addition to tracking resources, the software can help with formulating response plans and creating after-action reports. Moreover, software applications have been developed that allow first responders to query databases regarding hazardous substances (Figure 17.14). Among the information in these databases are recommendations as to protective clothing and first aid procedures.

Emergency Operations Centers

In larger disasters, organizations sometimes activate an emergency operations center (EOC). Recall from our chapter on communications dispatch centers (CDCs) that CDCs are becoming increasingly complex, adding dimensions like the Intelligent Traffic System (ITS). An EOC can be thought of as a complex dispatch center used for the management and control of the disaster. Moreover, an EOC may be supplemented by multiple ICPs in the field. An EOC would contain a representative from every department head in the jurisdiction or organization.[17] For instance, an EOC in a medium-sized city would probably have the mayor as the director.[18] The individual department heads such as the chief of police, fire chief, head of public works, and head of parks and recreation would be represented, and depending on the EOC configuration, they would have duties commensurate with their regular jobs. As an example, the chief of police might be the assistant director of the EOC.

The actual organizational structure of an EOC depends greatly upon the organization that it supports. A hospital EOC would have different components than a university EOC because of their missions and goals. The hospital would be concerned with the patients already in the hospital and the new arrivals. The university would be primarily concerned with the students on campus. Although they may have different missions and goals, most EOCs have an organizational structure similar to the ICS structure. At a minimum they would have:

- an operations section to implement responses to the unusual occurrence.
- a planning section to develop both long- and short-term responses.
- a logistics section that gathers, organizes, and allocates things like equipment, supplies, communications, food, and facilities.
- an administration section that maintains records of the unusual occurrence.

The job of the EOC is to coordinate all of the activities within a jurisdiction or to relieve some of the administrative burden from the incident commander. In the first instance, a major natural disaster is likely to have many locations where people are trapped, fires rage unchecked, and damaged buildings sway precariously. Many of these different situations within the larger natural disaster may require their own incident commanders. So if a jurisdiction suffers a disaster that causes six different "hot spots" that require an incident commander, the EOC is responsible for deciding, based on the information from the six incident commanders, which incidents should get which resources. Moreover, in a mutual aid situation where other jurisdictions are responding, the EOC can direct those resources to the incident commanders. This will prevent all of the resources from responding to one location; while another, equally important location receives little or no assistance. The job of the EOC is coordinating the response to the unusual occurrence on a wider scale.

Organizations that develop a permanent EOC and EOC staff often conduct disaster planning and disaster drills. For instance, in a municipal government setting, the different department heads along with the municipal government's chief executive (such as a city manager) may work together to plan a new budget. One of the planning processes that is unique to public safety organizations, like police and fire, is the need to create **contingent** or **standing plans**.[19] One of the recommended ways that these standing plans are designed is through a five-step process. The first step is to identify possible events that could have a major impact on public safety. This identification process might be considering which parts of a jurisdiction are in a flood plain, the identification of critical infrastructure sites that might be targets of terrorism, or planning for the annual Western Days Parade. The important point is that planning takes place for both unanticipated and anticipated events. The second and third steps involve determining the likely scope of an incident impact and at what point the standing or contingent plans would be implemented. The fourth step is the development of tactical and strategic responses to the incident (like predesignated ICPs). The fifth step in planning is to evaluate how the plan will mitigate the negative aspects of the anticipated incident.[20]

Planning for unusual occurrences is a critical function of both state and local law enforcement agencies. The ability to recover from an incident is directly impacted by the amount of planning done beforehand.[21]

Technological Considerations for the First Responder

As we have seen in the ICS model, when responding to a major incident or disaster, the police are often not the lead agency. For instance, when responding to almost any type of fire, the fire department supplies the incident commander, and the police officers work for the law enforcement branch under the operations section. Generally, a police officer's duties at a major incident or disaster include, but are not limited to: perimeter control, incident security, traffic control, crowd control, assisting with evacuations, the preservation and collection of evidence, and providing administrative support to the incident commander.

In our example of a tanker truck, law enforcement probably would not have remained the lead agency. However, law enforcement personnel do respond to incidents involving hazardous materials as in our tanker truck example. Many law enforcement agencies around the nation are pondering their response to potential terrorist attacks where biological, chemical, or nuclear materials are involved. In responding to any situation involving a hazardous material, the police officer's first job is to not become part of the problem by being exposed to the substance.

Unfortunately, most police officers do not have any protective gear that is suitable for situations involving hazardous materials. In fact, the gas masks that police officers are typically issued for crowd control situations offer little, if any, protection against hazardous materials. There are some law enforcement agencies around the nation that have trained and equipped specialized units within their organizations for response to situations involving hazardous materials. Today, in the post-9/11 era, the emphasis regarding hazardous materials has shifted somewhat from the danger of industrial accidents (like our tanker truck) to the threat of a terrorist attack involving a chemical, biological, or nuclear substance. But remember, the primary mission of the first responder is to avoid becoming part of the problem.

One of the ways that first responders can avoid becoming part of the problem is by understanding the limitations of their normal equipment. In past chapters, as we looked at communications equipment, we found that the various radio schemes have strengths and weakness. A first responder should consider that during a major unusual occurrence there may be communications problems, some of them as a direct result of the incident, others as a result of the weakness in the communications scheme. For instance, if an agency has a privately owned communications scheme, radio towers, transmitters, and even the primary dispatch site may become inoperative. This could create a total lack of communications or dead spots in communications coverage. If the agency relies on a vendor to supply a cellular-based communications system, the first responder can expect this to be more survivable than many government RF-based systems, but because many cellular-based systems do not give law enforcement personnel priority in frequency use, the unusual occurrence could cause heavy use of the cellular system and slow law enforcement communications. If voice systems are affected by the unusual occurrence, it is likely that data systems will be affected also. State and local police officers may find that they have limited or no access to outside sources of information during the unusual occurrence.

In addition to knowing the limitations of the system, first responders need to consider the limitations of their portable communications devices. There may be problems with building penetration, so first responders entering large buildings, malls, or collapsed structures (a very bad idea for police officers who lack training and equipment) may find that their radios do not work, especially on an overtaxed system.

Although some state and local law enforcement agencies have a hazardous materials or rescue response team, the primary jobs of most first responders remain

Figure 17.15 The Searchcam® EntryLink is a wireless video camera system that gives incident command personnel the ability to see and hear in real time what the entry team encounters in the exclusion zone. The EntryLink increases safety by allowing constant monitoring of the entry team's actions and provides a means to use technical experts from the safety of the support zone. The EntryLink reduces the number of entries required because technical experts can help provide solutions by viewing the video monitor. If additional entries are required, the backup team knows what to do because they have viewed the entry and have seen the problem. The EntryLink expedites the task and increases personnel safety. Most technologies like this are being used by specially trained firefighters and emergency medical services personnel. Under emergency operations configuration, it is the job of firefighters and emergency medical services personnel to enter hazardous zones to conduct cleanup, evidence collection, and rescue operations. *Photograph provided by Search Systems Inc.*

perimeter control, traffic control, and crime scene protection (Figure 17.15). This is all that most state and local police officers are equipped and trained for.

What's Not Included?

There is a huge variety of emergency and specialized equipment that we did not look at. We did not look at robots used for disarming explosive devices and searching dangerous areas. We did not look at specialized protection equipment designed to create a personal environment for the emergency worker. We did not look at these technologies because most state and local law enforcement police officers do not use this equipment on a routine basis, and they may not be the most important aspect of a first responders' duties at the scene of an unusual occurrence.

Chapter Summary

The Incident Command System (ICS) is an organizational technology that facilitates the command and control aspects of an unusual occurrence. The primary thing that can make state and local police departments more successful in handling unusual occurrences is someone taking charge. As a technology, ICS was designed to overcome many of the issues surrounding multiagency response to an unusual occurrence. As has been said throughout the text, state and local police agencies' technologies, equipment, procedures, and cultures are fragmented. Moreover, it is typical that in a response to a major unusual occurrence, many different types of government, nonprofit, and commercial firms will respond to the incident. By adding the different technologies, equipment, and procedures of outside agencies to the mix, the response to an unusual occurrence can be very disorganized. In keeping with our information technology theme, we looked at the ICS as IT that can give a common organizational structure, terminology, and goals to all the different entities that respond.

In larger unusual occurrences, many organizations activate an emergency operations center (EOC). The EOC is run by predesignated organizational members, in much the same manner that an incident command post is run in the field. The purpose of the EOC is to manage the wider resource allocation in an entire jurisdiction. The EOC may work with several field incident command posts, deciding where to apply existing resources and the mutual aid response.

Much of technology we looked at in earlier chapters has been combined into mobile command posts for use by incident commanders. Relational databases became important again when looking at technology that can assist in the management of an unusual occurrence. Software applications have been developed to assist with the management of resources and researching hazardous substances. Finally, with our grounding in technology, we are able to understand some of the potential challenges to using communications equipment during a major unusual occurrence. Radio systems may be disabled, they may be overloaded, or signal penetration factors may prevent their use in certain areas.

Discussion Questions

1. If you were involved in developing standing or contingent plans for a local law enforcement agency, what technologies that we have looked at thus far would be valuable in your planning? For instance, do you see a role for geographic information systems? If so, what would that role be?
2. How would you use technology to involve the community in disaster preparedness and response?
3. Visit either your campus emergency coordinator or local police agency. Do they have an emergency operations center? If so, is it different from their normal dispatch center. What kind of standing or contingent planning have they done?
4. Based on the technologies that you have explored in the text thus far, what potential problems do you see with the technologies during a major unusual occurrence?

Key Terms

2000 Emergency Response Guidebook
Action Plans
Contingent or Standing Plans
Disaster
Emergency Operation Center
Federal Emergency Management Agency (FEMA)

First Responder
Incident Command Post (ICP)
Incident Command System (ICS)
Major Incident
Modular Organization
Mutual Aid
Operations Section
Situation Estimate
Span of Control

Standardized Emergency Management System (SEMS)
Unified Command
Unusual Occurrence

End Notes

1. Buntin, "Disaster Master."
2. The National Interagency Incident Management System (NIIMS), which is operated by the United States Forest Service, is a system for responding to major disasters. One of the five components of NIIMS is the Incident Command System.
3. Cardwell, "Incident Command System."
4. Shafritz, *Public Policy and Administration*, 750.
5. See note 1 above.
6. Ibid.
7. See note 3 above.
8. "Emergency Planning Guide."
9. Federal Emergency Management Agency, Exemplary Practices.
10. See note 1 above.
11. Ibid.
12. A two-zone perimeter is fairly common in response to major incidents. In the example of the tanker truck, the inner zone would define the boundaries of the known hazards— the leaking substance. The outer zone would encompass the entire incident area. Most typically, police officers set up inner zone perimeters at crime scenes. This is the zone where no one, except those conducting the investigation, should enter. At a very well-maintained and controlled crime scene, the chief of police from the agency probably would not enter the inner zone because he or she is not actually involved in the investigation. The outer zone of any incident is the perimeter that regulates entry into the general area of operation. This keeps the outer operational area clear for the resources, and if needed, an expansion of the inner perimeter can be accomplished more easily.
13. See note 1 above.
14. See note 3 above.
15. See note 1 above.
16. There are any number of adaptations to the ICS forms around the nation. Some are designed based upon the primary mission of an organization (the USFS fights fires) or some variation based upon legislation. However, if you looked at them closely, you would see the basic ICS components, and you would find a common terminology.
17. Many large organizations, such as universities and hospitals, have an EOC.
18. See note 4 above.
19. Ibid., 514.
20. Ibid., 515.
21. Davies, "Reshaping the Information Era."

Chapter Eighteen
Technology in the Street

Learning Objectives

- The student will understand some of the Constitutional and case law that has motivated the development of **less-lethal use-of-force devices** and explore some of those devices.

- The student will explore the use of **radar** and **laser** technology in traffic enforcement.

- The student will explore technologies used in vehicle pursuits.

- The student will explore gunfire-reduction technology and some of the related evidence-gathering technology.

- The student will explore the use of **automated external defibrillators (AED)** by state and local police officers.

- The student will explore the technology of **body armor**.

Introduction

In the previous seventeen chapters we have concentrated on information technology (IT). We have seen that even the collection of evidence is an information-gathering function. But not all of the technologies that have been introduced into law enforcement have been IT based. Twenty-first century state and local police officers are safer today than they were in the not-too-distant past. Some of the increased level of personal safety has been because computer technology has given police officers ready access to critical information. But other technologies, like **body armor**, improved firearms, improved training, and other means to control combative offenders, have also added to their safety.[1] Moreover, as we shall see, much of the noninformation technology improvements have made the actions of police officers safer for the offender and the community.

As we have noted, the nightstick and revolver were the first technologies that police officers used to protect themselves. Both nightstick and firearm technology have matured. Today many state and local police officers no longer carry revolvers, they carry **semiautomatic handguns**. The semi-automatic handgun has a variety of features that make it a better firearm for police officers. A **semiautomatic handgun** is more compact; carries more ammunition; is significantly easier to reload under stress; and because of the reduced recoil, it can be a more accurate handgun.[2]

The second-most common firearm carried by state and local police officers is the **shotgun**. Shotguns are generally stored in the police vehicle and available for immediate deployment. Because the shotgun is carried in the vehicle, it is normally deployed when a police officer has some warning that a dangerous situation is about to occur. This warning is generally the type of call for service the officer is answering. For instance, a police officer responding to a bank robbery alarm call would probably have enough time to deploy the shotgun. The shotgun, if employed properly, can give a police officer several tactical advantages. For instance, it can have a psychological effect on an offender—it looks pretty scary.[3] One of the common misconceptions about a shotgun is that it is a weapon for less-than-proficient shooters. This is not true. Typical shotgun ammunition is a twelve-gauge round. This round consists of twelve ·32-caliber balls that are propelled forward by one cartridge.

When a revolver is fired, the hammer strikes the back of the ammunition causing the gunpowder in the shell casing of the ammunition to explode. This small explosion forces the bullet portion of the ammunition away from the shell casing and out the barrel of the revolver. The energy caused by the explosion goes in three basic directions. Most of it forces the bullet out of the barrel. Some of the energy forced back into the shooters hand, that is called recoil. The rest of the energy is expended in a flash that radiates away from the sides of the handgun, emanating from between the cylinder (where the ammunition is) and the barrel. With a semi-automatic handgun, some of the energy that would have gone backward into the shooters hand is used to push back the slide of the handgun. That is why these weapons are sometimes referred to as gas operated. As the slide moves back, it ejects the spent shell casing and a spring mechanism forces the next round of ammunition into the chamber. The energy dissipates rapidly and the slide moves forward and the handgun is ready to fire again. Now, there are a number of other features about a semi-automatic handgun, but the primary difference is that the revolver is purely mechanical and the semi-automatic handgun uses energy from the ammunition to operate.

Source: "Evolution and Development of Police Technology," 62.

When the balls leave the barrel of the shotgun, they are tightly packed together. However, the pattern expands at about a rate of one inch per foot and the effective range of the shotgun loaded with this type of ammunition is generally considered about 150 feet. So if the shotgun is not properly aimed at close range it is still a relatively tight pattern, and at longer ranges it is really spread out. If it is not aimed properly, the shooter will most likely miss the target. As we will see in the next section, the shotgun has also been modified to be a less-lethal weapon.

Less-Lethal Use-of-Force Devices

Before we examine some of the technologies that have been developed and implemented to assist state and local police officers in use-of-force situations, we should look at the how and why of use-of-force. Exact policies and procedures differ throughout the country. Just as technology is fragmented by community standards, budgets, and politics, so are policy areas, such as the use of force. That being said, there are some general guidelines that have been developed primarily from court cases.

The first concept to understand is that the offender's actions dictate the police officer's response.[4] Let's return to our traffic violator from Chapter One. If the violator is cooperative, we expect the police officer to be professional and courteous. But what if the traffic violator is uncooperative? What if he refuses to give the police officer his driver's license? The police officer can't just walk away. If police officers started walking away from people who refused to give them their licenses, society would probably fall apart in short order. We expect the police officer to use the appropriate and reasonable amount of force necessary to gain the compliance of the traffic violator.

Generally, when a traffic violator refuses the request to give the police officer his license, the refusal comes in the form of a question like, "Why did you stop me?" Of course, the traffic violator could just say no. In those instances, we expect the police officer to use her verbal skills. Perhaps the police officer's voice will become more forceful; perhaps she will offer an explanation. In any event, the police officer has probably developed some fairly standard responses designed to get people to cooperate.

Some agencies consider the situation where the traffic violator immediately complies with the officer to be a Level One, or positive and cooperative, encounter. In the second scenario, where the violator refuses, this would be considered a Level Two situation wherein the traffic violator is passively resisting the police officer, but no force is being used.[5]

Now let's say that our traffic violator exited his vehicle on his own, puts his fists in a fighting stance, and tells the police officer, "You want it; you take it." This offender would be considered physically defiant and threatening to assault the officer, or a Level Three situation. If the traffic violator actually swung his fists at the police officer, the situation would become a Level Four, or a situation where the traffic violator constitutes a threat of bodily harm to the police officer.[6] One of the problems with considering the use of force in levels or as part of a continuum is that when a use-of-force is reviewed, especially if the incident results in a trial, people tend to think that the police officer should have responded to the threat by trying every means between Level One and Level Four. This would make sense if altercations between police officers and offenders tended to escalate in some graduated or predictable pattern, but of course, they don't.

Consider a Level Five use-of-force. In a Level Five situation, a police officer is confronted by an offender who obviously intends to kill or inflict great bodily injury. For instance, presume our traffic violator, without saying anything, exited his vehicle and began shooting a handgun at the police officer. This is an all too common situation. In this instance, the situation has escalated immediately and without warning. The police officer's response is probably to defend herself with deadly force.

While situations involving deadly force do occur somewhat frequently, the overwhelming majority of use-of-force situations involve Levels One through Four. As we noted in Chapter Six, "A Brief History of Police Technology," for well over a hundred years, the only technology available to assist police officers in defending themselves was the handgun and nightstick, or baton. With Level One through Level Three, and sometimes Level Four uses of force, the use of the baton or handgun are inappropriate—and quite possibly criminal.

Policy and community standards are not the only things that control the use of force by law enforcement officials in our country. All state and local policy variations have foundations in Constitutional and case law. Recall in previous chapters we have discussed the Fourth Amendment as it relates to a variety of police technologies. The Fourth Amendment and associated case law guides our use of databases, the collection of evidence, and our use of electronic surveillance equipment. But it also is the foundation for the use of force by police officers. The Founders sure packed a lot into that one amendment. Think of it this way: the Fourth Amendment is about search and seizure; and the United States Supreme Court (Court) has properly decided that any time police officers stop someone, they are seizing that person.

This issue was further clarified by the Court in 1985 when they decided the case of ***Tennessee v. Garner***. In this case, Edward Garner, a fifteen-year-old boy, broke into a house and stole a purse and ten dollars. As he fled from the house, he was shot and killed by a police officer. The boy's father sued in federal district court on the grounds that the police officer violated his son's Constitutional rights when the police officer shot and killed him. That court ruled that the police officer's actions were authorized by the Tennessee law, which allowed the use of deadly force to stop a fleeing felon. The court of appeals found that the decision by the officer was within the law, but that the law was unconstitutional because the killing of a fleeing felon is a seizure under the Fourth Amendment, and

Two examples of less-lethal force options that have contributed to offender deaths and, therefore, have been severely restricted are the Hobble Technique (alternatively known as the Prone Maximum Restraint and Hog Tying) and Upper Body Control Holds (alternatively known as Choke Holds). Both techniques are effective in controlling combative offenders, and both are nonlethal under most conditions. However, under certain circumstances, the Hobble Technique has been found to cause positional asphyxia, which has contributed to offender deaths, and Upper Body Control Holds have also contributed to offender deaths.*

*Positional asphyxia is a term used to describe the placement of a body in a position that interferes with the ability to breathe. Breathing can be restricted by compression of the chest or abdomen as well as restricting or blocking the airway.

therefore could only be Constitutional if reasonable. The State of Tennessee appealed the ruling, but the Court affirmed the previous ruling—the use of deadly force against an offender who does not appear to pose a threat to police officers or others is unconstitutional. This ruling established the defense-of-life standard for the use of deadly force by police and introduced the concept that all force must be reasonably applied.[7] After the 1985 case, it was clear that police officers needed alternatives to deadly force.[8]

Because of Court decisions like *Tennessee v. Garner,* throughout the last two decades, an increasing amount of research and development has concentrated on finding alternative control methods for police officers.[9] At first, this search concentrated on finding nonlethal means of overcoming resistance, but as new ideas were field tested and old ideas improved upon, it was realized that just about any form of force can be deadly. Sometimes the offender's death results from a combination of factors outside the control of the police officer, such as the offender having already ingested a substance that overtaxed the physiological system. On other occasions, the use-of-force device was misapplied, causing death or serious injury. In still others, it wasn't realized that the force device could contribute to an offender's death. Subsequently, the research and development were refined to a search for **less-lethal use-of-force devices**. The concept is still a search for tools that can overcome offenders' resistance, with a minimum amount of force and minimal injury to the offenders and police officers, but contributing factors make just about any altercation between an offender and police officers potentially deadly.

Today police officers have more less-lethal tools at their disposal, but these tools and their limitations still leave gaps in a police officer's options. There have been devices proposed and in some instances tested, such as dart guns and paint balls that contain strong sedatives, giant nets, leg-grabbing hook devices on the ends of long poles, strobe lights that cause nausea, and sound generators.[10] For a variety of reasons, these devices were impractical or they did not work under field conditions. What researchers, scientists, and police officers are looking for are less-lethal weapons that minimize the risk of death and injury to police officers, offenders, and the community.[11] A second consideration is public reaction. Many use-of-force devices have been discontinued because of the community's reaction to the device, not its effectiveness.[12]

One positive outcome of the research has been a clarification of the features a less-lethal force device must have. Let's take a look at these features and then, in the following sections when we look at actual devices, you judge as to whether these devices meet the research criteria. The National Institute for Justice (NIJ) has

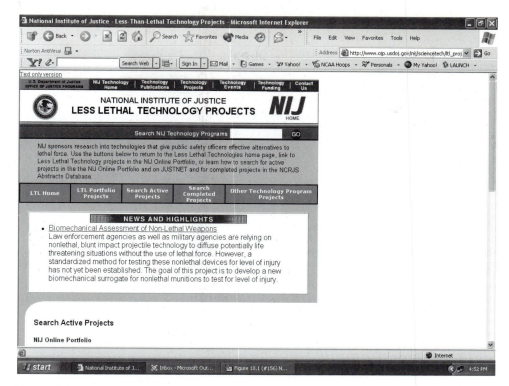

Figure 18.1 An important advisory panel is the NIJ's Less-Than-Lethal (LTL) Technology and Advisory Panel. This program develops and evaluates technology to give officers effective alternatives to lethal force.
Source: "Evolution and Development of Police Technology," 17.

laid out some commonsense guidelines for alternative force technologies (Figure 18.1). The first is that the technology must improve on a present practice because a technology that improves on a present practice is more likely to find acceptance in state and local police agencies in that it easily fits into current policies. Moreover, an improvement over something that is already done is more likely to gain community acceptance. As we have seen, situations requiring a police officer to use force generally happen without warning and tend to escalate in a matter of seconds. Any technology must be accessible to the police officer and yet not overburden the police officer. There is only so much equipment a police officer can carry on his or her person or in the police vehicle. Simply stated, whatever new force alternative technologies are developed cannot overburden the police officer.

As we have discussed throughout the text, state and local governments have limited budgets. Whatever force alternative technologies are developed must be relatively inexpensive. Part of the expense in the development of technologies for field police work is the ruggedization of the technology. So in addition to being inexpensive, it must work in the cold, rain, and heat and be able to take the daily abuse of a 24/7 police operation. In Chapter Nineteen, when we look at training, one of the overriding themes is keeping police officers up to date on perishable skills. Simply stated, if you don't do something frequently, your skill at doing the task degrades. In addition to being relatively infrequent, each use-of-force situation is different. So whatever alternative force technologies are developed, they cannot require intensive or frequent training. Moreover, most use-of-force situations occur between a single officer and a single offender, and the lion's share of local police agencies have very few police officers on duty at any one time, so technologies that require multiple officers are less useful than technologies readily available to a single police officer. Finally, the NIJ adds as a requirement that any force alternative technology must work. The primary caveat is the technology must work in the field, under adverse conditions.[13] A final note before you look at these technologies: they are ordered somewhat historically, but not completely. Many developments occurred nearly simultaneously, or there were steps forward and then back. Moreover, these devices are not listed in any way to correspond with the levels of force we previously discussed.

The Police Baton

The baton (alternately called the nightstick) is the most widely used and accepted impact/leverage tool used by police officers.[14] The original nightstick has developed into a **side-handle baton** that can be used as a striking instrument and for leverage holds that can cause pain (Figure 18.2). Batons are still in wide use because they are lightweight and versatile, and it is relatively easy to train a police officer in its use. The huge downside to the baton is that it can lead to significant offender injuries, the police officer must be within striking distance of the offender, and even when used properly and judiciously a baton strike can be distasteful. Moreover, the leverage holds that can be used with a side-handle baton were developed from martial arts techniques and are a perishable skill. Absent frequent training, the leverage holds are likely to fall into disuse or be used improperly.

Law enforcement officials realize that as a control tool, a baton may be inadequate for many use-of-force situations, so the search for alternatives continues.[15] In the next section of this chapter we will explore the three most commonly used less-lethal control devices—chemical agents, the **beanbag shotgun**, and the **Taser**.

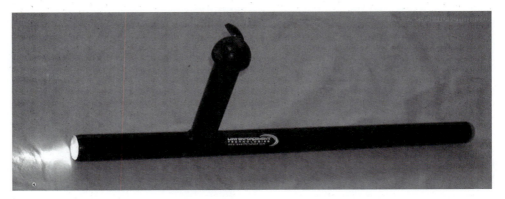

Figure 18.2 The nightstick, or baton, was the earliest form of technology used by police officers. In the 1980s side-handle batons gained increasing popularity in American law enforcement because they increased the number of force options available to the police officers on patrol. A side-handle baton can be used as both an impact weapon and for a number of leverage control holds. As with many of the technologies available to state and local police officers, the baton has continually developed, often incorporating other technologies. In this photograph, the ARB-4 Antiriot Baton comes equipped with a built-in high intensity flashlight on one end and a pepper spray dispenser on the other end. Both items are easily controlled through switches and a button intuitively located on the side handle.
Photograph provided by Law Enforcement Technologies, Inc.

Chemical Agents

Beginning in the mid-1960s, two chemical agents—**chloroacetophenone (CN) gas**, or as it is commonly called, tear gas, (CN is the chemical symbol for the compound) and **orthochlorobenzalmalononitrile (CS)**—were deployed in state and local police agencies around the country.[16] These chemical agents work on the central nervous system of the offender. They induce pain by activating receptor cells via neural transmitters within the brain. CN gas is designed to cause a burning pain in the eyes, nose, and throat, while CS causes pain in the nose, throat, and chest and can cause nausea and vomiting. Because these chemical agents work through the offender's central nervous system, any change in an offender's system can diminish or negate the effectiveness of the chemical agents. So if the offender is on drugs, or perhaps has a high level of endorphins in her system because of her excited state, chemical agents may not be effective.[17]

Generally speaking, offenders who physically engage police officers are not in their right mind. They may be mentally ill, on drugs or alcohol, or even so excited that they are not thinking clearly. If this sounds just like the offender with whom chemical agents would have no effect, you're right. Although they are ineffective on people who have some kind of altered central nervous system, the chemical agents are very effective on everyone else, especially the police. The problem was that after you had sprayed someone with the chemical agent and it had no effect, you now had to use some other method. If the baton was not appropriate and the chemical agent ineffective, the offender was often wrestled to the ground by multiple officers, who became immediately contaminated with the chemical agent and often incapacitated.[18]

In fact, when CN gas was first deployed in my agency (in the early 1980s—I am not that old), we used it several times. One night, after many disappointing and painful experiences, my partners and I hypothesized that the test subjects for the development of CN gas must have been police officers because it worked great on them. In addition to not working well on offenders, these chemical agents were designed to work on the human central nervous system; they did not work on dogs. Vicious dogs are a constant problem for police officers, especially those assigned to work the night watches. Also the delivery aerosol used with CN gas often had a very short shelf life, making replacement a relatively constant concern.

Chemical agents do work well in some crowd control situations. People who demonstrate, even when they choose to do so in an unlawful manner, usually are not the types of offenders with altered central nervous systems. Generally, chemical agents can be released in a crowd control situation via a gas grenade, 37 mm launcher, or even a specially developed shotgun round. They can also be used effectively in a barricaded offender situation; however, the delivery mechanism when released into a structure is often some type of munitions, which is activated by heat. Therefore, there is a risk of a collateral fire.

Many state and local agencies have relegated chemical agents to the tactical uses of crowd control and barricaded offenders. In its place, **oleoresin capsicum (OC)** gas is being used (Figure 18.3). OC is a natural substance found in cayenne pepper. Instead of working on the receptor cells of the central nervous system, OC is an inflammatory agent, not an irritant. Because it is an inflammatory agent, it causes a nearly immediate swelling of the eyes and breathing passages. Moreover, the swelling is accompanied by an intense burning sensation of any area that comes into contact with OC. Because it causes swelling, OC can cause the offender to experience a shortness of breath, involuntarily closing of

Figure 18.3 Oleoresin capsicum (OC), or pepper spray, has surpassed the use of tear gas by state and local law enforcement officers.
Source: "Evolution and Development of Police Technology," 55. *Photograph provided by ZARC International.*

the eyes, and coughing. Probably due to the restricted breathing and often intense coughing, the offender may experience a lack of upper body strength and coordination and even nausea.

In addition to being effective with offenders who have an altered central nervous system, OC is also effective as a means to control a vicious dog. Moreover, because it is more effective than chemical agents, there are fewer instances of police officers becoming contaminated. Finally, because OC is biodegradable and nonpersistent, decontamination and offender first aid only involves ventilation and the application of water.[19]

Beanbag Shotgun

By changing the ammunition fired from a traditional shotgun, the firearm is converted from a weapon solely used in deadly force situations to a less-lethal use-of-force device. Beginning in the 1960s, manufacturers began to experiment with alternatives to traditional firearms ammunition. Among the early developments were wooden and rubber bullets, which were intended to ricochet off the ground and strike an offender in the legs. Think of skipping a stone across a pond. If any type of ammunition is fired at an angle so as to produce a skip, or ricochet, the projectile (or round, or bullet), will rise to a level of about eighteen inches and continue at that height. It does not rise any farther than that. Moreover, by striking the ground first, some of the energy from the projectile is expended. Therefore, once it skips or ricochets, the projectile should continue with

Figure 18.4 All three of these less-lethal munitions are fired from a twelve-gauge shotgun. Each has specific tasks—the rubber pellets are a traditional ricochet round; the round on the right is a typical beanbag round; and the round in the middle is a new type of beanbag munition that has a tear-shaped design, improving aerodynamic efficiency and providing greater accuracy.
Photograph provided by Defense Technology Federal Laboratories.

less energy and at the level of the offender's legs. The problems with the scheme are fairly obvious. First, firing directly at an offender can be nearly as lethal as a traditional round of ammunition and in a stressful situation, aiming to strike a specific individual is problematic.

The solution was to change the projectile to a **beanbag**-like round (Figure 18.4). With this scheme, the device can be aimed directly at the offender's chest. As the beanbag round travels toward the offender, it loses some energy from friction. Furthermore, because of the projectile's design, it opens up, striking a larger area of the offender, and the energy from the projectile is dispersed, significantly diminishing the likelihood the projectile will penetrate the offender's skin.

In many instances this less-lethal use-of-force device has been very successful. In one instance, a man threatening bystanders with a knife was subdued with the **beanbag shotgun**. Had it not been for the beanbag shotgun, that incident would have likely ended with a use of deadly force. The beanbag shotgun has the advantage of being a conversion of a weapon already in use by most state and local police departments. Therefore, acquisition and training costs are reduced. Normally, a police agency will take existing shotguns and paint or modify them in such a manner as to ensure that police officers under stress know for certain which shotguns contain less-lethal rounds and which still contain the deadly ammunition (Figure 18.5).[20] The modified (in look only) shotgun is then segregated from the original version usually by being placed in a rack in the trunk of the vehicle. These weapons have their drawbacks. Although much more accurate than ricocheted rounds, these weapons can still injure bystanders. Moreover, if fired too close to the offender, they can still be fatal, especially if the offender is mistakenly struck in the head. Although the rounds are intended not to penetrate, there have

Try This

Take a piece of paper and a writing pen. Hold the paper in one hand and the pen in the other. With the writing point of the pen, stab the paper, penetrating it. Take a similar piece of paper, and use the nonwriting point of the pen to stab the paper with equal strength. The second time, using the flatter end of the pen, the pen should not penetrate the paper. This is because the point of the pen focuses the energy of your jab or stab, whereas the flat end disperses the energy over a wider area.

Figure 18.5 As a less-lethal technology, the beanbag shotgun is increasing in use by state and local law enforcement agencies. It has been effective primarily because it enable officers to select and isolate their targets.
Source: "Evolution and Development of Police Technology," 57. *Photograph provided by Defense Technology Federal Laboratories.*

been incidents of penetration. Finally, beyond sixty feet, the accuracy of the round deteriorates substantially.[21]

A close cousin of the beanbag shotgun is the foam baton round. It is a tactical crowd control less-lethal device. Generally, it is fired from a 37 mm launcher, and, like wooden or rubber bullets, it ricochets into a crowd. Because the device is intended to move large groups of hostile people, accuracy is not as much an issue as with a lone offender. Moreover, these devices tend to have a large psychological effect because their use creates a large amount of smoke, noise, and flash (Figure 18.6).

These types of less-lethal control devices help to fill the gap in available tools for police officers, but both have relatively limited applications. The ricocheted rounds are used for crowd control and the beanbag shotgun, in addition to having

Figure 18.6 In crowd control situations, chemical agents and less-lethal projectiles can be deployed from a 37 mm launcher.
Photograph provided by Defense Technology Federal Laboratories.

a limited range (not too close and not too far) must be obtained from the police vehicle in order to be used. So the search for alternatives continues.

Electrical Control Devices

Because of past police abuses with electrical cattle prod-like devices, state use of the electric chair for executions, and the use of electricity for torture, some communities are wary of police use of electrical devices as a less-lethal control device. However, there have still been advances in the technology of electrical control for use as less-lethal use-of-force devices. The most common of these is called the **Taser**.

Typically, these devices are handheld and shaped very much like a standard semiautomatic pistol. Compressed nitrogen is used to propel two projectiles, or probes, at a rate of 180 feet per second. The probes are attached to the handheld device by a thin, insulated wire. The probes themselves are sharp, hooklike devices that attach themselves to the offender's clothing or skin. An electrical charge is passed through the wire to the probes and ultimately to the offender. The result is the offender experiences an instantaneous loss of neuromuscular control.

The electrical charge essentially interferes with the electrical communication between the brain and the muscles. However, the electrical charge is insufficient to cause damage to the offender's nerves or other body parts. For instance, the charge, which is an electrical current of 1.76 Joules, is well below the 10–50 Joules required to cause cardiac ventricular fibrillation.

Depending on the type of cartridge used with the device, it has a range of between fifteen and twenty-one feet. It is shaped like a handgun primarily to facilitate use and aiming by state and local police officers. The first generations of these devices were relatively bulky and did not fit into a police officer's pocket, nor were they easily carried on the Sam Browne (gun or utility belt).[22] The later versions have been designed to resemble a semiautomatic pistol. Moreover, a variety of holsters have been created to allow state and local police officers to carry this device on the side opposite their firearms.

A Taser Dart

An offender hit with a Taser Dart will feel dazed for several seconds. However, recovery is quick and the effects stop the very instant the device is shut off. Some offenders may experience critical response amnesia and others might experience a tingling sensations afterwards. The pulsating electrical output of the TASER causes involuntary muscle contractions and a results in the offender experiencing a sense of vertigo. While the Taser can momentarily stun or render immobilized, low electrical amperage and short duration of pulsating current, ensure a non-lethal charge. Moreover, it does not cause permanent damage or long-term aftereffects to muscles, nerves or other body functions.

Traffic Enforcement

In Chapter Fifteen we looked at photographic traffic enforcement devices as surveillance systems. Both photored light and photographic radar were placed in that section because they are remote sensing devices used to conduct surveillance for traffic violations. Here we will take a more in-depth look at some of the technology used by state and local police officers for traffic enforcement. The traditional method of speed detection is to use **radar**, the acronym for the detection science radio detection and ranging. Radar was first used by the British to measure distance, speed, and the direction of enemy aircraft and navy vessels in World War II.[23] Recall from Chapters Five and Seven our discussions on time distance on arrival (TDOA) and angle on arrival (AOA) calculations. Early radar used a pulsed RF wave to determine distance to an object using the TDOA calculation, and the direction an object was traveling was calculated by using the AOA calculations.

The radar systems used by state and local police agencies work in very much the same manner. Police radar uses a constant RF wave instead of a pulsed RF wave. A police officer directs the radar at the potential traffic violator's vehicle, and an RF wave is sent toward the vehicle. When the wave hits the vehicle, part of the signal is reflected back to the police officer's radar device. We know that by using TDOA and AOA we can calculate the distance of the violator's vehicle from the police officer's radar gun, but we need some other science to actually determine the speed of the violator's vehicle.

Police radar, while essentially the same, uses constant wave signals instead of a pulse. A radar gun is a transceiver designed to pick up its own RF signals. Recall from Chapter Three that an RF transmitter contains an oscillator that creates a certain wavelength or frequency. The radar device, using a antenna that somewhat focuses the RF signals, broadcasts the signal toward the violator's vehicle. That same signal is reflected back but changed because the violator's car is moving. This change or shift in the frequency is due to what is called the Doppler effect.

You have probably been stuck at a train crossing and watched a slow-moving train go through the intersection. As the train passes, the engineer blows that obnoxious, loud whistle. If the train is moving slowly, the whistle sounds the same all throughout its use. It is one pitch or one constant tone. If the train is moving fast, the pitch of the whistle sounds as if it is changing, but the whistle is still blowing the one pitch. Sound, like RF transmissions, travels in waves. As the train approaches you, the waves have less distance to travel before they reach your ears. Therefore, the waves bunch up and the frequency, or pitch of the sound you hear, changes. Recall from Chapter Three that frequency is measured in the number of cycles in a wave during a specific period of time. If the number of waves in the time period increases, the frequency must also increase. As the train passes you, the sound of the whistle seems to get lower. This is because as the train moves farther away, the waves must travel a greater distance and they spread out, changing the frequency. When radio waves bounce or reflect off a moving object, the same frequency shift occurs.

So when the radar transmission comes back to the radar device, the frequency has been shifted. The speed of the vehicle is calculated by the amount of frequency shift. The faster the vehicle is moving, the greater the frequency shift. Radar has a disadvantage in that it cannot differentiate one vehicle from another when several cars are traveling together. It can only determine speed at a specific point, and exclusively targets the largest or the fastest vehicle.

An improvement over radar is **laser** speed dedication. The laser unit reflects light off the violator's vehicle then, using the TDOA formula, calculates the speed of the vehicle. Laser devices are more expensive, but they do allow the police officer to target specific vehicles. Moreover, a laser device has a dedication range of up to two thousand feet whereas radar typically is useful up to about one thousand feet. According to the Bureau of Justice Statistics, 6 percent of all local police departments, employing 15 percent of the local police officers in our country, use laser traffic-enforcement devices.[24]

Vehicle Pursuits

High-speed vehicle pursuits are very dangerous to the offender, the community, and the police officers. There is the danger of death or serious injury and the potential for expensive civil litigation. The first tool that state and local police agencies can have is a pursuit policy that guides the actions of police officers during stressful events. The basic technology for pursuits has not changed since the inception of radios in police vehicles. Police vehicles are equipped with emergency lights and sirens, but more often than not the emergency equipment is not seen by uninvolved motorists until the pursuit has nearly passed them by. Because offenders who are being pursued generally have no plan beyond eluding the police, it is difficult to anticipate their route and, therefore, difficult to radio ahead and have intersections closed and the community forewarned (Figure 18.7).

There are two common mechanical means employed by state and local police agencies to stop an offender's vehicle. The first is **tire deflation spikes**, which

Figure 18.7   A Look Ahead One means of training police officers to make good decisions during pursuit is through simulated training. The photograph here is a screen capture from a pursuit simulation training device that we will examine in the next chapter. Additionally, there are three basic means of stopping an offender's vehicle—mechanical, chemical, and electrical. There are no products on the market that offer viable chemical or electrical means of stopping an offender's vehicle. However, in Chapter Twenty-one, we will look at some promising future technologies.
Photograph provided by FAAC Incorporated.

are used by 26 percent of local agencies, who employ 36 percent of all local police officers.[25] The major difficulty associated with spikes is deployment. While the offender is being chased by one or more police vehicles, another police officer must anticipate the offender's route, get ahead of the pursuit, and deploy the spikes so that the offender cannot avoid them, but they do not interfere with other motorists. In addition to being difficult, it is dangerous. In 2003 two officers were killed deploying spikes.

A second option available to police officers is the **precision immobilization technique**, or PIT maneuver (this has been alternatively called the pursuit intervention technique and the precision intervention technique). The PIT maneuver involves the police officer striking the rear corner of the offender's vehicle, sending the offender's vehicle into an uncontrolled spin. In order to facilitate this technique, some state and local police agencies are outfitting their police vehicles with specially designed and reinforced, wrap-around front bumpers. The PIT maneuver requires that the police officer receive training in how to safely accomplish it and a willingness from the agency without special bumpers to incur around $1,500 in damage to the police vehicle each time the maneuver is employed. In those agencies that have them, police helicopters are often used in pursuits. If a police helicopter is over the pursuit, the police officer following the offender can slow down, and for them, the pursuit is less dangerous. However, even if the police vehicles back off, the offenders still tend to try to outrun the police helicopter.

Gunfire-Reduction Technology

Some areas of urban America are plagued by shootings and random gunfire. It is nearly as dangerous to fire a gun into the air as it is to fire a gun at someone. When the bullet returns to Earth, it has much the same energy that it did on the way up and can be fatal (Figure 18.8). Many states have drafted legislation that make it a felony to randomly discharge a firearm into the air. By combining a number of technologies that we have already looked at, there have been some unique developments aimed at curbing shootings and random gunfire.

In areas that experience a high volume of gunfire-related incidents, the number of calls to police dispatch centers seems to decrease as people become used to the sound. However, even in such an area, the sound of gunfire will often result in a call to the police. Typically, the caller will tell the dispatcher that he heard shots, and a general direction from which the caller believes they came. Of course, in an urban environment, sounds tend to echo, so except in those cases where the gunfire occurred right outside their homes, callers rarely give exact location information, but after examining GIS, we know that if the shots are heard in multiple locations and a general direction is known, we can calculate a fairly precise location for the source.

Some of the new technologies available to detect and locate gunfire use GIS principles to provide local police officers with precise information as to the location of gunfire. In one scheme, ten acoustic devices are placed on telephone poles, rooftops, and streetlamps within a one-square-mile area. These acoustic devices are sophisticated microphones that are connected to the police department's central dispatch either via standard telephone lines or some RF configuration.

The acoustic devices detect gunfire and feed information concerning the sound of the gunfire and its direction from the acoustic devices to a computer. If the gunfire is heard by at least four of the acoustic devices, the computer uses

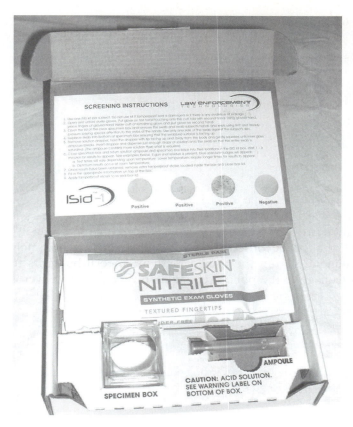

Figure 18.8 In most investigations, police officers concentrate on evidence the offender left at the crime scene. However, offenders often inadvertently pick up, take from, or are exposed to trace evidence during the commission of a crime. One technology that has continued to improve is field testing for gunshot residue. Often when an offender fires a handgun, minute particles of residue, particularly nitrocellulose, are deposited on the offender's hands. In this photograph, the Instant Shooter ID Kit (ISID™-1) provides police officers with immediate confirmation of recent gun use and can assist in rapidly focusing on key offenders. According to the Sandia National Laboratories, the test is able to detect as little as seven hundred nanograms of nitrocellulose; it is thereby able to detect if an offender has recently fired one shot from a handgun 75 percent of the time. If the offender fires multiple shots, the detection rate increases to more than 90 percent.
Source: Walker and Rodacy, "Gun Residue Detection." *Photograph provided by Law Enforcement Technologies.*

TDOA to determine the location of the gunfire. At this point in the scheme, there is human intervention. Once the computer calculates TDOA on the sounds the computer algorithm has identified as gunfire, a dispatcher is alerted. The dispatcher listens to a recording of the event and decides if the sound was actually gunfire (Figure 18.9).

Throughout the text, as we examined police technology, we were constantly cautioned that we were exploring the potentials of a fully integrated system and that most state and local agencies fall somewhere below full systems integration. However, for this **gunfire-reduction technology** to work, the police agency must have a relatively high level of systems integration.

Generally, once the dispatcher verifies that gunfire has occurred, the dispatcher uses a CAD-like system to translate the GIS information into a visual

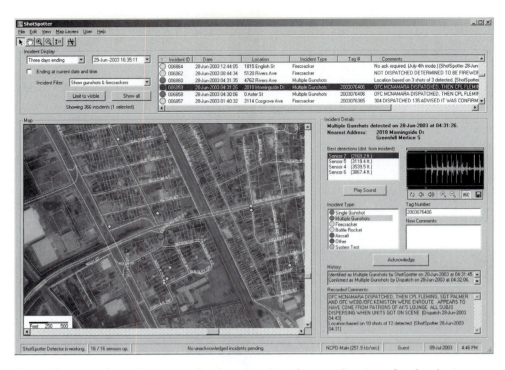

Figure 18.9 Gunfire-reduction technology involves the coordination of technologies examined in previous chapters, such as GIS and TDOA.
Screen capture provided by ShotSpotter, Inc.

display of the location. Moreover, gunfire technologies set up a database of shots fired, which can be referred to by the dispatcher or investigators. With the GIS and database information, the police officers in the field are dispatched to the location. Once at the location, the police officers' investigation depends on the circumstances they find. They may indeed find the victim of a shooting, just shell casings, a group loitering, or any combination of situations imaginable. While the police officers may uncover information that leads to an arrest, their dispatch to the exact location of the shooting when coupled with community knowledge of the system can have a deterrence effect. Rational choice theorists would probably argue that people who shoot randomly into the air because they don't fear the consequences of their actions and believe they are virtually undetectable because of their environment might think twice when the precision of the system is demonstrated.

Body Armor

Initially, soft body armor started out as tire treads. In 1972 the DuPont Corporation developed a fabric called Kevlar that was stronger than steel, yet lighter than nylon. It was first marketed to replace the steel belting in vehicle tires. At some point in the development, someone asked if Kevlar would stop bullets. No one knew for sure, so they folded a few pieces up and shot at it. The bullets bounced off. This revelation led to the NIJ sponsoring a project at the United States Land Warfare Laboratory. By 1998, soft body armor would be credited with saving the lives of more than two thousand police officers.[27]

There are two basic types of body armor—soft and hard. Hard body armor is made out of metal or ceramic plates. It works pretty much the same as it did for a medieval knight. In essence, hard body armor is designed to deflect gunfire. The drawbacks are that hard body armor is relatively heavy and it is inflexible. Therefore, hard body armor is usually worn either as a small supplement to soft body armor or during those situations wherein a state or local police officer believes there is a high likelihood of a deadly encounter. Typically, hard body armor would be worn by a SWAT team member. However, because it is designed to deflect bullets, hard body armor offers greater overall protection.

I hope you tried the earlier experiment with a pen and paper, because soft body armor works in a similar manner. Recall that the point of the pen focused the energy and allowed the pen to break the paper, whereas the flat end of the pen tended to disperse the energy and prevent penetration. Soft body armor is a series of tightly woven nylon threads that act to disperse the energy of a bullet striking it. Because the energy is dispersed, penetration is much less likely. The wearer is still going to feel the impact; there have been occasions were the bullet was stopped, but the impact stopped the wearer's heart. Moreover, soft body armor is primarily designed to stop handgun ammunition. It has less ability to stop high-powered ammunition from certain handguns and most rifles. Therefore, many state and local police officers supplement soft body armor with a ceramic plate that is placed in a cloth pocket between the soft body armor and the wearer. This plate is typically about eight inches by eight inches and covers the heart.

Automated External Defibrillator

Each year, more than 250,000 people collapse from a sudden cardiac arrest. More than two-thirds of these sudden incidents occur outside of a hospital, and between 45 percent and 85 percent of these victims have a reversible condition called ventricular fibrillation.[28] Your heartbeat is controlled by electrical impulses. Sometimes, these electrical impulses begin to beat out of synchronization, so instead of a coordinated beating, your heart contracts irregularly and does not pump blood throughout your body. This can rapidly cause you to die. According to studies, if your heart is defibrillated, or shocked, survival rates can be as high as 90 percent.[29] An **automated external defibrillator (AED)** is a device designed to allow first responders with minimal training to diagnosis and administer defibrillation. As these devices become more popular, first responders to these situations are becoming flight attendants, store clerks, and golf pros (Figure 18.10).

Essentially, the first responders place two prepackaged pads on the victim's chest. These pads send diagnostic information to the AED computer, and the computer tells the first responder, with simple voice commands, what to do. Sometimes people thought to be experiencing ventricular fibrillation have other medical problems, such as their hearts have stopped and they require cardiopulmonary resuscitation (CPR). If the AED does not detect the proper condition, the AED prevents the first responder from mistakenly delivering a shock to the victim. However, if the condition is present, the AED tells the first responder which of the three buttons to push and guides her through the process. After the AED delivers the shock, it continues to issue instructions to the first responder, such as to check the victim's pulse or breathing. Most experts agree that first responders who know CPR can learn to operate the AED in a few minutes.[30]

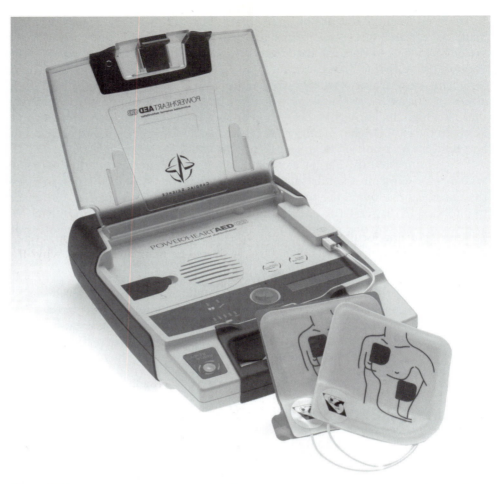

Figure 18.10 The automated external defibrillator pictured above, the Powerheart AED G3, includes features such as clear voice and written prompts that guide the state or local police officer through every step of the rescue process.
Photograph provided by Cardiac Science, Inc.

Chapter Summary

In this chapter we somewhat deviated from the exploration of information technologies to look at other technologies that affect the field police officer. One of the most important subjects for research and development into new technologies is in the area of less-lethal use-of-force devices. As we have seen, there have been a number of developments, but they have generally been restricted to improvements to the police baton, the improvement of irritants, the deployment of the beanbag shotgun, and the development and deployment of electrical control devices. As welcome as these improvements are, they still leave a gap for state and local police officers who are confronted with combative offenders.

Vehicle pursuits are one of the most dangerous incidents a police officer can become involved in. The only real technological developments have been in the area of the mechanical tire deflation devices. However, as we shall see in Chapter Twenty-one, there is some research into other methods.

We added to the devices that use radio waves, lasers, and TDOA when we looked at the radar and laser applications in traffic enforcement. We also saw how many technologies, such as TDOA, GIS, and relational databases, have come together in an effort to reduce gunfire. Finally, after a brief look at body armor, we examined automated external defibrillators. Police officers, who often arrive at medical emergencies before medical emergency services personnel, can assist in saving lives with this easy-to-use technology.

Discussion Questions

1. Compare the less-lethal devices with the level of force scale early in the chapter. Under what general circumstances do you think the less-lethal devices should be used?
2. Under what circumstances do you think police officers should engage in a vehicle pursuit?
3. Some state and local police agencies have designated soft body armor as optional police equipment. Do you think it should be mandatory? If so, why? If not, why?
4. In addition to including them in police vehicles, what other public locations would you recommend the deployment of AED?

Key Terms

Automated External
   Defibrillator (AED)
Beanbag
Beanbag Shotgun
Body Armor
Chloroacetophenone
   (CN)
Gunfire-reduction
   Technology

Laser
Less-Lethal Use-of-Force
   Devices
Oleoresin Capsicum
   (OC)
Orthochlorobenzal-
   malononitrile (CS)
Precision Immobilization
   Technique (PIT)

Radar
Semiautomatic Handgun
Shotgun
Side-handle Baton
Taser
Tennessee v. Garner
Tire Deflation Spikes

End Notes

1. "Evolution and Development of Police Technology," 62.
2. Ibid.
3. Ibid., 63.
4. Ibid., 49.
5. Ibid.
6. Ibid.
7. *Tennessee v. Gamer* et al. (1985)
8. "Evolution and Development of Police Technology," 57.
9. Onnen, "Oleoresin Capsicum."
10. "Evolution and Development of Police Technology," 58.
11. Lane, "New Technologies," 134.
12. "Evolution and Development of Police Technology," 50.
13. Ibid., 59.
14. Ibid., 58.
15. U.S. Congress, Office of Technology Assessment, Criminal Justice, "New Technologies," 21.
16. "Evolution and Development of Police Technology," 5.
17. See note 9 above.
18. Ibid.
19. Ibid.

20. "Evolution and Development of Police Technology," 57.
21. Ibid., 59.
22. The Sam Browne belt was named after General Sir Sam Browne VC, GCB, KCSI, (1849-98) of the British Army in India, the reported inventor of this style of utility belt. The accompanying strap was intended to help carry the weight of a heavy pistol or sword. The strap was dropped by many American state and local police agencies beginning in the early 1960s. As with so much of history, there are competing claims as to the actual origin of the design. There is some evidence to suggest that it was actually an American invention of the Revolutionary War. Nevertheless, the equipment belt worn by American state and local police officers is often referred to as the Sam Browne.
23. "Evolution and Development of Police Technology," 89.
24. Bureau of Justice Statistics, "2000 Local Law Enforcement Management Statistics."
25. Ibid.
26. Walker and Rodacy, "Gun Residue Detection."
27. "Evolution and Development of Police Technology," 45.
28. "Law Enforcement Agency Defibrillation," 273.
29. Ibid., 274.
30. Matarese, "Police and AEDs," 4.

POLICE
TECHNOLOGY

PART FOUR
Technology in Police Management

Chapter Nineteen
Personnel and Training

Learning Objectives

- The student will be exposed to a brief history of **scheduling** and **deployment** schemes in law enforcement.

- The student will explore some of the factors involved in the deployment and scheduling of police officers.

- The student will explore some of the theory behind the tracking of potential problem officers and some of the information technology that can be used.

- The student will understand the importance of continuous training in law enforcement and be exposed to some of the different technologies being use for training.

Introduction

This chapter begins the last section of the text. Here we are going to begin to concentrate on technologies used in the management of state and local law enforcement agencies. Although no new technological concepts will be introduced, we will see different combinations of the information technology (IT) we have previously explored.

Two of the major practices of good management are personnel and training. In the area of personnel management we will look at **scheduling** and **deployment**, case management, and the tracking of potential problem police officers. In the area of training we will examine training technologies that include interactive DVDs and situation simulators (Figure 19.1). As you read about these different technologies, remember that technology is not a substitute for good judgment or competent leadership.

During this chapter we will concentrate on uniformed, or patrol, operations because in a typical local law enforcement agency, patrol is the most visible and most expensive part of the operation. It is not unusual for a local agency to assign more than half of its personnel to the patrol operation. When supervisors and support personnel for patrol are accounted for, the patrol side of a police agency is probably the single biggest expense. Moreover, as we saw in previous chapters, upwards of 85 percent of the entire agency budget is dedicated to personnel costs. So management in scheduling, deployment, or training of these personnel resources can have a major positive or negative impact on the entire agency.[1]

Scheduling and Deployment

Scheduling and deployment are two different issues. For the police manager, deployment is the minimum operating force necessary to provide police services within the jurisdiction. Scheduling is the process of moving the personnel resources around to meet the deployment needs. Sometimes an agency does not have enough police officers to provide minimum coverage within a jurisdiction. For whatever reason, there are vacancies and consequently just not enough police officers. Unfortunately, an occurrence that is just as common is that there are enough police officers, but they are either deployed or scheduled inefficiently.[2]

Figure 19.1 A police officer using a driving simulator, such as the one pictured here, could experience a simulated fifty-square-mile area with eighty-seven miles of roadway. The simulator is programmed to react randomly to the police officer's virtual vehicle, making each session unique. Moreover, the simulator has more than sixty predefined sceneries and includes the ability to vary driving conditions such as lighting and weather conditions.
Photograph provided by FAAC Inc.

In this circumstance, the agency has either incorrectly determined when and what number of police officers should be working, or it has failed to schedule the police officers to work the appropriate shifts.

Beginning in the 1970s, researchers began to develop mathematical and computer models for the deployment of police officers. Two of these were the Patrol Car Allocation Model (PCAM) and the Hypercube Model.[3] Much of what we have looked at in police technology has been theories, systems, and devices that have been borrowed from other disciplines and adapted for use in the police service. One of the underlying theories of many police allocation schemes is **queuing theory** that, like rational choice theory, is borrowed from the field of economics.

Although the calculations and algorithms used to make predictions are fairly complex, the theory itself is relatively straightforward. Let's first look at the grocery store. If you are like me, when you first walk into a major grocery store, you look at how long the lines are to check out. Depending on what I have to do, I may decide the lines are too long and go somewhere else. Generally, you will see that there are fifteen or so check stands and two or three checkers working, and there are three or four people waiting in line to have their groceries checked and bagged and to pay their bills.

You walk about the grocery store, pick up the items you want, and return to the checkout line. During your travels, you noticed that the grocery store had employees completing other tasks throughout the store. There was an employee throwing cans on a shelf on aisle six, an employee in the fruits and vegetables arranging the plums, an employee cleaning a spill on aisle eleven, and one pushing a pallet of toilet paper toward aisle fourteen. Once you reach the checkout line, there are only two checkers and now you are the third person in line. You know that there are employees available to check your groceries and there are empty checkout registers, but the store has decided that it is an acceptable **level of service** to have you wait in line.

As you wait, three other people get in line behind you, and then your checker picks up the intercom and calls for another checker. He did this because the number of people in line, or queued, has exceeded their minimum level of service. The store could have called someone any time there was more than one person in line. You could have breezed through the line, but some waiting is acceptable. If the grocery store decided that the level of service was no one waits in line, they would have to hire more people. Cans still have to be thrown on to shelves, spills should be cleaned up, and no one likes disorganized fruit. Of course, if they hire more people, the groceries ultimately cost more. If the groceries cost more, we go elsewhere. Queuing theory is the mathematical model that combines the factors of circumstance (number of customers expected at any time) and the goal (level of service) to determine the number of resources (people and checkout stands) needed to attain the goal (level of service).

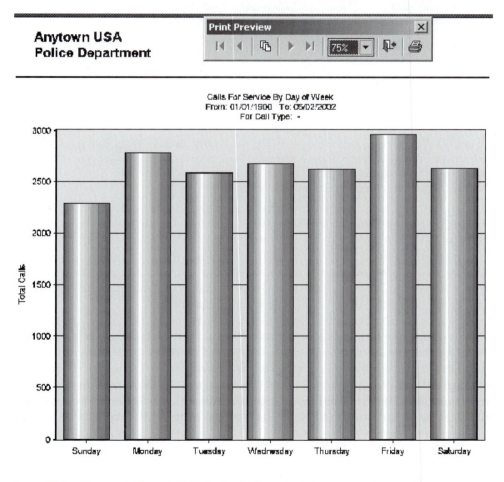

Figure 19.2 Figures 19.2 and 19.3 depict fairly typical documents that police managers use to make decisions on deployment. One displays the data in table format, while the other uses graphic format. A quick review of the calls for service by day of the week (above) might indicate that Friday is busy because of the number of social events and Monday is busier because when people return to work on Monday, they report crimes that happened over the weekend.
Screen capture provided by Crimestar Corporation.

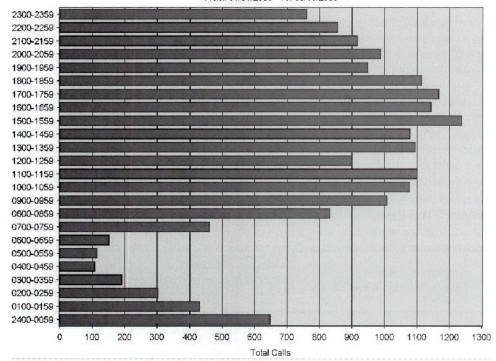
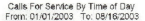

Calls For Service By Time of Day
From: 01/01/2003 To: 08/16/2003

Figure 19.3 This screen capture concerning the hourly distribution of calls is fairly consistent with the experience of most state and local law enforcement agencies—the day starts slow and becomes busier.
Screen capture provided by Crimestar Corporation.

That is a very simplified look at a fairly complex mathematical theory, but it is like any algebraic formula. If you know the level of service you want to provide and you have data about the circumstance, you can easily figure out the resources you are going to need to attain the goal (level of service). Conversely, if you know the goal and the probable circumstances, you can calculate the needed resources. If you know the level of service you have been providing and the number of resources you used, you can calculate the circumstances.

Our grocery stores know, based on sales, their peak times. They know that if they run a certain product on sale, there will be more customers. They know that other circumstances like weather, holidays, and sporting events directly impact the number of customers. They probably have a tremendous amount of historical data. The stores also know what other tasks have to be performed and generally how long those tasks should take. Since the stores generally know the workload, they can then determine the level of service they want their checkers to perform, or how many of us will be standing in line. For private industry, the queue, or the amount of time we stand in line, can affect their sales. If the lines are too long, we leave and don't buy. But the smart people running the grocery stores have done research to determine how long we will stand in line and still be satisfied. Through research, they know the level of service we will find acceptable. So with the historical data, the research on our tolerance for waiting, they know the number of people to have working at any one time. With some variation, this is how police deployment is commonly figured (Figures 19.2 & 19.3).[4]

There is one big difference. For the private firm, the goal is always to make a profit. While there are other things that a private firm does, if it doesn't turn a profit, it is not sustainable. It will go out of business and be replaced by someone who does make a profit. But for law enforcement (and government in general) the ultimate goals are much less tangible. Often the big question for police executives is what the ultimate goal is. Of course, the general answer is a reduction in crime.

While a reduction in crime or the prevention of crime is probably most agencies' answer to the ultimate goal, they still have to answer calls for service; they still have to provide an acceptable level of service in a myriad of ways that do not have a clear link to the mission of preventing crime. For instance, a common goal among police agencies is to answer an emergency call for service within a specific time limit. However, there isn't much scientific evidence that says the outcome of the response to an emergency call for service will be better if the police officers arrive in four minutes instead of seven. In many instances, the response times to calls for service are selected because they seem acceptable to the community.[5] The decisions on how fast we want police officers to respond, how much time we want them to spend working on crime and community problems, and how much time we want them to spend on administrative tasks are policy decisions.[6] Policy decisions are based on a number of factors often outside the control of the decision maker. As an example, while the local agency budget provides for only so many police officers, there may be programs or grant funding that restrict the use of certain personnel resources, and community expectations vary from jurisdiction to jurisdiction.

While police executives have difficult policy decisions to make, once those decisions are made, there are tools available to assist in deploying police officers so that policy goals can be met. In other words, state and local police agencies can be more efficient in meeting their operational goals, but questions remain as to the effectiveness of operational goals. Because questions about overall organization goals are complex and outside the venue of this text, we will look at how technology can assist in determining deployment in order to achieve operational goals.

Recall when we started this discussion on deployment we said that if you knew the operational goals (levels of service) desired and the workload, you could determine the number of police officers needed to attain the given level of service. Since the level of service is pretty much a policy issue, decided based upon factors that might or might not cause a reduction in crime, we will concentrate on how the workload is determined. So an agency could select any level of service, or operational goals, and if they knew the workload, they could determine how police officers should be deployed.

One of the primary considerations for workload in policing is geography, or space. Recall the discussion about the grocery store. There is no important spatial consideration—the work, the employees, and the customers are all in one central location. However, police work is often spread over a large area. Think about our imaginary city from the chapter on crime analysis. If you had a twenty five-square-mile area, and you said that all of the police officers working a particular shift should handle all calls in the city, you would eventually end up with police officers driving from routine call to routine call, wasting valuable time. Moreover,

In one agency, uniformed police officers have the operational goal of spending 47 percent of their time on calls for service, 33 percent of their time on community policing, and 20 percent of their time on administrative duties.
Source: Bair, et al., "Advanced Crime Mapping," 115.

one of the paramount concerns of the community policing model is that police officers develop a sense of ownership for the problems in their area and partnerships with the communities the police officers serve. If all police officers were trying to develop ownership and partnership citywide, it would be very ineffective. So, as has been discussed before, police agencies tend to divide their larger geographic area into beats or basic cars and then assign police officers responsibilities within those beats. The very large agency may divide a jurisdiction into bureaus or regions, then divide those bureaus or regions into geographic divisions. For the larger agency, a geographic division is generally the size of a medium-sized police agency. And of course, geographic divisions are further divided into beats or basic cars. Beats are also further subdivided into smaller, neighborhood-sized areas that are used to generally describe the location of a crime or call for service. Many agencies use United States Census tracts as their crime or call for service **reporting district (RD)**.[7] From the smallest to the largest division in a medium-sized local police agency we have: RD, beat, and citywide.

Since the purpose of a beat is to minimize time spent driving between calls for service and to enable problem ownership and partnership, beats tend to be varying sizes. The first question that must be answered is, "How many beats should there be?" Once that question has been answered the next question is, "What are boundaries of the individual beats?" Recall from our chapter on communications dispatch centers that computer-aided dispatch (CAD) collects a tremendous amount of information. Also, think about our crime analysis in Chapter Twelve. CAD is where we can get the data,[8] and the crime analyst is going to help us organize and interpret the data.[9]

Calls for service information is not the only information that is collected and referenced by RD. Most agencies include crime, arrest, and traffic citations in the information that is collected by RD. By analyzing this information, the workload in an RD and, thus, a beat can be determined. Sometimes this information is used to create visual displays by importing the CAD and records management system (RMS) (where crime and arrest data is commonly held) information into GIS software. By using all this information, referenced at the RD level, the workload in the individual beats can be analyzed, and if needed, the beats can be reorganized.[10]

Let's digress from the spatial analysis for a moment. If you know the total workload per day, you can also use the CAD information and some information from the daily logs that the police officers keep to determine how much time it takes to complete a certain task. How much time do they spend answering calls? How much time do the spend on self-initiated activities? How much time do they spend patrolling? How much time do they spend on administrative activities like training or paperwork? With this information, an estimate can be made of the number of officers who would be needed per day to handle the field workload. [11] This gives you a rough idea of how many beats are possible for the jurisdiction. In other words, if you need ten police officer per shift, and you create eleven beats, one beat will go without an assigned police officer every day.

The spatial factor in work load is not always done by just looking at and grouping the work together. As you can see, if beats are organized by workload, they probably take on different sizes. One part of a city may have a greater density of population, crime, and calls for service than other parts, but arranging beats just based on an even distribution of workload may be impractical for a number of reasons. Depending on the jurisdiction, any number of RDs could be in a beat. Presume that a busy beat in a city has fifteen RDs, and an adjacent beat has twenty RDs but not the same amount of work. It could be impractical to increase the size of the latter by decreasing the size of the former. There may be natural boundaries, like

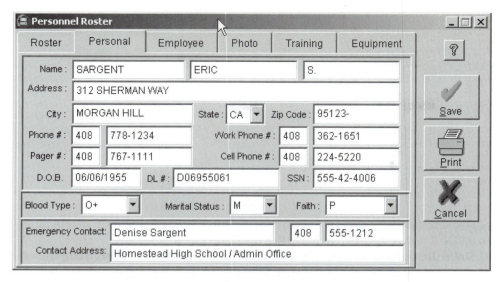

Figure 19.4 Offenders aren't the only ones ending up in an agency's relational database. Information about employees, from simple contact information to assigned equipment, is being tracked by agencies using relational databases and GUI-based software.
Screen capture provided by Crimestar Corp.

rivers or highways, that would make response time impractical. These RDs may be neighborhoods or communities in their own right and shaving a piece of them off and assigning them to another police beat may be politically impractical. Any local law enforcement official undertaking beat reorganization should realize that a beat reorganization can become a very volatile political subject. So far, by analyzing the data collected by CAD and RMS, workload estimates can be determined and beats organized as efficiently as possible, but the organization and workload we have examined thus far provides us with our minimum operating force. Typically, when beats are reorganized or developed, the agency looks at information from a large time frame. The sample that is used is typically one year, but law enforcement has daily, weekly, and seasonal cycles. Ignoring these cycles by fielding a constant number of police officers could endanger the public as well as the police officers. Moreover, by having a constant number of police officers deployed, you would have periods of not enough police officers for the workload and other periods where the number of calls for service didn't justify the deployment.[12] Recall the forecasting techniques from Chapter Twelve. By looking at the past pattern of calls for service and crime, we can get a general idea of the busy and slow periods. Deployment is determining how many police officers must be on duty at any one time to meet operational goals. Now that we know the number of police officers needed, the agency has to figure out who and how to schedule.

Most state and local police agencies operate twenty four hours a day, seven days a week. Depending on the size of the agency, there are a variety of possible shift schemes. The police officers may work a traditional five-day, forty-hour week, or they may work a modified schedule like four ten-hour days or three twelve-hour days. For some organizations these shift schemes are determined by union contracts (Figure 19.4).[13] The goal now is the fit the shift scheme into the proper deployment formula.

By looking at the data, most police agencies can determine which hours and days they need to deploy extra police officers. Into this formula are added special events, like parades, which may require the deployment of additional officers.

Deployment is usually determined by police managers, while scheduling is done by police supervisors. There is some software that can assist in scheduling, but there are so many issues, like seniority, union rules, holidays, vacation, and training, that many agencies find themselves doing scheduling manually.

Case Management

While the uniformed side of an agency's organization wrestles with deployment and scheduling issues, the investigative side usually is concerned with effectively managing the caseload of detectives or investigators (Figure 19.5). There are many ways that agencies manage their investigative caseload manually. One

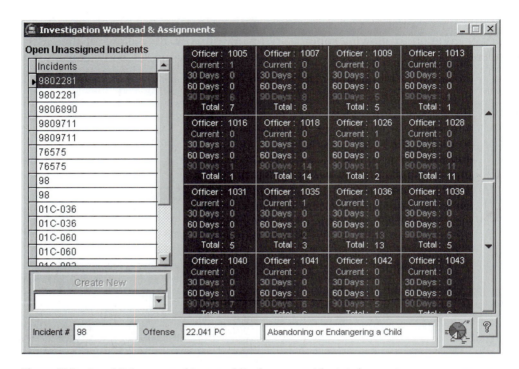

Figure 19.5 In addition to tracking workload agencywide, it is becoming more common to devise schemes whereby individual workload is tracked. This raises a number of questions for line employees, supervisors, and managers. Whenever the number of activities are tracked outside the context of those activities, a manager is only receiving a very small portion of the workload information. Generally, tracking systems that look at the number of something and the length of time it takes to complete a task, without looking at context, are considered gross indicators for the manager. In other words, think of your classes. If I told you that one professor was going to assign you seven books and one was going to assign you only two books for the semester, which would you choose? Based on the raw number, you might opt for the professor with two books. But, what if we put the information in context and I said, the seven books were paperback manuals, with no more than fifty pages per book (and lots of pictures), but the two-book professor was assigning one book with 400 pages and the second with 550 pages. Would that change your decision? It is thusly so for the police manager. Some investigations are complex and take an inordinate amount of time. Others are fairly simple. Indeed, we tend to give the complex stuff to the better employees. So we may see that one police officer handles far fewer cases, and takes a longer time, but a closer inspection might reveal that police officer is actually doing the better job.
Screen capture provided by Crimestar Corp.

common scheme calls for investigators to fill out a log that accounts for their time and states how they intend to investigate a case, or it is a chronological record of what they have done during an investigation. In addition to this log, investigators will often file follow-up reports to indicate their actions and what their investigations have discovered. With these two documents, the chronological record and follow-up reports, investigative supervisors could review what has been done, make suggestions or corrections, and give direction.

Many of these manual systems are being replaced by computerized case management systems that allow the investigators to record their efforts in a computer and allow investigative supervisors to monitor their efforts. An investigative caseload management system is another example of how relational databases and networks are being used in law enforcement.[14] At present, many of the caseload management programs are stand-alone configurations that are not linked directly to the agency's overall RMS. However, these systems share some general characteristics. In addition to allowing supervisory review of work, they allow for the cross-referencing of offenders and the tracking of evidence, witnesses, and victims.

Problem Officers

Just as it is believed that a small number of offenders commit the lion's share of crime, it is believed that a small percentage of police officers are responsible for a disproportionate share of citizen complaints. According to one report, there are police agencies where 2 percent of the police officers are responsible for 50 percent of the complaints.[15] One of the proposed solutions to this problem is to create a relational database of individual police officer activities in order to create an early-warning system on police officers.

One of the aspects of police work that was just discussed was the 24/7 nature of the job. Police officers often rotate shifts and assignment, many times ending with a different supervisor each time they complete a rotation, and on any particular shift, both police officers and sergeants take days off—in many instances different days off. Therefore, even in a small agency, it is possible for a police officer to have several supervisors. Moreover, in larger agencies, police officers can transfer from one geographic area to the next, sometimes never seeing their previous supervisors again. This is pointed out because the obvious question should be if there are police officers who are at the center of so many problems, where are their supervisors? Why is an early-warning relational database needed? Without being an apologist for poor or nonexistent supervision and leadership, there are circumstances that prevent any single supervisor from connecting the dots.

Proposed early-warning systems are designed to alert supervisors and managers of potential problems so that counseling and training can be provided to the police officer. The idea is to create a software program that recommends human intervention. There is debate as to what should be included in this program and how information should be weighed and interpreted. For instance, all recommended applications record and track citizen complaints, but many add internal complaints, traffic accidents, sick time usage, uses of force, and involvement in vehicle pursuits.

Although they are becoming increasingly popular, there is little research into the effectiveness of early-warning systems. However, one study indicated that 27 percent of the local law enforcement agencies that served a population of greater than fifty thousand employed some kind of early-warning system (Figure 19.6).[16] Proponents of early-warning systems believe they not only deter the negative behaviors of problem police officers through intervention, but may also act as

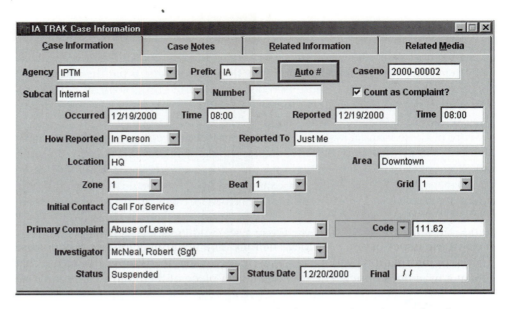

Figure 19.6 IA Trak allows agencies to keep track of personnel conduct and performance issues with ease. The system tracks Internal Affairs investigations as well as use of force, pursuits, employee crashes, prisoner injuries, and more. Alerts may be customized by the agency to have investigators warned when an employee reaches a minimum threshold, possibly averting potential problems. The system also comes with several reports designed to provide the investigative unit with investigative information as well as statistical analysis. Case investigations can be logged and tracked from beginning to end, maintaining a chronological order of all facets of the investigation time line.
Screen capture provided by the Institute of Police Technology and Management.

a general deterrence to all police officers. There is some evidence to suggest that the use of an early warning system has a positive effect, but a question remains as to whose behavior is more influenced. It could be that the early-warning-system creates a record forcing supervisors and managers to take action. It is likely that any deterrent effect is caused more by human intervention than by the presence of a computerized system. So the system changes the behavior of the supervisors and managers, forcing them to take action on troubled employees, which has the effect of modifying the police officer's behavior.[17]

There are a number of challenges to implementing an early-warning system. Depending on the amount and type of information that is entered into the system, it can be very data-entry intensive. This is because these systems collect information that is not normally collected by a standard RMS. In addition to having a high maintenance cost, there are often legal and union restrictions as to the amount and type of information that can be collected. When legal and police union restrictions are taken into account, questions as to the types of information that can be entered into an early-warning system become more complex. Do you enter all citizen complaints? What about complaints that are found to be false? Do you enter traffic accidents that have been determined not to be the police officer's fault? If you enter information related to field activities like use of force and pursuits, do you also enter productivity numbers? These questions aside, law enforcement is a difficult and complex task often undertaken by relatively young people. If an early-warning system has the effect of forcing supervisors and managers to provide intervention and training that is beneficial to police officers, it is probably overall worth the costs.

Training

Law enforcement is a complex and constantly changing profession. New technologies and laws are introduced; communities change, requiring police officers to adapt to new languages, cultures, and customs. Police officers answer millions of calls for service each year, and each one is different. Every change in the environment, from the changing of street names to the introduction of a new model car, requires a field police officer to learn a new piece of information. And yet, there are relatively few basic issues that constantly cause problems for police officers. By training and providing refresher training to police officers, the officers, supervisors, managers, and the community benefit because the police officers' responses to field situations can become more reliable.[18]

As we look at training in law enforcement there are three things to keep in mind. First, although the police officer's environment is constantly changing, most of the issues have a very long shelf life. The field police officer may not use a piece of information or tool every day, but he or she needs to be able to use that tool at a moment's notice. The tool could be a piece of technology or it could be information about how certain case law affects search and seizure. These issues are always there, in the background, but because they don't come up often, an individual's skills in applying a tool tend to diminish with time. Skills are perishable. We forget.

The second important issue with training is most people tend not to "rise to the occasion"; instead they default to the level of their training. Generally speaking, under stress people fall back on learned responses, and if skills have not been used recently, they will not have a basis for taking appropriate action. This leads to the third thing about law enforcement training: practice does not make a response perfect; it make a response automatic. In the field, police officers are required to convert what they have learned into appropriate actions in situations that may be similar, but are often vastly different. This may be the definition of common sense field police officers so often talk about—the ability to translate knowledge into appropriate actions. Can you teach that? I don't know. But what some technologies give law enforcement supervisors and managers the ability to do is teach and retrain on basic subjects and then using simulation and interaction, allow the police officer to apply that knowledge in a variety of different scenarios.

Most modern police training approaches divide training into two categories: knowledge and skill. Knowledge is learning specific information. It could be how to use a less-lethal force device, or it could be learning the organizational policy regarding the use of the device. Essentially, knowledge is all the information a police officer needs to perform his or her job. Skill, on the other hand, is the ability to apply what has been learned.[19] Training problems with police officers come in a variety of forms. They may not have been exposed to the information; they simply do not know. A police officer, like every other human being, could be exposed to information but not learn or understand the information. The police officer may learn a subject, but without practically applying it, the information does not develop into a skill, and as time passes the information that the police officer learned fades from memory, or the ability to perform the skill associated with the knowledge falls into disuse and the skill fades.

As law enforcement becomes more complex by the addition of new technologies, it will also become increasingly important to train with new equipment and procedures under field conditions. No matter how reliable a technology, if the user does not have the skill to use the technology under stressful conditions, the technology cannot add to overall public safety.[20] Moreover, even basic police skills, like techniques for searching an offender for weapons, become more reliably applied in the field when the skill is practiced under simulated field conditions.

For instance, in the previous chapter we examined the less-lethal force device of oleoresin capsicum (OC) gas. Even though you know what OC is, do you know how to use it? Do you know when to use it? Thorough training in OC should be comprehensive, going well beyond the technical aspects we looked at in Chapter Eighteen. Police officers should examine issues such as first-aid and decontamination protocols, legal issues, and tactical considerations in the use of OC.[21] OC should be included in situation simulations so that the police officer receives the knowledge and develops skills in the use of the device.

State and local law enforcement agencies are turning to **multimedia** forms of training as a means of imparting information and simulating field conditions for skill development. Whether video presentations, tactical simulators, or computer-based learning programs, technology is increasingly training the police officers. Multimedia education can be defined as using an electronic means to combine different visual and audio technologies in order to facilitate learning and skill development.[22]

Before we look at some of the multimedia applications, let's first consider the place of more traditional classroom educations. For imparting information to large groups of people, such as a college or police academy, classrooms with textbooks and lectures are still the most efficient means. The structure of the classroom and the limited feedback loop between the instructor and the student allow for knowledge to be gained. In smaller groups, such as a graduate seminar, there is considerably more feedback and discussion on issues surrounding the information. In smaller group settings, the students get to know each other and can talk about experiences about how the concepts and information have worked in the "real world." Because there is discussion on how concepts have actually worked, this type of education setting begins to bridge the gap between knowledge and skills.

New multimedia forms of education do not necessarily improve the quality of training.[23] The message, no matter the medium, still must be effectively delivered. What new forms of multimedia do give state and local police agencies is a variety of means to efficiently deliver the training. For instance, live training and role playing is probably one of the best methods for connecting knowledge to skills. Yet live role playing is expensive. As we look at the variety of technologies, there is an effort to use computer technology to create simulated environments. In effect, multimedia training attempts to re-create live role playing with a more efficient method of delivery. Whereas live role playing involves scheduling an instructor, training site, and students, interactive and simulated environments can be done virtually anywhere at any time. This may have the effect of police supervisors and managers becoming more likely to recommend training because of the reduced expense and loss of personnel time.[24]

The first application of technology in law enforcement training was probably videotaped lessons. This is probably still the most common technological application to training in law enforcement. These training videos started out as a simple taping of a lecture, often followed by a simple test using multiple choice or true/false questions. As the use of this technology matured, larger agencies and some state regulatory agencies like California Peace Officers Standards and Training (POST) began to produce video tapes that relayed the training through a story line.

The next generation of technology used for training was text-based interactive software applications. In essence, a standard lesson that could be delivered via textbook and pencil were converted to a computer program. This training scheme has the advantage of allowing the police officer to work at his own pace, and with the varying hours that police officers work, they can receive training that meets their personal and work schedule. If you signed up for the Federal Emergency Management Administration (FEMA) course from Chapter Seventeen, you know that these e-courses provide the user with continuous feedback and testing on key concepts and subjects.

The next step in the technological evolution of law enforcement training was to combine video technology with computer technology. One of the first efforts was by California POST several years ago. They produced several video-interactive computer-based programs. The initial format was laserdisc. We didn't look at laserdisc technology anywhere in the text because the technology has been replaced. A laserdisc can be thought of as the forerunner to DVDs. It worked with much the same basic technology, except laserdiscs were the size of long-play phonograph records (LPs), they could be easily damaged, and they held significantly less information than today's compact discs and DVDs. In this training the user would view a lesson and at certain points, much like the computer text-based program, review questions and tests would appear. The difference between computer text-based training and laserdisc training was laserdiscs provided audio-visual effects to supplement training.

Videotaped presentations of law enforcement training subjects are probably the most common use of technology. These videotaped presentations are increasing in quality and the methods of delivery are changing with technology. For instance, via satellite feed, police officers can receive training on subjects from domestic violence to pursuit driving. Generally, state and local law enforcement agencies pay a subscriber fee and these broadcasts are fed via satellite to the law enforcement agency twice in an eight-hour shift. Some agencies require officers to report for group viewing while other agencies allow the police officers to select the programs they want to watch (Figure 19.7).

The digital versatile disc (DVD), as a training technology, is a direct relative of the earlier laserdiscs. However, the DVD is much more portable and durable. Moreover, at the same time DVD technology has been evolving, video productions of law enforcement training subjects has matured. Both government-sponsored and commercially available products offer well-produced, interactive training. Moreover, DVDs can be viewed on many computers and with a relatively inexpensive home DVD system. Much like computer text-based training, the audiovisual training of the DVD is supplemented by tests, reviews, and decision making points.

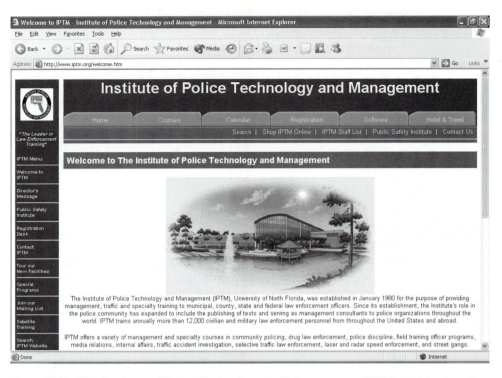

Figure 19.7 The Institute of Police Technology and Management (IPTM), University of North Florida, was established in January 1980 for the purpose of providing management, traffic, and specialty training to municipal, county, state, and federal law enforcement officers. Since its establishment, the Institute's role in the police community has expanded to include publishing texts and serving as management consultants to police organizations throughout the world. IPTM trains annually more than twelve thousand civilian and military law enforcement personnel from throughout the United States and abroad. IPTM offers a variety of management and specialty courses in community policing, drug law enforcement, police discipline, field training officer programs, media relations, internal affairs, traffic accident investigation, selective traffic law enforcement, laser and radar speed enforcement, and street gangs. Try this: visit their Web site and look at the training calendar **www.iptm.org/welcome.htm**.
Screen capture provided by the Institute of Police Technology and Management.

With most DVD systems, if a user provides the system with an incorrect answer to a question, the user can select the exact portion of the presentation for review. This is a distinct advantage over traditional video tape. Recall from Chapter Two that digital or analog information that is stored on tape must be viewed sequentially, whereas information stored on discs can be accessed in any order (Figure 19.8).

The most recent development in law enforcement training technologies is simulators. Currently, there are two basic subjects taught by simulator: the use of deadly force (or shooting) and driving. Commercial firms use analog and digital recordings of simulated events and computers to create judgment situations to which a police officer can react. These devices have become increasingly versatile and complex.

At first, shooting simulators projected a video presentation of a situation on a large screen. The screen was often ten feet tall and fifteen feet wide and contained electric sensors on a grid. The police officer receiving the training would be given a revolver that fired a low-velocity wax projectile at the screen. The computer was used to synchronize the video presentation with the screen. As the

Try This

Eventually, the Internet may surpass satellite technology as a means to deliver training programming. In the private sector, there is a move to create broadband, Internet-deliverable video programming by converting analog film productions into a digital format. While both analog and digital can be viewed via the Internet or digital television, converted analog video will give private firms the ability to make programming interactive. You can go to the Public Broadcasting Service (PBS) Web site and watch a Nova production on why the World Trade Center Towers failed at **www.pbs.org/wgbh/nova/wtc**. You can also watch a complete conversion on an analog program to a digital format, "Dying to Be Thin," at **www.pbs.org/wgbh/nova/thin/**.

Source: Christofferson and Gatzke, "Broadband Media," 49.

presentation unfolded, the police officer would be presented with a situation where he or she had to decide whether or not to shoot and at whom to shoot. If the police officer decided to fire the revolver, the wax projectiles struck the screen and the computer recorded when and where in the presentation the police officer discharged the weapon. Afterward, the presentation was replayed and stopped at the points the police officer could have fired and did fire. The

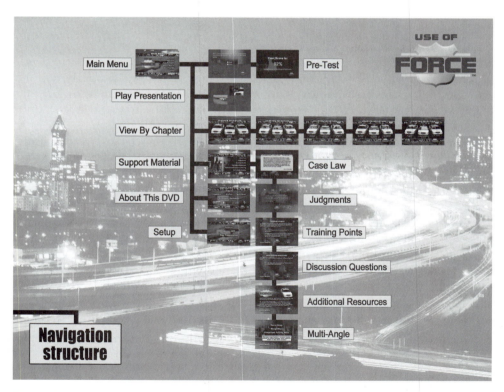

Figure 19.8   One way in which state and local police agencies are balancing the problems of perishable skills and 24/7 scheduling needs is by investing in technologies that allow either an individual police officer or group of police officers to receive critical training (like a preshift briefing, for instance). One of those technologies is through interactive DVDs. In this DVD police officers can take a pretest, review areas of concern, review supporting documentation and view hyperlinks to Web sites with additional information.
Photograph provided by Video I-D Teleproductions.

location of each round of ammunition was recorded and the police officer was able to review judgment and marksmanship.

These simulators have progressed along with technology (Figure 19.9). Now police officers enter the simulator and are given specially designed reproductions of their duty equipment, including a Sam Browne, semiautomatic handguns, and additional ammunition magazines. Instead of wax bullets, some of these systems use laser technology and sensors to record the police officers' actions. For instance, during a post-training debriefing, the exact moment the police officer drew his or her weapon is recorded. As with the wax bullets, the moment and location the firearm is discharged is recorded, but because the technology now relies on a digital medium, the screen interacts with the police officer. For instance, with the wax bullet simulator, if the police officer's rounds struck the offender during the presentation, the presentation did not change, the offender continued to shoot, take hostages, or flee. With the digital system, if the police officer's rounds strike the offender, the digital recording automatically changes to another scene wherein the offender drops as if shot.

Recall our discussion on semiautomatic handguns in the previous chapter. Although they have advantages over revolvers, they do have an occasional problem of malfunctioning. There are a variety of causes for the malfunction, but most malfunctions can be cleared in moments by the police officer—if he or she is adequately trained. One of the advantages of the new system is that the operator can signal the handguns the police officers are using for training to malfunction. If the police officers perform the proper malfunction drill, they are able to shoot back at the target. Finally, these systems allow for more than one shooter. Partner officers can go through the simulator together.

These training systems are very expensive. However, if used properly, not only can the police officers' shooting skills be evaluated, their judgment on drawing their weapons, use of verbal commands, and application of deadly force can be evaluated under simulated stressful conditions.

These systems are not without controversy. Some opponents of the system caution that they do not have decision-making or negotiating skills and do not provide instructors with the ability to teach a full range of force options. Others believe that these simulators may convey, especially to a newer police officer, the impression that every call for service or traffic stop contains a killer.[25] I think that these opponents only experienced the shooting scenes and not the briefing and debriefing that go along with these simulators. Many of these simulators have galleries from which police officers' peers can observe their actions. Having seen this in practice, they are a very tough audience when evaluating police officers' judgments and perceptions of threats. Moreover, just as these simulators can change scenes to depict an offender falling down, they often change the scenario so that when one police officer experiences the training the offender is armed and dangerous, reaching for a handgun, but for the next police officer, that offender reaches for a wallet and not a handgun. The critics of these devices have a point, simulated training that is not accompanied by a discussion on policy and ethics is just a video game.

The second type of simulator is a driving simulator. The advanced models of these simulators use computer technology to create an artificial environment. The simulators use a series of video screens to simulate the view outside of a police vehicle. The police officer receives training by sitting inside a mock-up of a typical police vehicle. These interactive scenarios could be simply patrol driving with a series of unexpected hazards, the involvement in a high-speed pursuit, or a routine traffic stop. Because of advancements in computer technology, driving simulators

Figure 19.9 One of the best ways to improve a police officer's perishable skills is through field simulations. While at the basic level this might involve partner officers talking through a series of "what if" situations, there are very advanced ways to simulate field situations. Some state and local law enforcement agencies are using state-of-the-art, interactive, large-screen theaters with broadcast-quality digital video scenarios. These interactive simulations are controlled by an instructor, and the police officer's action and judgment can be debriefed immediately. *Photograph provided by Advanced Interactive Systems.*

have become very lifelike and they have a wide variety of scenarios and options. If the police officer experiences a high-speed pursuit on a simulator, she can view her actions from a third-party, helicopter-like view. Officers can be scored on a variety of factors, and many of the factors can be adjusted to fit agency policy.

Chapter Summary

We looked at deployment as a means of determining the number of police officers needed to police a given area. As we looked at deployment, we found that most of the information needed to make calculations was recorded either by an agency's computer-aided dispatch or records management system. Once general deployment issues like a beat plan and minimum operating force have been determined, seasonal, cyclical, and special deployment needs can be gleaned from the same data. With this information, there are a variety of software programs that can assist supervisors or managers in scheduling police officers to meet deployment needs.

One of the newer applications of relational databases is for use in tracking problem police officers. These systems use information about citizen complaints, use of force, officer-involved traffic accidents, and high-speed pursuits to alert supervisory and management personnel of potential problem officers. Generally, this information is used for intervention and counseling of the potential problem officer. There is very little research into the effectiveness of these programs and less research into why they might be effective.

While technology cannot make up for poor judgment or compensate for inadequate training, it can provide law enforcement supervisors and managers with a wide variety of teaching tools.[26] The multimedia aspect of new technological applications not only makes them interactive and more lifelike, but also adds flexibility to applications. With some of the technologies, the training can be effective anywhere and any time.

Discussion Questions

1. Currently, deployment and scheduling data revolves around information collected by the CAD and RMS. However, this is very reminiscent of incident-driven policing. How would you include activities more in line with the community-oriented policing model, such as problem solving and establishing partnerships in deployment formulas? Can you think of a way to count these activities?
2. What other examples of queuing theory have you experienced?
3. What do you think of relational databases designed to track employee behavior for the purpose of intervention and counseling? Should college campuses have similar programs—tracking grades, timeliness of work submission, and absences—in order to provide intervention and counseling for potential problem students?
4. How could this textbook benefit from the interactive training technologies examined in this chapter?

Key Terms

Deployment

Level of Service

Multimedia

Queuing Theory

Reporting District (RD)

Scheduling

End Notes

1. Bair, et al., "Advanced Crime Mapping," 96.
2. Ibid.
3. Ibid., 104.
4. Ibid., 98.
5. Ibid., 96.
6. Ibid., 113.
7. Ibid., 101.
8. "Evolution and Development of Police Technology," 65.
9. Bair, et al., "Advanced Crime Mapping," 113.
10. Ibid., 101.
11. Ibid., 105.
12. Ibid., 112.
13. Ibid., 115.
14. Boyle, "Detective Case Management."
15. Walker, Alpert, and Kenny, "Early Warning Systems," 1.
16. Ibid.
17. Ibid., 3.
18. Kurke and Scrivner, "Police Psychology," 80.
19. Ibid.
20. Ibid., 83.
21. Onnen, "Oleoresin Capsicum."
22. Hasselbring and Glaser "Computer Technology," 102.
23. Ibid.
24. Halachmi, "Information Technology," 533.
25. "Evolution and Development of Police Technology," 102.
26. Ibid., 15.

Chapter Twenty
Implementing and Managing Technology

Learning Objectives

- The student will understand how a **steering committee** and **implementation team** are used during the planning process of a technology project.

- The student will understand the concept and use of **consultants**.

- The student will be exposed to the concept of **business process reengineering (BPR)**.

- The student will understand the concepts of **contracting out**, **outsourcing**, **pooled purchasing**, and **cooperative purchasing**.

- The student will be exposed to the government buying process, including the concepts of **request for proposal**, **request for quotation**, and **sole-source procurement**.

Introduction

In this chapter we are going to look at managing and/or implementing a technology project. If you have traveled through all of the preceding nineteen chapters, you are probably more prepared to discuss technology and technology-related projects than most law enforcement managers. Our primary purpose in this chapter is to pull all of the information technology (IT) together and see how it can be made to work. You probably realize now some of the potentials, limitations, and problems with technology. Now that you know the technology, it is time to take a look at how it can impact an organization and some of the concepts and techniques that can be used to make managing and implementing successful.[1]

As you will see, sound management and good leadership is often the key to the successful implementation of a new technology, and project failures are expensive. Consider that a medium-sized local agency that needs to outfit twenty-five police vehicles with radios and in-car computers would spend an estimated $1.14 million over the ten-year lifespan of the equipment.[2] What many don't consider is that initial purchase and installation of technology may be as little as 24 percent of the total cost. Organizers sometimes fail to factor in training, service, and upgrades.[3] Moreover, the poorer the planning, the higher the probability of additional costs during the life of the technology.

Projects don't work out as expected for a variety of reasons. As an example, some vendors are just not forthright about the failures of other projects. In other instances, technologies are new and there has been little research and evaluation. Sometimes projects and systems fail because the manager making the purchase decision does not do adequate research. Even if a manager does solid research, the purchasing schemes of many state and local governments require that low-bid systems are purchased. If you look at those four reasons, they come back to bad decisions made on imperfect knowledge.[4] Above all, if a manager is going to spend a million dollars, she ought to either be thoroughly familiar with the subject, develop the expertise in-house, or purchase expertise.

The fact is that new technologies are attractive. The potential of technology is continually touted by the news media, vendors, and even government managers. But the problem is that technology projects are often undertaken based

Vendors are private firms that manufacture, wholesale, or resell goods and services. Within this definition we have consultants, contract firms, and firms that sell specific products. As we explore this chapter further, we will look at the different types of vendors.

on information concerning the potential, not the reality. Decision makers go forward with projects and they simply have failed to take into account how a technology will effect their agencies. They haven't looked at the people, the existing systems, and sometimes most important their organizations' existing business practices.[5] Often success with IT projects comes down to having good management and sound leadership right from the beginning.[6]

Leadership and Technology

The need for leadership in implementing and managing technology is well established. For most projects, the critical question regarding leadership can concern whether or not the project requires a dedicated manager, someone whose full-time job is to manage the implementation of new technology or even the day-to-day running of an existing technology. While there is no definitive rule that says when a project becomes "this large," it must have a dedicated manager, there are some commonsense considerations. For instance, the expected length and complexity of a project are primary determinants of the need for a dedicated manager or leader.[7]

Presume that an IT project is sufficiently complex as to obviously need a dedicated manager. The question then becomes, "What skills should that manager have?" Traditionally, qualifications for IT managers have centered on their knowledge of technology.[8] The problem with relying on someone with solely a strong technology background is the impact technology has on organizations and in the wider law enforcement community. For instance, an IT project manager must have not only the ability to oversee the day-to-day operations, but also a background in criminal justice and public safety issues so that he or she can discuss policy issues with other managers.[9] In the past, IT managers have been hired for their abilities to work on issues like economic development and the implementation of e-government initiatives, but in the future, the new IT manager is likely to focus on how the technology impacts issues like police officer safety, crime reduction, and privacy.[10] The IT managers of the twenty-first century are still going to need a strong set of technological skills, but they must be matched by their managerial skills, policy skills, and knowledge of criminal justice issues.[11]

An IT manager can't possibly know everything. There aren't any superheroes available for IT project management. But even on smaller projects that don't require full-time IT managers, the project directors must know enough to know when they don't know. As you will see later in the chapter, successful IT implementation and management is a team effort, and sometimes the team is made up of people from outside the organization, people with specialized knowledge. Because the IT manager is working with expert or specialized knowledge, it is likely that a collaborative style of leadership will be the best fit. The manager will be supportive and innovative and yet strong enough to overcome resistance to change.[12] Perhaps not a superhero, but a tall order.

Planning

With larger IT projects it is likely that a **project manager** will be necessary.[13] The planning for the project should involve a very wide spectrum of people. While there are a number of methods for engendering involvement in a project, the development of a **steering committee** is often the first step. The purpose of the steering committee is to develop project goals and obtain political and financial support. This committee should include the project director, department heads from the involved jurisdictions, political stakeholders, community stakeholders, technical experts, and above all, end users.[14]

The involvement of end users seems so practical, and yet it is so often overlooked. The people who are ultimately responsible for using a system can have tremendous input on what they need.[15] A few end users involved in the beginning of the project often become the bridge between concept and implementation. They are the people who will ultimately sell their peers on the new technology. Moreover, if they are involved in the process of development, there will ultimately be a greater understanding among all end users on the capabilities and limitations of the IT project. If end users know what to expect from the beginning, they won't have unrealistic expectations. The project won't be deemed a failure because end users expected something that was not possible or practical.

While the steering committee develops goals and garners support, a secondary working group, an **implementation team**, is involved in the actual development of the project. The first job of the implementation team is to assess the agency's needs. They may ask questions like the following: What are the agency's current assets and resources? What does the current IT infrastructure look like? What are the end user requirements? This part of the planning process is critical because it helps to define the project's objectives. For instance, the steering committee may outline the general goal of "upgrading the current public safety radio communications system." The implementation team takes that general goal and further defines the problems with the old system, explores the possibility of upgrade or replacement, and looks at the potential future use and end user requirements. It then refines the overall goal to working objectives.

The implementation team, composed of managers, experts, and users, works out the details of the project's implementation. Their job is to implement the policies and goals of the steering committee. Generally speaking, the project manager is the head of the implementation team and a member of the steering committee. A larger agency might have the chief of police acting as the project manager. His or her implementation team might be composed of other agency managers, supervisors, and users. In the case of a smaller agency, the steering committee might be composed of the city manager, one or more representatives of the political leadership, the chief of police, experts, and users.

There are many ways to conduct the planning process on a major IT project. The implementation team may decide to break the tasks down and assign them to specific individuals or teams of individuals. The team may interview experts, interview vendors, or conduct site visits to other agencies who have completed similar projects.[16] One of the best ways to avoid failure is to learn from other people's mistakes. A site visit is much more valuable than reading about a project or even interviewing people on the telephone. Generally, people are more candid about an IT project when you speak to them in person.

An implementation team has three basic courses of action (Figure 20.1). They could elect to purchase predesigned software and hardware. They may find that an agency of similar size has an off-the-shelf product that is working very well. There are positives and negatives with an off-the-shelf product. On the positive side, they tend to be significantly less expensive, and if they fit the agency's needs, product upgrades and support from the vendor are often only a telephone call away. On the negative side, with IT and organizations, a one-size-fits-all product usually doesn't fit well. The agency may find itself in a position of having to modify practices to fit the technology.

The second option is to have the IT project custom designed. Obviously, this is more expensive, and the implementation team must work very closely with the designer so the final product resembles the original concept. If the team is vigilant, you may get what you asked for. I don't want to sound to harsh, but the reality is that law enforcement has a number of special needs that must be carefully designed. Think back to the issues we've already looked at—interoperability, durability, privacy, and the different requirements between tactical and strategic information needs. If the implementation team works closely with the designer, you can end up with an outstanding system; if the team is less than vigilant, you can end up with trash. Along this same line, a state or local law enforcement agency may want to consider developing in-house talent. An in-house design team, or technology unit, can create a technology career path inside the agency and in-house staff may tend to be more proactive in the development and maintenance of technology projects.

The final option is to turn the project completely over to a vendor. Some agencies contract their communications dispatch with a private firm or a larger agency. In that instance, it is like buying any other product. If you research it thoroughly, and like the way they do it, you can make the purchase. The success or failure of a project is directly attributable to the planning. The better the planning, the greater the possibility of success.[17]

Paving the Cow Path

The major north-south highway in California is Interstate 5. It basically starts at the border with Mexico and goes all the way into the state of Washington. Going north, as the interstate leaves Los Angeles County, it travels into a mountainous range and through the Tejon Pass. This section of the highway is often referred to as the Grapevine. It is said that long before humans inhabited the area, wildlife used the Tejon Pass as a natural migration route. Later Native Americans used the Tejon Pass as a trading route. Thousands of years after the Native Americans, the United States Cavalry built a fort in the pass to protect what had become a transportation link between upper and lower California. About a hundred years after that, the first two-lane highway, Highway 99 or the Ridge Route, was built. Several decades later, the four-lane interstate highway was built. If you stop at the historical museum at Fort Tejon in the Tejon Pass, guides will tell you that the interstate follows the Native American trade route. The museum will give the impression that we simply paved over where animals and humans found it convenient to walk over the mountains. That's not exactly true.

Throughout the years, as the technology changed, so did the path through the pass. The pass is still the most direct route, but within the expanse of the pass itself, there are a variety of choices. Wagons and early cars tended to take a more winding path that lessened the grade. Today, with our vehicles, the grade is as much a straight line as the terrain permits. It didn't make sense to simply widen the old road in parts. That is because the new technology afforded us the ability to go in a faster, more direct route.

Activity Steps for Implementing a New Technology Program

Process	Activity
Identify Project	Assess needs, develop justifications
Preliminary Approval	Develop steering committee and political support, identify funding sources
Refine Project	Develop project implementation team, refine specifications, obtain funding
Issue Request for Proposal	Identify potential vendors
Evaluate Responses	Compare products, prices, terms, and vendor histories
Select Vendor	Negotiate the contact, develop solid project completion time lines
Manage the Contract	Check for compliance, test system, accept completion

Table 20.1 By clearly planning a technology project from the beginning, an agency is more likely to be successful. Moreover, careful early planning can help prevent negative consequences, such as chasing useless grant money. Occasionally, organizations allow available grant money to drive project goals rather than find more appropriate funding. Changing organization technology goals solely to fit current grant funding is generally a bad idea.

For some reason, some IT projects are managed by people who haven't grasped the concept that technology changes business practices. Sure, you could build a winding four-lane highway and follow the previous path exactly, but you would be wasting the technology. More important, there are some portions of the old highway that you could make into a four-lane highway, but the engineering would probably be expensive and the trip dangerous. Technology can change an organization in unanticipated ways.[18] But, if the implementation team is careful in their planning, technology can be a positive enabler of change.[19]

One of the key tasks of the implementation team is to examine current organizational practices and determine how they will be affected by the new technology. An examination of practices generally begins with an examination of core functions.[20] For the law enforcement agency, the questions might be: How will this technology impact our ability to respond to calls for service? How will this technology affect our ability to perform crime analysis?

By looking at organizational goals, objectives, and functions, the implementation team can avoid having the new technology misapplied. By looking at how the new technology fits with old practices, the team may find that instead of using the technology to speed up or make tasks more efficient, they should use the technology to change the task in ways that may make it more efficient and effective. For instance, recall our examination of crime analysis. We know that much of the data used for crime analysis comes from CAD and RMS. Moreover, we know that most agencies are not fully integrated, so when crime analysis is performed, an analysis usually spends an inordinate amount of time collecting crime reports and entering data into a separate system. An example of paving the cow path would be upgrading the computer hardware and software in CAD, RMS, and crime analysis systems but not integrating the systems. Sure, all three functions are more efficient, but the organization would be much more efficient and effective if CAD, RMS, and crime analysis were upgraded and integrated. If the implementation team asked the right questions, the recommendation to the steering committee might be to delay upgrading the systems individually and working to integrate the existing hardware and software. The point is that organization goals should drive IT innovation; IT should not drive the organization.[21]

The intelligent use of technology can make state and local law enforcement agencies more efficient and more effective. The use of technology starts during the planning phase, when the implementation team is determining how the technology may change practices, systems, and policies. However, one of the most important tasks the team completes during planning is a consideration of how those changes affect the people in the organization. Even though the team is partially composed of users, the more a technology changes a system, practice, or policy, the more likely there is to be organizational and individual resistance to the technology.[22]

While the implementation team is planning the new technology, the goal of the chief executive of that organization is to prepare his or her organization for changes the technology will bring. If the organizational culture is prepared and acceptant of the changes, the likelihood of the success of the technology project increases.[23] If the organization is not prepared, the chief executive must take a strong leadership role and prepare the people in the organization for the changes.

The Use of Consultants

For most people, when thinking about a **consultant** and new technology, what comes to mind is a computer engineer or some type of software or hardware designer. In reality, depending on the magnitude of the technology, many different types of consultants may be employed. As an example, a chief executive of a state or local law enforcement agency who believes that a new technology will bring about profound change in organizational systems, policies, and procedures may choose to employ an organizational development consultant.

Sometimes state and local law enforcement agencies find themselves in a position to complete a task for which they do not have in-house expertise. They could go through the rather lengthy government hiring process and employ a person who has the expertise needed to complete the task, but since these are often unique, one-time situations, a more efficient means is to hire a consultant. Their are many different types of consultants used by law enforcement agencies. Their use is distinguished from contracting other services because they are generally hired for a limited time, to complete a specific task. On occasion, some consultants are retained over a fairly long period of time, but it is always task specific and there is an expectation that once the task is complete, the relationship between the consultant and agency ends. Many consultants are former government employees who leave government service because their skills, knowledge, and background are more valuable in the private sector.

For instance, an agency might hire a consultant with a background in CAD technology solely for the purpose of determining which CAD system best fits the agency. On the other hand, the consultant with CAD expertise could be hired to help the agency implement the CAD. Or the consultant could actually perform the job of the project director, overseeing the day-to-day activities involved in a technology plan.[24]

Consultants are "persons or firms who, pursuant to a contract, provide specific, often complex or technical reports, research, or services to government agencies." *Source:* Shafritz, *Public Policy and Administration*, 510.

One of the best uses of consultants might be in examining the potential effects a new technology could have on an organization. Typically, consultants with a strong background in criminal justice, organizational development, and possibly technology are often used to perform a **business process reengineering (BPR)** study.[25] A BPR study is looking at an organization's goals, processes, policies, and technologies with an eye toward making those four factors work together better. We looked at this earlier when we saw that one of the jobs of the implementation team is core organizational functions. Routinely, a BPR is something with which organizational members have little or no experience. In that case, the consultant can help guide the implementation team during their examination of the organization.

There are a few caveats when selecting and working with a consultant. First, the consultant should have experience completing a similar technology or organizational project.[26] Consultants can be contracted in two primary ways. They may be hired to perform a specific task for a fixed rate, or they may be hired on an hourly basis. Of course, to get a fixed-rate price, the agency has to know exactly what it wants done and have a reasonable idea of how long that task will take.

State and local agencies spend a lot of money on technology purchases, and as we noted in Chapter One, the rate at which agencies are disappointed with a technology acquisition is reportedly very high. Since the failure rate is high and costs are enormous, purchasing expert advice in the form of a consultant often makes good sense. A good consultant can assist an agency in getting the best price for the optimal equipment. Return to the purchase of a CAD system. Often buyers do not completely understand what they are getting. They will be shown a fully integrated CAD system and purchase that system, expecting it to fully integrate their agency's technology, but you know that while a CAD system may have the capability to be fully integrated, integration depends on all the other existing systems. Another common problem is that buyers will look at the fully integrated CAD system but opt for a less expensive version, not realizing the functions they have cut out of the purchase. Simply put, an experienced consultant can help an agency avoid these pitfalls.

Losing People

The reason that state and local law enforcement agencies use consultants is because they lack in-house expertise. The lack of expertise is particularly acute when it comes to personnel with a technology background. We find ourselves back in another economic theory—competition. The competition between the private sector and government service was more pronounced in the past decade, but the fact remains that highly skilled technical people are usually compensated better in the private sector. Making the problem worse is the situation where the employee leaves government service to pursue better compensation in the private sector.[27]

The drain of highly qualified people is not restricted to IT jobs. Other experts, such as those involved in criminal profiling and forgery, are also finding a place in the private sector.[28] It is very important to realize that when people leave government service, they often take just more than their skills sets. They also take their experience, judgment, and their institutional knowledge. Currently, there is not much a supervisor or manager can do to keep up with the higher compensation packages offered by private industry, but there are few things that can be done.

People are not solely motivated by money. Some argue that past a certain point, people aren't motivated all that much by money. What supervisors and managers can do to partially stem the flow of people out of government service is to provide good leadership and management. People will often stay if they feel they make a difference, they have the freedom to be creative and innovative, and they feel their work is appreciated. Shelf upon shelf of leadership and management books exist—so suffice it to say that good leadership and management skills can help to retain expertise.

Realizing that expertise may leave, managers should take an active interest in cultivating younger employees toward IT positions within an agency.[29] This idea has impact far beyond the potential of filling future vacancies. Most computer technology in state and local law enforcement is woefully underutilized. Sure, people use e-mail because it is like another telephone or memo, but how many use it to send files for review instead of killing trees? They use the computer for word processing but not for case management or crime analysis. By encouraging the use of technology, an agency can ensure the potential is explored and new IT-savvy employees are coming up through the ranks.

In addition to treating employees well and encouraging the use of IT, some agencies are trying to compete with the compensation packages of the private sector. In government service, compensation schemes are very hierarchal. The chief makes more than the captain, the captain makes more than the lieutenant, the lieutenant makes more than the detective, and so on. In some instances, you end up with an implementation team with a police officer and the chief of police, and the police officer, in this instance, has better technical skills, but he doesn't get paid any more. The chief can't pay him more and can't promote him to a classification that does pay more. He is a cop, no matter his skill, so he makes a cop's pay.

As a way of competing with the private sector, some organizations are considering **broadbanding**.[30] The concept of broadbanding started on the federal level with the Civil Service Reform Act of 1978. This act allowed federal agencies to conduct projects in order to find ways of reforming the hierarchal federal civil service pay system.[31] The first test project occurred in 1991 at the United States Navy's China Lake Weapons Testing facility. In this experiment, they reduced the number of civil service classifications from fifteen to five; they essentially merged pay grades. While there was a modest increase in personnel costs initially, turnover rate among high-performing employees was lower.[32] There isn't much research to indicate how effective this scheme was in the long run, but opponents would argue for another economic theory (I am not going to state it) that basically says government shouldn't try to compete with the private sector. In the private sector, competition causes compensation to follow the market, but once you increase a government employee's pay, you have increased their pay even if the market for their skill decreases. Probably the most viable option for the manager is to cultivate new talent within the organization or prepare to go outside the organization and contract or outsource the skill.

Contracting Out and Outsourcing

Contracting out is alternatively referred to as outsourcing, but there are a few subtle differences. Some of the literature on the two concepts merges them, but for our purposes we will demonstrate the subtlety. If you have a cellular telephone, you have agreed to a contract with an IT provider; you have contracted out. If your school pays for a guest lecturer to come teach a single class or series of classes, they have outsourced the teaching. The primary difference is that contracting tends to be for longer periods of time and for general services, whereas outsourcing is more like consulting; it is usually a shorter period of time and for a specific assignment. Of course, contracting out and outsourcing at the government level are more complex, but many of the issues are very similar.

Contracting out can be defined as a government organization, through a competitive process, contracting for a service with another organization. The organization with which a state or local government law enforcement agency contacts can be another government agency, a not-for-profit agency, or a typical private firm.[33]

Local governments often contract services.[34] One of the most common arrangements is for a small city to contract all law enforcement services with either the county sheriff or another city. In addition to contracting out all law enforcement services, a small city may contract out a portion of their law enforcement. A common IT arrangement is for a small city to contract its 9-1-1 Public Safety Answering Point (PSAP) and communications dispatch center with another law enforcement agency.

Did you sign a one-year contract with your cellular provider? What happens at the end of the year? In some cases, the great rate you got is no longer available. Do you just move to another provider? What if halfway through your one-year contract you find the service is not as dependable as you were led to believe? You and I can change providers at the end of the year, but then we have the hassle of changing the telephone number. Many people stay with service providers because of the hassle of changing telephone numbers. When a government contracts a service, it, too, loses some control over that service. What if the contract 9-1-1 employee is rude? The community doesn't blame the contract service; they blame the chief of police. In other instances, small communities have actually contracted PSAP and radio communications with the larger county agencies, only to find the fees continually increasing. In one instance, after five years the contract was so expensive the smaller communities bailed out of the contract. Of course, after five years they no longer had their communications equipment, so they incurred additional costs, as well as costs to break the agreement.

There are other hidden costs to contracting. For instance, late in this chapter we will take a brief look at the government purchasing process. If you include the costs of having to control the bidding, monitor the contract, and monitor the service, contracting out may ultimately be costing more.[35] Contracting out is a viable option, but one that should be exercised with care.

An example of outsourcing would be the use of a firm to train users on a new technology.[36] This task is specific and for a limited duration. Outsourcing differs from consulting in that an agency may have in-house talent that could complete the task, but the time and energy of the talent is better spent on other projects.[37] Indeed, it has been recommended that agencies only outsource tasks they know, so they can easily monitor performance.[38]

Both concepts, contracting out and outsourcing, are closely associated with the politics of government financing. Therefore, much of the focus on these two

At the time of the first draft of this book, cellular telephone numbers were not portable. In other words, you were stuck with the provider if you wanted to keep the number. However, proving the point that technology changes rapidly, by the time the book went to press, cellular numbers had become portable. You may now change providers and keep your number. The paragraph remains in the text as a good example of two things: First, that technology and the application of technology change rapidly (in this case, in less than a year). Second, to keep you current, updates to the book are posted at **www.hitechcj.com**, the book's companion website. At the website, in addition to receiving updates, you can provide input on revisions to future editions.

topics is on the potential monetary savings.[39] However, there are other public policy issues, and because state and local governments tend to focus on immediate savings (budgets are usually annual), there isn't much investigation into the long-term cost and effects of turning over a government service to the private sector. Some of the issues that are not fully addressed are loss of expertise, loss of control over the service, and privacy issues.

We briefly looked at the potential loss of expertise and loss of control, but what about privacy? Some outsource firms provide data warehousing, network services, and many IT-related functions for government agencies. Yet they are not government employees. Who knows which private firms actually have control over information about you and me.

Proponents of both outsourcing and contracting cite a number of valid points as to the efficiency and effectiveness of these two schemes. First, because private firms can have many customers, some of the costs of doing business are shared by all customers; therefore, government agencies who participate in outsourcing and contracting gain the benefit of economy of scale. Second, private firms are profit motivated, and profit comes from providing a good-quality product at a reasonable cost; therefore, governments benefit from a high quality. As has been alluded to, if government agencies contract or outsource a project, they can be expected to use their in-house talents to concentrate on their primary goals and objectives. Finally, private firms, again because they are profit motivated, can determine the exact costs associated with a good or service. Because of the private firms' abilities to account for all expenses related to an endeavor, government agencies are better able to understand the true costs of providing the good or service.[40]

All of the arguments put forth by the proponents of outsourcing and contracting are true, all other issues aside, but there is another way in which local law enforcement agencies may be able to garner some, if not all, of the benefits of contracting and outsourcing under certain circumstances. **Pooled purchasing** is when two or more agencies combine their needs and purchase goods together. For example, two adjacent local agencies both need to replace their radio systems. They decide on the features that they need and approach a vendor about buying the systems for both agencies. They are buying two different radio systems, but because their request is exactly the same and they are in close proximity to each other, the private firm can save money, passing that savings on to the agencies.

Pooled purchasing requires a tremendous amount of interagency cooperation, but it can be done. By using this scheme, the agencies reap some of the economic benefits, but don't surrender to some of the other issues. A close cousin of pooled purchasing is **cooperative purchasing**. When using a cooperative purchasing scheme, a local government makes purchases from the state's price list. State government buys thousands of items that are also used by local governments. Since the state is a larger purchaser, and because they produce an agreement list, they often are able to get fairly significant discounts.

The Government Buying Process

Our government spends a lot of money, and many of the items it spends money on it buys from the private sector. Recall in Chapters One and Six, we talked about the political era of policing. As we noted, policing did not develop in a vacuum. Our government had a very similar political period, a professional period, and there are efforts now to implement a community-governance model. Just as the political era in policing was rife with corruption, so too was the rest of government. Part of the corruption of government involves the purchase of

Try This

Surf the Internet for the terms "RFP law enforcement." You will undoubtedly find a number of RFP

examples. Take a good look at the complexity involved in some of these proposals.

goods and services. In the past, contracts have been handed out as political favors
and outright bribes. This behavior still takes place today.

In an effort to combat fraud and increase government efficiency in purchasing,
many state and local agencies use a competitive bid process. Usually, the implementation team would develop systems specifications then issue either a
request for quotation (RFQ) or a **request for proposal (RFP)**. An RFQ is
used for general items that are readily available from many private firms. A government entity might issue an RFQ for toilet paper. Generally speaking, the contract to supply the toilet paper is then awarded to the low bidder.

On the other hand, an RFP is used for more complex purchases, like IT systems. During the RFP process, the contract or purchase might be awarded to the
private firm based on things other than price. For instance, the private firm may
have recent references that impress the requesting agency or the product or system they propose for the price is so superior to the lower bid that the agency
spends more money.

Not every government purchase is made through the RFP and RFQ schemes.
Generally speaking, these procedures must be used on purchases that exceed a certain dollar amount, and that dollar amount varies around the country. But if a purchase is under a certain amount, it is generally made without going through the
RFQ or RFP process. What if you are a medium-sized agency whose rules require
that any purchase over $4,000 be completed through the RFP or RFQ process and
you need to purchase a software upgrade to a proprietary product for $4,100? If it is
proprietary, there is likely to be only one vendor. Do they bid against themselves?
Well, someone already figured this one out. This type of situation is handled through
what is called a **sole-source procurement**. Generally, the vendor is already providing the exact service or goods and no one else makes the exact product.

Another way around RFP and RFQ is with contract services. Most state and
local law enforcement budgets are annual. If you are paying for cellular telephone
service this year, it is likely you will budget it for next year. If your budget is approved, many agencies do not require that a new RFP or RFQ be used to extend
an existing service contract.

Because an RFP spells out in great detail what a state or local agency expects for
their money, these documents could be more than fifty pages in length. They are
very time consuming for the vendor to complete and submit as a bid only. While the
RFP and RFQ schemes may be ways of ensuring that government agencies get
the best-quality product they can afford, the cost of the RFP must be passed on to
the consumer. Moreover, since the vendor is agreeing to deliver a very specified
product, the implementation team (who usually authors the RFP) should take great
care in spelling out exactly what they want and how they expect it to perform.

Financing the Purchase

Government financing is a huge subject. That said, there are a few terms that
you should be familiar with as they relate to technology projects. Governments
are very much like you and me when it comes to purchasing. They can save their

Try This

Go to the National Criminal Justice Referral Service (NCJRS) grants and funding opportunities Web page at **www.ncjrs.org/fedgrant**. There are a variety of interesting grants at that location. Specifically, look at the requirements and forms required for a federal grant. Grant writing is an art form. Many state and local government agencies employ full-time people to write, monitor, and manage grants. Moreover, there are many consultants who assist in grant writing, preparation, and implementation.

money and make the purchase. There are local governments who set money aside each year because they realize that a piece of technology has a certain lifetime. In addition to budgeting funds to provide for maintenance, they set money aside for the ultimate replacement of the technology. Governments can also borrow the money in a number of ways. For major technology projects, the typical borrowing is done through the bond process. Finally, like you and I, state and local governments can go to their rich uncle—Uncle Sam. There are many different types of grants available to both state and local governments. Throughout the text we have referenced the amount of money spent by the federal government on state and local technology projects. Also, local governments often apply to the state government for grants.

Chapter Summary

Technology projects can be very expensive. In some instances, the failure and disappointment of technology projects is directly attributable to a lack of planning on the buyer's part. One way to ensure that proper planning takes place is to use a formal method that involves a steering committee and an implementation team. The job of the steering committee is to set overall project goals and gather political support for the project. On the other hand, the implementation team works out the details and guides the project through to completion. For both groups, membership is key to success. The steering committee is usually made up of high-level managers, and some political leadership, while the implementation team primarily consists of a project director, agency managers, and end users. However, in both groups, the involvement of end users is critical. End users bring the point of view of the line employee, the person ultimately responsible for working with the technology. Moreover, once a technology begins to be implemented, implementation team members who are also end users can act as an introduction bridge to other end users.

For a variety of reasons, state and local agencies often lack the in-house talent necessary to perform certain tasks. Rather than hire an employee to complete a specific task, in a relatively short duration of time, agencies will hire consultants. One of the tasks that consultants can assist an agency with is reviewing their systems, policies, and procedures in order to ensure they match the technologies being introduced. Sometimes a new technology changes the way in which a task is performed and impacts other tasks and goals so significantly that an agency must reengineer its practices. This type of thorough review of systems, policies, and procedures is often referred to as a business process reengineering.

In addition to using consultants, state and local governments will sometimes contract out or outsource goods and services. There are a variety of reasons that government agencies do this, but the primary reason is to garner some economic benefit by having a private firm or individual perform a task. State and local government agencies often use a somewhat complex set of competitive purchasing schemes. For more general and readily available goods and services, a state or local government agency may use a request for quotation where the low bid wins the contract. In the case of a complex purchase, like an information technology systems purchase, a state or local government may use a request for proposal scheme that very specifically details the agency's request. Sometimes RFP contracts are awarded based not on low bid, but rather on other factors like reputation, experience, and product quality.

Discussion Questions

1. The community oriented policing model calls for the decentralization of decision making, but new technologies give managers more information in real time. Do you think that with more real-time information, managers will attempt greater control over subordinates, or do you think that they will follow the model? Explain your position.
2. Can you think of an example of someone or some organization "paving the cow path"?
3. What should managers do to increase technological proficiency of their employees?
4. If your school, business, or agency were going to implement a major technology project, who would you place on the steering committee? Who would you place on the implementation team?

Key Terms

Broadbanding
Business Process Reengineering (BPR)
Consultant
Cooperative Purchasing

Implementation Team
Pooled Purchasing
Project Manager
Request For Proposal (RFP)

Request For Quotation (RFQ)
Sole-source Procurement
Steering Committee
Vendors

End Notes

1. Shafritz, *Public Policy and Administration*, 1340.
2. Imel and Hart, *Understanding Wireless Communications*, 9.
3. Dunn and Probstein, "Marketing High Tech," 10.
4. Coe and Wiesel, "Police Budgeting," 718.
5. Dawes, et al., "IT Innovation," 8.
6. Fletcher, "Government Paperwork Elimination Act," 723.
7. "Toward Improved Criminal Justice," 47.
8. Davies, "Information Era."
9. See note 7 above.
10. See note 8 above.
11. Brown and Brudney, "Geographic Information Systems," 335.
12. Korsching, Hipple, and Abbott, *All the Right Connections*, 150.
13. Cresswell et al., "Integrating Justice Information," 31.
14. Blumstein, Young, and Granholm, "Commentaries," 8.
15. Boyle, "Detective Case Management."
16. Cunningham, *B2B*, 161.
17. Imel and Hart, *Understanding Wireless Communications*, 11.

18. Jorgensen and Cable, "E-government," 15.
19. Dawes, et al., "IT Innovation," 3.
20. Imel and Hart, *Understanding Wireless Communications*, 7.
21. See note 19 above.
22. See note 12 above.
23. Ibid.
24. "Toward Improved Criminal Justice," 92.
25. Ibid., 47.
26. See note 17 above.
27. Korsching, Hipple, and Abbott, *All the Right Connections*, 168.
28. U.S. Congress, Office of Technology Assessment, Criminal Justice, New Technologies, 29.
29. Ford, "Can You Keep What You've Got?"
30. Ibid.
31. Hays and Kearny, *Public Personnel Management*, 62.
32. Ibid., 64.
33. Moore and Hudson, "Privatization Practices," 19.
34. Johnson and Walzer, *Local Government Innovation*, 2.
35. See note 11 above.
36. "Toward Improved Criminal Justice," 50.
37. Enos, "Outsourcing Technology."
38. See note 11 above.
39. Shafritz, *Public Policy and Administration*, 522.
40. See note 11 above.

Chapter Twenty-one
Emerging and Future Technologies

Learning Objectives

- The student will understand the importance of looking at possible future technologies.

- The student will be exposed to a variety of new and potential technological applications in law enforcement.

Introduction

A large portion of this book was devoted to looking at how scientific discoveries and technical innovations have led to technological progress in law enforcement. For instance, we started with a look at binary digits and radio waves so we could understand practical technologies like cellular digit packet data (CDPD). Our understanding of past developments made the digestion of what is going on in the present more understandable.

Our look at the present was also often a look at possible futures. Consider that in many instances we looked at fully intergrated systems, but we know that these are the exception and not the rule. For a variety of reasons, the implementation of technology in law enforcement has been significantly fragmented. Some agencies are very advanced, some are advanced in certain areas, but most are using technology that was available twenty or thirty years ago. Our view of past and present technologies should make us a better user of present technologies and a better decision maker about future implementations. Now we are at the point where we know enough about police technology to begin to think about possible futures.

Today you are likely to find major companies and government organizations employing consultants as futurists. These consultants forecast possible futures using a variety of quantitative and qualitative means. Their job is to provide information to organizations so they can chart their strategic course. While the title "futurist" is relatively new, the concept is very old. For instance, when human beings started to turn from hunter/gathers to farmers, they planted crops based upon their experiences with the fairly predictable cycle of the weather. You planted; it rained; you harvested. As things became more complex, humans looked at per-acre crop yields, transportation to market, transportation of water to increase yield, etc. We observed, recorded, and planned ahead. Our experience has been that most of the time, our predictions about the future when based upon the past are fairly good.

There are a number of techniques people use to predict the future. They may be qualitative such as Delphi surveys, questionnaires, and polls that use individuals with specialized or generalized knowledge.[1] Based upon the results of these qualitative measurements, the people looking at the future try to reach a consensus among those surveyed or who participated regarding the possible future. We have also seen in our chapter on crime analysis that there are statistical methods such as extrapolation, probability, variance, regression, and correlation techniques. Other people looking at the future look for analogies with existing systems. They use the development of the existing systems to explore the potential for new systems. Still others use role-playing and simulation games in an effort to make predictions about possible futures. Simply stated, there are many ways that we can look at the past and present in an effort to predict the future.

Thinking about the future is your job. In this chapter you will be provided with a number of brief descriptions or vignettes of technologies that are being field tested for law enforcement, have some potential for use in law enforcement, or are being discussed as potential law enforcement technologies. These technologies are on the horizon. They are in the near future and decisions about their use will have to be made by people like you and me. Looking at the future, we may be able to see how decisions on use and implementation today will affect state and local police agencies in the future.[2]

Finding Us

Since 1982, during emergency situations, aviators and mariners have made use of emergency location transmitters (ELTs) and emergency position indicating radio beacons (EPIRBs). In that time, these technologies have reportedly been used in more than fourteen thousand emergencies.[3] Recall in Chapter Five, on geographic information systems (GISs), we looked at how satellite technology was being used in automatic vehicle locator (AVL) devices. The ELT and EPIRB technologies are also satellite based. However, they are not true GPS devices. They do not use the GPS satellite constellation; instead they use a satellite constellation maintained by the National Oceanic and Atmospheric Administration (NOAA) called Search and Rescue Satellite-Aided Tracking System (SARSAT). The location determined by SARSAT is not as exact as the one that is generated by GPS satellites. When SARSAT receives a distress signal, the general geographic location of the signal is determined, and the appropriate search and rescue center is notified. Generally, this would be a United States Coast Guard (USCG) base. Aircraft and search vessels are then sent into the area where the signal is being transmitted. The signals generated by ELT and EPIRB can be monitored and triangulated by search and rescue aircraft and vessels. They home in on the signal and locate the beacon.

On July 1, 2003, the Federal Communications Commission (FCC) authorized the use of ELT and EPIRB technologies in the form of a **personal locator beacon (PLB)** for the general public. This type of technology will probably be useful for hikers, backpackers, and off-road vehicle users. When a PLB is activated, the SARSAT control center in Suitland, Maryland, notifies a designated contact point in the state wherein the PLB was activated.[4]

In the previous chapters we looked at AVL technology and we also briefly visited some of the commercial versions of AVL. It is likely that in the future commercial AVL systems, like the ones purchased for new cars, will include **automatic collision notification (ACN)** systems. These systems automatically contact Public Safety Answering Points (PSAP) if a privately owned vehicle equipped with ACN is involved in a traffic collision. Currently, some commercial AVL technology reports the activation of the airbag, but these new systems are likely to provide information about the collision. They would transmit not only the location of the traffic collision, but also information concerning the severity of the incident. With information concerning the severity of traffic collisions, the likely injuries could be extrapolated and the correct public safety response predetermined.[5]

Today if you walk through a department store, you will see that many of the high-value items within the store are tagged with a relatively large, often white, inventory control tag. Moreover, many preboxed items have a similar white tag that has a barcode (Figure 21.1), and inside the tag there is also an electronic inventory control device. If you walk past the threshold of the store without having the tag removed or demagnetized, a tone or disembodied voice directs you to return to the cash register. In the very near future, manufacturers are going to use

Figure 21.1 **Universal product code (UPC) barcodes** were created to facilitate the checkout process and inventory control in grocery stores, but like many successful technologies, UPC barcodes spread to use in many different situations, including law enforcement. Some agencies barcode evidence as a means of tracking it. For manufacturers and retailers, UPCs are granted by an organization called the Uniformed Code Council (**www.uc-council.org**). The manufacturers and retailers pay an annual fee to use a six-digit manufacturer identification number. So the first six digits on a barcode are the MIN, the next five are the product code, and the last is an error-checking digit, much like the error-checking digit we examined in packet data. A scanner reads the barcode by interpreting the widths of the black lines and spaces and the locations of the lines and spaces.

much smaller electronic tags embedded directly into the merchandise. Recall that your cellular telephone constantly broadcasts an electronic serial number (ESN). In the near future, nearly everything we purchase will contain a small microchip and RF transceiver that will broadcast the product's ESN.[6]

This process is referred to as **"chipping goods."** The transceiver located in the very small and inexpensive tag (there are estimates that the tags will cost less than four-tenths of a cent) does not contain a power source. It picks up energy from the scanner that is used to detect it and sends back its ESN, using the energy from the scanning device. Currently, these scanners can activate and detect the ESN from about five feet. For the store, this will enhance inventory control and loss prevention. For state and local law enforcement agencies, the potential and problems with these devices are vast.

What if a database of stolen tagged property was constructed? Every time a retailer or manufacturer suffered a theft, they could report the theft and the ESN. This information could be easily entered into a database. State and local police officers equipped with scanners could simply scan you and your vehicle during a traffic stop or at any other time you walked by a police officer. Is this a search? As these tags become commonplace and ridiculously inexpensive, will manufacturers tag every can of soda? In many states theft of an object with a value of less than $400 is a petty theft or a misdemeanor. However, possession of stolen property is often a felony. What if you buy something, like a lamp, at a garage sale, and it is stolen or at least reported stolen?

Another application of similar RF chips is embedding them into handguns. In 2001 5 percent of the police officers killed by firearms nationwide were killed with their own handguns. The NIJ is sponsoring a project designed to protect police officers from being killed by their own weapons. One of the ideas is to modify handguns so that they can be fired only by their owners. There are a number of schemes under consideration, such as the police officer wearing a ring that must come into contact with the weapon or, alternatively, a ring that must be in close proximity to the weapon.

Much like the personal locator beacons we looked at earlier, specific location devices are under development for police officers. One such idea is to have a transmitter worn in or around the collar of a police uniform. The transmitter would constantly provide information on the police officer's location and allow the police officer continuous communications contact with his or her dispatch center. In the future, you may see police officers using some derivative of the **remote control information system (RCIS)** which was originally developed for medics in the military. The RCIS is a highly compact communications system that provides videofeed, two-way communications, and vital signs monitoring, and has a GPS feature. With a system like this, the communications dispatch center would see and hear some of what the field police officer sees. More important, by having a real-time feed, it would be possible for the police officer to access real-time advice on field situations.

Our Homes as Prisons

As of 2003, more than two million people were in prison and federal, state, and local governments spent $40 billion dollars a year on corrections. A technological solution to the cost of the number of people in custody is being tested. It is estimated that approximately 20 percent, or four hundred thousand offenders, could qualify for some type of house arrest arrangement.[7] Currently, an offender who is under house arrest wears a bracelet with a **transponder**. At random intervals, the corrections agency calls the offender's home. The transponder responds to these telephone calls, and if the offender is not at home, he is in big trouble. It has been suggested that this transponder be replaced with technology similar to AVL technology. By incorporating GPS and a computer monitoring station, if the offender leaves his home, the corrections agency would be immediately notified. It is not too much of a jump to see the potential state and local law enforcement applications. First, if this arrangement were used and an offender violated the terms of his house arrest, the corrections agency could notify the local police jurisdiction.

But there are other potential applications. While there are a lot of people in jail, there are many more people on probation and parole. A condition of probation or parole could be the wearing of this AVL-like technology. In the future, a police officer may be driving down the street and be automatically alerted that he or she is in close proximity to someone who is on either parole or probation. With relational databases, GPS, AVL, and in-car computer technology, the police officer could receive the offender's photograph, physical description, and the terms of the parole or probation—in the car. Most offenders on parole and probation have surrendered their Fourth Amendment rights. They can be detained and searched without probable cause. Once alerted, a police officer might decide to stop and search the offender.

This technology also has potential applications for crime analysis and crime prevention. Since most crime is committed by repeat offenders, if offenders on parole or probation were wearing AVL technology, it could have a deterrent effect. Moreover, someday crime analysts might find themselves running comparisons between AVL-monitored offenders and crime patterns.

Scanning Us

There are a number of new scanning technologies that allow for very precise scanning for metallic objects and contraband on people. Two of these are **magnetic gradient measuring** and **passive millimeter wave (MMW) imaging**.[8] Fluxgate magnetometers measure changes in the Earth's magnetic field caused by metallic objects. As people walk through a portal, or gateway, they are scanned and the results of the scan are compared against a database that contains the magnetic disruption of the Earth's field by a certain weapon. This technology would be used to replace the large metal detectors that you must pass through on your way into many public buildings. It is predicted that this technology will be more reliable and accurate, speeding entry and reducing the number of false alarms. So unless your car keys meet the exact magnetic disruption of a handgun or knife, you walk on through.

Passive Millimeter Wave can see through your clothing. Fortunately, it cannot see your anatomical details, but it can detect weapons, plastic explosives, and other types of contraband. The technology uses the natural emissions from objects and, therefore, does not require that you be scanned. The NIJ is working on a project to mount MMW technology on a police vehicle for field use. This technology is probably a decade or so off, but think about the search and seizure issues involved. In addition to MMW, there are experiments underway to combine radar and ultrasound technology to allow for remote searching of people.

Using a video camera, an infrared light source, and optical character recognition (OCR) software, the text from a vehicle license plate can be read by a computer. The OCR software converts the text to a binary code and that code can be compared against many different relational databases. Although this can currently be done in real time, it has some limitations. The license plate on your car is made of a highly reflective material and is very good at reflecting infrared light. Of course, infrared is out of our visible light spectrum, so we never know when someone is shining an infrared light on us. The infrared image returns to the camera, and using an OCR-like algorithm, the license plate number of a vehicle is converted into computer code and can be stored and compared. These systems are being used in private industry for access control to parking structures, by quasi-governmental agencies for toll booths and at some border checkpoints. Currently, this technology has not be developed to the point where it can be installed in a police vehicle, but that is not far off. In the future, police officers will be alerted by their optical license plate reading (OLPR) system that the car in front of them is stolen or unregistered or the driver is wanted.

Dataviellance

Throughout the text we looked at a wide assortment of databases. We saw that the federal government alone has some two thousand databases, but so does your grocery store for their discount card, the bank for the ATM, the library, and the hospital. Just about every organization is creating relational databases. **Dataveillance** is the term coined to describe the use of data in the investigation and the monitoring of us.[9] It is watching us not by camera, not in person, but through our transactions.[10] As databases become more interconnected and cross-referenced, greater questions about personal privacy need to be asked. Think about combining any of the technologies in this chapter with dataveillance. For instance, when you go to the store, your discount card records your purchase and the chipped goods report exactly what you have purchased. You are driving down the street and OCR technology records your license plate as you travel. The potential and danger of any technology is increased by a relational database.

Using the Us of Us

Biometrics is the science of using technology to automatically identify an individual based on physical, biological, and behavioral characteristics. We have talked about a biometric science many times in this textbook. Think back to what made fingerprint evidence both strategic and tactical information. Fingerprints became tactical when it was possible to take a scan of a fingerprint, convert the fingerprint to binary code, and check the fingerprint against a database. That is the essence of biometrics—automatically identifying an individual based on characteristics.

There are two classifications of biometric information. First, there are physiological characteristics like your fingerprint, DNA, facial features, eye pattern, and **hand geometry**. Second, there are behavioral characteristics that are unique to people, such as voice and handwriting. Biometric information has the capacity to go even further. There is the way you walk, or your gait; your personal thermal pattern; and your personal magnetic resonance. Anything about us that is unique and can be converted to a digital format can be used to differentiate us from others automatically.

Currently, there are two broad categories of use for biometric information: access control and remote identification. Access control is used to prevent unauthorized individuals from gaining access to a location or to information. You probably don't know it, but you partially participate in biometric access control every day. Strict access control is a combination of three factors: what you are (biometrics), what you have (your ATM card), and what you know (your personal identification number, or PIN). Every time you use your ATM card, you gain access to your money by showing what you have (your ATM card) and telling what you know (your PIN). If you use a credit card, you show what you have (the card) and what you are (your signature), and often present picture identification (what you are) to gain access to your credit. The only reason a credit card is not a biometric transaction (yet), is because your picture or signature are not verified by comparing them to a relational database. However, there are many government locations and some private industry locations that may be accessed only through the use of biometric information. This happens when employees present identification (what they have), enter an access code (what they know), and verify their identities by fingerprint, retina scan, or hand geometry (what they are).

The other use of biometric information is to ascertain identity for purposes other than access control. The use of livescan devices by police officers is a prime example of using biometrics for a purpose other than access control. Although fingerprints have been known to be unique for more than a hundred years, the first biometric applications were with hand geometry. More than twenty years ago, the first biometric device was installed on Wall Street for timekeeping purposes. That device measured the length of the human fingers. Today, by taking a number of measurements, the hand geometry device can be found as an access control measure in a number of venues. For instance, hand geometry was used as identification equipment during the 1996 Olympics in Atlanta.

In addition to hand geometry and fingerprints, iris and retinal measurements are used to uniquely identify individuals. A retinal scan consists of a low-intensity beam of light directed into the individual's eyeball. The pattern of veins in the eyeball are recorded, converted to a digital format and then compared against a relational database. An iris eye measurement photographs the iris in the front of the eye. Retinal vein patterns can change over time, but the iris does not change and, like fingerprints, is unique to the individual.[11]

One of the most controversial biometric applications is **facial recognition technology (FRT)**. With FRT, a digital photograph of an individual's face is used to take measurements between nodal points, which are locations on every human face. For instance, the centers of the eyes, the tip of the nose, and the corners of the mouth are nodal points. While there are about eighty different nodal points, an FRT software algorithm requires only between fourteen and twenty-two of these points for comparison. Recall our examination of fingerprint technology in Chapter Six; FRT measurements and the subsequent conversion to a searchable database are somewhat similar. Facial recognition technology is being used in some jail management systems as a means of identifying people during the booking process and while they are in custody. This technology seems to work well as a supplement to the normal booking procedure. Although this software has been deployed at public events such as concerts with closed-circuit television cameras, there remains a considerable amount of technical and policy aspects that still need to be worked out.[12]

But of all the new biometric technologies, facial probably has the most promise and probably the most controversy. In Chapter Fifteen we found that you can't go anywhere without being videotaped. Moreover, you probably have seen a video on the news of a robbery or burglary where the offender is unidentified and the police are asking for assistance. In Pinellas County, Florida, and Los Angeles County, California, digital photographs are taken of offenders as they are being booked. Between these two agencies there are nearly one million photographs. If facial recognition algorithms and relational databases can be improved to the point where a million photographs can be filed and searchable by FRT, this biometric application may become a valuable investigative tool.

With improved FRT, once a first responder seizes a video as evidence, that video could go to a lab and the photographs of the offender can be compared against a database of known offenders. Since most are repeat offenders, there would be matches. Eventually, many offenders whose crimes were videotaped would be identified very quickly. Sometime in the future, when FTR algorithms, databases, and bandwidth issues mature further, we will probably see the in-car camera of a police vehicle being used for OCR of license plates and FRT for wanted offenders. Imagine a police officer driving down the street, his superintelligent police car scans for offenders on parole and probation with AVL, and his in-car camera scans back and forth, capturing licenses plates and the faces of people on the street. His supervisor is receiving real-time feed of the in-car camera and the camera and audio installed on the police officer's person. Of course, dispatch tracks the police officer's progress with AVL. It may be that some day the police officer will just ride in the car and it is preprogrammed to drive where and when the next crime is to be committed. You have seen all of this technology; it isn't far off.

Although a unique identifier, DNA is not yet fully under the biometric umbrella because of the way it must be collected and analyzed. However, consider that fingerprint evidence remained a nonbiometric science for more than a hundred years after its first use in law enforcement. As science and technology matures, it is quite likely that some day, perhaps decades off, DNA samples will be routinely "sniffed" from the air (recall we drop DNA everywhere) and like fingerprints, the police officer will know the offender's identity.

Voice recognition and handwriting are considered behavioral biometric sciences. Their applications in law enforcement are limited because of issues concerning conclusiveness. However, voice recognition biometrics probably could be used during wiretaps to provide insight into the identity of a caller.

Satellite Technology

If you asked most law enforcement managers what the potential use of satellite technology was for law enforcement, they would probably answer, "communications." Although it is not practical or economical to use satellite technology in law enforcement, the potential to relieve some of the problems associated with dead spots in communication exists.[13] Our look at satellite technology centered on its GPS capabilities, but there are other types of satellites—communications satellites probably being the most common. But what about using satellites for observations?

By combining infrared, visible light, and radar technology, a satellite can look down and see relatively small objects, very clearly. Who really knows how good the optics are on a military satellite? What if one were used to look down on an American city. Consider a real-time feed from a satellite to the communications dispatch center. When a burglary or robbery call comes in, the dispatcher could instruct the satellite to focus on the location. Currently, in many large cities, law enforcement uses helicopters for speedy response to emergencies. Helicopters have caught offenders leaving the scene of the crime many, many times, but helicopters make a lot of noise (warning offenders), and they, too, have a response time. But what if response was nearly immediate? What if the satellites fed information to ground stations and computers continually monitored for environmental changes, like sudden heat plumes. Could the fire department be dispatched before anyone even realized there was a fire? Perhaps the satellite relays images to a computer, and in the middle of the night, the computer continually looks for environmental changes, such as a thermal signature of burglars on the roof of a business? All of the technology exists, just not in this combination. However, what would be the public's reaction to this type of monitoring?

Pursuit Technology

As we saw in a previous chapter, the only means of pursuit termination are currently mechanical. One recent improvement has been the development of spiked barrier strips which have retractable and remotely operated spikes. Now the strip can be placed down even if other motorists are nearby, and only activated as the offender's vehicle passes over. There have been some interesting suggestions for technology: a small radio transmitter that is deployed to the offender's vehicle with a handheld launching device; a low-power radio transmitter that allows the police to talk to the offender; spiked balls on a chain to be shot across the roadway; and a giant parachute that would be launched as a package from an aircraft and once it attaches to the vehicle, it causes slowing by increased drag. I didn't make any of those up.

One electric solution that has been suggested is the use of a very strong electromagnetic pulse directed at the offender's vehicle. The pulse would burn out the computer chips that run the car, causing it to stop. There might be a problem with offender's braking and steering the vehicle after it shuts down in such a manner, and issues abound concerning accidentally hitting another vehicle with the pulse. One promising solution is the use of a laser device that allows police to specifically target a vehicle, if that vehicle has a preinstalled computer chip. When the laser strikes the vehicle, the chip slows the vehicle to fifteen miles per hour and eventually shuts if off by restricting the flow of gasoline.[14] Another similar technology proposes that a chip be preinstalled that allows police officers to shut the vehicle off after it has been reported stolen. For either of these technologies to work, they would have to be legislatively mandated into new vehicle construction.

That solution probably isn't far from what will eventually happen. Manufacturers are increasingly including GPS systems that enable AVL. There isn't much to engineering the remote shutoff chip. While commercial AVL is a consumer choice, a mandated product would not only help to reduce police pursuits, it would probably decrease new car theft, or at least minimize damage to newer cars because the AVL would allow the police to track down the stolen cars. Of course, there are privacy issues.

With the difficulties associated with driving during a high-speed pursuit, it is unlikely that we are going to see a device actually deployed from the chasing vehicle. If anything, like the spike strips, police officers may be able to anticipate the offender's route and deploy some electrical device. Deployment of external charges or pulses from a helicopter seem unlikely, because of aiming and the potential effects it might have on the helicopter. In reality, the only viable near-term solution seems to be the internally installed chips.

AVL

As AVL technology in police vehicles becomes more commonplace, we are likely to see a continued integration of AVL into any number of other systems. One suggestion has been combining AVL with traffic management systems. So if you are a police officer and you activate your emergency equipment, AVL gives you the route to your call and gives you green traffic lights all the way there. This has applications for all of public safety. It would likely speed up police, fire, and emergency medical services response in urban areas.[15]

Less-Lethal Use of Force

Through the National Institute for Justice, the Oak Ridge National Laboratory in Tennessee is involved in the research and development of less-lethal force devices. They are looking at a variety of exotic tools that can cause temporary physiological responses like nausea. They are investigating how the human body responds to sound, light, and different types of electromagnetic waves. What they are looking for is a less-lethal force device that incapacitates the offender without causing injury. One of the things they have experimented with is using RF energy to raise the body temperature of an offender. This RF energy, or thermal, gun would cause an offender to become disorientated. They have also experimented with using electromagnetic energy to produce a seizure in the offender, another energy beam weapon that causes the offender to "see stars."

Getting Smaller

One of the operational strategies often associated with community-oriented policing is the deployment of police officers on foot or bicycle patrol. Police officers assigned to these duties can carry only a limited amount of equipment. Unlike most police officers assigned to vehicle patrol, these police officers did not have ready access to databases via a computer. With the introduction of personal digital assistants (PDAs) police officers assigned any detail have computer access to databases from motor vehicle departments and the National Crime Information Center.[16] Recall from Chapter Two, a PDA is a handheld personal computer (Figure 21.2).

Figure 21.2 PDAs like the one in this photograph give police officers in special details, like bicycle patrols or footbeats, a method to easily record information as well as access to federal, state, and local databases.
Photograph provided by CyberCop-Software.

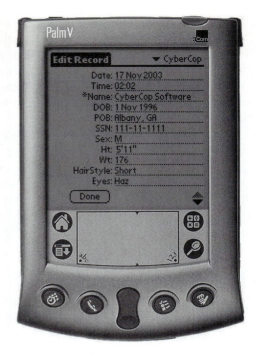

Chapter Summary

Some of the technologies mentioned in this chapter are very far from deployment in the field and others are examples of interesting but not quite useful ideas. An underlying theme of this chapter is how different technologies are being combined to make them more effective or to be used for a completely different purpose.

New technologies also bring new questions about policy. As was stated in the beginning, most of police work is about gathering information. Therefore, it is not surprising that most of the technology being introduced into law enforcement enables the collection, organization, and analysis of information. Moreover, since the police and technology are focused on information, the primary community concerns usually center around issues of privacy and the Fourth Amendment.

Technology is making police work more complex. Certainly, in some instances it is making police work efficient, but technology adds to the information a police officer must know. A police officer must still know how to communicate with a wide variety of people often under stressful circumstances; a police officer still must exercise basic tactical skills like standing with the gun leg back; a police officer must still know how to use their traditional tools like the radio, vehicle, baton, and firearm. Added on top of the basics is new technology—a computer in the car, AVL, and two thousand federal databases.

Discussion Questions

1. If you were in charge of nationwide development of new police technologies, which of the new technologies or areas of technological development would you emphasize? Why?
2. Which of the emerging and future technologies do you think will have the most difficulty with community acceptance? Why?

3. Based on what you've read, what combinations of technology do you think would be useful for police officers?
4. Based on all of the technology you've read about, how can technology enable or enhance community-oriented policing?

Key Terms

Automatic Collision Notification (ACN)
Biometrics
Chipping Goods
Dataveillance
Facial Recognition Technology (FRT)

Hand Geometry
Magnetic Gradient Measuring
Passive Millimeter Wave (MMW) Imaging
Personal Locator Beacon (PLB)

Remote Control Information System (RCIS)
Transponder
Universal Product Code (UPC) Barcodes

End Notes

1. Halal, Kull, and Leffmann, "Emerging Technologies," 20.
2. Kenney and McNamara *Police and Policing,* 52.
3. Scarper, "Personal Locator Beacons."
4. In California, the contact point for PLB alerts will be the Governor's Office of Emergency Services Warning Center.
5. McEwhn, "Public Safety Support."
6. Blumstein, Young, and Granholm "Commentaries," 13.
7. Ibid., 3.
8. Moore, *Mass Communication Law,* 384.
9. Clarke, "Information Technology and Dataveillance."
10. Solove, "Privacy and Power," 1393.
11. U.S. Congress, Office of Technology Assessment, Criminal Justice, "New Technologies," 2.
12. See note 6 above.
13. Imel and Hart, *Understanding Wireless Communications,* 94.
14. "Giant Techno Leaps," 1.
15. See note 5 above.
16. Newcombe, "PCs in Pocket."

Bibliography

Adams, Dwight E. *Statement for the Record, The Federal Bureau of Investigation's CODIS Program before the Senate Judiciary Committee, Subcommittee on Crime and Drugs.* **www.ojp.usdoj.gov/nij/dnamtgtrans9/trans-k.html** (accessed May 14, 2002).

Al-Kibsi, Gassan, et al. "Putting Citizens On-line, Not in Line." *McKinsey Quarterly* 65 (2001) **www.questia.com** (accessed March 28, 2004).

Bair, Sean, et al. "Advanced Crime Mapping Topics." (Denver, Colo.: National Law Enforcement and Corrections Technology Center, Rocky Mountain Region, April, 2002). **www.nlectc.org/cmap/cmap_adv_topics_symposium.pdf** (accessed March 18, 2004).

Bakewell, Eric J., Michelle Koldaro, and Jennifer M. Tjia. "Computer Crimes." *American Criminal Law Review* 38, no. 3 (2001).

Band, Jonathan and Masanobu Katoh. *Interfaces on Trial: Intellectual Property and Interoperability in the Global Software Industry.* Boulder, Colo.: Westview Press, 1995.

Banks, Christopher J. "The Third Generation of Wireless Communications: The Intersection of Policy, Technology, and Popular Culture." *Law and Policy in International Business* 32, no. 3 (2001).

Bayley, David H., and Clifford D. Shearing. "The Future of Policing." *Law & Society Review* 30, no. 3 (1996): 585–606.

Bielski, Lauren. "Peer-to-Peer Technology." *ABA Banking Journal* 93, no. 6 (2001).

Bielski, Lauren. "So, What Ever Happened to the Paperless Office?" *ABA Banking Journal* 94, no. 6 (2002): 57+.

Blumstein, Alfred, Peter Young, and Jennifer Granholm. "Commentaries on Development of Policy Governing the Use of Technology in the Criminal Justice System." National Criminal Justice Reference Service **www.ncjrs.org/pdffiles1/nij/189106-3a.pdf** (accessed June 15, 2003).

Bonnett, Thomas W. "Is ISP-Bound Traffic Local or Interstate?" *Federal Communications Law Journal* 53, no. 2 (2001): 187.

Bovens, Mark, and Stavros Zouridis. "From Street-Level to System-Level Bureaucracies: How Information and Communication Technology Is Transforming Administrative Discretion and Constitutional Control." *Public Administration Review* 62, no. 2 (2002): 174.

Boyle, John P. "Detective Case Management—How to Make It Work for Your Department." *Police Chief Magazine* (April, 1997).

Brown, Mary Maureen and Jeffrey L. Brudney. "A Smarter, Better, Faster, and Cheaper Government: Contracting and Geographic Information Systems." *Public Administration Review* 58, no. 4 (1998).

Buckler, Marylin. "NCIC 2000: More Than Just Images." *Police Chief Magazine* (April, 1998).

Buntin, John. "Disaster Master." *Governing Magazine* (December, 2001) **www.governing.com/archive/2001/dec/disaster.txt** (accessed August 6, 2003).

Burges, Audrey J. "*Patterson v. Commonwealth:* An Illustration of the Legal Complexity of DNA Databases." *Richmond Journal of Law and Technology* 9, no. 2 (Winter 2002–2003) **law.richmond.edu/jolt/v9i2/Note2.html** (accessed July 20, 2003).

California Governor's Office of Emergency Services. "Definitions and Terminology." Auxiliary Communications Service **acs.oes.ca.gov/Pages/acs_definitions.html** (accessed June 25, 2003).

California Penal Code Section 502. (2003) **www.leginfo.ca.gov/cgi-bin/displaycode?section=pen&group=00001–01000&file=484–502.9.**

California High Technology Crime Advisory Committee. "Annual Report on High Technology Crime in California." **www.ocjp.ca.gov/publications/pub_htk1.doc** (accessed May 1, 2003).

Cardwell, Michael D. "Nationwide Application of the Incident Command System Is the Key." *The FBI Law Enforcement Bulletin* (October, 2000).

Christofferson, Scott A. and Michael A. Gatzke. "Broadband Media: Look Before You Leap." *McKinsey Quarterly* 49 (2001) **www.questia.com** (accessed March 28, 2004).

Cisar, Jim. "Enhancing the Police Department Website" *Police Chief Magazine* (May, 2003).

Clarke, Irvine. "Emerging Value Propositions for M-Commerce." *Journal of Business Strategies* 18, no. 2 (2001): 133.

Coe, Charles K., and Deborah Lamm Wiesel. "Police Budgeting: Winning Strategies." *Public Administration Review* 61, no. 6 (2001).

"Computer-Aided Dispatch." Public Safety Wireless Network **www.pswn.gov** (accessed May 20, 2003).

Cresswell, Anthony, et al. *And Justice for All: Designing Your Business Case for Integrating Justice Information.* Albany, N.Y.: Center for Technology in Government, State University at Albany, New York, 2000.

Cunningham, Michael J. *B2B: How to Build a Profitable E-Commerce Strategy.* Cambridge, Mass.: Perseus, 2001.

Danziger, James N. and Kim Viborg Andersen. "The Impacts of Information Technology on Public Administration: An Analysis of Empirical Research from the 'Golden Age' of Transformation." *International Journal of Public Administration* 25, no. 5 (2002).

Davies, Thomas R. "Reshaping the Information Era." *Governing Magazine* (December, 2001) **www.governing.com/archive/2001/dec/tech.txt** (accessed August 6, 2003).

Dawes, Sharon S., et al. *Four Realities of IT Innovation in Government.* Albany, N.Y.: Center for Technology in Government, State University at Albany, 2000.

Department of Justice. "The Nation's Two Crime Measures." (May, 2003).

Department of Justice. Community-Oriented Policing Services Website **www.cops.usdoj.gov** (accessed May 14, 2003).

Department of Justice, Administrative Office of the United States Courts. "2001 Annual Wiretap Report." (2001) **www.uscourts.gov/wiretap01.contents.html**

Department of Justice, Bureau of Justice Statistics. "Effects of the Redesign on Victimization Estimates." National Crime Victimization Survey. (April, 1997) **www.ojp.usdoj.gov/bjs/pub/pdf/erve.pdf**

Department of Justice, Computer Crime and Intellectual Property Section, Criminal Division. "Searching and Seizing Computers and Obtaining Electronic Evidence in Criminal Investigations." (January, 2001) 9.

Department of Justice, Bureau of Justice Statistics. *Law Enforcement Management and Administrative Statistics.* "Local Police Departments." (1999) **www.ojp.gov/bjs/pub/pdf/lpd99.pdf**

Department of Justice, Bureau of Justice Statistics. "2000 Law Enforcement Management and Administrative Statistics (LEMAS) 2000."

Department of Justice, Bureau of Justice Statistics. "The Nation's Two Crime Measures." Department of Justice, **www.ojp.usdoj.gov/bjs/pub/ascii/ntcm.txt** (accessed June 7, 2003)

Department of Transportation, "2000 Emergency Response Guide," **www.tc.gc.ca/canutec/erg_gmu/en/User's_guide.htm** (accessed July 1, 2003).

Drummond, William J. "Address Matching: GIS Technology for Mapping Human Activity Patterns." *Journal of the American Planning Association* 61, no. 2 (1995).

Dunham, Griffin S. "Carnivore, the FBI's E-mail Surveillance System: Devouring Criminals, Not Privacy." *Federal Communications Law Journal* 54, no. 3 (2002).

Dunn, Dan T., and Sidney C. Probstein. "Marketing High Tech Services." *Review of Business* 24, no. 1 (2003): 10.

Electronic Crime Needs Assessment for State and Local Law Enforcement." National Institute for Justice Research Report, NCJ 186276 (March, 2001) **www.ncjrs.org/pdffiles1/nij/186276.pdf**

"Emergency Planning Guide." California Governor's Office of Emergency Services **http://acs.oes.ca.gov** (accessed June 25, 2003).

Enos, Gary. "Guide to Outsourcing Technology." *Governing Magazine* (July, 2001) **www.governing.com/archive/2001/jul/out.txt** (accessed August 6, 2003).

Enos, Gary. "A Guide to Technology Mega-Deals." *Governing Magazine* (January, 1997) **www.governing.com/archive/1997/jan/techdeal.txt**

"The Evolution and Development of Police Technology: A Technical Report Prepared for the National Committee on Criminal Justice Technology, National Institute of Justice." *SEASKATE, Inc.* July 1, 1998.

Farrel, Greg. "$50M 'Pump-and-Dump' Scam Nets 20 Arrests." *USA Today* (March 9, 2001) **www.usatoday.com/money/general/2001-03-09-pump-and-dump.htm** (accessed July 14, 2003).

Federal Bureau of Investigation. "Crime Reporting in the Age of Technology: The National Incident-Based Reporting System." *Criminal Justice Information Services Newsletter* 4, no.1.

Federal Bureau of Investigation. *Uniform Crime Report Handbook.* Clarksburg, W. V. Criminal Justice Information Services Division, 2000.

Federal Bureau of Investigation. "Uniform Crime Reporting Statistics: Their Proper Use." Criminal Justice Information Services Division. **www.fbi .gov/hq/cjisd/ucrstat.htm**

Federal Emergency Management Agency. *Exemplary Practices in Emergency Management, Standardized Emergency Management System (SEMS)* **www.fema.gov/rrr/exp_06.shtm** (accessed May 2, 2003).

Fletcher, Patricia Diamond. "The Government Paperwork Elimination Act: Operating Instructions for an Electronic Government." *International Journal of Public Administration* 25, no. 5 (2002): 723.

Foerstel, Herbert N. "Freedom of Information and the Right to Know: The Origins and Applications of the Freedom of Information Act." Westport, Conn.: Greenwood Press, 1999.

Ford, Robert E. "Can You Keep What You've Got?—Retaining the Technically Savvy Officer. *Police Chief Magazine* (May, 1999).

Frank, Diana. "E-Gov XML Committee Formed." *Federal Computer Week* (December 2, 2002).

Gaines, Larry and Roger Leroy Miller. *Criminal Justice in Action: The Core.* Belmont, Calif.: Thomson Wadsworth, 2d ed 2004.

Garipoli, Michael A. "Offender Identification and Central Booking Project Integrates Three Technologies." *Police Chief Magazine* (October, 2001).

Geerken, Michael R. *Consequences of Inadequately Integrated Justice Information System.* Metairie, La.: Center for Society, Law and Justice, University of New Orleans, March, 2002.

Geisler, Eliezer and Everett M. Rogers. *Methodology, Theory, and Knowledge in the Managerial and Organizational Sciences: Actions and Consequences.* Westport, Conn.: Quorum Books, 1999.

"Giant Techno Leaps in Small Packages." *Law Enforcement News* 27, no. 567–568 (December 15/31, 2001) 1.

Gottlieb, Steven, Sheldon Arenberg, and Raj Singh. *Crime Analysis: From First Report to Final Arrest.* Montclair, Calif.: Alpha Publishing, 1998.

"Guidance for Using Red Light Cameras." Federal Highway Administration, National Highway Traffic Safety Administration. **safety.fhwa.dot.gov/rlcguide** (accessed March 20, 2003).

"Guide for the Selection of Communications Equipment for Emergency First Responders." National Institute for Justice, Law Enforcement and Corrections Standards and Testing Program. *NIJ Guide 104-00* I (February, 2002).

Halachmi, Arie. "The Brave New World of Information Technology," *Public Personnel Management* 21, no. 4 (1992).

Halal, William E., Michael D. Kull, and Ann Leffmann. "Emerging Technologies: What's Ahead for 2001–2030. Scholars Assemble a Comprehensive Forecast of Coming Technologies." *The Futurist* (November/December, 1997) 20.

Hampon, Rick. "Digital Times, Private Lives Are Breaking Up Party Lines." *USA Today Information Network* (October 23, 2000).

Hasselbring, Ted S. and Candyce H. Williams Glaser. "Use of Computer Technology to Help Students with Special Needs." *The Future of Children* 10, no. 2 (2000).

Hays, Steven W. and Richard C. Kearny. *Public Personnel Management: Problems and Prospects* Upper Saddle River, N. J.: Prentice Hall, 1995.

Heffernan, William C. "Fourth Amendment Privacy Interests." *Journal of Criminal Law and Criminology* (2001) **www.questia.com** (accessed March 28, 2004).

Henderson, Nathan C. "The Patriot Act's Impact on the Government's Ability to Conduct Electronic Surveillance of Ongoing Domestic Communications." *Duke Law Journal* 52, no. 1 (2002): 179+.

Higgins, Daniel. "A Crime Analyst's Guide to Mapping." Illinois Criminal Justice Authority, Illinois State University, Chicago, IL, April 2003.

Hittle, Byron D. "An Uphill Battle: The Difficulty of Deterring and Detecting Perpetrators of Internet Stock Fraud." *Federal Communications Law Journal* 54, no. 1 (2001).

Huey, Laura J. "Policing the Abstract: Some Observations on Policing Cyberspace." *Canadian Journal of Criminology* 44, no. 3 (2002).

"Implementing the National Incident-Based Reporting System: A Project Status Report–A Joint Project of the Bureau of Justice Statistics and the Federal Bureau of Investigation." United States Department of Justice, Office of Justice Programs, Bureau of Justice Statistics. NCJ-165581 (July, 1997) **www.ojp.gov/bjs/pub/ascii/inibrs.txt**

Imel, Kathy J. and James W. Hart, P.E. *Understanding Wireless Communications in Public Safety: A Guidebook to Technology, Issues, Planning, and Management, 2nd ed.* National Law Enforcement and Corrections Technology Center (January, 2003). **draco.aspensys.com/scripts/ rwisapi.dll/@JUSTNET.env?CQ_SESSION_KEY=CTIOVGANKELQ& CQ_TPT_VIEW_DOC=YES&CQDOC_NUM=Z**

Ismail, Ayman, Samir Patil, and Suneel Saigal. "When Computers Learn to Talk: A Web Services Primer." *The McKinsey Quarterly* (2002): 71+.

Jacobson, Heather and Rebecca Green. "Computer Crimes." *American Criminal Law Review* 39, no. 2 (2002).

Johnson, Robin A. and Norman Walzer, eds. *Local Government Innovation: Issues and Trends in Privatization and Managed Competition*. Westport, Conn.: Quorum Books, 2000.

Jorgensen, Daniel J. and Susan Cable. "Facing the Challenges of E-Goverment: A Case Study of the City of Corpus Christi, Texas." *SAM Advanced Management Journal* 67, no. 3 (2002).

Judd, Damon. "Database Management and GIS: What's the Connection?" *Earth Observation Magazine* **www.eomoline.com** (accessed June 1, 2003).

Kaluta, Roman W. "New Developments in Interjurisdictional Communications Technology." *Police Chief Magazine* (January, 2001).

Kay, David H. and George F. Sensabaugh, Jr. "Reference Guide on DNA Evidence." *Reference Manual on Scientific Evidence*. Federal Judicial Center. (2000) **air.fjc.gov/public/fjcweb.nsf/pages/16**

Keeline, James D. "Who Invented Tom Swift's Electric Rifle?" **www.keeline.com/Electric_Rifle.pdf** (accessed August 10, 2003).

Kenney, Dennis Jay and Robert P. McNamara, eds. *Police and Policing: Contemporary Issues, 2d ed.* Westport, Conn.: Praeger, 1999.

Kimmelman, Jonathan. "Risking Ethical Insolvency: A Survey of Trends in Criminal DNA Databanking." *Journal of Law, Medicine & Ethics* 28, no. 3 (2000): 209.

Korsching, Peter F., Patricia C. Hipple, and Eric A. Abbott. *Having All the Right Connections: Telecommunications and Rural Viability*. Westport, Conn.: Praeger, 2000.

Kurke, Martin I. and Ellen M. Scrivner. *Police Psychology into the Twenty-first Century*. Hillsdale, N.J.: Lawrence Erlbaum Associates, 1995.

Kyllo v. United States, 533 U.S. 27 (2001).

Laidler, Keith J. *To Light Such a Candle: Chapters in the History of Science and Technology*. Oxford, England: Oxford University Press, 1998.

Lane, Cason. "New Technologies Protect Officers and Inmates." *Corrections Today*, (August, 1999).

Leonard, Matarese. "Police and AEDs: A Chance to Save Thousands of Lives Each Year." *Public Management* 79, no. 6 (June 1997).

Lichtveld, Maureen, et al. "Preparedness on the Frontline: What's Law Got to Do with It?" *Journal of Law, Medicine and Ethics* 30, no. 3 (2002): 184.

Lipton, Robert and Paul Gruenewald. "The Spatial Dynamics of Violence and Alcohol Outlets." *Journal of Studies on Alcohol* 63, no. 2 (2002).

Mansell, Robin and Uta Wehn. *Knowledge Societies: Information Technology for Sustainable Development*. Oxford, England: Oxford University Press, 1998.

"Mapping and Analysis for Public Safety." National Institute for Justice **www.ojp.usdoj.gov/nij/maps/briefingbook.html** (accessed June 1, 2003).

Markowitz, Kenneth J. "Legal Challenges and Market Rewards to the Use and Acceptance of Remote Sensing and Digital Information as Evidence." *Duke Environmental Law and Policy Forum* 12, no. 2 (2002).

McCarthy, Bill. "New Economics of Sociological Criminology." *Annual Review of Sociology* (2002) **www.questia.com** (accessed March 28, 2004).

McCullagh, Declan. "Technology as Security." *Harvard Journal of Law & Public Policy* 25, no. 1 (2001): 129+.

McEntire, David A., et al. "A Comparison of Disaster Paradigms: The Search for a Holistic Policy Guide." *Public Administration Review* 62, no. 3 (2002): 267.

McEwhn, Harlin R. "Public Safety Support for Intelligent Transportation Systems." *Police Chief Magazine* (February, 2003).

Mellon, Jennifer N. "Manufacturing Convictions: Why Defendants Are Entitled to the Data Underlying Forensic DNA Kits." *Duke Law Journal* 51, no. 3 (2001).

Miller, Wilbur. "The Good, the Bad and the Ugly: Policing America." *History Today* (August, 2000) 29.

Miranda v. Arizona, 384 U.S. 436 (1966).

"Money Laundering." *American Criminal Law Review* 39, no. 2 (2002): 839.

Moore Adrian and Wade Hudson, "The Evolution of Privatization Practices and Strategies." In *Local Government Innovation: Issues and Trends in Privatization and Managed Competition*. Edited by Robin A. Johnson and Norman Walzer. (Westport, Conn.: Quorum Books, 2000), 19.

Moore, Roy L. *Mass Communication Law and Ethics*. Mahwah, N.J.: Lawrence Erlbaum Associates, 1999.

Mosesso, Vincent N., Jr., et al. "Law Enforcement Agency Defibrillation (LEA-D): Proceedings of the National Center for Early Defibrillation of Police AED Issues Forum." *Prehospital Emergency Care* 6, no. 3 (July–September, 2002) 273-282.

Myers, Michael D. and Leigh Miller. "Ethical Dilemmas in the Use of Information Technology: An Aristotelian Perspective." *Ethics and Behavior* 6, no. 2 (1996): 153-160.

Newcombe, Ted. "Cops Put PC's in Pocket: New Devices Improve Access to Law Enforcement Data." *Government Technology* (February, 2003).

Nichols, Lavra J. "The Use of CCTV/Video Cameras in Law Enforcement." International Association of Chiefs of Police, Executive Brief, (March, 2001) **www.theiacp.org/documents/pdfs/Publications/UseofCCTV%2Epdf**

Nunn, Samuel. "Police Information Technology: Assessing the Effects of Computerization on Urban Police Functions." *Public Administration Review* 61, no. 2 (2001).

Olmstead v. United States, 48 S. Ct. 564, 277 U.S. 438.

Onnen, Jami. "Oleoresin Capsicum." *Police Chief Magazine* (June, 1993).

Oscar, Kenneth J. "A Common E-Commerce Architecture for the Federal Procurement System." *The Public Manager* 30, no. 1 (2001): 11.

"Overview of NIBRS." Association of State Uniform Crime Reporting Programs **www.asucrp.orgs/index.html** (accessed June 6, 2003).

Pastore, Ann L. and Kathleen Maguire. "Sourcebook of Criminal Justice Statistics." **www.albany.edu/sourcebook** (accessed June 1, 2003).

Perlman, Ellen. "Can We Talk?" *Governing Magazine* (May, 2003).

Peterson, Rebecca Sasser. "DNA Databases: When Fear Goes Too Far." *American Criminal Law Review* 37, no. 3 (2000): 1219.

Phipps, Steven. "Order out of Chaos: A Reexamination of the Historical Basis for the Scarcity of Channels Concept." *Journal of Broadcasting and Electronic Media* 45, no. 1 (2001): 57.

"PSWN Program Releases National Interoperability Scorecard: Study Shows Efforts to Improve Public Safety Communications Are Making Headway." *Public Safety Wireless Network Newsletter* (Summer 2003) **www.pswn.gov/admin/librarydocs12/Newsletter_Summer_2003.pdf** (accessed August 6, 2003).

"A Public Safety Answering Point Managers' Guide to Geographic Information Technology." A National Emergency Number Association White Paper (October, 2002) **www.nena.org/wireless911/PDF/PSAPGuidetoGIS.pdf**

"Putting Web Services in a 'No Spin Zone.'" *ABA Banking Journal* 94, no. 11 (2002): 16+.

Qureshi, Anique A., Stephen Hartman, and Joel Siegel. "What the CPA Must Know About Computer Networks." *CPA Journal* 67, no. 3 (1997).

Ramstack, Tom. "Justices Rule Heat-Sensing Is Search." *The Washington Times* (June 12, 2001) 3.

Raskin, Xan and Jeannie Schaldach-Paiva. "Computer Crimes." *American Criminal Law Review* 33, no. 3 (1996): 541–573.

"Report of the National Task Force on Privacy, Technology, and Criminal Justice Information." U.S. Department of Justice, Office of Justice Programs, Bureau of Justice Statistics. *NCJ 187669* (August, 2001) **www.ojp.gov/bjs/pub/pdf/rntfptcj.pdf**

Roberts, David J. "Integration in the Context of Justice Information Systems: A Common Understanding." SEARCH, The National Consortium for Justice Information and Statistics (2001) **www.search.org/integration/pdf/Integration%20def.pdf**

Robinson, Brian. "Solving the XML Enigma." *Federal Computer Week* (January 13, 2003).

Russell-Chamberlin, June. "Where the Bad Guys Are." *Mercator's World* (January, 2001) 34.

Scarper, Matt. "Personal Locator Beacons in California." *California Governor's Office of Emergency Services Information Bulletin* (June 25, 2003) **www.oes.ca.gov/Operational/OESHome.nsf/PDF/IB-PLB062503/$file/IB-PLB062503.pdf**

Shafritz, Jay M. *International Encyclopedia of Public Policy and Administration*, vol. 4. Boulder, Colo.: Westview Press, 1998.

Siegel, Larry J. *Criminology*. Albany, N.Y.: Wadsworth. 1998.

Simon, Jonathan. "Governing Through Crime." In *The Crime Conundrum: Essays on Criminal Justice*. Edited by Lawrence M. Friedman and George Fisher. Boulder, Colo.: Westview Press, 1997, 171–184.

Skogan, Wesley G., et al. *On the Beat: Police and Community Problem Solving*. Boulder, Colo.: Westview Press, 1999.

Smith, Brad. "Police Grapple with CDPD Roadblock: Anticipated Shutdown of Network Leaves Officer with Complex Issues" *Wireless Week* (November 18, 2002).

Smith, Kimberly. "Integrated Automated Fingerprint Identification System: Twenty-first Century Technology for Law Enforcement." *Police Chief Magazine* (May, 1998).

Solove, Daniel J. "Privacy and Power: Computer Databases and Metaphors for Information Privacy." *Stanford Law Review* 53, no. 6 (2001).

Spykerman, Ron. "Is E-mail Monitoring Legal?" **www.policypatrol.com/docs/Email monitoring-article.pdf** (July 13, 2003).

Staley, David J. "From Writing to Associative Assemblages: 'History' in an Electronic Culture." In *Writing, Teaching, and Researching History in the Electronic Age: Historians and Computers*. Edited by Dennis A. Trinkle. Armonk, N.Y.: M. E. Sharpe, 1998.

Steele, Jeffery. "Investment Scams Find a New Home: Internet Fraud Is a Major Problem." *Chicago Tribune* (January 28, 2003).

Steins, Chris and Abhijeet Chavan. "Technology Trends for 2001: A Report from COMDEX." *Planning* (January, 2001) 28.

Sullivan, Bob. "FBI Software Cracks Encryption Wall Magic Lantern Part of New Carnivore Project." **msnbc.com/news/660096.asp?cp1=1** (accessed June 24, 2003).

Swope, Christopher. "Guide to Wireless Security: WI-FI Anxiety." *Governing Magazine* (March, 2003) **www.governing.com/archive/2003/mar/wireless.txt** (accessed August 4, 2003).

Taslitz, Andrew E. "The Fourth Amendment in the Twenty-First Century: Technology, Privacy, and Human Emotions." *Law and Contemporary Problems* 65, no. 2 (2002).

Thomas, John Clayton and Gregory Streib. "The New Face of Government: Citizen-Initiated Contacts in the Era of E-government." *Journal of Public Administration Research and Theory* 13, no. 1 (2003): 83.

Tonry, Michael. *The Handbook of Crime and Punishment*. New York: Oxford University Press, 1998.

"Toward Improved Criminal Justice Information Sharing: An Information Integration Planning Model." International Association of Chiefs of Police (April, 2002) **www.theiacp.org/documents/pdfs/Publications/cjinfosharing.pdf** (accessed August 6, 2003).

Trinkle, Dennis A. *Writing, Teaching, and Researching History in the Electronic Age: Historians and Computers*. Armonk, N.Y.: M. E. Sharpe, 1998.

Turner, Marlene E. *Groups at Work: Theory and Research*. Mahwah, N.J.: Lawrence Erlbaum Associates, 2001.

"Understanding Classic SoundEx Algorithms." Creativyst, Inc. **www.creativyst.com** (accessed August 20, 2003).

U.S. Congress, Office of Technology Assessment. *Criminal Justice, New Technologies, and the Constitution, OTA-CIT-366*. (Washington, D.C.: U.S. Government Printing Office, 1988).

U.S. Congress, Office of Technology Assessment. *Electronic Surveillance in a Digital Age, OTA-BP-ITC-149*. (Washington, D.C.: U.S. Government Printing Office, 1995).

United States Constitution, Fourth Amendment.

Vila, Bryan and Cynthia Morris. *The Role of Police in American Society: A Documentary History*. Westport, Conn.: Greenwood Press, 1999.

Walker, Pamela K. and Philip J. Rodacy. *Field Test Kit for Gun Residue Detection*. Albuquerque, N. M.: Sandia National Laboratories, January, 2002.

Walker, Samuel, Geoffrey P. Alpert, and Dennis J. Kenny. "Early Warning Systems: Responding to the Problem Police Officer." U.S. Department of Justice, Office of Justice Programs, National Institute for Justice (July, 2001) **www.ncjrs.org**

Watson, Nathan. "The Private Workplace and the Proposed Notice of Electronic Monitoring Act: Is Notice Enough?" *Federal Communications Law Journal* 54, no. 1 (2001): 79.

"Wireless Data Networking Support Report: Public Safety Applications for Handheld Computing Devices." Public Safety Wireless Network (April, 2002) **www.pswn.gov/admin/librarydocsIL/Pda-final-7_02.pdf**

Wood, Stearns J. "A Practitioner's Guide to GIS Terminology." **www.techweb.com** (accessed June 1, 2003).

"XML Specification for Interstate Rap Sheets." Justice Standards Clearing House (September 22, 2000) **it.ojp.gov/jst/public/viewDetail.jsp?sub_id=177#stat**

"Your Papers, Please: From the State Driver's License to a National Identification System: Watching the Watchers." Electronic Privacy Information Center—Policy Report No. One: (February, 2002) **www.epic.org/privacy/id_cards/yourpapersplease.pdf**

Zhu, Xuan. "Developing Web-Based Mapping Applications Through Distributed Object Technology." *Cartography and Geographic Information Science* 28, no. 4 (2001): 249+.

Index

Note: Pages in italic indicate a table or figure is on that page.